HIGH
POINTS
IN
ANTHROPOLOGY

HIGH POINTS IN ANTHROPOLOGY

Edited,
with Introductions, by
Paul Bohannan
NORTHWESTERN UNIVERSITY

and
Mark Glazer
PURDUE UNIVERSITY

ALFRED A. KNOPF   NEW YORK

Preface

The aegis of this book is, we believe, unusual. About 1967, when Glazer was a graduate student at Northwestern University, he undertook a reading course with Bohannan in the important historical writings in anthropology. A few years later he was teaching a course in the history of anthropology at Purdue at about the same time Bohannan was taking over that course at Northwestern. We compared notes whenever we met—and found we both had the same problem. Although we admired Marvin Harris' accomplishment in *The Rise of Anthropological Theory*, and although we would continue to use it, we disagreed with some of its interpretations and felt that there could be no substitute for reading the original materials. But our classes were so large that there weren't enough of those materials in the libraries of our universities for everyone to read.

We decided to do something about the problem. And while our solution, this book of readings, is obviously a compromise—because the professional student, at least, needs a library and not a book of readings—both of us have found that using these readings has vastly increased the effectiveness of our courses.

Bohannan wrote the first draft of the introduction and (with the help of Cathleen Weigley and Candice Phillips as research assistants) the background sketches. Glazer wrote the first draft of the introductions to each of the sections.

Contents

PART FOUR | **EVOLUTION AND STRUCTURALISM**

Introduction

       History has no beginning. Neither has anthropology. But historians of anthropology have to start somewhere. There is a grave temptation to say that anthropology "begins" with Tylor—or Helvetius, or Aristotle. The beginning of anthropology is very like the beginning of mankind itself— the only way to deal with such an ill-considered question is to create false entities and make declarations by scholarly fiat.

       There is no event, no person, before which there was no anthropology and after which there was. Rather, there are human curiosities and activities that we today think of as anthropological—and we extend our conceptualizations into the past, to periods before the word was even coined, and certainly to periods when the word meant something very different from what we mean by it today.

       It would be possible to go back to, say, the Greek and Roman historians. Xenophon, Herodotus, and Tacitus have a great deal to say about strange and barbarian peoples that, in a later day, would pass for ethnographic descriptions. It would be just as sensible to begin with the observations of the great medieval Arab geographer and scholar Ibn Khaldun, whose descriptions of African and Asian peoples are vivid and, as near as we can judge, accurate. But was Ibn Khaldun an anthropologist? Was *Australopithecus* a man?

       Yet a book must have a beginning. And its authors or editors should know, and should tell their readers, why they began where they did. Moreover, since compiling a history of anything involves being highly selective of data and requires an "angle," whether it be admitted or not, the angle and the bases for selectivity should be made overt.

PHILOSOPHICAL POSITION FOR A HISTORY OF ANTHROPOLOGY

       Anthropologists, engaged in either ethnography or self-study through history, can do no better than to read Marc Bloch's *Apologie pour l'histoire* to find the essential method and problems of their subject. If they add to this book R. G. Collingwood's *The Idea of History* and E. H. Carr's *What Is History?* they will be well armed, not merely to study history, but also to make any ethnographic study. Especially in Carr's book is one struck by the similarity of the two pursuits.

Although the methodology of data gathering in history and that in anthropology are wildly different, the modes of judgment in the two fields are the same. And astonishingly enough, the purpose is the same: to bring to the attention of our contemporaries and congeners the ways in which people from other places and other times have ordered their lives. We are interested both in the common humanity and in the vastly different kinds of lives that human beings can lead—in the common problems as well as the different solutions.

Anthropologists should be among the first to grasp the essentials of the Collingwood position. He claimed that the philosophy of history is concerned neither with the past, with itself, nor even with what historians think about the past, but rather with the relationship between the past and the way the historian thinks about it. As he put it, "The past which a historian studies is not a dead past, but a past which in some sense is still living in the present" (quoted in Carr 1961:22). In the specific case in hand we must, in studying the history of anthropology, search for the meanings that anthropologists of various times and places have found in anthropology. These meanings are products of the times in which they lived, but they have relevance for us today.

We are studying, therefore, not what anthropology was, but what it is and what it will be. For what it *was* necessarily changes with the changes in what it is *becoming*.

We are thus adopting straightforwardly a view that some historians call—not always as a compliment—"presentistic." Indeed, for a scientist to adopt any other view is questionable. This is not to imply that we cannot detect anachronisms or that we are not interested in what Spencer meant in Spencer's day. Obviously we cannot fully understand Spencer's work without knowing something about the ignorances and enthusiasms of his readers. But if Spencer had no meaning in today's world, there would be no point in reading him.

We have found significance for today's anthropology in all of the selections we have made. We shall enumerate some of these significances in short introductions to each selection, but what we find there is necessarily limited by our vision as well as by the practical matter of space. Any person who goes over this material in the light of his knowledge is likely to find things that we did not recognize.

A study of the history of anthropology can save the anthropological present a lot of trouble. Gunnar Myrdal is said to have noted that Lord Keynes, since he knew no Swedish and hence could not read the writings of many of Sweden's most illustrious economists, was doomed to "unnecessary Anglo-Saxon originality." Knowing the history of one's discipline can save one a good deal of unnecessary originality. It can also give one a great many good ideas, for the past never says things quite in the way the present needs them said. With new culture, old passages accrete new meaning—or else lose meaning altogether. We think that the passages we have selected have accreted new meaning, and that they are significant for the future of the subject.

THE "ANGLE"

We have chosen to structure this book around the emergence of several "big ideas," each of which had a decided impact on whatever was called anthropology before it. Each of these ideas has a continuing life in anthropology, which we have tried to point out as we come forward through time.

Obviously, the background or milieu into which a concept falls (or from which it emerges—it is the same thing) is also an essential thing to know about its reception and use by a discipline. It seems to us that some of the most important "external" forces in the history of anthropology were such occurrences as the loss of the first British and French empires and the establishment and ultimate loss of their second empires; the French Revolution and the Napoleonic upheavals not only provided a turning point in intellectual as well as political history, but had the further effect of bringing a large German population to America, a population that provided the heart of the American educational system and the American liberal tradition, both of which were vital factors in the development of anthropology. Then, with the eclipse of the liberal tradition and the floundering of the educational system, anthropology changed again.

Another such point is that minorities are an inherent part of the organization known as the nation-state, whether these be "outside," as in Central Europe (the Tyrolese are a good example), or "inside," as in Russia (the Volga Germans or the Armenians) and the United States (Indians, blacks, and the rest). National states, because of the built-in "minorities" issue, create somewhat different kinds of colonial imperialism than others, such as the Roman Empire or Ottoman Empire, created. They also create a special kind of anthropology.

Two major thinkers have been omitted from this book on the ground that they had an impact on the general milieu of anthropology rather than on anthropology itself. They are Marx and Freud. Both are part of the *Zeitgeist,* and only in that sense part of anthropology. Both were interested in anthropology, although Marx lived before the word meant what it does today; Freud read extensively in it. Both misused it as grossly as anyone ever has—that is, used anthropological materials to nonanthropological ends, and to ends of which people who called themselves anthropologists tended to disapprove.

The importance of Freud to anthropology is not, interestingly enough, to be found in a work such as *Totem and Tabu,* which purports to deal with anthropology; neither is his importance to be found in a later work such as *Civilization and Its Discontents,* which is so often assigned to undergraduates in social science survey courses. Rather, it comes from his early writings—his book with Breuer, *On Hysteria;* his masterpiece, *The Interpretation of Dreams;* and the *Three Contributions.* These books could not possibly be excerpted in such a way as to provide a step in a developing anthropological history—although Chapter 7 of *The Interpretation of Dreams* may well be one of the seminal documents of all time for anthropology (in spite of the fact that comparatively few anthropologists have read it).

The same kind of thing can be said of Marx: his work has been so jousted about since his death, its implications have been made so vast, that to excerpt any part of Marx and put it into a book of this sort is to encourage a misunderstanding of the whole. Anthropologists must at one level or another deal with Marx, as they must deal with Freud, but as part of the environing milieu, not as a distinct contribution to their own discipline.

This is not to say that anthropology has made no major contributions to the milieu of other disciplines. After all, Marx was influenced by Lewis H. Morgan, and Freud was vastly influenced by many anthropologists. And the tone of the late twentieth century would be very different indeed without anthropological ideas like culture. Our young would be reared very differently if Margaret Mead had not gone to the Pacific in the 1920s.

Obviously, then, many historical events and trends, many thinkers and many actors, have set the stage for the emergence of the ideas that we today call anthropology. Detailing all of them, of course, would require another book. But such trends nevertheless provide a set of factors that must not be ignored when we investigate the past of our discipline. Anthropology, like any other pursuit, is set into time, place, and culture. Our insights apply to ourselves as much as to any other group. If they do not, something is awry.

It is far easier to set forth some "big ideas" of anthropology and let our students and our critics argue about which ones we have left out. We expect and seek controversy on this point.

The three "big ideas" we want to deal with here are evolution, culture, and structure.

EVOLUTION

The idea of evolution was in the air in the early nineteenth century. Goethe, for example, was an evolutionist. But the first scholar to set forth the idea in a form that is recognizable today was Herbert Spencer. In the 1840s he created a theory of evolution that allowed him to take the best features of geographical determinism and some of the features of the biology current at the time and to explain it all in terms of "the survival of the fittest." But Spencer was only peripherally talking about the fittest animals; he was focusing on the fittest social and cultural institutions.

When Spencer set forward the idea of cultural evolution, it was calmly received. There was intellectual objection from some quarters, but no moral indignation. The idea of evolution became controversial only when Darwin applied it to biology. It is ironic that the Western world made a big thing of the centennial publication of Darwin's *The Origin of Species*, whereas the centenary of Spencer's work went unnoticed—certainly uncelebrated. Only after Darwin, under the impact of the misnomer "social Darwinism," did the idea of cultural evolution become anathema to some schools of anthropology in the early part of the twentieth century—especially those schools whose foundations lay in the German liberal tradition.

Thus we begin our book with Herbert Spencer. Spencer is not fully "modern"—and reading him means dealing with writing that utilizes a vocabulary predating most social science as we know it. In reading Spencer one must constantly keep two things in mind. First, that he is working with an extremely limited vocabulary and hence falls back on analogies, false concretizations, and even common sense (little changes faster than common sense). Second, Spencer when he is understood seems, like Shakespeare, to be full of truisms —*everybody* knows that! But everybody knows that because Spencer and his colleagues figured it out.

There is, of course, continuity between the pre-evolutionary and evolutionary forms of anthropology. But (to take one eminent pre-evolutionary example) the "Anthropology" of Immanuel Kant is dead, for all that continuity. It is the victim of superior knowledge and more developed ratiocination. Blumenbach's *On the Natural Variety of Mankind* (1775) is a better book but is equally dead, and for the same reason.

The only thing that connects pre-evolutionary and evolutionary anthropology is the insistence of some anthropologists on explaining human cultural differences biologically—what Harris (1968), following many others, calls "racism"—which means that after the "evolution revolution" they used racism to explain cultural changes and even cultural evolution.

The early nineteenth century stood desperately in need of a new world view. The entire culture of the day was struggling toward what Spencer, Darwin, Alfred Russell Wallace, Lewis H. Morgan, Marx, and Engels ultimately provided; a theory that would explain the past and the future of biotic and cultural forms. What was really new about evolution was that it explained the future as well as the past; obviously, we cannot know the "stages" of future evolution, but we do know that evolution is all around us, that each of us (and our very subject) is an integral part of it. And as Teilhard du Chardin (1959) has pointed out, framing the theory of evolution was itself a major step in evolution.

Concern with evolution has peaked twice in anthropology—once with Spencer and Morgan in the early part of the nineteenth century and once again with Leslie White and his followers and his now-routed adversaries in the twentieth. Between these times was a period in which anthropologists sought to avoid the subject—always with truths that turned out to be irrelevant. They decried reconstruction of history on the basis of inadequate information. So do we—but the argument doesn't even touch on the basis of an evolutionary theory. The foes of evolution turned to the detailed trivia of diffusion and the truisms of functionalism only to learn that both could be seen to underwrite the theory of evolution.

CULTURE

The second big idea to alter the very fundamentals of anthropology is the idea of culture. This idea is a very simple one—so simple, in fact, that for decades it was hard to understand. And so simple that, like "life," it seems self-evident enough, and varied enough, that definitions of it became stylish in order to pin it down. And, like "life," it defies mere definition: it is a realm of living, and it is one of the systems, as is life, for beating entropy in the short run (for all that both of them speed up entropy in the long run).

Discovering culture was as important to evolution as discovering the cell. The century after 1865 or so, when the idea of culture began to be taken into social science from the German romantic literary tradition, saw the beginning of a professional anthropology—the emergence of people who called themselves anthropologists rather than people who did anthropology as an avocation because it was an interesting and significant thing for a gentleman or a philosopher to occupy himself with. These new professionals investigated the way the new ideas of culture fitted into every other dimension of their worlds: religion was among the earliest subjects to be culturized by Edward Burnett Tylor and many lesser scholars. But culture had to be fitted ultimately to ideas about psyche, biology, economy, polity, family, ecology. To ideas about everything.

Different scholars have thought that one or more of these "fitting together" notions was the core of the subject. There have been economic determinists, psychic determinists, sexual determinists, ecological determinists—even cultural determinists.

Today we have culture just about digested—we seem to know what it "is." We have not, however, discovered the "secret" of culture, in the sense that DNA and the double helix are the "secret" of life. Although a number of anthropologists (A. R. Radcliffe-Brown is probably the most celebrated), have banished the word "culture" at various stages in their careers, they nevertheless (like Émile Durkheim and Marcel Mauss) were talking about culture without using the word.

Without the concept of culture it is too easy—perhaps inevitable—to fall back on some notion of a "folk memory." This is what Seán O'Faolain did in *The Irish* (1947). It is what Freud did in *Totem and Tabu*. It is what Marvin Harris (1968) accused Durkheim of doing, with some—but not entire—justification. For Durkheim did have the concept of the "representation"—it is in the "collective" that the difficulty arises. The notion of the "group mind" is but a step—actually a serious misstep—from the *representation collective*; the "ancestral mind" is but another misstep beyond that.

The concept of culture is an important one because it gets us out of this particular kind of mysticism (not to say sentimentality). Indeed, that is the trouble. We switch uncomprehendingly from culture to "a culture," get "a culture" confused with ancestry, give the whole a mystical aura that is fundamentally narcissistic—and we are back in the racist ages that the idea of culture should have saved us from.

Interestingly enough, the idea of culture has never had a serious hiatus since it was first developed—unless we are now entering into one. That is to say, the idea of evolution went through a longish period when it was rejected by anthropologists, then re-emerged into anthropological thinking. No major school of anthropology, being "the science of culture" in the eyes of some of its practitioners, has ever turned its back on culture. Yet.

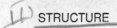 STRUCTURE

The idea of structure is as old as the problem of whether the sum of the parts is greater or less than the whole. But structure in the form in which the idea was to emerge in the twentieth century is found in Herbert Spencer—perhaps well before.

It is still too early to say whether the idea of structure will be a seminal idea like evolution and culture. But it is very much in the air now, and its *Anlagen* are to be found throughout the selections in this book.

The idea of structure, in its modern dominant avatar, came into anthropology via British social anthropologists. To them it did not and does not mean culture structure, but rather social structure. But *human* social structure, no matter how "innate" some of it may be, no matter how easily distinguished from culture, must be played out in cultural terms. Thus culture—as an idiom for the expression of the relationships that are "structured" into a social organization—was never absent. We have heard British social anthropologists of twenty years ago say, "Oh, that isn't important—that is only culture." They were not denying culture—they merely wanted to move it out of a central position and give structure that role.

A little later the word "structure" came also to be applied to what Noam Chomsky has referred to as the "deep structure" that underlies language and to what Claude Lévi-Strauss was doing with his study of myth and his *pensées sauvages*, being a set of cultural universals but representing nevertheless something that is infracultural in the human perceptual and conceptual apparatus. In the last section of the book we have included Lévi-Strauss' piece on "Social Structure" and his short article "The Structural Study of Myth."

We repeat: Even ten years from now the matter of "structure" may look very different—that is, it may be even more important than we think. But it seems just as likely that it will be less important than our giving it this much space in this particular company would suggest. In other words, this third "big idea" is being set forth with a certain tentativeness.

BEING AN ANTHROPOLOGIST TODAY

There is a myth in anthropology that it is a "young science." It is not. The problems that concern anthropologists today have been around for a long time—since, indeed, the eleventh chapter of Genesis, which tells how God divided mankind into language groups and thus set them to participating in mutually unintelligible cultural traditions. The point of this book is that, even from a formal standpoint, anthropology as we know it today goes back a hundred and fifty years. Had we chosen to go into earlier periods we could have reached the Middle Ages. And if we had gone back to speculation about cultural differences and their meanings, we could have begun with the creation of the written word.

Anthropology is not new. But it does not have an impressive past. The reason is that, like the other bodies of knowledge we in today's jargon call behavioral sciences, anthropology attacks our common sense—and then forms the basis for a new common sense. Insofar as anthropology is any good, it changes—by exposing silliness and error—the myths and values of the cultures that spawn it. Indeed, anthropologists may be the very poets that Plato wanted to throw out of his Republic. They ask embarrassing questions. And once asked, those questions (at least the good ones) do not go away. Nor are most of them solved. Some of them are, however, made obsolete by our next questions.

The history of anthropology, then, is really the history of values in the world, particularly the Western world. Some might even add, the middle-class world. Yet in a narrower sense it is the history of how some of today's most telling values in the field of "the human sciences" got to be what they are, of the missteps we took along the way.

Our selections stop with the year 1960. Obviously, one is less sure of one's position in recent times, which one has one's self lived through. But 1960 is an important year in anthropology—a sort of watershed—and for many reasons. First of all, it was the year in which anthropologists began, metaphorically at least, to outnumber natives. Second, it was the year of African independence, and hence of the demise of political colonialism (whatever leftovers or new forces there are that may be called the likes of economic colonialism or neocolonialism). The 1960s saw a progressive erosion of the liberal ethic until, late in the decade, the subject of anthropology (along with everything else) was involved in a paroxysm of ethical doubt. If things settle down in the 1970s, anthropology will be about something else.

Anthropology today is at a crossroads, which is no mere figure of speech. Anthropologists are facing the need for adjustment as a consequence of two developments. First, the absorption of the concept of "culture" and the activities of field work by all disciplines have to a degree undermined our conceptions of ourselves, and the necessity of sharing the notion of structure with all behavioral sciences makes it harder to maintain an identity than it once was. Second, colonialism is disappearing—not fast enough, perhaps, but the trend is clear—with the result that anthropologists are being integrated into a new contextual milieu.

The first development means that anthropology is being absorbed by everything and everybody—from history to biology. Its "integrity" is being threatened by its very successes. The second means that anthropologists can no longer do what they were doing before 1960. A field trip to New Guinea or Africa has quite a different meaning both to the anthropologists and to the informants now than it had then.

Therefore anthropology, like love, is where you find it—and today it is all over the place. It is a fascinating time to be an anthropologist.

REFERENCES

Carr, E. H.
  1961   *What Is History?* London: Macmillan.
Harris, Marvin
  1968   *The Rise of Anthropological Theory.* New York: Thomas Y. Crowell.
O'Faolain, Seán
  1947   *The Irish.* Harmondsworth: Pelican Books.
Teilhard du Chardin, Pierre
  1959   *The Phenomenon of Man.* New York: Harper & Row.

PART
ONE
EVOLUTION
and the
COMPARATIVE
METHOD

Herbert Spencer 1820–1903

BACKGROUND

Two ideas dominated the life of Herbert Spencer: that of evolution, for which he invented the term "survival of the fittest," and that of personal freedom. His contemporaries described him as opinionated, independent, and intellectually overambitious. Spencer, however, was always unwavering in his convictions. He was a man of little pretense; he refused to attend funerals, scorned academic honors, and disdained government pomp. His lifelong obsession was to explain all of nature as one synchronized materialistic system.

Born in Derby, England, Herbert was the only child of his parents to live beyond early childhood. His father was a schoolteacher of progressive social and religious views; his mother was a quiet, conforming woman. Spencer was encouraged to pursue his interest in science, particularly natural history, physics, and chemistry, to the exclusion of history and the classics. Therefore, his contemporaries thought him undereducated.

He was sixteen when he completed his formal schooling. He returned home and became an assistant schoolmaster for a while. Then he became a railroad construction engineer, during which time he tinkered about inventing things and published a few technical articles. From the railroad he turned his interest to political theory—his main concern being to limit the functions of the state and to achieve universal suffrage and total separation of church and state.

When he was twenty-eight, Spencer became subeditor of a journal, *The Economist,* and soon after published his first book, *Social Statics.* The book's main points were (1) that "every man has freedom to do all that he wills, provided he infringes not the equal freedom of any other man"; (2) that the functions of any state should be limited to domestic police duties and protection from foreign aggression through armed services; and (3) that it is natural for an individual, through his "adaptive capacity" to move endlessly toward a state of "perfect adjustment." He claimed that "progress . . . is not an accident but a necessity."

Spencer published an anonymous article in 1852—seven years before the publication of Darwin's *Origin of Species*—defending the theory of organic evolution. In 1855 came the *Principles of Psychology,* in which he based mental conditions on particular chemical and physical properties. Since this view was unpopular (not to say shocking), and since it did indeed show his narrow scope of education and his distaste for reading, it was universally condemned.

3

Two years later Spencer began to formulate his system of philosophy. It was based on evolution, and he envisioned—at least eight decades before it was finally accepted—that a theory of evolution could encompass all the phenomena of nature. In order to finance publication of his writing, he sold 600 subscriptions to a series called *Descriptive Sociology.* The first work in the series, *First Principles,* appeared in 1862. Meanwhile he had published *Education,* another "shocking" book, in which he advocated the natural development of a child's intelligence, the importance of the learner's interest, and the idea that training a child through freedom and experience works better than through command and punishment.

Principles of Biology, which appeared in 1864, was a result of direct collaboration with Thomas Huxley. In it he argued for direct environmental influences on the organism and a tendency of evolution toward equilibrium.

Spencer, often ill, was always a hypochondriac. After 1866 his life came more and more to consist only of intellectual associations and a yearly trip to Scotland. Suffering some sort of "mental overload"—he was a Victorian's Victorian who wore his suffering on his sleeve—Spencer saw himself as continuously forced to seek diversion. But he dictated during breaks when he was out rowing, compiled a huge autobiography, helped to found the Anti-Aggression League, visited the United States, and wrote *Man Versus the State*—all despite his apparently delicate health.

Spencer was periodically destitute; he lived by such windfalls as legacies from his father and uncle and gifts from loyal followers. He started to realize some profits on his work about 1871. There were later periods of destitution, but when he died he left a considerable sum to carry on *Descriptive Sociology.*

Spencer hired three scholars when he began to write his monumental *Principles of Sociology.* Their task was to read and compile data on primitive peoples from which Spencer could write. During the same period he was involved in using this material for his many-volumed *Descriptive Sociology* and was writing the *Study of Sociology,* which considers some of the problems confronting a social scientist. *Principles of Sociology* finally began to appear in 1877; the last volume was published in 1896.

Spencer was well known for his comparison of society to an organism—his driving belief that the state should be maintained only in the interests of its citizens. He postulated two types of society. One was the military (structured on status), and the other was the industrial (based on contract), to which the military gave way in some places.

Increasing misrepresentation of his views embittered Spencer's last years. After his death in 1903 his reputation went into a long decline from which it was to emerge only in the last third of the twentieth century.

INTRODUCTION

Spencer is regarded as the philosopher of evolution. This idea about him has been so overwhelming that his other contributions to the theory of the social sciences are usually ignored. Indeed, his "synthetic philosophy" has largely been forgotten. That an author such as Spencer can be so thoroughly relegated to our unconscious is truly paradoxical—the more so because he formulated many of the terms in use today. It was he who first used as technical terms such words as "superorganic," "function," "structure," and "system." The origins of structural functionalism are also to be found in Spencer—a fact that was over-looked during the many decades when it was assumed that evolution and function-alism were opposites.

Spencer as a synthetic philosopher was not interested in the social sciences alone; he was interested in all the sciences. He had a very special interest in biol-ogy. It was Spencer, not Darwin, who formulated "the survival of the fittest"—although it was indeed Wallace and Darwin who spelled out the biological mech-anisms at work.

More important for the anthropologist, Spencer retained the model of the bio-logical organism as the basis for understanding the social realm. Spencer saw the organism as a model for society in two ways: (1) a society represents a system that has structures and functions; and (2) a society represents a certain level of social evolution, determined on the basis of its structural differentiation. This approach to society obviously represents thinking by analogy—the organic analogy, which treats society as a biological organism. Processes that hold for biology—evolution, function, structure, and homeostasis—are said to hold in social logic. Yet analogy is not identity.

According to Spencer the universe can be explained only in evolutionary terms. Society, he claimed, began as an undifferentiated and simple system (organism). Through evolution, societies (note the change from singular to plural—it is Spencer's) developed specialized structures (e.g., government) to perform special-ized functions (e.g., coordinating the whole system). The more structurally and functionally differentiated a society is, the more advanced a place it has in an evolutionary taxonomy.

From this kind of reasoning Spencer developed two distinct and separate schemes of social taxonomy. They are worse than inadequate, both theoretically and from the point of view of data utilization. But they were an important beginning.

As noted, Spencer also used the term "superorganic," which has its own place in anthropological theory as developed in the writings of such authors as Edward Sapir and Alfred Louis Kroeber. In Spencer's writings the superorganic refers to ideas that exceed the individual. It is through the superorganic, according to Spencer, that coordinated human action is possible. With this idea Spencer is reach-ing for the concept of culture; indeed, if the word "culture" is substituted in the previous sentence, the meaning of that sentence becomes clear. The term, of course, is a first cousin of Émile Durkheim's "conscience collective," another great struggle to talk about culture without a culture concept.

It must be noted that, in spite of Spencer's total dedication to evolutionary con-ceptualization, modern evolutionary theory stems from Morgan more directly than from Spencer. But today's structural functionalism appears to have strong roots in Spencer's views of structure, function, organism, and evolution.

1 THE EVOLUTION OF SOCIETY

WHAT IS A SOCIETY?

This question has to be asked and answered at the outset. Until we have decided whether or not to regard a society as an entity, and until we have decided whether, if regarded as an entity, a society is to be classed as absolutely unlike all other entities or as like some others, our conception of the subject matter before us remains vague.

It may be said that a society is but a collective name for a number of individuals. Carrying the controversy between nominalism and realism into another sphere, a nominalist might affirm that just as there exist only the members of a species while the species considered apart from them has no existence, so the units of a society alone exist, while the existence of the society is but verbal. Instancing a lecturer's audience as an aggregate which by disappearing at the close of the lecture proves itself to be not a thing but only a certain arrangement of persons, he might argue that the like holds of the citizens forming a nation.

But without disputing the other steps of his argument, the last step may be denied. The arrangement, temporary in the one case, is permanent in the other; and it is the permanence of the relations among component parts which constitutes the individuality of a whole as distinguished from the individualities of its parts. A mass broken into fragments ceases to be a thing, while conversely, the stones, bricks, and wood, previously separate, become the thing called a house if connected in fixed ways.

Thus we consistently regard a society as an entity because, though formed of discrete units, a certain concreteness in the aggregate of them is implied by the general persistence of the arrangements among them throughout the area occupied. And it is this trait which yields our idea of a society. . . .

But now, regarding a society as a thing, what kind of thing must we call it? It seems totally unlike every object with which our senses acquaint us. Any likeness it may possibly have to other objects cannot be manifest to perception, but can be discerned only by reason. If the constant relations among its parts make it an entity, the question arises whether these constant relations among its parts are akin to the constant relations among the parts of other entities. Between a society and anything else, the only conceivable resemblance must be one due to *parallelism of principle in the arrangement of components*.

There are two great classes of aggregates with which the social aggregate may be compared—the inorganic and the organic. Are the attributes of a society in any way like those of a non-living body—or are they in any way like those of a living body? or are they entirely unlike those of both?

Reprinted from Robert L. Carneiro, ed., *The Principles of Sociology* (Chicago: University of Chicago Press, 1967), by permission of the publisher.

The first of these questions needs only to be asked to be answered in the negative. A whole of which the parts are alive cannot, in its general characters, be like lifeless wholes. The second question, not to be thus promptly answered, is to be answered in the affirmative. The reasons for asserting that the permanent relations among the parts of a society are analogous to the permanent relations among the parts of a living body we have now to consider.

A SOCIETY IS AN ORGANISM

When we say that growth is common to social aggregates and organic aggregates we do not thus entirely exclude community with inorganic aggregates. Some of these, as crystals, grow in a visible manner, and all of them, on the hypothesis of evolution, have arisen by integration at some time or other. Nevertheless, compared with things we call inanimate, living bodies and societies so conspicuously exhibit augmentation of mass that we may fairly regard this as characterizing them both. Many organisms grow throughout their lives and the rest grow throughout considerable parts of their lives. Social growth usually continues either up to times when the societies divide or up to times when they are overwhelmed.

Here, then, is the first trait by which societies ally themselves with the organic world and substantially distinguish themselves from the inorganic world.

It is also a character of social bodies, as of living bodies, that while they increase in size they increase in structure. Like a low animal, the embryo of a high one has few distinguishable parts, but while it is acquiring greater mass, its parts multiply and differentiate. It is thus with a society. At first the unlikenesses among its groups of units are inconspicuous in number and degree, but as population augments, divisions and subdivisions become more numerous and more decided. Further, in the social organism as in the individual organism, differentiations cease only with that completion of the type which marks maturity and precedes decay.

Though in inorganic aggregates also, as in the entire solar system and in each of its members, structural differentiations accompany the integrations, yet these are so relatively slow and so relatively simple that they may be disregarded. The multiplication of contrasted parts in bodies politic and in living bodies is so great that it substantially constitutes another common character which marks them off from inorganic bodies.

This community will be more fully appreciated on observing that progressive differentiation of structures is accompanied by progressive differentiation of functions.

The divisions, primary, secondary, and tertiary, which arise in a developing animal, do not assume their major and minor unlikenesses to no purpose. Along with diversities in their shapes and compositions go diversities in the actions they perform: they grow into unlike organs having unlike duties. Assuming the entire function of absorbing nutriment at the same time that it takes on its structural characters, the alimentary system becomes gradually marked off into contrasted portions, each of which has a special function forming part of the general function. A limb, instrumental to locomotion or prehension, acquires divisions and subdivisions which perform their leading and their subsidiary shares in this office.

So is it with the parts into which a society divides. A dominant class arising does not simply become unlike the rest, but assumes control over the rest; when this class separates into the more and the less dominant, these again begin to discharge distinct parts of the entire control. With the classes whose actions are controlled it is the same. The various groups into which they fall have various occupations: each of such groups also, within itself, acquiring minor contrasts of parts along with minor contrasts of duties.

And here we see more clearly how the two classes of things we are comparing distinguish themselves from things of other classes, for such differences of structure as slowly arise in inorganic aggregates are not accompanied by what we can fairly call differences of function.

Why in a body politic and in a living body these unlike actions of unlike parts are properly regarded by us as functions, while we cannot so regard the unlike actions of unlike parts in an inorganic body, we shall perceive on turning to the next and most distinctive common trait.

Evolution establishes in them both, not differences simply, but definitely connected differences—differences such that each makes the others possible. The parts of an inorganic aggregate are so related that one may change greatly without appreciably affecting the rest. It is otherwise with the parts of an organic aggregate or of a social aggregate. In either of these, the changes in the parts are mutually determined, and the changed actions of the parts are mutually dependent. In both, too, this mutuality increases as the evolution advances. The lowest type of animal is all stomach, all respiratory surface, all limb. Development of a type having appendages by which to move about or lay hold of food can take place only if these appendages, losing power to absorb nutriment directly from surrounding bodies, are supplied with nutriment by parts which retain the power of absorption. A respiratory surface to which the circulating fluids are brought to be aerated can be formed only on condition that the concomitant loss of ability to supply itself with materials for repair and growth is made good by the development of a structure bringing these materials.

Similarly in a society. What we call with perfect propriety its organization, necessarily implies traits of the same kind. While rudimentary, a society is all warrior, all hunter, all hut-builder, all tool-maker: every part fulfils for itself all needs. Progress to a stage characterized by a permanent army can go on only as there arise arrangements for supplying that army with food, clothes, and munitions of war by the rest. If here the population occupies itself solely with agriculture and there with mining—if these manufacture goods while those distribute them—it must be on condition that in exchange for a special kind of service rendered by each part to other parts, these other parts severally give due proportions of their services.

This division of labor, first dwelt on by political economists as a social phenomenon, and thereupon recognized by biologists as a phenomenon of living bodies, which they called the "physiological division of labor," is that which in the society, as in the animal, makes it a living whole. Scarcely can I emphasize enough the truth that in respect of this fundamental trait a social organism and an individual organism are entirely alike. When we see that in a mammal arresting the lungs quickly brings the heart to a stand, that if the stomach fails absolutely in its office all other parts by-and-by cease to act, that paralysis of its limbs entails on the body at large death from want of food or inability to escape, that loss of even such small organs as the eyes deprives the rest of a service essential to their preservation, we cannot but admit that mutual dependence of parts is an essential characteristic. And when, in a society, we see that the workers in iron stop if the miners do not supply materials, that makers of clothes cannot carry on their business in the absence of those who spin and weave textile fabrics, that the manufacturing community will cease to act unless the food-producing and food-distributing agencies are acting, that the controlling powers, governments, bureaus, judicial officers, police, must fail to keep order when the necessaries of life are not supplied to them by the parts kept in order, we are obliged to say that this mutual dependence of parts is similarly rigorous. Unlike as the two kinds of aggregate otherwise are, they are alike in respect of this fundamental character, and the characters implied by it.

How the combined actions of mutually dependent parts constitute life of the whole, and how there hence results a parallelism between social life and animal life, we see still more clearly on learning that the life of every visible organism is constituted by the lives of units too minute to be seen by the unaided eye.

An undeniable illustration is furnished by the strange order *Myxomycetes.* The spores or germs produced by one of these forms become ciliated monads which, after a time of active locomotion, change into shapes like those of amoebae, move about, take in nutriment, grow, multiply by fission. Then these amoeba-form individuals swarm together, begin to coalesce into groups, and these groups to coalesce with one another, making a mass sometimes barely visible, sometimes as big as the hand. This *plasmodium*, irregular, mostly reticulated, and in substance gelatinous, itself exhibits movements of its parts like those of a gigantic rhizopod, creeping slowly over surfaces of decaying matters, and even up the stems of plants. Here, then, union of many minute living individuals to form a relatively vast aggregate in which their individualities are apparently lost but the life of which results from combination of their lives, is demonstrable. . . .

The relation between the lives of the units and the life of the aggregate has a further character common to the two cases. By a catastrophe the life of the aggregate may be destroyed without immediately destroying the lives of all its units, while, on the other hand, if no catastrophe abridges it, the life of the aggregate is far longer than the lives of its units.

In a cold-blooded animal, ciliated cells perform their motions with perfect regularity long after the creature they are part of has become motionless. Muscular fibers retain their power of contracting under stimulation. The cells of secreting organs go on pouring out their product if blood is artificially supplied to them. And the components of an entire organ, as the heart, continue their cooperation for many hours after its detachment.

Similarly, arrest of those commercial activities, governmental coordinations, etc., which constitute the corporate life of a nation may be caused, say by an inroad of barbarians, without immediately stopping the actions of all the units. Certain classes of these, especially the widely diffused ones engaged in food-production, may long survive and carry on their individual occupations.

On the other hand, the minute living elements composing a developed animal severally evolve, play their parts, decay, and are replaced, while the animal as a whole continues. In the deep layer of the skin, cells are formed by fission which, as they enlarge, are thrust outwards, and, becoming flattened to form the epidermis, eventually exfoliate, while the younger ones beneath take their places. Liver-cells, growing by imbibition of matters from which they separate the bile, presently die, and their vacant seats are occupied by another generation. Even bone, though so dense and seemingly inert, is permeated by blood vessels carrying materials to replace old components by new ones. And the replacement, rapid in some tissues and in others slow, goes on at such rate that during the continued existence of the entire body each portion of it has been many times over produced and destroyed.

Thus it is also with a society and its units. Integrity of the whole as of each large division is perennially maintained, notwithstanding the deaths of component citizens. The fabric of living persons which, in a manufacturing town, produces some commodity for national use, remains after a century as large a fabric, though all the masters and workers who a century ago composed it have long since disappeared. Even with minor parts of this industrial structure the like holds. A firm that dates from past generations, still carrying on business in the name of its founder, has had all its members and employees changed one by one, perhaps several times over, while the firm has continued to occupy the same place and to maintain like relations with buyers and sellers. Throughout we find this. Governing bodies, general and local, ecclesiastical corporations, armies, institutions of all orders down to guilds, clubs, philanthropic associations, etc., show us a continuity of life exceeding that of the persons constituting them. Nay, more. As part of the same law, we see that the existence of the society at large exceeds in duration that of some of the compound parts. Private unions, local public bodies, secondary national institutions, towns carrying on special industries, may decay, while the nation, maintaining its integrity, evolves in mass and structure.

In both cases, too, the mutually dependent functions of the various divisions, being severally made up of the actions of many units, it results that these units dying one by one, are replaced without the function in which they share being sensibly affected. In a muscle, each sarcous element wearing out in its turn, is removed and a substitution made while the rest carry on their combined contractions as usual; the retirement of a public official or death of a shopman perturbs inappreciably the business of the department, or activity of the industry, in which he had a share.

Hence arises in the social organism, as in the individual organism, a life of the whole quite unlike the lives of the units, though it is a life produced by them.

From these likenesses between the social organism and the individual organism we must now turn to an extreme unlikeness. The parts of an animal form a concrete whole, but the parts of a society form a whole which is discrete. While the living units composing the one are bound together in close contact, the living units composing the other are free, are not in contact, and are more or less widely dispersed. How, then, can there be any parallelism? . . .

Though coherence among its parts is a prerequisite to that cooperation by which the life of an individual organism is carried on, and though the members of a social organism, not forming a concrete whole, cannot maintain cooperation by means of physical influences directly propagated from part to part, yet they can and do maintain cooperation by another agency. Not in contact, they nevertheless affect one another through intervening spaces, both by emotional language and by the language, oral and written, of the intellect. For carrying on mutually dependent actions it is requisite that impulses, adjusted in their kinds, amounts, and times, shall be conveyed from part to part. This requisite is fulfilled in living bodies by molecular waves that are indefinitely diffused in low types and in high types are carried along definite channels (the function of which has been significantly called *internuncial*). It is fulfilled in societies by the signs of feelings and thoughts conveyed from person to person, at first in vague ways and only through short distances, but afterwards more definitely and through greater distances. That is to say, the internuncial function, not achievable by stimuli physically transferred, is nevertheless achieved by language—emotional and intellectual.

That mutual dependence of parts which constitutes organization is thus effectually established. Though discrete instead of concrete, the social aggregate is rendered a living whole. . . .

Let us now . . . sum up the reasons for regarding a society as an organism.

It undergoes continuous growth. As it grows, its parts become unlike: it exhibits increase of structure. The unlike parts simultaneously assume activities of unlike kinds. These activities are not simply different, but their differences are so related as to make one another possible. The reciprocal aid thus given causes mutual dependence of the parts. And the mutually dependent parts, living by and for one another, form an aggregate constituted on the same general principle as is an individual organism. The analogy of a society to an organism becomes still clearer on learning that every organism of appreciable size is a society, and on further learning that in both, the lives of the units continue for some time if the life of the aggregate is suddenly arrested, while if the aggregate is not destroyed by violence, its life greatly exceeds in duration the lives of its units. Though the two are contrasted as respectively discrete and concrete, and though there results a difference in the ends subserved by the organization, there does not result a difference in the laws of the organization: the required mutual influences of the parts, not transmissible in a direct way, being, in a society, transmitted in an indirect way.

Having thus considered in their most general forms the reasons for regarding a society as an organism, we are prepared for following out the comparison in detail.

SOCIAL GROWTH

Societies, like living bodies, begin as germs—originate from masses which are extremely minute in comparison with the masses some of them eventually reach. That out of small wandering hordes have arisen the largest societies, is a conclusion not to be contested. The implements of prehistoric peoples, ruder even than existing savages use, imply absence of those arts by which alone great aggregations of men are made possible. Religious ceremonies that survived among ancient historic races pointed back to a time when the progenitors of those races had flint knives, and got fire by rubbing together pieces of wood, and must have lived in such small clusters as are alone possible before the rise of agriculture.

The implication is that by integrations, direct and indirect, there have in course of time been produced social aggregates a million times in size the aggregates which alone existed in the remote past. Here, then, is a growth reminding us, by its degree, of growth in living bodies.

Between this trait of organic evolution and the answering trait of superorganic evolution, there is a further parallelism: the growths in aggregates of different classes are extremely various in their amounts.

Glancing over the entire assemblage of animal types, we see that the members of one large class, the *Protozoa*, rarely increase beyond the microscopic size with which every higher animal begins. Among the multitudinous kinds of *Coelenterata*, the masses range from that of the small hydra to that of the large medusa. The annulose and molluscous types respectively show us immense contrasts between their superior and inferior members. And the vertebrate animals, much larger on the average than the rest, display among themselves enormous differences.

Kindred unlikenesses of size strike us when we contemplate the entire assemblage of human societies. Scattered over many regions there are minute hordes—still extant samples of the primordial type of society. We have Wood Veddas living sometimes in pairs, and only now and then assembling; we have Bushmen wandering about in families, and forming larger groups but occasionally; we have Fuegians clustered by the dozen or the score. Tribes of Australians, of Tasmanians, of Andamanese, are variable within the limits of perhaps twenty to fifty. And similarly, if the region is inhospitable, as with the Eskimos, or if the arts of life are undeveloped, as with the Digger Indians, or if adjacent higher races are obstacles to growth, as with Indian Hill tribes like the Juangs, this limitation to primitive size continues. Where a fruitful soil affords much food, and where a more settled life, leading to agriculture, again increases the supply of food, we meet with larger social aggregates: instance those in the Polynesian Islands and in many parts of Africa. Here a hundred or two, here several thousands, here many thousands, are held together more or less completely as one mass. And then in the highest societies, instead of partially aggregated thousands, we have completely aggregated millions.

The growths of individual and social organisms are allied in another respect. In each case size augments by two processes which go on sometimes separately, sometimes together. There is increase by simple multiplication of units, causing enlargement of the group; there is increase by union of groups, and again by union of groups of groups. The first parallelism is too simple to need illustration but the facts which show us the second must be set forth.

Organic integration, treated of at length in the *Principles of Biology*, must be here summarized to make the comparison intelligible. . . . The smallest animal, like the smallest plant, is essentially a minute group of living molecules. There are many forms and stages showing us the clustering of such smallest animals. Sometimes, as in the compound *Vorticellae* and in the sponges, their individualities are scarcely at all masked; but as evolution of the composite aggregate advances, the individualities of the component aggregates become less distinct. In some *Coelenterata*, though they retain considerable independence, which they show by moving about like amoebae when separated, they have their individualities mainly merged in that of the aggregate formed of them: instance the common hydra. Tertiary aggregates similarly result from the massing of secondary ones. . . .

Social growth proceeds by an analogous compounding and recompounding. The primitive social group, like the primitive group of living molecules with which organic evolution begins, never attains any considerable size by simple increase. Where, as among Fuegians, the supplies of wild food yielded by an inclement habitat will not enable more than a score or so to live in the same place—where, as among Andamanese, limited to a strip of shore backed by impenetrable bush, forty is about the number of individuals who can find prey without going too far from their temporary abode (Mouat 1863:300)—where, as among Bushmen, wandering over barren tracts, small hordes are alone possible and even families "are sometimes obliged to separate, since the same spot will not afford sufficient sustenance for all" (Lichtenstein 1812–

1815, II:194), we have extreme instances of the limitation of simple groups, and the formation of migrating groups when the limit is passed.

Even in tolerably productive habitats, fission of the groups is eventually necessitated in a kindred manner. Spreading as its number increases, a primitive tribe presently reaches a diffusion at which its parts become incoherent, and it then gradually separates into tribes that become distinct as fast as their continually diverging dialects pass into different languages. Often nothing further happens than repetition of this. Conflicts of tribes, dwindlings or extinctions of some, growths and spontaneous divisions of others, continue.

The formation of a larger society results only by the joining of such smaller societies, which occurs without obliterating the divisions previously caused by separations. This process may be seen now going on among uncivilized races, as it once went on among the ancestors of the civilized races. Instead of absolute independence of small hordes, such as the lowest savages show us, more advanced savages show us slight cohesions among larger hordes. In North America each of the three great tribes of Comanches consists of various bands having such feeble combination only as results from the personal character of the great chief (Schoolcraft 1853–1856, I:260; Bollaert 1850:267). So of the Dakotas there are, according to Burton (1861:116), seven principal bands, each including minor bands, numbering altogether, according to Catlin, forty-two (1876, I:209). And in like manner the five Iroquois nations had severally eight tribes.

Closer unions of these slightly coherent original groups arise under favorable conditions, but they only now and then become permanent. A common form of the process is that described by Mason as occurring among the Karens (1868:130). "Each village, with its scant domain, is an independent state, and every chief a prince; but now and then a little Napoleon arises, who subdues a kingdom to himself, and builds up an empire. The dynasties, however, last only with the controlling mind." The like happens in Africa. Livingstone says, "Formerly all the Maganja were united under the government of their great Chief, Undi; . . . but after Undi's death it fell to pieces. . . . This has been the inevitable fate of every African Empire from time immemorial" (ref. lost).

Only occasionally does there result a compound social aggregate that endures for a considerable period, as Dahomey or as Ashanti, which is "an assemblage of states owing a kind of feudal obedience to the sovereign" (Beecham 1841:86). The histories of Madagascar and of sundry Polynesian islands also display these transitory compound groups, out of which at length come in some cases permanent ones. During the earliest times of the extinct civilized races, like stages were passed through. In the words of Maspero, Egypt was "divided at first into a great number of tribes, which at several points simultaneously began to establish small independent states, every one of which had its laws and its worship" (1878:18). The compound groups of Greeks first formed were those minor ones resulting from the subjugation of weaker towns by stronger neighboring towns. And in northern Europe during pagan days the numerous German tribes, each with its cantonal divisions, illustrated this second stage of aggregation.

After such compound societies are consolidated, repetition of the process on a larger scale produces doubly compound societies which, usually cohering but feebly, become in some cases quite coherent. Maspero infers that the Egyptian nomes described above as resulting from integrations of tribes, coalesced into the two great principalities, Upper Egypt and Lower Egypt, which were eventually united, the small states becoming provinces. The boasting records of Mesopotamian kings similarly show us this union of unions going on. So, too, in Greece the integration at first occurring locally, began afterwards to combine the minor societies into two confederacies. During Roman days there arose for defensive purposes federations of tribes which eventually consolidated, and subsequently these were compounded into still larger aggregates. Before and after the Christian era, the like happened throughout northern Europe. Then after a period of vague and varying combinations, there came, in later times, as is well illustrated by French history, a massing of small feudal territories into provinces, and a subsequent massing of these into kingdoms.

So that in both organic and superorganic growths we see a process of compounding and recompounding carried to various stages. In both cases, after some consolidation of the smallest aggregates there comes the process of forming larger aggregates by union of them; in both cases repetition of this process makes secondary aggregates into tertiary ones.

Organic growth and superorganic growth have yet another analogy. As above said, increase by multiplication of individuals in a group and increase by union of groups may go on simultaneously, and it does this in both cases.

The original clusters, animal and social, are not only small, but they lack density. Creatures of low types occupy large spaces considering the small quantities of animal substance they contain, and low-type societies spread over areas that are wide relatively to the numbers of their component individuals. But as integration in animals is shown by concentration as well as by increase of bulk, so that social integration which results from the clustering of clusters is joined with augmentation of the number contained by each cluster. If we contrast the sprinklings in regions inhabited by wild tribes with the crowds filling equal regions in Europe or if we contrast the density of population in England under the Heptarchy with its present density, we see that besides the growth produced by union of groups there has gone on interstitial growth. Just as the higher animal has become not only larger than the lower but more solid, so, too, has the higher society.

Social growth, then, equally with the growth of a living body, shows us the fundamental trait of evolution under a twofold aspect. Integration is displayed both in the formation of a larger mass and in the progress of such mass towards that coherence due to closeness of parts.

It is proper to add, however, that there is a model of social growth to which organic growth affords no parallel—that caused by the migration of units from one society to another. Among many primitive groups and a few developed ones this is a considerable factor but, generally, its effect bears so small a ratio to the effects of growth by increase of population and coalescence of groups that it does not much qualify the analogy.

SOCIAL STRUCTURES

to complete

In societies, as in living bodies, increase of mass is habitually accompanied by increase of structure. Along with that integration which is the primary trait of evolution, both exhibit in high degrees the secondary trait, differentiation.

The association of these two characters in animals was described in the *Principles of Biology*, § 44. Excluding certain low kinds of them whose activities are little above those of plants, we recognized the general law that large aggregates have high organizations. The qualifications of this law which go along with differences of medium, of habitat, of type, are numerous but when made they leave intact the truth that for carrying on the combined life of an extensive mass, involved arrangements are required.

So, too, is it with societies. As we progress from small groups to larger, from simple groups to compound groups, from compound groups to doubly compound ones, the unlikenesses of parts increase. The social aggregate, homogeneous when minute, habitually gains in heterogeneity along with each increment of growth, and to reach great size must acquire great complexity. Let us glance at the leading stages.

Naturally in a state like that of the Cayaguas or Wood-Indians of South America, so little social that "one family lives at a distance from another," social organization is impossible and even where there is some slight association of families, organization does not arise while they are few and wandering (Southey 1810–1819, II:373). Groups of Eskimos, of Australians, of Bushmen, of Fuegians, are without even that primary contrast of parts implied by settled chieftainship. Their members are subject to no control but such as is temporarily acquired by the stronger, or more cunning, or more experienced; not even a permanent nucleus is present. Habitually where larger simple groups exist, we find some kind of head. Though not a uniform rule (for, as we shall hereafter see, the genesis of a controlling agency depends on the nature of the social activities), this is a general rule. The headless clusters, wholly ungoverned, are incoherent, and separate before they acquire considerable sizes; but along with maintenance of an aggregate approaching to, or exceeding, a hundred, we ordinarily find a simple or compound ruling agency—one or more men claiming and exercising authority that is natural, or supernatural, or both. This is the first social differentiation.

Soon after it there frequently comes another, tending to form a division between regulative and operative parts. In the lowest tribes this is rudely represented only by the contrast in status between the sexes: the men, having unchecked control, carry on such external activities as the tribe shows us, chiefly in war, while the women are made drudges who perform the less skilled parts of the process of sustentation. But that tribal growth, and establishment of chieftainship, which gives military superiority, presently causes enlargement of the operative part by adding captives to it. This begins unobtrusively. While in battle the men are killed, and often afterwards eaten, the noncombatants are enslaved. Patagonians, for example, make slaves of women and children taken in war (Fitzroy 1839, II:166). Later, and especially when cannibalism ceases, comes the enslavement of male captives, whence results, in some cases, an operative part clearly marked off from the regulative part. Among the Chinooks, "slaves do all the laborious work" (Ross 1849:92). We read that the Beluchi, avoiding the hard labor of cultivation, impose it on the Jutts, the ancient inhabitants whom they have subjugated (Postans 1848:112). Beecham says it is usual on the Gold Coast to make the slaves clear the ground for cultivation (1841:136). And among the Felatahs "slaves are numerous: the males are employed in weaving, collecting wood or grass, or on any other kind of work; some of the women are engaged in spinning . . . in preparing the yarn for the loom, others in pounding and grinding corn, etc." (Denham *et al.* 1828, II:94).

Along with that increase of mass caused by union of primary social aggregates into a secondary one, a further unlikeness of parts arises. The holding together of the compound cluster implies a head of the whole as well as heads of the parts, and a differentiation analogous to that which originally produced a chief, now produces a chief of chiefs. Sometimes the combination is made for defense against a common foe, and sometimes it results from conquest by one tribe of the rest. In this last case the predominant tribe, in maintaining its supremacy, develops more highly its military character, thus becoming unlike the others.

After such clusters of clusters have been so consolidated that their united powers can be wielded by one governing agency, there come alliances with, or subjugations of, other clusters of clusters, ending from time to time in coalescence. When this happens there results still greater complexity in the governing agency, with its king, local rulers, and petty chiefs; and at the same time, there arise more marked divisions of classes—military, priestly, slave, etc. Clearly, then, complication of structure accompanies increase of mass.

This increase of heterogeneity, which in both classes of aggregates goes along with growth, presents another trait in common. Beyond unlikenesses of parts due to development of the coordinating agencies, there presently follow unlikenesses among the agencies coordinated—the organs of alimentation, etc., in the one case, and the industrial structures in the other.

When animal-aggregates of the lowest order unite to form one of a higher order, and when, again, these secondary aggregates are compounded into tertiary aggregates, each component is at first similar to the other components, but in the course of evolution dissimilarities arise and become more and more decided. Among the *Coelenterata* the stages are clearly indicated. From the sides of a common hydra bud out young ones which, when fully developed, separate from their parent. In the compound hydroids the young polyps produced in like manner remain permanently attached and, themselves repeating the process, presently form a branched aggregate. When the members of the compound group lead similar and almost independent lives, as in various rooted genera, they remain similar save those of them which become reproductive organs. But in the floating and swimming clusters, formed by a kindred process, the differently conditioned members become different, while assuming different functions.

It is thus with the minor social groups combined into a major social group. Each tribe originally had within itself such feebly marked industrial divisions as sufficed for its low kind of life, and these were like those of each other tribe. But union facilitates exchange of commodities and if, as mostly happens, the component tribes severally occupy localities favorable to unlike kinds of production, unlike occupations are initiated, and there result unlikenesses of industrial structures. Even between tribes not united, as those of Australia, barter of products furnished by their respective habitats goes on so long as war does not hinder. And evidently when there is reached such a stage of integration as in Madagascar, or as in the chief Negro states of Africa, the internal peace that follows subordination to one government makes commercial intercourse easy. The like parts being permanently held together, mutual dependence becomes possible and along with growing mutual dependence the parts grow unlike.

The advance of organization which thus follows the advance of aggregation, alike in individual organisms and in social organisms, conforms in both cases to the same general law: differentiations proceed from the more general to the more special. First broad and simple contrasts of parts, then within each of the parts primarily contrasted, changes which make unlike divisions of them, then within each of these unlike divisions, minor unlikenesses, and so on continually.

The successive stages in the development of a vertebrate column illustrate this law in animals. At the outset an elongated depression of the blastoderm, called the "primitive groove," represents the entire cerebrospinal axis; as yet there are no marks of vertebrae, nor even a contrast between the part which is to become head and the part which is to become backbone. Presently the ridges bounding this groove, growing up and folding over more rapidly at the anterior end, which at the same time widens, begin to make the skull distinguishable from the spine, and the commencement of segmentation in the spinal part, while the cephalic part remains unsegmented, strengthens the contrast. Within each of these main divisions minor divisions soon arise. The rudimentary cranium, bending forward, simultaneously acquires three dilatations indicating the contained nervous centers, while the segmentation of the spinal column, spreading to its ends, produces an almost-uniform series of "proto-vertebrae." At first these proto-vertebrae not only differ very little from one another, but each is relatively simple—a quadrate mass. Gradually this almost-uniform series falls into unlike divisions—the cervical group, the dorsal group, the lumbar group; and while the series of vertebrae is thus becoming specialized in its different regions, each vertebra is changing from that general form which it at first had in common with the rest, to the more special form eventually distinguishing it from the rest. Throughout the embryo there are, at the same time, going on kindred processes which, first making each large part unlike all other large parts, then make the parts of that part unlike one another.

During social evolution analogous metamorphoses may everywhere be traced. The rise of the structure exercising religious control will serve as an example. In simple tribes, and in clusters of tribes during their early stages of aggregation, we find men who are at once sorcerers, priests, diviners, exorcists, doctors—men who deal with supposed supernatural beings in all the various possible ways: propitiating them, seeking knowledge and aid from them, commanding them, subduing them. Along with advance in social integration, there come both differences of function and differences of rank. In Tanna "there are rain makers . . . and a host of other 'sacred men' " (Turner 1861:89); in Fiji there are not only priests, but seers (Williams and Calvert 1858, I:229); among the Hawaiian Islanders there are diviners as well as priests (Ellis 1826:118); among the New Zealanders, Thomson distinguishes between priests and sorcerers (1859, I:116); and among the Kaffirs, besides diviners and rain makers, there are two classes of doctors who respectively rely on supernatural and on natural agents in curing their patients (Backhouse 1844:230).

More advanced societies, as those of ancient America, show us still greater multiformity of this once-uniform group. In Mexico, for example, the medical class, descending from a class of sorcerers who dealt antagonistically with the supernatural agents supposed to cause disease, were distinct from the priests, whose dealings with supernatural agents were propitiatory. Further, the sacerdotal class included several kinds, dividing the religious offices among them—sacrificers, diviners, singers, composers of hymns, instructors of youth; and then there were also gradations of ranks in each (Clavigero 1787, I:272).

This progress from general to special in priesthoods has, in the higher nations, led to such marked distinctions that the original kinships are forgotten. The priest-astrologers of ancient races were initiators of the scientific class, now variously specialized; from the priest-doctors of old have come the medical class with its chief division and minor divisions; while within the clerical class proper have arisen not only various ranks from pope down to acolyte, but various kinds of functionaries—dean, priest, deacon, chorister, as well as others classed as curates and chaplains. Similarly if we trace the genesis of any industrial structure, as that which from primitive blacksmiths who smelt their own iron as well as make implements from it, brings us to our iron-manufacturing districts, where preparation of the metal is separated into smelting, refining, puddling, rolling, and where turning this metal into implements is divided into various businesses.

The transformation here illustrated is, indeed, an aspect of that transformation of the homogeneous into the heterogeneous which everywhere characterizes evolution; but the truth to be noted is that it characterizes the evolution of individual organisms and of social organisms in especially high degrees.

Closer study of the facts shows us another striking parallelism. Organs in animals and organs in societies have internal arrangements framed on the same principle.

Differing from one another as the viscera of a living creature do in many respects, they have several traits in common. Each viscus contains appliances for conveying nutriment to its parts, for bringing it materials on which to operate, for carrying away the product, for draining off waste matters, as also for regulating its activity. Though liver and kidneys are unlike in their general appearances and minute structures, as well as in the offices they fulfil, the one as much as the other has a system of arteries, a system of veins, a system of lymphatics—has branched channels through which its excretions escape, and nerves for exciting and checking it. In large measure the like is true of those higher organs which, instead of elaborating and purifying and distributing the blood, aid the general life by carrying on external actions—the nervous and muscular organs. These, too, have their ducts for bringing prepared materials, ducts for drafting off vitiated materials, ducts for carrying away effete matters; as also their controlling nerve cells and fibers. So that, along with the many marked differences of structure, there are these marked communities of structure.

It is the same in a society. The clustered citizens forming an organ which produces some commodity for national use, or which otherwise satisfies national wants, has within it subservient structures substantially like those of each other organ carrying on each other function. Be it a cotton-weaving district or a district where cutlery is made, it has a set of agencies which bring the raw material, and a set of agencies which collect and send away the manufactured articles; it has an apparatus of major and minor channels through which the necessaries of life are drafted out of the general stocks circulating through the kingdom, and brought home to the local workers and those who direct them; it has appliances, postal and other, for bringing those impulses by which the industry of the place is excited or checked; it has local controlling powers, political and ecclesiastical, by which order is maintained and healthful action furthered. So, too, when, from a district which secretes certain goods we turn to a seaport which absorbs and sends out goods, we find the distributing and restraining agencies are mostly the same. Even where the social organ, instead of carrying on a material activity, has, like a university, the office of preparing certain classes of units for social functions of particular kinds, this general type of structure is repeated: the appliances for local sustentation and regulation, differing in some respects, are similar in essentials—there are like classes of distributors, like classes for civil control, and a specially-developed class for ecclesiastical control.

On observing that this community of structure among social organs, like the community of structure among organs in a living body, necessarily accompanies mutual dependence, we shall see even more clearly than hitherto how great is the likeness of nature between individual organization and social organization.

One more structural analogy must be named. The formation of organs in a living body proceeds in ways which we may distinguish as primary, secondary, and tertiary, and, paralleling them, there are primary, secondary, and tertiary ways in which social organs are formed. We will look at each of the three parallelisms by itself.

In animals of low types, bile is secreted, not by a liver, but by separate cells imbedded in the wall of the intestine at one part. These cells individually perform their function of separating certain matters from the blood, and individually pour out what they separate. No organ, strictly so-called, exists, but only a number of units not yet aggregated into an organ.

This is analogous to the incipient form of an individual structure in a society. At first each worker carries on his occupation alone, and himself disposes of the product to consumers. The arrangement still extant in our villages, where the cobbler at his own fireside makes and sells boots, and where the blacksmith single-handed does what iron-work is needed by his neighbors, exemplifies the primitive type of every producing structure. Among savages slight differentiations arise from individual aptitudes. Even of the degraded Fuegians, Fitzroy tells us that "one becomes an adept with the spear; another with the sling; another with a bow and arrow" (1839, II:186). As like differences of skill among members of primitive tribes cause some to become makers of special things, it results that necessarily the industrial organ begins as a social unit. Where, as among the Shasta Indians of California, arrow-making is a distinct profession, it is clear that manipulative superiority being the cause of the differentiation, the worker is at first single (Bancroft 1875–1876, I:343). And during subsequent periods of growth, even in small settled communities, this type continues. The statement that among the Coast Negroes "the most ingenious man in the village is usually the blacksmith; joiner, architect, and weaver" (Winterbottom 1803, I:89), while it shows us artisan functions in an undifferentiated stage, also shows us how completely individual is the artisan structure; the implication being that as the society grows, it is by the addition of more such individuals, severally carrying on their occupations independently, that the additional demand is met.

By two simultaneous changes an incipient secreting organ in an animal reaches that higher structure with which our next comparison may be made. The cells pass from a scattered cluster into a compact cluster, and they severally become compound. In place of a single cell elaborating and emitting its special product we now have a small elongated sac containing a family of cells, and this, through an opening at one end, gives exit to their products. At the same time there is formed an integrated group of such follicles, each containing secreting units and having its separate orifice of discharge.

To this type of individual organ we find, in semi-civilized societies, a type of social organ closely corresponding. In one of these settled and growing communities the demands upon individual workers, now more specialized in their occupations, have become unceasing, and each worker, occasionally pressed by work, makes helpers of his children. This practice, beginning incidentally, establishes itself, and eventually it grows into an imperative custom that each man shall bring up his boys to his own trade. Illustrations of this stage are numerous. Skilled occupation, "like every other calling and office in Peru, always descended from father to son. The division of castes, in this particular, was as precise as that which existed in Egypt or Hindostan" (Prescott 1847, I:138). In Mexico, too, "the sons in general learned the trades of their fathers, and embraced their professions" (Clavigero 1787, I:338). The like was true of the industrial structures of European nations in early times. By the Theodosian code a Roman youth "was compelled to follow the employment of his father . . . and the suitor who sought the hand of the daughter could only obtain his bride by becoming wedded to the calling of her family" (Palgrave 1832, I:332).

In medieval France handicrafts were inherited, and the old English periods were characterized by a like usage. Branching of the family through generations into a number of kindred families carrying on the same occupation, produced the germ of the guild, and the related families who monopolized each industry formed a cluster habitually occupying the same quarter. Hence the still extant names of many streets in English towns—"Fellmonger, Horsemonger, and Fleshmonger, Shoewright and Shieldwright, Turner and Salter Streets" (Kemble 1849, II:340), a segregation like that which still persists in Oriental bazaars.

And now, on observing how one of these industrial quarters was composed of many allied families, each containing sons working under direction of a father, who while sharing in the work sold the produce, and who, if the family and business were large, became mainly a channel taking in raw material and giving out the manufactured article, we see that there existed an anology to the kind of glandular organ described above, which consists of a number of adjacent cell-containing follicles having separate mouths.

A third stage of the analogy may be traced. Along with that increase of a glandular organ necessitated by the more active functions of a more developed animal there goes a change of structure consequent on augmentation of bulk. If the follicles multiply while their ducts have all to be brought to one spot, it results that their orifices, increasingly numerous, occupy a larger area of the wall of the cavity which receives the discharge, and if lateral extension of this area is negatived by the functional requirements, it results that the needful area is gained by formation of a caecum. Further need of the same kind leads to secondary caeca diverging from this main caecum, which hence becomes, in part, a duct. Thus is at length evolved a large viscus, such as a liver, having a single main duct with ramifying branches running throughout its mass.

Now we rise from the above-described kind of industrial organ by parallel stages to a higher kind. There is no sudden leap from the household type to the factory type, but a gradual transition. The first step is shown us in those rules of trade guilds under which, to the members of the family, might be added an apprentice (possibly at first a relation) who, as Brentano (1870: 129–130) says, "became a member of the family of his master, who instructed him in his trade, and who, like a father, had to watch over his morals, as well as his work"; practically an adopted son. This modification having been established, there followed the employing of apprentices who had changed into journeymen. With development of this modified household group the master grew into a seller of goods made, not by his own family only, but by others and, as his business enlarged, necessarily ceased to be a worker, and became wholly a distributor—a channel through which went out the products, not of a few sons, but of many unrelated artisans. This led the way to establishments in which the employed far outnumber the members of the family, until at length, with the use of mechanical power, came the factory—a series of rooms, each containing a crowd of producing units, and sending its tributary stream of product to join other streams before reaching the single place of exit. Finally, in greatly developed industrial organs, we see many factories clustered in the same town, and others in adjacent towns, to and from which, along branching roads, come the raw materials and go the bales of cloth, calico, etc.

There are instances in which a new industry passes through these stages in the course of a few generations, as happened with the stocking-manufacture. In the Midland counties, fifty years ago, the rattle and burr of a solitary stocking-frame came from a roadside cottage every here and there; the single worker made and sold his product. Presently arose workshops in which several such looms might be heard going: there was the father and his sons, with perhaps a journeyman. At length grew up the large building containing many looms driven by a steam engine; and finally many such large buildings in the same town.

These structural analogies reach a final phase that is still more striking. In both cases there is a contrast between the original mode of development and a substituted later mode.

In the general course of organic evolution from low types to high, there have been passed through by insensible modifications all the stages above described; but now, in the individual evolution of an organism of high type, these stages are greatly abridged, and an organ is produced by a comparatively direct process. Thus the liver of a mammalian embryo is formed by the accumulation of numerous cells, which presently grow into a mass projecting from the wall of the intestine, while simultaneously there dips down into it a caecum from the intestine. Transformation of this caecum into the hepatic duct takes place at the same time that within the mass of cells there arise minor ducts, connected with this main duct and there meanwhile go on other changes which, during evolution of the organ through successively higher types, came one after another.

In the formation of industrial organs the like happens. Now that the factory system is well-established—now that it has become ingrained in the social constitution—we see direct assumptions of it in all industries for which its fitness has been shown. If at one place the discovery of ore prompts the setting up of iron-works, or at another a special kind of water facilitates brewing, there is no passing through the early stages of single worker, family, clustered families, and so on, but there is a sudden drafting of materials and men to the spot, followed by formation of a producing structure of the advanced type. Nay, not one large establishment only is thus evolved after the direct manner, but a cluster of large establishments. At Barrow-in-Furness we see a town with its iron-works, its importing and exporting businesses, its extensive docks and means of communication, all in the space of a few years framed after that type which it has taken centuries to develop through successive modifications.

An allied but even more marked change in the evolutionary process is also common to both cases. Just as in the embryo of a high animal various organs have their important parts laid down out of their original order, in anticipation, as it were, so, with the body at large, it happens that entire organs which, during the serial genesis of the type, came comparatively late, come in the evolving individual comparatively soon. This, which Prof. Haeckel has called heterochrony, is shown us in the early marking out of the brain in a mammalian embryo, though in the lowest vertebrate animal no brain ever exists; or, again, in the segmentation of the spinal column before any alimentary system is formed, though, in a proto-vertebrate, even when its alimentary system is completed, there are but feeble signs of segmentation.

The analogous change of order in social evolution is shown us by new societies which inherit the confirmed habits of old ones. Instance the United States, where a town in the far west, laid down in its streets and plots, has its hotel, church, post-office, built while there are but few houses, and where a railway is run through the wilderness in anticipation of settlements. Or instance Australia, where a few years after the huts of gold diggers begin to cluster round new mines there is established a printing-office and journal, though, in the mother-country, centuries passed before a town of like size developed a like agency.

SOCIAL FUNCTIONS

Changes of structures cannot occur without changes of functions. Much that was said [previously] might, therefore, be said here with substituted terms. Indeed, as in societies many changes of structure are more indicated by changes of function than directly seen, it may be said that these last have been already described by implication.

There are, however, certain functional traits not manifestly implied by traits of structure. To these a few pages must be devoted.

If organization consists in such a construction of the whole that its parts can carry on mutually dependent actions, then in proportion as organization is high there must go a dependence of each part upon the rest so great that separation is fatal; and conversely. This truth is equally well shown in the individual organism and in the social organism.

The lowest animal-aggregates are so constituted that each portion, similar to every other in appearance, carries on similar actions, and here spontaneous or artificial separation interferes scarcely at all with the life of either separated portion. When the faintly differentiated speck of protoplasm forming a rhizopod is accidentally divided, each division goes on as before. So, too, it is with those aggregates of the second order in which the components remain substantially alike. The ciliated monads clothing the horny fibers of a living sponge need one another's aid so little that, when the sponge is cut in two, each half carries on its processes without interruption. Even where some unlikeness has arisen among the units, as in the familiar polyp, the perturbation caused by division is but temporary: the two or more portions resulting need only a little time for the units to rearrange themselves into fit forms before resuming their ordinary simple actions.

The like happens for the like reason with the lowest social aggregates. A headless wandering group of primitive men divides without any inconvenience. Each man, at once warrior, hunter, and maker of his own weapons, hut, etc., with a squaw who has in every case the like drudgeries to carry on, needs concert with his fellows only in war and to some extent in the chase, and, except for fighting, concert with half the tribe is as good as concert with the whole. Even where the slight differentiation implied by chieftainship exists, little inconvenience results from voluntary or enforced separation. Either before or after a part of the tribe migrates, some man becomes head, and such low social life as is possible recommences.

With highly organized aggregates of either kind it is very different. We cannot cut a mammal in two without causing immediate death. Twisting off the head of a fowl is fatal. Not even a reptile, though it may survive the loss of its tail, can live when its body is divided. And among annulose creatures it similarly happens that though in some inferior genera bisection does not kill either half, it kills both in an insect, an arachnid, or a crustacean.

If in high societies the effect of mutilation is less than in high animals, still it is great. Middlesex separated from its surroundings would in a few days have all its social processes stopped by lack of supplies. Cut off the cotton-district from Liverpool and other ports and there would come arrest of its industry followed by mortality of its people. Let a division be made between the coal-mining populations and adjacent populations which smelt metals or make broadcloth by machinery, and both, forthwith dying socially by arrest of their actions, would begin to die individually. Though when a civilized society is so divided that part of it is left without a central controlling agency it may presently evolve one, yet there is meanwhile much risk of dissolution, and before reorganization is efficient, a long period of disorder and weakness must be passed through.

So that the consensus of functions becomes closer as evolution advances. In low aggregates, both individual and social, the actions of the parts are but little dependent on one another, whereas in developed aggregates of both kinds that combination of actions which constitutes the life of the whole makes possible the component actions which constitute the lives of the parts.

Another corollary, manifest a priori and proved a posteriori, must be named. Where parts are little differentiated they can readily perform one another's functions, but where much differentiated they can perform one another's functions very imperfectly, or not at all.

Again the common polyp furnishes a clear illustration. One of these sack-shaped creatures admits of being turned inside out, so that the skin becomes stomach and the stomach becomes skin, each thereupon beginning to do the work of the other. The higher we rise in the scale of organization the less practicable do we find such exchanges. Still, to some extent, substitutions of functions remain possible in highly developed creatures. Even in man the skin shows a trace of its original absorptive power, now monopolized by the alimentary canal: it takes into the system certain small amounts of matter rubbed on to it. Such vicarious actions are, however, most manifest between parts having functions that are still allied. If, for instance, the bile-excreting function of the liver is impeded, other excretory organs, the kidneys and the skin, become channels through which bile is got rid of. If a cancer in the esophagus prevents swallowing, the arrested food, dilating the esophagus, forms a pouch in which imperfect digestion is set up. But these small abilities of the differentiated parts to discharge one another's duties are not displayed where they have diverged more widely. Though mucous membrane, continuous with skin at various orifices, will, if everted, assume to a considerable extent the characters and powers of skin, yet serous membrane will not; nor can bone or muscle undertake, for any of the viscera, portions of their functions if they fail.

In social organisms, low and high, we find these relatively great and relatively small powers of substitution. Of course, where each member of the tribe repeats every other in his mode of life, there are no unlike functions to be exchanged; and where there has arisen only that small differentiation implied by the barter of weapons for other articles, between one member of the tribe skilled in weapon-making and others less skilled, the destruction of this specially-skilled member entails no great evil, since the rest can severally do for themselves that which he did for them, though not quite so well. Even in settled societies of considerable sizes we find the like holds to a great degree. Of the ancient Mexicans, Zurita says, "Every Indian knows all handicrafts which do not require great skill or delicate instruments" (1840:183), and in Peru each man "was expected to be acquainted with the various handicrafts essential to domestic comfort" (Prescott 1847, I:138): the parts of the societies were so slightly differentiated in their occupations that assumption of one another's occupations remained practicable.

But in societies like our own, specialized industrially and otherwise in high degrees, the actions of one part which fails in its function cannot be assumed by other parts. Even the relatively unskilled farm laborers, were they to strike, would have their duties very inadequately performed by the urban population; and our iron manufacturers would be stopped if their trained artisans, refusing to work, had to be replaced by peasants or hands from cotton factories. Still less could the higher functions, legislative, judicial, etc., be effectually performed by coal miners and navvies.

Evidently the same reason for this contrast holds in the two cases. In proportion as the units forming any part of an individual organism are limited to one kind of action, as that of absorbing, or secreting, or contracting, or conveying an impulse, and become adapted to that action, they lose adaptation to other actions; and in the social organism the discipline required for effectually discharging a special duty causes unfitness for discharging special duties widely unlike it.

Beyond these two chief functional analogies between individual organisms and social organisms, that when they are little evolved, division or mutilation causes small inconvenience, but when they are much evolved it causes great perturbation or death, and that in low types of either kind the parts can assume one another's functions, but cannot in high types, sundry consequent functional analogies might be enlarged on did space permit.

There is the truth that in both kinds of organisms the vitality increases as fast as the functions become specialized. In either case, before there exist structures severally adapted for the unlike actions, these are ill-performed and in the absence of developed appliances for furthering it, the utilization of one another's services is but slight. But along with advance of organization, every part, more limited in its office, performs its office better; the means of exchanging benefits become greater; each aids all, and all aid each with increasing efficiency; and the total activity we call life, individual or national, augments.

REFERENCES

Backhouse, J.
    1844   A Narrative of a Visit to the Mauritius and South Africa. London.
Bancroft, H. H.
    1875–1876   The Native Races of the Pacific States of North America. 5 vols.
                London.
Beecham, J.
    1841   Ashanti and the Gold Coast. London.
Bollaert, W.
    1850   "Observations of the Indian Tribes in Texas." Journal of the
                Ethnological Society of London, Old Series, 2:262–283.
Brentano, L.
    1870   Preliminary Essay on Gilds: English Gilds. London.
Burton, R. F
    1861   The City of Saints and Across the Rocky Mountains to California.
                London.
Catlin, G.
    1876   Illustrations of the American Indians, with Letters and Notes.
                2 vols. London.
Clavigero, F. J.
    1787   The History of Mexico. Translated from the Spanish. 2 vols.
                London.
Denham, D., H. Clapperton and Dr. Oudney
    1828   Travels in Northern and Central Africa. 3rd ed., 2 vols. London.

Ellis, Rev. W.
  1826   *Tour Through Hawaii.* London.

Fitzroy, R.
  1839   *Narrative of the Surveying Voyages of His Majesty's Ships Adventurer and Beagle Between the Years 1826 and 1836.* 3 vols. London.

Kemble, J. M.
  1849   *The Saxons in England.* 2 vols. London.

Lichtenstein, H.
  1812–1815   *Travels in Southern Africa.* Translated from the German. 2 vols. London.

Mason, Rev. F.
  1868   "On Dwellings, Works of Art, Laws, etc., of the Karens." *Journal of the Asiatic Society of Bengal* 37:125–169.

Maspero, Sir G. C. C.
  1878   *Histoire ancienne des peuples de l'Orient.* Paris.

Mouat, F. J.
  1863   *Adventures and Researches among the Andaman Islanders.* London.

Palgrave, F.
  1832   *The Rise and Progress of the English Commonwealth: Anglo-Saxon Period.* 2 vols. London.

Postans, T.
  1848   "On the Biluchi Tribes Inhabiting Sindh in the Lower Valley of the Indus and the Cutchi." *Journal of the Ethnological Society of London.* Old Series I:103–127.

Prescott, W. H.
  1847   *History of the Conquest of Peru.* 2 vols. London.

Ross, A.
  1849   *Adventures of the First Settlers on the Oregon.* 2 vols. London.

Schoolcraft, H. R.
  1853–1856   *Information Respecting the Indian Tribes of the United States.* 5 vols. London.

Southey, R.
  1810–1819   *History of Brazil.* 2 vols. London.

Thomson, A. S.
  1859   *The Story of New Zealand: Past and Present—Savage and Civilized.* 2 vols. London.

Turner, Rev. G.
  1861   *Nineteen Years in Polynesia.* London.

Williams, T., and J. Calvert
  1858   *Fiji and Fijians.* 2 vols. London.

Winterbottom, T. M.
  1803   *Account of the Native Africans in the Neighborhood of Sierra Leone.* 2 vols. London.

Zurita, A. de
  1840   "Rapports sur les différentes classes de chefs de la Nouvelle-Espagne." Translated from the Spanish. In H. Ternaux-Compans, *Voyages, Relations et Mémoires Originaux pour Servir à l'Histoire de la Découverte de l'Amerique.* Vol. 11. Paris.

Lewis Henry Morgan 1818–1881

BACKGROUND

Lewis Henry Morgan was one of the most influential thinkers of the nineteenth century—not just for the future of anthropology, but for the future of world politics. For his work as interpreted by Marx and Engels led these men to some of their most telling points. Morgan was a middle-class bourgeois Christian lawyer and businessman. He was interested in the Industrial Revolution and certainly not in any other. But never did an age so badly need a new world view. It was not Morgan's overt purpose to provide one. Nevertheless, his research both grew out of, and laid an important part of, the foundation for the evolutionary world view that emerged.

He was one of thirteen children, a member of an old Massachusetts family that had "gone west" to upper New York State. He did well in school—so well that he entered Union College with junior standing. In college he was a skilled orator and clever debater. After graduation in 1840, he spent four years studying law. It was during this period that he began his lifelong study of the American Indian, particularly the Iroquois. He founded a secret society, "The Gordian Knot," patterned after the Iroquois Federation. The members held meetings at night, around campfires, in authentic costume. The group grew to become the "Grand Order of the Iroquois," its stated goals being to study and promote Indian lore, to educate the Indians, and to defend Indian rights against an aggressive and unfair government policy. In 1847, after successfully representing their interests against land claims, Morgan was made an honorary member of the Seneca nation. When the interests of too many members of the "Grand Order" degenerated into revelry, Morgan left the organization and found other means for helping the Indians.

After his bar examinations, an economic recession and an overabundance of lawyers in western New York kept him working on the family farm near Aurora for three years. He gave some lectures related to the "classic revival," supported temperance activities, and continued to read.

In 1851 Morgan moved to Rochester, New York, and established a law firm with his old classmate and friend George F. Danforth; the practice was hugely successful. He also married Mary Elizabeth Steele and published his *League of the Iroquois* that year. The book was the product of years of research in collaboration with his friend Ely S. Parker, a Seneca. It is considered to be "the first scientific account" of an Indian people, and it still holds its own as a valuable ethnography.

Traveling as a representative of New York Central Railways and intending to look after his own investments as well, Morgan went to upper Michigan in 1858. While there he developed an interest in the beaver, which led to a decade of study and, in 1868, to publication of *The American Beaver and His Works*. The book is still an important source of knowledge about that animal.

He also discovered in Michigan that the kinship system of the Ojibwa Indians was precisely like that of the Iroquois. The idea that he could generalize the concepts put forward in his Iroquois book fired Morgan's imagination. He traveled through Kansas, Nebraska, Missouri, and north as far as Hudson Bay, studying almost seventy tribes and formulating a theory that one kinship system was typical of all North American Indians. Then, with help from the Smithsonian Institution, he developed and circulated worldwide a questionnaire to gather the kinship terminologies of hundreds of peoples. Morgan published the data and conclusions of this study in 1871, entitling it *Systems of Consanguinity and Affinity of the Human Family*. It remains a monument and a major source of data.

Morgan's best known work is *Ancient Society*. Since it was first published in 1877, it has never been out of print. His scheme concerning the evolution of the family and his analysis of the unilineal descent group were put forward in this book. Although anthropologists today doubt that there has been any evolution in family form since human beings originally became "familying animals" in the early stages of their own evolution, and although the cultural markers of Morgan's stages of cultural evolution have been questioned, the core of the book remains unassailable. Indeed, reading it today in the light of the succeeding years of anthropology is a humbling experience.

Morgan's last book was *Houses and House-Life of the American Aborigines*. It is still an important idea book in the study of the proxemics of domestic groups.

Morgan retained his early interest in law and politics and, as a conservative, served in the New York assembly and later in the state senate from 1861 to 1869. Only one of his books, *League of the Iroquois*, ever paid for itself. Morgan's considerable prosperity was based on his investments and his law practice. His life in Rochester was a quiet one, dominated by Presbyterianism and marked by family tragedy.

A man of enviable energy, Morgan belonged to many literary groups, to the National Academy of Sciences, and to the American Association for the Advancement of Science. He was the creative force behind the development of the Anthropology Branch in the latter organization, and he served as the AAAS president during 1879–1880. His library was well known for its size and content—and for the book cabinets that he carved himself.

As late as 1880 Morgan supported the creation of an archaeological expedition to study the Pueblo areas. The study, led by A. F. Bandalier, was to last for many years. Morgan died in December of 1881, leaving a large part of his fortune in trust for the creation of a college for women at the University of Rochester.

INTRODUCTION

Three aspects of Morgan's work still live: (1) his discovery of the classificatory system of kinship; (2) his analytical distinction between family and household, especially his careful analysis of the way the two fit together in American Indian society; and (3) his contributions to broader anthropological theory. The discovery that American Indians, as well as a large number of other people in all parts of the world, use classificatory kinship terminology (i.e., they use the same word for mother and mother's sister, etc.) is an extremely important one. As a result, many anthropologists since Morgan have specialized in kinship or kinship systems. The classificatory system of kinship is part of the subject matter of all of Morgan's works, but it is handled most thoroughly in his *Systems of Consanguinity and Affinity of the Human Family* (1871). The household is examined in *Houses and House-Life of the American Aborigines* (1881).

However, Morgan's main contribution to broader anthropological theory is in what has been called the "materialist" approach to evolution and society. As we have said, *Ancient Society* (1877) is one of the most important and influential works in evolutionary thinking. Because Morgan was a materialist, he has found favor in widely differing camps. When Engels discovered this book, he made an interpretation of it that is one of the canons of dialectical materialism. Morgan's influence on archaeology, both in Marxist and non-Marxist circles, has been considerable because of this materialist approach. His greatest influence today is to be found in what Marvin Harris (1968) calls "cultural materialism." On the other hand, because of its careless use of the comparative method (for a critique see the Boas article later in this book) and the noncritical use of data by lesser practitioners, such comparativism and evolutionism were almost totally ignored in American anthropology from roughly 1900 to 1949 (the date of publication of Leslie White's *The Science of Culture*).

It is through his attempt in *Ancient Society* to understand society via technology and economy that Morgan has made his major impact on Engels, Gordon Childe, Leslie White, and Marvin Harris. Morgan's data were not always the best—and some of it may have been misused—but that does not take anything away from the valuable principles that underlie his theory.

In *Ancient Society* Morgan proposes an evolutionary scheme in which every evolutionary stage corresponds with certain types of technology and subsistence. For example, his stage of "Middle Barbarism" starts with the development of the bow and arrow and terminates with the use of pottery. In other words, every stage of evolution must have a technology specific to it, as well as a type of sociocultural life that corresponds to the technology. Today we know that Morgan's stages, with their particular technological indicators, are wrong. But we also know—and Morgan was right about this—that technological inventions and discoveries alter social homeostasis in such a way as to make the development of new sociocultural traits a necessity for survival.

2 ANCIENT SOCIETY

ETHNICAL PERIODS

The latest investigations respecting the early condition of the human race are tending to the conclusion that mankind commenced their career at the bottom of the scale and worked their way up from savagery to civilization through the slow accumulations of experimental knowledge.

As it is undeniable that portions of the human family have existed in a state of savagery, other portions in a state of barbarism, and still other portions in a state of civilization, it seems equally so that these three distinct conditions are connected with each other in a natural as well as necessary sequence of progress. Moreover, that this sequence has been historically true of the entire human family, up to the status attained by each branch respectively, is rendered probable by the conditions under which all progress occurs, and by the known advancement of several branches of the family through two or more of these conditions.

An attempt will be made in the following pages to bring forward additional evidence of the rudeness of the early condition of mankind, of the gradual evolution of their mental and moral powers through experience, and of their protracted struggle with opposing obstacles while winning their way to civilization. It will be drawn, in part, from the great sequence of inventions and discoveries which stretches along the entire pathway of human progress; but chiefly from domestic institutions, which express the growth of certain ideas and passions.

As we re-ascend along the several lines of progress toward the primitive ages of mankind, and eliminate one after the other, in the order in which they appeared, inventions and discoveries on the one hand, and institutions on the other, we are enabled to perceive that the former stand to each other in progressive, and the latter in unfolding relations. While the former class have had a connection, more or less direct, the latter have been developed from a few primary germs of thought. Modern institutions plant their roots in the period of barbarism, into which their germs were transmitted from the previous period of savagery. They have had a lineal descent through the ages, with the streams of the blood, as well as a logical development.

Two independent lines of investigation thus invite our attention. The one leads through inventions and discoveries, and the other through primary institutions. With the knowledge gained therefrom, we may hope to indicate the principal stages of human development. The proofs to be adduced will be drawn chiefly from domestic institutions; the references to achievements more strictly intellectual being general as well as subordinate.

The facts indicate the gradual formation and subsequent development of certain ideas, passions, and aspirations. Those which hold the most promi-

Reprinted from Lewis H. Morgan, *Ancient Society* (Cambridge, Mass.: The Belknap Press of Harvard University Press, 1964). © 1964 by the President and Fellows at Harvard College.

nent positions may be generalized as growths of the particular ideas with which they severally stand connected. Apart from inventions and discoveries they are the following:

I.	*Subsistence,*	V.	*Religion,*
II.	*Government,*	VI.	*House Life and Architecture,*
III.	*Language,*	VII.	*Property.*
IV.	*The Family,*		

First. Subsistence has been increased and perfected by a series of successive arts, introduced at long intervals of time, and connected more or less directly with inventions and discoveries.

Second. The germ of government must be sought in the organization into gentes in the Status of savagery; and followed down, through the advancing forms of this institution, to the establishment of political society.

Third. Human speech seems to have been developed from the rudest and simplest forms of expression. Gesture or sign language, as intimated by Lucretius,[1] must have preceded articulate language, as thought preceded speech. The monosyllabical preceded the syllabical, as the latter did that of concrete words. Human intelligence, unconscious of design, evolved articulate language by utilizing the vocal sounds. This great subject, a department of knowledge by itself, does not fall within the scope of the present investigation.

Fourth. With respect to the family, the stages of its growth are embodied in systems of consanguinity and affinity, and in usages relating to marriage, by means of which, collectively, the family can be definitely traced through several successive forms.

Fifth. The growth of religious ideas is environed with such intrinsic difficulties that it may never receive a perfectly satisfactory exposition. Religion deals so largely with the imaginative and emotional nature, and consequently with such uncertain elements of knowledge, that all primitive religions are grotesque and to some extent unintelligible. This subject also falls without the plan of this work excepting as it may prompt incidental suggestions.

Sixth. House architecture, which connects itself with the form of the family and the plan of domestic life, affords a tolerably complete illustration of progress from savagery to civilization. Its growth can be traced from the hut of the savage, through the communal houses of the barbarians, to the house of the single family of civilized nations, with all the successive links by which one extreme is connected with the other. This subject will be noticed incidentally.

Lastly. The idea of property was slowly formed in the human mind, remaining nascent and feeble through immense periods of time. Springing into life in savagery, it required all the experience of this period and of the subsequent period of barbarism to develop the germ, and to prepare the human brain for the acceptance of its controlling influence. Its dominance as a passion over all other passions marks the commencement of civilization. It not only led mankind to overcome the obstacles which delayed civilization, but to establish political society on the basis of territory and of property. A critical knowledge of the evolution of the idea of property would embody, in some respects, the most remarkable portion of the mental history of mankind.

It will be my object to present some evidence of human progress along these several lines, and through successive ethnical periods, as it is revealed by inventions and discoveries, and by the growth of the ideas of government, of the family, and of property.

It may be here premised that all forms of government are reducible to two general plans, using the word plan in its scientific sense. In their bases the two are fundamentally distinct. The first, in the order of time, is founded upon persons, and upon relations purely personal, and may be distinguished as a society (*societas*). The gens is the unit of this organization; giving as the successive stages of integration, in the archaic period, the gens, the phratry, the tribe, and the confederacy of tribes, which constituted a people or nation (*populus*). At a later period a coalescence of tribes in the same area into a nation took the place of a confederacy of tribes occupying independent areas. Such, through prolonged ages, after the gens appeared, was the substantially universal organization of ancient society; and it remained among the Greeks and Romans after civilization supervened. The second is founded upon territory and upon property, and may be distinguished as a state (*civitas*). The township or ward, circumscribed by metes and bounds, with the property it contains, is the basis or unit of the latter, and political society is the result. Political society is organized upon territorial areas, and deals with property as well as with persons through territorial relations. The successive stages of integration are the township or ward, which is the unit of organization; the county or province, which is an aggregation of townships or wards; and the national domain or territory, which is an aggregation of counties or provinces; the people of each of which are organized into a body politic. It taxed the Greeks and Romans to the extent of their capacities, after they had gained civilization, to invent the deme or township and the city ward; and thus inaugurate the second great plan of government, which remains among civilized nations to the present hour. In ancient society this territorial plan was unknown. When it came in it fixed the boundary line between ancient and modern society, as the distinction will be recognized in these pages.

It may be further observed that the domestic institutions of the barbarous, and even of the savage ancestors of mankind, are still exemplified in portions of the human family with such completeness that, with the exception of the strictly primitive period, the several stages of this progress are tolerably well preserved. They are seen in the organization of society upon the basis of sex, then upon the basis of kin, and finally upon the basis of territory; through the successive forms of marriage and of the family, with the systems of consanguinity thereby created; through house life and architecture; and through progress in usages with respect to the ownership and inheritance of property.

The theory of human degradation to explain the existence of savages and of barbarians is no longer tenable. It came in as a corollary from the Mosaic cosmogony, and was acquiesced in from a supposed necessity which no longer exists. As a theory, it is not only incapable of explaining the existence of savages, but it is without support in the facts of human experience.

The remote ancestors of the Aryan nations presumptively passed through an experience similar to that of existing barbarous and savage tribes. Though the experience of these nations embodies all the information necessary to illustrate the periods of civilization, both ancient and modern, together with a part of that in the Later period of barbarism, their anterior experience must be deduced, in the main, from the traceable connection between the elements of their existing institutions and inventions, and similar elements still preserved in those of savage and barbarous tribes.

It may be remarked finally that the experience of mankind has run in nearly uniform channels; that human necessities in similar conditions have been substantially the same; and that the operations of the mental principle have been uniform in virtue of the specific identity of the brain of all the races of mankind. This, however, is but a part of the explanation of uniformity in results. The germs of the principal institutions and arts of life were developed while man was still a savage. To a very great extent the experience of the subsequent periods of barbarism and of civilization have been expended in the further development of these original conceptions. Wherever a connection can be traced on different continents between a present institution and a common germ, the derivation of the people themselves from a common original stock is implied.

The discussion of these several classes of facts will be facilitated by the establishment of a certain number of Ethnical Periods; each representing a distinct condition of society, and distinguishable by a mode of life peculiar to itself. The terms "Age of *Stone*," "of *Bronze*," and "of *Iron*," introduced by Danish archaeologists, have been extremely useful for certain purposes, and will remain so for the classification of objects of ancient art; but the progress of knowledge has rendered other and different subdivisions necessary. Stone implements were not entirely laid aside with the introduction of tools of iron, nor of those of bronze. The invention of the process of smelting iron ore created an ethnical epoch, yet we could scarcely date another from the production of bronze. Moreover, since the period of stone implements overlaps those of bronze and of iron, and since that of bronze also overlaps that of iron, they are not capable of a circumscription that would leave each independent and distinct.

It is probable that the successive arts of subsistence which arose at long intervals will ultimately, from the great influence they must have exercised upon the condition of mankind, afford the most satisfactory bases for these divisions. But investigation has not been carried far enough in this direction to yield the necessary information. With our present knowledge the main result can be attained by selecting such other inventions or discoveries as will afford sufficient tests of progress to characterize the commencement of successive ethnical periods. Even though accepted as provisional, these periods will be found convenient and useful. Each of those about to be proposed will be found to cover a distinct culture, and to represent a particular mode of life.

The period of savagery, of the early part of which very little is known, may be divided, provisionally, into three sub-periods. These may be named respectively the *Older,* the *Middle,* and the *Later* period of savagery; and the condition of society in each, respectively, may be distinguished as the *Lower,* the *Middle,* and the *Upper Status* of savagery.

In like manner, the period of barbarism divides naturally into three sub-periods, which will be called, respectively, the *Older,* the *Middle,* and the *Later* period of barbarism; and the condition of society in each, respectively, will be distinguished as the *Lower,* the *Middle,* and the *Upper Status* of barbarism.

It is difficult, if not impossible, to find such tests of progress to mark the commencement of these several periods as will be found absolute in their application, and without exceptions upon all the continents. Neither is it necessary, for the purpose in hand, that exceptions should not exist. It will be sufficient if the principal tribes of mankind can be classified, according to the degree of their relative progress, into conditions which can be recognized as distinct.

I. *Lower Status of Savagery.* This period commenced with the infancy of the human race, and may be said to have ended with the ·acquisition of a fish subsistence and of a knowledge of the use of fire. Mankind were then living in their original restricted habitat, and subsisting upon fruits and nuts. The commencement of articulate speech belongs to this period. No exemplification of tribes of mankind in this condition remained to the historical period.

II. *Middle Status of Savagery.* It commenced with the acquisition of a fish subsistence and a knowledge of the use of fire, and ended with the invention of the bow and arrow. Mankind, while in this condition, spread from their original habitat over the greater portion of the earth's surface. Among tribes still existing it will leave in the Middle Status of savagery; for example, the Australians and the greater part of the Polynesians when discovered. It will be sufficient to give one or more exemplifications of each status.

III. *Upper Status of Savagery.* It commenced with the invention of the bow and arrow, and ended with the invention of the art of pottery. It leaves in the Upper Status of savagery the Athapascan tribes of the Hudson's Bay Territory, the tribes of the valley of the Columbia, and certain coast tribes of North and South America; but with relation to the time of their discovery. This closes the period of Savagery.

IV. *Lower Status of Barbarism.* The invention or practice of the art of pottery, all things considered, is probably the most effective and conclusive test that can be selected to fix a boundary line, necessarily arbitrary, between savagery and barbarism. The distinctness of the two conditions has long been recognized, but no criterion of progress out of the former into the latter has hitherto been brought forward. All such tribes, then, as never attained to the art of pottery will be classed as savages, and those possessing this art but who never attained a phonetic alphabet and the use of writing will be classed as barbarians.

The first sub-period of barbarism commenced with the manufacture of pottery, whether by original invention or adoption. In finding its termination, and the commencement of the Middle Status, a difficulty is encountered in the unequal endowments of the two hemispheres, which began to be influential upon human affairs after the period of savagery had passed. It may be met, however, by the adoption of equivalents. In the Eastern hemisphere, the domestication of animals, and in the Western, the cultivation of maize and plants by irrigation, together with the use of adobe-brick and stone in house building have been selected as sufficient evidence of progress to work a transition out of the Lower and into the Middle Status of barbarism. It leaves, for example, in the Lower Status, the Indian tribes of the United States east of the Missouri River, and such tribes of Europe and Asia as practiced the art of pottery, but were without domestic animals.

V. *Middle Status of Barbarism.* It commenced with the domestication of animals in the Eastern hemisphere, and in the Western with cultivation by irrigation and with the use of adobe-brick and stone in architecture, as shown. Its termination may be fixed with the invention of the process of smelting iron ore. This places in the Middle Status, for example, the Village Indians of New Mexico, Mexico, Central America and Peru, and such tribes in the Eastern hemisphere as possessed domestic animals, but were without a knowledge of iron. The ancient Britons, although familiar with the use of iron, fairly belong in this connection. The vicinity of more advanced continental tribes had advanced the arts of life among them far beyond the state of development of their domestic institutions.

VI. *Upper Status of Barbarism.* It commenced with the manufacture of iron, and ended with the invention of a phonetic alphabet, and the use of writing in literary composition. Here civilization begins. This leaves in the Upper Status, for example, the Grecian tribes of the Homeric age, the Italian tribes shortly before the founding of Rome, and the Germanic tribes of the time of Caesar.

VII. *Status of Civilization.* It commenced, as stated, with the use of a phonetic alphabet and the production of literary records, and divides into *Ancient* and *Modern*. As an equivalent, hieroglyphical writing upon stone may be admitted.

RECAPITULATION

PERIODS	CONDITIONS
I. *Older Period of Savagery*	I. *Lower Status of Savagery*
II. *Middle Period of Savagery*	II. *Middle Status of Savagery*
III. *Later Period of Savagery*	III. *Upper Status of Savagery*
IV. *Older Period of Barbarism*	IV. *Lower Status of Barbarism*
V. *Middle Period of Barbarism*	V. *Middle Status of Barbarism*
VI. *Later Period of Barbarism*	VI. *Upper Status of Barbarism*

VII. *Status of Civilization*

I. *Lower Status of Savagery,*   *from the infancy of the human race to the commencement of the next period*

II. *Middle Status of Savagery,*   *from the acquisition of a fish subsistence and a knowledge of the use of fire, to etc.*

III. *Upper Status of Savagery,*   *from the invention of the bow and arrow, to etc.*

IV. *Lower Status of Barbarism,*   *from the invention of the art of pottery, to etc.*

V. *Middle Status of Barbarism,*   *from the domestication of animals on the Eastern hemisphere, and in the Western from the cultivation of maize and plants by irrigation, with the use of adobe-brick and stone, to etc.*

VI. *Upper Status of Barbarism,*   *from the invention of the process of smelting iron ore, with the use of iron tools, to etc.*

VII. *Status of Civilization,*   *from the invention of a phonetic alphabet, with the use of writing, to the present time*

Each of these periods has a distinct culture and exhibits a mode of life more or less special and peculiar to itself. This specialization of ethnical periods renders it possible to treat a particular society according to its condition of relative advancement, and to make it a subject of independent study and discussion. It does not affect the main result that different tribes and nations on the same continent, and even of the same linguistic family, are in different conditions at the same time, since for our purpose the *condition* of each is the material fact, the *time* being immaterial.

Since the use of pottery is less significant than that of domestic animals, of iron, or of a phonetic alphabet, employed to mark the commencement of subsequent ethnical periods, the reasons for its adoption should be stated. The manufacture of pottery presupposes village life, and considerable progress in the simple arts.[2] Flint and stone implements are older than pottery, remains of the former having been found in ancient repositories in numerous instances unaccompanied by the latter. A succession of inventions of greater need and adapted to a lower condition must have occurred before the want of pottery would be felt. The commencement of village life, with some degree of control over subsistence, wooden vessels and utensils, finger weaving with filaments of bark, basket making, and the bow and arrow make their appearance before the art of pottery. The Village Indians who were in the Middle Status of barbarism, such as the Zuñians, the Aztecs and the Cholulans, manufactured pottery in large quantities and in many forms of considerable excellence; the partially Village Indians of the United States, who were in the Lower Status of barbarism, such as the Iroquois, the Choctas and the Cherokees, made it in smaller quantities and in a limited number of forms; but the Non-horticultural Indians, who were in the Status of savagery, such as the Athapascans, the tribes of California, and of the valley of the Columbia, were ignorant of its use.[3] In Lubbock's *Pre-Historic Times,*[4] in Tylor's *Early History of Mankind,* and in Peschel's *Races of Man,*[5] the particulars respecting this art, and the extent of its distribution, have been collected with remarkable breadth of research. It was unknown in Polynesia (with the exception of the Islands of the Tongans and Fijians), in Australia, in California, and in the Hudson's Bay Territory. Mr. Tylor remarks that "the art of weaving was unknown in most of the Islands away from Asia," and that "in most of the South Sea Islands there was no knowledge of pottery."[6] The Rev. Lorimer Fison, an English missionary residing in Australia, informed the author in answer to inquiries, that "the Australians had no woven fabrics, no pottery, and were ignorant of the bow and arrow." This last fact was also true in general of the Polynesians. The introduction of the ceramic art produced a new epoch in human progress in the direction of an improved living and increased domestic conveniences. While flint and stone implements— which came in earlier and required long periods of time to develop all their uses—gave the canoe, wooden vessels and utensils, and ultimately timber and plank in house architecture,[7] pottery gave a durable vessel for boiling food, which before that had been rudely accomplished in baskets coated with clay, and in ground cavities lined with skin, the boiling being effected with heated stones.[8]

Whether the pottery of the aborigines was hardened by fire or cured by the simple process of drying has been made a question. Prof. E. T. Cox,[9] of Indianapolis, has shown by comparing the analyses of ancient pottery and hydraulic cements, "that so far as chemical constituents are concerned it (the pottery) agrees very well with the composition of hydraulic stones." He remarks further that "all the pottery belonging to the mound-builders' age, which I have seen, is composed of alluvial clay and sand, or a mixture of the former with pulverized fresh-water shells. A paste made of such a mixture possesses in a high degree the properties of hydraulic Puzzuolani and Portland cement, so that vessels formed of it hardened without being burned, as is customary with modern pottery. The fragments of shells served the purpose of gravel or fragments of stone as at present used in connection with hydraulic lime for the manufacture of artificial stone."[10] The composition of Indian pottery in analogy with that of hydraulic cement suggests the difficulties in the way of inventing the art, and tends also to explain the lateness of its introduction in the course of human experience. Notwithstanding the ingenious suggestion of Prof. Cox, it is probable that pottery was hardened by artificial heat. In some cases the fact is directly attested. Thus Adair, speaking of the Gulf Tribes, remarks that "they make earthern pots of very different sizes, so as to contain from two to ten gallons, large pitchers to carry water, bowls, dishes, platters, basins, and a prodigious number of other vessels of such antiquated forms as would be tedious to describe, and impossible to name. Their method of glazing them is, they place them over a large fire of smoky pitch-pine, which makes them smooth, black and firm."[11]

Another advantage of fixing definite ethnical periods is the direction of special investigation to those tribes and nations which afford the best exemplification of each status, with the view of making each both standard and illustrative. Some tribes and families have been left in geographical isolation to work out the problems of progress by original mental effort; and have, consequently, retained their arts and institutions pure and homogeneous; while those of other tribes and nations have been adulterated through external influence. Thus, while Africa was and is an ethnical chaos of savagery and barbarism, Australia and Polynesia were in savagery, pure and simple, with the arts and institutions belonging to that condition. In like manner, the Indian family of America, unlike any other existing family, exemplified the condition of mankind in three successive ethnical periods. In the undisturbed possession of a great continent, of common descent, and with homogeneous institutions, they illustrated, when discovered, each of these conditions, and especially those of the Lower and of the Middle Status of barbarism, more elaborately and completely than any other portion of mankind. The far northern Indians and some of the coast tribes of North and South America were in the Upper Status of savagery; the partially Village Indians east of the Mississippi were in the Lower Status of barbarism, and the Village Indians of North and South America were in the Middle Status. Such an opportunity to recover full and minute information of the course of human experience and progress in developing their arts and institutions through these successive conditions has not been offered within the historical period. It must be added that it has been indifferently improved. Our greatest deficiencies relate to the last period named.

Differences in the culture of the same period in the Eastern and Western hemispheres undoubtedly existed in consequence of the unequal endowments of the continents; but the condition of society in the corresponding status must have been, in the main, substantially similar.

The ancestors of the Grecian, Roman, and German tribes passed through the stages we have indicated, in the midst of the last of which the light of history fell upon them. Their differentiation from the undistinguishable mass of barbarians did not occur, probably, earlier than the commencement of the Middle Period of barbarism. The experience of these tribes has been lost, with the exception of so much as is represented by the institutions, inventions and discoveries which they brought with them, and possessed when they first came under historical observation. The Grecian and Latin tribes of the Homeric and Romulian periods afford the highest exemplification of the Upper Status of barbarism. Their institutions were likewise pure and homogeneous, and their experience stands directly connected with the final achievement of civilization.

Commencing, then, with the Australians and Polynesians, following with the American Indian tribes, and concluding with the Roman and Grecian, who afforded the highest exemplifications respectively of the six great stages of human progress, the sum of their united experiences may be supposed fairly to represent that of the human family from the Middle Status of savagery to the end of ancient civilization. Consequently, the Aryan nations will find the type of the condition of their remote ancestors, when in savagery, in that of the Australians and Polynesians; when in the Lower Status of barbarism in that of the partially Village Indians of America; and when in the Middle Status in that of the Village Indians, with which their own experience in the Upper Status directly connects. So essentially identical are the arts, institutions and mode of life in the same status upon all the continents, that the archaic form of the principal domestic institutions of the Greeks and Romans must even now be sought in the corresponding institutions of the American aborigines. . . . This fact forms a part of the accumulating evidence tending to show that the principal institutions of mankind have been developed from a few primary germs of thought; and that the course and manner of their development was predetermined, as well as restricted within narrow limits of divergence, by the natural logic of the human mind and the necessary limitations of its powers. Progress has been found to be substantially the same in kind in tribes and nations inhabiting different and even disconnected continents, while in the same status, with deviations from uniformity in particular instances produced by special causes. The argument when extended tends to establish the unity of origin of mankind.

In studying the condition of tribes and nations in these several ethnical periods we are dealing, substantially, with the ancient history and condition of our own remote ancestors.

ARTS OF SUBSISTENCE

The important fact that mankind commenced at the bottom of the scale and worked up is revealed in an expressive manner by their sucessive arts of subsistence. Upon their skill in this direction the whole question of human supremacy on the earth depended. Mankind are the only beings who may be said to have gained an absolute control over the production of food; which at the outset they did not possess above other animals. Without enlarging the basis of subsistence, mankind could not have propagated themselves into other areas not possessing the same kinds of food, and ultimately over the whole surface of the earth; and lastly, without obtaining an absolute control over both its variety and amount, they could not have multiplied into populous nations. It is accordingly probable that the great epochs of human progress have been identified, more or less directly, with the enlargement of the sources of subsistence.

We are able to distinguish five of these sources of human food created by what may be called as many successive arts, one superadded to the other, and brought out at long separated intervals of time. The first two originated in the period of savagery, and the last three, in the period of barbarism. They are the following stated in the order of their appearance:

I. *Natural Subsistence upon Fruits and Roots on a Restricted Habitat.*

This proposition carries us back to the strictly primitive period of mankind, when few in numbers, simple in subsistence, and occupying limited areas, they were just entering upon their new career. There is neither an art nor an institution that can be referred to this period; and but one invention, that of language, which can be connected with an epoch so remote. The kind of subsistence indicated assumes a tropical or subtropical climate. In such a climate, by common consent, the habitat of primitive man has been placed. In fruit and nutbearing forests under a tropical sun, we are accustomed, and with reason, to regard our progenitors as having commenced their existence.

The races of animals preceded the race of mankind, in the order of time. We are warranted in supposing that they were in the plenitude of their strength and numbers when the human race first appeared. The classical poets pictured the tribes of mankind dwelling in groves, in caves and in forests, for the possession of which they disputed with wild beasts[12]—while they sustained themselves with the spontaneous fruits of the earth. If mankind commenced their career without experience, without weapons, and surrounded with ferocious animals, it is not improbable that they were, at least partially, tree-livers, as a means of protection and security.

The maintenance of life, through the constant acquisition of food, is the great burden imposed upon existence in all species of animals. As we descend in the scale of structural organization, subsistence becomes more and more simple at each stage, until the mystery finally vanishes. But, in the ascending scale, it becomes increasingly difficult until the highest structural form, that of man, is reached, when it attains the maximum. Intelligence from henceforth becomes a more prominent factor. Animal food, in all probability, entered from a very early period into human consumption; but whether it was actively sought when mankind were essentially frugivorous in practice, though omnivorous in structural organization, must remain a matter of conjecture. This mode of sustenance belongs to the strictly primitive period.

II. *Fish Subsistence*. In fish must be recognized the first kind of artificial food, because it was not fully available without cooking. Fire was first utilized, not unlikely, for this purpose. Fish were universal in distribution, unlimited in supply, and the only kind of food at all times attainable. The cereals in the primitive period were still unknown, if in fact they existed, and the hunt for game was too precarious ever to have formed an exclusive means of human support. Upon this species of food mankind became independent of climate and of locality; and by following the shores of the seas and lakes, and the courses of the rivers could, while in the savage state, spread themselves over the greater portion of the earth's surface. Of the fact of these migrations there is abundant evidence in the remains of flint and stone implements of the Status of Savagery found upon all the continents. In reliance upon fruits and spontaneous subsistence a removal from the original habitat would have been impossible.

Between the introduction of fish, followed by the wide migrations named, and the cultivation of farinaceous food, the interval of time was immense. It covers a large part of the period of savagery. But during this interval there was an important increase in the variety and amount of food. Such, for example, as the bread roots cooked in ground ovens, and in the permanent addition of game through improved weapons, and especially through the bow and arrow. This remarkable invention, which came in after the spear and war club, and gave the first deadly weapon for the hunt, appeared late in savagery.[13] It has been used to mark the commencement of its Upper Status. It must have given a powerful upward influence to ancient society, standing in the same relation to the period of savagery, as the iron sword to the period of barbarism, and fire-arms to the period of civilization.

From the precarious nature of all these sources of food, outside of the great fish areas, cannibalism became the dire resort of mankind. The ancient universality of this practice is being gradually demonstrated.

III. *Farinaceous Subsistence through Cultivation.* We now leave savagery and enter the Lower Status of barbarism. The cultivation of cereals and plants was unknown in the Western hemisphere except among the tribes who had emerged from savagery; and it seems to have been unknown in the Eastern hemisphere until the tribes of Asia and Europe had passed through the Lower, and had drawn near to the close of the Middle Status of barbarism. It gives us the singular fact that the American aborigines in the Lower Status of barbarism were in possession of horticulture one entire ethnical period earlier than the inhabitants of the Eastern hemisphere. It was a consequence of the unequal endowments of the two hemispheres; the Eastern possessing all the animals adapted to domestication, save one, and a majority of the cereals; while the Western had only one cereal fit for cultivation, but that the best. It tended to prolong the older period of barbarism in the former, to shorten it in the latter; and with the advantage of condition in this period in favor of the American aborigines. But when the most advanced tribes in the Eastern hemisphere, at the commencement of the Middle Period of barbarism, had domesticated animals which gave them meat and milk, their condition, without a knowledge of the cereals, was much superior to that of the American aborigines in the corresponding period, with maize and plants, but without domestic animals. The differentiation of the Semitic and Aryan families from the mass of barbarians seems to have commenced with the domestication of animals.

That the discovery and cultivation of the cereals by the Aryan family was subsequent to the domestication of animals is shown by the fact that there are common terms for these animals in the several dialects of the Aryan language, and no common terms for the cereals or cultivated plants. Mommsen, after showing that the domestic animals have the same names in the Sanskrit Greek and Latin (which Max Müller afterwards extended to the remaining Aryan dialects[14]) thus proving that they were known and presumptively domesticated before the separation of these nations from each other, proceeds as follows: "On the other hand, we have as yet no certain proofs of the existence of agriculture at this period. Language rather favors the negative view. Of the Latin-Greek names of grain none occur in the Sanskrit with the single exception of ζέα, which philologically represents the Sanskrit *yavas,* but denotes in Indian, barley; in Greek, *spelt.* It must indeed be granted that this diversity in the names of cultivated plants, which so strongly contrasts with the essential agreement in the appellations of domestic animals, does not absolutely preclude the supposition of a common original agriculture. The cultivation of rice among the Indians, that of wheat and spelt among the Greeks, and that of rye and oats among the Germans and Celts, may all be traceable to a common system of original tillage."[15] This last conclusion is forced. Horticulture preceded field culture, as the garden (*hortos*) preceded the field (*ager*); and although the latter implies boundaries, the former signifies directly an "inclosed space." Tillage, however, must have been older than the inclosed garden; the natural order being first, tillage of patches of open alluvial land, second of inclosed spaces or gardens, and third, of the field by means of the plow drawn by animal power. Whether the cultivation of such plants as the pea, bean, turnip, parsnip, beet, squash and melon, one or more of them, preceded the cultivation of the cereals, we have at present no means of knowing. Some of these have common terms in Greek and Latin; but I am assured by our eminent philologist, Prof. W. D. Whitney[16] that neither of them has a common term in Greek or Latin and Sanskrit.

Horticulture seems to have originated more in the necessities of the domestic animals than in those of mankind. In the Western hemisphere it commenced with maize. This new era, although not synchronous in the two hemispheres, had immense influence upon the destiny of mankind. There are reasons for believing that it required ages to establish the art of cultivation, and render farinaceous food a principal reliance. Since in America it led to localization and to village life, it tended, especially among the Village Indians, to take the place of fish and game. From the cereals and cultivated plants, moreover, mankind obtained their first impression of the possibility of an abundance of food.

The acquisition of farinaceous food in America and of domestic animals in Asia and Europe were the means of delivering the advanced tribes, thus provided, from the scourge of cannibalism, which as elsewhere stated, there are reasons for believing was practiced universally throughout the period of savagery upon captured enemies, and, in time of famine, upon friends and kindred. Cannibalism in war, practiced by war parties in the field, survived among the American aborigines, not only in the Lower, but also in the Middle Status of barbarism, as, for example, among the Iroquois and the Aztecs; but the general practice had disappeared. This forcibly illustrates the great importance which is exercised by a permanent increase of food in ameliorating the condition of mankind.

IV. *Meat and Milk Subsistence.* The absence of animals adapted to domestication in the Western hemisphere, excepting the llama,[17] and the specific differences in the cereals of the two hemispheres exercised an important influence upon the relative advancement of their inhabitants. While this inequality of endowments was immaterial to mankind in the period of savagery, and not marked in its effects in the Lower Status of barbarism, it made an essential difference with that portion who had attained to the Middle Status. The domestication of animals provided a permanent meat and milk subsistence which tended to differentiate the tribes which possessed them from the mass of other barbarians. In the Western hemisphere, meat was restricted to the precarious supplies of game. This limitation upon an essential species of food was unfavorable to the Village Indians; and doubtless sufficiently explains the inferior size of the brain among them in comparison with that of Indians in the Lower Status of barbarism. In the Eastern hemisphere, the domestication of animals enabled the thrifty and industrious to secure for themselves a permanent supply of animal food, including milk; the healthful and invigorating influence of which upon the race, and especially upon children, was undoubtedly remarkable. It is at least supposable that the Aryan and Semitic families owe their pre-eminent endowments to the great scale upon which, as far back as our knowledge extends, they have identified themselves with the maintenance in numbers of the domestic animals. In fact, they incorporated them, flesh, milk, and muscle, into their plan of life.[18] No other family of mankind have done this to an equal extent, and the Aryan have done it to a greater extent than the Semitic.

The domestication of animals gradually introduced a new mode of life, the pastoral, upon the plains of the Euphrates and of India, and upon the steppes of Asia; on the confines of one or the other of which the domestication of animals was probably first accomplished. To these areas, their oldest traditions and their histories alike refer them. They were thus drawn to regions which, so far from being the cradle lands of the human race, were areas they would not have occupied as savages, or as barbarians in the Lower Status of barbarism, to whom forest areas were natural homes. After becoming habituated to pastoral life, it must have been impossible for either of these families to re-enter the forest areas of Western Asia and of Europe with their flocks and herds, without first learning to cultivate some of the cereals with which to subsist the latter at a distance from the grass plains. It seems extremely probable, therefore, as before stated, that the cultivation of the cereals originated in the necessities of the domestic animals, and in connection with these western migrations; and that the use of farinaceous food by these tribes was a consequence of the knowledge thus acquired.

In the Western hemisphere, the aborigines were enabled to advance generally into the Lower Status of barbarism, and a portion of them into the Middle Status, without domestic animals, excepting the llama in Peru, and upon a single cereal, maize, with the adjuncts of the bean, squash and tobacco, and in some areas, cacoa, cotton and pepper. But maize, from its growth in the hill—which favored direct cultivation—from its useableness both green and ripe, and from its abundant yield and nutritive properties, was a richer endowment in aid of early human progress than all other cereals put together. It serves to explain the remarkable progress the American aborigines had made without the domestic animals; the Peruvians having produced bronze, which stands next, and quite near, in the order of time, to the process of smelting iron ore.

V. *Unlimited Subsistence through Field Agriculture.* The domestic animals supplementing human muscle with animal power contributed a new factor of the highest value. In course of time, the production of iron gave the plow with an iron point, and a better spade and axe. Out of these, and the previous horticulture, came field agriculture; and with it, for the first time, unlimited subsistence. The plow drawn by animal power may be regarded as inaugurating a new art. Now, for the first time, came the thought of reducing the forest, and bringing wide fields under cultivation.[19] Moreover, dense populations in limited areas now became possible. Prior to field agriculture it is not probable that half a million people were developed and held together under one government in any part of the earth. If exceptions occurred, they must have resulted from pastoral life on the plains, or from horticulture improved by irrigation, under peculiar and exceptional conditions.

In the course of these pages it will become necessary to speak of the family as it existed in different ethnical periods; its form in one period being sometimes entirely different from its form in another. . . . These several forms of the family . . . will be frequently mentioned. . . . They are the following:

I. *The Consanguine Family.* It was founded upon the intermarriage of brothers and sisters in a group. Evidence still remains in the oldest of existing systems of consanguinity, the Malayan, tending to show that this, the first form of the family, was anciently as universal as this system of consanguinity which it created.

II. *The Punaluan Family.* Its name is derived from the Hawaiian relationship of *Punalua.* It was founded upon the intermarriage of several brothers to each other's wives in a group; and of several sisters to each other's husbands in a group. But the term brother, as here used, included the first, second, third, and even more remote male cousins, all of whom were considered brothers to each other, as we consider own brothers; and the term sister included the first, second, third, and even more remote female cousins, all of whom were sisters to each other, the same as own sisters. This form of the family supervened upon the consanguine. It created the Turanian and Ganowánian systems of consanguinity. Both this and the previous form belong to the period of savagery.

III. *The Syndyasmian Family.* The term is from συνδυάζω, to pair, συνδυασμός, a joining two together. It was founded upon the pairing of a male with a female under the form of marriage, but without an exclusive cohabitation. It was the germ of the monogamian family. Divorce or separation was at the option of both husband and wife. This form of the family failed to create a system of consanguinity.

IV. *The Patriarchal Family.* It was founded upon the marriage of one man to several wives. The term is here used in a restricted sense to define the special family of the Hebrew pastoral tribes, the chiefs and principal men of which practiced polygamy. It exercised but little influence upon human affairs for want of universality.

V. *The Monogamian Family.* It was founded upon the marriage of one man with one woman, with an exclusive cohabitation, the latter constituting the essential element of the institution. It is pre-eminently the family of civilized society, and was therefore essentially modern. This form of the family also created an independent system of consanguinity.

Evidence will elsewhere be produced tending to show both the existence and the general prevalence of these several forms of the family at different stages of human progress.

RATIO OF HUMAN PROGRESS

It is well to obtain an impression of the relative amount and of the ratio of human progress in the several ethnical periods named, by grouping together the achievements of each, and comparing them with each other as distinct classes of facts. This will also enable us to form some conception of the relative duration of these periods. To render it forcible, such a survey must be general, and in the nature of a recapitulation. It should, likewise, be limited to the principal works of each period.

Before man could have attained to the civilized state it was necessary that he should gain all the elements of civilization. This implies an amazing change of condition, first from a primitive savage to a barbarian of the lowest type, and then from the latter to a Greek of the Homeric period, or to a Greek of the time of Abraham. The progressive development which history records in the period of civilization was not less true of man in each of the previous periods.

By re-ascending along the several lines of human progress toward the primitive ages of man's existence, and removing one by one his principal institutions, inventions and discoveries, in the order in which they have appeared, the advance made in each period will be realized.

The principal contributions of modern civilization are the electric telegraph, coal gas, the spinning-jenny, and the power loom; the steam-engine with its numerous dependent machines, including the locomotive, the railway, and the steam-ship; the telescope; the discovery of the ponderability of the atmosphere and of the solar system; the art of printing; the canal lock; the mariner's compass; and gunpowder. The mass of other inventions, such, for example, as the Ericsson propeller, will be found to hinge upon one or another of those named as antecedents: but there are exceptions, as photography, and numerous machines not necessary to be noticed. With these also should be removed the modern sciences; religious freedom and the common schools; representative democracy; constitutional monarchy with parliaments; the feudal kingdom; modern privileged classes; international, statute and common law.

Modern civilization recovered and absorbed whatever was valuable in the ancient civilizations; and although its contributions to the sum of human knowledge have been vast, brilliant and rapid, they are far from being so disproportionately large as to overshadow the ancient civilizations and sink them into comparative insignificance.

Passing over the mediaeval period, which gave Gothic architecture, feudal aristocracy with hereditary titles of rank, and a hierarchy under the headship of a pope, we enter the Roman and Grecian civilizations. They will be found deficient in great inventions and discoveries, but distinguished in art, in philosophy, and in organic institutions. The principal contributions of these civilizations were imperial and kingly government; the civil law; Christianity; mixed aristocratical and democratical government, with a senate and consuls; democratical government with a council and popular assembly; the organization of armies into cavalry and infantry, with military discipline; the establishment of navies, with the practice of naval warfare; the formation of great cities, with municipal law; commerce on the seas; the coinage of money; and the state, founded upon territory and upon property; and among inventions, fire-baked brick, the crane,[20] the water-wheel for driving mills, the bridge, aqueduct and sewer; lead pipe used as a conduit with the faucet; the arch, the balance scale; the arts and sciences of the classical period, with their results, including the orders of architecture; the Arabic numerals and alphabetic writing.

These civilizations drew largely from, as well as rested upon, the inventions and discoveries and the institutions of the previous period of barbarism. The achievements of civilized man, although very great and remarkable, are nevertheless very far from sufficient to eclipse the works of man as a barbarian. As such he had wrought out and possessed all the elements of civilization, excepting alphabetic writing. His achievements as a barbarian should be considered in their relation to the sum of human progress; and we may be forced to admit that they transcend, in relative importance, all his subsequent works.

The use of writing, or its equivalent in hieroglyphics upon stone, affords a fair test of the commencement of civilization.[21] Without literary records neither history nor civilization can properly be said to exist. The production of the Homeric poems, whether transmitted orally or committed to writing at the time, fixes with sufficient nearness the introduction of civilization among the Greeks. These poems, ever fresh and ever marvelous, possess an ethnological value which enhances immensely their other excellences. This is especially true of the *Iliad,* which contains the oldest as well as the most circumstantial account now existing of the progress of mankind up to the time of its composition. Strabo compliments Homer as the father of geographical science;[22] but the great poet has given, perhaps without design, what was infinitely more important to succeeding generations: namely, a remarkably full exposition of the arts, usages, inventions and discoveries, and mode of life of the ancient Greeks. It presents our first comprehensive picture of Aryan society while still in barbarism, showing the progress then made, and of what particulars it consisted. Through these poems we are enabled confidently to state that certain things were known among the Greeks before they entered upon civilization. They also cast an illuminating light far backward into the period of barbarism.

Using the Homeric poems as a guide and continuing the retrospect into the Later Period of barbarism, let us strike off from the knowledge and experience of mankind the invention of poetry; the ancient mythology in its elaborate form, with the Olympian divinities; temple architecture; the knowledge of the cereals, excepting maize and cultivated plants, with field agriculture;[23] cities encompassed with walls of stone, with battlements, towers and gates; the use of marble in architecture;[24] ship-building with plank and probably with the use of nails;[25] the wagon and the chariot;[26] metallic plate armor;[27] the copper-pointed spear and embossed shield;[28] the iron sword;[29] the manufacture of wine, probably;[30] the mechanical powers excepting the screw; the potter's wheel and the hand-mill for grinding grain;[31] woven fabrics of linen and woolen from the loom;[32] the iron axe and spade;[33] the iron hatchet and adz;[34] the hammer and the anvil;[35] the bellows and the forge;[36] and the side hill furnace for smelting iron ore, together with a knowledge of iron. Along with the above-named acquisitions must be removed the monogamian family; military democracies of the heroic age; the later phase of the organization into gentes, phratries and tribes; the agora or popular assembly, probably; a knowledge of individual property in houses and lands; and the advanced form of municipal life in fortified cities. When this has been done, the highest class of barbarians will have surrendered the principal portion of their marvelous works, together with the mental and moral growth thereby acquired.

From this point backward through the Middle Period of barbarism the indications become less distinct, and the relative order in which institutions, inventions and discoveries appeared is less clear; but we are not without some knowledge to guide our steps even in these distant ages of the Aryan family. For reasons previously stated, other families, besides the Aryan, may now be resorted to for the desired information.

Entering next the Middle Period, let us, in like manner, strike out of human experience the process of making bronze; flocks and herds of domestic animals;[37] communal houses with walls of adobe, and of dressed stone laid in courses with mortar of lime and sand; cyclopean walls; lake dwellings constructed on piles; the knowledge of native metals,[38] with the use of charcoal and the crucible for melting them; the copper axe and chisel; the shuttle and embryo loom; cultivation by irrigation, causeways, reservoirs and irrigating canals; paved roads; osier suspension bridges; personal gods, with a priesthood distinguished by a costume, and organized in a hierarchy; human sacrifices; military democracies of the Aztec type; woven fabrics of cotton and other vegetable fibre in the Western hemisphere, and of wool and flax in the Eastern; ornamental pottery; the sword of wood, with the edges pointed with flints; polished flint and stone implements; a knowledge of cotton and flax; and the domestic animals.

The aggregate of achievements in this period was less than in that which followed; but in its relations to the sum of human progress it was very great. It includes the domestication of animals in the Eastern hemisphere, which introduced in time a permanent meat and milk subsistence, and ultimately field agriculture; and also inaugurated those experiments with the native metals which resulted in producing bronze,[39] as well as prepared the way for the higher process of smelting iron ore. In the Western hemisphere it was signalized by the discovery and treatment of the native metals, which resulted in the production independently of bronze; by the introduction of irrigation in the cultivation of maize and plants, and by the use of adobe-brick and stone in the construction of great joint tenement houses in the nature of fortresses.

Resuming the retrospect and entering the Older Period of barbarism, let us next remove from human acquisitions the confederacy, based upon gentes, phratries and tribes under the government of a council of chiefs which gave a more highly organized state of society than before that had been known. Also the discovery and cultivation of maize and the bean, squash and tobacco, in the Western hemisphere, together with a knowledge of farinaceous food; finger weaving with warp and woof; the kilt, moccasin and leggin of tanned deer-skin; the blow-gun for bird shooting; the village stockade for defense; tribal games; element worship, with a vague recognition of the Great Spirit; cannibalism in time of war; and lastly, the art of pottery.

As we ascend in the order of time and of development, but descend in the scale of human advancement, inventions become more simple, and more direct in their relations to primary wants; and institutions approach nearer and nearer to the elementary form of a gens composed of consanguinei, under a chief of their own election, and to the tribe composed of kindred gentes, under the government of a council of chiefs. The condition of Asiatic and European tribes in this period (for the Aryan and Semitic families did not probably then exist) is substantially lost. It is represented by the remains of ancient art between the invention of pottery and the domestication of animals; and includes the people who formed the shell-heaps on the coast of the Baltic, who seem to have domesticated the dog, but no other animals.

In any just estimate of the magnitude of the achievements of mankind in the three sub-periods of barbarism, they must be regarded as immense, not only in number and in intrinsic value, but also in the mental and moral development by which they were necessarily accompanied.

Ascending next through the prolonged period of savagery, let us strike out of human knowledge the organization into gentes, phratries and tribes; the syndyasmian family; the worship of the elements in its lowest form; syllabical language; the bow and arrow; stone and bone implements; cane and splint baskets; skin garments; the punaluan family; the organization upon the basis of sex; the village, consisting of clustered houses; boat craft, including the bark and dug-out canoe; the spear pointed with flint, and the war club; flint implements of the ruder kinds; the consanguine family; monosyllabical language; fetishism; cannibalism; a knowledge of the use of fire; and lastly, gesture language.[40] When this work of elimination has been done in the order in which these several acquisitions were made, we shall have approached quite near the infantile period of man's existence, when mankind were learning the use of fire, which rendered possible a fish subsistence and a change of habitat, and when they were attempting the formation of articulate language. In a condition so absolutely primitive, man is seen to be not only a child in the scale of humanity, but possessed of a brain into which not a thought or conception expressed by these institutions, inventions and discoveries had penetrated—in a word, he stands at the bottom of the scale, but potentially all he has since become.

With the production of inventions and discoveries, and with the growth of institutions, the human mind necessarily grew and expanded; and we are led to recognize a gradual enlargement of the brain itself, particularly of the cerebral portion. The slowness of this mental growth was inevitable, in the period of savagery, from the extreme difficulty of compassing the simplest invention out of nothing, or with next to nothing to assist mental effort; and of discovering any substance or force in nature available in such a rude condition of life. It was not less difficult to organize the simplest form of society out of such savage and intractable materials. The first inventions and the first social organizations were doubtless the hardest to achieve, and were consequently separated from each other by the longest intervals of time. A striking illustration is found in the successive forms of the family. In this law of progress, which works in a geometrical ratio, a sufficient explanation is found of the prolonged duration of the period of savagery.

That the early condition of mankind was substantially as above indicated is not exclusively a recent, nor even a modern opinion. Some of the ancient poets and philosophers recognized the fact that mankind commenced in a state of extreme rudeness from which they had risen by slow and successive steps. They also perceived that the course of their development was registered by a progressive series of inventions and discoveries, but without noticing as fully the more conclusive argument from social institutions.

The important question of the ratio of this progress, which has a direct bearing upon the relative length of the several ethnical periods, now presents itself. Human progress, from first to last, has been in a ratio not rigorously but essentially geometrical. This is plain on the face of the facts; and it could not, theoretically, have occurred in any other way. Every item of absolute knowledge gained became a factor in further acquisitions, until the present complexity of knowledge was attained. Consequently, while progress was slowest in time in the first period, and most rapid in the last, the relative amount may have been greatest in the first, when the achievements of either period are considered in their relations to the sum. It may be suggested, as not improbable of ultimate recognition, that the progress of mankind in the period of savagery, in its relations to the sum of human progress, was greater in degree than it was afterwards in the three sub-periods of barbarism; and that the progress made in the whole period of barbarism was, in like manner, greater in degree than it has been since the entire period of civilization.

What may have been the relative length of these ethnical periods is also a fair subject of speculation. An exact measure is not attainable, but an approximation may be attempted. On the theory of geometrical progression, the period of savagery was necessarily longer in duration than the period of barbarism, as the latter was longer than the period of civilization. If we assume a hundred thousand years as the measure of man's existence upon

the earth in order to find the relative length of each period—and for this purpose, it may have been longer or shorter—it will be seen at once that at
least sixty thousand years must be assigned to the period of savagery. Three-
fifths of the life of the most advanced portion of the human race, on this
apportionment, were spent in savagery. Of the remaining years, twenty thousand, or one-fifth, should be assigned to the Older Period of barbarism. For
the Middle and Later Periods there remain fifteen thousand years, leaving
five thousand, more or less, for the period of civilization.

The relative length of the period of savagery is more likely under- than
overstated. Without discussing the principles on which this apportionment is
made, it may be remarked that in addition to the argument from the geometrical progression under which human development of necessity has
occurred, a graduated scale of progress has been universally observed in
remains of ancient art, and this will be found equally true of institutions. It
is a conclusion of deep importance in ethnology that the experience of mankind in savagery was longer in duration than all their subsequent experience,
and that the period of civilization covers but a fragment of the life of the race.

Two families of mankind, the Aryan and Semitic, by the commingling of
diverse stocks, superiority of subsistence or advantage of position, and
possibly from all together, were the first to emerge from barbarism. They were
substantially the founders of civilization.[41] But their existence as distinct families was undoubtedly, in a comparative sense, a late event. Their progenitors
are lost in the undistinguishable mass of earlier barbarians. The first ascertained appearance of the Aryan family was in connection with the domestic
animals, at which time they were one people in language and nationality. It
is not probable that the Aryan or Semitic families were developed into individuality earlier than the commencement of the Middle Period of barbarism,
and that their differentiation from the mass of barbarians occurred through
their acquisition of the domestic animals.

The most advanced portion of the human race were halted, so to express
it, at certain stages of progress, until some great invention or discovery, such
as the domestication of animals or the smelting of iron ore, gave a new and
powerful impulse forward. While thus restrained, the ruder tribes, continually
advancing, approached in different degrees of nearness to the same status;
for wherever a continental connection existed, all the tribes must have shared
in some measure in each other's progress. All great inventions and discoveries propagate themselves; but the inferior tribes must have appreciated their
value before they could appropriate them. In the continental areas certain
tribes would lead; but the leadership would be apt to shift a number of times
in the course of an ethnical period. The destruction of the ethnic bond and
life of particular tribes, followed by their decadence, must have arrested for
a time, in many instances and in all periods, the upward flow of human
progress. From the Middle Period of barbarism, however, the Aryan and
Semitic families seem fairly to represent the central threads of this progress,
which in the period of civilization has been gradually assumed by the Aryan
family alone.

The truth of this general position may be illustrated by the condition of the American aborigines at the epoch of their discovery. They commenced their career on the American continent in savagery; and, although possessed of inferior mental endowments, the body of them had emerged from savagery and attained to the Lower Status of barbarism; whilst a portion of them, the Village Indians of North and South America, had risen to the Middle Status. They had domesticated the llama, the only quadruped native to the continent which promised usefulness in the domesticated state, and had produced bronze by alloying copper with tin. They needed but one invention, and that the greatest, the art of smelting iron ore, to advance themselves into the Upper Status. Considering the absence of all connection with the most advanced portion of the human family in the Eastern hemisphere, their progress in unaided self-development from the savage state must be accounted remarkable. While the Asiatic and European were waiting patiently for the boon of iron tools, the American Indian was drawing near to the possession of bronze, which stands next to iron in the order of time. During this period of arrested progress in the Eastern hemisphere, the American aborigines advanced themselves, not to the status in which they were found, but sufficiently near to reach it while the former were passing through the last period of barbarism, and the first four thousand years of civilization. It gives us a measure of the length of time they had fallen behind the Aryan family in the race of progress: namely, the duration of the Later Period of barbarism, to which the years of civilization must be added. The Aryan and Ganowánian families together exemplify the entire experience of man in five ethnical periods, with the exception of the first portion of the Later Period of savagery.

Savagery was the formative period of the human race. Commencing at zero in knowledge and experience, without fire, without articulate speech, and without arts, our savage progenitors fought the great battle, first for existence, and then for progress, until they secured safety from ferocious animals, and permanent subsistence. Out of these efforts there came gradually a developed speech, and the occupation of the entire surface of the earth. But society from its rudeness was still incapable of organization in numbers. When the most advanced portion of mankind had emerged from savagery, and entered the Lower Status of barbarism, the entire population of the earth must have been small in numbers. The earliest inventions were the most difficult to accomplish because of the feebleness of the power of abstract reasoning. Each substantial item of knowledge gained would form a basis for further advancement; but this must have been nearly imperceptible for ages upon ages, the obstacles to progress nearly balancing the energies arrayed against them. The achievements of savagery are not particularly remarkable in character, but they represent an amazing amount of persistent labor with feeble means continued through long periods of time before reaching a fair degree of completeness. The bow and arrow afford an illustration.

The inferiority of savage man in the mental and moral scale, undeveloped, inexperienced, and held down by his low animal appetites and passions, though reluctantly recognized, is, nevertheless, substantially demonstrated by the remains of ancient art in flint stone and bone implements, by his cave life in certain areas, and by his osteological remains. It is still further illustrated by the present condition of tribes of savages in a low state of development, left in isolated sections of the earth as monuments of the past. And yet to this great period of savagery belongs the formation of articulate language and its advancement to the syllabical stage, the establishment of two forms of the family and possibly a third, and the organization into gentes which gave the first form of society worthy of the name. All these conclusions are involved in the proposition, stated at the outset, that mankind commenced their career at the bottom of the scale; which "modern science claims to be proving by the most careful and exhaustive study of man and his works."[42]

In like manner, the great period of barbarism was signalized by four events of pre-eminent importance: namely, the domestication of animals, the discovery of the cereals, the use of stone in architecture, and the invention of the process of smelting iron ore. Commencing probably with the dog as a companion in the hunt, followed at a later period by the capture of the young of other animals and rearing them, not unlikely, from the merest freak of fancy, it required time and experience to discover the utility of each, to find means of raising them in numbers, and to learn the forbearance necessary to spare them in the face of hunger. Could the special history of the domestication of each animal be known, it would exhibit a series of marvelous facts. The experiment carried, locked up in its doubtful chances, much of the subsequent destiny of mankind. Secondly, the acquisition of farinaceous food by cultivation must be regarded as one of the greatest events in human experience. It was less essential in the Eastern hemisphere, after the domestication of animals, than in the Western, where it became the instrument of advancing a large portion of the American aborigines into the Lower, and another portion into the Middle Status of barbarism. If mankind had never advanced beyond this last condition, they had the means of a comparatively easy and enjoyable life. Thirdly, with the use of adobe-brick and of stone in house building, an improved mode of life was introduced, eminently calculated to stimulate the mental capacities, and to create the habit of industry—the fertile source of improvements. But, in its relations to the high career of mankind, the fourth invention must be held the greatest event in human experience, preparatory to civilization. When the barbarian, advancing step by step, had discovered the native metals, and learned to melt them in the crucible and to cast them in moulds; when he had alloyed native copper with tin and produced bronze; and, finally, when by a still greater effort of thought he had invented the furnace, and produced iron from the ore, nine-tenths of the battle for civilization was gained.[43] Furnished with iron tools capable of holding both an edge and a point, mankind were certain of attaining to civilization. The production of iron was the event of events in human experience, without a parallel, and without an equal, beside which all other inventions and discoveries were inconsiderable, or at least subordinate. Out of it came the metallic hammer and anvil, the axe and the chisel, the plow with an iron point, the iron sword;

in fine, the basis of civilization, which may be said to rest upon this metal. The want of iron tools arrested the progress of mankind in barbarism. There they would have remained to the present hour had they failed to bridge the chasm. It seems probable that the conception and the process of smelting iron ore came but once to man. It would be a singular satisfaction could it be known to what tribe and family we are indebted for this knowledge, and with it for civilization. The Semitic family were then in advance of the Aryan, and in the lead of the human race. They gave the phonetic alphabet to mankind and it seems not unlikely the knowledge of iron as well.

At the epoch of the Homeric poems, the Grecian tribes had made immense material progress. All the common metals were known, including the process of smelting ores, and possibly of changing iron into steel; the principal cereals had been discovered, together with the art of cultivation, and the use of the plow in field agriculture; the dog, the horse, the ass, the cow, the sow, the sheep and the goat had been domesticated and reared in flocks and herds, as has been shown. Architecture had produced a house constructed of durable materials, containing separate apartments,[44] and consisting of more than a single story;[45] ship building, weapons, textile fabrics, the manufacture of wine from the grape, the cultivation of the apple, the pear, the olive and the fig,[46] together with comfortable apparel, and useful implements and utensils, had been produced and brought into human use.[47] But the early history of mankind was lost in the oblivion of the ages that had passed away. Tradition ascended to an anterior barbarism through which it was unable to penetrate. Language had attained such development that poetry of the highest structural form was about to embody the inspirations of genius. The closing period of barbarism brought this portion of the human family to the threshold of civilization, animated by the great attainments of the past, grown hardy and intelligent in the school of experience, and with the undisciplined imagination in the full splendor of its creative powers. Barbarism ends with the production of grand barbarians. Whilst the condition of society in this period was understood by the later Greek and Roman writers, the anterior state, with its distinctive culture and experience, was as deeply concealed from their apprehension as from our own; except as occupying a nearer stand-point in time, they saw more distinctly the relations of the present with the past. It was evident to them that a certain sequence existed in the series of inventions and discoveries, as well as a certain order of development of institutions, through which mankind had advanced themselves from the status of savagery to that of the Homeric age; but the immense interval of time between the two conditions does not appear to have been made a subject even of speculative consideration.

NOTES

1. . . . and for womankind
    And children they would claim kind treatment, pleading
    With cries and gestures inarticulately

That all men ought to have pity on the weak.

> Lucretius, *De rerum natura* 5.1019–1021 [trans. R. C. Trevelyan (New York: Cambridge University Press, 1937).]

2. Mr. Edward B. Tylor observes that Goquet "first propounded, in the last century, the notion that the way in which pottery came to be made, was that people daubed such combustible vessels as these with clay to protect them from fire, till they found the clay alone would answer the purpose and thus the art of pottery came into the world" (*Researches into the Early History of Mankind,* 2nd ed., London, 1870, p. 273). Goquet relates of Capt. Gonneville who visited the southeast coast of South America in 1503, that he found "their household utensils of wood, even their boiling pots, but plastered with a kind of clay, a good finger thick, which prevented the fire from burning them" (*ibid.,* p. 273). [Edward Burnett Tylor (1832–1917), eminent English anthropologist, was the keeper of the University Museum and Professor of Anthropology at Oxford University.]

3. Pottery has been found in aboriginal mounds in Oregon within a few years past (J. W. Foster, *Pre-Historic Races of the United States,* Chicago, 1874, pp. 151–154). The first vessels of pottery among the aborigines of the United States seem to have been made in baskets of rushes or willows used as moulds which were burned off after the vessel hardened (Charles C. Jones, Jr., *Antiquities of the Southern Indians,* New York, 1873, p. 461; Charles Rau, "Indian Pottery," *Annual Report of the Board of Regents of the Smithsonian Institution . . . for 1866,* Washington, D.C., 1867, p. 352).

4. [New York, 1873. The author, Sir John Lubbock (1834–1913), was an English banker and anthropologist. While on his European tour in 1871, Morgan visited Lubbock at his country estate in England (Leslie A. White, ed., "Extracts from the European Travel Journal of Lewis H. Morgan," *Rochester Historical Society Publications,* vol. XVI (Rochester, N.Y., 1937), pp. 371–374; see also pp. 339, 368.]

5. [*The Races of Men* (London, 1876) is the title of the English translation of *Völkerkunde* (Leipzig, 1874), by Oscar Peschel (1826–1875), German geographer.]

6. Tylor, *Early History of Mankind,* p. 181; see also Lubbock, *Pre-Historic Times,* pp. 437, 441, 462, 477, 533, 542.

7. Lewis and Clarke (1805) found plank in use in houses among the tribes of the Columbia River (Meriwether Lewis and George Rogers Clarke, *Travels to the Source of the Missouri River and Across the American Continent to the Pacific Ocean,* 3 vols., London, 1815, II, 241). Mr. John Keast Lord found "cedar plank chipped from the solid tree with chisels and hatchets made of stone," in Indian houses on Vancouver's Island (*The Naturalist in Vancouver Island and British Columbia,* 2 vols., London, 1866, I: 165).

8. Tylor, *Early History of Mankind,* pp. 265–272.

9. [Edward Travers Cox (1821–1907), American geologist and archaeologist.]

10. E. T. Cox, "Geological Report of Indiana," in the *Fifth Annual Report of the Geological Survey of Indiana* (Indianapolis, 1874), pp. 119–120. He gives the following analysis:

Ancient Pottery, "Bone Bank," Posey Co., Indiana.

Moisture at 212 F.,	1.00	Peroxide of Iron,	5.50
Silica,	36.00	Sulphuric Acid,	.20
Carbonate of Lime,	25.50	Organic matter	
Carbonate of Magnesia,	3.20	(alkalies and loss),	23.60
Alumina,	5.00		
			100.00

[The percentages, as changed, now add up to 100.00.]

11. James Adair, *The History of the American Indians* (London, 1775), pp. 424–425. The Iroquois affirm that in ancient times their forefathers cured their pottery before a fire.

12. Not yet they knew of fire, not yet to use
The skins of wild beasts, and to clothe their frame
With spoils won from them; in the groves and woods
And mountain caves they lived, and in the brush
Sheltered their squalid limbs, when
Forced to fly the stormy winds and rain.
 Lucretius, *De rerum natura,* 5.950–954 [trans. Sir Robert Allison (London: Hatchards, 1925)].

13. As a combination of forces it is so abstruse that it not unlikely owed its origin to accident. The elasticity and toughness of certain kinds of wood, the tension of a cord of sinew or vegetable fibre by means of a bent bow, and finally their combination to propel an arrow by human muscle, are not very obvious suggestions to the mind of a savage. As elsewhere noticed, the bow and arrow are unknown to the Polynesians in general, and to the Australians. From this fact alone it is shown that mankind were well advanced in the savage state when the bow and arrow made their first appearance.

14. Max Müller, *Chips from a German Workshop,* 2 vols. (New York, 1869), II, 42. [When Morgan was in England in 1870 he called upon Müller at the latter's home in Oxford; see White, ed., "Extracts from the European Travel Journal of Lewis H. Morgan," pp. 243–245. Rochester Historical Society Publications, XVII, 221–389 (Rochester, N.Y., 1937).]

15. Theodor Mommsen, *The History of Rome,* trans. Rev. William P. Dickson, 4 vols. (New York, 1870), I, 38.

16. [William Dwight Whitney (1827–1894), distinguished American philologist, professor of Sanskrit at Yale University. He was one of three members of a committee to whom the manuscript of *Systems of Consanguinity and Affinity of the Human Family* was submitted by Joseph Henry, Secretary of the Smithsonian Institution, for evaluation with a view to publication in the Smithsonian Contributions to Knowledge.]

17. The early Spanish writers speak of a "dumb dog" found domesticated in the West India Islands, and also in Mexico and Central America. (See figures of the Aztec dog in Pl. iii, vol. I of Clavigero's *History of Mexico.*) I have seen no identification of the animal. They also speak of poultry as well as turkeys on the continent. The aborigines had domesticated the turkey, and the Nahuatlac tribes some species of wild fowl.

18. We learn from the *Iliad* that the Greeks milked their sheep, as well as their cows and goats: "Even as ewes stand in throngs past counting in the court of a man of much substance to be milked of their white milk," Homer, *Iliad* 4.433 [trans. A. T. Murray, 2 vols. (Loeb Classical Library)].

19. And they would force the forests day by day
To retreat higher up the mountain-sides
And yield the ground below to husbandry,
That so meadows and ponds, rivulets, crops
And glad vineyards might cover hill and plain.
 Lucretius, *De rerum natura,* 5.1368–1371 [trans. R. C. Trevelyan (New York: Cambridge University Press, 1937)].

20. The Egyptians may have invented the crane (see *Herodotus* 2.125). They also had the balance scale.

21. The phonetic alphabet came, like other great inventions, at the end of successive efforts. The slow Egyptian, advancing the hieroglyph through its several forms, had reached a syllabus composed of phonetic characters, and at this stage

was resting upon his labors. He could write in permanent characters upon stone. Then came in the inquisitive Phoenician, the first navigator and trader on the sea, who, whether previously versed in hieroglyphs or otherwise, seems to have entered at a bound upon the labors of the Egyptian, and by an inspiration of genius to have mastered the problem over which the latter was dreaming. He produced that wondrous alphabet of sixteen letters which in time gave to mankind a written language and the means for literary and historical records.

22. Strabo 1.2.

23. Barley, white barley.—*Iliad* 5.196; 8.564: barley flour.—*Iliad* 11.631: barley meal, made of barley and salt, and used as an oblation.—*Iliad* 1.449: wheat.—*Iliad* 10.756: rye.—*Iliad* 5.196, 7.564: bread.—*Iliad* 24.625: an inclosed 50 acres of land.—*Iliad* 9.579: a fence.—*Iliad* 5.90: a field.—*Iliad* 5.90: stones set for a field boundary.—*Iliad* 21.405: plow.—*Iliad* 10.353; 13.703.

24. The house or mansion.—*Iliad* 6.390: odoriferous chambers of cedar, lofty roofed.—*Iliad* 6.390: house of Priam, in which were fifty chambers of polished stones.—*Iliad* 6.243.

25. Ship.—*Iliad* 1.485: white sail.—*Iliad* 1.480: cable or hawser.—*Iliad* 1.476: oar.—*Odyssey* 4.782: mast.—*Odyssey* 4.781: keel.—*Iliad* 1.482: ship plank.—*Iliad* 3.61: long plank.—*Odyssey* 5.162: nail.—*Iliad* 11.633: golden nail.—*Iliad* 11.633.

26. Chariot or vehicle.—*Iliad* 8.389, 565: four-wheeled wagon.—*Iliad* 24.324: chariot.—*Iliad* 5.727, 837; 8.403: the same.—*Iliad* 2.775; 7.426.

27. Helmet.—*Iliad* 18.611; 20.398: cuirass or corselet.—*Iliad* 16.133; 18.610: greaves.—*Iliad* 16.131.

28. Spear.—*Iliad* 15.712; 16.140: shield of Achilles.—*Iliad* 18.478, 609: round shield.—*Iliad* 13.611.

29. Sword.—*Iliad* 7.303; 11.29: silver-studded sword.—*Iliad* 7.303: the sword.—*Iliad* 23.807; 15.713: a double-edged sword. *Iliad* 10.256.

30. Wine.—*Iliad* 8.506: sweet wine.—*Iliad* 10.579.

31. Potter's wheel.—*Iliad* 18.600: hand-mill for grinding grain.—*Odyssey* 7.104; 20.106.

32. Linen.—*Iliad* 18.352; 23.254: linen corselet.—*Iliad* 2.529: robe of Minerva.—*Iliad* 5.734: tunic.—*Iliad* 10.131: woolen cloak.—*Iliad* 10.133; 24.280: rug or coverlet.—*Iliad* 24.280, 645: mat.—*Iliad* 24.644: veil.—*Iliad* 22.470.

33. Axe.—*Iliad* 3.60; 23.114, 875: spade or mattock.—*Iliad* 21.259.

34. Hatchet or battle-axe.—*Iliad* 13.612; 15.711: knife.—*Iliad* 11.844; 19.252: chip-axe or adz.—*Odyssey* 5.273.

35. Hammer.—*Iliad* 18.477: anvil.—*Iliad* 18.476: tongs.—*Iliad* 18.477.

36. Bellows.—*Iliad* 18.372, 468: furnace, the boshes.—*Iliad* 18.470.

37. Horse.—*Iliad* 11.680: distinguished into breeds: Thracian.—*Iliad* 10.588; Trojan, 5.265: Erechthonius owned three thousand mares.—*Iliad* 20.221: collars, bridles and reins.—*Iliad* 19.339: ass.—*Iliad* 11.558: mule.—*Iliad* 10.352; 7.333: ox.—*Iliad* 11.678; 8.333: bull; cow.—*Odyssey* 20.251: goat.—*Iliad* 11.679: dog. 5.476; 8.338; 22.509: sheep.—*Iliad* 11.678: bear or sow.—*Iliad* 11.679; 8.338: milk.—*Iliad* 16.643: pails full of milk.—*Iliad* 16.642.

38. Homer mentions the native metals; but they were known long before his time, and before iron. The use of charcoal and the crucible in melting them prepared the way for smelting iron ore. Gold.—*Iliad* 2.229: silver.—*Iliad* 18.475: copper, called brass.—*Iliad* 3.229; 18.460: tin, possibly pewter.—*Iliad* 11.25; 20.271; 21.292: lead.—*Iliad* 11.237: iron.—*Iliad* 8.473: iron axle-tree.—*Iliad* 5.723: iron club.—*Iliad* 7.141: iron wagon-tire.—*Iliad* 23.505.

39. The researches of Beckmann have left a doubt upon the existence of a true bronze earlier than a knowledge of iron among the Greeks and Latins. He thinks *electrum,* mentioned in the *Iliad,* was a mixture of gold and silver (John Beckmann, *A History of Inventions, Discoveries, and Origins,* 4th ed., trans. William Johnston, 2 vols., London, 1846, II, 212); and that the *stannum* of the Romans, which consisted of silver and lead, was the same as the *kassiteron* of Homer (*ibid.,* II, 217). This word has usually been interpreted as tin. In commenting upon the composition called bronze, he remarks: "In my opinion the greater part of these things were made of *stannum,* properly so called, which by the admixture of the noble metals, and some difficulty of fusion, was rendered fitter for use than pure copper" (*ibid.,* II, 213). These observations were limited to the nations of the Mediterranean, within whose areas tin was not produced. Axes, knives, razors, swords, daggers and personal ornaments discovered in Switzerland, Austria, Denmark, and other parts of Northern Europe, have been found, on analysis, composed of copper and tin, and therefore fall under the strict definition of bronze. They were also found in relations indicating priority to iron.

40. The origin of language has been investigated far enough to find the grave difficulties in the way of any solution of the problem. It seems to have been abandoned, by common consent, as an unprofitable subject. It is more a question of the laws of human development and of the necessary operations of the mental principle, than of the materials of language. Lucretius remarks that with sounds and with gesture, mankind in the primitive period intimated their thoughts stammeringly to each other (Vocibus, et gestu, cum balbe significarent.—5.1021). He assumes that thought preceded speech, and that gesture language preceded articulate language. Gesture or sign language seems to have been primitive, the elder sister of articulate speech. It is still the universal language of barbarians, if not of savages, in their mutual intercourse when their dialects are not the same. The American aborigines have developed such a language, thus showing that one may be formed adequate for general intercourse. As used by them it is both graceful and expressive, and affords pleasure in its use. It is a language of natural symbols, and therefore possesses the elements of a universal language. A sign language is easier to invent than one of sounds; and, since it is mastered with greater facility, a presumption arises that it preceded articulate speech. The sounds of the voice would first come in, on this hypothesis, in aid of gesture; and as they gradually assumed a conventional signification, they would supersede, to that extent, the language of signs, or become incorporated in it. It would also tend to develop the capacity of the vocal organs. No proposition can be plainer than that gesture has attended articulate language from its birth. It is still inseparable from it; and may embody the remains, by survival, of an ancient mental habit. If language were perfect, a gesture to lengthen out or emphasize its meaning would be a fault. As we descend through the gradations of language into its ruder forms, the gesture element increases in the quantity and variety of its forms until we find language so dependent upon gestures that without them they would be substantially unintelligible. Growing up and flourishing side by side through savagery, and far into the period of barbarism, they remain, in modified forms, indissolubly united. Those who are curious to solve the problem of the origin of language would do well to look to the possible suggestions from gesture language.

41. The Egyptians are supposed to affiliate remotely with the Semitic family.

42. William W. Whitney, *Oriental and Linguistic Studies* (New York, 1873), p. 341.

43. M. Quiquerez, a Swiss engineer, discovered in the canton of Berne the remains of a number of side-hill furnaces for smelting iron ore; together with tools, fragments of iron and charcoal. To construct one, an excavation was made in the

side of a hill in which a bosh was formed of clay, with a chimney in the form of a dome above it to create a draft. No evidence was found of the use of the bellows. The boshes seem to have been charged with alternate layers of pulverized ore and charcoal, combustion being sustained by fanning the flames. The result was a spongy mass of partly fused ore which was afterwards welded into a compact mass by hammering. A deposit of charcoal was found beneath a bed of peat twenty feet in thickness. It is not probable that these furnaces were coeval with the knowledge of smelting iron ore; but they were, not unlikely, close copies of the original furnace. *Vide,* Louis Figuier, *Primitive Man,* rev. ed., trans. Edward Burnett Tylor (New York, 1871), p. 301.

44. Palace of Priam.—*Iliad* 6.242.

45. House of Ulysses.—*Odyssey* 16.448.

46. *Odyssey* 7.115.

47. In addition to the articles enumerated in the previous notes the following may be added from the *Iliad* as further illustrations of the progress then made: The shuttle.—22.448: the loom.—22.440: a woven fillet.—22.469: silver basin.—23.741: goblet, or drinking cup.—24.285: golden goblet.—24.285: basket, made of reeds.—24.626: ten talents in gold.—19.247: a harp.—9.186 and 13.731: a shepherd's pipe.—18.526: sickle, or pruning knife.—13.551: fowler's net.—5.487: mesh of a net.—5.487: a bridge.—5.89: also a dike.—21.245: rivets. 18.379: the bean.—13.589: the pea.—13.589: the onion.—21.245: rivets. —18.561: a vineyard.—18.561: wine.—8.506; 10.579: the tripod.—9.122: a copper boiler or caldron.—9.123: a brooch.—14.180: ear-ring.—14.183: a sandal or buskin.—14.186: leather.—16.636: a gate.—21.537: bolt for fastening gate.—21.537. And in the *Odyssey:* a silver basin.—1.137: a table.—1.138: golden cups.—*Odyssey* 1.142: rye.—4.41: a bathing tub.—4.48: cheese; milk. —4.88: distaff or spindle.—4.131; 7.105; 17.97: silver basket.—4.125: bread.—4.623; 14.456: tables loaded with bread, meat and wine.—15.333: shuttle.—5.62: bed.—8.337: brazier plunging an axe or adz in cold water for the purpose of tempering it.—9.391: salt.—11.123; 23.270: bow.—21.31, 53: quiver.—21.54: sickle.—18.368.

Edward Burnett Tylor 1832–1917

BACKGROUND

For many of the later years of the nineteenth century, anthropology was said in England to be "Mr. Tylor's science." Herbert Spencer had never used the word "anthropologist" of himself. But Edward Tylor, under the influence of Matthew Arnold and other literati of the day, came to adopt the word and the study of "culture" from the German, and to apply the word "anthropology" to the study of man and his cultural works. The word "anthropology" as it applies to the biological study of the human animal is much older; but Tylor was among the first to see the unity in the subject and to seek to demonstrate the point by constant interreferences of man's body and his culture.

Tylor was born in Camberwell, England, in 1832. His father was a prosperous brass founder. The Tylors were Quakers—a middle-class people in England, made strong and rich by opposition and persistence, in those days as today. Because the universities in England were open only to members of the established church, Tylor was unable to study in a university, so he went to work for his father. After seven years, however, he became ill. As part of his efforts to regain his health he traveled to the tropics of the New World. In the course of his journey, in Cuba, he met Henry Christy. Christy was also a Quaker, tho generation of Tylor's father. Tylor had met him before but had not known him well. Christy was an enthusiastic amateur ethnologist who was able to show Tylor what one missed when traveling without understanding the way of life one was seeing from the standpoint of those who were living it. The two of them undertook a six-months' trip to Mexico. Tylor's first book was *Anahuac, Or Mexico and the Mexicans, Ancient and Modern*, written about his experiences on this trip. It is a good nineteenth-century travel book, an attempt to see the present in terms of the past in Mexican Indian history. The author's enthusiasm is still infectious, but the book shows little of the vast but easy erudition that was to become Tylor's mark. However, this trip allowed Tylor to read ethnography with a critical and sympathetic mien that was always denied to Herbert Spencer.

In 1856, on his return to England, Tylor married Anna Fox. It was a fortunate match. Anna remained his most enthusiastic supporter. Later in his life, when he lectured at Oxford, she attended his lectures (it is said that he sometimes began a lecture: "And now, my dear Anna, as I was saying last week . . . ."). Described by contemporary friends as "ideal," the marriage apparently approached that state.

61

Tylor's travels in the New World set him to reading and note taking. He became the best-informed person of his age on ethnographic facts. His hard work and the breadth of his study—all of primitive society, much of classical society, and the storehouses of fact known to history—were evident; for all that, his prose was always smooth, and he wore his great erudition lightly.

In 1865 Tylor published his first scientific study, *Researches into the Early History of Mankind.* It contains reports on his own field work among the deaf of England and Germany (he was among the first to point out that "gesture order" among the deaf does not alter with the language spoken around these people). It contains what is still the best comparative description of fire-making techniques around the world, as well as much else of lasting significance.

However, it was in 1871 that Tylor published his masterpiece, *Primitive Culture.* The first few lines of the first chapter of this book, reprinted below, are now a "definition" of culture—the only one most anthropologists can quote correctly, and the one they fall back on when others prove too cumbersome.

There are two main ideas in *Primitive Culture.* The first is that it is possible to reconstruct the past cultures of peoples through a close study of the present and the "survivals" of past cultural states that they encapsulate. Basically, the idea is that anything that is nonfunctional in a present-day culture must be a leftover or "survival" of a previous stage. Although the idea is no longer used in the simplistic sense in which Tylor used it, he was among the first to set anthropology safely on the road toward sensible interpretation of culture—it was not he who turned the method into a caricature by not being critical when it was misapplied. The other main idea in *Primitive Culture* is the concept of animism: the most fundamental religious idea being the inevitability of a belief in the existence of spirits.

Tylor's last book, published in 1881, was *Anthropology,* a sort of proto-textbook that is also a credo.

Tylor was the first English anthropologist to be honored with a university appointment. He was given an honorary D.C.L. by Oxford in 1875, which made it possible some years later for him to be appointed a University Lecturer. He became Oxford's first professor of anthropology in 1896, but the appointment was a "personal" one, and after his retirement no new appointment to a professorship in anthropology at Oxford was made for over four decades (although there were distinguished anthropologists such as Marrett there). Tylor was instrumental in establishing anthropology as a branch of the British Association, becoming the first president of the branch; he became president of the Anthropological Society (later made "Royal" by recognition by the monarchs) in 1891. He was knighted in 1912.

Sir Edward Tylor was the first "compleat anthropologist" as we today think of an "all-round anthropologist." The existence of our concepts and our university departments reiterates the faith we maintain in "Mr. Tylor's science."

INTRODUCTION

Several aspects of Tylor's work should be noted: his definition of culture, his ideas of cognitive evolution, and his attempts to use statistical analysis in comparative studies.

Tylor's famous anthropological definition of culture is found in the first sentence in the following selection from his work: "that complex whole which includes knowledge, belief, art, morals, law, custom and any other capabilities and habits acquired by man as a member of society." Today's anthropologists find this definition inadequate to some of their most sophisticated needs, but it is the first definition of culture from an anthropological perspective, and in teaching it is as useful as any later definition.

Tylor's evolutionism will be seen to be very different from either Spencer's or Morgan's. Both Spencer and Morgan were interested in the development of social organization and the complexity attached to such development. Tylor's interest is centered more on problems of culture than on society, and particularly on the development of religion through animism. His treatment is strictly on a cognitive basis. His main argument traces the evolution of religion—on a cognitive basis—in three basic stages: animism, polytheism, and monotheism. Trying to establish cognitive patterns of evolution is even more difficult than attempting a materalist or organizational theory of evolution, because deciding what is cognitively later involves making value judgments: in fact, short of documentation there is no other way to do it. Tylor believed in the basic similarity of all human minds—in every land, in every culture—the so-called doctrine of the psychic unity of mankind. His evolutionary theory of animism is not a racist theory claiming that people with simpler religions have simpler minds; it claims only that they have less complex religions. He also claimed that societies with more advanced cultures could retain primitive items within their culture; he called such items "survivals." However, the argument for the existence of "survivals" within cultural traditions is not a very good one. What counts is the viability of a culture and not the fact that some of its traditions are apparently meaningless and merely left over from earlier times.

In 1899 Tylor published an article entitled "On a Method of Investigating the Development of Institutions Applied to Laws of Marriage and Descent." This article is as original as his definition of culture. It was the first use of a statistical method within anthropology, and it initiated cross-cultural studies that today form an important sub-branch of the subject.

3 PRIMITIVE CULTURE

THE SCIENCE OF CULTURE

Culture or Civilization, taken in its wide ethnographic sense, is that complex whole which includes knowledge, belief, art, morals, law, custom, and any other capabilities and habits acquired by man as a member of society. The condition of culture among the various societies of mankind, in so far as it is capable of being investigated on general principles, is a subject apt for the study of laws of human thought and action. On the

Reprinted from Edward B. Tylor, *Primitive Culture* (London: J. Murray, 1871).

one hand, the uniformity which so largely pervades civilization may be ascribed, in great measure, to the uniform action of uniform causes; while on the other hand its various grades may be regarded as stages of development or evolution, each the outcome of previous history, and about to do its proper part in shaping the history of the future. To the investigation of these two great principles in several departments of ethnography, with especial consideration of the civilization of the lower tribes as related to the civilization of the higher nations, the present volumes are devoted.

Our modern investigators in the sciences of inorganic nature are foremost to recognize, both within and without their special fields of work, the unity of nature, the fixity of its laws, the definite sequence of cause and effect through which every fact depends on what has gone before it, and acts upon what is to come after it. They grasp firmly the Pythagorean doctrine of pervading order in the universal Kosmos. They affirm, with Aristotle, that nature is not full of incoherent episodes, like a bad tragedy. They agree with Leibnitz in what he calls "my axiom, that nature never acts by leaps (la nature n'agit jamais par saut)," as well as in his "great principle, commonly little employed, that nothing happens without its sufficient reason." Nor, again, in studying the structure and habits of plants and animals, or in investigating the lower functions even of man, are these leading ideas unacknowledged. But when we come to talk of the higher processes of human feeling and action, of thought and language, knowledge and art, a change appears in the prevalent tone of opinion. The world at large is scarcely prepared to accept the general study of human life as a branch of natural science, and to carry out, in a large sense, the poet's injunction to "Account for moral as for natural things." To many educated minds there seems something presumptuous and repulsive in the view that the history of mankind is part and parcel of the history of nature, that our thoughts, wills, and actions accord with laws as definite as those which govern the motion of waves, the combination of acids and bases, and the growth of plants and animals.

The main reasons of this state of the popular judgment are not far to seek. There are many who would willingly accept a science of history if placed before them with substantial definiteness of principle and evidence, but who not unreasonably reject the systems offered to them, as falling too far short of a scientific standard. Through resistance such as this, real knowledge always sooner or later makes its way, while the habit of opposition to novelty does such excellent service against the invasions of speculative dogmatism, that we may sometimes even wish it were stronger than it is. But other obstacles to the investigation of laws of human nature arise from considerations of metaphysics and theology. The popular notion of free human will involves not only freedom to act in accordance with motive, but also a power of breaking loose from continuity and acting without cause,—a combination which may be roughly illustrated by the simile of a balance sometimes acting in the usual way, but also possessed of the faculty of turning by itself without or against its weights. This view of an anomalous action of the will, which it need hardly be said is incompatible with scientific argument, subsists as an opinion patent or latent in men's minds, and strongly affecting their theoretic views of history, though it is not, as a rule, brought prominently forward in systematic reasoning. Indeed the definition of human will, as strictly according with motive, is the only possible scientific basis in such enquiries. Happily, it is not needful to add here yet another to the list of dissertations on supernatural intervention and natural causation, on liberty, predestination, and accountability. We may hasten to escape from the regions of transcendental philosophy and theology, to start on a more hopeful journey over more practicable ground. None will deny that, as each man knows by the evidence of his own consciousness, definite and natural cause does, to a great extent, determine human action. Then, keeping aside from considerations of extra-natural interference and causeless spontaneity, let us take this admitted existence of natural cause and effect as our standing-ground, and travel on it so far as it will bear us. It is on this same basis that physical science pursues, with ever-increasing success, its quest of laws of nature. Nor need this restriction hamper the scientific study of human life, in which real difficulties are the practical ones of enormous complexity of evidence, and imperfection of methods of observation.

Now it appears that this view of human will and conduct, as subject to definite law, is indeed recognized and acted upon by the very people who oppose it when stated in the abstract as a general principle, and who then complain that it annihilates man's free will, destroys his sense of personal responsibility, and degrades him to a soulless machine. He who will say these things will nevertheless pass much of his own life in studying the motives which lead to human action, seeking to attain his wishes through them, framing in his mind theories of personal character, reckoning what are likely to be the effects of new combinations, and giving to his reasoning the crowning character of true scientific enquiry, by taking it for granted that in so far as his calculation turns out wrong, either his evidence must have been false or incomplete, or his judgment upon it unsound. Such a one will sum up the experience of years spent in complex relations with society, by declaring his persuasion that there is a reason for everything in life, and that where events look unaccountable, the rule is to wait and watch in hope that the key to the problem may some day be found. This man's observation may have been as narrow as his inferences are crude and prejudiced, but nevertheless he has been an inductive philosopher "more than forty years without knowing it." He has practically acknowledged definite laws of human thought and action, and has simply thrown out of account in his own studies of life the whole fabric of motiveless will and uncaused spontaneity. It is assumed here that they should be just so thrown out of account in wider studies, and that the true philosophy of history lies in extending and improving the methods of the plain people who form their judgments upon facts, and check them upon new facts. Whether the doctrine be wholly or but partly true, it accepts the very condition under which we search for new knowledge in the lessons of experience, and in a word the whole course of our rational life is based upon it.

"One event is always the son of another, and we must never forget the parentage," was a remark made by a Bechuana chief to Casalis the African missionary. Thus at all times historians, so far as they have aimed at being more than mere chroniclers, have done their best to show not merely succession, but connexion, among the events upon their record. Moreover, they have striven to elicit general principles of human action, and by these to explain particular events, stating expressly or taking tacitly for granted the existence of a philosophy of history. Should any one deny the possibility of thus establishing historical laws the answer is ready with which Boswell in such a case turned on Johnson: "Then, sir, you would reduce all history to no better than an almanack." That nevertheless the labours of so many eminent thinkers should have as yet brought history only to the threshold of science need cause no wonder to those who consider the bewildering complexity of the problems which come before the general historian. The evidence from which he is to draw his conclusions is at once so multifarious and so doubtful that a full and distinct view of its bearing on a particular question is hardly to be attained, and thus the temptation becomes all but irresistible to garble it in support of some rough and ready theory of the course of events. The philosophy of history at large, explaining the past and predicting the future phenomena of man's life in the world by reference to general laws, is in fact a subject with which, in the present state of knowledge, even genius aided by wide research seems but hardly able to cope. Yet there are departments of it which, though difficult enough, seem comparatively accessible. If the field of inquiry be narrowed from History as a whole to that branch of it which is here called Culture, the history, not of tribes or nations, but of the condition of knowledge, religion, art, custom, and the like among them, the task of investigation proves to lie within far more moderate compass. We suffer still from the same kind of difficulties which beset the wider argument, but they are much diminished. The evidence is no longer so wildly heterogeneous, but may be more simply classified and compared, while the power of getting rid of extraneous matter, and treating each issue on its own proper set of facts, makes close reasoning on the whole more available than in general history. This may appear from a brief preliminary examination of the problem, how the phenomena of Culture may be classified and arranged, stage by stage, in a probable order of evolution.

Surveyed in a broad view, the character and habit of mankind at once display that similarity and consistency of phenomena which led the Italian proverb-maker to declare that "all the world is one country," "tutto il mondo è paese." To general likeness in human nature on the one hand, and to general likeness in the circumstances of life on the other, this similarity and consistency may no doubt be traced, and they may be studied with especial fitness in comparing races near the same grade of civilization. Little respect need be had in such comparisons for date in history or for place on the map; the ancient Swiss lake-dweller may be set beside the mediaeval Aztec, and the Ojibwa of North America beside the Zulu of South Africa. As Dr. Johnson contemptuously said when he had read about Patagonians and South Sea Islanders in Hawkesworth's Voyages, "one set of savages is like another." How true a generalization this really is, any Ethnological Museum may show.

Examine for instance the edged and pointed instruments in such a collection; the inventory includes hatchet, adze, chisel, knife, saw, scraper, awl, needle, spear and arrow-head, and of these most or all belong with only differences of detail to races the most various. So it is with savage occupations; the wood-chopping, fishing with net and line, shooting and spearing game, fire-making, cooking, twisting cord and plaiting baskets, repeat themselves with wonderful uniformity in the museum shelves which illustrate the life of the lower races from Kamchatka to Tierra del Fuego, and from Dahome to Hawaii. Even when it comes to comparing barbarous hordes with civilized nations, the consideration thrusts itself upon our minds, how far item after item of the life of the lower races passes into analogous proceedings of the higher, in forms not too far changed to be recognized, and sometimes hardly changed at all. Look at the modern European peasant using his hatchet and his hoe, see his food boiling or roasting over the log-fire, observe the exact place which beer holds in his calculation of happiness, hear his tale of the ghost in the nearest haunted house, and of the farmer's niece who was bewitched with knots in her inside till she fell into fits and died. If we choose out in this way things which have altered little in a long course of centuries, we may draw a picture where there shall be scarce a hand's breadth difference between an English ploughman and a negro of Central Africa. These pages will be so crowded with evidence of such correspondence among mankind, that there is no need to dwell upon its details here, but it may be used at once to override a problem which would complicate the argument, namely, the question of race. For the present purpose it appears both possible and desirable to eliminate considerations of hereditary varieties or races of man, and to treat mankind as homogeneous in nature, though placed in different grades of civilization. The details of the enquiry will, I think, prove that stages of culture may be compared without taking into account how far tribes who use the same implement, follow the same custom, or believe the same myth may differ in their bodily configuration and the colour of their skin and hair.

A first step in the study of civilization is to dissect it into details, and to classify these in their proper groups. Thus, in examining weapons, they are to be classed under spear, club, sling, bow and arrow, and so forth; among textile arts are to be ranged matting, netting, and several grades of making and weaving threads; myths are divided under such headings as myths of sunrise and sunset, eclipse-myths, earthquake-myths, local myths which account for the names of places by some fanciful tale, eponymic myths which account for the parentage of a tribe by turning its name into the name of an imaginary ancestor; under rites and ceremonies occur such practices as the various kinds of sacrifice to the ghosts of the dead and to other spiritual beings, the turning to the east in worship, the purification of ceremonial or moral uncleanness by means of water or fire. Such are a few miscellaneous examples from a list of hundreds, and the ethnographer's business is to classify such details with a view to making out their distribution in geography and history, and the relations which exist among them.

What this task is like may be almost perfectly illustrated by comparing these details of culture with the species of plants and animals as studied by the naturalist. To the ethnographer, the bow and arrow is a species, the habit of flattening children's skulls is a species, the practice of reckoning numbers by tens is a species. The geographical distribution of these things, and their transmission from region to region, have to be studied as the naturalist studies the geography of his botanical and zoological species. Just as certain plants and animals are peculiar to certain districts, so it is with such instruments as the Australian boomerang, the Polynesian stick-and-groove for fire-making, the tiny bow and arrow used as a lancet or phleme by tribes about the Isthmus of Panama, and in like manner with many an art, myth, or custom found isolated in a particular field. Just as the catalogue of all the species of plants and animals of a district represents its Flora and Fauna, so the list of all the items of the general life of a people represents that whole which we call its culture. And just as distant regions so often produce vegetables and animals which are analogous, though by no means identical, so it is with the details of the civilization of their inhabitants. How good a working analogy there really is between the diffusion of plants and animals and the diffusion of civilization comes well into view when we notice how far the same causes have produced both at once. In district after district, the same causes which have introduced the cultivated plants and domesticated animals of civilization, have brought in with them a corresponding art and knowledge. The course of events which carried horses and wheat to America carried with them the use of the gun and the iron hatchet, while in return the old world received not only maize, potatoes, and turkeys, but the habit of smoking and the sailor's hammock.

It is a matter worthy of consideration that the accounts of similar phenomena of culture, recurring in different parts of the world, actually supply incidental proof of their own authenticity. Some years since, a question which brings out this point was put to me by a great historian—"How can a statement as to customs, myths, beliefs, &c., of a savage tribe be treated as evidence where it depends on the testimony of some traveller or missionary, who may be a superficial observer, more or less ignorant of the native language, a careless retailer of unsifted talk, a man prejudiced or even wilfully deceitful?" This question is, indeed, one which every ethnographer ought to keep clearly and constantly before his mind. Of course he is bound to use his best judgment as to the trustworthiness of all authors he quotes, and if possible to obtain several accounts to certify each point in each locality. But it is over and above these measures of precaution that the test of recurrence comes in. If two independent visitors to different countries, say a mediaeval Mohammedan in Tartary and a modern Englishman in Dahome, or a Jesuit missionary in Brazil and a Wesleyan in the Fiji Islands, agree in describing some analogous art or rite or myth among the people they have visited, it becomes difficult or impossible to set down such correspondence to accident or wilful fraud. A story by a bushranger in Australia may, perhaps, be objected to as a mistake or an invention, but did a Methodist minister in

Guinea conspire with him to cheat the public by telling the same story there? The possibility of intentional or unintentional mystification is often barred by such a state of things as that a similar statement is made in two remote lands, by two witnesses, of whom A lived a century before B, and B appears never to have heard of A. How distant are the countries, how wide apart the dates, how different the creeds and characters of the observers, in the catalogue of facts of civilization, needs no farther showing to any one who will even glance at the foot-notes of the present work. And the more odd the statement, the less likely that several people in several places should have made it wrongly. This being so, it seems reasonable to judge that the statements are in the main truly given, and that their close and regular coincidence is due to the cropping up of similar facts in various districts of culture. Now the most important facts of ethnography are vouched for in this way. Experience leads the student after a while to expect and find that the phenomena of culture, as resulting from widely-acting similar causes, should recur again and again in the world. He even mistrusts isolated statements to which he knows of no parallel elsewhere, and waits for their genuineness to be shown by corresponding accounts from the other side of the earth, or the other end of history. So strong, indeed, is this means of authentication that the ethnographer in his library may sometimes presume to decide, not only whether a particular explorer is a shrewd and honest observer, but also whether what he reports is conformable to the general rules of civilization. *Non quis, sed quid.*

To turn from the distribution of culture in different countries to its diffusion within these countries. The quality of mankind which tends most to make the systematic study of civilization possible is that remarkable tacit consensus or agreement which so far induces whole populations to unite in the use of the same language, to follow the same religion and customary law, to settle down to the same general level of art and knowledge. It is this state of things which makes it so far possible to ignore exceptional facts and to describe nations by a sort of general average. It is this state of things which makes it so far possible to represent immense masses of details by a few typical facts, while, these once settled, new cases recorded by new observers simply fall into their places to prove the soundness of the classification. There is found to be such regularity in the composition of societies of men that we can drop individual differences out of sight, and thus can generalize on the arts and opinions of whole nations, just as, when looking down upon an army from a hill, we forget the individual soldier, whom, in fact, we can scarce distinguish in the mass, while we see each regiment as an organized body, spreading or concentrating, moving in advance or in retreat. In some branches of the study of social laws it is now possible to call in the aid of statistics, and to set apart special actions of large mixed communities of men by means of taxgatherers' schedules, or the tables of the insurance-office. Among modern arguments on the laws of human action, none have had a deeper effect than generalizations such as those of M. Quetelet, on the regularity, not only of such matters as average stature and the annual rates of birth and death, but of the recurrence, year after year, of such obscure and seemingly incalculable products of national life as the numbers of murders and suicides, and the proportion of the very weapons of crime. Other striking cases are the annual regularity of persons killed accidentally in the London streets, and of undirected letters dropped into post-office letter-boxes. But in examining the culture of the lower races, far from having at command the measured arithmetical facts of modern statistics, we may have to judge of the condition of tribes from the imperfect accounts supplied by travellers or missionaries, or even to reason upon relics of prehistoric races of whose very names and languages we are hopelessly ignorant. Now these may seem at the first glance sadly indefinite and unpromising materials for a scientific enquiry. But in fact they are neither indefinite nor unpromising, but give evidence that is good and definite, so far as it goes. They are data which, for the distinct way in which they severally denote the condition of the tribe they belong to, will actually bear comparison with the statistician's returns. The fact is that a stone arrow-head, a carved club, an idol, a grave-mound where slaves and property have been buried for the use of the dead, an account of a sorcerer's rites in making rain, a table of numerals, the conjugation of a verb are things which each express the state of a people as to one particular point of culture, as truly as the tabulated numbers of deaths by poison, and of chests of tea imported, express in a different way other partial results of the general life of a whole community.

That a whole nation should have a special dress, special tools and weapons, special laws of marriage and property, special moral and religious doctrines is a remarkable fact, which we notice so little because we have lived all our lives in the midst of it. It is with such general qualities of organized bodies of men that ethnography has especially to deal. Yet, while generalizing on the culture of a tribe or nation, and setting aside the peculiarities of the individuals composing it as unimportant to the main result, we must be careful not to forget what makes up this main result. There are people so intent on the separate life of individuals that they cannot grasp a notion of the action of a community as a whole—such an observer, incapable of a wide view of society, is aptly described in the saying that he "cannot see the forest for the trees." But, on the other hand, the philosopher may be so intent upon his general laws of society as to neglect the individual actors of whom that society is made up, and of him it may be said that he cannot see the trees for the forest. We know how arts, customs, and ideas are shaped among ourselves by the combined actions of many individuals, of which actions both motive and effect often come quite distinctly within our view. The history of an invention, an opinion, a ceremony, is a history of suggestion and modification, encouragement and opposition, personal gain and party prejudice, and the individuals concerned act each according to his own motives, as determined by his character and circumstances. Thus sometimes we watch individuals acting for their own ends with little thought of their effect on society at large, and sometimes we have to study movements of national life as a whole, where the individuals co-operating in them are utterly beyond our observation. But seeing that collective social action is the mere resultant of many individual actions, it is clear that these two methods of enquiry, if rightly followed, must be absolutely consistent.

In studying both the recurrence of special habits or ideas in several districts and their prevalence within each district, there come before us ever-reiterated proofs of regular causation producing the phenomena of human life, and of laws of maintenance and diffusion according to which these phenomena settle into permanent standard conditions of society, at definite stages of culture. But, while giving full importance to the evidence bearing on these standard conditions of society, let us be careful to avoid a pitfall which may entrap the unwary student. Of course the opinions and habits belonging in common to masses of mankind are to a great extent the results of sound judgment and practical wisdom. But to a great extent it is not so. That many numerous societies of men should have believed in the influence of the evil eye and the existence of a firmament, should have sacrificed slaves and goods to the ghosts of the departed, should have handed down traditions of giants slaying monsters and men turning into beasts—all this is ground for holding that such ideas were indeed produced in men's minds by efficient causes, but it is not ground for holding that the rites in question are profitable, the beliefs sound, and the history authentic. This may seem at the first glance a truism, but, in fact, it is the denial of a fallacy which deeply affects the minds of all but a small critical minority of mankind. Popularly, what everybody says must be true, what everybody does must be right— "Quod ubique, quod semper, quod ab omnibus creditum est, hoc est vere proprieque Catholicum"—and so forth. There are various topics, especially in history, law, philosophy, and theology, where even the educated people we live among can hardly be brought to see that the cause why men do hold an opinion, or practise a custom, is by no means necessarily a reason why they ought to do so. Now collections of ethnographic evidence, bringing so prominently into view the agreement of immense multitudes of men as to certain traditions, beliefs, and usages, are peculiarly liable to be thus improperly used in direct defence of these institutions themselves, even old barbaric nations being polled to maintain their opinions against what are called modern ideas. As it has more than once happened to myself to find my collections of traditions and beliefs thus set up to prove their own objective truth, without proper examination of the grounds on which they were actually received, I take this occasion of remarking that the same line of argument will serve equally well to demonstrate, by the strong and wide consent of nations, that the earth is flat, and nightmare the visit of a demon.

It being shown that the details of Culture are capable of being classified in a great number of ethnographic groups of arts, beliefs, customs, and the rest, the consideration comes next how far the facts arranged in these groups are produced by evolution from one another. It need hardly be pointed out that the groups in question, though held together each by a common character, are by no means accurately defined. To take up again the natural history illustration, it may be said that they are species which tend to run widely into varieties. And when it comes to the question what relations some of these groups bear to others, it is plain that the student of the habits of mankind has a great advantage over the student of the species of plants and animals. Among naturalists it is an open question whether a theory of development from species to species is a record of transitions which actually took place or a mere ideal scheme serviceable in the classification of species whose origin was really independent. But among ethnographers there is no such question as to the possibility of species of implements or habits or beliefs being developed one out of another, for development in culture is recognized by our most familiar knowledge. Mechanical invention supplies apt examples of the kind of development which affects civilization at large. In the history of fire-arms, the clumsy wheel-lock, in which a notched steel wheel was turned by a handle against the flint till a spark caught the priming, led to the invention of the more serviceable flint-lock, of which a few still hang in the kitchens of our farm-houses, for the boys to shoot small birds with at Christmas; the flint-lock in time passed by an obvious modification into the percussion-lock, which is just now changing its old-fashioned arrangement to be adapted from nuzzle-loading to breech-loading. The mediaeval astrolabe passed into the quadrant, now discarded in its turn by the seaman, who uses the more delicate sextant, and so it is through the history of one art and instrument after another. Such examples of progression are known to us as direct history, but so thoroughly is this notion of development at home in our minds, that by means of it we reconstruct lost history without scruple, trusting to general knowledge of the principles of human thought and action as a guide in putting the facts in their proper order. Whether chronicle speaks or is silent on the point, no one comparing a long-bow and a cross-bow would doubt that the cross-bow was a development arising from the simpler instrument. So among the savage fire-drills for igniting by friction, it seems clear on the face of the matter that the drill worked by a cord or bow is a later improvement on the clumsier primitive instrument twirled between the hands. That instructive class of specimens which antiquaries sometimes discover, bronze celts modelled on the heavy type of the stone hatchet, are scarcely explicable except as first steps in the transition from the Stone Age to the Bronze Age, to be followed soon by the next stage of progress, in which it is discovered that the new material is suited to a handier and less wasteful pattern. And thus, in the other branches of our history, there will come again and again into view series of facts which may be consistently arranged as having followed one another in a particular order of development, but which will hardly bear being turned round and made to follow in reversed order.

. . .

Among evidence aiding us to trace the courses which the civilization of the world has actually followed is that great class of facts to denote which I have found it convenient to introduce the term "survivals." These are processes, customs, opinions, and so forth, which have been carried on by force of habit into a new state of society different from that in which they had their original home, and they thus remain as proofs and examples of an older condition of culture out of which a newer has been evolved. Thus, I know an old Somersetshire woman whose hand-loom dates from the time before the introduction of the "flying shuttle," which new-fangled appliance she has never even learnt to use, and I have seen her throw her shuttle from hand to hand in true classic fashion; this old woman is not a century behind her times, but she is a case of survival. Such examples often lead us back to the habits of hundreds and even thousands of years ago. The ordeal of the Key and Bible, still in use, is a surival; the Midsummer bonfire is a survival; the Breton peasants' All Souls' supper for the spirits of the dead is a survival. The simple keeping up of ancient habits is only one part of the transition from old into new and changing times. The serious business of ancient society may be seen to sink into the sport of later generations, and its serious belief to linger on in nursery folk-lore, while superseded habits of old-world life may be modified into new-world forms still powerful for good and evil. Sometimes old thoughts and practices will burst out afresh, to the amazement of a world that thought them long since dead or dying; here survival passes into revival, as has lately happened in so remarkable a way in the history of modern spiritualism, a subject full of instruction from the ethnographer's point of view. The study of the principles of survival has, indeed, no small practical importance, for most of what we call superstition is included within survival, and in this way lies open to the attack of its deadliest enemy, a reasonable explanation. Insignificant, moreover, as multitudes of the facts of survival are in themselves, their study is so effective for tracing the course of the historical development through which alone it is possible to understand their meaning, that it becomes a vital point of ethnographic research to gain the clearest possible insight into their nature. This importance must justify the detail here devoted to an examination of survival, on the evidence of such games, popular sayings, customs, superstitions, and the like, as may serve well to bring into view the manner of its operation.

Progress, degradation, survival, revival, modification are all modes of the connexion that binds together the complex network of civilization. It needs but a glance into the trivial details of our own daily life to set us thinking how far we are really its originators, and how far but the transmitters and modifiers of the results of long past ages. Looking round the rooms we live in, we may try here how far he who only knows his own time can be capable of rightly comprehending even that. Here is the honeysuckle of Assyria, there the fleur-de-lis of Anjou, a cornice with a Greek border runs round the ceiling, the style of Louis XIV and its parent the Renaissance share the looking-glass between them. Transformed, shifted, or mutilated, such elements of art still carry their history plainly stamped upon them; and if the history yet farther behind is less easy to read, we are not to say that because we cannot clearly discern it there is therefore no history there. It is thus even with the fashion of the clothes men wear. The ridiculous little tails of the German postilion's coat show of themselves how they came to dwindle to such absurd rudiments; but the English clergyman's bands no longer so convey their history to the eye, and look unaccountable enough till one has seen the intermediate stages through which they came down from the more serviceable wide collars, such as Milton wears in his portrait, and which gave their name to the "band-box" they used to be kept in. In fact, the books of costume, showing how one garment grew or shrank by gradual stages and passed into another, illustrate with much force and clearness the nature of the change and growth, revival and decay, which go on from year to year in more important matters of life. In books, again, we see each writer not for and by himself, but occupying his proper place in history; we look through each philosopher, mathematician, chemist, poet, into the background of his education—through Leibnitz into Descartes, through Dalton into Priestley, through Milton into Homer. The study of language has, perhaps, done more than any other in removing from our view of human thought and action the ideas of chance and arbitrary invention, and in substituting for them a theory of development by the co-operation of individual men, through processes ever reasonable and intelligible where the facts are fully known. Rudimentary as the science of culture still is, the symptoms are becoming very strong that even what seem its most spontaneous and motiveless phenomena will, nevertheless, be shown to come within the range of distinct cause and effect as certainly as the facts of mechanics. What would be popularly thought more indefinite and uncontrolled than the products of the imagination in myths and fables? Yet any systematic investigation of mythology, on the basis of a wide collection of evidence, will show plainly enough in such efforts of fancy at once a development from stage to stage, and a production of uniformity of result from uniformity of cause. Here, as elsewhere, causeless spontaneity is seen to recede farther and farther into shelter within the dark precincts of ignorance; like chance, that still holds its place among the vulgar as a real cause of events otherwise unaccountable, while to educated men it has long consciously meant nothing but this ignorance itself. It is only when men fail to see the line of connexion in events that they are prone to fall upon the notions of arbitrary impulses, causeless freaks, chance and nonsense, and indefinite unaccountability. If childish games, purposeless customs, absurd superstitions are set down as spontaneous because no one can say exactly how they came to be, the assertion may remind us of the like effect that the eccentric habits of the wild rice-plant had on the philosophy of a Red Indian tribe, otherwise disposed to see in the harmony of nature the effects of one controlling personal will. The Great Spirit, said these Sioux theologians, made all things except the wild rice; but the wild rice came by chance.

"Man," said Wilhelm von Humboldt, "ever connects on from what lies at hand (der Mensch knüpft immer an Vorhandenes an)." The notion of the continuity of civilization contained in this maxim is no barren philosophic principle, but is at once made practical by the consideration that they who wish to understand their own lives ought to know the stages through which their opinions and habits have become what they are. Auguste Comte scarcely overstated the necessity of this study of development, when he declared at the beginning of his "Positive Philosophy" that "no conception can be understood except through its history," and his phrase will bear extension to culture at large. To expect to look modern life in the face and comprehend it by mere inspection is a philosophy whose weakness can easily be tested. Imagine any one explaining the trivial saying, "a little bird told me," without knowing of the old belief in the language of birds and beasts, to which Dr. Dasent, in the introduction to the Norse Tales, so reasonably traces its origin. To ingenious attempts at explaining by the light of reason things which want the light of history to show their meaning, much of the learned nonsense of the world has indeed been due. Sir H. S. Maine, in his "Ancient Law," gives a perfect instance. In all the literature which enshrines the pretended philosophy of law, he remarks, there is nothing more curious than the pages of elaborate sophistry in which Blackstone attempts to explain and justify that extraordinary rule of English law, only recently repealed, which prohibited sons of the same father by different mothers from succeeding to one another's land. To Sir H. S. Maine, knowing the facts of the case, it was easy to explain its real origin from the "Customs of Normandy," where according to the system of agnation, or kinship on the male side, brothers by the same mother but by different fathers were of course no relations at all to one another. But when this rule "was transplanted to England, the English judges, who had no clue to its principle, interpreted it as a general prohibition against the succession of the half-blood, and extended it to consanguineous brothers, that is to sons of the same father by different wives." Then, ages after, Blackstone sought in this blunder the perfection of reason, and found it in the argument that kinship through both parents ought to prevail over even a nearer degree of kinship through but one parent.[1] Such are the risks that philosophers run in detaching any phenomenon of civilization from its hold on past events, and treating it as an isolated fact, to be simply disposed of by a guess at some plausible explanation.

In carrying on the great task of rational ethnography, the investigation of the causes which have produced the phenomena of culture, and the laws to which they are subordinate, it is desirable to work out as systematically as possible a scheme of evolution of this culture along its many lines. In the following chapter [of *Primitive Culture*], on the Development of Culture, an attempt is made to sketch a theoretical course of civilization among mankind, such as appears on the whole most accordant with the evidence. By comparing the various stages of civilization among races known to history, with the aid of archaeological inference from the remains of pre-historic tribes, it seems possible to judge in a rough way of an early general condition of man, which from our point of view is to be regarded as a primitive condition, whatever yet earlier state may in reality have lain behind it. This hypothetical primitive condition corresponds in a considerable degree to that of modern savage tribes, who, in spite of their difference and distance, have in common certain elements of civilization, which seem remains of an early state of the human race at large. If this hypothesis be true, then, notwithstanding the continual interference of degeneration, the main tendency of culture from primaeval up to modern times has been from savagery towards civilization. On the problem of this relation of savage to civilized life, almost every one of the thousands of facts discussed in the succeeding chapters has its direct bearing. Survival in Culture, placing all along the course of advancing civilization way-marks full of meaning to those who can decipher their signs, even now sets up in our midst primaeval monuments of barbaric thought and life. Its investigation tells strongly in favour of the view that the European may find among the Greenlanders or Maoris many a trait for reconstructing the picture of his own primitive ancestors. Next comes the problem of the Origin of Language. Obscure as many parts of this problem still remain, its clearer positions lie open to the investigation whether speech took its origin among mankind in the savage state, and the result of the enquiry is that, consistently with all known evidence, this may have been the case. From the examination of the Art of Counting a far more definite consequence is shown. It may be confidently asserted that not only is this important art found in a rudimentary state among savage tribes, but that satisfactory evidence proves numeration to have been developed by rational invention from this low stage up to that in which we ourselves possess it. The examination of Mythology contained in the first volume is for the most part made from a special point of view, on evidence collected for a special purpose, that of tracing the relation between the myths of savage tribes and their analogues among more civilized nations. The issue of such enquiry goes far to prove that the earliest myth-maker arose and flourished among savage hordes, setting on foot an art which his more cultured successors would carry on, till its results came to be fossilized in superstition, mistaken for history, shaped and draped in poetry, or cast aside as lying folly.

Nowhere, perhaps, are broad views of historical development more needed than in the study of religion. Notwithstanding all that has been written to make the world acquainted with the lower theologies, the popular ideas of their place in history and their relation to the faiths of higher nations are still of the mediaeval type. It is wonderful to contrast some missionary journals with Max Müller's Essays, and to set the unappreciating hatred and ridicule that is lavished by narrow hostile zeal on Brahmanism, Buddhism, Zoroastrism, beside the catholic sympathy with which deep and wide knowledge can survey those ancient and noble phases of man's religious consciousness; nor, because the religions of savage tribes may be rude and primitive compared with the great Asiatic systems, do they lie too low for interest and even for respect. The question really lies between understanding and misunderstanding them. Few who will give their minds to master the general principles of savage religion will ever again think it ridiculous, or the knowledge of it superfluous to the rest of mankind. Far from its beliefs and practices being a rubbish-heap of miscellaneous folly, they are consistent and logical in so high a degree as to begin, as soon as even roughly classified, to display the principles of their formation and development; and these principles prove to be essentially rational, though working in a mental condition of intense and inveterate ignorance. It is with a sense of attempting an investigation which bears very closely on the current theology of our own day, that I have set myself to examine sytematically, among the lower races, the development of Animism; that is to say, the doctrine of souls and other spiritual beings in general. More than half of the present work is occupied with a mass of evidence from all regions of the world, displaying the nature and meaning of this great element of the Philosophy of Religion, and tracing its transmission, expansion, restriction, modification, along the course of history into the midst of our own modern thought. Nor are the questions of small practical moment which have to be raised in a similar attempt to trace the development of certain prominent Rites and Ceremonies—customs so full of instruction as to the inmost powers of religion, whose outward expression and practical result they are.

In these investigations, however, made rather from an ethnographic than a theological point of view, there has seemed little need of entering into direct controversial argument, which indeed I have taken pains to avoid as far as possible. The connexion which runs through religion, from its rudest forms up to the status of an enlightened Christianity, may be conveniently treated of with little recourse to dogmatic theology. The rites of sacrifice and purification may be studied in their stages of development without entering into questions of their authority and value, nor does an examination of the successive phases of the world's belief in a future life demand a discussion of the arguments adduced for or against the doctrine itself. The ethnographic results may then be left as materials for professed theologians, and it will not perhaps be long before evidence so fraught with meaning shall take its legitimate place. To fall back once again on the analogy of natural history, the time may soon come when it will be thought as unreasonable for a scientific student of theology not to have a competent acquaintance with the principles of the religions of the lower races, as for a physiologist to look with the contempt of fifty years ago on evidence derived from the lower forms of life, deeming the structure of mere invertebrate creatures matter unworthy of his philosophic study.

Not merely as a matter of curious research, but as an important practical guide to the understanding of the present and the shaping of the future, the investigation into the origin and early development of civilization must be pushed on zealously. Every possible avenue of knowledge must be explored, every door tried to see if it is open. No kind of evidence need be left untouched on the score of remoteness or complexity, of minuteness or triviality. The tendency of modern enquiry is more and more toward the conclusion that if law is anywhere, it is everywhere. To despair of what a conscientious collection and study of facts may lead to, and to declare any problem insoluble because difficult and far off, is distinctly to be on the wrong side in science; and he who will choose a hopeless task may set himself to discover the limits of discovery. One remembers Comte starting in his account of astronomy with a remark on the necessary limitation of our knowledge of the stars: we conceive, he tells us, the possibility of determining their form, distance, size, and movement, whilst we should never by any method be able to study their chemical composition, their mineralogical structure, &c. Had the philosopher lived to see the application of spectrum analysis to this very problem, his proclamation of the dispiriting doctrine of necessary ignorance would perhaps have been recanted in favour of a more hopeful view. And it seems to be with the philosophy of remote human life somewhat as with the study of the nature of the celestial bodies. The processes to be made out in the early stages of our mental evolution lie distant from us in time as the stars lie distant from us in space, but the laws of the universe are not limited with the direct observation of our senses. There is vast material to be used in our enquiry; many workers are now busied in bringing this material into shape, though little may have yet been done in proportion to what remains to do; and already it seems not too much to say that the vague outlines of a philosophy of primaeval history are beginning to come within our view.

NOTE

1. Blackstone, "Commentaries." "As every man's own blood is compounded of the bloods of his respective ancestors, he only is properly of the whole or entire blood with another, who hath (so far as the distance of degrees will permit), all the same ingredients in the composition of his blood that the other hath," etc.

PART
TWO
PARTICULARISM— ETHNOGRAPHIC and OTHERWISE

Franz Boas 1858–1942

BACKGROUND

Although there were many American anthropologists before Franz Boas, it was he who founded the first university department in America (at Clark University in 1888), and he was himself a sort of funnel through which all anthropology passed between its nineteenth-century juniority and its twentieth-century maturity.

Boas (like many American anthropologists of the time) was born and brought up in Germany—a fact that is not unimportant in the history of the subject, dictating as it did that French influences came late into American anthropology. His family was actively liberal, inactively Jewish. His father was a successful businessman, his "very idealistic"—his own description—mother active in civic affairs. His first nineteen years were spent in local schools, where he developed strong interests in natural history and botany and became an accomplished pianist. Throughout his life he maintained close family ties.

At twenty Boas began university, moving from Heidelberg to Bonn and finally to Kiel, where he received his doctorate in 1881. He studied physics, then math, and finished in geography—his dissertation was "Contributions to the Understanding of the Color of Water." There are conflicting stories about the scars on his face—some people said they were acquired from dueling while at the university; on at least one occasion he himself attributed them to polar-bear clawing.

A staunch believer in the value of first-hand information, he decided in 1883 to undertake a geological expedition to investigate seawater under Arctic conditions. His year-long stay with the whalers and Eskimos turned Boas into an ethnographer and convinced him that knowledge gained by mere observation is useless without understanding the traditions that condition the perceiver. This realization, along with the warm friendships of his Arctic hosts, precipitated what was to become his lifelong interest—field research as a royal road to anthropology.

He spent the winter of 1884–1885 in New York, then returned to Germany to the Museum für Völkerkunde, where he first met trained ethnologists. In 1886 he accepted an appointment in geography at the University of Berlin. Then, inspired by a group of visiting Bella Coola Indians, he set out to begin his lifelong study of the Indians of the British Columbia coast. When he returned to Germany a year later, he married, decided to become an American, and resigned his University of Berlin position.

In 1888 he returned to British Columbia and began his period of teaching and research at Clark University, which was marked by many publications on linguistics, ethnological theory, anthropometry, folklore, and the aims of ethnology.

Boas left Clark in 1892 to become chief assistant in anthropology at the Chicago Exposition. When the Field Museum grew out of the exposition, he became curator of anthropology. Forced to resign because of personal conflicts—he was a stickly man—Boas moved to the American Museum of Natural History in New York and soon began lecturing at Columbia.

In 1899 Boas became a tenured professor, and from 1901 to 1905 he was also curator of the American Museum. Because of further personality conflicts, he was forced to leave the museum. However, by this time he was well established and ready to devote his entire efforts to teaching and research. He built a home on the New Jersey palisades that was to remain a gathering spot for the Boas children and grandchildren throughout his life.

There are starkly contrasting opinions about the quality of Boas' teaching, but it is generally agreed that he was "the founder of modern field work in America" and that he trained a generation of brilliant and productive anthropologists. Boas was not a good lecturer. He introduced little concrete data into his lectures (and little else into his ethnographic books). He took the students' prior background and language ability for granted, to the dismay of some of them. However, to the inspired and responsible student, Boas was a magnificent teacher. The personal warmth that his family knew was reserved for the small, intimate group of his most talented students.

In 1910 Boas helped to establish the International School of American Archaeology and Ethnology in Mexico. Serving as resident-director in 1911–1912, he was influential in the introduction of new stratigraphic methods of excavation. He published what may be his most famous book, *The Mind of Primitive Man,* in 1911 in an effort to help clarify the relationship—or lack of it—between culture and human physical types. His revolutionary approach to language in the study of culture was seminal in the creation of the field of comparative linguistics.

In 1914 cancer involving a main facial nerve led to permanent paralysis of half of his face but did not damage his sturdy constitution, and six weeks after surgery he left to do field work in Puerto Rico. The 1920s were marred by the deaths of his wife and two of his children. Despite his losses, he continued research and teaching, maintained his interest in race problems and civil rights, and expressed alarm over the rise of German Nazism. When Hitler came to power, all of Boas' writings were publicly burned in Kiel.

He retired from Columbia in 1936 but continued to write and lecture at public meetings. He had published more than six hundred articles, as well as what many people call his "five-foot shelf" of Kwakiutl ethnography.

Boas—the man whose tough spirit had scientized American anthropology—died while giving a luncheon for his friends and associates at the University Club of Columbia on December 21, 1942.

INTRODUCTION

Trying to select representative pieces from the immense *oeuvre* of Franz Boas makes one poignantly aware of how very much he contributed to the discipline through the students he trained and the oral tradition. His writings tend to be so specific as to be suitable only in a very narrow context; to get the good of most of Boas' work one must be immersed in it. Therefore we have picked two pieces that we think focus on his most important contribution: one discusses the professionalization of field research and the other attacks sloppy use of the comparative method. That leaves out much—such as his continuing attack on racism, which he synthesized in *The Mind of Primitive Man* (1911). His analysis concludes that the range of cultures, to be found in association with any race, is so wide as to prove any relationship between race and culture nonexistent. He also concluded that the variation of phenotypes within a race makes it impossible to speak of inferior or superior races.

Boas held this position on race all through his life. In an article in 1932 he stated that the difference between populations is independent of racial characteristics while being a function of cultural differences. The date of that article is important, and so is the fact that it was published in German. It was just a year before Hitler's domination of Germany.

Boas published his attack on the comparative method in 1896. That article, "The Limitations of the Comparative Method of Anthropology," was the first expression of cultural relativism, which Boas did so much to create and which is still a strongly held position in anthropology. According to the tenets of cultural relativism, all cultures are equal and comparable; there are no inferior or superior cultures. It is therefore impossible, Boas said, to order cultures in an evolutionary scheme. A better way to say this would have been to say that whenever we make judgments of good or bad, better or worse, about cultures, we necessarily do so on the basis of certain overt or covert premises. Such premises are certainly culture-bound and probably are ethnocentric. Therefore, whether a trait is the same from one culture to the next is a difficult question, and whether one culture is "better" than another is a silly question. Put that way, we can see that sentimentality rather than evolution is the enemy of cultural relativism.

Here are some of the limitations of the comparative method according to Boas:

1. It is impossible to account for all the types of culture by claiming that they are similar because of the similarity of the human mind.

2. The discovery of similar traits in different societies is not as important as the comparative school would have it.

3. Similar traits may well have developed for very different reasons in differing cultures.

4. The view that cultural differences are minute is groundless—it is the cultural differences that are of major ethnographic importance.

Boas tried to replace the comparative method with a method that stressed the following points:

1. Customs have to be studied in detail and as a part of the cultural whole.

2. The distribution of a custom within neighboring cultures should also be analyzed.

According to Boas this method would enable the student (1) to reveal the environmental factors that influenced a culture, (2) to clarify the psychological aspects that shape the culture, and (3) to clarify the history of the local development of a custom.

This, obviously, is a call for the inductive method in anthropology. Boas taught that the first task of anthropology was to study individual societies and that comparative generalizations could come only on the basis of accumulated data. His importance within the discipline is precisely this view—that anthropology should become a discipline using the scientific method of induction. In an age when the scientific method was crucially important in intellectual circles, it is not surprising that Boas' idea was found to be the right alternative to the comparative method, whose use of crosscultural data had been carried to excess.

4 THE LIMITATIONS OF THE COMPARATIVE METHOD OF ANTHROPOLOGY[1]

Modern anthropology has discovered the fact that human society has grown and developed everywhere in such a manner that its forms, its opinions and its actions have many fundamental traits in common. This momentous discovery implies that laws exist which govern the development of society; that they are applicable to our society as well as to those of past times and of distant lands; that their knowledge will be a means of understanding the causes furthering and retarding civilization; and that, guided by this knowledge, we may hope to govern our actions so that the greatest benefit to mankind will accrue from them. Since this discovery has been clearly formulated, anthropology has begun to receive that liberal share of public interest which was withheld from it as long as it was believed that it could do no more than record the curious customs and beliefs of strange peoples; or, at best, trace their relationships, and thus elucidate the early migrations of the races of man and the affinities of peoples.

While early investigators concentrated their attention upon this purely historical problem, the tide has now completely turned, so that there are even anthropologists who declare that such investigations belong to the historian, and that anthropological studies must be confined to researches on the laws that govern the growth of society.

A radical change of method has accompanied this change of views. While formerly identities or similarities of culture were considered incontrovertible proof of historical connection, or even of common origin, the new school declines to consider them as such, but interprets them as results of the uniform working of the human mind. The most pronounced adherent of this view in our country is Dr. D. G. Brinton, in Germany the majority of the followers of Bastian, who in this respect go much farther than Bastian himself. Others, while not denying the occurrence of historical connections, regard them as significant in results and in theoretical importance as compared to

Reprinted from *Science* 4, no. 103 (December 18, 1896), courtesy of Charles C Thomas, Publisher, Springfield, Illinois.

the working of the uniform laws governing the human mind. This is the view of by far the greater number of living anthropologists.

This modern view is founded on the observation that the same ethnical phenomena occur among the most diverse peoples, or, as Bastian says, on the appalling monotony of the fundamental ideas of mankind all over the globe. The metaphysical notions of man may be reduced to a few types which are of universal distribution; the same is the case in regard to the forms of society, laws and inventions. Furthermore, the most intricate and apparently illogical ideas and the most curious and complex customs appear among a few tribes here and there in such a manner that the assumption of a common historical origin is excluded. When studying the culture of any one tribe, more or less close analoga of single traits of such a culture may be found among a great diversity of peoples. Instances of such analoga have been collected to a vast extent by Tylor, Spencer, Bastian, Andree, Post and many others, so that it is not necessary to give here any detailed proof of this fact. The idea of a future life, the one underlying shamanism; inventions such as fire and the bow; certain elementary features of grammatical structure —these will suggest the classes of phenomena to which I refer. It follows from these observations that when we find an analogon of single traits of culture among distant peoples, the presumption is not that there has been a common historical source, but that they have arisen independently.

But the discovery of these universal ideas is only the beginning of the work of the anthropologist. Scientific inquiry must answer two questions in regard to them: First, what is their origin? and second, how do they assert themselves in various cultures?

The second question is the easier one to answer. The ideas do not exist everywhere in identical form, but they vary. Sufficient material has been accumulated to show that the causes of these variations are either external, that is founded in environment—taking the term environment in its widest sense—or internal, that is founded on psychological conditions. The influence of external and internal factors upon elementary ideas embodies one group of laws governing the growth of culture. Therefore, our endeavors must be directed to showing how such factors modify elementary ideas.

The first method that suggests itself and which has been generally adopted by modern anthropologists is to isolate and classify causes by grouping the variants of certain ethnological phenomena according to external conditions under which the people live, among whom they are found, or to internal causes which influence their minds; or inversely, by grouping these variants according to their similarities. Then the correlated conditions of life may be found.

By this method we begin to recognize even now with imperfect knowledge of the facts what causes may have been at work in shaping the culture of mankind. Friedrich Ratzel and W. J. McGee have investigated the influence of geographical environment on a broader basis of facts than Ritter and Guyot were able to do at their time. Sociologists have made important studies on the effects of the density of population and of other simple social causes. Thus the influence of external factors upon the growth of society is becoming clearer.

The effects of psychical factors are also being studied in the same manner. Stoll has tried to isolate the phenomena of suggestion and of hypnotism and to study the effects of their presence in the cultures of various peoples. Inquiries into the mutual relations of tribes and peoples begin to show that certain cultural elements are easily assimilated while others are rejected; and the time-worn phrases of the imposition of culture by a more highly civilized people upon one of lower culture that has been conquered are giving way to more thorough views on the subject of exchange of cultural achievements. In all these investigations we are using sound, inductive methods in order to isolate the causes of observed phenomena.

The other question in regard to the universal ideas, namely, that of their origin, is much more difficult to treat. Many attempts have been made to discover the causes which have led to the formation of ideas "that develop with iron necessity wherever man lives." This is the most difficult problem of anthropology and we may expect that it will baffle our attempts for a long time to come. Bastian denies that it is possible to discover the ultimate sources of inventions, ideas, customs and beliefs which are of universal occurrence. They may be indigenous, they may be imported, they may have arisen from a variety of sources, but they are there. The human mind is so formed that it invents them spontaneously or accepts them whenever they are offered to it. This is the much misunderstood elementary idea of Bastian.

To a certain extent the clear enunciation of the elementary idea gives us the psychological reason for its existence. To exemplify: the fact that the land of the shadows is so often placed in the west suggests the endeavor to localize it at the place where the sun and the stars vanish. The mere statement that primitive man considers animals as gifted with all the qualities of man shows that the analogy between many of the qualities of animals and human qualities has led to the generalization that all the qualities of animals are human. In other cases the causes are not so self-evident. Thus the question why all languages distinguish between the self, the person addressed and the person spoken of, and why most languages do not carry out this sharp, logical distinction in the plural is difficult to answer. The principle when carried out consistently requires that in the plural there should be a distinction between the "we" expressing the self and the person addressed and the "we" expressing the self and the person spoken of, which distinction is found in comparatively few languages only. The lesser liability to misunderstandings in the plural explains this phenomenon partly but hardly adequately. Still more obscure is the psychological basis in other cases, for instance, in that of widely spread marriage customs. Proof of the difficulty of this problem is the multitude of hypotheses that have been invented to explain it in all its varied phases.

In treating this, the most difficult problem of anthropology, the point of view is taken that if an ethnological phenomenon has developed independently in a number of places its development has been the same everywhere;

or, expressed in a different form, that the same ethnological phenomena are always due to the same causes. This leads to the still wider generalization that the sameness of ethnological phenomena found in diverse regions is proof that the human mind obeys the same laws everywhere. It is obvious that if different historical developments could lead to the same results, that then this generalization would not be tenable. Their existence would present to us an entirely different problem, namely, how it is that the developments of culture so often lead to the same results. It must, therefore, be clearly understood that anthropological research which compares similar cultural phenomena from various parts of the world, in order to discover the uniform history of their development, makes the assumption that the same ethnological phenomenon has everywhere developed in the same manner. Here lies the flaw in the argument of the new method, for no such proof can be given. Even the most cursory review shows that the same phenomena may develop in a multitude of ways.

I will give a few examples: Primitive tribes are almost universally divided into clans which have totems. There can be no doubt that this form of social organization has arisen independently over and over again. The conclusion is certainly justified that the psychical conditions of man favor the existence of a totemistic organization of society, but it does not follow that totemistic society has developed everywhere in the same manner. Dr. Washington Matthews has shown that the totems of the Navajo have arisen by association of independent clans. Capt. Bourke has pointed out that similar occurrences gave origin to the Apache clans, and Dr. Fewkes has reached the same conclusion in regard to some of the Pueblo tribes. On the other hand, we have proof that clans may originate by division. I have shown that such events took place among the Indians of the North Pacific coast. Association of small tribes, on the one hand, and disintegration of increasing tribes, on the other, has led to results which appear identical to all intents and purposes.

Here is another example. Recent investigations have shown that geometrical designs in primitive art have originated either from naturalistic forms which were gradually conventionalized or from technical motives, or that they were primarily geometrical or that they were derived from symbols. From all these sources the same forms have developed. Out of designs representing diverse objects grew in course of time frets, meanders, crosses and the like. Therefore the frequent occurrence of these forms proves neither common origin nor that they have always developed according to the same psychical laws. On the contrary, the identical result may have been reached on four different lines of development and from an infinite number of starting points.

Another example may not be amiss: The use of masks is found among a great number of peoples. The origin of the custom of wearing masks is by no means clear in all cases, but a few typical forms of their use may easily be distinguished. They are used for deceiving spirits as to the identity of the wearer. The spirit of a disease who intends to attack the person does not recognize him when he wears a mask, and the mask serves in this manner as a protection. In other cases the mask represents a spirit which is personified by the wearer, who in this shape frightens away other hostile spirits. Still other masks are commemorative. The wearer personifies a deceased person whose memory is to be recalled. Masks are also used in theatrical performances illustrating mythological incidents (Andree 1889:107 ff.).

These few data suffice to show that the same ethnical phenomenon may develop from different sources. The simpler the observed fact, the more likely it is that it may have developed from one source here, from another there.

Thus we recognize that the fundamental assumption which is so often made by modern anthropologists cannot be accepted as true in all cases. We cannot say that the occurrence of the same phenomenon is always due to the same causes, and that thus it is proved that the human mind obeys the same laws everywhere. We must demand that the causes from which it developed be investigated and that comparisons be restricted to those phenomena which have been proved to be effects of the same causes. We must insist that this investigation be made a preliminary to all extended comparative studies. In researches on tribal societies those which have developed through association must be treated separately from those that have developed through disintegration. Geometrical designs which have arisen from conventionalized representations of natural objects must be treated separately from those that have arisen from technical motives. In short, before extended comparisons are made, the comparability of the material must be proved.

The comparative studies of which I am speaking here attempt to explain customs and ideas of remarkable similarity which are found here and there. But they pursue also the more ambitious scheme of discovering the laws and the history of the evolution of human society. The fact that many fundamental features of culture are universal, or at least occur in many isolated places, interpreted by the assumption that the same features must always have developed from the same causes, leads to the conclusion that there is one grand system according to which mankind has developed everywhere; that all the occurring variations are no more than minor details in this grand uniform evolution. It is clear that this theory has for its logical basis the assumption that the same phenomena are always due to the same causes. To give an instance: We find many types of structure of family. It can be proved that paternal families have often developed from maternal ones. Therefore, it is said, all paternal families have developed from maternal ones. If we do not make the assumption that the same phenomena have everywhere developed from the same causes, then we may just as well conclude that paternal families have in some cases arisen from maternal institutions, in other cases in other ways. To give another example: Many conceptions of the future life have evidently developed from dreams and hallucinations. Consequently, it is said, all notions of this character have had the same origin. This is also true only if no other causes could possibly lead to the same ideas.

We have seen that the facts do not favor the assumption of which we are speaking at all; that they much rather point in the opposite direction. Therefore we must also consider all the ingenious attempts at constructions of a grand system of the evolution of society as of very doubtful value, unless at the same time proof is given that the same phenomena could not develop by any other method. Until this is done, the presumption is always in favor of a variety of courses which historical growth may have taken.

It will be well to restate at this place one of the principal aims of anthropological research. We agreed that certain laws exist which govern the growth of human culture, and it is our endeavor to discover these laws. The object of our investigation is to find the *processes* by which certain stages of culture have developed. The customs and beliefs themselves are not the ultimate objects of research. We desire to learn the reasons why such customs and beliefs exist—in other words, we wish to discover the history of their development. The method which is at present most frequently applied in investigations of this character compares the variations under which the customs or beliefs occur and endeavors to find the common psychological cause that underlies all of them. I have stated that this method is open to a very fundamental objection.

We have another method, which in many respects is much safer. A detailed study of customs in their bearings to the total culture of the tribe practicing them, and in connection with an investigation of their geographical distribution among neighboring tribes, affords us almost always a means of determining with considerable accuracy the historical causes that led to the formation of the customs in question and to the psychological processes that were at work in their development. The results of inquiries conducted by this method may be three-fold. They may reveal the environmental conditions which have created or modified cultural elements; they may clear up psychological factors which are at work in shaping the culture; or they may bring before our eyes the effects that historical connections have had upon the growth of the culture.

We have in this method a means of reconstructing the history of the growth of ideas with much greater accuracy than the generalizations of the comparative method will permit. The latter must always proceed from a hypothetical mode of development, the probability of which may be weighed more or less accurately by means of observed data. But so far I have not yet seen any extended attempt to prove the correctness of a theory by testing it at the hand of developments with whose histories we are familiar. This method of starting with a hypothesis is infinitely inferior to the one in which by truly inductive processes the actual history of definite phenomena is derived. The latter is no other than the much ridiculed historical method. Its way of proceeding is, of course, no longer that of former times when slight similarities of culture were considered proofs of relationships, but it duly recognizes the results obtained by comparative studies. Its application is based, first of all, on a well-defined, small geographical territory, and its comparisons are not extended beyond the limits of the cultural area that forms the basis of the study. Only when definite results have been obtained in regard to this area is it permissible to extend the horizon beyond its limits, but the greatest care must be taken not to proceed too hastily in this, as else the fundamental proposition which I formulated before might be overlooked, viz.: that when we find an analogy of single traits of culture among distant peoples the presumption is not that there has been a common historical source, but that they have arisen independently. Therefore the investigation must always demand continuity of distribution as one of the essential conditions for proving historical connection, and the assumption of lost connecting links must be applied most sparingly. This clear distinction between the new and the old historical methods is still often overlooked by the passionate defenders of the comparative method. They do not appreciate the difference between the indiscriminate use of similarities of culture for proving historical connection and the careful and slow detailed study of local phenomena. We no longer believe that the slight similarities between the cultures of Central America and of eastern Asia are sufficient and satisfactory proof of a historical connection. On the contrary, analogy of other similarities makes such a connection improbable. But, on the other hand, no unbiased observer will deny that there are very strong reasons for believing that a limited number of cultural elements found in Alaska and in Siberia have a common origin. The similarities of inventions, customs and beliefs, together with the continuity of their distribution through a comparatively small area, are a satisfactory proof of this opinion. But it is not possible to extend this area safely beyond the limits of Columbia River in America and northern Japan in Asia. This method of anthropological research is represented in our country by Prof. F. W. Putnam and Prof. Otis T. Mason; in England by Dr. E. B. Tylor; in Germany by Friedrich Ratzel and his followers.

It seems necessary to say a word here in regard to an objection to my arguments that will be raised by investigators who claim that similarity of geographical environment is a sufficient cause for similarity of culture, that is to say, that, for instance, the geographical conditions of the plains of the Mississippi basin necessitate the development of a certain culture. There are those who would even go so far as to believe that similarity of form of language may be due to environmental causes. Environment has a certain limited effect upon the culture of man, but I do not see how the view that it is the primary moulder of culture can be supported by any facts. A hasty review of the tribes and peoples of our globe shows that people most diverse in culture and language live under the same geographical conditions, as proof of which may be mentioned the ethnography of East Africa or of New Guinea. In both these regions we find a great diversity of customs in small areas. But much more important is this: Not one observed fact can be brought forward in support of this hypothesis which cannot be much better explained by the well known facts of diffusion of culture; for archaeology as well as ethnography teaches us that intercourse between neighboring tribes has always existed and has extended over enormous areas. In the Old World the products of the Baltic found their way to the Mediterranean and the works of art of the eastern Mediterranean reached Sweden. In America the shells of the ocean found their way into the innermost parts of the continent and the obsidians of the West were carried to Ohio. Intermarriages, war, slavery, trade, have been so many sources of constant introduction of foreign cultural elements, so that an assimilation of culture must have taken place over continuous areas. Therefore, it seems to my mind that where among neighboring tribes an immediate influence of environment cannot be shown to exist, the presumption must always be in favor of historical connection. There has been a time of isolation during which the principal traits of diverse cultures developed according to the character and environment of the tribes. But the stages of culture representing this period have been covered with so much that is new and that is due to contact with foreign tribes that they cannot be discovered without the most painstaking isolation of foreign elements.

The immediate results of the historical method are, therefore, histories of the cultures of diverse tribes which have been the subject of study. I fully agree with those anthropologists who claim that this is not the ultimate aim of our science, because the general laws, although implied in such a description, cannot be clearly formulated nor their relative value appreciated without a thorough comparison of the manner in which they assert themselves in different cultures. But I insist that the application of this method is the indispensable condition of sound progress. The psychological problem is contained in the results of the historical inquiry. When we have cleared up the history of a single culture and understand the effects of environment and the psychological conditions that are reflected in it we have made a step forward, as we can then investigate in how far the same causes or other causes were at work in the development of other cultures. Thus by comparing histories of growth general laws may be found. This method is much safer than the comparative method, as it is usually practiced, because instead of a hypothesis on the mode of development actual history forms the basis of our deductions.

The historical inquiry must be considered the critical test that science must require before admitting facts as evidence. By its means the comparability of the collected material must be tested, and uniformity of processes must be demanded as proof of comparability. It may also be mentioned that when historical connection between two phenomena can be proved, they must not be admitted as independent evidence.

In a few cases the immediate results of this method are of so wide a scope that they rank with the best results that can be attained by comparative studies. Some phenomena have so immense a distribution that the discovery of their occurrence over very large continuous areas proves at once that certain phases of the culture in these areas have sprung from one source. Thus are illuminated vast portions of the early history of mankind. When Prof. Morse showed that certain methods of arrow release are peculiar to whole continents it became clear at once that the common practice that is found over a vast area must have had a common origin. When the Polynesians employ a method of fire making consisting in rubbing a stick along a groove, while almost all other peoples use the fire drill, it shows their art of fire making has a single origin. When we notice that the ordeal is found all over

Africa in certain peculiar forms, while in those parts of the inhabited world that are remote from Africa it is found not at all or in rudimentary forms only, it shows that the idea as practiced in Africa had one single origin.

The great and important function of the historical method of anthropology is thus seen to lie in its ability to discover the processes which in definite cases led to the development of certain customs. If anthropology desires to establish the laws governing the growth of culture it must not confine itself to comparing the results of the growth alone, but whenever such is feasible it must compare the processes of growth, and these can be discovered by means of studies of the cultures of small geographical areas.

Thus we have seen that the comparative method can hope to reach the grand results for which it is striving only when it bases its investigations on the historical results of researches which are devoted to laying clear the complex relations of each individual culture. The comparative method and the historical method, if I may use these terms, have been struggling for supremacy for a long time, but we may hope that each will soon find its appropriate place and function. The historical method has reached a sounder basis by abandoning the misleading principle of assuming connections wherever similarities of culture were found. The comparative method, notwithstanding all that has been said and written in its praise, has been remarkably barren of definite results, and I believe it will not become fruitful until we renounce the vain endeavor to construct a uniform systematic history of the evolution of culture, and until we begin to make our comparisons on the broader and sounder basis which I ventured to outline. Up to this time we have too much reveled in more or less ingenious vagaries. The solid work is still all before us.

NOTE

1. Paper read at the meetings of the American Association for the Advancement of Science, Buffalo, New York.

REFERENCE

Andree, Richard
    1889   *Ethnographische Parallelen und Vergleiche.* Neue Folge.

5 THE METHODS OF ETHNOLOGY

During the last ten years the methods of inquiry into the historical development of civilization have undergone remarkable changes. During the second half of the last century evolutionary thought held almost

Reprinted by permission of the American Anthropological Association from *American Anthropologist* 22, no. 4 (October–December, 1920): 311–321.

complete sway and investigators like Spencer, Morgan, Tylor, Lubbock, to mention only a few, were under the spell of the idea of a general, uniform evolution of culture in which all parts of mankind participated. The newer development goes back in part to the influence of Ratzel, whose geographical training impressed him with the importance of diffusion and migration. The problem of diffusion was taken up in detail particularly in America, but was applied in a much wider sense by Foy and Graebner, and finally seized upon in a still wider application by Elliot Smith and Rivers, so that at the present time, at least among certain groups of investigators in England and also in Germany, ethnological research is based on the concept of migration and dissemination rather than upon that of evolution.

A critical study of these two directions of inquiry shows that each is founded on the application of one fundamental hypothesis. The evolutionary point of view presupposes that the course of historical changes in the cultural life of mankind follows definite laws which are applicable everywhere, and which bring it about that cultural development is, in its main lines, the same among all races and all peoples. This idea is clearly expressed by Tylor in the introductory pages of his classic work "Primitive Culture." As soon as we admit that the hypothesis of a uniform evolution has to be proved before it can be accepted, the whole structure loses its foundation. It is true that there·are indications of parallelism of development in different parts of the world, and that similar customs are found in the most diverse and widely separated parts of the globe. The occurrence of these similarities, which are distributed so irregularly that they they cannot readily be explained on the basis of diffusion, is one of the foundations of the evolutionary hypothesis, as it was the foundation of Bastian's psychologizing treatment of cultural phenomena. On the other hand, it may be recognized that the hypothesis implies the thought that our modern Western European civilization represents the highest cultural development towards which all other more primitive cultural types tend, and that, therefore, retrospectively, we construct an orthogenetic development towards our own modern civilization. It is clear that if we admit that there may be different ultimate and coexisting types of civilization, the hypothesis of one single general line of development cannot be maintained.

Opposed to these assumptions is the modern tendency to deny the existence of a general evolutionary scheme which would represent the history of the cultural development the world over. The hypothesis that there are inner causes which bring about similarities of development in remote parts of the globe is rejected and in its place it is assumed that identity of development in two different parts of the globe must always be due to migration and diffusion. On this basis historical contact is demanded for enormously large areas. The theory demands a high degree of stability of cultural traits such as is apparently observed in many primitive tribes, and it is furthermore based on the supposed correlation between a number of diverse and mutually independent cultural traits which reappear in the same combinations in distant parts of the world. In this sense, modern investigation takes up anew Gerland's theory of the persistence of a number of cultural traits which were developed in one center and carried by man in his migrations from continent to continent.

It seems to me that if the hypothetical foundations of these two extreme forms of ethnological research are broadly stated as I have tried to do here, it is at once clear that the correctness of the assumptions has not been demonstrated, but that arbitrarily the one or the other has been selected for the purpose of obtaining a consistent picture of cultural development. These methods are essentially forms of classification of the static phenomena of culture according to two distinct principles, and intepretations of these classifications as of historical significance, without, however, any attempt to prove that this interpretation is justifiable. To give an example: It is observed that in most parts of the world there are resemblances between decorative forms that are representative and others that are more or less geometrical. According to the evolutionary point of view, their development is explained in the following manner: the decorative forms are arranged in such order that the most representative forms are placed at the beginning. The other forms are so placed that they show a gradual transition from representative forms to purely conventional geometric forms, and this order is then interpreted as meaning that geometric designs originated from representative designs which gradually degenerated. This method has been pursued, for instance, by Putnam, Stolpe, Balfour, and Haddon, and by Verworn and, in his earlier writings, by von den Steinen. While I do not mean to deny that this development may have occurred, it would be rash to generalize and to claim that in every case the classification which has been made according to a definite principle represents an historical development. The order might as well be reversed and we might begin with a simple geometric element which, by the addition of new traits, might be developed into a representative design, and we might claim that this order represents an historical sequence. Both of these possibilities were considered by Holmes as early as 1885. Neither the one nor the other theory can be established without actual historical proof.

The opposite attitude, namely, origin through diffusion, is exhibited in Heinrich Schurtz's attempt to connect the decorative art of Northwest America with that of Melanesia. The simple fact that in these areas elements occur that may be interpreted as eyes, induced him to assume that both have a common origin, without allowing for the possibility that the pattern in the two areas—each of which shows highly distinctive characteristics—may have developed from independent sources. In this attempt Schurtz followed Ratzel, who had already tried to establish connections between Melanesia and Northwest America on the basis of other cultural features.

While ethnographical research based on these two fundamental hypotheses seems to characterize the general tendency of European thought, a different method is at present pursued by the majority of American anthropologists. The difference between the two directions of study may perhaps best be summarized by the statement that American scholars are primarily interested in the dynamic phenomena of cultural change, and try to elucidate cultural history by the application of the results of their studies; and that they relegate the solution of the ultimate question of the relative importance of parallelism of cultural development in distant areas, as against worldwide diffusion, and stability of cultural traits over long periods to a future time when the actual conditions of cultural change are better known. The American ethnological methods are analogous to those of European, particularly of Scandinavian, archaeology, and of the researches into the prehistoric period of the eastern Mediterranean area.

It may seem to the distant observer that American students are engaged in a mass of detailed investigations without much bearing upon the solution of the ultimate problems of a philosophic history of human civilization. I think this interpretation of the American attitude would be unjust because the ultimate questions are as near to our hearts as they are to those of other scholars, only we do not hope to be able to solve an intricate historical problem by a formula.

First of all, the whole problem of cultural history appears to us as an historical problem. In order to understand history it is necessary to know not only how things are, but how they have come to be. In the domain of ethnology, where, for most parts of the world, no historical facts are available except those that may be revealed by archaeological study, all evidence of change can be inferred only by indirect methods. Their character is represented in the researches of students of comparative philology. The method is based on the comparison of static phenomena combined with the study of their distribution. What can be done by this method is well illustrated by Dr. Lowie's investigations of the military societies of the Plains Indians, or by the modern investigation of American mythology. It is, of course, true that we can never hope to obtain incontrovertible data relating to the chronological sequence of events, but certain general broad outlines can be ascertained with a high degree of probability, even of certainty.

As soon as these methods are applied, primitive society loses the appearance of absolute stability which is conveyed to the student who sees a certain people only at a certain given time. All cultural forms rather appear in a constant state of flux and subject to fundamental modifications.

It is intelligible why in our studies the problem of dissemination should take a prominent position. It is much easier to prove dissemination than to follow up developments due to inner forces, and the data for such a study are obtained with much greater difficulty. They may, however, be observed in every phenomenon of acculturation in which foreign elements are remodeled according to the patterns prevalent in their new environment, and they may be found in the peculiar local developments of widely spread ideas and activities. The reason why the study of inner development has not been taken up energetically is not due to the fact that from a theoretical point of view it is unimportant, it is rather due to the inherent methodological difficulties. It may perhaps be recognized that in recent years attention is being drawn to this problem, as is manifested by the investigations on the processes of acculturation and of the interdependence of cultural activities which are attracting the attention of many investigators.

The further pursuit of these inquiries emphasizes the importance of a feature which is common to all historic phenomena. While in natural sciences we are accustomed to consider a given number of causes and to study their effects, in historical happenings we are compelled to consider every phenomenon not only as effect but also as cause. This is true even in the particular application of the laws of physical nature, as, for instance, in the study of astronomy in which the position of certain heavenly bodies at a given moment may be considered as the effect of gravitation, while, at the same time, their particular arrangement in space determines future changes. This relation appears much more clearly in the history of human civilization. To give an example: a surplus of food supply is liable to bring about an increase of population and an increase of leisure, which gives opportunity for occupations that are not absolutely necessary for the needs of every day life. In turn the increase of population and of leisure, which may be applied to new inventions, gives rise to a greater food supply and to a further increase in the amount of leisure, so that a cumulative effect results.

Similar considerations may be made in regard to the important problem of the relation of the individual to society, a problem that has to be considered whenever we study the dynamic conditions of change. The activities of the individual are determined to a great extent by his social environment, but in turn his own activities influence the society in which he lives, and may bring about modifications in its form. Obviously, this problem is one of the most important ones to be taken up in a study of cultural changes. It is also beginning to attract the attention of students who are no longer satisfied with the systematic enumeration of standardized beliefs and customs of a tribe, but who begin to be interested in the question of the way in which the individual reacts to his whole social environment, and to the differences of opinion and of mode of action that occur in primitive society and which are the causes of far-reaching changes.

In short then, the method which we try to develop is based on a study of the dynamic changes in society that may be observed at the present time. We refrain from the attempt to solve the fundamental problem of the general development of civilization until we have been able to unravel the processes that are going on under our eyes.

Certain general conclusions may be drawn from this study even now. First of all, the history of human civilization does not appear to us as determined entirely by psychological necessity that leads to a uniform evolution the world over. We rather see that each cultural group has its own unique history, dependent partly upon the peculiar inner development of the social group, and partly upon the foreign influences to which it has been subjected. There have been processes of gradual differentiation as well as processes of leveling down differences between neighboring cultural centers, but it would be quite impossible to understand, on the basis of a single evolutionary scheme, what happened to any particular people. An example of the contrast between the two points of view is clearly indicated by a comparison of the treatment of Zuñi civilization by Frank Hamilton Cushing on the one hand, on the other by modern students, particularly by Elsie Clews Parsons, A. L. Kroeber and Leslie Spier. Cushing believed that it was possible to explain Zuñi culture entirely on the basis of the reaction of the Zuñi mind to its geographical environment, and that the whole of Zuñi culture could be explained as the development which followed necessarily from the position in which the people were placed. Cushing's keen insight into the Indian mind and his thorough knowledge of the most intimate life of the people gave great plausibility to his interpretations. On the other hand, Dr. Parsons' studies prove conclusively the deep influence which Spanish ideas have had upon Zuñi culture, and, together with Professor Kroeber's investigations, give us one of the best examples of acculturation that have come to our notice. The psychological explanation is entirely misleading, notwithstanding its plausibility, and the historical study shows us an entirely different picture, in which the unique combination of ancient traits (which in themselves are undoubtedly complex) and of European influences has brought about the present condition.

Studies of the dynamics of primitive life also show that an assumption of long continued stability such as is demanded by Elliot Smith is without any foundation in fact. Wherever primitive conditions have been studied in detail, they can be proved to be in a state of flux, and it would seem that there is a close parallelism between the history of language and the history of general cultural development. Periods of stability are followed by periods of rapid change. It is exceedingly improbable that any customs of primitive people should be preserved unchanged for thousands of years. Furthermore, the phenomena of acculturation prove that a transfer of customs from one region into another without concomitant changes due to acculturation are very rare. It is, therefore, very unlikely that ancient Mediterranean customs could be found at the present time practically unchanged in different parts of the globe, as Elliot Smith's theory demands.

While on the whole the unique historical character of cultural growth in each area stands out as a salient element in the history of cultural development, we may recognize at the same time that certain typical parallelisms do occur. We are, however, not so much inclined to look for these similarities in detailed customs but rather in certain dynamic conditions which are due to social or psychological causes that are liable to lead to similar results. The example of the relation between food supply and population to which I referred before may serve as an example. Another type of example is presented in those cases in which a certain problem confronting man may be solved by a limited number of methods only. When we find, for instance, marriage as a universal institution, it may be recognized that marriage is possible only between a number of men and a number of women; a number of men and one woman; a number of women and one man; or one man and one woman. As a matter of fact, all these forms are found the world over and it is, therefore, not surprising that analogous forms should have been adopted quite independently in different parts of the world, and, considering both the general economic conditions of mankind and the character of sexual instinct in the higher animals, it also does not seem surprising that group marriage and polyandrous marriages should be comparatively speaking rare. Similar considerations may also be made in regard to the philosophical views held by mankind. In short, if we look for laws, the laws relate to the effects of physiological, psychological, and social conditions, not to sequences of cultural achievement.

In some cases a regular sequence of these may accompany the development of the psychological or social status. This is illustrated by the sequence of industrial inventions in the Old World and in America, which I consider as independent. A period of food gathering and of the use of stone was followed by the invention of agriculture, of pottery and finally of the use of metals. Obviously, this order is based on the increased amount of time given by mankind to the use of natural products, of tools and utensils, and to the variations that developed with it. Although in this case parallelism seems to exist on the two continents, it would be futile to try to follow out the order in detail. As a matter of fact, it does not apply to other inventions. The domestication of animals, which, in the Old World must have been an early achievement, was very late in the New World, where domesticated animals, except the dog, hardly existed at all at the time of discovery. A slight beginning had been made in Peru with the domestication of the llama, and birds were kept in various parts of the continent.

A similar consideration may be made in regard to the development of rationalism. It seems to be one of the fundamental characteristics of the development of mankind that activities which have developed unconsciously are gradually made the subject of reasoning. We may observe this process everywhere. It appears, perhaps, most clearly in the history of science which has gradually extended the scope of its inquiry over an ever-widening field and which has raised into consciousness human activities that are automatically performed in the life of the individual and of society.

I have not heretofore referred to another aspect of modern ethnology which is connected with the growth of psycho-analysis. Sigmund Freud has attempted to show that primitive thought is in many respects analogous to those forms of individual psychic activity which he has explored by his psycho-analytical methods. In many respects his attempts are similar to the interpretation of mythology by symbolists like Stucken. Rivers has taken hold of Freud's suggestion as well as of the interpretations of Graebner and Elliot Smith, and we find, therefore, in his new writings a peculiar disconnected application of a psychologizing attitude and the application of the theory of ancient transmission.

While I believe some of the ideas underlying Freud's psycho-analytic studies may be fruitfully applied to ethnological problems, it does not seem to me that the one-sided exploitation of this method will advance our understanding of the development of human society. It is certainly true that the influence of impressions received during the first few years of life has been entirely underestimated and that the social behavior of man depends to a great extent upon the earliest habits which are established before the time when connected memory begins, and that many so-called racial or hereditary traits are to be considered rather as a result of early exposure to a certain form of social conditions. Most of these habits do not rise into consciousness and are, therefore, broken with difficulty only. Much of the difference in the behavior of adult male and female may go back to this cause. If, however, we try to apply the whole theory of the influence of suppressed desires to the activities of man living under different social forms, I think we extend beyond their legitimate limits the inferences that may be drawn from the observation of normal and abnormal individual psychology. Many other factors are of greater importance. To give an example: The phenomena of language show clearly that conditions quite different from those to which psycho-analysts direct their attention determine the mental behavior of man. The general concepts underlying language are entirely unknown to most people. They do not rise into consciousness until the scientific study of grammar begins. Nevertheless, the categories of language compel us to see the world arranged in certain definite conceptual groups which, on account of our lack of knowledge of linguistic processes, are taken as objective categories and which, therefore, impose themselves upon the form of our thoughts. It is not known what the origin of these categories may be, but it seems quite certain that they have nothing to do with the phenomena which are the subject of psycho-analytic study.

The applicability of the psycho-analytic theory of symbolism is also open to the greatest doubt. We should remember that symbolic interpretation has occupied a prominent position in the philosophy of all times. It is present not only in primitive life, but the history of philosophy and of theology abounds in examples of a high development of symbolism, the type of which depends upon the general mental attitude of the philosopher who develops it. The theologians who interpreted the Bible on the basis of religious symbolism were no less certain of the correctness of their views, than the psycho-analysts are of their interpretations of thought and conduct based on sexual symbolism. The results of a symbolic interpretation depend primarily upon the subjective attitude of the investigator who arranges phenomena according to his leading concept. In order to prove the applicability of the symbolism of psycho-analysis, it would be necessary to show that a symbolic interpretation from other entirely different points of view would not be equally plausible, and that explanations that leave out symbolic significance or reduce it to a minimum would not be adequate.

While, therefore, we may welcome the application of every advance in the method of psychological investigation, we cannot accept as an advance in ethnological method the crude transfer of a novel, one-sided method of psychological investigation of the individual to social phenomena the origin of which can be shown to be historically determined and to be subject to influences that are not at all comparable to those that control the psychology of the individual.

Alfred Louis Kroeber 1876–1960

BACKGROUND

For years before his death in 1960, Alfred Kroeber was called "the dean of American anthropologists." Since then there has been no dean. Kroeber's good looks, charm, and scholarly mien made him the commanding figure in every room he entered.

He was born in Hoboken, New Jersey, and grew up in New York. His father had come from Cologne, Germany, twenty-five years before and had developed a prosperous wholesale clock business. The household was totally bilingual, and the children were given the finest of educations. Alfred had a German private tutor and went to Sachs, a prominent New York prep school.

At Columbia, Kroeber made many friends who were to share an interest in or to influence his life's work. He also joined some students to create *Morningside* magazine in protest against existing student publications and to pull off such tricks as painting Central Park statues blue and white (the Columbia colors) and giving them red hair and mustaches. Linkage of social protest and the absurd recurred in his life and his talk.

Kroeber got his B.A. and M.A. in literature in 1896 and 1897. This was a crucial period both in Kroeber's life and in the history of anthropology. Franz Boas had come to Columbia in 1896, and Kroeber was one of the three who elected to take his seminar in American Indian languages, which met around the Boas dining room table. As a result, Kroeber decided to take his doctorate in anthropology. In 1899 a Columbia fellowship enabled him to spend the summer among the Arapaho in Wyoming. He went back again in 1900, extending his study to include the Shoshone, Ute, and Bannock.

The Academy of Sciences in San Francisco, taking note of its rapidly expanding collection of California Indian artifacts, wrote to Boas, asking for someone to fill the newly created position of curator. Kroeber took the job. Since the collection contained obvious gaps, Kroeber hustled two small grants to finance field expeditions to take notes and collect artifacts. But when the academy board had to tell him they couldn't afford him, he returned to New York to finish his dissertation, part of which appeared in the *American Anthropologist* (3 [1901]: 308–336) as "Decorative Symbolism of the Arapaho."

In the fall of 1901 Kroeber joined the faculty of the University of California. A full professor by 1919, he stayed at Berkeley until his retirement in 1946. In 1903 he once again became curator of the Academy of Sciences Museum, continuing until 1911, and in 1908 he was made director of the university's Museum of Anthropology, a post he held until his retirement.

In 1907 Kroeber married Henriette Rothschild, the educated and artistic only daughter of a wealthy San Francisco businessman. She died in 1913 after a long illness, and Kroeber, exhausted, the tempo of his academic activity slowing, found some diversion in friendship and study of Ishi, the last Yana Indian, who, exhausted and starving, had been found in 1910 and brought to the museum, where as a kind of "living exhibit" as well as janitorial worker he spent a number of happy and useful years. Ishi's death in 1916 also saddened Kroeber.

In these years Kroeber suffered from an ear infection that sometimes affected his balance. When the condition was misdiagnosed as psychosomatic, Kroeber went into psychoanalysis. The correct diagnosis was finally made, but he finished his analysis nevertheless, took training in the subject, and treated patients until 1922. There are a few articles and reviews that arose from this association, but Kroeber chose not to develop the area of psychoanalytic anthropology (at that time a province of analysts, largely untrained in anthropology).

Kroeber published a comprehensive and influential textbook, *Anthropology*, in 1923 and did an almost unbelievable amount of ethnography. In 1925 he published *The Handbook of the Indians of California*, one of the monumental primary source books in American ethnology. He was the recognized authority on the cultures of California, and he also did ethnological work in New Mexico, Mexico, Peru, India, most of the Orient, and Southeast Asia.

In 1926 Kroeber remarried: Theodora Kracow Brown, a young widow with two small sons, who had enrolled in one of his courses. The marriage, which produced two more children, was a close and rich one until his death. Mrs. Kroeber's book *Ishi* has joined the ranks of world literature, and her biography *Alfred Kroeber: A Personal Configuration*, is a work of scholarship and love.

Kroeber was an early observer and recorder of the close relationship of ecology and culture and civilization. *Configurations of Culture Growth*, published in 1944, was the result of thirteen years' work. It was an elaboration of his ideas on civilization, culture areas, and ecology. In contrast to his ethnography, which stands undisputed, his theories of cultural history are debated and questioned.

Kroeber led a long and busy life as a teacher and scholar. He was disciplined, orderly—and always curious. In 1946, when he retired from Berkeley, he was visiting professor at a number of universities. The new building that houses the anthropology department at Berkeley was called Kroeber Hall, and he kept an office there. He took an active part in numerous associations and societies until his sudden death, at the age of eighty-four, on a vacation in Paris just after serving as chairman of an international conference in Austria.

INTRODUCTION

The period of cultural realism in American anthropology reflects not only a great poverty of theory but also the difficulties of antitheory. Following Boas and his emphasis on studying as many societies as possible, the best-known anthropologists of the period produced a good deal of ethnography.

They did not fail to produce viable theory. Most of them positively eschewed producing it. It is with this realization that we must approach Kroeber, Lowie, and most of the other major figures of this era.

In Kroeber's case, if one theoretical problem has to be singled out as being most important to him, it is the problem of the superorganic. We have already seen that Spencer struggled with this idea in the absence of a culture concept. Kroeber, on the other hand, used the idea to explain something about culture. He approached this theoretical problem from a variety of vantage points all through his life, and his emphasis on it during a period when anthropology was mainly interested in ethnography and with psychological approaches makes him astonishingly close to Émile Durkheim, with an emphasis on the social during the most blatant cultural relativist period in American anthropology.

The importance of the superorganic in Kroeber's work can be seen as early as his "Eighteen Professions" (1915). Here he makes a series of points about the importance of social facts. He states that (1) civilization is an entity apart from the individuals who carry it, (2) the individual has no historical value, and (3) there are no minds. In the same essay, which is a credo, Kroeber also affirms some of the basic tenets of cultural relativism: (1) all men are totally civilized, and (2) there are no higher and lower stages of civilization.

One of the best five-finger exercises for any anthropologist of our own time is to examine Kroeber's professions—to restate them for his age and for himself. Some hold up, some must be restated, some must be discarded and replaced. But these professions provide an excellent view of both the times and the man.

 EIGHTEEN PROFESSIONS

Anthropology today includes two studies which fundamental differences of aim and method render irreconcilable. One of these branches is biological and psychological; the other, social or historical.

There is a third field, the special province of anthropology, concerned with the relation of biological and social factors. This is no-man's-land, and therefore used as a picnic-ground by whosoever prefers pleasure excursions to the work of cultivating a patch of understanding. Some day this tract will also be surveyed, fenced, and improved. Biological science already claims it; but the title remains to be established. For the present, the labor in hand is the delimitation of the scope of history from that of science.

In what follows, historical anthropology, history, and sociology are referred to as history. Physical anthropology and psychology are included in biology.

1. *The aim of history is to know the relations of social facts to the whole of civilization.*

Reprinted by permission of the American Anthropological Association from *American Anthropologist* 17, no. 2 (1915): 283–288.

Civilization means civilization itself, not its impulses. Relation is actual connection, not cause.

2. *The material studied by history is not man, but his works.*

It is not men, but the results of their deeds, the manifestations of their activities, that are the subject of historical inquiry.

3. *Civilization, though carried by men and existing through them, is an entity in itself, and of another order from life.*

History is not concerned with the agencies producing civilization, but with civilization as such. The causes are the business of the psychologist. The entity civilization has intrinsically nothing to do with individual men nor with the aggregates of men on whom it rests. It springs from the organic, but is independent of it. The mental processes of groups of men are, after all, only the collected processes of individuals reacting under certain special stimuli. Collective psychology is therefore ultimately resolvable into individual human psychology, just as this in turn is resolvable into organic psychology and physiology. But history deals with material which is essentially non-individual and integrally social. History is not concerned with the relations of civilization to men or organisms, but with the interrelations of civilization. The psychic organization of man in the abstract does not exist for it, save as something given directly and more or less completely to the student's consciousness. The uncivilized man does not exist; if he did, he would mean nothing to the historian. Even civilized man is none of history's business; its sphere is the civilization of which man is the necessary basis but which is inevitable once this basis exists.

4. *A certain mental constitution of man must be assumed by the historian, but may not be used by him as a resolution of social phenomena.*

The historian can and should obtain for himself the needed interpretation of man's mind from familiarity with social facts and the direct application to them of his own psychic activities. This interpretation is likely to be of service in proportion as it emanates immediately from himself and not from the formulated laws of the biological psychologist. Whether an understanding of civilization will or will not help the psychologist is for the latter to determine.

5. *True instincts lie at the bottom and origin of social phenomena, but cannot be considered or dealt with by history.*

History begins where instincts commence to be expressed in social facts.

6. *The personal or individual has no historical value save as illustration.*

Ethnological genealogies are valuable material. So are the actions of conspicuous historical personages. But their dramatic, anecdotic, or biographic recital is biographic or fictional art, or possibly psychology, not history.

7. *Geography, or physical environment, is material made use of by civilization, not a factor shaping or explaining civilization.*

Civilization reacts to civilization, not to geography. For the historian, geography does not act on civilization, but civilization incorporates geographical circumstances. Agriculture presupposes a climate able to sustain agriculture, and modifies itself according to climatic conditions. It is not caused by climate. The understanding of agricultural activity is to be sought in the other phenomena of civilization affecting it.

8. *The absolute equality and identity of all human races and strains as carriers of civilization must be assumed by the historian.*

The identity has not been proved nor has it been disproved. It remains to be established, or to be limited, by observations directed to this end, perhaps only by experiments. The historical and social influences affecting every race and every large group of persons are closely intertwined with the alleged biological and hereditary ones, and have never yet been sufficiently separated to allow demonstration of the actual efficiency of either. All opinions on this point are only convictions falsely fortified by subjectively interpreted evidence. The biologist dealing with man must assume at least some hereditary differences, and often does assume biological factors as the only ones existent. The historian, until such differences are established and exactly defined, must assume their non-existence. If he does not base his studies on this assumption, his work becomes a vitiated mixture of history and biology.

9. *Heredity cannot be allowed to have acted any part in history.*

Individual hereditary differences undoubtedly exist, but are not historical material because they are individual. Hereditary differences between human groups may ultimately be established, but like geography must in that event be converted into material acted upon by the force of civilization, not treated as causes of civilization.

10. *Heredity by acquirement is equally a biological and historical monstrosity.*

This naive explanation may be eliminated on the findings of biology; but should biology ever determine that such heredity operates through a mechanism as yet undiscovered, this heredity must nevertheless be disregarded by history together with congenital heredity. In the present stage of understanding, heredity by acquirement is only too often the cherished inclination of those who confuse their biological thinking by the introduction of social aspects, and of those who confound history by deceiving themselves that they are turning it into biology.

11. *Selection and other factors of organic evolution cannot be admitted as affecting civilization.*

It is actually unproved that the processes of organic evolution are materially influencing civilization or that they have influenced it. Civilization obviously introduces an important factor which is practically or entirely lacking in the existence of animals and plants, and which must at least largely neutralize the operation of any kind of selection. Prehistoric archeology shows with certainty that civilization has changed profoundly without accompanying material alterations in the human organism. Even so far as biological evolution may ultimately be proved in greater or less degree for man, a correspondence between organic types and civilizational forms will have to be definitely established before history can concern itself with these organic types or their changes.

12. *The so-called savage is no transition between the animal and the scientifically educated man.*

All men are totally civilized. All animals are totally uncivilized because they are almost totally uncivilizable. The connecting condition, which it is universally believed must have existed, is entirely unknown. If ever it becomes known, it can furnish to the historian only an introduction to history. There is no higher and lower in civilization for the historian. The ranging of the portions of civilization in any sequence, save the actual one of time, place, and connection, is normally misleading and always valueless. The estimation of the adult savage as similar to the modern European child is superficial and prevents his proper appreciation either biologically or historically.

13. *There are no social species or standard cultural types or stages.*

A social species in history rests on false analogy with organic species. A stage in civilization is merely a preconception made plausible by arbitrarily selected facts.

14. *There is no ethnic mind, but only civilization.*

There are only individual minds. When these react on each other cumulatively, the process is merely physiological. The single ethnic or social existence is civilization, which biologically is resolvable purely into a product of physiological forces, and historically is the only and untranscendable entity.

15. *There are no laws in history similar to the laws of physicochemical science.*

All asserted civilizational laws are at most tendencies, which, however determinable, are not permanent quantitative expressions. Nor are such tendencies the substitute which history has for the laws of science. History need not deny them and may have to recognize them, but their formulation is not its end.

16. *History deals with conditions sine qua non, not with causes.*

The relations between civilizational phenomena are relations of sequence, not of effect. The principles of mechanical causality, emanating from the underlying biological sciences, are applicable to individual and collective psychology. Applied to history, they convert it into psychology. An insistence that all treatment of civilizational data should be by the methods of mechanical causality is equivalent to a denial of the valid existence of history as a subject of study. The only antecedents of historical phenomena are historical phenomena.

17. *The causality of history is teleological.*

Psychological causes are mechanical. For history, psychology is assumable, not demonstrable. To make the object of historical study the proving of the fundamental identity of the human mind by endless examples is as tedious as barren. If the process of civilization seems the worth-while end of knowledge of civilization, it must be sought as a process distinct from that of mechanical causality, or the result will be a reintegration that is not history. Teleology of course does not suggest theology to those free from the influence of theology. The teleology of history involves the absolute conditioning of historical events by other historical events. This causality of history is as completely unknown and unused as chemical causality was a thousand and physical causality three thousand years ago.

18. *In fine, the determinations and methods of biological, psychological, or natural science do not exist for history, just as the results and the manner of operation of history are disregarded by consistent biological practice.*

Most biologists have implicitly followed their aspect of this doctrine, but their consequent success has tempted many historians, especially sociologists, anthropologists, and theorists, to imitate them instead of pursuing their proper complementary method.

INTRODUCTION

Kroeber also had a long-term interest in the nature of culture and the way culture formed recognizable and persistent patterns. He associated this idea with the superorganic, which he came back to a number of times (1917, 1919, and 1940). It is interesting to note that Kroeber showed the importance of the superorganic, as well as pattern, by investigating changes in women's fashions. He found that women's fashions, rather than merely showing personal choice, show cultural patterns (1919, 1940). He also found examples of culture patterns in philosophy, the arts, and other subjects to demonstrate that individual genius is part of a cultural era and not an independent agent.

The interest Kroeber showed in cultural patterns culminated in his *Configurations of Culture Growth* (1944), in which he tried to account for culture growth in some historical societies of Europe, the Near East, and the Far East. The basic tenet was that societies frequently develop cultural configurations "spasmodically": when culture patterns develop, geniuses cluster within certain periods in relationship to cultural growth. Kroeber discussed the growth of philosophy, science, philology, sculpture, drama, painting, literature, music, and finally the growth of nations, in his configuration. It was an enormous project, bold—and probably a failure. But perhaps to state such a judgment is only to say that the people who have taken up Kroeber's ideas about the history of civilization have not been anthropologists; most anthropologists have ignored this work.

Kroeber's summary views of culture themselves, which are to be found in his giant works, are vastly instructive. This 1949 article is as good a summary of the state of the art, from his view, as was the "Eighteen Professions" of thirty years earlier.

7 THE CONCEPT OF CULTURE IN SCIENCE

I propose to discuss the concept of culture—its origin and validity, its use and limitations. Like every concept, this one is a tool; and as a tool the concept of culture is two-edged. It ties some phenomena and interpretations together; it dissimilates and distinguishes others—about which more later.

Like all important ideas, that of culture was the realization of many minds, and it developed gradually. There are still great civilized nations—the French, for instance—who refuse to admit the word "culture" into their intellectual vocabulary. On the other hand, the ancients knew, and modern primitives are aware of, some of the phenomena of culture—as, for instance, distinctive customs. "We don't do that way, we do like this"—such a statement, which every human being is likely to make at some time, is a recognition of a cultural phenomenon.

Phenomena have a way of occurring composite in nature, intricately blended. Their qualities, still more their conceptualized general aspects, can be extricated only gradually from the welter of appearances. Until well into the nineteenth century and in certain situations and contexts until today, the concept of culture has remained unextricated from that of society. When Comte founded sociology and coined its name more than a century ago, he stamped on it the impress of the social. But his famous three stages of mythology, metaphysics, and positivism are stages primarily of ideology, and therefore of culture. Only incidentally are they stages of specifically social or interpersonal relations. Still more does this essential reference to culture instead of society hold of Comte's differentiating characterizations of Catholicism and Protestantism and hundreds of other special dicta.

When so original and penetrating a thinker as Durkheim hypostasized society as that by which early groups were impressed, which they worshiped, and thus originated religion, he put forth a view which has generally seemed far-fetched and, to many, mystical. But as soon as we substitute for his nondifferentium of "society" the customs and beliefs which hold together primitive societies and seem to help them to survive—in another word, their "culture"—then the Durkheim interpretation begins to assume reasonableness. It seems fair to assume that that is what Durkheim "meant," what he would say today.

That nondifferentiation of the two aspects should continue up to a certain point is expectable, since culture by definition includes, or at least presupposes, society. As something shared and supraindividual, culture can exist only when a society exists; and conversely every human society is accompanied by a culture. This converse, to be sure, is not complete: it applies only to *human* societies. In principle, however, the limitation is extremely important. The existence of cultureless or essentially cultureless subhuman socie-

Reprinted from Alfred Louis Kroeber, *The Nature of Culture* (Chicago: University of Chicago Press, 1952), pp. 118–135, by permission of the publisher.

ties, especially the highly elaborate ones of the social insects, serves as an irrefutable touchstone for the significant discrimination of the concepts of the social and the cultural: they *can* exist separately. At any rate, one of them does exist separately.

The word "social" is itself a relatively late appellation. The Roman term was *civilis, civitas,* from *civis,* a "citizen," corresponding to Aristotle's definition of man as a *zoon politicon* or "political animal"—a civil animal to the Romans, a social animal to us. Of course, institutions were implied in the term "political animal," and therewith culture was implied, but not as a segregated, coagulated concept. These ancient Mediterranean terms are illuminative of how abstract ideas originate in a matrix of the concrete. When Aristotle wanted to talk generically of what we call "society" and "culture," he used the word *polis*, which still carried full implication and imagery of citadel and city wall, of free citizens entitled to vote and to fight.

The word "culture" in its modern scientific sense, as, for instance, any anthropologist would use it with assurance that every other anthropologist would know what he meant, and not something else—this modern meaning of "culture" is still more recent. The first definition of "culture" in this broad but definite sense of its current social science usage—as distinct from cultivation and refinement, from nurture, from agriculture and pearl culture and test-tube cultures—the first definition I have found in an English dictionary dates from the late twenties. The first deliberate usage in a book was by Tylor when in 1871 he published *Primitive Culture* and formulated that most-quoted of definitions of culture which begins: "that complex whole which includes . . ." It is clear that Tylor was conscious of establishing the term, just as he was aware of using "culture" and "civilization" as synonyms in his discourse. To be exact, he already had used the word "culture" a few times as a hesitant alternative for "civilization," and in the same sense but without definition, six years earlier in his *Researches*, as if trying it out on the British public. He may have got it from the German ethnographer Klemm, whom he read and cited. Klemm spells the word with a *C—Cultur*—in his 1843 as well as his 1854 book. The word appears to have been in general German usage at that period with its modern meaning, and was in no sense handled then like a new coinage. I do not know precisely how far back the German word *Cultur* goes with its modern scientific meaning. Kant uses it repeatedly in his *Anthropologie*, but it is mostly difficult to say whether he is thinking of culture in our sense or of "becoming more cultured." Arciniegas quotes Paul Hazard as saying that the word first appears in the German dictionary of 1793.

Let us take a long step back from both culture and its undifferentiated immediate matrix, which we would today call "sociocultural"—a step back to the psychosomatic. Just as culture presupposes society, so society presupposes persons. It is an assemblage of individuals—plus something additional—that something which we and termite societies share. Well, here, then, are three elements or sets of factors: culture, society, persons, each resting upon, or preconditioned by, the next. In fact, we can immediately go one step further and separate persons into bodies and minds as two aspects which in some situations at least it is profitable to deal with separately—in all strictly psychological situations, for instance. That the separation is warranted, when it is useful, is clear not only from the current distinction of biological science from psychology but also from the fact that plants, though possessing somas, are generally conceded as showing no evidence of having psyches.

So now we are already facing four superposed aspects—four "levels," let us call them: body, psyche, society, culture. By now it is obvious where the line of thought is leading us; the next step prefaces the inorganic as underlying the somatic, the psychic, the social, and the cultural.

De facto phenomena of the inorganic level can also be split up, when, as, and if useful—and in many situations, perhaps most, it is useful—into physical and chemical. Indeed, we can split finer and laminate off a subatomic level and perhaps another for supermolecular virus phenomena or for crystal manifestations. All these segregations, however, fall within the larger inorganic or suborganic end of the scale; and, as our particular concern here is with the ultraorganic, with the most superorganic at the opposite end, it would be digressive and distracting to enter here into these finer distinctions at the bottom of the hierarchy.

It has become customary of late to designate these hierarchical planes as "levels of organization" and, alternatively, as "dimensions." The latter term is appropriate in certain contexts, as when it is said that every human situation has environmental, organic, social, and cultural dimensions. The word "dimension" here is equivalent to "aspects" or to "class of impinging factors." It definitely avoids even implication of hierarchy. Dimensions crosscut one another, levels imply parallelism. In a so-called "field approach" to a limited phenomenal area, such as a personality, where emphasis is on the interaction of factors converging at a single point, it is natural to see cultural, social, organic, and physical factors as so many dimensions "radiating" out from the point under observation. By contrast, as the approach is macroscopic, or even telescopic, as in the tracing of large historic patterns or their interrelations, the dimensions automatically segregate themselves into parallel and superposed layers, and the term "levels" is more appropriate.

However, it is necessary not to confound "levels of organization" with "levels of abstraction." It is true that, while we are focusing on cultural aspects, we are in a technical sense "abstracting" from the organic and physical aspects pertaining to the same phenomena. "Abstracting" here means removing our consideration from, ignoring; it is temporary, shifting, reversible. But cultural phenomena are *not* more abstract than physical or organic phenomena in the sense of being more abstruse, rarefied, unconcrete, or conceptualized. The surge of anger is as concrete a phenomenon as is a contracted eyebrow or a constricted blood vessel. The custom of headhunting or of catching the bride's bouquet is certainly thoroughly concrete. It is only culture as a generalized concept that is abstract; but so are society, psyche, body, matter, and energy abstract. What is much more significant than abstractness is that cultural phenomena occur organized on different principles from social phenomena, social phenomena from psychic, and so on down the series.

What is clearest about the levels is that certain properties or qualities of the phenomena of each are peculiar to it. Presumably this is due to a difference in arrangement or organization. That which is specifically characteristic and distinctively significant of phenomena of a level is intelligible only in terms of the other phenomena, qualities, or regularities of that same level. The most characteristic qualities or phenomena are never explained by what we know of another level: they are not really reached by other-level knowledge, especially when the levels are well separated. The findings of a study of lower-level phenomena do indeed *apply* to those of higher level, but they apply with decreasing significance.

Thus gravitation, electrical conductivity, and element valence apply to organic bodies as well as to inorganic ones. But principles or laws such as these are the only ones which apply to inorganic bodies; and yet they do not to any serious degree explain the specific organic phenomena of hereditary repetition, of conception and death, of adaptability. These specifically organic processes *conform* to established physicochemical processes; they cannot be *derived* from them. Laws of a lower level set the frame within which phenomena of a higher level operate; they do not per se produce those phenomena. The lower-level laws will explain the constants, universals, and uniformities of phenomena on an upper level. They will explain or describe those qualities or properties which an upper level shares with a lower—that an organic body has mass or conductivity, for instance. They fail to explain or even describe those properties that are specific of a level, distinctive of it— as how an organic body repeats itself in its offspring.

In short, it appears that the total work of science must be done on a series of levels which the experience of science gradually discovers. To reduce everything in the universe to a monistic set of principles, mechanical or otherwise, may be a legitimate philosophy—or may not be; it is certainly not an adequate operational method of science. It involves using the hard-won earnings of physics for verbal extensions into biology or sociology, and thereby short-circuiting genuine problem solution in those very domains. Apparently, true progress is made when every science is autonomous in its procedures, while also realizing its relation of dependence on the subjacent ones and of support to the independent overlying ones. It is investigation on autonomous levels that is a precondition of most extensions of our understanding of the world. After enough such extensions have been made, it is valid reductionism that gradually integrates and consolidates them. Premature reductionism is just verbal forcing.

This does not mean that a new entity is hypostasized as the unique substance of each level. Life, mind, society, and culture are not outside matter and energy, not outside space and time and free of them. They are in and of nature with matter and energy. They are different organizations of matter and energy, if one will, which physicists and chemists cannot, in virtue of their physical and chemical methods, deal with fruitfully; and similarly all the way up the scale.

This is where the modern level-approach differs from the older segregation of spirit from matter, of soul from body. In this the higher substance was reserved from the operations of nature, was excluded from its sphere. The body perished, but the soul went on; matter was subject to mechanical laws, but the spirit was free of them—it stood outside nature. On the contrary, the scientific point of view is that every phenomenon is in nature and part of it. The levels represent empirically found segmentations of the total field of nature, in each of which somewhat distinctive intellectual procedures or operations seem to be most productive. The whole recognition of levels is, in one sense, an affair of scientific methodology, is wholly internal to science. It does not portend the reintroduction of vitalism, mentalism, spirit, or *Geisteswissenschaften*.

Philosophically, cognizance of a system of levels seems to have been recent and rather perfunctory. Bergson has been reckoned a proponent of the view of emergence of the new; but, so far as his *élan vital* is extra-natural, his emergents would be something more than levels. Alexander's *Space, Time, and Deity* (1920) is often credited with being the fullest exposition in English of the point of view by a professional philosopher. Alexander works from space and time successively through matter, life, and mind toward God. This view may stem partly from scientific experience but is used to transcend science and nature. C. Lloyd Morgan's *Emergent Evolution*, three years later, is perhaps the most-cited work on the subject. "There is more in the events that occur in the living organism," he says (p. 20), "than can adequately be interpreted in terms of physics and chemistry, though physico-chemical events are always involved." Vital relatedness—organization on the organic level—is effective because changes occur under it "the like of which do not occur when life is absent." Morgan credits Lewes with the word "emergent," and Wundt with the term "principle of creative resultants," namely, that psychical products are more than a mere summation of elements and represent a new formation. J. Needham and William Morton Wheeler have expressed similar views, which Koestler's second *Yogi and Commissar* essay also sets forth with charm and originality.

Two things hold about most of these formulations. First, they concentrate on biological and psychological autonomy from the physicochemical and fail to pursue the principle onto the social and cultural level, at any rate explicitly so. (Wheeler does go on up to the social level but not to the cultural. Warden in 1936 did explicitly recognize culture as an emergent.) Second, the stress is on an evolving universe and on emergences in the course of this. Evolution is therefore a primary postulate, and emphasis is on emergences within this—in other words, on innovating changes. Logically, however, a hierarchical series of levels of phenomena could exist in a static world. How they successively emerged to become graded as they are is a separate problem, which logically need not obtrude. My point is not to combat or deny that there may have been cosmic evolution but to assert that the concept of evolution and the concept of levels are not necessarily involved or implied with each other. Emergence is no longer contained in the idea of levels as soon as levels are separated from evolution. New levels leap into appearance only if one has already assumed an evolutionary and progressive process. I would contend that the whole linkage with evolution has happened because our generation silently takes evolution for granted, as most former generations assumed deity: evolution is a compulsion culturally and emotionally difficult for us to escape from. A scientific methodology based as purely as possible on scientific experience is perhaps really better off without emergence, because unencumbered.

More fruitful is Koestler's metaphor and diagram of a staircase. Viewed from above, from the angle of strictly scientific exploration, this staircase looks like a plane surface, like a flat continuum to which everything is already reduced and in which everything therefore appears explainable. Viewed from the front, however, by phenomenal contemplation, it is the rise of the series of steps, and the nonpredictabilities between them, that are impressive. In short, primary organizing relations are operative within levels rather than translevel.

There is another aspect of the levels which scientists have generally not noted and philosophers have fumbled when they did note. This is a fact which is not yet fully explained, but nevertheless it is indubitable on the basis of the overwhelming run of empirical experience to date. This fact is that the more basic a level is in the hierarchy, the more successfully do its phenomena lend themselves to manipulation by the methods of science in the strict sense —methods resulting in uniformities, repetitive regularities, and therefore predictability. But, on the contrary, the higher the level, the more recalcitrant are its phenomena to treatment by methods homologous or perhaps even analogous to those of physics and chemistry; whereas they yield readily—and with significance, though of a somewhat different kind—to intellectual treatment similar in principle to that which historians follow. The neo-Kantian philosophers have long since pointed out that, while a strictly scientific approach is generalizing and nomothetic, a historical approach is idiographic, in that it remains much more attached to the particular phenomena per se. Instead of dissolving them away into laws or generalizations, the historical approach preserves its phenomena, on whatever level it happens to be operating, and finds its intellectual satisfaction in putting each preserved phenomenon into a relation of ever widening context with the phenomenal cosmos.

From here, however, the neo-Kantians have not gone on to take the next steps which would seem compelled by a judicial inspection of the actual practices obtaining in the entire study of nature. These further steps are two. First, the contextual relations which a historical approach determines involve relations of absolute space equally with absolute time—not of time alone or primarily, as is so often asserted for history. Also, context involves relations of form, including function but perhaps excluding cause; and therewith it involves relations of value. The question of cause has its complexities, in part because scientists proper are also beginning to challenge and repudiate causality, especially in prestige-laden ultraphysics. However, it is notorious that, in the three uppermost levels of mind, society, and culture, specific causality is extremely difficult to determine. Presumably, this is because the phenomena of these levels are at least in part epiphenomena to phenomena of lower levels. It is therefore probably by translevel reductionism that the complex causes of upper-level phenomena will be found, if at all. However, relations of absolute space and time, of form, structure, and function, and of value do remain characteristic of the historical approach.

Second, while it is obvious that the great triumphs of strictly scientific method have been won on the lower levels and the ready development of the historical approach has taken place on the levels of man's mind, society, and culture, nevertheless it does not follow that a dichotomy of levels corresponds in a one-to-one manner to the dichotomy of intellectual procedures. Rather should it be assumed, on trial at least, that the correspondence is only partial and that the historical approach is applicable also on the basal levels—though with certain considerable difficulties—and the strictly scientific approach on the upper levels—again with difficulties. Such a view is not strange, nor is it paradoxical, when one remembers that astronomers admit astronomy to be a historical science; that much of geology is on its very face avowedly historical; and that evolutionary biology, from palaeontology through comparative morphology to systematics, professes to be the grand history of life on earth. Until this situation has been met by explicit and straightforward counterargument— which it has not been, so far as my knowledge goes—we must then assume that both the fundamental methods of intellectual understanding—the scientific and the historical—are applicable to all levels of phenomena, though with a sliding degree of fruitfulness.

After brilliantly showing that the *Geisteswissenschaften*, as so called in nineteenth-century Germany, were really disciplines dealing not with spirit or soul as such but with culture and that their *de facto* approach was essentially historical, the neo-Kantian Rickert blocked his farther progress with a simplistic dichotomy, to wit: Culture, historically intelligible, versus Nature, scientifically intelligible. Here the antithesis, culture : nature, is a relic of the older idealistic antithesis, spirit : nature, as this in its turn had been a softening modernization of theological soul : body opposition. And it is the same sharp antithesis which led Rickert to misappraise thoroughly the genuinely historical component in the sciences of astronomy, geology, and biology.

In any event, it is cultural phenomena—or, let us say, phenomena organizable in cultural terms and relations—that constitute the very top level of our hierarchy. If it seem rash to affirm this when the concept of culture is of as recent emergence into consciousness as we have seen it to be, we can modify the statement to say: culture is the top level recognized to date. Personally, I would not have the glimmering of a suspicion as to what a level of organization higher than that of culture might be like. Yet a future generation may see more clearly. For the present, however, let us examine the consequences of this top-level position of our subject matter.

First of all, while culture is underlain and preconditioned by social and psychosomatic factors, the enormous influence of culture on the behavior and activity of individual men and of men in groups has become fully recognized. So heavy is this overlay that "human nature," as that which is biologically given before culture begins to operate, has receded into a remote background in the social sciences and is maintained by biologists as a citadel of principle rather than with specific effectiveness. Now, in general, it is the lower levels that condition the upper: life conforms to physicochemical laws, not the reverse, and so on. There is, accordingly, something anomalous to the general scheme of things in the degree to which the human hereditary organism, individually and in groups, conforms to the sway of the culture to which it happens to be exposed. It is doubtful whether there is another instance of factors on a higher level influencing events on a lower to so great a degree as this. Even the physical world is not immune from the agency of the restless human beavers operating with their cultural activities and artifacts: canals, dams, bridges; river diversions and soil erosion; deforestation and reforestation; pilfering of coal, gas, and other resources of the earth's crust; even attempts at artificial weather.

However, it is only the degree of the influencing and its special manipulative quality that are new as regards culture. There is at best only a trend in nature, not a rigorous law, making lower-level factors the prevailingly influencing ones on upper. A moment's reflection reveals that purely organic agents also have perceptibly modified the surface and outer shell of this physical planet: coral reefs, limestones, coal beds, domes of hydrocarbon oil and gas are among their residues.

Second, it is reasonable to assume that the findings of the top level will differ considerably in kind from those of the bottom levels. All our experience to date corroborates this. The revolutionary extension of physicochemical science by speculation and devised trial during the last fifty years centers around subatomic particles. In the same half-century we have also become much more aware and informed of the domain of culture. But this better understanding of culture has given no sign, until now, of including anything corresponding to the subatomic particles or the geneticists' genes. There is nothing in sight which suggests that we shall discover in culture any invariable elemental units, or even definite relations of integral number or fixed association.

Reflection confirms this negative appraisal. Context, significant of the historical approach which is dominant in the apprehension of culture, concerns external relations viewed as widely as possible—ultimately, in total relations. By contrast, the primary problem of physics, as of genetics and physiology, is to isolate or extricate valid simplicities, recurrent regularities, from the amorphous confusion of nature's phenomena. We may be reasonably confident that nothing corresponding to allelomorphic unit-characters or genes, to protons or neutrons, even to atoms or molecules, is likely to be discovered on the level of culture. Whatever such elemental units may be operative on culture—if any—we may expect to be elements of a lower level.

Indeed, such more or less recurrent near-regularities of form or process as have to date been formulated for culture are actually mainly subcultural in nature. They are limits set to culture by physical or organic factors. The so-called "cultural constants" of family, religion, war, communications, and the like appear to be biopsychological frames variably filled with cultural content, so far as they are more than categories reflecting the compartmenting of our own Occidental logicoverbal culture. Of processes, diffusion and socialization are both only psychological learning, imitation, and suggestion under special conditions. Custom is psychobiological habit on a social scale and carrying cultural values. And so on.

What evidently takes the place of the formulation of law, in intellectual operations on the cultural level, is the recognition of significances, including values. At any rate this holds in the degree that the approach to consideration of the phenomena is historical in kind, in the sense in which a historical approach has already been referred to as distinct from (though complementary to) the more narrowly scientific or nomothetic one. This becomes clear on consideration of history in its specific sense, the history studied by historians. This is indeed mixed as to its content: a jumble of pieces of individual biographies, more or less dramatic events, social contacts and clashes, definition of or implicit reference to institutions, that is, cultural forms and their succession, with perhaps occasional recognition of dashes of influence from inanimate nature or organic race. Now the recognized failure of history to discover laws may perhaps be due partly to the fact that it operates with its materials nearly as mixed as they come to hand, without consistently selecting them according to one or another aspect or principle. But the notorious weakness of historians in successfully assigning causes—they can ordinarily deal best with minute and immediate ones: why the Bastille fell on July 14 and not 15, as against the causes of the French Revolution—this failure of the historians is compensated for by their ability to express significances. And both the failure and the ability seem to be due to the considerable upper-level, sociocultural component in the materials of intellectual history which attempts more than representational dramatization.

That this is so becomes more evident as soon as consideration is given to bodies of sociocultural and especially cultural materials least contaminated by admixture with individual personalities and particular events. In the study of English as a language it does not matter whether "Give me Liberty" was uttered by Patrick Henry or by any other Anglo-Saxon speaker; whether in the eighteenth, nineteenth, or twentieth century; or whether the occasion was historically momentous or not. (Note the term "historically momentous": that is, historically effective or significant—significant to a larger pattern of events, to a context of currents of events and of institutional forms.) To the linguist all this is irrelevant. What he sees in the phrase "Give me Liberty" is data bearing on the form, structure, and relations of certain sounds and meanings. And these sounds and meanings, as well as their form and structure, are constant and repetitive, thoroughly social, and yet anonymous—are therefore anonymous, we might say. The phrase is always uttered by an individual; but by which individual and from what motivation and with what consequences in which circumstances are irrelevant to the linguist.

We have here a clear-cut instance of the selective extrication of upper-level phenomena—in this case linguistic phenomena—from the welter of events in which they occur, and of their intellectual treatment purely as phenomena of that level. What eventuates in such a case is, in popular phraseology, an English grammar. Such a grammar is an organized analysis and resynthesized description of the phenomenal appearance, the structure, and the internal relations and functioning of a language. Such a synthesized description makes sense precisely because it is self-contained and self-sufficient. It deals with superindividual forms and relations; and therefore, while it does not deny the necessary participation of individuals in the phenomena, linguistic science normally and basically suppresses the individual, "holds him constant," "abstracts from him." Why this is so needs no elaborate proof.

It is clear that to operate successfully as a linguist one does not have either to personify or reify languages or to endow them with a substance of their own. One analyzes and synthesizes so long as results are forthcoming, *as if* one's data constituted a self-contained system. That ultimately they are not wholly self-contained is obvious. But it is a truism that the scientist's concern as scientist is not with ultimates—certainly not to begin with.

It is also clear that linguistic science is consistently backward and weak in ascertaining causality but that its particular selective concentration is what enables it to determine significant relations of form and structure—patterns and their interrelations. The causes of linguistic phenomena such as changes of form or meaning of words—the causes of these in the ordinary sense of "efficient" causes—evidently lie below the linguistic-cultural level itself and presumably are numerous, obscure, conflicting, and determined by still more remote causes. But it will be noted that the linguistic phenomena which result from these sublinguistic causes come highly regularized, formalized, patterned, and definitely interrelated, as soon as we look for the forms contained in them. The phenomena even contain a great deal of predictability, which we are ordinarily neglectful of because it is so commonplace in experience. For instance, the next Anglo-Saxon uttering Henry's sentiment would also say "Give me Liberty" and not "Gave mine liberting." In short, intellectual order and intellectual significance are most readily and successfully attained on the linguistic level by directing attention to form-patterns and form-relations and not toward causal relations.

Finally, as regards approach being "historic" in the larger sense in which the word has been used here, the linguist can operate synchronically and descriptively, or again he can operate diachronically and historically in the narrower, conventional sense. This, however, is a detail and an incident. In both cases the linguist deals with forms and form-relations which have significance to him; and he deals with them to an equal degree in the two cases. In both instances his material remains essentially superindividual, anonymous, patterned, predictive as to its repetitiveness, and almost unconcerned with cause. What this likeness of method of synchronic descriptive linguistics and of diachronic linguistics imports is this: The differentiation into synchronic and diachronic treatment being secondary, the approach which I call the "historic" one, in contrast with the nomothetic approach, is thereby shown to be characterized primarily not by accentuation of the time element and succession in time, as is still so often supposed, but is characterized rather by its other properties that have been enumerated. It is these other properties—superindividuality, patterning, relative nonconcern with cause—that are fundamental to the generic historic approach.

Language has been chosen here as illustration because it is somewhat narrower, somewhat more set off and self-contained, than the rest of culture and therefore somewhat more clear cut. But the difference is only of degree. To understand cultural manifestations, we must also seek for idiosyncratic and physiognomic forms and seek for their significances first within a coherent, largely self-sufficient system of forms such as a particular civilization; and beyond that in a great context of total forms achieved in human history. We must also expect to discover in our material little of causality in the sense of the physicist's causality. We must be ready, where we get further by it, to ignore and suppress the individual, who from the angle of the understanding of culture is perhaps more often irrelevant and distracting than helpful. The ordering or relating which yields understanding in the study of culture is basically best defined, perhaps, as a process of perceiving significant interrelations of forms as forms.

It is evident that the ultimate relating of cultural forms to their largest possible context, in order to bring out their fullest significance, carries in it an element of weighting of the large relation, of the long-range view. And this, in turn, is akin to diachronic interest, to unwillingness to remain restricted to the moment. The moment is sufficient in interest when it is typical of repetitive totality, when it contains totality, as it were, as it does in physics. When the moment or spot is not containing or representative of a larger whole, as when it is uniquely idiosyncratic, then intellectual interest pushes on from it to the whole. Therewith the view tends to become diachronic, and the approach is characterizable as historic in nature, whether or not it succeeds in becoming actually chronological.

In the entire realm of style the superpersonal flow of form is obviously strong. The word itself—*stylus*, the "pencil"—originally had anthropomorphic reference to the particular quality or manner of writing of an individual. The word "style" tends nowadays to be used for a group similarity, for what is the manner common to a school or series of writers or artists, for a superindividual quality. We can still speak of Shakespeare's "style": we more often speak of "Elizabethan style." And we successfully trace and analyze styles which we cannot, for lack of knowledge, segregate into the contributions of individuals. This holds, for instance, of much of Greek vase painting and of much of Romanesque and Gothic architecture, not to mention the beginnings of most arts and all primitive ones.

Allied to styles are the courses of dress fashion or mode—that which to the unsophisticated the word "style" is in fact most likely to denote. Names of individuals—Prince Albert, Empress Eugénie—are now and then applied to such fashions, but secondarily and arbitrarily, as picturesque handles. Actually, dress fashions arise obscurely, are due to undetermined causes, and are almost wholly shaped and executed, as well as accepted and used anonymously, by the great nameless throng—superindividually in short.

Even in the fine arts it is only when these become a self-conscious cult that real interest in the individual artist arises and that he is sought after and his work prized as peculiarly his, as Chambers has set forth in *Cycles of Taste*. In most of human history, and to most men, it is objects and styles that are meaningful; the artist is only a personal exemplification and a passing incident.

It is much the same with inventions. Today we think in terms of inventors. But the discoveries and inventions of other lands, of the past, of our own Middle Ages, are anonymous. Metalworking, blacksmithing; plows, screws, shears; stirrups, horseshoes, harnesses, wheels, axles; clocks, levels, lamps, candles; glass and pots; fertilizing, irrigating, castrating, riding—the whole basis of mechanical civilization has no personally known authors. They were never recorded or have been long forgotten, because they did not matter.

When finally this condition changes and legend or history gives us, first, imagined inventors and then documentarily authenticated ones, a strange persistence of the ancient condition nevertheless continues. The inventors now come in contemporary pairs or triplets or teams of competitors. Wallace synchronizes with Darwin, Leverrier with Adams, De Vries with Correns and Tschermak; Langley's flight with Wright's; Bell anticipated Gray by a day; Fulton contests with Symington, Fitch, Rumsey, and Stevens. That the making of inventions is normally multiple and simultaneous is by now a fairly well-established fact. From the angle of the individual, the inventors operate independently. From that of the culture, it is the trend, the antecedents, the moment, that unite to force the invention; within its setting it has become, as it were, inevitable; which person is the vehicle of discovery matters little to the society and to the growth of the culture.

Another long-noted phenomenon points the same way, if one will see it so. This is the clustering of great men in certain epochs of certain civilizations and their rarity elsewhere. Nothing now known in biological heredity, nothing in the laws of chance, can account for these tremendous variations in the frequency and intensity of genius. The only explanation yet advanced which is not wholly speculative or arbitrary sees a correlation between realized genius and opportunity given by stage of a civilization's development—the stage where its productive cultural patterns are defined and mature but where their inherent potentialities have not yet begun to be exhausted. By this view, it is the phase of developing culture patterns that is primarily determinative of greatness and fineness of human achievement; geniuses are the index of such development of pattern. What we are wont to call "great men" are those among many more individuals of above-average ability who happen to get born in a time and place and society the patterns of whose culture have formed with sufficient potential value and have developed to sufficient ripeness to allow the full capacities of these individuals to be realized and expressed. This is not really a revolutionary view. It should not even be disturbing to anyone who has apprehended the strength and fulness with which culture holds us all. It ought certainly not upset him who has read and absorbed Sumner's *Folkways* of more than forty years ago and has made the inevitable short extrapolation from the folk to the sophisticates and has realized that we are all in the grip of our ways and our mores—in the grip of our culture.

I have just spoken of greatness and fineness, of potential and realized achievements. Therewith we are plumb in the field of that which the scientist has long said is not for him to touch: values—human values which are cultural values, whether moral, aesthetic, sensory, intellectual, or what not.

One must grant that human cultural values have nothing to do with physics, have no place in it or in any science that models itself on the plan and rules of physics. But how is it possible, without the most sterile stultification, to make intellectual study of social man who is cultural man, and yet permanently to leave out of consideration his product, culture, and that essence of culture, its forms and its values?

This is not to affirm that all study which has man for its subject need take cognizance of values. It is possible to investigate responses of learning or the mechanism of propagandizing or the structure and size of social groupings and never tread on a value. But that it is possible to skirt values and yet not touch them is not per se a moral mandate to do only that. It is evident that we shall have to admit two nonconcurrent plans or ways of investigation into what are called "social phenomena." One approach tries to follow as best it may the methods of the physicist or to find near-surrogates for them, to measure and experiment, and to dispense with consideration of values. The second approach accepts values as inherent in culture and characteristic of it, as thus being part of nature and therefore susceptible of study like any other set of phenomena in nature, and of study by methods analogous to those used in the study of the other parts of nature, though not necessarily identical with those of physics. Values, along with the culture forms to which they attach, can obviously be described; their differential qualities as well as common characteristics can be compared; their developmental phases, sequential relations, and connections can be investigated. This has, in fact, been done in every study of the history of an art, in every attempt to present a religion, in all ethnographic accounts that rise above mechanical itemization, in all writings on culture history that are more than atomistic.

It is true that it is customary to relegate many such studies to what are named the "humanities" and therewith to read them out of the so-called "social sciences." But what of that—provided that the phenomena considered and the forces in them are regarded as natural, as part of the rest of nature and in no sense supernatural? And provided also that they are subjected to dissection, recombination, and inference according to the basic rules of evidence followed in the investigation of other parts or realms of nature, without admittance of bias, personal advantage, self-superiority or ethnocentricity.

In the past the trouble has been that values were claimed and regarded as direct products of deity, which stood outside nature and above it, or as emanating from the soul, whose spirituality, first protected by separation from the body, was further preserved by exclusion from the domain of nature and nature's matter and energy. But surely those days are over. It is difficult to imagine a ground on which contemporary natural scientists would deny validity to any endeavor to understand any set of manifestations occurring in nature, provided that the endeavor is free of reservations, overt or concealed, as to exclusions from nature.

Cultural values, along with cultural forms and cultural content, surely exist only through men and reside in men. As the products of human bodies and minds and their functionings and as a specialized extension of them, cultural values thus form a wholly "natural" part of nature. Here the concept of the hierarchy of levels helps. Not only are the levels separated into steps; their superposition one on the other also ties them together, though not into an undifferentiated unity.

Values, like all sociocultural manifestations, are largely superpersonal. That is, far more of any individual's values are instilled into him from outside, directly or indirectly from his society, than he produces within and by himself. Hence values participate in what used to be called the "collective" or "mass" origin—what I prefer to call the "essential anonymity" of origin—or phenomena like customs, morals, ideologies, fashions, and speech. Sumner's "folkways" excellently conveys this same quality except for its false implication that there also exists a social intelligentsia exempt from being folk. It is possible to exalt collectivity into something self-containedly mystical, as shown by the example of Jung and perhaps of Durkheim. But it is not necessary to be mystical in dealing with collectivity, and we shall therefore assume that we are concerned with the collective only as something completely in relation with the remainder of nature.

Now the collective or anonymous, being everybody's, is also nobody's: there is a quality of the impersonal about it. The things that are everyone's enter individuality more diffusely than those which a person has sweated out for or by himself. These latter he is likely to prize, almost certain to be well aware of, and to have a conscious history and highlighted reasons for, whether these reasons be true or false. But what he shares with the collectivity is more massive and extensive, often more firmly rooted, and also more obscure; it tends to be less in the focus of consciousness. Hence what has been called the "covertness" of many patterns of culture; they have been set aside from the overt patterns as "configurations" by Kluckhohn. "Covertness" here does not imply intent of concealment, as it does so often in interpersonal motivations, rather only lack of awareness. It is probably a case of cultural forms being relatively more and less in focus of awareness along a sliding scale partly of occasion and partly of generic situation. Thus rules of conduct, which serve as protections to personality, are likely to be formulated with awareness and explicitness, though also subject to attempted warpings by self-interest. At the other end of the scale, rules of grammar in speech, which normally serves to connect personalities when they feel relaxed and in least need of protection, are unformulated, except as a result of the highly sophisticated curiosity of linguists, and can properly be described as having grown up both anonymously and unconsciously. Breaches of grammatical rule, though instantly observed, are ordinarily not resented, because they invade nothing particular to the individual, but are accepted with tolerance, amusement, or contempt.

Allied to this unawareness or unconsciousness of cultural form and organization is the irrationality of much of the collective in culture. "Irrationality" is what it is sometimes called. I have used the term myself. It covers a variety of happenings in culture which have in common a factor of inconsistency. The totality of a situation or way of doing comes out less regular and less coherent than it might have been under rational planning. Daylight saving; the letter *Double-U* after *U* and *V*; mannered mediaeval instead of classic Roman script; ideographs when an alphabet is available; the spellings "ought" and "eight"; the plural "oxen" instead of "oxes," will serve as examples. The point, of course, is that such irregularities and inefficiencies *were* not thought out but are the result of long and complex histories, with quite different factors often impinging successively. Established individual habits, prestige values, change in one part of a system with lag in another, actual economic cost, mere inertia or nostalgia—all sorts of reasons, mostly rational enough in the concrete situation, have been at work; and the resulting system shows the effect of compromises and patches. Any fool could devise a more consistent system than exists, but even a despot rarely can institute one. In one sense the outcome is "irrational" indeed, in that the institution lacks the full reasonableness which its defenders claim for it. Actually, it rather is nonrational, and only partly that. Most strictly, it is that the institutional pattern is irregular, not wholly consistent.

These considerations rather foreshadow what might be said of the integratedness of the cultures of particular societies. Cultures tend toward integration and, in the main, largely achieve some degree of it, though never total integration. This latter is an ideal condition invented by a few anthropologists not well versed in history. It is hard to imagine any historian—other than a propagandist—bringing himself to advance such a claim as the complete integration of any culture, in the face of his professional experience.

That values constitute an essential element of cultures leads to another consideration. A first account of a new culture, having necessarily to seize and portray the values which help to give it organization and orientation, is likely to emerge as a somewhat idealized account, since the values of the culture are reflected in the society's ideals. Of course, no society is ideal in its behavior. The society aims to conform to the value standards; but we are all more or less lazy, mean, self-centered, cowardly, spiteful, motivated by personal interest. There is thus an unavoidable gap between the ideal or "pure" picture of the culture and the actuality of how this ideal is lived out by the average adherent of the culture. The psychologically minded analyst of behavior, the student of personality and culture, for whom culture is less an end than a take-off of interest, will accentuate the actuality; and between personality stresses and strains, traumas and frustrations, the ideal values of conduct which the "culturologist" has built up into such gleaming, streamlined patterns will emerge tarnished and battered or even cracked. This is a difference to be aware of without worrying too much over it. He who is really interested in the phenomena of culture knows that their ideal values always suffer in actual human living of them. But, at the same time, he knows that in apprehending cultures the most essential thing to apprehend is their values, because without these he will not know either toward what the cultures are slanted or around what they are organized.

Incidentally, it seems to be with reference to this value-ideal content that the full study of culture has sometimes been called "normative" and "humanistic." Not that we should study cultures merely in order to learn proper conduct in life but that, without cognizance of their norms, we are studying only their shells.

Its extraordinary variability or plasticity is one of the most marked properties of culture. Living organisms are also adaptable and modifiable but do repeat their basic plan of structure closely in successive generations of individuals. There is almost nothing in culture to correspond to this organic repetitiveness. Allegations of regular recurrences in culture refer to shadowy, large resemblances which are only dubiously substantiable because they are not precisely definable. Itemized bits of culture content may persist with tenacity for long periods. Functioning organizations of cultural material apparently always change, even if they persist, until it is often difficult to say whether we are still within the original complex, form, or pattern or have slid into a new one. This inherent plasticity is evident as soon as one is in position to follow any one institution in detail through the centuries; or, equally, to follow an institution or custom through its provincial or regional variants, or through its appearances among a series of nonliterate tribes that are geographically contiguous.

The reason for this strong propensity of culture to vary seems to lie in the following fact: All cultural phenomena are invariably related to certain other cultural phenomena to which they are similar and which precede or succeed them or occur near them contemporaneously; and their fullest understanding can be attained only through cognizance of these relations. While these relations are indisputable, they are relations of form, value, and significance. They are not, directly, relations of cause in the ordinary sense of efficient cause. The efficient causes of cultural phenomena are the actions or behavior of men—of psychosomatic individual human beings. A denial of this proposition seems to leave no alternative but admission of a set of insulated, self-contained cultural forces operating in and on a self-sufficient cultural substance. This would be a large assumption and would immediately incur the charge, from scientists, of being a mystical tenet aiming to exclude a particular domain of phenomena from the sway of the remainder of the cosmos as studied by total science.

Now, as soon as the efficient causality of culture is admitted to lie essentially on the psychobiological level, it is evident that cultural phenomena are, in the strict sense, only by-products of organic activities, epiphenomena of primary organic phenomena. This conclusion, in turn, would seem to explain the irregularity, unpredictability, variability, and "plasticity" of cultural phenomena. They may once be the large cultural products of inconsequential subcultural forces or, again, the relatively insignificant side-effects of organic causes whose primary expression is in organic consequences. It cannot be doubted that single individuals occasionally affect the stream of culture perceptibly: Napoleon with his Code, Caesar on the Calendar, Shi Hwang-ti with the Burning of the Books, Copernicus with his revolution—not to mention religious leaders. Even suborganic influence on culture must be admitted: catastrophes that wipe out one society, obliterating its culture, but spare another, leaving its culture intact; changes in climate favorable to prosperity and increase of particular populations, with consequent dominance of their cultures over those of disadvantaged peoples. It is evident that the greater the number and variety of these subcultural causes, the greater the variability or "plasticity" of cultural phenomena is likely to be.

Of course, the total outcome is not utter cultural randomness but only a high degree of what may properly be called plasticity; and this for the following reason.

Predominantly it will be the psychosomatic actions of human beings that contain the immediate causality of cultural phenomena. But human beings, with their extraordinarily high symbolizing faculties, which means cultural faculties, are always culturalized. That is, they are culturally determined—and heavily determined—by the time they reach the age at which they become potential causes of culture. What is therefore operative is a powerful system of circular causality. The human beings who influence culture and make new culture are themselves molded; and they are molded through the intervention of other men who are culturalized and thus products of previous culture. So it is clear that, while human beings are always the *immediate* causes of cultural events, these human causes are themselves the result of antecedent culture situations, having been fitted to the existing cultural forms which they encounter. There is thus a continuity of indirect causation from culture event to culture event through the medium of human intermediaries. These intermediaries are concerned, first of all, with relieving their own tensions and achieving their personal gratification; but in so doing they also transmit, and to some degree modify, the culture which they carry, because they have been conditioned to it. In a sense, accordingly, a kind of cultural causality is also operative. However, compared with the immediate efficient causality of men on culture, the causation of culture on culture is indirect, remote, and largely a functional relation of form to form. At any rate, as long as one's interest is in what happens in culture, it is the cultural antecedents that become significant. The human transmitters and carriers and modifiers are likely to average pretty much alike. As causes they tend to average uniform and constant, except so far as cultural exposure has differentiated them.

The inquirer, if his interest is really in culture, tends therefore to omit the human agents. He operates *as if* individual personalities did not have a hand in cultural events. In the main he is justified in this procedure. He is certainly justified in proportion as his view is long-range. On telescopic inspection of

the greater cultural currents, even the greatest and most influential personalities shrink to minuteness.

As the range contracts and the segment of culture examined begins to be
minute, the role of individuals, under the microscopic dissection being carried
on, looms correspondingly larger. Here is an equally legitimate method of
study; but, of course, it yields results of a quite different order. It gives insight
into the interaction of persons and culture: on how individuals get caught in
the net of their culture; of how some kinds of them stretch the net or tear
rents in it; how others, meanwhile, are weaving new ranges of mesh. The
value of such studies is as examples of the close-up mechanism of the change
which culture is always tending to undergo. An additional value is in the illu-
mination thrown on the reactions of human beings, viewed as integral personalities, to their enveloping culture. These are certainly important fields of
knowledge. But they are obviously different from straight culture history or
from the analytic comparison of cultural forms and values as such.

What "culture and personality" as a field of study seems to be, in its
purest form, is what has just been described as the interaction of persons and
their enveloping culture. Really to pursue this study, it is obviously first necessary to understand pretty well what the culture is and what the persons are like.
It would be vain to hope that worth-while results will eventuate from operating
with an indeterminately variable X matched against an indeterminately variable
Y. Kluckhohn, prominently identified with the "culture-and-personality" movement, has recently proposed shifting its focus from the mutual interaction of
the two factors, as just described, to a focus within personality, as this is
affected by hereditary constitution, by social environment, by society, and
by culture. This would make personality the real subject of investigation, and
culture only one of several factors impinging on it. This is less, and rather
more one-sided, than a true culture-and-personality field as it has just been
envisaged. But such an evenly balanced field is an especially difficult one to
investigate until both the contributing fields or levels, whose relation is being
investigated, are fairly thoroughly understood. And that can as yet hardly be
affirmed of either culture or personality. The danger is therefore of a Scylla of
inconclusiveness faced by a Charybdis of forced verbalistic conclusions.
Nevertheless, whichever approach is used, the entire legitimacy of the translevel subject of culture-personality interaction is unquestionable.

Of course, some personality study and attempted culture-and-personality
study is motivated primarily by a lack of interest in culture or understanding of
it—in short, by a desire to escape from dealing with it. There is no valid
quarrel with this attitude, only with the nonavowal of its motivation.

Allied are productions like Chapple and Coon's *Principles of Anthropology*,
from which even the word "culture" has been expunged except for a few oversights. This is a seemingly conscious attempt, at any rate a *de facto* one, to
explain culture away into phenomena and factors of lower level. In short, the
purpose is outright reductionist.

The problem remains unresolved of how far general forms, therefore recurrent forms, can be demonstrated in culture. The difficulty has been that the

recurrent forms are lax and ill defined. With strict analysis, the stable content of concepts like feudalism, clan, mana, soul, and taboo shrinks increasingly. This seems to be because the actual cultural content of such general concepts has been acquired by them during their historical development, which is always complex and always tending toward the unique, as historians have long ago learned to take for granted. The general or recurrent remnant in these seemingly recurrent phenomena is usually not cultural but of lower level, especially psychological. What is common to clans is that they function as associations of people felt to be kindred, toward whom one has or develops kinsman attitudes. This is essentially a finding in social psychology. More specific recurrences show this even more clearly. The tendency of writing systems to devise or revert to symbols for syllables is quite evidently the result of a psychosomatic inclination to syllabify when speech is being rendered very distinctly or analytically. Psychologists are generally not concerned with any finding so concrete and specific as this one, so they have not announced it. But, so far as it is a little "law," it is a psychosomatic one explanative of cultural phenomena.

Another feature of these partial recurrences or resemblances is that they cut across resemblances due to historical connection and are therefore left without benefit of explanation of similarity as due to community of origin. If, then, the recurrence is due to some deeper-seated, generic factor, the question arises why the results of this are not universal, as they almost always fail to be. The situation is like one familiar in botany. Trees have quite evidently been independently developed in a whole series of families, even orders, of plants. Likewise vines; likewise herbs; and so on. The botanist does not therefore put all trees into one order, all vines into another. Neither does he discard the common-knowledge concepts of categories of tree, vine, bush, herb, altogether; he uses them as a more or less useful adjunct or supplement in description. It would seem that this would turn out to be about the proper function of the corresponding categories of recurrences in culture, such as feudalism, caste, shaman, taboo, totem.

There is also no agreement as yet as to the most general forms among which the totality of culture could be distributed, so far as recurrences or regularities do hold water. The earliest such attempts took the shape of stages and suffered from intellectual naïveté. There was the hunting-herding-farming stage sequence; the mythologic-religious-positive one; even the chipped stone–polished stone-bronze-iron classification.

Of more promise is the concept of recurrent functional nexuses of internal relations: say, of feudalism, piety, and mediaevalistic economy. This Weberian approach is still rather inadequately explored.

Finally, there is the question of how far the maximum nexuses or totalities which we call "civilizations" show recurrences in their developmental phases —in other words, show a recurrent pattern of growth. If they do, empirically, show such a recurrent pattern, civilizations would provide an actual and natural segmentation which would help us to organize intellectually the otherwise variable tossing and endlessly stretching sea of the variable continuum of culture as a whole. There is a growing recognition of the probable reality of such segmentation, as well as of its specific limits and inclusions—in other words, of what each civilization takes in.

As to what is at work in the formation of these great units, however, there is wide divergence. Spengler sees immanent predestination, Toynbee moral free will, Sorokin a pendulum beat between sensate and ideational proclivities. This area of inquiry will unquestionably undergo considerable further cultivation, if for no other reason than that our thinking of history has until recently been too ethnocentrically weighted, too "auto-culturo-centric," for the large problems in this area to be effectively conceived or framed.

The question remains whether the concept of culture will serve as a mechanism for integrating more closely the several social sciences. The answer is both Yes and No. There is no doubt that cultural aspects can be recognized and followed through all human areas commonly recognized as social. Economics and government *are* only segments of culture. The data of formal sociology are so intertwined with cultural ones that subjects like family, kinship, associations, the state, are claimed and treated equally by sociologists and by cultural anthropologists. Formal history, even at its most biographical, cannot wholly avoid institutional implications; and, at the opposite end of its range, history is institutional, and thus *de facto* cultural. Psychology can pretty much eliminate cultural factors by narrowing its analysis and by holding the cultural factors constant in selective experiment. Yet, as soon as it rewidens its activity to take in total personalities, a flood of cultural considerations inevitably pours in on it.

However, what all this means is that if one is interested in cultural manifestations, one can recognize them and deal with them selectively in every scientific study that has man for its subject. And such a selective pursuit will yield certain understandings unattainable by any other and less differentiated method. But it *is* selective; that is a fact that must not be forgotten. There are other bases of selection, and each has its own kind of fruitfulness. Economic theory, though validated by empirical techniques rather than derived from them, seems reasonably to satisfy economists and is not likely to be given up by them for any more generalized theory of culture. Historians presumably will continue to prefer their accustomed mixed diet of events, persons, and institutional forms, with its maximum of adherence to raw phenomena, opportunities for stirring dramatic representation in narrative, and minimum necessity of generalization—and then generalization merely as incidental commentary. We have already considered the translevel or interlevel studies of fields like personality in culture, which, though still groping and unsure of method and occasionally confusing hope with fulfilment, are certainly legitimate and to be counted on to grow.

In summary, it is evident that the cultural approach, now that it is well isolated and developed, will continue to be used because it yields distinctive results. Yet it is equally clear that the cultural approach is not exclusively valid within the area of superorganic phenomena; nor, of course, is it a panacea. It is a selective approach, fruitful because of its selectiveness, but, for the same reason, not unlimited in its scope.

Robert H. Lowie 1883–1957

BACKGROUND

Alfred Kroeber and Robert Lowie were colleagues for many years at the University of California. If Kroeber was the "dean" of American anthropologists, Lowie was certainly their "grand old man." The two disagreed on many points—often in print—but never allowed their differences to affect their colleagueship.

Robert Lowie, born in Vienna in 1883, was brought to the United States when he was ten years old. Although he lived in New York City for the next twenty-four years, the atmosphere in which he lived and grew up was completely Austrian. "To all intents and purposes," his boyhood friend Paul Radin wrote, "the United States was a foreign and somewhat shadowy land, with which one came in contact when leaving the house and with which one lost contact when reentering it."

The influence of this turn-of-the-century Viennese culture stayed with Lowie all his life. Like so many anthropologists, he was bicultural even before he became an anthropologist. An old-world kind of education gave him a lifelong interest in philosophy and literature. His scientific work showed the influence of German philosophers like Wilhelm Dilthey and later Ernst Mach. An admiration for Boas' German scholarly virtues was one of the things that attracted Lowie to Boas.

At City College he concentrated on Latin and Greek for two years, then switched to science. He earned his B.A. in 1901, when he was only eighteen, and taught for three years in the New York public school system. He intended to continue his studies in chemistry—but then he met Franz Boas. He was quickly converted to anthropology and began graduate work at Columbia in 1904.

In those days Boas assigned subjects for doctoral dissertations (a practice that Lowie himself took over). Lowie's assignment was a topic in American Indian mythology—a subject in which he was not interested. However, since that was the assigned task, he set about it with his usual thoroughness and competence. He turned out an excellent thesis on "The Test Theme in North American Mythology," and he was awarded his Ph.D. in 1907.

While at Columbia, Lowie volunteered his services to Clark Wissler at the American Museum of Natural History. It was Wissler who sent him on his first field trip—to the Lemhi Shoshone in 1906. He remained at the museum until 1917, filling various posts, writing monographs on Indians and articles on classificatory systems of kinship. During this part of his career, Lowie was interested in general problems of culture and psychology (the psychology of Wilhelm Wundt and Hermann Ebbinghaus), in problems of culture and environment, and in totemism. A small book, *Culture and Ethnology* (1917), and contributions to a symposium on totemism in *Anthropos* (1917) characterize this period.

The year 1917 also saw Lowie's departure for the University of California, where he stayed until his retirement in 1950. Soon after he got there, a publisher asked him to write a book on primitive society. He said it was not one of his special interests, but he accepted the commission—and 1920 saw the production of a classic, *Primitive Society.* In this book Lowie rejected Lewis H. Morgan's evolutionary scheme of social organization and emphasized diffusion. When he was accused of being destructive and too little concerned with reconstruction, he responded that ethnology was a science and its theories must be supported by facts. Indeed, it is the strong supporting evidence in *Primitive Society* that allowed it to dominate the field of social organization for twenty-five years.

Primitive Society was followed by *Primitive Religion* (1924) and *The Origin of the State* (1927). Lowie was editor of the *American Anthropologist* from 1924 to 1933. In 1933 he married Louella Cole, a psychologist.

History of Ethnological Theory appeared in 1937. Although he had mellowed by this time, his views were basically unchanged: distaste for the extreme diffusionist views and evolutionary sequences of the German Kulturkreis school, equally great distaste for the general laws of A. R. Radcliffe-Brown—which were not, he said, based on facts.

During World War II, Lowie's involvement with German culture led him to teach a course on Germany and the Balkans at Berkeley; in 1945 he published *The German People: A Social Portrait to 1914.* After his retirement he spent a couple of years in Germany, Austria, and Switzerland and wrote *Toward Understanding Germany* (1954). Like many anthropologists, in straightening out his own life and cultural position, he left cultural analyses of lasting value.

Lowie wrote until his death in 1957. Several articles appeared in *American Anthropologist* in 1956 and 1957; his autobiography, *Robert H. Lowie, Ethnologist,* was edited by Mrs. Lowie and published posthumously in 1959.

INTRODUCTION

The most difficult single task we had in editing this book was finding a selection from Lowie that does him sufficient credit. As a whole, Lowie's is one of the most significant bodies of work in the history of anthropology. It does not break easily into self-contained short units.

Lowie probably came closer to Boas' program for anthropology than any of his contemporaries. He was deeply rooted in the philosophy of science, and he regarded cultural anthropology as a science. His theoretical arguments, as well as his refutations of authors such as Morgan, derive from his scientific world view. In spite of his nontheoretical outlook, Lowie often wrote on subjects of theoretical concern. He addressed himself to evolutionary theory, geographical determinism, the relationship of culture to race and psychology, and finally to diffusion as an explanation of culture.

Lowie's criticism of Morgan's evolutionary theory is epistemological. He claimed that Morgan's scheme of the evolution of kinship could not be proved and that the data used by Morgan was often erroneous. Lowie found Morgan's basic contributions to be in social organization, and more particularly in the development of kinship terminology. Since he would not accept evolutionism as a determinant of culture, Lowie was obliged to seek other explanations for such a determinant. He never saw race as a determinant of culture—all his life he argued against racial explanations of culture.

Culture cannot be reduced to psychology, according to Lowie, for psychology is the science of innate attitudes and behavior of individuals. Or, put into different words, psychology is "what is not culture" in man. For Lowie, the plasticity of the human organism had been well demonstrated (by Boas), making the relationship of psychology to anthropology a one-sided affair. Psychological reductionism cannot possibly explain ethnographic facts, nor can culture be reduced to psychology.

According to Lowie, diffusion or cultural contact is extremely important, and borrowing is always easier than originating. Cultural contact is a very important reason for cultural development. In the exchange of ideas that makes up cultural contact, both simple and complex societies participate, both as donors and recipients.

8 THE DETERMINANTS OF CULTURE

Psychology, racial differences, geographical environment, have all proved inadequate for the interpretation of cultural phenomena. The inference is obvious. Culture is a thing *sui generis* which can be explained only in terms of itself. This is not mysticism but sound scientific method. The biologist, whatever metaphysical speculations he may indulge in as to the ultimate origin of life, does not depart in his workaday mood from the principle that every cell is derived from some other cell. So the ethnologist will do well to postulate the principle, *Omnis cultura ex cultura* (Rivers 1914:92). This means that he will account for a given cultural fact by merging it in a group of cultural facts or by demonstrating some other cultural fact out of which it has developed. The cultural phenomenon to be explained may either have an antecedent within the culture of the tribe where it is found or it may have been imported from without. Both groups of determinants must be considered.

The extraneous determinants of culture summed up under the heading of "diffusion" or "contact of peoples" have been repeatedly referred to in the preceding pages. A somewhat detailed examination seems desirable, for it is difficult to exaggerate their importance.

"Civilization," says Tylor, "is a plant much oftener propagated than developed" (Tylor 1889a:53), and the latest ethnographic memoir that comes

Reprinted from Chapter Four of *Culture and Ethnology* by Robert H. Lowie, © 1966 by Basic Books, Inc., Publishers, New York.

to hand voices the same sentiment: "It is and has always been much easier to borrow an idea from one's neighbors than to originate a new idea; and transmission of cultural elements, which in all ages has taken place in a great many different ways, is and has been one of the greatest promoters of cultural development" (Hatt 1916:246).

A stock illustration of cultural assimilation is that of the Japanese, who in the nineteenth century adopted our scientific and technological civilization ready-made, just as at an earlier period they had acquired wholesale the culture of China. It is essential to note that it is not always the people of lower culture who remain passive recipients in the process of diffusion. This is strikingly shown by the spread of Indian corn. The white colonist "did not simply borrow the maize seed and then in conformity with his already established agricultural methods, or on original lines, develop a maize culture of his own," but "took over the entire material complex of maize culture" as found among the aborigines (Wissler 1916:656–661). The history of Indian corn also illustrates the remarkable rapidity with which cultural possessions may travel over the globe. Unknown in the Old World prior to the discovery of America, it is mentioned as known in Europe in 1539 and had reached China between 1540 and 1570 (Boas 1911:167).

The question naturally arises here, whether this process of diffusion, which in modern times is a matter of direct observation, could have been of importance during the earlier periods of human history when means of communication were of a more primitive order. So far as this point is concerned, we must always remember that methods of transportation progressed very slightly from the invention of the wheeled cart until the most recent times. As Montelius suggests, the periods of 1700 B.C. and A.D. 1700 differed far less in this regard than might be supposed on superficial consideration. Yet we know the imperfection of facilities for travel did not prevent dissemination of culture in historic times.

The great Swedish archaeologist has, indeed, given us a most fascinating picture of the commercial relations of northern Europe in earlier periods and their effect on cultural development (Montelius 1910:249–291). We learn with astonishment that in the ninth and tenth centuries of our era, trade was carried on with great intensity between the North of Europe and the Mohammedan culture sphere since tens of thousands of Arabic coins have been found on Swedish soil. But intercourse with remote countries dates back to a far greater antiquity. One of the most powerful stimuli of commercial relations between northern and southern Europe was the desire of the more southern populations to secure amber, a material confined to the Baltic region and occurring more particularly about Jutland and the mouth of the Vistula. Amber beads have been found not only in Swiss pile-dwellings (Forrer 1908:197) but also in Mycenaean graves of the second millennium B.C. Innumerable finds of amber work in Italy and other parts of southern Europe prove the importance attached to this article, which was exchanged for copper and bronze. The composition of Scandinavian bronzes indicates that their material was imported not from England but from the faraway regions of central Europe. That bronze was not of indigenous manufacture is certain because tin does not occur in Sweden at all while the copper deposits of northern Scandinavia remained untouched until about 1500 years after the end of the Bronze Age. Considering the high development of the bronze technique in Scandinavia and the fact that every pound of bronze had to be imported from without, it would be difficult to exaggerate the extent of contact with the southern populations. But intercourse was not limited to the South. For example, Swedish weapons and implements have been discovered in Finland. Again, crescent-shaped gold ornaments of Irish provenance have been found in Denmark, while a Swedish rock-painting represents with painstaking exactness a type of bronze shield common at a certain prehistoric period of England.

Montelius shows that historical connections of the type so amply attested for the Bronze Age also obtained in the preceding Neolithic era. Swedish hammers of stone dating back to the third pre-Christian millennium and flint daggers have been found in Finland, and earthenware characteristic of Neolithic Scandinavia also turns up on the Baltic coast of Russia. Stone burial cists with a peculiar oval opening at one end occur in a limited section of southwestern Sweden and likewise in England. Since such monuments have been discovered neither in other parts of Sweden nor in Jutland or the Danish islands, they point to a direct intercourse between Britain and western Sweden at about 2000 B.C. A still older form of burial unites Scandinavia with other parts of the continent. Chambers built up of large stones set up edgewise and reaching from the floor to the roof, the more recent ones with and the older without a long covered passage, are highly characteristic of Sweden, Denmark, the British Isles, and the coasts of Europe from the Vistula embouchure to the coasts of France and Portugal, of Italy, Greece, the Crimea, North Africa, Syria, and India. Specific resemblances convince the most competent judges that some, at least, of these widely diffused 'dolmens' are historically connected with their Swedish equivalents, and since the oldest of these Northern chambers go back 3,000 years before our era, we thus have evidence of cultural diffusion dating back approximately five millennia.

It is highly interesting to trace under Montelius' guidance the development of culture as it seems to have actually taken place in southern Sweden. Beginning with the earliest periods, we find the coastal regions inhabited by a population of fishermen and hunters. At a subsequent stage coarse pottery appears with articles of bone and antler, and there is evidence that the dog has become domesticated. In the later Neolithic era perfectly polished stone hammers and exquisitely chipped flint implements occur, together with indications that cattle, horses, sheep and pigs are domesticated and that the cultivation of the soil has begun. Roughly speaking, we may assume that the culture of Scandinavia at the end of the Stone Age resembled in advancement that of the agricultural North American and Polynesian tribes as found by the first European explorers. We may assume a long period of essentially indigenous cultural growth followed towards its close by intimate relations with alien populations. Nevertheless, it was the more extensive contact of the Bronze period that rapidly raised the ancestral Swedes to a cultural position high above a primitive level, with accentuation of agriculture, the use of woolen clothing, and a knowledge of metallurgy. It was again foreign influence that later brought the knowledge of iron and in the third century of our era transformed the Scandinavians into a literary people, flooded their country with art products of the highest then existing Roman civilization, and ultimately introduced Christianity.

The case of Scandinavian culture is fairly typical. We have first a long-continued course of leisurely and relatively undisturbed development, which is superseded by a tremendously rapid assimilation of cultural elements from without. Through contact with tribes possessing a higher civilization the ancient Scandinavians came to participate in its benefits and even to excel in special departments of it, such as bronze work, which from lack of material, they would have been physically incapable of developing unaided. Diffusion was the determinant of Scandinavian cultural progress from savagery to civilization.

It is obvious that this insistence on contact of peoples as a condition of cultural evolution does not solve the ultimate problem of the origin of culture. The question naturally obtrudes itself: If the Scandinavians obtained their civilization from the Southeast, how did the Oriental cultures themselves originate? Nevertheless, when we examine these higher civilizations of the Old World, we are again met with indubitable evidence that one of the conditions of development is the contact of peoples and the consequent diffusion of cultural elements. This appears clearly from a consideration of the ancient civilizations of Egypt, Babylonia, and China.

We now have abundant evidence for a later Stone Age in Egypt with an exceptionally high development of the art of chipping, as well as specimens of pottery and other indications of a sedentary mode of life. About 5000 B.C. this undisturbed evolution began to suffer from a series of migrations of West Asiatic tribes, bringing in their wake a number of cultivated plants and domesticated animals, as well as various other features which possibly included the art of smelting copper, while the ceramic ware of the earlier period agrees so largely with that of Elam in what is now southern Persia that a cultural connection seems definitely established.

If from Egypt we turn to the most probable source of alien culture elements found there, *viz.,* to the region of Mesopotamia, possibly the oldest seat of higher civilization in Asia, we find again that the culture of Babylonia under the famous lawgiver Hammurabi (about 2000 B.C.) is not the product of purely indigenous growth but represents the resultant of at least two components, that of the Sumerian civilization of southern Babylonia and the Accadian culture of the North. It is certain that the Accadians adopted the art of writing from the Sumerians and were also stimulated by this contact in their artistic development. The evolution of Sumerian civilization is lost in obscurity but on the basis of well-established historical cases we should hesitate to assign to them an exclusively creative, and to other populations an exclusively receptive, rôle. We may quite safely assume that the early splendor of Sumerian civilization was also in large part due to stimuli received through foreign relations. That cultural elements of value may be borrowed from an inferior as well as from a higher level has already been exemplified by the case of maize. It is also, among other things, illustrated by the history of the Chinese.

The Chinese have generally been represented as developing in complete isolation from other peoples. This traditional conception, however, breaks down with more intimate knowledge. Dr. Laufer has demonstrated that Chinese civilization, too, is a complex structure due to the conflux of distinct cultural streams. As an originally inland people inhabiting the middle and lower course of the Yellow River, they gradually reached the coast and acquired the art of navigation through contact with Indo-Chinese seafarers. Acquaintance with the northern nomads of Turkish and Tungus stock led to the use of the horse, donkey and camel, as well as the practice of felt and rug weaving, possibly even to the adoption of furniture and the iron technique (Laufer 1909:212–223). Most important of all, it appears that essentials of agriculture, cattle-raising, metallurgy and pottery, as well as less tangible features of civilization are common to ancient China and Babylonia, which forces us to the conclusion that both the Chinese and Babylonian cultures are ramifications from a common Asiatic sub-stratum. It would be idle to speculate as to the relative contributions of each center to this ancient cultural stock. The essential point is that the most ancient Asiatic civilizations of which we have any evidence already indicate close contact of peoples and the dispersal of cultural elements.

Contact of peoples is thus an extraordinary promoter of cultural development. By the free exchange of arts and ideas among a group of formerly independent peoples, a superiority and complexity is rendered possible which without such diffusion would never have occurred. The part played in this process by the cruder populations must not be underestimated. They may contribute both actively and passively; actively, by transmitting knowledge independently acquired, as in the case of the felt technique the Chinese learned from the northern nomads; passively, by forming a lower caste on which the economic labors devolve and thus liberating their conquerors for an enlarged activity in the less utilitarian spheres of culture.

Nevertheless, before peoples can communicate their cultures to others with whom they come into contact, they must first evolve these cultures. The question thus remains, What determines this evolution? In order to gain a proper perspective in this matter, we must for a moment consider the progress of human civilization as a whole. Archaeological research shows that the modern era of steel and iron tools was preceded by an age of bronze and copper implements, which in turn was preceded by a stone age subdivided into a more recent period of polished, and an earlier of merely chipped, stone tools. Now the chronological relations of these epochs are extremely suggestive. The very lowest estimate by any competent observer of the age of Palaeolithic man in Europe sets it at 50,000 years (Obermaier, n.d.:337); since this is avowedly the utmost minimum value that can be assigned on geological grounds, we may reasonably assume twice that figure for the age of human culture generally. Using the rough estimate permissible in discussions of this sort, we may regard the end of the Palaeolithic era as dating back about 15,000 years ago. In short, for more than eight-tenths of its existence, the human species remained at a cultural level at best comparable with that of the Australian. We may assume that it was during this immense space of time that dispersal over the face of the globe took place and that isolation fixed the broader diversities of language and culture, over and above what may have been the persisting cultural sub-stratum common to the earliest undivided human group. The following Neolithic period of different parts of the globe terminated at different times and had not been passed at all by most of the American aborigines and the Oceanians at the time of their discovery. However, from the broader point of view here assumed, it was not relieved by the age of metallurgy until an exceedingly recent past. The earliest estimate I have seen does not put the event back farther than 6000 B.C. even in Mesopotamia. During nine-tenths of his existence, then, man was ignorant of the art of smelting copper from the ore. Finally, the iron technique does not date back 4,000 years; it took humanity ninety-six hundredths of its existence to develop this art.

We may liken the progress of mankind to that of a man a hundred years old, who dawdles through kindergarten for eighty-five years of his life, takes ten years to go through the primary grades, then rushes with lightning rapidity through grammar school, high school and college. Culture, it seems, is a matter of exceedingly slow growth until a certain 'threshhold' is passed, when it darts forward, gathering momentum at an unexpected rate. For this peculiarity of culture as a whole, many miniature parallels exist in special subdivisions of culture history. Natural science lay dormant until Kepler, Galileo and Newton stirred it into unexampled activity, and the same holds for applied science until about a century ago.

This discontinuity of development receives strong additional illustration from a survey of special subdivisions of ancient culture. Though the Palaeolithic era certainly preceded the later Stone Age, archaeologists have hitherto failed to show the steps by which the later could develop out of the earlier. This gap may, of course, be due merely to our lack of knowledge. Yet when we take subdivisions of the Palaeolithic period, the same fact once more confronts us. There is no orderly progression from Solutrean to Magdalenian times. The highly developed flint technique of the former dwindles away in the latter and its place is taken by what seems a spontaneous generation of bone and ivory work, with a high development of realistic art.

In view of the evidence, it seems perfect nonsense to say that early European civilization, by some law inherent in the very nature of culture, developed in the way indicated by archaeological finds. Southern Scandinavia could not possibly have had a bronze age without alien influence. In this case, discontinuity was the result of cultural contact. It may be that the lack of definite direction observed throughout the Stone Age may in part be due to similar causes, the migrations and contact of different peoples, as Professor Sollas suggests. But it is important to note that discontinuity is a necessary feature of cultural progress. It does not matter whether we can determine the particular point in the series at which the significant trait was introduced. It does not matter whether, as I have suggested in the discussion of racial features, the underlying *causes* of the phenomena proceed with perfect continuity. Somewhere in the observed cultural *effects* there is the momentous innovation that leads to a definite break with the past. From a broad point of view, for example, it is immaterial whether the doctrine of evolution clings to the name of the younger or the elder Darwin, to Lamarck or St. Hilaire; the essential thing is that somehow the idea originated, and that when it had taken root it produced incalculable results in modern thought.

If culture, even when uninfluenced by foreign contact, progresses by leaps and bounds, we should naturally like to ascertain the determinants of such 'mutations.' In this respect, the discontinuity of indigenous evolution differs somewhat from that connected with cultural development due to diffusion. It was absolutely impossible that Scandinavia should produce bronze in the absence of tin. But *a priori* it is conceivable that an undisturbed culture might necessarily develop by what biologists call 'orthogenetic evolution', *i.e.*, in a definite direction through definite stages. This is, indeed, what is commonly known as the classical scheme of cultural evolution, of which men like Morgan are the protagonists. Now, how do the observed facts square with this theoretical possibility?

As Professor Boas and American ethnologists generally have maintained (Boas 1911:182 ff.), many facts are quite inconsistent with the theory of unilinear evolution. That theory can be tested very simply by comparing the sequence of events in two or more areas in which independent development has taken place. For example, has technology in Africa followed the lines ascertained for ancient Europe? We know today that it has not. Though unlike southern Scandinavia, the Dark Continent is not lacking in copper deposits, the African Stone Age was not superseded by a Copper Age, but directly by a period of Iron. Similarly, I have already pointed out that the possession of the same domesticated animals does not produce the same economic utilization of them: while the Tungus rides his reindeer, other Siberians harness their animals to a sledge; the Chinaman will not milk his cattle, while the Zulu's diet consists largely of milk. That a particular innovation occurred at a given time and place is, of course, no less the result of definite causes than any other phenomenon of the universe. But often it seems to have been caused by an accidental complex of conditions rather than in accordance with some fixed principle.

For example, the invention of the wheel revolutionized methods of transportation. Now, why did this idea develop in the Old World and never take root among the American Indians? We are here face to face with one of those ultimate data that must simply be accepted like the physicist's fact that water expands in freezing while other substances contract. So far as we can see, the invention might have been made in America as well as not; and for all we know it would never have been made there until the end of time. This introduces a very important consideration. A given culture is, in a measure, at least, a unique phenomenon. In so far as this is true it must defy generalized treatment, and the explanation of a cultural phenomenon will consist in referring it back to the particular circumstances that preceded it. In other words, the explanation will consist in a recital of its past history; or, to put it negatively, it cannot involve the assumption of an organic law of cultural evolution that would necessarily produce the observed effect.

Facts already cited in other connections may be quoted again by way of illustration. When a copper implement is fashioned not according to the requirements of the material, but in direct imitation of preëxisting stone patterns, we have an instance of cultural inertia: it is only the past history of technology that renders the phenomena conceivable. So the unwieldy Chukchee tent, which adheres to the style of a pre-nomadic existence, is explained as soon as the past history of the tribe comes to light.

Phenomena that persist in isolation from their original context are technically known as 'survivals', and form one of the most interesting chapters of ethnology. One or two additional examples will render their nature still clearer. The boats of the Vikings were equipped for rowing as well as for sailing. Why the superfluous appliances for rowing, which were later dropped? As soon as we learn that the Norse boats were originally rowboats and that sails were a later addition, the rowing equipment is placed in its proper cultural setting and the problem is solved. Another example may be offered from a different phase of life. Among the Arapaho Indians there is a series of dance organizations graded by age. Membership is acquired by age-mates at the same time, each receiving the requisite ceremonial instructions from some older man who passed through the dance in his day. These older men, who are paid for their services by the candidates, may belong to any and all of the higher organizations. Oddly enough, each group of dancers is assisted by a number of 'elder brothers', all of whom rank them by *two* grades in the series of dancers. This feature is not at all clear from the Arapaho data alone. When, however, we turn to the Hidatsa Indians, with whom there is evidence this system of age-societies originated, we find that here the youngest group of men does not buy instructions from a miscellaneous assemblage of older men, but buys the dance outright from the whole of the second grade; this group, in order to have the privilege of performing a dance, must buy that of the third grade, and so on. In all these purchases the selling group seeks to extort the highest possible price while the buyers try to get off as cheaply as possible and are aided by the second higher group, *i.e.,* the group just ranking the sellers. Here the sophomore-senior versus freshman-junior relationship is perfectly intelligible; both the freshman and the junior, to pursue the analogy, bear a natural economic hostility against the sophomore, and vice versa. The Arapaho usage is intelligible as a survival from this earlier Hidatsa condition.

Our own civilization is shot through with survivals, so that further illustrations are unnecessary. They suggest, however, another aspect of our general problem. Of course, in every culture different traits are linked together without there being any essential bond between them. An illustration of this type of association is that mentioned by Dr. Laufer for Asiatic tribes, *viz.*, that all nations which use milk for their diet have epic poems, while those which abstain from milk have no epic literature. This type of chance association, due to historical causes, has been discussed by Dr. Wissler (1914:447–605) and Professor Czekanowski (1911:71–75). But survivals show that there may be an *organic* relation between phenomena that have become separated and are treated as distinct by the descriptive ethnologist. In such cases, one trait is the determinant of the other, possibly as the actually preceding cause, possibly as part of the same phenomenon in the sense in which the side of a triangle is correlated with an angle.

A pair of illustrations will elucidate the matter. Primitive terms of relationship often reveal characteristic differences of connotation from their nearest equivalents in European languages. On the other hand, they are remarkably similar not only among many of the North American Indians but also in many other regions of the globe, such as Australia, Oceania, Africa. The most striking peculiarity of this system of nomenclature lies in the inclusiveness of certain terms. For example, the word we translate as 'father' is applied indiscriminately to the father, all his brothers, and some of his male cousins; while the word for 'mother' is correspondingly used for the mother's sisters and some of their female cousins. On the other hand, paternal and maternal uncle or aunt are rigidly distinguished by a difference in terminology. As Morgan divined and Tylor clearly recognized, this system is connected with the one-sided exogamous kin organization by which an individual is reckoned as belonging to the exogamous social group of one, and only one, of his parents. The terminology that appears so curious at first blush then resolves itself very simply into the method of calling those members of the tribe who belong to the father's social group and generation by the same term as the father, while the maternal uncles, who must belong to another group because of the exogamous rule, are distinguished from the father. In short, the terminology simply expresses the existing social organization. In a world-wide survey of the field Tylor found that the number of peoples who use the type of nomenclature I have described and are divided into exogamous groups is about three times that to be expected on the doctrine of chances: in other words, the two apparently distinct phenomena are causally connected (Tylor 1889b:245–272). This interpretation has recently been forcibly advocated by Dr. Rivers, and I have examined the North American data from this point of view. It developed, as a matter of fact, that practically all the tribes with exogamous 'clans', *i.e.*, matrilineal kin groups, or exogamous 'gentes', *i.e.*, patrilineal kin groups, had a system of the type described, while most of the tribes lacking such groups also lacked the nomenclature in question. Accordingly, it follows that there is certainly a functional relation between these phenomena, although it is conceivable that both are functionally related to still other phenomena, and that the really significant relationship remains to be determined.

As a linked illustration, the following phenomena may be presented. Among the Crow of Montana, the Hopi of Arizona, and some Melanesian tribes, the same term is applied to a father's sister and to a father's sister's daughter; indeed, among the Crow and the Hopi the term is extended to all the female descendants through females of the father's sister *ad infinitum.* Such a usage is at once intelligible from the tendency to call females of the father's group belonging to his and younger generations by a single term, regardless of generation, *if* descent is reckoned through the mother, for in that case, and that case only, will the individuals in question belong to the same group. And the fact is that in each of the cases mentioned, group affiliation is traced through the mother, while I know of not a single instance in which paternal descent coexists with the nomenclatorial disregard of generations in the form described.

My instances show, then, that cultural traits may be functionally related, and this fact renders possible a parallelism, however limited, of cultural development in different parts of the globe. The field of culture, then, is not a region of complete lawlessness. Like causes produce like effects here as elsewhere, though the complex conditions with which we are grappling require unusual caution in definitely correlating phenomena. It is true that American ethnologists have shown that in several instances like phenomena can be traced to diverse causes; that, in short, unlike antecedents converge to the same point. However, at the risk of being anathematized as a person of utterly unhistorical mentality, I must register my belief that this point has been overdone and that the continued insistence on it by Americanists is itself an illustration of cultural inertia. Indeed, the vast majority of so-called convergencies are not genuine, but false analogies due to our throwing together diverse facts from ignorance of their true nature, just as an untutored mind will class bats with birds, or whales with fish. When, however, rather full knowledge reveals not superficial resemblance but absolute identity of cultural features, it would be miraculous, indeed, to assume that such equivalence somehow was shaped by different determinants. When a Zulu of South Africa, an Australian, and a Crow Indian all share the mother-in-law taboo imposing mutual avoidance on the wife's mother and the daughter's husband, with exactly the same psychological correlate, it is, to my mind, rash to decree without attempt to produce evidence that this custom must, in each case, have developed from entirely distinct motives. To be sure, this particular usage has not yet, in my opinion, been satisfactorily accounted for. Nevertheless, in contradistinction to some of my colleagues and to the position I myself once shared, I now believe that it is pusillanimous to shirk the real problem involved, and that in so far as any explanation admits the problem, any explanation is preferable to the flaunting of fine phrases about the unique character of cultural phenomena. When, however, we ask what sort of explanation could be given, we find that it is by necessity a *cultural* explanation. Tylor, *e.g.,* thinks that the custom is correlated with the social rule that the husband takes up his abode with the wife's relatives and that the taboo merely marks the difference between him and the rest of the family. We have here clearly one cultural phenomenon as the determinant of another.

It is not so difficult as might at first appear to harmonize the principle that a cultural phenomenon is explicable only by a unique combination of antecedent circumstances with the principle that like phenomena are the product of like antecedents. The essential point is that in either case we have past history as the determinant. It is not necessary that certain things should happen; but if they do happen, then there is at least a considerable likelihood that certain other things will also happen. Diversity occurs where the particular thing of importance, say the wheel, has been discovered or conceived in one region but not in another. Parallelism tends to occur when the same significant phenomenon is shared by distinct cultures. It remains true that in culture history we are generally wise after the event. *A priori*, who would not expect that milking must follow from the domestication of cattle?

When we find that a type of kinship terminology is determined by exogamy or matrilineal descent, we have, indeed, given a cultural explanation of a cultural fact; but for the ultimate problems how exogamy or maternal descent came about, we may be unable to give a solution. Very often we cannot ascertain an anterior or correlated cultural fact for another cultural fact, but can merely group it with others of the same kind. Of this order are many of the parallels that figure so prominently in ethnological literature. For example, that primitive man everywhere believes in the animation of nature seems an irreducible datum which we can, indeed, paraphrase and turn hither and thither for clearer scrutiny but can hardly reduce to simpler terms. All we can do is to merge any particular example of such animism in the general class after the fashion of all scientific interpretation. That certain tendencies of all but universal occurrence are characteristic of culture, no fair observer can deny, and it is the manifest business of ethnology to ascertain all such regularities so that as many cultural phenomena as possible may fall into their appropriate categories. Only those who would derive each and every trait similar in different communities of human beings from a single geographical source can ignore such general characteristics of culture, which may, in a sense, be regarded as determinants of specific cultural data or rather, as the principles of which these are particular manifestations.

Recently I completed an investigation of Plains Indian societies begun on the most rigorous of historical principles, with a distinct bias in favor of the unique character of cultural data. But after smiting hip and thigh the assumption that the North American societies were akin to analogous institutions in Africa and elsewhere, I came face to face with the fact that, after all, among the Plains Indians, as among other tribes, the tendency of age-mates to flock together had formed social organizations and thus acted as a cultural determinant.

Beyond such interpretative principles for special phases of civilization, there are still broader generalizations of cultural phenomena. One has been repeatedly alluded to under the caption of cultural inertia, or survival—the irrational persistence of a feature when the context in which it had a place has vanished. But culture is not merely a passive phenomenon but a dynamic one as well. This is strikingly illustrated in the assimilation of an alien cultural stimulus. As I have already pointed out, it is not sufficient to bring two cultures into contact in order to have a perfect cultural interpenetration. The element of selection enters in a significant way. Not everything that is offered by a foreign culture is borrowed. The Japanese have accepted our technology but not our religion and etiquette. Moreover, what is accepted may undergo a very considerable change. While the whole range of phenomena is extremely wide and cannot be dismissed with a few words, it appears fairly clear that generally the preëxisting culture at once seizes upon a foreign element and models it in accordance with the *native* pattern. Thus, the Crow Indians, who had had a pair of rival organizations, borrowed a society from the Hidatsa where such rivalry did not exist. Straightway, the Crow imposed on the new society their own conception, and it became the competitor of another of their organizations. Similarly, the Pawnee have a highly developed star cult. Their folklore is in many regards similar to that of other Plains tribes, from which some tales have undoubtedly been borrowed. Yet in the borrowing these stories became changed and the same episodes which elsewhere relate to human heroes now receive an astral setting. The preëxisting cultural pattern synthetizes the new element with its own preconceptions.

Another tendency that is highly characteristic of all cultures is the rationalistic explanation of what reason never gave rise to. This is shown very clearly in the justification of existing cultural features or of opinions acquired as a member of a particular society. Hegel's notion that whatever exists is rational and Pope's 'whatever is, is right' have their parallels in primitive legend and the literature of religious and political partisanship. In the special form of justification employed we find again the determining influence of the surrounding cultural atmosphere. Among the Plains Indians almost everything is explained as the result of supernatural revelation; if a warrior has escaped injury in battle it is because he wore a feather bestowed on him in a vision; if he acquires a large herd of horses it is in fulfilment of a spiritistic communication during the fast of adolescence. In a community where explanations of this type hold sway, we are not surprised to find that the origin of rites, too, is almost uniformly traced to a vision and that even the most trivial alteration in ceremonial garb is not claimed as an original invention but ascribed to supernatural promptings. Thus, the existing culture acts doubly as the determinant of the explanation offered for a particular cultural phenomenon. It evokes the search for its own *raison d'être;* and the type of interpretation called forth conforms to the explanatory pattern characteristic of the culture involved.

Culture thus appears as a closed system. We may not be able to explain all cultural phenomena or at least not beyond a certain point; but inasmuch as we *can* explain them at all, explanation must remain on the cultural plane.

What are the determinants of culture? We have found that cultural traits may be transmitted from without and in so far forth are determined by the culture of an alien people. The extraordinary extent to which such diffusion has taken place proves that the actual development of a given culture does not conform to innate laws necessarily leading to definite results, such hypothetical laws being overridden by contact with foreign peoples. But even where a culture is of relatively indigenous growth comparison with other cultures suggests that one step does not necessarily lead to another, that an invention like the wheel or the domestication of an animal occurs in one place and does not occur in another. To the extent of such diversity we must abandon the quest for general formulae of cultural evolution and recognize as the determinant of a phenomenon the unique course of its past history. However, there is not merely discontinuity and diversity but also stability and agreement in the sphere of culture. The discrete steps that mark culture history may not determine one another, but each may involve as a necessary or at least probable consequence other phenomena which in many instances are simply new aspects of the same phenomenon, and in so far forth one cultural element as isolated in description is the determinant or correlate of another. As for those phenomena which we are obliged to accept as realities without the possibility of further analysis, we can, at least, classify a great number of them and merge particular instances in a group of similar facts. Finally, there are dominant characteristics of culture, like cultural inertia or the secondary rationalization of habits acquired irrationally by the members of a group, which serve as broad interpretative principles in the history of civilization.

In short, as in other sciences, so in ethnology there are ultimate, irreducible facts, special functional relations, and principles of wider scope that guide us through the chaotic maze of detail. And as the engineer calls on the physicist for a knowledge of mechanical laws, so the social builder of the future who should seek to refashion the culture of his time and add to its cultural values will seek guidance from ethnology, the science of culture, which in Tylor's judgment is 'essentially a reformer's science.'

REFERENCES

Boas, F.
  1911   *The Mind of Primitive Man.* New York.

Czekanowski, Jan
  1911   "Objektive Kriterien in der Ethnologie," *Korrespondenzblatt der Deutschen Gesellschaft für Anthropologie, Ethnologie und Urgeschichte,* XLII, pp. 71–75.

Forrer, R.
  1908   *Urgeschichte des Europäers von der Menschwerdung zum Anbruch der Geschichte.* Stuttgart.

Hatt, Gudmund
  1916   "Moccasins and their Relation to Arctic Footwear," *Memoirs, American Anthropological Association,* Vol. 3, No. 3.

Laufer, B.
  1909   *Chinese Pottery of the Han Dynasty.* Leiden.

Montelius, O.
  1910   "Der Handel in der Vorzeit," *Praehistorische Zeitschrift,* II, pp. 249–291.

Obermaier, H.
    n.d.   *Der Mensch der Vorzeit.* Berlin.
Rivers, W. H. R.
    1914   *Kinship and Social Organization.* London.
Tylor, E. B.
    1889a   *Primitive Culture.* New York.
    1889b   "On a Method of Investigating the Development of Institutions; Applied to the Laws of Marriage and Descent," *Journal of the Anthropological Institute,* Vol. 18, pp. 245–272.
Wissler, C.
    1914   "Material Cultures of the North American Indians," *American Anthropologist* 16:477–505.
    1916   "Aboriginal Maize Culture as a Typical Culture-Complex," *American Journal of Sociology,* pp. 656–661.

Edward Sapir 1884–1939

BACKGROUND

Edward Sapir was born in Germany. His family emigrated to America when he was five years old. His father's first job was as a cantor in Richmond, Virginia, where Edward started school, but the family soon moved to New York and settled on the Lower East Side. Sapir was raised in the strict tradition of Orthodox Judaism. As a young man he discarded what he felt to be the restrictions of orthodoxy, but he retained much of its outlook throughout his life.

Although his family was very poor, he managed to continue his schooling; he won a scholarship to Horace Mann School and then a Pulitzer fellowship to Columbia.

After graduation in 1904, he did a year of graduate work in Germanics and Semitics at Columbia. His interest in language brought him in touch with Franz Boas, who fired his interest in unwritten languages—and extended it to the rest of anthropology. From that time on his principal work was in linguistic anthropology.

Having completed his M.A. in 1905, Sapir, with Boas' support, left for the lower Columbia River to study the Wishram. The next year he worked out a grammar of the Takelma language of Oregon. This grammar was presented as his doctoral dissertation in 1907 and published in 1912. His Wishram studies had been published in 1909.

Sapir spent the academic year 1907–1908 as Alfred Kroeber's research assistant at the new Department of Anthropology at the University of California at Berkeley. Since the university was unable to give him a permanent job, he went on to the University of Pennsylvania, where he stayed for two years, first as fellow and then as instructor. Although little of his work on the Paiute language of the Shoshonean family was published until 1930, the main body of it was done during this period in Philadelphia. This study verified the theory of the Uto-Aztecan family of languages.

Sapir soon established his versatility, his interests including psychiatry, psychology, sociology, ethnology, folklore, and religion. He read profusely and remembered monumentally—he could recall huge quantities of information whenever he needed to give an example or back up a theory.

In 1910 he married and went to Ottawa as chief of the newly established Division of Anthropology of the Geological Survey of Canada. This job provided him with fine opportunities for field work. In his first years there he produced a succession of descriptive ethnographies and summaries of large bodies of data with demonstrations of underlying principles, such as "The Social Organization of the West Coast Tribes" (1915) and "Time Perspective in Aboriginal American Culture: A Study in Method" (1916). An article written in reply to Kroeber's reformulation of Spencer's concept of the superorganic was called "Do We Need a Superorganic?" (1917), and was the first of many statements in which Sapir emphasized the importance of the individual in the study of culture. In 1921 he published his only book, *Language*.

However, Sapir felt isolated in Ottawa. His intellectual interests centered more and more on psychological problems of culture—an interest shared by none of his colleagues. His wife died after suffering a long illness, leaving him with three children. When he was asked to join the Department of Anthropology in Chicago in 1925, he accepted eagerly.

In Chicago, where the department had only recently been established by Fay-Cooper Cole, Sapir could train serious students in linguistic theory and practice and, for the first time, make use of his great talents as a lecturer. He was also popular outside the university and was in great demand as a lecturer. He led a busy life in Chicago: he remarried, maintained a heavy lecture schedule, and did such things as studying an African language through a young immigrant he found working in a bowling alley.

His interests in problems of personality and culture continued to grow. He incorporated ideas from such books as Jung's *Psychological Types* and Ogden's and Richards' *Meaning of Meaning* into a course that he gave at Columbia the summer before he went to Chicago, and that he realized more fully at the University of Chicago. At this time he also began to take a major interest in semantics, which involved him in intensive study of English language and communication.

To Sapir, sociological approaches were either self-evident or threatening to the autonomy of the self. He continually insisted on the importance of the person. He objected to conventional ethnographic statements as inadequate on the grounds that they were generalized formulations that said little about variation, conflict, denial, or emotion. The solution, he believed, lay in the use of the techniques of individual psychology, particularly psychotherapy. Anthropology, he insisted, was interested in the similarities among people.

Sapir's primary work, however, was always language. The articles he did on culture and personality were often responses to requests or offshoots of his linguistic studies. With Leonard Bloomfield, he was considered to be the founder of formal descriptive linguistics and the distributional method that characterized it. He also worked in historical and comparative linguistics, mostly with American Indian languages, particularly Navajo, Yana, Nootka, Tlingit, Sarcee, Kutche, Chinook, and Southern Paiute. He is also remembered for a series of intricate analyses of the earliest stages of Indo-European.

In 1931 Sapir accepted a Sterling Professorship at Yale and, with the help of a young man named George Peter Murdock, who had been temporarily housed in the sociology department, founded the Department of Anthropology there. He continued to occupy himself with psychological problems, setting up a year's seminar to study the impact of culture on personality, establishing a committee on personality and culture for the National Research Council, and writing articles on "Cultural Anthropology and Psychiatry" (1932) and "The Contribution of Psychiatry to an Understanding of Behavior" (1937).

Sapir did more with language than just study it. He was a poet, and for many years his poetry appeared regularly in *The New Republic, The Nation, Poetry,* and other magazines. He carried on an extensive correspondence with Ruth Benedict (who also wrote poetry and on whose anthropology he had a decisive influence) in which he showed sharp insight into a world that to others seemed far removed from the technical universe of linguistic analysis.

In 1937 Sapir suffered a series of heart attacks and, after a long illness, died early in 1939. His death cut short a number of projects, including the analysis of a large body of ethnographic data and extensive studies in Indo-European and Semitic languages.

INTRODUCTION

Edward Sapir, although very much an anthropologist of the Boasian mold, was also one of the founders of the science of linguistics. His contributions to linguistics, which are mostly technical, are of a permanent and basic nature. Like most of his contemporaries (except Kroeber, who had more psychological training than any of them), Sapir had an interest in the place of the individual in culture, and therefore in studies of culture and personality. His interest in the individual seems, however, to have been from a cognitive rather than an emotional approach to the human psyche.

Sapir came to anthropological linguistics from Germanic philology. His greatest gift to anthropology and to linguistics was his stress on the importance of culture and the analogy of language and culture. He lived when it was still necessary to argue that the type of language a people or an individual spoke has nothing to do with race, and that to call any language primitive is to misunderstand—that all languages are fully developed within their own cultural goals.

Sapir argued that there is no causal link between a language and a culture. He regarded a culture as what a social group does and thinks, and he regarded a language as a way of thinking. He also regarded language as the "symbolic guide to culture." This approach to language led, through the work of his student Benjamin Lee Whorf, to the development of the Sapir-Whorf hypothesis, which posits a very close relationship between cultural categories and language. Sapir, along with Boas, was one of the earlier students of linguistics to see the difference between the universal and particular aspects of language. His formulation of the universal aspects of language makes him one of the earliest in anthropological and linguistic theory to stress the deep structures of language that later became an important foundation of French structuralism.

9 THE STATUS OF LINGUISTICS AS A SCIENCE

Linguistics may be said to have begun its scientific career with the comparative study and reconstruction of the Indo-European languages. In the course of their detailed researches Indo-European linguists have gradually developed a technique which is probably more nearly perfect than that of any other science dealing with man's institutions. Many of the formulations of comparative Indo-European linguistics have a neatness and a regularity which recall the formulae, or the so-called laws, of natural science. Historical and comparative linguistics has been built up chiefly on the basis of the hypothesis that sound changes are regular and that most morphological readjustments in language follow as by-products in the wake of these regular phonetic developments. There are many who would be disposed to deny the psychological necessity of the regularity of sound change, but it remains true, as a matter of actual linguistic experience, that faith in such regularity has been the most successful approach to the historic problems of language. Why such regularities should be formed and why it is necessary to assume regularity of sound change are questions that the average linguist is perhaps unable to answer satisfactorily. But it does not follow that he can expect to improve his methods by discarding well tested hypotheses and throwing the field open to all manner of psychological and sociological explanations that do not immediately tie up with what we actually know about the historical behavior of language. A psychological and a sociological interpretation of the kind of regularity in linguistic change with which students of language have long been familiar are indeed desirable and even necessary. But neither psychology nor sociology is in a position to tell linguistics what kinds of historical formulations the linguist is to make. At best these disciplines can but urge the linguist to concern himself in a more vital manner than heretofore with the problem of seeing linguistic history in the larger framework of human behavior in the individual and in society.

The methods developed by the Indo-Europeanists have been applied with marked success to other groups of languages. It is abundantly clear that they apply just as rigorously to the unwritten primitive languages of Africa and America as to the better known forms of speech of the more sophisticated peoples. It is probably in the languages of these more cultured peoples that the fundamental regularity of linguistic processes has been most often crossed by the operation of such conflicting tendencies as borrowing from other languages, dialectic blending, and social differentiations of speech. The more we devote ourselves to the comparative study of the languages of a primitive linguistic stock, the more clearly we realize that phonetic law and analogical leveling are the only satisfactory key to the unraveling of the development of dialects and languages from a common base. Professor

Reprinted from *Language* 5, no. 4 (December 1929): 207–214, by permission of the Linguistic Society of America.

Leonard Bloomfield's experiences with Central Algonkian and my own with Athabaskan leave nothing to be desired in this respect and are a complete answer to those who find it difficult to accept the large scale regularity of the operation of all those unconscious linguistic forces which in their totality give us regular phonetic change and morphological readjustment on the basis of such change. It is not merely theoretically possible to predict the correctness of specific forms among unlettered peoples on the basis of such phonetic laws as have been worked out for them—such predictions are already on record in considerable number. There can be no doubt that the methods first developed in the field of Indo-European linguistics are destined to play a consistently important rôle in the study of all other groups of languages, and that it is through them and through their gradual extension that we can hope to arrive at significant historical inferences as to the remoter relations between groups of languages that show few superficial signs of a common origin.

It is the main purpose of this paper, however, not to insist on what linguistics has already accomplished, but rather to point out some of the connections between linguistics and other scientific disciplines, and above all to raise the question in what sense linguistics can be called a 'science'.

The value of linguistics for anthropology and culture history has long been recognized. As linguistic research has proceeded, language has proved useful as a tool in the sciences of man and has itself required and obtained a great deal of light from the rest of these sciences. It is difficult for a modern linguist to confine himself to his traditional subject matter. Unless he is somewhat unimaginative, he cannot but share in some or all of the mutual interests which tie up linguistics with anthropology and culture history, with sociology, with psychology, with philosophy, and, more remotely, with physics and physiology.

Language is becoming increasingly valuable as a guide to the scientific study of a given culture. In a sense, the network of cultural patterns of a civilization is indexed in the language which expresses that civilization. It is an illusion to think that we can understand the significant outlines of a culture through sheer observation and without the guide of the linguistic symbolism which makes these outlines significant and intelligible to society. Some day the attempt to master a primitive culture without the help of the language of its society will seem as amateurish as the labors of a historian who cannot handle the original documents of the civilization which he is describing.

Language is a guide to 'social reality'. Though language is not ordinarily thought of as of essential interest to the students of social science, it powerfully conditions all our thinking about social problems and processes. Human beings do not live in the objective world alone, nor alone in the world of social activity as ordinarily understood, but are very much at the mercy of the particular language which has become the medium of expression for their society. It is quite an illusion to imagine that one adjusts to reality essentially without the use of language and that language is merely an incidental means of solving specific problems of communication or reflection. The fact of the matter is that the 'real world' is to a large extent unconsciously built up on the language habits of the group. No two languages are ever sufficiently similar to be considered as representing the same social reality. The worlds in which different societies live are distinct worlds, not merely the same world with different labels attached.

The understanding of a simple poem, for instance, involves not merely an understanding of the single words in their average significance, but a full comprehension of the whole life of the community as it is mirrored in the words, or as it is suggested by their overtones. Even comparatively simple acts of perception are very much more at the mercy of the social patterns called words than we might suppose. If one draws some dozen lines, for instance, of different shapes, one perceives them as divisible into such categories as 'straight', 'crooked', 'curved', 'zigzag' because of the classificatory suggestiveness of the linguistic terms themselves. We see and hear and otherwise experience very largely as we do because the language habits of our community predispose certain choices of interpretation.

For the more fundamental problems of the student of human culture, therefore, a knowledge of linguistic mechanisms and historical developments is certain to become more and more important as our analysis of social behavior becomes more refined. From this standpoint we may think of language as the *symbolic guide to culture*. In another sense too linguistics is of great assistance in the study of cultural phenomena. Many cultural objects and ideas have been diffused in connection with their terminology, so that a study of the distribution of culturally significant terms often throws unexpected light on the history of inventions and ideas. This type of research, already fruitful in European and Asiatic culture history, is destined to be of great assistance in the reconstruction of primitive cultures.

The value of linguistics for sociology in the narrower sense of the word is just as real as for the anthropological theorist. Sociologists are necessarily interested in the technique of communication between human beings. From this standpoint language facilitation and language barriers are of the utmost importance and must be studied in their interplay with a host of other factors that make for ease or difficulty of transmission of ideas and patterns of behavior. Furthermore, the sociologist is necessarily interested in the symbolic significance, in a social sense, of the linguistic differences which appear in any large community. Correctness of speech or what might be called 'social style' in speech is of far more than aesthetic or grammatical interest. Peculiar modes of pronunciation, characteristic turns of phrase, slangy forms of speech, occupational terminologies of all sorts—these are so many symbols of the manifold ways in which society arranges itself and are of crucial importance for the understanding of the development of individual and social attitudes. Yet it will not be possible for a social student to evaluate such phenomena unless he has very clear notions of the linguistic background against which social symbolisms of a linguistic sort are to be estimated.

It is very encouraging that the psychologist has been concerning himself more and more with linguistic data. So far it is doubtful if he has been able to contribute very much to the understanding of language behavior beyond what the linguist has himself been able to formulate on the basis of his data. But the feeling is growing rapidly, and justly, that the psychological explanations of the linguists themselves need to be restated in more general terms, so that purely linguistic facts may be seen as specialized forms of symbolic behavior. The psychologists have perhaps too narrowly concerned themselves with the simple psychophysical bases of speech and have not penetrated very deeply into the study of its symbolic nature. This is probably due to the fact that psychologists in general are as yet too little aware of the fundamental importance of symbolism in behavior. It is not unlikely that it is precisely in the field of symbolism that linguistic forms and processes will contribute most to the enrichment of psychology.

All activities may be thought of as either definitely functional in the immediate sense, or as symbolic, or as a blend of the two. Thus, if I shove open a door in order to enter a house, the significance of the act lies precisely in its allowing me to make an easy entry. But if I 'knock at the door', a little reflection shows that the knock in itself does not open the door for me. It serves merely as a sign that somebody is to come to open it for me. To knock on the door is a substitute for the more primitive act of shoving it open of one's own accord. We have here the rudiments of what might be called language. A vast number of acts are language acts in this crude sense. That is, they are not of importance to us because of the work they immediately do, but because they serve as mediating signs of other more important acts. A primitive sign has some objective resemblance to what it takes the place of or points to. Thus, knocking at the door has a definite relation to intended activity upon the door itself. Some signs become abbreviated forms of functional activities which can be used for reference. Thus, shaking one's fist at a person is an abbreviated and relatively harmless way of actually punching him. If such a gesture becomes sufficiently expressive to society to constitute in some sort the equivalent of an abuse or a threat, it may be looked on as a symbol in the proper sense of the word.

Symbols of this sort are primary in that the resemblance of the symbol to what it stands for is still fairly evident. As time goes on, symbols become so completely changed in form as to lose all outward connection with what they stand for. Thus, there is no resemblance between a piece of bunting colored red, white, and blue, and the United States of America—itself a complex and not easily definable notion. The flag may therefore be looked upon as a secondary or referential symbol. The way to understand language psychologically, it seems, is to see it as the most complicated example of such a secondary or referential set of symbols that society has evolved. It may be that originally the primal cries or other types of symbols developed by man had some connection with certain emotions or attitudes or notions. But a connection is no longer directly traceable between words, or combinations of words, and what they refer to.

Linguistics is at once one of the most difficult and one of the most fundamental fields of inquiry. It is probable that a really fruitful integration of linguistic and psychological studies lies still in the future. We may suspect that linguistics is destined to have a very special value for configurative psychology ('Gestalt psychology'), for, of all forms of culture, it seems that language is that one which develops its fundamental patterns with relatively the most complete detachment from other types of cultural patterning. Linguistics may thus hope to become something of a guide to the understanding of the 'psychological geography' of culture in the large. In ordinary life the basic symbolisms of behavior are densely overlaid by cross-functional patterns of a bewildering variety. It is because every isolated act in human behavior is the meeting point of many distinct configurations that it is so difficult for most of us to arrive at the notion of contextual and non-contextual form in behavior. Linguistics would seem to have a very peculiar value for configurative studies because the patterning of language is to a very appreciable extent self-contained and not significantly at the mercy of intercrossing patterns of a non-linguistic type.

It is very notable that philosophy in recent years has concerned itself with problems of language as never before. The time is long past when grammatical forms and processes can be naïvely translated by philosophers into metaphysical entities. The philosopher needs to understand language if only to protect himself against his own language habits, and so it is not surprising that philosophy, in attempting to free logic from the trammels of grammar and to understand knowledge and the meaning of symbolism, is compelled to make a preliminary critique of the linguistic process itself. Linguists should be in an excellent position to assist in the process of making clear to ourselves the implications of our terms and linguistic procedures. Of all students of human behavior, the linguist should by the very nature of his subject matter be the most relativist in feeling, the least taken in by the forms of his own speech.

A word as to the relation between linguistics and the natural sciences. Students of linguistics have been greatly indebted for their technical equipment to the natural sciences, particularly physics and physiology. Phonetics, a necessary prerequisite for all exact work in linguistics, is impossible without some grounding in acoustics and the physiology of the speech organs. It is particularly those students of language who are more interested in the realistic details of actual speech behavior in the individual than in the socialized patterns of language who must have constant recourse to the natural sciences. But it is far from unlikely that the accumulated experience of linguistic research may provide more than one valuable hint for the setting up of problems of research to acoustics and physiology themselves.

All in all, it is clear that the interest in language has in recent years been transcending the strictly linguistic circles. This is inevitable, for an understanding of language mechanisms is necessary for the study of both historical problems and problems of human behavior. One can only hope that linguists will become increasingly aware of the significance of their subject in the general field of science and will not stand aloof behind a tradition that threatens to become scholastic when not vitalized by interests which lie beyond the formal interest in language itself.

Where, finally, does linguistics stand as a science? Does it belong to the natural sciences, with biology, or to the social sciences? There seem to be two facts which are responsible for the persistent tendency to view linguistic data from a biological point of view. In the first place, there is the obvious fact that the actual technique of language behavior involves very specific adjustments of a physiological sort. In the second place, the regularity and typicality of linguistic processes lead to a quasi-romantic feeling of contrast with the apparently free and undetermined behavior of human beings studied from the standpoint of culture. But the regularity of sound change is only superficially analogous to a biological automatism. It is precisely because language is as strictly socialized a type of human behavior as anything else in culture and yet betrays in its outlines and tendencies such regularities as only the natural scientist is in the habit of formulating, that linguistics is of strategic importance for the methodology of social science. Behind the apparent lawlessness of social phenomena there is a regularity of configuration and tendency which is just as real as the regularity of physical processes in a mechanical world, though it is a regularity of infinitely less apparent rigidity and of another mode of apprehension on our part. Language is primarily a cultural or social product and must be understood as such. Its regularity and formal development rest on considerations of a biological and psychological nature, to be sure. But this regularity and our underlying unconsciousness of its typical forms do not make of linguistics a mere adjunct to either biology or psychology. Better than any other social science, linguistics shows by its data and methods, necessarily more easily defined than the data and methods of any other type of discipline dealing with socialized behavior, the possibility of a truly scientific study of society which does not ape the methods nor attempt to adopt unrevised the concepts of the natural sciences. It is peculiarly important that linguists, who are often accused, and accused justly, of failure to look beyond the pretty patterns of their subject matter, should become aware of what their science may mean for the interpretation of human conduct in general. Whether they like it or not, they must become increasingly concerned with the many anthropological, sociological, and psychological problems which invade the field of language.

Benjamin Lee Whorf 1897–1941

BACKGROUND

Benjamin Lee Whorf was born into an old New England family whose ancestors had settled in Provincetown soon after the landing of the Pilgrims. His father, Harry Church Whorf, was a commercial artist (whose work included the design for the Old Dutch Cleanser can) and a man of many interests —photography, stage designing, and play writing and directing.

Benjamin and his two younger brothers (both of whom became famous—John, an artist noted for his watercolors, and Richard, an actor and director for stage and screen) grew up in an atmosphere of drama, books, drawings, manuscripts, chemicals, and photography equipment. Indeed, many of the interests that led him into linguistics developed when Whorf was a boy. He read and reread Prescott's *Conquest of Mexico*; his father did stage designs for a play Benjamin had written about a Mayan princess—his research took him into Mayan archaeology. Botany and astrology, ciphers and codes were also big interests. He was especially intrigued by chemicals and photography, and in 1914 he went to the Massachusetts Institute of Technology to study chemical engineering.

After his graduation from MIT he became a trainee in fire prevention engineering and in 1919 joined the Hartford Insurance Company, where he was valued for his ability to attract business as well as his technical skill. He was appointed a special agent in 1928 and elected assistant secretary of the company in 1940. He remained a full-time employee of this company for the rest of his life, although at times his scholarly output was equal to that of many full-time research professors. He refused many offers of academic posts, saying that his business situation offered him a more comfortable living and a freer opportunity to develop his intellectual interests in his own way.

After settling in Hartford, he wrote a "book of religious philosophy in the form of a novel." It was rejected by every publisher who saw it. At the same time he finished a shorter manuscript, "Why I Have Rejected Evolution"; his conclusions were that the key to the contradictions of Biblical and scientific cosmologies lay in the linguistic interpretation of the Old Testament. In 1924 he began to study Hebrew. A major influence was the work of a French dramatist, philologist, and mystic of the early nineteenth century, Antoine Fabre d'Olivet, especially *La langue hebraïque restituée* (1815–1816), which tried to show the hidden meaning of the Bible through an analysis of the structure of the triliteral Hebrew root.

So stimulated, Whorf read more widely on the subject of linguistics. In the process he made use of the collections of the Watkinson Library, whose collection of American Indian ethnology, folklore, and language reawakened his old interests in Mexican antiquities. In 1926 he began seriously studying Aztec; in 1928, Mayan.

Whorf began an extensive correspondence with A. M. Tozzer of Harvard, who encouraged him to translate a page of old Mexican manuscript, a copy of which was in the Peabody Museum. This resulted in the paper that he read before the Twenty-third International Congress of Americanists in 1928 and that later was published as "An Aztec Account of the Period of the Toltec Decline."

By the end of 1928 his work on the familial relations between Tepecano, Piman, and Aztec had progressed to the point that he sought a research fellowship from the Social Science Research Council to enable him to do more intensive work. In the next few years, he visited Mexico City and published a major series of works concerning Mayan hieroglyphs.

In 1931 Whorf enrolled in Edward Sapir's course in American Indian linguistics at Yale—his first formal training in linguistics. His time at Yale brought him into contact with a small band of first-rate students—Morris Swadesh, George Trager, Carl Voeglin, Mary Haas, and William Dyk—and tempered his enthusiasm for bizarre linguistic theories. In 1937–1938 he was a lecturer in anthropology at Yale.

Sapir was influential in encouraging Whorf to take up the study of Hopi, distantly related to Aztec. Utilizing research methods learned from Sapir, he worked mostly with a Hopi informant living in New York. By 1935 he had prepared a tentative grammar and dictionary, but except for a brief sketch of Hopi grammar in Harry Hoijer's *Linguistic Structure of Native America* and two technical articles, these studies were never published.

Whorf's major importance to anthropology is his work on the relationship between language and thought. "An American Indian Model of the Universe" (probably written in 1936 but not published until 1950) explored the implications of the Hopi verb system with regard to the Hopi conception of space and time. Also at this time he published his best known article, "The Relation of Habitual Thought and Behavior to Language" (1939).

During this time he was coping constantly with a long and lingering illness, to which he finally succumbed on July 26, 1941, at the age of forty-four.

INTRODUCTION

Whorf had a deep impact on both linguistics and cultural anthropology through a very simple set of ideas: meaning is essential, he claimed, to the study of linguistics, and the categories of meaning change from one cultural tradition to another.

Whorf's views are put in a way that is unstylish today because he claimed that language reflects and constrains "thought." But we can at least agree that the language one learns necessarily constrains and structures what it is that one says. Presumably one also "thinks" in terms of one's language. For this reason, the categories of "thought" are the categories of a particular culture. Whorf's examples are vivid—the time dimensions of the Hopi language are, he claimed, different from those of English. Therefore Hopi culture and American culture are at odds on at least one important dimension of perception.

Whorf's thesis has been called "linguistic relativism," a very unfortunate phrase that contains all the unsavory aspects of cultural relativism without its simple truths, at the same time that it allows some people to interpret Whorf as a linguistic determininst, which surely is to misread him.

Whorf's underlying problem was that of finding the hidden aspects of linguistic categories. One of his favorite examples (although we cannot find that he published it) was to point out the two plurals in English for different kinds of fish—the s-plural and the zero-plural. The difference between the two is to be found only in cultural custom. If we eat it, it takes a zero-plural (tuna, herring, perch); if we do not, it takes an s-plural (sharks, suckers, etc.). There are exceptions (eel—we are insecure both about its plural and its edibility), but the rule seems to hold in most cases. Whorf's claim is that there may be dozens of such "grammatical rules" that are thus bound up with culture.

Certainly, in America of the 1970s we are struggling with the fact that English does not have a third-person singular pronoun, either nominative or objective, that does not code for sex; and with the fact that English does not have a common noun for many species (dog, cow, man) that does not code for sex. Whorf would have been in the middle of the search for words for the chairperson or the shaperson.

Two things have happened to Whorf. On the one hand, he was "operationalized," scientized, and his work called "ethnoscience." On the other, he was misunderstood and turned into a determinist. However, it should be remembered that Whorf was a naïve but trained, unshackled but disciplined man with an enviable "cultural imagination." Whorf is, in our opinion, to be read for his ideas about culture, not just linguistics, and for his evocativeness as much as for his results. And seldom has anyone written such deliciously exciting anthropology.

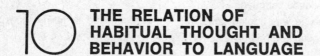 # THE RELATION OF HABITUAL THOUGHT AND BEHAVIOR TO LANGUAGE

There will probably be general assent to the proposition that an accepted pattern of using words is often prior to certain lines of thinking and forms of behavior, but he who assents often sees in such a statement nothing more than a platitudinous recognition of the hypnotic power of philosophical and learned terminology on the one hand or of catchwords, slogans, and rallying-cries on the other. To see only thus far is to miss the point of one of the important interconnections which Sapir saw between language,

Reprinted from Leslie Spier, ed., *Language, Culture and Personality: Essays in Memory of Edward Sapir* (Menasha, Wisc.: Sapir Memorial Publication Fund, 1941), pp. 75–93, by permission of the publisher.

culture, and psychology, and succinctly expressed in the introductory quotation. It is not so much in these special uses of language as in its constant ways of arranging data and its most ordinary every-day analysis of phenomena that we need to recognize the influence it has on other activities, cultural and personal.

THE NAME OF THE SITUATION AS AFFECTING BEHAVIOR

I came in touch with an aspect of this problem before I had studied under Dr. Sapir, and in a field usually considered remote from linguistics. It was in the course of my professional work for a fire insurance company, in which I undertook the task of analyzing many hundreds of reports of circumstances surrounding the start of fires, and in some cases, of explosions. My analysis was directed toward purely physical conditions, such as defective wiring, presence or lack of air spaces between metal flues and woodwork, etc., and the results were presented in these terms. Indeed it was undertaken with no thought that any other significances would or could be revealed. But in due course it became evident that not only a physical situation *qua* physics, but the meaning of that situation to people, was sometimes a factor, through the behavior of the people, in the start of the fire. And this factor of meaning was clearest when it was a *linguistic meaning,* residing in the name or the linguistic description commonly applied to the situation. Thus around a storage of what are called "gasoline drums" behavior will tend to a certain type, that is, great care will be exercised; while around a storage of what are called "empty gasoline drums" it will tend to be different—careless, with little repression of smoking or of tossing cigarette stubs about. Yet the "empty" drums are perhaps the more dangerous, since they contain explosive vapor. Physically the situation is hazardous, but the linguistic analysis according to regular analogy must employ the word "empty," which inevitably suggests lack of hazard. The word "empty" is used in two linguistic patterns: (1) as a virtual synonym for "null and void, negative, inert," (2) applied in analysis of physical situations without regard to, e.g., vapor, liquid vestiges, or stray rubbish, in the container. The situation is named in one pattern (2) and the name is then "acted out" or "lived up to" in another (1); this being a general formula for the linguistic conditioning of behavior into hazardous forms.

In a wood distillation plant the metal stills were insulated with a composition prepared from limestone and called at the plant "spun limestone." No attempt was made to protect this covering from excessive heat or the contact of flame. After a period of use the fire below one of the stills spread to the "limestone," which to everyone's great surprise burned vigorously. Exposure to acetic acid fumes from the stills had converted part of the limestone (calcium carbonate) to calcium acetate. This when heated in a fire decomposes, forming inflammable acetone. Behavior that tolerated fire close to the covering was induced by use of the name "limestone," which because it ends in "stone" implies noncombustibility.

A huge iron kettle of boiling varnish was observed to be overheated, nearing the temperature at which it would ignite. The operator moved it off the fire and ran it on its wheels to a distance, but did not cover it. In a minute or so the varnish ignited. Here the linguistic influence is more complex; it is due to the metaphorical objectifying (of which more later) of "cause" as contact or the spatial juxtaposition of "things"—to analyzing the situation as "on" versus "off" the fire. In reality the stage when the external fire was the main factor had passed; the overheating was now an internal process of convection in the varnish from the intensely heated kettle, and still continued when "off" the fire.

An electric glow heater on the wall was little used, and for one workman had the meaning of a convenient coat-hanger. At night a watchman entered and snapped a switch, which action he verbalized as "turning on the light." No light appeared, and this result he verbalized as "light is burned out." He could not see the glow of the heater because of the old coat hung on it. Soon the heater ignited the coat, which set fire to the building.

A tannery discharged waste water containing animal matter into an outdoor settling basin partly roofed with wood and partly open. This situation is one that ordinarily would be verbalized as "pool of water." A workman had occasion to light a blow-torch nearby, and threw his match into the water. But the decomposing waste matter was evoking gas under the wood cover, so that the setup was the reverse of "watery." An instant flare of flame ignited the woodwork, and the fire quickly spread into the adjoining building.

A drying room for hides was arranged with a blower at one end to make a current of air along the room and thence outdoors through a vent at the other end. Fire started at a hot bearing on the blower, which blew the flames directly into the hides and fanned them along the room, destroying the entire stock. This hazardous setup followed naturally from the term "blower" with its linguistic equivalence to "that which blows," implying that its function necessarily is to "blow." Also its function is verbalized as "blowing air for drying," overlooking that it can blow other things, e.g., flames and sparks. In reality a blower simply makes a current of air and can exhaust as well as blow. It should have been installed at the vent end to *draw* the air over the hides, then through the hazard (its own casing and bearings) and thence outdoors.

Beside a coal-fired melting pot for lead reclaiming was dumped a pile of "scrap lead"—a misleading verbalization, for it consisted of the lead sheets of old radio condensers, which still had paraffin paper between them. Soon the paraffin blazed up and fired the roof, half of which was burned off.

Such examples, which could be greatly multiplied, will suffice to show how the cue to a certain line of behavior is often given by the analogies of the linguistic formula in which the situation is spoken of, and by which to some degree it is analyzed, classified, and allotted its place in that world which is "to a large extent unconsciously built up on the language habits of the group." And we always assume that the linguistic analysis made by our group reflects reality better than it does.

GRAMMATICAL PATTERNS AS INTERPRETATIONS OF EXPERIENCE

The linguistic material in the above examples is limited to single words, phrases, and patterns of limited range. One cannot study the behavioral compulsiveness of such material without suspecting a much more far-reaching compulsion from large-scale patterning of grammatical categories, such as plurality, gender and similar classifications (animate, inanimate, etc.), tenses, voices, and other verb forms, classifications of the type of "parts of speech," and the matter of whether a given experience is denoted by a unit morpheme, an inflected word, or a syntactical combination. A category such as number (singular vs. plural) is an attempted interpretation of a whole large order of experience, virtually of the world or of nature; it attempts to say how experience is to be segmented, what experience is to be called "one" and what "several." But the difficulty of appraising such a far-reaching influence is great because of its background character, because of the difficulty of standing aside from our own language, which is a habit and a cultural *non est disputandum,* and scrutinizing it objectively. And if we take a very dissimilar language, this language becomes a part of nature, and we even do to it what we have already done to nature. We tend to think in our own language in order to examine the exotic language. Or we find the task of unraveling the purely morphological intricacies so gigantic that it seems to absorb all else. Yet the problem, though difficult, is feasible; and the best approach is through an exotic language, for in its study we are at long last pushed willy-nilly out of our ruts. Then we find that the exotic language is a mirror held up to our own.

In my study of the Hopi language, what I now see as an opportunity to work on this problem was first thrust upon me before I was clearly aware of the problem. The seemingly endless task of describing the morphology did finally end. Yet it was evident, especially in the light of Sapir's lectures on Navaho, that the description of the *language* was far from complete. I knew for example the morphological formation of plurals, but not how to use plurals. It was evident that the category of plural in Hopi was not the same thing as in English, French, or German. Certain things that were plural in these languages were singular in Hopi. The phase of investigation which now began consumed nearly two more years.

The work began to assume the character of a comparison between Hopi and western European languages. It also became evident that even the grammar of Hopi bore a relation to Hopi culture, and the grammar of European tongues to our own "Western" or "European" culture. And it appeared that the interrelation brought in those large subsummations of experience by language, such as our own terms "time," "space," "substance," and "matter." Since with respect to the traits compared there is little difference between English, French, German, or other European languages with the *possible* (but doubtful) exception of Balto-Slavic and non-Indo-European, I have lumped these languages into one group called SAE, or "Standard Average European."

That portion of the whole investigation here to be reported may be summed up in two questions: (1) Are our own concepts of "time," "space," and "matter" given in substantially the same form by experience to all men, or are they in part conditioned by the structure of particular languages? (2) Are there traceable affinities between (a) cultural and behavioral norms and (b) large-scale linguistic patterns? (I should be the last to pretend that there is anything so definite as "a correlation" between culture and language, and especially between ethnological rubrics such as "agricultural," "hunting," etc., and linguistic ones like "inflected," "synthetic," or "isolating.")[1] When I began the study the problem was by no means so clearly formulated and I had little notion that the answers would turn out as they did.

PLURALITY AND NUMERATION IN SAE AND HOPI

In our language, that is SAE, plurality and cardinal numbers are applied in two ways: to real plurals and imaginary plurals. Or more exactly if less tersely: perceptible spatial aggregates and metaphorical aggregates. We say "ten men" and also "ten days." Ten men either are or could be objectively perceived as ten, ten in one group-perception[2]—ten men on a street corner, for instance. But "ten days" cannot be objectively experienced. We experience only one day, to-day; the other nine (or even all ten) are something conjured up from memory or imagination. If "ten days" be regarded as a group it must be as an "imaginary," mentally constructed group. Whence comes this mental pattern? Just as in the case of the fire-causing errors, from the fact that our language confuses the two different situations, has but one pattern for both. When we speak of ten steps forward, ten strokes on a bell, or any similarly described cyclic sequence, "times" of any sort, we are doing the same thing as with "days." *Cyclicity* brings the response of imaginary plurals. But a likeness of cyclicity to aggregates is not unmistakably given by experience prior to language, or it would be found in all languages, and it is not.

Our *awareness* of time and cyclicity does contain something immediate and subjective—the basic sense of "becoming later and later." But in the habitual thought of us SAE people this is covered under something quite different, which though mental should not be called subjective. I call it *objectified*, or imaginary, because it is patterned on the *outer* world. It is this that reflects our linguistic usage. Our tongue makes no distinction between numbers counted on discrete entities and numbers that are simply counting itself. Habitual thought then assumes that in the latter case the numbers are just as much counted on *something* as in the former. This is objectification. Concepts of time lose contact with the subjective experience of "becoming later" and are objectified as counted *quantities*, especially as lengths, made up of units as a length can be visibly marked off into inches. A "length of time" is envisioned as a row of similar units, like a row of bottles.

In Hopi there is a different linguistic situation. Plurals and cardinals are used only for entities that form or can form an objective group. There are no imaginary plurals, but instead ordinals used with singulars. Such an expression as "ten days" is not used. The equivalent statement is an operational one that reaches one day by a suitable count. "They stayed ten days" becomes "they stayed until the eleventh day" or "they left after the tenth day." "Ten days is greater than nine days" becomes "the tenth day is later than the ninth." Our "length of time" is not regarded as a length but as a relation between two events in lateness. Instead of our linguistically promoted objectification of that datum of consciousness we call "time," the Hopi language has not laid down any pattern that would cloak the subjective "becoming later" that is the essence of time.

NOUNS OF PHYSICAL QUANTITY IN SAE AND HOPI

We have two kinds of noun denoting physical things: individual nouns, and mass nouns; e.g., water, milk, wood, granite, sand, flour, meat. Individual nouns denote bodies with definite outlines: a tree, a stick, a man, a hill. Mass nouns denote homogeneous continua without implied boundaries. The distinction is marked by linguistic form; e.g., mass nouns lack plurals,[3] in English drop articles, and in French take the partitive article *du; de la, des.* The distinction is more widespread in language than in the observable appearance of things. Rather few natural occurrences present themselves as unbounded extents; air of course, and often water, rain, snow, sand, rock, dirt, grass. We do not encounter butter, meat, cloth, iron, glass, or most "materials" in such kind of manifestation, but in bodies small or large with definite outlines. The distinction is somewhat forced upon our description of events by an unavoidable pattern in language. It is so inconvenient in a great many cases that we need some way of individualizing the mass noun by further linguistic devices. This is partly done by names of body-types: stick of wood, piece of cloth, pane of glass, cake of soap; also, and even more, by introducing names of containers though their contents be the real issue: glass of water, cup of coffee, dish of food, bag of flour, bottle of beer. These very common container-formulas, in which "of" has an obvious, visually perceptible meaning ("contents"), influence our feeling about the less obvious type-body formulas: stick of wood, lump of dough, etc. The formulas are very similar: individual noun plus a similar relator (English "of"). In the obvious case this relator denotes contents. In the inobvious one it *suggests* contents. Hence the lumps, chunks, blocks, pieces, etc., seem to contain something, a "stuff," "substance," or "matter" that answers to the water, coffee, or flour in the container formulas. So with SAE people the philosophic "substance" and "matter" are also the naive idea; they are instantly acceptable, "common sense." It is so through linguistic habit. Our language patterns often require us to name a physical thing by a binomial that splits the reference into a formless item plus a form.

Hopi is again different. It has a formally distinguished class of nouns. But this class contains no formal sub-class of mass nouns. All nouns have an individual sense and both singular and plural forms. Nouns translating most nearly our mass nouns still refer to vague bodies or vaguely bounded extents. They imply indefiniteness, but not lack, of outline and size. In specific statements "water" means one certain mass or quantity of water, not what we call "the substance water." Generality of statement is conveyed through the verb or predicator, not the noun. Since nouns are individual already they are not individualized either by type-bodies or names of containers, if there is no special need to emphasize shape or container. The noun itself implies a suitable type-body or container. One says, not "a glass of water" but kǝ·yi "a water," not "a pool of water" but pa·hǝ,[4] not "a dish of corn-flour" but ŋǝmni "a (quantity of) corn-flour," not "a piece of meat" but sikʷi "a meat." The language has neither need for nor analogies on which to build the concept of existence as a duality of formless item and form. It deals with formlessness through other symbols than nouns.

PHASES OF CYCLES IN SAE AND HOPI

Such terms as summer, winter, September, morning, noon, sunset, are with us nouns, and have little formal linguistic difference from other nouns. They can be subjects or objects, and we say "at" sunset or "in" winter just as we say at a corner or in an orchard.[5] They are pluralized and numerated like nouns of physical objects, as we have seen. Our thought about the referents of such words hence becomes objectified. Without objectification it would be a subjective experience of real time, i.e., of the consciousness of "becoming later and later"—simply a cyclic phase similar to an earlier phase in that ever-later-becoming duration. Only by imagination can such a cyclic phase be set beside another and another in the manner of a spatial (i.e., visually perceived) configuration. But such is the power of linguistic analogy that we do so objectify cyclic phasing. We do it even by saying "a phase" and "phases" instead of, e.g., "phasing." And the pattern of individual and mass nouns, with the resulting binomial formula of formless item plus form, is so general that it is implicit for all nouns, and hence our very generalized formless items like "substance," "matter," by which we can fill out the binomial for an enormously wide range of nouns. But even these are not quite generalized enough to take in our phase nouns. So for the phase nouns we have made a formless item, "time." We have made it by using "a time," i.e., an occasion or a phase, in the pattern of a mass noun, just as from "a summer" we make "summer" in the pattern of a mass noun. Thus with our binomial formula we can say and think "a moment of time," "a second of time," "a year of time." Let me again point out that the pattern is simply that of "a bottle of milk" or "a piece of cheese." Thus we are assisted to imagine that "a summer" actually contains or consists of such-and-such a quantity of "time."

In Hopi, however, all phase terms, like summer, morning, etc., are not nouns but a kind of adverb, to use the nearest SAE analogy. They are a formal part of speech by themselves, distinct from nouns, verbs, and even other Hopi "adverbs." Such a word is not a case form or a locative pattern, like "des Abends" or "in the morning." It contains no morpheme like one of "in the house" or "at the tree."[6] It means "when it is morning" or "while morning-phase is occurring." These "temporals" are not used as subjects or objects, or at all like nouns. One does not say "it's a hot summer" or "summer is hot"; summer is not hot, summer is only *when* conditions are hot, *when* heat occurs. One does not say "*this* summer," but "summer now" or "summer recently." There is no objectification, as a region, an extent, a quantity, of the subjective duration-feeling. Nothing is suggested about time except the perpetual "getting later" of it. And so there is no basis here for a formless item answering to our "time."

TEMPORAL FORMS OF VERBS IN SAE AND HOPI

The three-tense system of SAE verbs colors all our thinking about time. This system is amalgamated with that larger scheme of objectification of the subjective experience of duration already noted in other patterns—in the binomial formula applicable to nouns in general, in temporal nouns, in plurality and numeration. This objectification enables us in imagination to "stand time units in a row." Imagination of time as like a row harmonizes with a system of *three* tenses; whereas a system of *two,* an earlier and a later, would seem to correspond better to the feeling of duration as it is experienced. For if we inspect consciousness we find no past, present, future, but a unity embracing complexity. *Everything* is in consciousness, and everything in consciousness *is,* and is together. There is in it a sensuous and a non-sensuous. We may call the sensuous—what we are seeing, hearing, touching—the "present" while in the non-sensuous the vast image-world of memory is being labelled "the past" and another realm of belief, intuition, and uncertainty "the future"; yet sensation, memory, foresight, all are in consciousness together—one is not "yet to be" nor another "once but no more." Where real time comes in is that all this in consciousness is "getting later," changing certain relations in an irreversible manner. In this "latering" or "durating" there seems to me to be a paramount contrast between the newest, latest instant at the focus of attention and the rest—the earlier. Languages by the score get along well with two tense-like forms answering to this paramount relation of later to earlier. We can of course *construct and contemplate in thought* a system of past, present, future, in the objectified configuration of points on a line. This is what our general objectification tendency leads us to do and our tense system confirms.

In English the present tense seems the one least in harmony with the paramount temporal relation. It is as if pressed into various and not wholly congruous duties. One duty is to stand as objectified middle term between objectified past and objectified future, in narration, discussion, argument, logic, philosophy. Another is to denote inclusion in the sensuous field: "I *see* him." Another is for nomic, i.e., customarily or generally valid, statements: "We *see* with our eyes." These varied uses introduce confusions of thought, of which for the most part we are unaware.

Hopi, as we might expect, is different here too. Verbs have no "tenses" like ours, but have validity-forms ("assertions"), aspects, and clause-linkage forms (modes), that yield even greater precision of speech. The validity-forms denote that the speaker (not the subject) reports the situation (answering to our past and present) or that he expects it (answering to our future)[7] or that he makes a nomic statement (answering to our nomic present). The aspects denote different degrees of duration and different kinds of tendency "during duration." As yet we have noted nothing to indicate whether an event is sooner or later than another when both are *reported.* But need for this does not arise until we have two verbs, i.e., two clauses. In that case the "modes" denote relations between the clauses, including relations of later to earlier and of simultaneity. Then there are many detached words that express similar relations, supplementing the modes and aspects. The duties of our three-tense system and its tripartite linear objectified "time" are distributed among various verb categories, all different from our tenses; and there is no more basis for an objectified time in Hopi verbs than in other Hopi patterns; although this does not in the least hinder the verb forms and other patterns from being closely adjusted to the pertinent realities of actual situations.

DURATION, INTENSITY, AND TENDENCY IN SAE AND HOPI

To fit discourse to manifold actual situations all languages need to express durations, intensities, and tendencies. It is characteristic of SAE and perhaps of many other language-types to express them metaphorically. The metaphors are those of spatial extension, i.e., of size, number (plurality), position, shape, and motion. We express duration by long, short, great, much, quick, slow, etc.; intensity by large, great, much, heavy, light, high, low, sharp, faint, etc.; tendency by more, increase, grow, turn, get, approach, go, come, rise, fall, stop, smooth, even, rapid, slow, and so on through an almost inexhaustible list of metaphors that we hardly recognize as such since they are virtually the only linguistic media available. The non-metaphorical terms in this field, like early, late, soon, lasting, intense, very, tending, are a mere handful, quite inadequate to the needs.

It is clear how this condition "fits in." It is part of our whole scheme of *objectifying*—imaginatively spatializing qualities and potentials that are quite non-spatial (so far as any spatially-perceptive senses can tell us). Noun-meaning (with us) proceeds from physical bodies to referents of far other sort. Since physical bodies and their outlines in *perceived space* are denoted by size and shape terms and reckoned by cardinal numbers and plurals, these patterns of denotation and reckoning extend to the symbols of non-spatial meanings, and to suggest an *imaginary space*. Physical shapes move, stop, rise, sink, approach, etc., in perceived space; why not these other referents in their imaginary space? This has gone so far that we can hardly refer to the simplest non-spatial situation without constant resort to physical metaphors. I "grasp" the "thread" of another's arguments, but if its "level" is "over my head" my attention may "wander" and "lose touch" with the "drift" of it, so that when he "comes" to his "point" we differ "widely," our "views" being indeed so "far apart" that the "things" he says "appear" "much" too arbitrary, or even "a lot" of nonsense!

The absence of such metaphor from Hopi speech is striking. Use of space terms when there is no space involved is *not there*—as if on it had been laid the taboo teetotal! The reason is clear when we know that Hopi has abundant conjugational and lexical means of expressing duration, intensity, and tendency directly as such, and that major grammatical patterns do not, as with us, provide analogies for an imaginary space. The many verb "aspects" express duration and tendency of manifestations, while some of the "voices" express intensity, tendency, and duration of causes or forces producing manifestations. Then a special part of speech, the "tensors," a huge class of words, denotes only intensity, tendency, duration, and sequence. The function of the tensors is to express intensities, "strengths," and how they continue or vary, their rate-of-change; so that the broad concept of intensity, when considered as necessarily always varying and/or continuing, includes also tendency and duration. Tensors convey distinctions of degree, rate, constancy, repetition, increase and decrease of intensity, immediate sequence, interruption or sequence after an interval, etc., also *qualities* of strengths, such as we should express metaphorically as smooth, even, hard, rough. A striking feature is their lack of resemblance to the terms of real space and movement that to us "mean the same." There is not even more than a trace of apparent derivation from space terms.[8] So while Hopi in its nouns seems highly concrete, here in the tensors it becomes abstract almost beyond our power to follow.

HABITUAL THOUGHT IN SAE AND HOPI

The comparison now to be made between the habitual thought worlds of SAE and Hopi speakers is of course incomplete. It is possible only to touch upon certain dominant contrasts that appear to stem from the linguistic differences already noted. By "habitual thought" and "thought world" I mean more than simply language, i.e., than the linguistic patterns themselves. I include all the analogical and suggestive value of the patterns (e.g., our "imaginary space" and its distant implications), and all the give-and-take between language and the culture as a whole, wherein is a vast amount that is not linguistic yet shows the shaping influence of language. In brief, this "thought world" is the microcosm that each man carries about within himself, by which he measures and understands what he can of the macrocosm.

The SAE microcosm has analyzed reality largely in terms of what it calls "things" (bodies and quasi-bodies) plus modes of extensional but formless existence that it calls "substances" or "matter." It tends to see existence through a binomial formula that expresses any existent as a spatial form plus a spatial formless continuum related to the form as contents is related to the outlines of its container. Non-spatial existents are imaginatively spatialized and charged with similar implications of form and continuum.

The Hopi microcosm seems to have analyzed reality largely in terms of *events* (or better "eventing"), referred to in two ways, objective and subjective.

Objectively, and only if perceptible physical experience, events are expressed mainly as outlines, colors, movements, and other perceptive reports. Subjectively, for both the physical and non-physical, events are considered the expression of invisible intensity-factors, on which depend their stability and persistence, or their fugitiveness and proclivities. It implies that existents do not "become later and later" all in the same way; but some do so by growing, like plants, some by diffusing and vanishing, some by a procession of metamorphoses, some by enduring in one shape till affected by violent forces. In the nature of each existent able to manifest as a definite whole is the power of its own mode of duration; its growth, decline, stability, cyclicity, or creativeness. Everything is thus already "prepared" for the way it now manifests by earlier phases, and what it will be later, partly has been, and partly is in act of being so "prepared." An emphasis and importance rest on this preparing or being prepared aspect of the world that may to the Hopi correspond to that "quality of reality" that "matter" or "stuff" has for us.

HABITUAL BEHAVIOR FEATURES OF HOPI CULTURE

Our behavior, and that of Hopi, can be seen to be coordinated in many ways to the linguistically-conditioned microcosm. As in my fire case-book, people act about situations in ways which are like the ways they talk about them. A characteristic of Hopi behavior is the emphasis on preparation. This includes announcing and getting ready for events well beforehand, elaborate precautions to insure persistence of desired conditions, and stress on good will as the preparer of right results. Consider the analogies of the day-counting pattern alone. Time is mainly reckoned "by day" (taLk, -tala) or "by night" (tok), which words are not nouns but tensors, the first formed on a root "light, day," the second on a root "sleep." The count is by *ordinals*. This is not the pattern of counting a number of different men or things, even though they appear successively, for even then they *could* gather into an assemblage. It is the pattern of counting successive reappearances of the *same* man or thing, incapable of forming an assemblage. The analogy is not to behave about day-cyclicity as to several men ("several days"), which is what *we* tend to do, but to behave as to the successive visits of the *same man*. One does not alter several men by working upon just one, but one can prepare and so alter the later visits of the same man by working to affect the visit he is making now. This is the way the Hopi deal with the future—by working within a present situation which is expected to carry impresses, both obvious and occult, forward into the future event of interest. One might say that Hopi society understands our proverb "Well begun is half done," but not "To-morrow is another day." This may explain much in Hopi character.

This Hopi preparing behavior may be roughly divided into announcing, outer preparing, inner preparing, covert participation, and persistence. Announcing, or preparative publicity, is an important function in the hands of a special official, the Crier Chief. Outer preparing is preparation involving much visible activity, not all necessarily directly useful within our understanding. It includes ordinary practising, rehearsing, getting ready, introductory formalities, preparing of special food, etc. (all of these to a degree that may seem over-elaborate to us), intensive sustained muscular activity like running, racing, dancing, which is thought to increase the intensity of development of events (such as growth of crops), mimetic and other magic, preparations based on esoteric theory involving perhaps occult instruments like prayer sticks, prayer feathers, and prayer meal, and finally the great cyclic ceremonies and dances, which have the significance of preparing rain and crops. From one of the verbs meaning "prepare" is derived the noun for "harvest" or "crop": na'twani "the prepared" or the "in preparation."[9]

Inner preparing is use of prayer and meditation, and at lesser intensity good wishes and good will, to further desired results. Hopi attitudes stress the power of desire and thought. With their "microcosm" it is utterly natural that they should. Desire and thought are the earliest, and therefore the most important, most critical and crucial, stage of preparing. Moreover, to the Hopi, one's desires and thoughts influence not only his own actions, but all nature. This too is wholly natural. Consciousness itself is aware of work, of the feel of effort and energy, in desire and thinking. Experience more basic than language tells us that if energy is expended effects are produced. *We* tend to believe that our bodies can stop up this energy, prevent it from affecting other things until we will our *bodies* to overt action. But this may be only because we have our own linguistic basis for a theory that formless items like "matter" are things in themselves, malleable only by similar things, by more matter, and hence insulated from the powers of life and thought. It is no more unnatural to think that thought contacts everything and pervades the universe than to think, as we all do, that light kindled outdoors does this. And it is not unnatural to suppose that thought, like any other force, leaves everywhere traces of effect. Now when *we* think of a certain actual rose-bush, we do not suppose that our thought goes to that actual bush, and engages with it, like a searchlight turned upon it. What then do we suppose our consciousness is dealing with when we are thinking of that rose-bush? Probably we think it is dealing with a "mental image" which is not the rose-bush but a mental surrogate of it. But why should it be *natural* to think that our thought deals with a surrogate and not with the real rose-bush? Quite possibly because we are dimly aware that we carry about with us a whole imaginary space, full of mental surrogates. To us, mental surrogates are old familiar fare. Along with the images of imaginary space, which we perhaps secretly know to be imaginary only, we tuck the thought-of actually existing rose-bush, which may be quite another story, perhaps just because we have that very convenient "place" for it. The Hopi thought-world has no imaginary space. The corollary to this is that it may not locate thought dealing with real space anywhere but in real space, nor insulate real space from the effects of thought. A Hopi would naturally suppose that his thought (or he himself) traffics with the actual rose-bush—or more likely, corn-plant—that he is thinking about. The thought then should leave some trace of itself with the plant in the field. If it is a good thought, one about health and growth, it is good for the plant; if a bad thought, the reverse.

The Hopi emphasize the intensity-factor of thought. Thought to be most effective should be vivid in consciousness, definite, steady, sustained, charged with strongly-felt good intentions. They render the idea in English as "concentrating," "holding it in your heart," "putting your mind on it," "earnestly hoping." Thought power is the force behind ceremonies, prayer sticks, ritual smoking, etc. The prayer pipe is regarded as an aid to "concentrating" (so said my informant). Its name, na'twanpi, means "instrument of preparing."

Covert participation is mental collaboration from people who do not take part in the actual affair, be it a job of work, hunt, race, or ceremony, but direct their thoughts and good will toward the affair's success. Announcements often seek to enlist the support of such mental helpers as well as of overt participants, and contain exhortations to the people to aid with their active good will.[10] A similarity to our concepts of a sympathetic audience or the cheering section of a football game should not obscure the fact that it is primarily the power of directed thought, and not merely sympathy or encouragement, that is expected of covert participants. In fact these latter get in their deadliest work before, not during the game! A corollary to the power of thought is the power of wrong thought for evil; hence one purpose of covert participation is to obtain the mass force of many good wishers to offset the harmful thought of ill wishers. Such attitudes greatly favor cooperation and community spirit. Not that the Hopi community is not full of rivalries and colliding interests. Against the tendency to social disintegration in such a small, isolated group, the theory of "preparing" by the power of thought, logically leading to the great power of the combined, intensified and harmonized thought of the whole community, must help vastly toward the rather remarkable degree of cooperation that in spite of much private bickering the Hopi village displays in all the important cultural activities.

Hopi "preparing" activities again show a result of their linguistic thought background in an emphasis on persistence and constant insistent repetition. A sense of the cumulative value of innumerable small momenta is dulled by an objectified, spatialized view of time like ours, enhanced by a way of thinking close to the subjective awareness of duration, of the ceaseless "latering" of events. To us, for whom time is a motion on a space, unvarying repetition seems to scatter its force along a row of units of that space, and be wasted. To the Hopi, for whom time is not a motion but a "getting later" of everything that has ever been done, unvarying repetition is not wasted but accumulated. It is storing up an invisible charge that holds over into later events.[11] As we have seen, it is as if the return of the day were felt as the return of the same person, a little older but with all the impresses of yesterday, not as "another day," i.e., like an entirely different person. This principle joined with that of thought-power and with traits of general Pueblo culture is expressed in the theory of the Hopi ceremonial dance for furthering rain and crops, as well as in its short, piston-like tread, repeated thousands of times, hour after hour.

SOME IMPRESSES OF LINGUISTIC HABIT IN WESTERN CIVILIZATION

It is harder to do justice in few words to the linguistically-conditioned features of our own culture than in the case of the Hopi, because of both vast scope and difficulty of objectivity—because of our deeply ingrained familiarity with the attitudes to be analyzed. I wish merely to sketch certain characteristics adjusted to our linguistic binomialism of form plus formless item or "substance," to our metaphoricalness, our imaginary space, and our objectified time. These, as we have seen, are linguistic.

From the form-plus-substance dichotomy the philosophical views most traditionally characteristic of the "Western world" have derived huge support. Here belong materialism, psycho-physical parallelism, physics—at least in its traditional Newtonian form—and dualistic views of the universe in general. Indeed here belongs almost everything that is "hard, practical common sense." Monistic, holistic, and relativistic views of reality appeal to philosophers and some scientists, but they are badly handicapped for appealing to the "common sense" of the Western average man. This is not because nature herself refutes them (if she did, philosophers could have discovered this much) but because they must be talked about in what amounts to a new language. "Common sense," as its name shows, and "practicality," as its name does not show, are largely matters of talking so that one is readily understood. It is sometimes stated that Newtonian space, time, and matter are sensed by everyone intuitively, whereupon relativity is cited as showing how mathematical analysis can prove intuition wrong. This, besides being unfair to intuition, is an attempt to answer offhand question (1) put at the outset of this paper, to answer which this research was undertaken. Presentation of the findings now nears its end, and I think the answer is clear. The offhand answer, laying the blame upon intuition for our slowness in discovering mysteries of the cosmos, such as relativity, is the wrong one. The right answer is: Newtonian space, time, and matter are no intuitions. They are recepts from culture and language. That is where Newton got them.

Our objectified view of time is, however, favorable to historicity and to everything connected with the keeping of records, while the Hopi view is unfavorable thereto. The latter is too subtle, complex, and ever-developing, supplying no ready-made answer to the question of when "one" event ends and "another" begins. When it is implicit that everything that ever happened still is, but is in a necessarily different form from what memory or record reports, there is less incentive to study the past. As for the present, the incentive would be not to record it but to treat it as "preparing." But *our* objectified time puts before imagination something like a ribbon or scroll marked off into equal blank spaces, suggesting that each be filled with an entry. Writing has no doubt helped toward our linguistic treatment of time, even as the linguistic treatment has guided the uses of writing. Through this give-and-take between language and the whole culture we get, for instance:

1. Records, diaries, book-keeping, accounting, mathematics stimulated by accounting;
2. Interest in exact sequence, dating, calendars, chronology, clocks, time wages, time graphs, time as used in physics;
3. Annals, histories, the historical attitude, interest in the past, archaeology, attitudes of introjection towards past periods, e.g., classicism, romanticism.

Just as we conceive our objectified time as extending in the future like the way it extends in the past, so we set down our estimates of the future in the same shape as our records of the past, producing programs, schedules, budgets. The formal equality of the space-like units by which we measure and conceive time leads us to consider the "formless item" or "substance" of time to be homogeneous and in ratio to the number of units. Hence our pro rata allocation of value to time, lending itself to the building up of a commercial structure based on time–pro rata values: time wages (time work constantly supersedes piece work), rent, credit, interest, depreciation charges, and insurance premiums. No doubt this vast system once built would continue to run under any sort of linguistic treatment of time; but that it should have been built at all, reaching the magnitude and particular form it has in the Western world, is a fact decidedly in consonance with the patterns of the SAE languages. Whether such a civilization as ours would be possible with widely different linguistic handling of time is a large question—in our civilization our linguistic patterns and the fitting of our behavior to the temporal order are what they are, and they are in accord. We are of course stimulated to use calendars, clocks, and watches, and to try to measure time ever more precisely; this aids science, and science in turn, following these well-worn cultural grooves, gives back to culture an ever-growing store of applications, habits, and values, with which culture again directs science. But what lies outside this spiral? Science is beginning to find that there is something in the cosmos that is not in accord with the concepts we have formed in mounting the spiral. It is trying to frame a *new language* by which to adjust itself to a wider universe.

It is clear how the emphasis on "saving time" which goes with all the above and is very obvious objectification of time, leads to a high valuation of "speed," which shows itself a great deal in our behavior.

Still another behavioral effect is that the character of monotony and regularity possessed by our image of time as an evenly scaled limitless tape measure persuades us to behave as if that monotony were more true of events than it really is. That is, it helps to routinize us. We tend to select and favor whatever bears out this view, to "play up to" the routine aspects of existence. One phase of this is behavior evincing a false sense of security or an assumption that all will always go smoothly, and a lack in foreseeing and protecting ourselves against hazards. Our technique of harnessing energy does well in routine performance, and it is along routine lines that we chiefly strive to improve it—we are, for example, relatively uninterested in stopping the energy from causing accidents, fires, and explosions, which it is doing constantly and on a wide scale. Such indifference to the unexpectedness of life would be disastrous to a society as small, isolated, and precariously poised as the Hopi society is, or rather once was.

Thus our linguistically determined thought-world not only collaborates with our cultural idols and ideals, but engages even our unconscious personal reactions in its patterns and gives them certain typical characters. One such character, as we have seen, is *carelessness*, as in reckless driving or throwing cigarette stubs into waste paper. Another of different sort is *gesturing* when we talk. Very many of the gestures made by English-speaking people at least, and probably by all SAE speakers, serve to illustrate by a movement in space, not a real spatial reference but one of the non-spatial references that our language handles by metaphors of imaginary space. That is, we are more apt to make a grasping gesture when we speak of grasping an elusive idea than when we speak of grasping a doorknob. The gesture seeks to make a metaphorical and hence somewhat unclear reference more clear. But if a language refers to non-spatials without implying a spatial analogy, the reference is not made any clearer by gesture. The Hopi gesture very little, perhaps not at all in the sense we understand as gesture.

It would seem as if kinesthesia, or the sensing of muscular movement, though arising prior to language, should be made more highly conscious by linguistic use of imaginary space and metaphorical images of motion. Kinesthesia is marked in two facets of European culture: art and sport. European sculpture, an art in which Europe excels, is strongly kinesthetic, conveying great sense of the body's motions; European painting likewise. The dance in our culture expresses delight in motion rather than symbolism or ceremonial, and our music is greatly influenced by our dance forms. Our sports are strongly imbued with this element of the "poetry of motion." Hopi races and games seem to emphasize rather the virtues of endurance and sustained intensity. Hopi dancing is highly symbolic and is performed with great intensity and earnestness, but has not much movement or swing.

Synesthesia, or suggestion by certain sense receptions of characters belonging to another sense, as of light and color by sounds and vice versa, should be made more conscious by a linguistic metaphorical system that refers to non-spatial experiences by terms for spatial ones, though undoubtedly it arises from a deeper source. Probably in the first instance metaphor arises from synesthesia and not the reverse, yet metaphor need not become firmly rooted in linguistic pattern, as Hopi shows. Non-spatial experience has one well-organized sense, *hearing*—for smell and taste are but little organized. Non-spatial consciousness is a realm chiefly of thought, feeling, and *sound*. Spatial consciousness is a realm of light, color, sight, and touch, and presents shapes and dimensions. Our metaphorical system, by naming non-spatial experiences after spatial ones, imputes to sounds, smells, tastes, emotions, and thoughts qualities like the colors, luminosities, shapes, angles, textures, and motions of spatial experience. And to some extent the reverse transference occurs; for after much talking about tones as high, low, sharp, dull, heavy, brilliant, slow, the talker finds it easy to think of some factors in spatial experience as like factors of tone. Thus we speak of "tones" of color, a gray "monotone," a "loud" necktie, a "taste" in dress: all spatial metaphor in reverse. Now European art is distinctive in the way it seeks deliberately to play with synesthesia. Music tries to suggest scenes, color, movement, geometric design; painting and sculpture are often consciously guided by the analogies of music's rhythm; colors are conjoined with feeling for the analogy to concords and discords. The European theatre and opera seek a synthesis of many arts. It may be that in this way our metaphorical language that is in some sense a confusion of thought is producing, through art, a result of far-reaching value—a deeper esthetic sense leading toward a more direct apprehension of underlying unity behind the phenomena so variously reported by our sense channels.

HISTORICAL IMPLICATIONS

How does such a network of language, culture, and behavior come about historically? Which was first, the language patterns or the cultural norms? In main they have grown up together, constantly influencing each other. But in this partnership the nature of the language is the factor that limits free plasticity and rigidifies channels of development in the more autocratic way. This is because a language is a system, not just an assemblage of norms. Large systemic outlines can change to something really new only very slowly, while many other cultural innovations are made with comparative quickness. Language thus represents the mass mind; it is affected by inventions and innovations, but affected little and slowly, whereas *to* inventors and innovators it legislates with the decree immediate.

The growth of the SAE language-culture complex dates from ancient times. Much of its metaphorical reference to the non-spatial by the spatial was already fixed in the ancient tongues, and more especially in Latin. It is indeed a marked trait of Latin: If we compare, say Hebrew, we find that while Hebrew has some allusion to not-space as space, Latin has more. Latin terms for non-spatials, like *educo, religio, principia, comprehendo*, are usually metaphorized physical references: lead out, tying back, etc. This is not true of all languages—it is quite untrue of Hopi. The fact that in Latin the direction of development happened to be from spatial to non-spatial (partly because of secondary stimulation to abstract thinking when the intellectually crude Romans encountered Greek culture), and that later tongues were strongly stimulated to mimic Latin, seems a likely reason for a belief which still lingers on among linguists that this is the natural direction of semantic change in all languages, and for the persistent notion in Western learned circles (in strong contrast to Eastern ones) that objective experience is prior to subjective. Philosophies make out a weighty case for the reverse, and certainly the direction of development is sometimes the reverse. Thus the Hopi word for "heart" can be shown to be late formation within Hopi from a root meaning think or remember. Or consider what has happened to the word "radio" in such a sentence as "he bought a new radio," as compared to its prior meaning," science of wireless telephony."

In the middle ages the patterns already formed in Latin began to interweave with the increased mechanical invention, industry, trade, and scholastic and scientific thought. The need for measurement in industry and trade, the stores and bulks of "stuffs" in various containers, the type-bodies in which various goods were handled, standardizing of measure and weight units, invention of clocks and measurement of "time," keeping of records, accounts, chronicles, histories, growth of mathematics and the partnership of mathematics and science, all cooperated to bring our thought and language world into its present form.

In Hopi history, could we read it, we should find a different type of language and a different set of cultural and environmental influences working together. A peaceful agricultural society isolated by geographic features and nomad enemies in a land of scanty rainfall, arid agriculture that could be made successful only by the utmost perseverance (hence the value of persistence and repetition), necessity for collaboration (hence emphasis on the psychology of teamwork and on mental factors in general), corn and rain as primary criteria of value, need of extensive *preparations* and precautions to assure crops in the poor soil and precarious climate, keen realization of dependence upon nature favoring prayer and a religious attitude toward the forces of nature, especially prayer and religion directed toward the ever-needed blessing, rain—these things interacted with Hopi linguistic patterns to mold them, to be molded again by them, and so little by little to shape the Hopi world-outlook.

To sum up the matter, our first question asked in the beginning is answered thus: Concepts of "time" and "matter" are not given in substantially the same form by experience to all men but depend upon the nature of the language or languages through the use of which they have been developed. They do not depend so much upon *any one system* (e.g., tense, or nouns) within the grammar as upon the ways of analyzing and reporting experience which have become fixed in the language as integrated "fashions of speaking" and which cut across the typical grammatical classifications, so that such a "fashion" may include lexical, morphological, syntactic, and otherwise systematically diverse means coordinated in a certain frame of consistency. Our own "time" differs markedly from Hopi "duration." It is conceived as like a space of strictly limited dimensions, or sometimes as like a motion upon such a space, and employed as an intellectual tool accordingly. Hopi "duration" seems to be inconceivable in terms of space or motion, being the mode in which life differs from form, and consciousness *in toto* from the spatial elements of consciousness. Certain ideas born of our own time-concept, such as that of absolute simultaneity, would be either very difficult to express or impossible and devoid of meaning under the Hopi conception, and would be replaced by operational concepts. Our "matter" is the physical sub-type of "substance" or "stuff," which is conceived as the formless extensional item that must be joined with form before there can be real existence. In Hopi there seems to be nothing corresponding to it; there are no formless extensional items; existence may or may not have form, but what it also has, with or without form, is intensity and duration, these being non-extensional and at bottom the same.

But what about our concept of "space," which was also included in our first question? There is no such striking difference between Hopi and SAE about space as about time, and probably the apprehension of space is given in substantially the same form by experience irrespective of language. The experiments of the Gestalt psychologists with visual perception appear to establish this as a fact. But the *concept of space* will vary somewhat with language, because as an intellectual tool[12] it is so closely linked with the concomitant employment of other intellectual tools, of the order of "time" and "matter," which are linguistically conditioned. We see things with our eyes in the same space forms as the Hopi, but our idea of space has also the property of acting as a surrogate of non-spatial relationships like time, intensity, tendency, and as a void to be filled with imagined formless items, one of which may even be called "space." Space as sensed by the Hopi would not be connected mentally with such surrogates, but would be comparatively "pure," unmixed with extraneous notions.

As for our second question: There are connections but not correlations or diagnostic correspondences between cultural norms and linguistic patterns. Although it would be impossible to infer the existence of Crier Chiefs from the lack of tenses in Hopi, or vice versa, there is a relation between a language and the rest of the culture of the society which uses it. There are cases where the "fashions of speaking" are closely integrated with the whole general culture, whether or not this be universally true, and there are connections within this integration, between the kind of linguistic analyses employed and various behavioral reactions and also the shapes taken by various cultural developments. Thus the importance of Crier Chiefs does have a connection, not with tenselessness itself, but with a system of thought in which categories different from our tenses are natural. These connections are to be found not so much by focusing attention on the typical rubrics of linguistic, ethnographic, or sociological description as by examining the culture and the language (always and only when the two have been together historically for a considerable time) as a whole in which concatenations that run across these departmental lines may be expected to exist, and if they do exist, eventually to be discoverable by study.

NOTES

1. We have plenty of evidence that this is not the case. Consider only the Hopi and the Ute, with languages that on the overt morphological and lexical level are as similar as, say, English and German. The idea of "correlation" between language and culture, in the generally accepted sense of correlation, is certainly a mistaken one.

2. As we say, "ten at the *same time,*" showing that in our language and thought we restate the fact of group-perception in terms of a concept "time," the large linguistic component of which appears in the course of this paper.

3. It is no exception to this rule of lacking a plural that a mass noun may sometimes coincide in lexeme with an individual noun that of course has a plural; e.g., "stone" (no pl.) with "a stone" (pl. "stones"). The plural form denoting varieties, e.g., "wines" is of course a different sort of thing from the true plural; it is a curious outgrowth from the SAE mass nouns, leading to still another sort of imaginary aggregate, which will have to be omitted from this paper.

4. Hopi has two words for water-quantities: kə·yi and pa·hə. The difference is something like that between "stone" and "rock" in English, pa·hə implying greater

    size and "wildness"; flowing water, whether or not outdoors or in nature, is pa·hə, so is "moisture." But unlike "stone" and "rock," the difference is essential, not pertaining to a connotative margin, and the two can hardly ever be interchanged.

5. To be sure there are a few minor differences from other nouns, in English for instance in the use of the articles.

6. "Year" and certain combinations of "year" with name of season, rarely season names alone, can occur with a locative morpheme "at," but this is exceptional. It appears like historical detritus of an earlier different patterning, or the effect of English analogy, or both.

7. The expective and reportive assertions contrast according to the "paramount relation." The expective expresses anticipation existing *earlier* than objective fact, and coinciding with objective fact *later* than the status quo of the speaker, this status quo, including all the subsummation of the past therein, being expressed by the reportive. Our notion "future" seems to represent at once the earlier (anticipation) and the later (afterwards, what will be), as Hopi shows. This paradox may hint of how elusive the mystery of real time is, and how artificially it is expressed by a linear relation of past-present-future.

8. One such trace is that the tensor "long in duration," while quite different from the adjective "long" of space, seems to contain the same root as the adjective "large" of space. Another is that "somewhere" of space used with certain tensors means "at some indefinite time." Possibly, however, this is not the case and it is only the tensor that gives the time element, so that "somewhere" still refers to space and that under these conditions indefinite space means simply general applicability regardless of either time or space. Another trace is that in the temporal (cycle word) "afternoon" the element meaning "after" is derived from the verb "to separate." There are other such traces, but they are few and exceptional, and obviously not like our own spatial metaphorizing.

9. The Hopi verbs of preparing naturally do not correspond neatly to our "prepare"; so that na'twani could also be rendered "the practised-upon," "the tried-for," and otherwise.

10. See, e.g., Ernest Beaglehole, *Notes on Hopi Economic Life* (Yale University Publications in Anthropology, No. 15, 1937), especially the reference to the announcement of a rabbit hunt, and on p. 30, description of the activities in connection with the cleaning of Toreva Spring—announcing, various preparing activities, and finally, preparing the continuity of the good results already obtained and the continued flow of the spring.

11. This notion of storing up power, which seems implied by much Hopi behavior, has an analogue in physics, acceleration. It might be said that the linguistic background of Hopi things equips it to recognize naturally that force manifests not as motion or velocity, but as cumulation or acceleration. Our linguistic background tends to hinder in us this same recognition, for having legitimately conceived force to be that which produces change, we then think of change by our linguistic *metaphorical* analogue, motion, instead of by a pure motionless changingness concept, i.e., accumulation or acceleration. Hence it comes to our naïve feeling as a shock to find from physical experiments that it is not possible to define force by motion, that motion and speed, as also "being at rest," are wholly relative, and that force can be measured only by acceleration.

12. Here belong "Newtonian" and "Euclidean" space, etc.

Ruth Fulton Benedict 1887–1948

BACKGROUND

Ruth Benedict was a magnetic person. Since she was slightly deaf in childhood, and more than that in the later part of her life, she became a skilled lipreader. Her large eyes, and her tendency to keep them intently on your face as you spoke, gave you a feeling of real importance. She was quiet, gracious, occasionally satirical, and—very rarely—even sarcastic, and about her there seemed to be an aura of sadness, although she was lively and interested.

She was born of old American farming stock—six ancestors had fought in the Revolution. Her father was a doctor who died before she was two; her childhood was rigorous and poor, but she got a good education. In 1905 she went to Vassar, where her major interest was English literature. She graduated in 1909—a Phi Beta Kappa, but nevertheless disquieted, feeling that her education had given little intellectual or social meaning to her life. The next year she spent in Europe with two classmates from Vassar. When she returned, she taught secondary school for three years and did research on women who had become literary figures. In 1914 she married Stanley Benedict, a biochemist teaching at Cornell Medical College.

Benedict was over thirty when she found anthropology—a discipline that she felt allowed her for the first time to place in perspective contrasts between different peoples and different historical periods. From 1919 to 1921 she was a student of Alexander Goldenweiser and Elsie Clews Parsons at the New School for Social Research. Through them she met Franz Boas, who had great influence on her work. The influence of Robert Lowie, from whom she took a course at the American Museum of Natural History, is also apparent; she said that her first published paper, "The Vision in Plains Culture" (1922), was written for him and at his behest.

She did her first field work in the summer of 1922 among the Serrano, under the direction of Alfred Kroeber. Field work was not easy for Benedict, because she could not hear and found it ultimately impossible to learn to lipread new phonetic patterns. She completed her doctoral dissertation, "The Concept of the Guardian Spirit in North America," in 1923, and her first teaching appointment was as an assistant to Boas in an undergraduate class at Barnard in 1922–1923 (imagine having Boas and Benedict together in a single class!). The next year she began teaching at the graduate school of Columbia.

Benedict's commitment to anthropology was not complete until she knew definitely that she would not have children; after that it was total. She had been trained as a scholar and had become a first-rate comparative ethnologist without experiencing any shift of role.

In 1927, when she was in the field with the Pima Indians, she was struck by the tremendous contrast between them and the Pueblo cultures, which she had known earlier. The Pueblo emphasized harmony; the Pima extremism. She began to view culture not merely as the matrix in which personalities develop, but as being like a personality on a larger scale. The theory that underlay *Patterns of Culture* was worked out for a paper for the Twenty-third Congress of Americanists in 1928, but the book was not written until 1931. She drew on Nietzsche for the terms "Apollonian" and "Dionysian" to describe differences between Pueblo culture and other American Indian culture. She called Dobuan culture "paranoid" and the Kwakiutl culture "megalomaniac." She was strongly taken to task by some of her colleagues, but the book has become a classic, although seldom read outside anthropology today because of its very success—all her good points have become truisms.

After Boas' retirement, Benedict served as acting chairman for several years—still an assistant professor. During these Depression years, she struggled to help her students get funds for field work, write-up money, and jobs. She edited the *Journal of American Folklore* (1928–1939) and directed summer field work trips—one to the Apache in 1930, another to the Blackfoot in 1938. Her first sabbatical, in 1938–1939, she devoted to *Race: Science and Politics,* which grew out of a pamphlet she had written for the army. It had been printed but not distributed because it offended some congressmen. In response, she wrote a book that contains what is still one of the best discussions of the history of racism. During all this time Benedict also wrote poetry, which was later published under the name of Anne Singleton.

World War II opened up an entirely new area of study for Benedict—the application of anthropological thought to contemporary societies, based not on field work but on interviews and documents. Her work was a research post in Washington, where she worked consecutively on Romania, Siam, Germany, and Holland, near the end of the war turning her attention to Japan. The summer immediately after the war she had planned to go to Germany to set up and supervise a series of cultural studies of German communities, but the military authorities refused to let her go—they said because of her health, she said rather scornfully because they were afraid she would get hurt and cause a scandal.

She returned to Columbia in 1946 after finishing *The Chrysanthemum and the Sword,* which some anthropologists consider her masterpiece. It is a book about Japan that remains more or less unique in the annals of anthropology. In the spring of 1947 she undertook a large research project on contemporary cultures, out of which came studies of France, Germany, Poland, Russia, pre-Communist China, and the eastern European *shtetl.* She helped develop a manual, *The Study of Culture at a Distance,* which, among other things, discusses and illustrates applied anthropology as it is relevant to the relations of national governments.

The following year, 1948, she was tardily made full professor. That summer she lectured at a UNESCO summer school in Prague, then toured the countries she had been studying: Czechoslovakia, Poland, France, Belgium, and Holland. Five days after she returned from this tour, she became ill, and five days after that she died of coronary thrombosis.

INTRODUCTION

Ruth Benedict was a one-issue theoretician: she dealt with the relationship of cultural configuration to individual behavior. According to Benedict, every culture is an integrated whole that has its own configuration. In turn, every individual in that cultural configuration carries the characteristic of that culture and behaves according to that pattern.

The best exposition of Benedict's views can be found in her *Patterns of Culture* (1934). Here she defines anthropology as the discipline that studies the differences between cultural traditions. Two extremely important points accrue from such an outlook. First, the "s" that was added to "culture" by Boas and others, becomes central—we are no longer so interested in culture as we are in cultures and what they do to you. Second, "a culture" is integrated. Every culture, in this view, is made by man, is in a given place, and is different from other cultures. This means that every culture is more or less integrated, which in turn implies that a culture is more than the sum of its parts.

The emphasis on whole cultures is very much a part of the cultural relativist position that cultures should be studied rather than culture on the one hand or culture traits on the other. The cultural configuration emphasized by Benedict does, however, take the Boasian program a step ahead. Where Boas emphasizes the collection of information, Benedict proposes a way to improve understanding of the cultures being studied by integrating pertinent data around the concept of cultural configurations.

The use of cultural patterns by Benedict represents an extreme reductionism of cultural characteristics. When, for example, she characterizes the Zuñi as being "Apollonian"—a culture in which moderation prevails—she reduces cultural patterns to such a degree as to try to explain human behavior by them. A logical point of view this may be—but it is also oversimplification. Benedict, unlike so many of her predecessors, was trying to understand the behavior of individuals in society. Her device for such an understanding was to use her oversimplified cultural patterns as the central concept to explain individual behavior. The pattern "causes" behavior. The problem with this approach is its failure to allow for the range of possible behaviors that any culture allows.

However, it must be emphasized that, in spite of its extreme reductionism, Ruth Benedict's theory of culture patterns represents the first theory—nonevolutionary, noncomparative, nonbiological—that attempts to understand human behavior on the basis of cultural integration.

11 THE INTEGRATION OF CULTURE

The diversity of cultures can be endlessly documented. A field of human behaviour may be ignored in some societies until it barely exists; it may even be in some cases unimagined. Or it may almost monopolize the whole organized behaviour of the society, and the most alien situations be manipulated only in its terms. Traits having no intrinsic relation one with the other, and historically independent, merge and become inextricable, providing the occasion for behaviour that has no counterpart in regions that do not make these identifications. It is a corollary of this that standards, no matter in what aspect of behaviour, range in different cultures from the positive to the negative pole. We might suppose that in the matter of taking life all peoples would agree in condemnation. On the contrary, in a matter of homicide, it may be held that one is blameless if diplomatic relations have been severed between neighbouring countries, or that one kills by custom his first two children, or that a husband has right of life and death over his wife, or that it is the duty of the child to kill his parents before they are old. It may be that those are killed who steal a fowl, or who cut their upper teeth first, or who are born on a Wednesday. Among some peoples a person suffers torments at having caused an accidental death; among others it is a matter of no consequence. Suicide also may be a light matter, the recourse of anyone who has suffered some slight rebuff, an act that occurs constantly in a tribe. It may be the highest and noblest act a wise man can perform. The very tale of it, on the other hand, may be a matter for incredulous mirth, and the act itself impossible to conceive as a human possibility. Or it may be a crime punishable by law, or regarded as a sin against the gods.

The diversity of custom in the world is not, however, a matter which we can only helplessly chronicle. Self-torture here, head-hunting there, pre-nuptial chastity in one tribe and adolescent license in another, are not a list of unrelated facts, each of them to be greeted with surprise wherever it is found or wherever it is absent. The tabus on killing oneself or another, similarly, though they relate to no absolute standard, are not therefore fortuitous. The significance of cultural behaviour is not exhausted when we have clearly understood that it is local and man-made and hugely variable. It tends also to be integrated. A culture, like an individual, is a more or less consistent pattern of thought and action. Within each culture there come into being characteristic purposes not necessarily shared by other types of society. In obedience to these purposes, each people further and further consolidates its experience, and in proportion to the urgency of these drives the heterogeneous items of behaviour take more and more congruous shape. Taken up by a well-integrated culture, the most ill-assorted acts become characteristic of its peculiar goals, often by the most unlikely metamorphoses. The form that these acts take we can understand only by understanding first the emotional and intellectual mainsprings of that society.

Such patterning of culture cannot be ignored as if it were an unimportant detail. The whole, as modern science is insisting in many fields, is not merely the sum of all its parts, but the result of a unique arrangement and interrelation of the parts that has brought about a new entity. Gunpowder is not merely the sum of sulphur and charcoal and saltpeter, and no amount of knowledge even of all three of its elements in all the forms they take in the natural world will demonstrate the nature of gunpowder. New potentialities have come into being in the resulting compound that were not present in its elements, and its mode of behaviour is indefinitely changed from that of any of its elements in other combinations.

Cultures, likewise, are more than the sum of their traits. We may know all about the distribution of a tribe's form of marriage, ritual dances, and puberty initiations, and yet understand nothing of the culture as a whole which has used these elements to its own purpose. This purpose selects from among the possible traits in the surrounding regions those which it can use, and discards those which it cannot. Other traits it recasts into conformity with its demands. The process of course need never be conscious during its whole course, but to overlook it in the study of the patternings of human behaviour is to renounce the possibility of intelligent interpretation.

This integration of cultures is not in the least mystical. It is the same process by which a style in art comes into being and persists. Gothic architecture, beginning in what was hardly more than a preference for altitude and light, became, by the operation of some canon of taste that developed within its technique, the unique and homogeneous art of the thirteenth century. It discarded elements that were incongruous, modified others to its purposes, and invented others that accorded with its taste. When we describe the process historically, we inevitably use animistic forms of expression as if there were choice and purpose in the growth of this great art form. But this is due to the difficulty in our language forms. There was no conscious choice, and no purpose. What was at first no more than a slight bias in local forms and techniques expressed itself more and more forcibly, integrated itself in more and more definite standards, and eventuated in Gothic art.

What has happened in the great art styles happens also in cultures as a whole. All the miscellaneous behaviour directed toward getting a living, mating, warring, and worshipping the gods, is made over into consistent patterns in accordance with unconscious canons of choice that develop within the culture. Some cultures, like some periods of art, fail of such integration, and about many others we know too little to understand the motives that actuate them. But cultures at every level of complexity, even the simplest, have achieved it. Such cultures are more or less successful attainments of integrated behaviour, and the marvel is that there can be so many of these possible configurations.

Anthropological work has been overwhelmingly devoted to the analysis of culture traits, however, rather than to the study of cultures as articulated wholes. This has been due in great measure to the nature of earlier ethnological descriptions. The classical anthropologists did not write out of first-hand knowledge of primitive people. They were armchair students who had at their disposal the anecdotes of travellers and missionaries and the formal and schematic accounts of the early ethnologists. It was possible to trace from these details the distribution of the custom of knocking out teeth, or of divination by entrails, but it was not possible to see how these traits were embedded in different tribes in characteristic configurations that gave form and meaning to the procedures.

Studies of culture like *The Golden Bough* and the usual comparative ethnological volumes are analytical discussions of traits and ignore all the aspects of cultural integration. Mating or death practices are illustrated by bits of behaviour selected indiscriminately from the most different cultures, and the discussion builds up a kind of mechanical Frankenstein's monster with a right eye from Fiji, a left from Europe, one leg from Tierra del Fuego, and one from Tahiti, and all the fingers and toes from still different regions. Such a figure corresponds to no reality in the past or present, and the fundamental difficulty is the same as if, let us say, psychiatry ended with a catalogue of the symbols of which psychopathic individuals make use, and ignored the study of patterns of symptomatic behaviour—schizophrenia, hysteria, and manic-depressive disorders—into which they are built. The rôle of the trait in the behaviour of the psychotic, the degree to which it is dynamic in the total personality, and its relation to all other items of experience differ completely. If we are interested in mental processes, we can satisfy ourslves only by relating the particular symbol to the total configuration of the individual.

There is as great an unreality in similar studies of culture. If we are interested in cultural processes, the only way in which we can know the significance of the selected detail of behaviour is against the background of the motives and emotions and values that are institutionalized in that culture. The first essential, so it seems today, is to study the living culture, to know its habits of thought and the functions of its institutions, and such knowledge cannot come out of post-mortem dissections and reconstructions.

The necessity for functional studies of culture has been stressed over and over again by Malinowski. He criticizes the usual diffusion studies as post-mortem dissections of organisms we might rather study in their living and functioning vitality. One of the best and earliest of the full-length pictures of a primitive people which have made modern ethnology possible is Malinowski's extended account of the Trobriand Islanders of Melanesia. Malinowski, however, in his ethnological generalizations is content to emphasize that traits have a living context in the culture of which they are a part, that they function. He then generalizes the Trobriand traits—the importance of reciprocal obligations, the local character of magic, the Trobriand domestic family—as valid for the primitive world instead of recognizing the Trobriand configuration as one of many observed types, each with its characteristic arrangements in the economic, the religious, and the domestic sphere.

The study of cultural behaviour, however, can no longer be handled by equating particular local arrangements with the generic primitive. Anthropologists are turning from the study of primitive culture to that of primitive cultures, and the implications of this change from the singular to the plural are only just beginning to be evident.

The importance of the study of the whole configuration as over against the continued analysis of its parts is stressed in field after field of modern science. Wilhelm Stern has made it basic in his work in philosophy and psychology. He insists that the undivided totality of the person must be the point of departure. He criticizes the atomistic studies that have been almost universal both in introspective and experimental psychology, and he substitutes investigation into the configuration of personality. The whole *Struktur* school has devoted itself to work of the kind in various fields. Worringer has shown how fundamental a difference this approach makes in the field of aesthetics. He contrasts the highly developed art of two periods, the Greek and the Byzantine. The older criticism, he insists, which defined art in absolute terms and identified it with the classical standards, could not possibly understand the processes of art as they are represented in Byzantine painting or mosaic. Achievement in one cannot be judged in terms of the other, because each was attempting to achieve quite different ends. The Greeks in their art attempted to give expression to their own pleasure in activity; they sought to embody their identification of their vitality with the objective world. Byzantine art, on the other hand, objectified abstraction, a profound feeling of separation in the face of outside nature. Any understanding of the two must take account, not only of comparisons of artistic ability, but far more of differences of artistic intention. The two forms were contrasting, integrated configurations, each of which could make use of forms and standards that were incredible in the other.

The *Gestalt* (configuration) psychology has done some of the most striking work in justifying the importance of this point of departure from the whole rather than from its parts. *Gestalt* psychologists have shown that in the simplest sense-perception no analysis of the separate percepts can account for the total experience. It is not enough to divide perceptions up into objective fragments. The subjective framework, the forms provided by past experience, are crucial and cannot be omitted. The 'wholeness-properties' and the 'wholeness-tendencies' must be studied in addition to the simple association mechanisms with which psychology has been satisfied since the time of Locke. The whole determines its parts, not only their relation but their very nature. Between two wholes there is a discontinuity in kind, and any understanding must take account of their different natures, over and above a recognition of the similar elements that have entered into the two. The work in *Gestalt* psychology has been chiefly in those fields where evidence can be experimentally arrived at in the laboratory, but its implications reach far beyond the simple demonstrations which are associated with its work.

In the social sciences the importance of integration and configuration was stressed in the last generation by Wilhelm Dilthey. His primary interest was in the great philosophies and interpretations of life. Especially in *Die Typen der Weltanschauung* he analyzes part of the history of thought to show the relativity of philosophical systems. He sees them as great expressions of the variety of life, moods, *Lebensstimmungen*, integrated attitudes the fundamental categories of which cannot be resolved one into another. He argues vigorously against the assumption that any one of them can be final. He does not formulate as cultural the different attitudes he discusses, but because he takes for discussion great philosophical configurations, and historical periods like that of Frederick the Great, his work has led naturally to more and more conscious recognition of the rôle of culture.

This recognition has been given its most elaborate expression by Oswald Spengler. His *Decline of the West* takes its title not from its theme of destiny ideas, as he calls the dominant patterning of a civilization, but from a thesis which has no bearing upon our present discussion, namely, that these cultural configurations have, like any organism, a span of life they cannot overpass. This thesis of the doom of civilizations is argued on the basis of the shift of cultural centres in Western civilization and the periodicity of high cultural achievement. He buttresses this description with the analogy, which can never be more than an analogy, with the birth- and death-cycle of living organisms. Every civilization, he believes, has its lusty youth, its strong manhood, and its disintegrating senescence.

It is this latter interpretation of history which is generally identified with *The Decline of the West,* but Spengler's far more valuable and original analysis is that of contrasting configurations in Western civilization. He distinguishes two great destiny ideas: the Apollonian of the classical world and the Faustian of the modern world. Apollonian man conceived of his soul 'as a cosmos ordered in a group of excellent parts.' There was no place in his universe for will, and conflict was an evil which his philosophy decried. The idea of an inward development of the personality was alien to him, and he saw life as under the shadow of catastrophe always brutally threatening from the outside. His tragic climaxes were wanton destructions of the pleasant landscape of normal existence. The same event might have befallen another individual in the same way and with the same results.

On the other hand, the Faustian's picture of himself is as a force endlessly combatting obstacles. His version of the course of individual life is that of an inner development, and the catastrophes of existence come as the inevitable culmination of his past choices and experiences. Conflict is the essence of existence. Without it personal life has no meaning, and only the more superficial values of existence can be attained. Faustian man longs for the infinite, and his attempts to reach out toward it. Faustian and Apollonian are opposed interpretations of existence, and the values that arise in the one are alien and trivial to the other.

The civilization of the classical world was built upon the Apollonian view of life, and the modern world has been working out in all its institutions the implications of the Faustian view. Spengler glances aside also at the Egyptian, 'which saw itself as moving down a narrow and inexorably prescribed life-path to come at last before the judges of the dead,' and at the Magian with its strict dualism of body and soul. But his great subjects are the Apol-

Ionian and the Faustian, and he considers mathematics, architecture, music, and painting as expressing these two great opposed philosophies of different periods of Western civilization.

The confused impression which is given by Spengler's volumes is due only partially to the manner of presentation. To an even greater degree it is the consequence of the unresolved complexities of the civilizations with which he deals. Western civilizations, with their historical diversity, their stratification into occupations and classes, their incomparable richness of detail, are not yet well enough understood to be summarized under a couple of catchwords. Outside of certain very restricted intellectual and artistic circles, Faustian man, if he occurs, does not have his own way with our civilization. There are the strong men of action and the Babbitts as well as the Faustians, and no ethnologically satisfactory picture of modern civilization can ignore such constantly recurring types. It is quite as convincing to characterize our cultural type as thoroughly extrovert, running about in endless mundane activity, inventing, governing, and as Edward Carpenter says, 'endlessly catching its trains,' as it is to characterize it as Faustian, with a longing for the infinite.

Anthropologically speaking, Spengler's picture of world civilizations suffers from the necessity under which he labours of treating modern stratified society as if it had the essential homogeneity of a folk culture. In our present state of knowledge, the historical data of western European culture are too complex and the social differentiation too thorough-going to yield to the necessity analysis. However suggestive Spengler's discussion of Faustian man is for a study of European literature and philosophy, and however just his emphasis upon the relativity of values, his analysis cannot be final because other equally valid pictures can be drawn. In retrospect it may be possible to characterize adequately a great and complex whole like Western civilization, but in spite of the importance and the truth of Spengler's postulate of incommensurable destiny ideas, at the present time the attempt to interpret the Western world in terms of any one selected trait results in confusion.

It is one of the philosophical justifications for the study of primitive peoples that the facts of simpler cultures may make clear social facts that are otherwise baffling and not open to demonstration. This is nowhere more true than in the matter of the fundamental and distinctive cultural configurations that pattern existence and condition the thoughts and emotions of the individuals who participate in those cultures. The whole problem of the formation of the individual's habit-patterns under the influence of traditional custom can best be understood at the present time through the study of simpler peoples. This does not mean that the facts and processes we can discover in this way are limited in their application to primitive civilizations. Cultural configurations are as compelling and as significant in the highest and most complex societies of which we have knowledge. But the material is too intricate and too close to our eyes for us to cope with it successfully.

The understanding we need of our own cultural processes can most economically be arrived at by a détour. When the historical relations of human beings and their immediate forbears in the animal kingdom were too involved to use in establishing the fact of biological evolution, Darwin made use instead of the structure of beetles, and the process, which in the complex physical organization of the human is confused, in the simpler material was transparent in its cogency. It is the same in the study of cultural mechanisms. We need all the enlightenment we can obtain from the study of thought and behaviour as it is organized in the less complicated groups.

I have chosen three primitive civilizations to picture in some detail [in subsequent chapters of *Patterns of Culture*]. A few cultures understood as coherent organizations of behaviour are more enlightening than many touched upon only at their high spots. The relation of motivations and purposes to the separate items of cultural behaviour at birth, at death, at puberty, and at marriage can never be made clear by a comprehensive study of the world. We must hold ourselves to the less ambitious task, the many-sided understanding of a few cultures.

REFERENCES

Dilthey, Wilhelm
    1914–1931   *Gesammelte Schriften,* Band 2; 8. Leipzig.
Koffka, Kurt
    1927   *The Growth of the Mind.* New York.
Köhler, Wilhelm
    1929   *Gestalt Psychology.* New York.
Malinowski, Bronislaw
    1922   *Argonauts of the Western Pacific.* London.
    1926a   *Crime and Custom in Savage Society.* London.
    1926b   *Myth in Primitive Psychology.* New York.
    1927   *Sex and Repression in Savage Society.* London.
    1929   *The Sexual Life of Savages.* London.
Murphy, Gardner
    1932   *Approaches to Personality.* New York.
Spengler, Oswald
    1927–1928   *The Decline of the West.* New York.
Stern, Wilhelm
    1921   *Die differentielle Psychologie in ihren Grundlagen.* Leipzig.
Worringer, Wilhelm
    1927   *Form in Gothic.* London.

Ralph Linton 1893–1953

> . . . I consider as my greatest accomplishment that I am an
> adopted member of the Comanche tribe, was accepted as a
> master carver by the Marquesan natives and executed com-
> missions for them in their own art, am a member of the Native
> Church of North America (Peyote) according to Quapaw rite,
> became a properly accredited ombiasy nkazo (medicine man) in
> Madagascar and was even invited to join the Rotary Club of a
> middle western city.—RALPH LINTON

BACKGROUND

Ralph Linton, besides having a very original turn of thought
and being a master wordmonger, had a great synthesizing mind. By the time he
wrote, anthropology had become so diffuse that getting it all under one skull was
becoming increasingly difficult, while at the same time it had not yet developed
far enough that each of its branches could create the kind of generalizations that
could turn being a "generalist" into a specialty.

Linton was born into an old Philadelphia Quaker family with few overt scientific or intellectual interests. His father, a successful businessman, believed that
growing boys should spend their spare time working and earning their own spending money, so from the age of ten Linton's vacations were spent working in one or
another of a chain of restaurants his father owned in Philadelphia.

He went to a Quaker high school, where he found little inspiration to study,
but he was encouraged to continue his education. His undergraduate work was at
Swarthmore College, which, at that time, offered no anthropology; Linton worked
in natural sciences and was an omnivorous reader in history and literature. While
at Swarthmore he came under the influence of Spencer Trotter, whose courses in
general science inspired him with the notion of seeking a synthesis of the many
points of view he had encountered. His search for a synthesis eventually led him
to anthropology.

Linton's early career in anthropology centered around archaeology—as a boy
he had systematically collected arrowheads. In 1912–1913, while he was still an
undergraduate, he joined field expeditions to the American Southwest and Guate-
mala. In 1915, just after he received his B.A., he discovered an Archaic site near
Haddonfield, New Jersey—the first such culture identified south of New England.
His publications about this excavation led to considerable controversy.

In World War I Linton was a corporal in the 149th Field Artillery, 42nd (Rainbow) Division, and was mildly gassed on the front in France. He showed a typical dry whimsicality about all this, writing an article called "Totemism and the A.E.F. [American Expeditionary Force]" that is very funny—indeed, he often broke into irreverent humor in his writing. His straight-faced "proof," using "the best scientific methods," that corn had to have been domesticated in Africa is not only funny, but a telling critique of the diffusionist school of anthropology.

In 1920 he undertook field work in the Marquesas Islands. During his two years in Polynesia, his interests changed direction. He continued to work in archaeology, but he became more and more interested in contemporary peoples. In 1922, when he returned from Polynesia, he joined the staff of the Field Museum of Natural History in Chicago, where he wrote a large number of short papers on Oceanic and American Indian material culture.

His second field trip was to Madagascar in 1925–1927. When he returned, he accepted a job at the University of Wisconsin—and his interests continued to shift toward "anthropology-on-the-hoof." Within a few years he had become known as one of America's leading social scientists.

Linton was a magnificent teacher. He soon acquired a following of young scholars who did undergraduate work at Wisconsin—John Dollard, John Gillen, E. Adamson Hoebel, Clyde Kluckhohn, Lauriston Sharp, and Sol Tax, among others. Linton in turn was greatly influenced by some of his colleagues at Wisconsin: Kimball Young, the social psychologist; psychologists Clark Hull and Harry Harlow; and ethicists F. C. Sharp and Eliseo Vivas.

Linton spent several summers while at Wisconsin doing archaeological field work in the northern part of the state, in cooperation with the Milwaukee Public Museum. In the summer of 1934 he was in charge of the Laboratory of Anthropology training expeditions to study the Comanche Indians of Oklahoma.

In the 1930s American anthropology was changing rapidly—and Linton was one of the leaders of the change. Archaeology and physical anthropology were separating; new developments in psychiatry and psychology were having a real impact; European sociology and ideas of functionalism were undermining the established viewpoints. In such a milieu, Linton's interests and capacity to synthesize became of utmost importance—he also had the rare ability to express his ideas and syntheses in pure and simple English. He never found it necessary to impose a closed system; total consistency was not one of his goals. He was thoroughly open-ended.

During the 1930s Radcliffe-Brown came to teach at the University of Chicago. Linton deplored his influence on young anthropologists, because he saw the larger concern of a unity of anthropology disappearing before the narrow specializations of social anthropology. His public debates with Radcliffe-Brown led Linton to improve his functional analyses, which took culture and historical factors more fully into account.

In 1936 Linton published *The Study of Man*, which he considered his major contribution to anthropology. (We consider it the major book of the decade.) In it he developed the concepts of status and role, which are now used by all social scientists, summarized a sensible view of functionalism, and saw his next goal: a bridge over the gap between the individual and culture.

Linton went to Columbia in 1937 and the next year became chairman of the anthropology department. There, continued contact with psychologists stimulated his interest in culture and personality and led to a series of joint seminars with Abram Kardiner. They collaborated on *The Psychological Frontiers of Society* (1945). Linton also published *The Cultural Background of Personality,* which contains some views divergent from those of Kardiner.

In 1946 he was invited to Yale as Sterling Professor of Anthropology. It was at this time that he turned to the problems of cultural relativism and universal ethical values.

Linton died Christmas Eve, 1953, from the final of a series of heart attacks that afflicted him over a period of eight years. At the time of his death he left a draft of *The Tree of Culture* with only two chapters missing. From notes, outlines, and tapes the book was finished by Mrs. Linton with the help of several of his colleagues.

INTRODUCTION

Ralph Linton must be regarded as one of the key authors of culture and personality studies. However, his contributions to anthropology are far more extensive than that. Linton's approach to anthropology is overall cultural, and one of the foremost characteristics of his work is the importance he attributes to the individual in all cultural and social studies. It is as a culturist and an individualist that Linton must be seen.

The book from which the first selection is taken is Linton's *The Study of Man* (1936). It is the earliest book represented here that seems absolutely modern to today's readers. Indeed, it is a temptation to reprint the whole thing. We have selected the chapter on status and role—and have had to omit Linton's ideas about functionalism. Such ideas should nevertheless be examined so that we can fit Linton not only into the past but into the work of the people who came later.

For most authors, functionalism has two basic meanings: (1) purpose, so that there is a teleological dimension to functionalism; and (2) the mathematical idea that two things change together, each dependent on change in the other. Linton could not be so simplistic.

Although Linton was writing at a time when functionalism was regarded as an important new development in anthropology, he refused to emphasize the systemic aspect of functionalism, which stressed the interrelationship of institutions, ignoring the individuals. To Linton the term "function" refers to the interrelationship of individuals and nothing else. He attributes to cultural elements four characteristics: form, meaning, use, and function. Form to Linton refers to the total arrangement of behavior patterns; meaning refers to the associations given to a cultural element by members of a society, and it may be subjective and sometimes unconscious; use refers to the utilization of a trait within a cultural context. It follows from this multifaceted approach to cultural elements that Linton was opposed to exclusive or one-sided explanations of cultural reality. Indeed, he once stated that true advancement in anthropology would not come from functionalism alone, but through the synthesis of all perspectives.

The idea of role from the same book is reprinted in the selection that follows.

It has become so much a part of our general culture that it is difficult to realize that it was formulated as a technical term only in the 1930s.

Linton was a great synthesizer—the very quality that made Spencer outstanding. In bringing ideas into new contexts he exposed new meanings. In order to maintain the values he placed on the individual and develop his ideas about the relationship of the individual to culture, Linton had to create a way of associating the individual with society. His sharpening of the concept of status (although Max Weber and many others had written about that) and his development of the concept of role allowed him to talk about human society as being "supra-individual" and still retain his notion of individuals, with their personalities, playing out their roles in a culture.

The workings of a society, according to Linton, depend on the existence of configurations of reciprocity between members of a society. Status refers to positions within structures of reciprocity and can be regarded as the sum of an individual's rights and duties within a society. On the other hand, role refers to the behavioral aspect of status. When rights and duties are acted out, an individual plays his role in society. It follows that role and status cannot be separated—the two terms represent different aspects of the same phenomenon. Role as a concept refers to experienced behavior; and status, to the cognitive aspect of society. This approach, which distinguishes meaning from action, is typical in the works of Linton. We shall see that he also makes use of it in his discussion of cultural elements.

12 STATUS AND ROLE

The functioning of societies depends upon the presence of patterns for reciprocal behavior between individuals or groups of individuals. The polar positions in such patterns of reciprocal behavior are technically known as *statuses*. The term *status*, like the term *culture*, has come to be used with a double significance. *A status*, in the abstract, is a position in a particular pattern. It is thus quite correct to speak of each individual as having many statuses, since each individual participates in the expression of a number of patterns. However, unless the term is qualified in some way, *the status* of any individual means the sum total of all the statuses which he occupies. It represents his position with relation to the total society. Thus the status of Mr. Jones as a member of his community derives from a combination of all the statuses which he holds as a citizen, as an attorney, as a Mason, as a Methodist, as Mrs. Jones's husband, and so on.

A status, as distinct from the individual who may occupy it, is simply a collection of rights and duties. Since these rights and duties can find expres-

---

sion only through the medium of individuals, it is extremely hard for us to maintain a distinction in our thinking between statuses and the people who hold them and exercise the rights and duties which constitute them. The relation between any individual and any status he holds is somewhat like that between the driver of an automobile and the driver's place in the machine. The driver's seat with its steering wheel, accelerator, and other controls is a constant with ever-present potentialities for action and control, while the driver may be any member of the family and may exercise these potentialities very well or very badly.

A *role* represents the dynamic aspect of a status. The individual is socially assigned to a status and occupies it with relation to other statuses. When he puts the rights and duties which constitute the status into effect, he is performing a role. Role and status are quite inseparable, and the distinction between them is of only academic interest. There are no roles without statuses or statuses without roles. Just as in the case of *status,* the term *role* is used with a double significance. Every individual has a series of roles deriving from the various patterns in which he participates and at the same time *a role,* general, which represents the sum total of these roles and determines what he does for his society and what he can expect from it.

Although all statuses and roles derive from social patterns and are integral parts of patterns, they have an independent function with relation to the individuals who occupy particular statuses and exercise their roles. To such individuals the combined status and role represent the minimum of attitudes and behavior which he must assume if he is to participate in the overt expression of the pattern. Status and role serve to reduce the ideal patterns for social life to individual terms. They become models for organizing the attitudes and behavior of the individual so that these will be congruous with those of the other individuals participating in the expression of the pattern. Thus if we are studying football terms in the abstract, the position of quarterback is meaningless except in relation to the other positions. From the point of view of the quarter-back himself it is a distinct and important entity. It determines where he shall take his place in the line-up and what he shall do in various plays. His assignment to this position at once limits and defines his activities and establishes a minimum of things which he must learn. Similarly, in a social pattern such as that for the employer-employee relationship the statuses of employer and employee define what each has to know and do to put the pattern into operation. The employer does not need to know the techniques involved in the employee's labor, and the employee does not need to know the techniques for marketing or accounting.

It is obvious that, as long as there is no interference from external sources, the more perfectly the members of any society are adjusted to their statuses and roles the more smoothly the society will function. In its attempt to bring about such adjustments every society finds itself caught on the horns of a dilemma. The individual's formation of habits and attitudes begins at birth, and, other things being equal, the earlier his training for a status can begin the more successful it is likely to be. At the same time, no two individuals are alike, and a status which will be congenial to one may be quite uncongenial to another. Also, there are in all social systems certain roles which require more than training for their successful performance. Perfect technique does not make a great violinist, nor a thorough book knowledge of tactics an efficient general. The utilization of the special gifts of individuals may be highly important to society, as in the case of the general, yet these gifts usually show themselves rather late, and to wait upon their manifestation for the assignment of statuses would be to forfeit the advantages to be derived from commencing training early.

Fortunately, human beings are so mutable that almost any normal individual can be trained to the adequate performance of almost any role. Most of the business of living can be conducted on a basis of habit, with little need for intelligence and none for special gifts. Societies have met the dilemma by developing two types of statuses, the *ascribed* and the *achieved*. Ascribed statuses are those which are assigned to individuals without reference to their innate differences or abilities. They can be predicted and trained for from the moment of birth. The *achieved* statuses are, as a minimum, those requiring special qualities, although they are not necessarily limited to these. They are not assigned to individuals from birth but are left open to be filled through competition and individual effort. The majority of the statuses in all social systems are of the ascribed type and those which take care of the ordinary day-to-day business of living are practically always of this type.

In all societies certain things are selected as reference points for the ascription of status. The things chosen for this purpose are always of such a nature that they are ascertainable at birth, making it possible to begin the training of the individual for his potential statuses and roles at once. The simplest and most universally used of these reference points is sex. Age is used with nearly equal frequency, since all individuals pass through the same cycle of growth, maturity, and decline, and the statuses whose occupation will be determined by age can be forecast and trained for with accuracy. Family relationships, the simplest and most obvious being that of the child to its mother, are also used in all societies as reference points for the establishment of a whole series of statuses. Lastly, there is the matter of birth into a particular socially established group, such as a class or caste. The use of this type of reference is common but not universal. In all societies the actual ascription of statuses to the individual is controlled by a series of these reference points which together serve to delimit the field of his future participation in the life of the group.

The division and ascription of statuses with relation to sex seems to be basic in all social systems. All societies prescribe different attitudes and activities to men and to women. Most of them try to rationalize these prescriptions in terms of the physiological differences between the sexes or their different roles in reproduction. However, a comparative study of the statuses ascribed to women and men in different cultures seems to show that while such factors may have served as a starting point for the development of a division the actual ascriptions are almost entirely determined by culture. Even the psychological characteristics ascribed to men and women in different societies vary so much that they can have little psychological basis. Our own idea of women as ministering angels contrasts sharply with the ingenuity of women as torturers among the Iroquois and the sadistic delight they took in the process. Even the last two generations have seen a sharp change in the psychological patterns for women in our own society. The delicate, fainting lady of the middle eighteen-hundreds is as extinct as the dodo.

When it comes to the ascription of occupations, which is after all an integral part of status, we find the differences in various societies even more marked. Arapesh women regularly carry heavier loads than men "because their heads are so much harder and stronger." In some societies women do most of the manual labor; in others, as in the Marquesas, even cooking, housekeeping, and baby-tending are proper male occupations, and women spend most of their time primping. Even the general rule that women's handicap through pregnancy and nursing indicates the more active occupations as male and the less active ones as female has many exceptions. Thus among the Tasmanians seal-hunting was women's work. They swam out to the seal rocks, stalked the animals, and clubbed them. Tasmanian women also hunted opossums, which required the climbing of large trees.

Although the actual ascription of occupations along sex lines is highly variable, the pattern of sex division is constant. There are very few societies in which every important activity has not been definitely assigned to men or women. Even when the two sexes coöperate in a particular occupation, the field of each is usually clearly delimited. Thus in Madagascar rice culture the men make the seed beds and terraces and prepare the fields for transplanting. The women do the work of transplanting, which is hard and backbreaking. The women weed the crop, but the men harvest it. The women then carry it to the threshing floors, where the men thresh it while the women winnow it. Lastly, the women pound the grain in mortars and cook it.

When a society takes over a new industry, there is often a period of uncertainty during which the work may be done by either sex, but it soon falls into the province of one or the other. In Madagascar pottery is made by men in some tribes and by women in others. The only tribe in which it is made by both men and women is one into which the art has been introduced within the last sixty years. I was told that during the fifteen years preceding my visit there had been a marked decrease in the number of male potters, many men who had once practised the art having given it up. The factor of lowered wages, usually advanced as the reason for men leaving one of our own occupations when women enter it in force, certainly was not operative here. The field was not overcrowded, and the prices for men's and women's products were the same. Most of the men who had given up the trade were vague as to their reasons, but a few said frankly that they did not like to compete with women. Apparently the entry of women into the occupation had robbed it of a certain amount of prestige. It was no longer quite the thing for a man to be a potter, even though he was a very good one.

The use of age as a reference point for establishing status is as universal as the use of sex. All societies recognize three age groupings as a minimum: child, adult, and old. Certain societies have emphasized age as a basis for assigning status and have greatly amplified the divisions. Thus in certain African tribes the whole male population is divided into units composed of those born in the same years or within two- or three-year intervals. However, such extreme attention to age is unusual, and we need not discuss it here.

The physical differences between child and adult are easily recognizable, and the passage from childhood to maturity is marked by physiological events which make it possible to date it exactly for girls and within a few months for boys. However, the physical passage from childhood to maturity does not necessarily coincide with the social transfer of the individual from one category to the other. Thus in our own society both men and women remain legally children until long after they are physically adult. In most societies this difference between the physical and social transfer is more clearly marked than in our own. The child becomes a man not when he is physically mature but when he is formally recognized as a man by his society. This recognition is almost always given ceremonial expression in what are technically known as puberty rites. The most important element in these rites is not the determination of physical maturity but that of social maturity. Whether a boy is able to breed is less vital to his society than whether he is able to do a man's work and has a man's knowledge. Actually, most puberty ceremonies include tests of the boy's learning and fortitude, and if the aspirants are unable to pass these they are left in the child status until they can. For those who pass the tests, the ceremonies usually culminate in the transfer to them of certain secrets which the men guard from women and children.

The passage of individuals from adult to aged is harder to perceive. There is no clear physiological line for men, while even women may retain their full physical vigor and their ability to carry on all the activities of the adult status for several years after the menopause. The social transfer of men from the adult to the aged group is given ceremonial recognition in a few cultures, as when a father formally surrenders his official position and titles to his son, but such recognition is rare. As for women, there appears to be no society in which the menopause is given ceremonial recognition, although there are a few societies in which it does alter the individual's status. Thus Comanche women, after the menopause, were released from their disabilities with regard to the supernatural. They could handle sacred objects, obtain power through dreams and practise as shamans, all things forbidden to women of bearing age.

The general tendency for societies to emphasize the individual's first change in age status and largely ignore the second is no doubt due in part to the difficulty of determining the onset of old age. However, there are also psychological factors involved. The boy or girl is usually anxious to grow up, and this eagerness is heightened by the exclusion of children from certain activities and knowledge. Also, society welcomes new additions to the most active division of the group, that which contributes most to its perpetuation and well-being. Conversely, the individual who enjoys the thought of growing old is atypical in all societies. Even when age brings respect and a new measure of influence, it means the relinquishment of much that is pleasant.

We can see among ourselves that the aging usually refuse to recognize the change until long after it has happened.

In the case of age, as in that of sex, the biological factors involved appear to be secondary to the cultural ones in determining the content of status. There are certain activities which cannot be ascribed to children because children either lack the necessary strength or have not had time to acquire the necessary technical skills. However, the attitudes between parent and child and the importance given to the child in the family structure vary enormously from one culture to another. The status of the child among our Puritan ancestors, where he was seen and not heard and ate at the second table, represents one extreme. At the other might be placed the status of the eldest son of a Polynesian chief. All the *mana* (supernatural power) of the royal line converged upon such a child. He was socially superior to his own father and mother, and any attempt to discipline him would have been little short of sacrilege. I once visited the hereditary chief of a Marquesan tribe and found the whole family camping uncomfortably in their own front yard, although they had a good house on European lines. Their eldest son, aged nine, had had a dispute with his father a few days before and had tabooed the house by naming it after his head. The family had thus been compelled to move out and could not use it again until he relented and lifted the taboo. As he could use the house himself and eat anywhere in the village, he was getting along quite well and seemed to enjoy the situation thoroughly.

The statuses ascribed to the old in various societies vary even more than those ascribed to children. In some cases they are relieved of all heavy labor and can settle back comfortably to live off their children. In others they perform most of the hard and monotonous tasks which do not require great physical strength, such as the gathering of firewood. In many societies the old women, in particular, take over most of the care of the younger children, leaving the younger women free to enjoy themselves. In some places the old are treated with consideration and respect; in others they are considered a useless incumbrance and removed as soon as they are incapable of heavy labor. In most societies their advice is sought even when little attention is paid to their wishes. This custom has a sound practical basis, for the individual who contrives to live to old age in an uncivilized group has usually been a person of ability and his memory constitutes a sort of reference library to which one can turn for help under all sorts of circumstances.

In certain societies the change from the adult to the old status is made more difficult for the individual by the fact that the patterns for these statuses ascribe different types of personality to each. This was the case among the Comanche, as it seems to have been among most of the Plains tribes. The adult male was a warrior, vigorous, self-reliant, and pushing. Most of his social relationships were phrased in terms of competition. He took what he could get and held what he had without regard to any abstract rights of those weaker than himself. Any willingness to arbitrate differences or to ignore slights was a sign of weakness resulting in loss of prestige. The old man, on the other hand, was expected to be wise and gentle, willing to overlook slights and, if need be, to endure abuse. It was his task to work for the welfare of the tribe, giving sound advice, settling feuds between the warriors, and even preventing his tribe from making new enemies. Young men strove for war and honor, old men strove for peace and tranquillity. There is abundant evidence that among the Comanche the transition was often a difficult one for the individual. Warriors did not prepare for old age, thinking it a better fate to be killed in action. When waning physical powers forced them to assume the new rôle, many of them did so grudgingly, and those who had strong magic would go on trying to enforce the rights which belonged to the younger status. Such bad old men were a peril to young ones beginning their careers, for they were jealous of them simply because they were young and strong and admired by the women. The medicine power of these young men was still weak, and the old men could and did kill them by malevolent magic. It is significant that although benevolent medicine men might be of any age in Comanche folklore, malevolent ones were always old.

Before passing on, it might be well to mention still another social status which is closely related to the foregoing. This is the status of the dead. We do not think of the dead as still members of the community, and many societies follow us in this, but there are others in which death is simply another transfer, comparable to that from child to adult. When a man dies, he does not leave his society; he merely surrenders one set of rights and duties and assumes another. Thus a Tanala clan has two sections which are equally real to its members, the living and the dead. In spite of rather half-hearted attempts by the living to explain to the dead that they are dead and to discourage their return, they remain an integral part of the clan. They must be informed of all important events, invited to all clan ceremonies, and remembered at every meal. In return they allow themselves to be consulted, take an active and helpful interest in the affairs of the community, and act as highly efficient guardians of the group's mores. They carry over into their new status the conservatism characteristic of the aged, and their invisible presence and constant watchfulness do more than anything else to ensure the good behavior of the living and to discourage innovations. In a neighboring tribe there are even individual statuses among the dead which are open to achievement. Old Betsileo men and women will often promise that, after their deaths, they will give the living specific forms of help in return for specific offerings. After the death of one of these individuals, a monument will be erected and people will come to pray and make offerings there. If the new ghost performs his functions successfully, his worship may grow into a cult and may even have a priest. If he fails in their performance, he is soon forgotten.

Biological relationships are used to determine some statuses in all societies. The mere fact of birth immediately brings the individual within the scope of a whole series of social patterns which relate him to his parents, either real or ascribed, his brothers and sisters, and his parents' relatives. The biological basis for the ascription of these family statuses is likely to blind us to the fact that the physiological factors which may influence their content are almost exactly the same as those affecting the content of sex and age statuses. While there is a special relationship between the young child and its mother, based on the child's dependence on nursing, even this is soon broken off. After the second year any adult woman can do anything for the child that its mother can do, while any adult male can assume the complete role of the father at any time after the child is conceived. Similarly, the psychological factors which might affect the statuses of uncle and nephew, uncle and niece, or brother and sister are identical with those affecting the relations of persons in different age or sex groupings. This lack of physiological determinants may be responsible in part for the extraordinarily wide range of variation in the contents of the statuses ascribed on the basis of biological relationships in various societies.

Actually, the statuses associated with even such a close biological relationship as that of brother and sister are surprisingly varied. In some societies the two are close intimates. In others they avoid each other carefully and cannot even speak to each other except in the presence of a third party who relays the questions and answers. In some systems the eldest child ranks the others regardless of sex and must be respected and obeyed by them. In others the question of dominance is left to be settled by the children themselves, while in still others the youngest child ranks all those who preceded him. Practically every possible arrangement is represented in one society or another, suggesting that we have here a free field for variation, one in which one arrangement will work quite as well as another. The same sort of wide variation is found in the content of all the other statuses based on blood relationship with the exception of those relating to mother and child, and even here there is a fair degree of variation. There are a number of societies in which there is a more or less conscious attempt to break up the child's habits of dependence upon the mother and to alienate the child from her in order to bring it into closer association with its father's relatives. The child is taught that its mother really is not a member of the family, and hostility between mother and child is encouraged.

Not only do the statuses assigned by different societies to persons standing in the same blood relationships vary markedly, but there is also a high degree of variation in the sorts of blood relationships which are recognized and used as reference points for the assignment of status. Some societies, like our own, tend to recognize only close relatives and to be vague as to the reciprocal rights and duties of any relationships more remote than first cousin. Others select the line of the mother or the father and utilize relationships in this line to remote degrees while ignoring all but the closest relationships in the other line. In a very few cases, relationship in both lines is recognized to remote degrees, with a consequent assignment of status. Where this is the case the statuses based on relationship may actually include a whole tribe and determine the mutual rights and duties of all its members. Thus in certain Australian groups recognized blood relationships are extended to include not only the whole tribe but numerous individuals in other tribes as well. It is said that when a stranger visits such a tribe the old men investigate his genealogy until they find some point in common with one of the genealogies within their own group. When such a point of contact has been established, they can determine the relationship of the newcomer to all the various members of their own group and assign him a series of statuses which immediately fit him into the social body. If they are unable to find such a common point of relationship, they usually kill the stranger simply because they do not know what else to do with him. They have no reference points other than blood relationships by which statuses might be assigned to him.

There is another type of biologically conditioned relationship which is recognized in practically all societies. This is the relationship arising from the more or less continuous sexual association of individuals, i.e., marriage. The real importance of such associations lies in their continuity, in social recognition, and in the new series of blood relationships to which they give rise through the offspring which they produce. Casual or temporary sexual associations usually receive only a negative recognition from society, being ignored when not actually reprehended. Patterns may be developed to govern the behavior of individuals in such casual associations, but these patterns are usually extremely limited in their scope. They only affect the individuals who are directly involved and do not establish new statuses for the members of the families to which the contracting parties belong. Marriage, on the other hand, always establishes a series of such statuses. Thus the parents of a man and his mistress do not become parties to any reciprocal pattern of rights and duties, while the parents of a man and his wife always do become parties to such a pattern.

While relationships arising from sexual association are intrinsically different from those deriving from blood relationships, the two types have become interrelated in all societies. Blood relationships are everywhere used as reference points for delimiting the group of individuals within which marriage relationships may be contracted. This regulation is usually of a negative sort, certain blood relatives being prohibited from marrying but at the same time permitted freedom of choice among individuals not standing in these relationships. However, there are a fair number of societies in which such regulations assume a positive aspect. In such societies a man is not only forbidden to marry certain female relatives, such as his mother or sister, but is also enjoined to marry within a particular group of female relatives, as his mother's brother's or father's sister's daughters. In some cases these prescriptions are so strong that a man may have no alternatives except to marry a particular woman or remain a bachelor.

The causes which underlie such limitations on marriage, technically known as incest regulations, are very imperfectly understood. Since these regulations are of universal occurrence, it seems safe to assume that their causes are everywhere present, but biological factors can be ruled out at once. Close inbreeding is not necessarily injurious. Even when hereditary defects in the strain may make it so, its deleterious results require a long time to manifest themselves. Moreover, the average uncivilized group is small and rarely marries with outsiders. Within a few generations the heredity of its members becomes so uniform that there is little if any biological difference between marriage with a first cousin and marriage with a fourth cousin. Neither are purely social explanations of incest regulations altogether satisfactory, since the forms which these regulations assume are extremely varied. The prohibition of marriage between mother and son is the only one universally present. Marriage between father and daughter is permitted in at least one society, the Azande, while several societies have recognized or even required marriage between brother and sister. This last seems to occur mainly in small ruling groups and seems to be designed to keep privilege and rank rigidly within the group. Thus in Hawaiian royal families brother and sister were required to marry and to cohabit until an heir had been born, although after this they might separate. It seems possible that there are certain psychological factors involved, but these can hardly be strong enough or constant enough to account for the institutionalization of incest regulations. This is proved by the fact that cases of incest between all the prohibited degrees do occur in all societies and that all societies have certain preventive regulations which would be unnecessary if the rules were self-enforcing. Incest regulations, once developed, are a valuable tool for preventing conflicts in the statuses held by individuals, but it is a little hard to imagine their invention for this purpose. They have probably originated from a combination of all these factors.

The bulk of the ascribed statuses in all social systems are parceled out to individuals on the basis of sex, age, and family relationships. However, there are many societies in which purely social factors are also used as a basis of ascription. There seems to be a general tendency for societies to divide their component individuals into a series of groups or categories and to ascribe to such categories differing degrees of social importance. Such divisions may originate in many different ways. They may grow out of individual differences in technical skill or other abilities, as in the case of craft groups or the aristocracies of certain Indian tribes, membership in which was determined by the individual's war record. They may also originate through the conscious formation of some social unit, such as the first college fraternity or the first business men's club, which is usually followed by the formation of a series of similar units organized upon nearly the same lines. Lastly, such divisions may originate through the subjugation of one society by another society, with the subsequent fusion of both into a single functional unit, as in the case of Old World aristocracies deriving from conquest. Even when the social divisions originate in individual differences of ability, there seems to be a strong tendency for such divisions to become hereditary. The members of a socially favored division try to transmit the advantages they have gained to their offspring and at the same time to prevent the entry into the division of individuals from lower divisions. In many cases these tendencies result in the organization of the society into a series of hereditary classes or castes. Such hereditary units are always used as reference points for the ascription of status.

The factor of social class or caste rarely if ever replaces the factors of sex, age, and biological relationship in the determination of status. Rather, it supplements these, defining the roles of individuals still more clearly. Where the class system is strong, each class becomes almost a society in itself. It will have a series of sex, age, and relationship statuses which are peculiar to its members. These will differ from the statuses of other classes even when both are determined by the same biological factors. Not only is the commoner debarred from the occupation of aristocratic statuses, but the aristocrat is similarly debarred from the occupation of common statuses. It may be mentioned in passing that this arrangement is not always entirely to the advantage of the members of the upper class. During the nineteenth century the aristocratic prohibition against engaging in trade condemned many aristocrats to genteel poverty.

Feudal Europe offers an excellent example of the ascription of statuses on the basis of social class. A man born into the noble class could look forward to being a bachelor, in the technical sense of a boy beginning his training for knighthood, a squire, and lastly a knight and lord of a manor. The performance of the roles connected with the final status required a long and arduous training both in the use of arms and in administration. The woman born into the same class could also look forward to being lady of a manor, a task which entailed special knowledge and administrative ability fully on a par with that of her husband. A man born into the peasant class could look forward only to becoming a tiller of the soil. He would pass through no statuses corresponding to those of bachelor or squire, and although he might be trained to the use of weapons, these would be different weapons from those used by the knight. The woman born in this class could only look forward to becoming a simple housewife, and her necessary training for this status was limited to a knowledge of housekeeping and baby-tending. The third class in medieval society, the burghers, also had its own series of statuses, the boy looking forward to becoming first an apprentice and then a master training apprentices in turn. All these divergent, class-determined statuses were mutually interdependent, and all contributed to the successful functioning of medieval society. The noble provided protection and direction, the peasant provided food, and the burgher took care of trade and manufactures.

Ascribed statuses, whether assigned according to biological or to social factors, compose the bulk of all social systems. However, all these systems also include a varying number of statuses which are open to individual achievement. It seems as though many statuses of this type were primarily designed to serve as baits for socially acceptable behavior or as escapes for the individual. All societies rely mainly on their ascribed statuses to take care of the ordinary business of living. Most of the statuses which are thrown open to achievement do not touch this business very deeply. The honored ones are extremely satisfying to the individuals who achieve them, but many of them are no more vital to the ordinary functioning of the society than are honorary degrees or inclusions in "Who's Who" among ourselves.

Most societies make only a grudging admission of the fact that a limited number of statuses do require special gifts for their successful performance.

Since such gifts rarely manifest themselves in early childhood, these statuses are, of necessity, thrown open to competition. At the same time, the pattern of ascribing all vital statuses is so strong that all societies limit this competition with reference to sex, age, and social affiliations. Even in our own society, where the field open to individual achievement is theoretically unlimited, it is strictly limited in fact. No woman can become President of the United States. Neither could a Negro nor an Indian, although there is no formal rule on this point, while a Jew or even a Catholic entering the presidential race would be very seriously handicapped from the outset. Even with regard to achievable statuses which are of much less social importance and which, perhaps, require more specific gifts, the same sort of limited competition is evident. It would be nearly if not quite impossible for either a woman or a Negro to become conductor of our best symphony orchestra, even if better able to perform the duties involved than any one else in America. At the same time, no man could become president of the D.A.R., and it is doubtful whether any man, unless he adopted a feminine *nom de plume*, could even conduct a syndicated column on advice to the lovelorn, a field in which our society assumes, *a priori*, that women have greater skill.

These limitations upon the competition for achieved statuses no doubt entail a certain loss to society. Persons with special talents appear to be mutants and as such are likely to appear in either sex and in any social class. At the same time, the actual loss to societies through this failure to use their members' gifts to the full is probably a good deal less than persons reared in the American tradition would like to believe. Individual talent is too sporadic and too unpredictable to be allowed any important part in the organization of society. Social systems have to be built upon the potentialities of the average individual, the person who has no special gifts or disabilities. Such individuals can be trained to occupy almost any status and to perform the associated role adequately if not brilliantly. The social ascription of a particular status, with the intensive training that such ascription makes possible, is a guarantee that the role will be performed even if the performance is mediocre. If a society waited to have its statuses filled by individuals with special gifts, certain statuses might not be filled at all. The ascription of status sacrifices the possibility of having certain roles performed superlatively well to the certainty of having them performed passably well.

When a social system has achieved a good adjustment to the other sectors of the group's culture and, through these, to the group's environment, it can get along very well without utilizing special gifts. However, as soon as changes within the culture or in the external environment produce maladjustments, it has to recognize and utilize these gifts. The development of new social patterns calls for the individual qualities of thought and initiative, and the freer the rein given to these the more quickly new adjustments can be arrived at. For this reason, societies living under new or changing conditions are usually characterized by a wealth of achievable statuses and by very broad delimitations of the competition for them. Our own now extinct frontier offered an excellent example of this. Here the class lines of the European societies from which the frontier population had been drawn were completely discarded and individuals were given an unprecedented opportunity to find their place in the new society by their own abilities.

As social systems achieve adjustment to their settings, the social value of individual thought and initiative decreases. Thorough training of the component individuals becomes more necessary to the survival and successful functioning of society than the free expression of their individual abilities. Even leadership, which calls for marked ability under conditions of change, becomes largely a matter of routine activities. To ensure successful training, more and more statuses are transferred from the achieved to the ascribed group, and the competition for those which remain is more and more rigidly delimited. To put the same thing in different terms, individual opportunities decrease. There is not an absolute correlation between the degree of adjustment of a social system to its setting and the limitation of individual opportunity. Thus if the group attaches a high value to individual initiative and individual rights, certain statuses may be left open to competition when their ascription would result in greater social efficiency. However, well-adjusted societies are, in general, characterized by a high preponderance of ascribed over achieved statuses, and increasing perfection of adjustment usually goes hand in hand with increasing rigidity of the social system.

Americans have been trained to attach such high values to individual initiative and achievement that they tend to look down upon societies which are rigidly organized and to pity the persons who live in them. However, the members of a society whose statuses are mainly prescribed are no less happy than ourselves and considerably more at peace. It would never occur to an orthodox Hindu that he was to be pitied because he could not change his caste. His whole life is arranged and oriented in terms of caste, and if he ever envies the members of other castes the emotion is on a par with our own envy of some animal's obvious comfort or satisfaction. His religion provides him with rationalizations of the whole system and with an explanation of his presence in the caste as a result of his soul's evolutionary status. It also holds out the hope of a better position in his next incarnation if his work in this is properly done. As a caste member his social and even emotional needs are amply provided for. There are even a small series of achievable statuses open to him if he is ambitious. He may become a member of the caste's governing body or the best goldsmith in a group of goldsmiths, admired by those whose admiration is based on a thorough knowledge of the work. In any struggle for advancement he knows exactly who his competitors are and what it is he wants to attain. He is much less likely to be disappointed than a man living under our own system, where every other man may be a rival and where the limits for ambition are not socially defined.

In India the idea of ceremonial pollution makes social intercourse between the castes difficult; but in societies which have strong class lines, without this idea, the presence of classes actually makes for ease of social intercourse. Here also, classes serve to delimit fields of competition. Where there can be no rivalry in vital matters and no social climbing, snubbing becomes unnecessary and indeed meaningless. Social status is something fixed and understood by both parties, so it can be ignored under circumstances where it has no direct bearing. Members of different classes can form friendships which are the stronger because their interests can never clash and they can evaluate each other as human beings with a clarity unclouded by fear of rivalry. Membership in a rigidly organized society may deprive the individual of opportunities to exercise his particular gifts, but it gives him an emotional security which is almost unknown among ourselves. Which of these is best or which makes for the greatest happiness to the greatest number the reader must decide for himself.

INTRODUCTION

The main focus of Linton's work was always on the idea of culture and the individual creating and reacting to it. His work with Abram Kardiner on the modal personality was of primary importance.

Yet, in spite of his close association with studies of culture and personality and the neo-Freudianism of Kardiner, Linton was strong in his assertions of the primacy of culture. In Linton's view, most of the problems an individual has to face in life have previously been solved by his culture. All the individual does is learn these solutions—every generation molds its cultural configurations all over again. Basically, however, an individual is shaped by his culture, not only in his cognitive abilities, but also in his personality. It is culture, according to Linton, that shapes the basic type of personality in every society and that molds the statuses typical of a society within certain ranges.

13 CULTURE AND NORMALITY[1]

THE NATURE OF CULTURE

Culture has often been defined as "the sum total of human achievement." This is a philosophical definition which is of no use for the purposes of this book. Moreover, it is hardly necessary to say that the concept of culture used here does not refer to the ordinary usage. designating "the finer things of life" such as reading Browning and playing the piano. Throughout this book I will use the concept of culture in its technical, anthropological sense.

Since the old and long-established definition of culture as "the sum total of human achievement" is operationally useless for the anthropologist, he

---

Reprinted from George Devereux, ed., *Culture and Mental Disorders* (Springfield, Ill.: Charles C Thomas, 1956), pp. 3–14, courtesy of the publisher and the editor.

speaks of cultures, in the plural. When the anthropologist uses culture in the singular, he refers to processes which are to be found in many cultures and can therefore be regarded as characteristic of Culture as a distinct phenomenon.

Each society has its own culture, which can be defined briefly as its "way of life." The tendency which some social scientists and historians fall into of using the terms "society" and "culture" interchangeably is regrettable, and results in considerable confusion. Actually, society is simply an organized group of individuals. Culture, on the other hand, is an organized group of ideas, habits and conditioned emotional responses shared by the members of a society. In practice, society and culture are always linked, since, without culture, a group of individuals is not a society but merely an aggregate. A big football game may bring together thousands of people united by a common interest and reacting in unison to stimuli, such as long end runs or a touchdown, but when the game is over, the aggregate dissolves. Societies must be together long enough to develop techniques of living and working together. The organization of *all* societies and the existence of *any* society as such depends upon culture. It is the sharing of ideas, habits, attitudes, etc., which makes it possible for a group of individuals to organize and to function as a society. To keep this distinction quite clear, we might say that the agencies involved are different. Societies are people, while cultures exist on a psychological and behavioral level. Both societies and cultures are continua. They persist through time and have normally a much longer life span than any individual. Both are largely self-perpetuating. This persistence of both society and culture is, from the point of view of society, based upon the *training* of the individuals; when viewed from the point of vantage of the individual, it is based upon *learning.* Hence learning mechanisms are of tremendous importance in any attempt to correlate personality and culture. This point should be borne in mind in anticipation of our subsequent discussion of certain basic problems in the formation of the ethnic or basic personality.

The structuring of society is actually an aspect of culture, since society, as a continuing organization, is made up of positions, or statuses, which are occupied by a series of successive individuals or groups of individuals, whose relations to other positions, or other statuses, can only be defined in terms of the reciprocal rights and duties that exist between the holders of statuses.

We may say, then, that cultures have both content and organization, both of which are present at every point in time and also throughout the entire time dimension. The content of cultures consists of the ideas and behavior of society's members, though this is not what we think of when we are dealing with Culture as a concept. We must therefore stop for a moment and consider the manner in which this concept comes into being, or is constructed. Since there are no identities anywhere in the universe, no two situations, no two behaviors, etc., are identical. In fact, the general semanticists will even point out that no one is the same individual at any two instants of his life. Yet, even though there is no real identity anywhere, neither is there infinite variety. What we do observe is a wide range of similarities. Thus, although no two situations which serve as stimuli to individual behavior are ever identical, many situations are very much alike, and it is in terms of these similarities that human beings operate by equating different situations with the forms of behavior that, customarily, go with them.[2] Briefly stated, while the behavior of the members of a society will vary with respect to a particular type of situation, these variations will be within a definite and finite range. This *range* is what we call the *real* culture pattern, as distinct from Culture as a construct.

The generalized picture which the ethnographer gets from a series of behaviors, or responses to a particular situation, is what I call the *culture construct pattern.* I hasten to add that I am using the term "pattern" in accordance with its long-established usage, which is more limited than is the way in which it was used by Dr. Ruth Benedict in her *Patterns of Culture* (1934). The sum total of these construct patterns, which we record as "the culture," is what we anthropologists mean when we are talking about the culture of a particular society. These construct patterns represent the *modes of variation* in the behavior of the members of that group in response to what *they* consider similar situations.[3]

The point to be retained is that the *real pattern* of behavior is, in every case, not a single point; it is a *range* within which observed behaviors fall. This range is a *particular finite range*, and, by falling within this range, behavior becomes effective socially and realistically, with respect to a particular type of situation.

It is this generalized picture which I call the *culture construct pattern*, and what is included in it is the *mode of the range of variations at the point of maximum frequency*. As we shall see, these construct patterns are of great importance for personality studies.[4]

Except for a few brief references to the problems of status and position, I spoke in the preceding pages as though all members of a society were mutually interchangeable, i.e., as if all of them defined situations by and large in the same manner and responded to them more or less similarly. This, needless to say, is not the case. The individual participates in the culture of his society to the extent required by his social roles. Every culture includes a series of ideas, values, and patterns of behavior with which all members of the culture must be familiar. Language is one of these.[5]

In addition to such patterns, familiar to all members of a society or culture, there are many other skills which are known only to a limited number of individuals, even though these skills contribute materially to the well-being of the entire society. The skill of the physician is an example of such special knowledge, possessed by one group of persons within a culture.

The content of the culture of any homogeneous society can be divided into three categories, on the basis of the extent to which the elements within each category are shared by the society's members.

First, there are those ideas, habits and conditioned emotional responses which are common to all sane, adult members of the society. We will call these *Universals*. It must be understood that this terminology applies only to the content of a particular culture. An element classed as a Universal in one culture may be completely lacking in another. To this category belong such elements as the use of a particular language, the tribal patterns of costume and housing, and the ideal patterns for social relationships. This category also includes the associations and values which lie, for the most part, below the level of consciousness but which are, at the same time, an integral part of the culture.

Second, we have those elements of culture which are shared by the members of certain socially recognized categories of individuals but which are not shared by the total population. We will call these *Specialties*. Under this head come the patterns for all those varied but mutually interdependent activities which have been assigned to various sections of the society in the course of its division of labor. In all societies certain things are done by, or known to, only a designated part of the population, although they contribute to the well-being of the whole. Thus all women within the tribe will be familiar with certain occupations and techniques, while the men will be familiar with a different series. As a rule, the men will have only a rather vague general knowledge of the things which belong in the women's province and vice versa. Under this head there can also be classed the activities which the society has assigned to special craftsmen or functionaries, such as the smith, carpenter, doctor and priest. . . . The uninstructed do not know the full details of procedure, but everyone has a general knowledge of how [these things are done] and will be resentful of inferior workmanship and suspicious of innovations. Any departure from the accustomed procedure or failure to achieve the expected results brings an emotional reaction.

Third, there are in every culture a considerable number of traits which are shared by certain individuals but which are not common to all the members of the society or even to all the members of any one of the socially recognized categories. We will call these *Alternatives*. The elements of culture which may be included in this class have a wide range, varying from the special and often quite atypical ideas and habits of a particular family to such things as different schools of painting or sculpture. Aside from the nature of participation in them, all these Alternatives have this in common: they represent different reactions to the same situations or different techniques of achieving the same ends. The cultures of small societies living under primitive conditions usually include only a moderate number of such *Alternatives* while in a culture such as our own they are plentiful. Examples of such *Alternatives* for ourselves would be such things as the use of horses, bicycles, railroad, automobiles and airplanes for the single purpose of transportation; our variety of teaching techniques, or our wide range of beliefs and attitudes toward the supernatural.

Beyond the limits of culture there lies still a fourth category of habits, ideas and conditioned emotional responses; that of *Individual Peculiarities*. These include such things as one person's abnormal fear of fire, due perhaps to some accident of his early experience. . . . Every individual has certain peculiarities of this sort, whether he is a member of a primitive tribe or a modern urban community, and the sum total of such individual differences within any society is enormous. Individual Peculiarities cannot be classed as a part of culture, in the sense in which the term is ordinarily used, since they are not shared by the society's members (Linton 1936: 272–274).

It is obvious from the foregoing that the relation between the individual and the culture of his society is a reciprocal one. He is both shaped by it and, in turn, contributes to its shaping. We shall, first of all, consider in some detail the cultural influences exerted upon the developing individual—in other words, how the behavior of *other* individuals, acting in a culturally prescribed way, influences the development of the growing child.

Broadly speaking, the influences can be grouped under three headings:

(1) *What other people do to the individual.* This category includes, first and foremost, techniques of child care and child training.

(2) *What other people consciously teach the individual.* This category includes the whole range of what is commonly referred to as "instruction."

(3) *The behavior of other people, as observed by the individual.* This category is frequently ignored in studies of child development, especially in those which focus their attention too exclusively upon actual, observed technical procedures in child care. Devereux (1945), in particular, has systematically stressed the ability of the child to compare the treatment *he* receives with that received by *others*, and he has emphasized that not the least important aspect of this comparison is the emotional tone characteristic of the adult who performs a culturally standardized child training manipulation.[6] It seems self-evident that the child's comparison between his experiences and those of other children is an important factor in the development of its self-evaluation and in determining the emotional affect characteristic of concrete parent-child relationships.

Cultural influences on the formation of the normal ethnic or basic personality are particularly important in the early years of life, though the exact period during which the maximum influence is exerted is still undetermined. Recent research seems to indicate that the predominant role assigned to early infantile experiences by certain schools of psychoanalysis is not supported by evidence: nursing, toilet training, etc., seem to be much less significant as determinants of personality than was formerly supposed. Such at least appear to be the conclusions to be drawn from the findings of Sewell (1952), and Orlansky (1949). However, it should be stressed that these studies were focussed primarily on actual *technical operations,* without a correspondingly detailed study of the maternal attitudes which accompanied these performances. Unobserved or ignored differences in attitudes accompanying the motor acts of nursing, weaning or toilet training may, as Devereux suggests, be far more crucially important than are actual nursing schedules, the date at which the baby is weaned, or the suddenness with which it is toilet trained. In addition, the conformity or nonconformity of the infantile experiences of a given child with the usual experiences of other children in a given society probably also has a deep-going influence on the manner in which actual nursing, weaning and toilet training experiences affect the child's development. Thus, I recall Devereux telling me that a Plains Indian analytic patient of his, who, by Western standards, was weaned late—i.e., at the age of one year—felt a savage resentment over having been denied the breast too soon, since by the standards of the culture children are nursed longer than this (1951).

Directly related to this problem is the matter of the critical period in development during which cultural factors exert the greatest influence on personality formation. Many anthropologists have agreed with certain schools of psychoanalysis that the crucial time in personality formation is early childhood. However, I am inclined to agree with Devereux's recent views (1953) that cultural influences may have their greatest effect during the oedipal period, at least with regard to the formation of the *socially most relevant segment* of personality. He states his views on this point as follows:

The effort to understand the basic personality *primarily* in terms of *baby* and *infant* care techniques is a futile one. In stressing almost exclusively the experiences of the pre-oedipal stage of psychosexual development, one tends to disregard the very crucial experiences of the oedipal periods, and, *a fortiori,* of the pubertal period, during which the oedipal conflict is once more faced and, in many cases, more or less successfully resolved. Indeed, the oedipal and pubertal stages of life are of special significance for the adjustment of the individual to society, since the manner in which the oedipus complex comes into being and is resolved determines to a large extent not merely man's manipulation of his culture, but, above all, the nature of his relation to other human beings, *as real persons and not merely as sources of purely narcissistic pre-oedipal gratification.* In addition, it is self evident that, as the child matures, the segments of the culture pattern mediated to it through cultural experience expand rather rapidly. Thus the child becomes increasingly capable of seeing—or, at least, of effectively sensing—the cultural forest behind the trees of discrete, atomistic experiences with individual culture traits. In other words, only the broadening of the child's cultural experiences enables it to detect the pattern, ethos, value system, means-end schema, etc., which give a meaning and a structure to his discrete experiences. When seen in this context, the thesis that baby, infant, and child-care techniques exert an *appreciable* influence on the personality only if they are closely connected with, and easily derivable from, the tribal ethos, ceases to be merely an axiom and becomes susceptible of verification. Indeed, the adaptation and adjustment of the baby, infant or child to the expectations and training techniques of its environment, and its response both to its training and to those who train it, can, during the pre-oedipal period, only be narcissistic and sadomasochistic. Hence, they can lead neither to genuine relations to real human beings, nor to a meaningful and constructive manipulation of the segments of culture which these persons mediate to the infant. Only after the child is old enough for these early impressions, expectations, rules, etc., to acquire a meaning and reveal a pattern, can they be *accepted*—though with certain pregenitally determined distortions—instead of being merely *endured,* and only then can the human beings who reared it become *persons,* instead of remaining "partial objects" which are merely sources of narcissistic gratifications, or of blows to the infant's self-esteem.

It is therefore felt that the decisive force in personality formation is the ethos, which gives meaning to discrete culture traits, rather than the individual culture traits, e.g., training techniques, themselves. The determining force of the latter depends primarily on the extent to which they reflect the over-all ethos and pattern of the total culture. This means that the basic personality is formed *primarily* during the oedipal and pubertal periods, *whose resolving eliminates or sublimates earlier pregenital traits and urges* (1953:45–46).

Another point of importance is whether the original start given the budding personality in childhood is, or is not, supported by subsequent experiences. Some types of influence unquestionably continue throughout life. In a stable culture this influence is rather toward the reinforcement of already established personality patterns than toward the evolving of new patterns. By contrast, in a rapidly changing culture, the change in influences and the difference between the personality-shaping influences experienced in childhood as contrasted with those experienced in adulthood, as a result of cultural change, can be an appreciably disorganizing factor, as all acculturation studies tend to show.

It is implicit in what we just said that cultural influences upon the individual are paralleled by the influence which the individual exerts on culture. This latter type of influence manifests itself chiefly through the acceptance or rejection of new cultural items. Indeed, it is chiefly in adulthood that the individual is free and able to accept or reject new ideas, new appliances, etc., thus determining whether or not these new cultural items will be integrated into his society's culture.[7]

NOTES

1. Much of the research for [*Culture and Normality*] was done under a grant given by the Wenner-Gren Foundation for Anthropological Research to the Institute of Human Relations at Yale University to be administered by Dr. Linton. Grateful acknowledgment is made for this generous aid in the study of personality and culture.

2. The classical example is, of course, the legal process, which operates extensively in terms of precedent, though no two legal situations arising in life are truly identical.

3. A very homely example of this is the initial way in which some of the Plains Indian tribes dealt with the newly imported horse. The Crow called it "the magic dog" [the dog being their only real domestic animal] and promptly hitched the horse to the travois, a means of transporting goods which consisted of two poles, the ends of which dragged on the ground, while the tops were crossed over the back of the beast of burden. This device was designed for the dog as a transport animal. Likewise, when the horse was first imported into the Near East, where the long established beast of burden was the ox, the horse was primarily used as a draft animal and therefore, as we learn from Homer, was driven not with a whip but with a goad.

4. The logical problems involved in the *construction* of these patterns from observed behavior has been discussed in some detail by Devereux (1945, 1953).

5. It may be argued, of course, that in some societies there is a special "women's language" or "children's language," or else "directional speech," the vocabulary and structure of which are determined by whether one addresses a superior, an equal or an inferior. These facts are correct, of course, but do not invalidate the thesis that language is shared by all members of a society. Indeed, even though a culture may contain special vocabularies for the use of women, this language must be understandable to the men. The most obvious example is the fact that even though, ordinarily, the American *male* has no occasion to *use* the expression "my husband," he understands it perfectly well.

6. In a recent paper, written in response to criticisms of her views on swaddling, Margaret Mead (1954) likewise reaches the conclusion that the impact of child care is greatly influenced by the attitude of those who perform these technical operations.

7. Needless to say, this applies quite as much to new items borrowed from other cultures through acculturation as to new items resulting from the internal development or progress of the individual's own culture.

REFERENCES

Benedict, Ruth
    1934   *Patterns of Culture*. Boston: Houghton Mifflin.

Devereux, G.
  1945   "Logical Foundations of Culture and Personality Studies," *Transactions of the New York Academy of Sciences,* Series 2, 7:110–130.
  1951   *Reality and Dream: The Psychotherapy of a Plains Indian.* New York: International Universities Press.
  1953   "Cultural Factors in Psychoanalytic Theory," *Journal of the American Psychoanalytic Association,* 1:629–655.

Linton, R.
  1936   *The Study of Man.* New York: Appleton-Century.
  1940   *Acculturation in Seven American Indian Tribes* (ed.). New York: Appleton-Century.

Mead, M.
  1954   "The Swaddling Hypothesis: Its Reception," *American Anthropologist,* 56:395–409.

Orlansky, H.
  1949   "Infant Care and Personality," *Psychological Bulletin,* 46:1–48.

Sewell, W. H.
  1952   "Infant Training and the Personality of the Child," *American Journal of Sociology,* 58:150–159.

Abram Kardiner 1891–

BACKGROUND

Abram Kardiner was born in New York City and educated in its schools. He received his B.A. from City College in 1912. Going on to Cornell, he earned his M.D. in 1917, the same year that he married.

After World War I, Kardiner served an apprenticeship with Freud. He returned to the United States to join the faculty at the New York Psychoanalytic Institute in 1922, remaining there until 1944. In 1923 he took a post at Cornell as instructor in psychiatry, which he held for six years before moving to a similar post at Columbia University.

During the 1930s Kardiner engaged primarily in the clinical practice of therapeutic psychoanalysis. In the course of his work he developed an interest in the interrelations of personality and culture, particularly in the effects of particular projective systems on the development and perpetuation of particular cultural institutions. He published some of his results in such papers as "The Role of Economic Security in the Adaptation of the Individual" (1936) and "Security, Cultural Restraints, Intra-Social Dependences and Hostilities" (1937).

In 1936 he organized a seminar at the New York Psychoanalytic Institute in which Edward Sapir, Ruth Benedict, and Ruth Bunzel were participants. They analyzed a number of cultures from the literature and one, the Zuñi, from verbal accounts of Benedict and Bunzel. In 1937 the seminar moved to Columbia University, where it was joined by Linton, Cora DuBois, and Carl Withers, all of whom submitted ethnographic data for Kardiner's psychocultural analysis. The seminar resulted in two major publications—*The Individual and His Society* (1939), which attempted to forge a technique for synthesizing the material gathered at the seminars; and, with Linton, *The Psychological Frontiers of Society* (1945), which described a set of techniques for studying reciprocal relations between culture and personality. Kardiner sought to demonstrate, for example, that religious institutions of tribal peoples were projections of a "basic personality structure" formed, not by the action of an unconsciously remembered historical trauma (as Jung and some of Freud's followers would have it), but by the more observable traumas produced by child-training practices. This approach was later extended and cast into quantitative form by John Whiting.

In 1939 Kardiner was made associate professor in the Department of Anthropology at Columbia, a post he retained until 1952 at the same time that he was assistant clinical professor of psychiatry and then, after 1949, full clinical professor.

In 1951, together with Lionel Ovesey, another New York psychiatrist, he published *The Mark of Oppression,* a book based on the psychodynamic investigation of twenty-five biographies and conceived and written on the premise that group characteristics are adaptive in nature and therefore not inborn but acquired.

Sex and Morality was published in 1954, and the following year Kardiner became director of his own psychoanalytic clinic. He had not lost his interest in anthropology, however; in 1961 he wrote *They Studied Man* with Edward Preble. This book presents, through biographies, the birth and growth of the social scientific tradition within an adaptive framework, focusing on Charles Darwin, Herbert Spencer, Edward Tylor, James Frazer, Émile Durkheim, Franz Boas, Bronislaw Malinowski, Alfred Kroeber, and Ruth Benedict. The major hypotheses of these innovators were related—of course, but the documentation is important—to the ethos of the times and their specific personal experiences.

In 1961 Kardiner left New York for Emory University, where he was a research professor in psychiatry until he retired in 1968.

INTRODUCTION

We pointed out in our introduction that we have considered Freud to be part of the *Zeitgeist* of a period of anthropological development rather than a direct contributor to anthropology. Although Freud's impact has been manifold—in the work of such scholars as Geza Roheim, Warner Munsterberger, Erik Erikson, Margaret Mead, and Bronislaw Malinowski—Abram Kardiner must be credited more than any other author for detaching Freudian theory from its Western base and its theoretical emphasis on the sex drive. Kardiner, unlike Roheim, emphasized the importance of personal adaptation over drives as a basis from which to approach psychodynamics.

According to Kardiner there are four Freudian approaches to social phenomena, which have been developed by a variety of authors. The first of these approaches, held by Freud himself as well as Roheim, Theodor Reik, and Munsterberger, claims that what is unconscious for modern man was part of the conscious for primitive man. Kardiner holds that this is an untenable position. The second approach, the libido theory, claims that the sexual drive shapes man in basically the same manner in all societies. Kardiner finds this view devoid of environmental and cultural context, and therefore unacceptable. The third Freudian approach discussed by Kardiner is the work of Harry Stack Sullivan, Karen Horney, and Erich Fromm—and this he dismisses far too cavalierly.

The fourth school is Kardiner's own. His approach stresses adaptation of the individual to the culture and environment.

The concrete contributions Kardiner made to anthropology are his concept of basic personality structure and his views on primary and secondary institutions. The relationship between personality and culture had puzzled students for a long time before Kardiner, and the most commonly accepted solution to the problem had been the idea that the pattern of "a culture" influences the behavior of individuals. This vague and reductionist view was replaced by Kardiner's concept of the basic personality structure, which refers to the common tools of adaptation that a society extends to its members. These, which are to be found in all members of a society and are culture specific, are acquired through basically standardized child-rearing techniques, differing in each society. Common childhood experiences mean that the basic personality structure of a culture becomes manifest.

14 THE TECHNIQUE OF PSYCHODYNAMIC ANALYSIS

Psychology can be of use to the social sciences only if its use can be reduced to a technique which is verifiable, teachable, and can be corrected or changed in the face of new evidence. Systematized opinions in technical language are no more binding in psychology than in any other field. Generalizations which codify the obvious are not techniques capable of yielding new information.

The predecessor of this book was an adventure in technique. This technique was the outgrowth of a few simple observations. After a culture like that of Tanala had been presented in detail, certain correspondences were noted. In Tanala the relation of the individual to the ancestral gods seemed strikingly like the relation of the child to the parent in this culture. There was the same emphasis on obedience. The first conclusion was that obedience to a duty was universal. We found as we studied the same correlation in Marquesas there was no emphasis on childhood obedience. The folklore in Tanala showed a typical father-son relationship, in which jealousy was repressed and a passive feminine attitude appeared in its place. In Marquesas myths father-hatred was absent, and in lieu of this father-hatred there was strong fear, hatred, and distrust of the woman. In other words, according as the experiences varied, so did the products of the *projective systems* in folklore and religion. This gave us our first clue, and the same procedure was used on more and more phenomena.

As we proceeded we found it necessary to have a cultural unit to describe the various practices and customs, and for this purpose the concept *institution* could be used operationally. The institutions were therefore treated as the vehicle through which specific influences were brought to bear on the growing individual. If therefore we again look at the correlation in the previous paragraph, we find that if childhood disciplines constitute one order of institutions then religion and folklore comprise another. We called the former primary and the latter secondary. Also there was something created in the individual by his childhood experiences which formed the basis for the projective systems subsequently used to create folklore and religion. This group

Reprinted from Abram Kardiner, *The Psychological Frontiers of Society* (New York: Columbia University Press, 1945), pp. 23–46, by permission of the publisher.

of nuclear constellations in the individual was designated the *basic personality structure.* This concept proved to be only a refinement of a concept long since used descriptively by Herodotus and Caesar and known as *national character.* The term *basic personality structure* was chosen to obviate the lack of clarity in the terms group, national, or social character, because a group can no more have a common character than it can have a common soul or pair of lungs. Moreover the constellations identified in basic personality structure were not finished character traits, but a matrix in which these character traits develop. For example, in Alor we find distrust as a permanent feature of basic personality; but this distrust may show itself in any number of different character traits. What was new and important about this concept was not its name, but the technique of its derivation and the introduction of a genetic viewpoint into sociology. The concept of basic personality structure thus became a powerful operational implement, for through it we acquired a precise means of delineating the interrelationship of various social practices through their compatibility or incompatibility with certain constant identifiable human needs and drives.

Whereas this operational scheme was made possible by the ability to identify remote derivations of basic experiences through the use of projections, further experience with new cultures and new material in the form of biographies showed this scheme to be oversimplified and decidedly incomplete.

The first difficulty arose in connection with the use of the concept *institution.* This concept was originally defined to connote "a fixed mode of thought or behavior which can be communicated, which enjoys common acceptance and the infringement of or deviation from which creates some disturbance in the individual or group." This definition did not work in practice. It was found that in some societies (e.g., Alor) some of the most important sources of projective systems were not institutionalized but were related to other practices which were. Poor maternal care in Alor was an accident resulting from the mother's having to work all day in her fields. The basic institution is that the mother works in the fields all day; the neglect of the children is not institutionalized, though almost universal. There are no sanctions against good care of the children. We can therefore amend the concept primary institution to read: *primary institution or related practices, whether institutionalized or not.* To substitute the word *practices* for institutions would not be any more satisfactory than either *institutions* or *mores.* Moreover the latter terms would imply the backing by a specific rationale, which, though often the case, is not universal. Institutions should be defined to mean what people do, think, believe, or feel. Their locus is within the human personality; and they have an accommodative or adaptive function. In connection with primary institutions, the question frequently arose concerning their origin. This question could never be answered. Linton[1] pointed out that this question was not pertinent to the present endeavor. The primary institution is treated as the taking-off point for the individual, not for the culture. The origin of an institution has nothing to do with the effect it creates on the growing individual.

A second technical difficulty arose in connection with the identification of the products of the projective systems, called secondary institutions. Here much confusion arose because many institutions could not be classified as either primary or secondary. This fact alone, that there were institutions outside and independent of the projective system, indicates either that our formulation of the determinants of basic personality structure is incomplete or that institutions exist outside its range. This is very likely to be the case with institutions or practices of purely rational origin.

The important point about this classification into primary and secondary institutions is that it is closely bound to the concept of basic personality structure. It means that institutions cannot be compared with each other or establish relations with each other directly. This relationship is mediated by the personality.

In the earlier work we' had no opportunity to check the validity of basic personality against actual biographical material and social changes. The only cultures that have a long recorded history and plenty of biographical material are the oriental cultures and our own. But these could not be confidently approached until certain elementary problems had been solved.

The use of the concept basic personality structure therefore includes the following questions: (1) What are the key integrational systems and their institutional background? (2) Are the effects of normative institutions the only sources of basic personality structure? (3) How can the concept be tested against biographies and how could the inevitable variations of personal character in the same culture be reconciled with it? (4) What are the effects of knowledge empirically derived and verified by criteria outside the range of the "common sense" of the culture upon institutions of projective origin? In other words, what are the relations of scientific knowledge to the basic personality? The last is of course significant for the study of our own society, where science has so evidently altered the social utility of the projective systems employed in religion.

THE KEY INTEGRATIONAL SYSTEMS

Any selection of key situations which influence personality formation is bound to be incomplete. We are prejudiced in our selection by our experience with individuals in our society and particularly by the constellations which predominate in neuroses. This is admittedly a bias. We have already surveyed a sufficient number of cultures to know that constellations important in our society are not universal, and some situations in our society are overlooked because they do not act as impediments to development in our culture but do in others. If we had no opportunity to examine any culture other than our own, we would never surmise that maternal care and nurture are exceedingly important to the cohesiveness of the society and so would never look to maternal care as a key situation. This we can learn only by comparison with other cultures where maternal care is inadequate. By this time we have studied ten cultures intensively and have a sufficient number of contrasts to indicate a workable list.[2]

Maternal care
    Constancy of attention—or abandonment
    Feeding regularity
    Surrogate parents—activities of
    Help in learning processes—walking, talking
    Pre-walking and post-walking care
    Weaning—age, methods
    Sphincter control—when inducted, associated ideas (cleanliness, obedience, etc.)
Induction of affectivity
    Solicitation of response; handling, play, fondling
    Maternal attitudes to child—care or neglect, honesty to children or practice of deception
    Insistence on obedience and presence or absence of reward systems—superego formation
Early disciplines
    Consistency
    Punishment—reward systems—when punishment is inflicted, place of choice for inflicting bodily pain, etc.
Sexual disciplines
    Masturbation, interdicted or permitted, attitudes of elders—neglect, ridicule, castration threats, tolerance, or used as placebo
    Playing with opposite sex—permitted openly or tacitly, attitude of elders
Institutionalized sibling attitudes
    Rivalries encouraged or suppressed
    Aggression—controls
Induction into work
    Age—duties, rewards, degree of participation
    Differences between sexes
    Attitudes to work—division of economic responsibilities
Puberty
    Alteration of participation in society
    Premature or deferred.
    Parental aid in preparation for marital status
Marriage
    Mating mores
        Difficulties in mating created by parents
    Position of woman, freedom of choice
    Economic status requirements
    Fidelity requirements, freedom of divorce
Character of participation in society
    Status differentiation
    Function differentiation
    Life goals
Factors that keep the society together
    Superego formation

Coöperative and antagonistic phases
Permitted and controlled activities—sanctions
Projective systems
Religion
Folklore
Reality systems, derived from empirical or projective sources
Arts, crafts, and techniques
Techniques of production
Differentiation of function
Participation in distributed products—status differentiation, degrees and controls of prestige

The technique of applying these principles can be illustrated by taking a particular combination of conditions. Society A is one in which the mother cares diligently for the infant for two weeks after birth, and thereafter only two hours in the morning and two hours in the evening, the rest of her time being spent in the gardens raising vegetable food. For the major portion of the day the care of the infant is left to older siblings or others. The child probably is given enough food, but many tensions are unsatisfied for long periods. No systematic teaching of talking or walking occurs. The child shifts for itself. It is masturbated to keep it quiet. Add to this, teasing and later deliberate misrepresentation. To this situation someone may say: "What does a child or infant know, and therefore what difference does it make? It gets enough food, doesn't it?" This view overlooks the fact that the infant has no ready-made reactions; that by the conditions described a specific environment is created for the child; that its needs and tensions are constant, and if they are relieved with little effort or discomfort on the part of the child, one integrational system will follow; while if the tensions are unrelieved, the resulting constellation will be different. The child will eventually develop a definite attitude to the parent, to itself, and to the tensions which cause it so much discomfort. These attitudes are adapted to the particular conditions and tend to become habitual, automatic, and compounded. Moreover the constellations formed under these conditions can be predicted with a fair degree of accuracy. The constellations thus created will not all be alike, but the range can be predicted.

A child under these conditions cannot develop an undivided feeling or attitude to the mother. He must feel some hatred, some distrust, some isolation, a sense of having no one whom he can positively count on. Moreover the functions which develop under the influence of good care, confidence in himself, interest in the outer world, enterprise—these will all suffer. Sexuality is stimulated, but it is detached from the image of an affectionate person who stimulates it.

The next question that arises is whether these attitudes need remain permanent. They need not, if other factors are introduced into the child's life which would tend to counteract them. However, if they are not counteracted, they tend to continue. If the child as he grows encounters influences which tend to reinforce these reactions, by the time he is an adult they constitute his character. By that time there is formed a definite pattern (for perceiving human relationships and dealing with them) which is totally unconscious, and a definite and specific system of projections is likely to spring from these early experiences. When adult he may invent a story, a pure fabrication, in which he may detect the operation of these constellations formed in childhood. These constellations may be recovered in dreams in distorted forms.

We have had up to this point a series of inferences about the probable effects of certain formative institutions. How can this guess be substantiated or contradicted? If our hypothesis is correct, namely that these conditions in childhood become consolidated and form a basis for subsequent projective use, then we can expect to find some evidence of it in all projective systems —religious, folklore, and perhaps other institutions. In other words, if we know how the basic personality is established, we can make certain predictions about the institutions this personality is likely to invent. If we follow the particular personality created by the above mentioned conditions, we expect to find folk tales dealing with parental hatred, with desertion by parents; we expect to find a religion devoid of any concepts dealing with reward for good deeds or punishment for bad ones. We expect no emphasis on the idea of reinstatement into the good graces of the deity through suffering. We expect no idealization of the deity.

The utility of the concept of basic personality structure does not end here. We find institutions other than folklore and religion derived from that same source. If we could do no more than predict types of religion and folklore, the usefulness of this procedure would be very limited and would be entirely inadequate for our society where the projective systems have been largely deflected from use in religion. Since the personality has in it elements of distrust toward parents, we could not expect this lack of trust to be limited to the parents, but extended to others. When the whole chain of elements entering into this particular integrational system is completed, we would also expect to find bad relations between the sexes, frequency of divorce, and also institutionalized obstacles against divorce.

The more the ethnographer tells us about the traits of these people, the greater the number of institutions that we can place as derivatives of this *basic personality structure*. For example, we hear that the people discussed above have no interest in the arts and their skills rate very low. We also hear that they surrender easily to illness. These traits fall easily into place once we know the basic personality structure; but these particular traits *could not be predicted*, and there are likely to be some that cannot be accounted for even when we know the basic personality.

We cannot therefore maintain that the prediction value of the concept of the basic personality structure is its chief merit; we do not know the possibilities of early conditionings accurately enough to make predictions on a large scale. We may be able to do so when we have comparative studies on about fifty cultures, and even then original and unique details are likely to surprise us.

The chief merit of this concept is that it offers us a basis for examining the structuralizations in society and for relating institutions to each other, not directly but through the medium of the individuals who compose it.

This is as far as our procedure can take us, given only the accurate description of institutions. Conclusions made from this source alone can have but the status of guesses, more or less approximate. There is another way not only to check on our conclusions but to furnish us with a fresh source of information—that is, the biographies of the individuals in the society.

WHAT ADDITIONAL FACTORS ENTER INTO BASIC PERSONALITY STRUCTURE?

If we were to stop our consideration of basic personality structure with those systems which, though they originate in actual experience, become the unconscious basis for projective systems, we could be justly accused of omitting several very important sources of "learning," which play a prominent role in the adaption of the individual. There is a large contingent of data imparted to the child by direct tuition.[3] To this group belong all explanations about the outer world, how to deal with it, and the relations of man to it, and the conventionalized attitudes which govern the relations of people to each other. These systems are consciously inducted, much of their content being subject to demonstrations of a kind, and in some instances are modifiable.[*]

The introduction of this category of "learned" systems brings with it unavoidable difficulty. In the previous section [of *The Psychological Frontiers of Society*] we described an aspect of common sense derived from actual experiences in interpersonal relationships which form the basis of projective systems, some of which are used to explain the outer world. Now we introduce a system taught directly. These two systems cannot possibly be incompatible if they are used to explain the outer world. If they were, one would tend to disappear, and the system eliminated would of necessity be the one most amenable to change, the conscious system. More likely than not a taught system at complete variance with the projective system could not be accepted. This simple idea can be illustrated as follows: Suppose that a missionary attempts to convey to a primitive people the idea of redemption through suffering and atonement. This is presented as a bit of reality, and hence it is "taught" as such. Whether or not this idea has any significance to a primitive man depends on whether it has a certain plausibility according to his own experience. If he has not himself experienced the logical sequence of committing an act interpreted as a misdeed, being punished for it, and then being reinstated, the proposition as stated must remain meaningless. For it is merely a projection, rationalization, and generalization from the basic experience.

What we are saying therefore is that the entire projective system tends to exercise a polarizing influence over all taught reality systems that are presented to the individual; there are bound to be inconsistencies and exceptions.[4] But all aspects of the reality systems do not by any means fall under the influence of the system. One can in fact establish a series in which the projective system has less and less influence. It naturally has the least influence on manipulation of crafts and techniques. But other systems, which are taught also, fall decidedly under the influence of the projective system. Let us take two instances, one in which a drive is involved and another in which no drive is concerned.

The first can be taken from a very common injunction in both primitive and civilized society. It is the proposition: "If you masturbate then you will become insane" (or some other dire consequence). For the moment we are less concerned about the disposition of the somatically determined tensions than we are about the form in which the injunction is implemented. The consequence of insanity is stated as a fact, which is a ready-made rationalization to justify the prohibition. The impulse to masturbate is thus accompanied by an anxiety which is channelized into a specific direction. The danger is made to appear as a real danger, for if it did not arouse terror it would hardly act as a deterrent.

This reality aspect occupies an important place in the conflict which centers about masturbation. If the activity in question is abandoned, it may undergo repression, and the only manifestation of its existence may be the anxiety about insanity. This can be represented graphically thus:

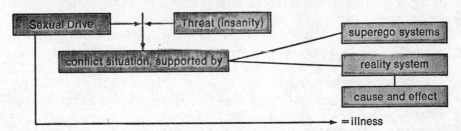

Thus the fear of illness may emerge as the only manifestation of the original impulse to satisfy a somatic sexual tension. The place of the reality aspect (masturbation causes insanity) is therefore shown to be related to the super-ego (conscience) systems created in a society.

This is an opportune place to discuss how extensively such as idea as the one described above can become systematized. This belief about the pernicious effects of masturbation persisted until about a half century ago. Before the advent of bacteriology almost every illness was attributed to masturbation, and long treatises based on "scientific" empirical observations were written in proof. This is an illustration of scientific rationalization. The unknown factor in this complex rationalization is the unconscious insistence that masturbation should be punished. The scientific data were merely organized to support this assumption.

There are other types of reality systems taught by direct induction which are unrelated to any drive. The Pomo and Navaho are both taught at an early age to bury excreta lest they be used as bait. This is an anxiety which can cling to the individual for a lifetime. But it is natural to assume that an anxiety of this kind would be reinforced by strong interpersonal tensions. In childhood, however, this belief becomes a part of the reality system, and the anxiety is controlled by appropriate defenses and precautions which become institutionalized. Thus the excretory function becomes associated with a special set of ideas laden with anxiety. These ideas are different from those we encountered in Tanaia, where the associated idea was neither cleanliness nor fear of poisoning, but obedience. Several tension-release systems depend on which of these ideas becomes associated with the excretory function. The anxiety system just described can be represented thus:

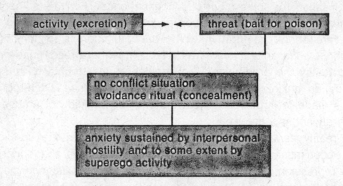

A system like the one described can outlive by centuries the original circumstances that gave it origin, whose meaning can no longer be reconstructed. Among certain tribes of the Navaho the practice of concealing excreta has disappeared owing to the influence of whites. It would be interesting to know whether the disappearance was facilitated by the diminution of interpersonal hostilities and mutual suspicion.

In relation to these systems the question of the place of primitive taboo systems arises. The taboo systems may differ in origin. For the greater part they are taught as a part of the external reality system, in much the same way as we are taught to avoid a live electric wire. The relation of taboo systems to the culture as a whole cannot be precisely defined. We would expect them to be compatible with the basic personality structure. At the same time, as in our culture, many taboos are likely to persist in spite of the fact that no precise relationship to basic personality structure can be established.

In this hierarchy of systems in the basic personality structure there are the purely rational or scientific systems, subject to direct demonstration and discarded when proven wrong. This hierarchy of systems in basic personality structure can be arranged as follows:

1. Projective systems based on experience with the aid of rationalizations, generalizations, systematization and elaboration. To this category belongs the security system of the individual and superego systems, that is, those dealing with conscience and ideals.
2. Learned systems connected with drives.
3. Learned systems in which no drives are involved but ideas associated with activities.
   Groups 2 and 3 lay the basis for specific psychosomatic tension release routes.
4. Taboo systems, all learned as part of reality.[5]

5. Pure empirical reality systems, subject to demonstration.
6. Value systems and ideologies (which cut across all the previous systems).

At this point it is important to decide the position of *value systems.* They cannot be placed in any of the categories above. Some value systems belong to ideals, for example, honesty; some value systems derive from ideas associated with activities and hence directly taught, for example, cleanliness. Others derive from a social complex which precipitates out qualities having a high value at one time and not at another. Such a value is "freedom," which can never be defined in absolute terms but only in relation to the particular conditions which create an issue about it. No Comanche or Alorese would have any conception of freedom in the sense in which it is commonly used today in our society.

The question of ideologies presents the same difficulties as value systems. They are compounds of projective systems, in the interest of which empirical evidence is mobilized, and have therefore the same structure as rationalizations.

These are all constituents of the basic personality structure but they are not homogeneous; they vary in the degree of conscious representability and in the degree to which they are modifiable. Group 1 is completely unconscious and can only be identified through its projective manifestations, from which source it can be traced back to the institutions which gave it origin. This system is least susceptible to modification except by way of the institutions which gave it origin. All the other systems are subject to validation by some kind of empirical demonstration. Group 5 is subject to direct demonstration; the others are held in place by a chain of rationalizations of which the following is typical. A native of Alor tells us that his younger brother falls ill and is given appropriate medicine. The boy does not recover. His father, a seer, divines that he has failed to get well because a pair of carabao horns were stolen from the hearth. The carabao horns are replaced and the boy gets well. This is a closed system of rationalizations that cannot be beaten. If the boy had failed to get well with the replacement of the horns, some other explanation would have been offered. The manner in which these rationalizations are defended by the natives is fantastic in its tenacity. The commonest of all rationalizations used is that "everything was done right, but it was too late." This leaves the system intact. Why are these systems maintained on such "flimsy evidence" concerning their efficacy? Because they cannot be readily replaced and because a bad system has better anxiety-staying powers than no system at all. Systems like this present a never-ending, vicious logical cycle.

The viability and modifiability of these systems (1 to 5) are indicated in the order they are presented. This order is important in attempting to evaluate the extent to which diffusion of culture can take place. The most easily diffused are the manipulative and purely empirically derived reality systems, and manipulative techniques whose utility value is directly discernible. The least modifiable are those systems which are unconscious and those in which only parts are conscious, the rest being maintained by deep-rooted emotional interests.

THE BIOGRAPHY AS SOCIAL SOURCE MATERIAL

Constructing a biography is one of the most difficult of psychological enterprises. As in the description of a society, we have here a wide range of things to look for. Dollard[6] has demonstrated several points of view from which the life history can be documented, each varying in emphasis and selection. This much is certain: we cannot leave to chance or to the narrator's discretion or prejudices the selection of material he gives us. Dollard defines this undertaking as "a deliberate attempt to define the growth of a person in a cultural milieu and to make theoretical sense out of it." Taking an adequate biography involves a knowledge of the culture in which the subject lives; the pattern of his personal accommodations to it, created by the specific circumstances of his environment throughout life; and finally some theoretical scheme for arranging the data.

It is important to know the culture in which the individual lives because everything he tells us is attuned to its values and emphases. The subject does not, however, know his own culture as an arbitrary arrangement of institutions. He is a product of it and he has no insight into what made him what he is. He is only aware of those places in his cultural milieu which gave him specific frustrations, gratifications, or other vicissitudes. Much that he tells us he takes for granted. For example, he has a working conception of the outer world which he began to learn about in his earliest perceptions. He has been "taught" certain ready-made interpretations of its nature and how to deal with it. This is what may be called his "reality system," and this he has in common with all other members of his society. Much of what he tells us is in terms of this particular reality system. If we do not understand this, we can never follow what he is trying to impart to us. We must, in other words, understand the particular environment in which he operates and the particular methods he has for dealing with it.

The vicissitudes he describes to us as his life story include much about the human beings in his milieu and the specific relations he has with them. We also note that this individual has a specific *character*; he has specific links and antipathies, aptitudes, sympathies, avoidances, etc. We may also note that when similar circumstances arise in his life he tends to react to them always in a similar way. Thus Mangma whenever he encounters a difficult situation runs away from it. He has a specific attitude toward women, not always contingent on the specific attributes of the woman. He has specific interests, such as gardening, and we note this fact because it is an unusual interest for a man in Alorese society. He has certain attitudes toward himself; he is sensitive, and tends to impress us with abilities he does not have. When we describe his character we are describing attitudes toward himself and toward others and behavior patterns which tend to be repetitive; so when we know his character, we know his idiosyncratic traits, what to expect of him, and how to get on with him when we need to.

But we cannot be guided exclusively by what he tells us about himself. We must observe him in the actual process of living from day to day. If we do not, we shall miss some very important data. Moreover we must try not only to follow him in his daily activities, we must know, if it is possible, what he dreams at night. We must assume that our subject will try to put as good a face on his story as possible, and hide all he regards as damaging. If possible, he must be given an incentive to tell about himself honestly. And if an interpreter is present who is a member of the same society as the subject, we are bound to get a highly edited account. However if we observe his day-to-day activity, note his reactions to the ethnographer, and cross-check on his dreams, we can distill from all this a reliable story of his life and a dynamic picture of his personality.

When we have all this data we face the most difficult task of all, the theoretical framework in which it will be encompassed. We cannot use a purely descriptive scheme, for a string of qualifying epithets like "sensitive," "anxious," will not help us much. We must use a dynamic scheme and use it genetically so that we can consistently trace the growth of the individual and so appreciate his motivations. We must know the experiences he had which made him adopt certain modes of behavior and not others. In a large measure we have dealt with this problem in the derivation of the basic personality structure, and there is not much need to repeat it.

For the purpose of substantiating the thesis of this book one biography in a culture will hardly suffice. We must have an adequate sampling of sex, age, and status differentiations, and no arbitrary number can be regarded as adequate. We need a sufficient number to make adequate comparisons, but it is more important to find where the deviations are. As we progress in our study of biographies we note the banal fact that no two in the same culture are alike. But the deviants are as important to us as the norms.

The uses of the biographies are numerous. Here is our first chance to see whether our guess about the kind of personality a given set of institutions will create is at all approximated in reality. We can reverse the procedure and operate from personalities to institutions. It is only in a biography that we can see how the various institutions are functionally articulated.

Next comes the question of comparing the results of the biographies. The comparison with the basic personality structure will establish a sufficient number of points at which aberrations may appear. These aberrations do not vitiate but rather confirm the procedure of deriving basic personality structure. If, for example, we study eight biographies in a comparative way and discover that no two describe the same situation with respect to parental care, then we expect these differences to be registered in the personality structure in a very specific way. If Rilpada has in his character structure a few uncommon traits, such as a delicate conscience, a willingness to get on with his friends, a tendency to forgive and forget, and a tendency to idealize his father, we know that some influence not typical in this culture has been operating. We can locate this in the form of a powerful, solicitous, and intelligent father who devoted much time to his son.

The points at which we note character variations indicate not only differences in personal fate, but also differences in cultural practices. In a culture where maternal neglect is the rule, the exceptional case who gets good maternal care will show distinctive characteristics. This comparative aspect of biographical analysis is likely to be most informative where status differentiations include not only differences in the dominant interests of the individual but also differences in the factors which make for specific character formations. Thus in studying basic personality structure in our culture new differentiations must be made not only for sex and age, but especially for status. Current struggles in the modern world cannot be understood without a study of specific tensions arising out of the anxieties and claims of each status.

REALITY SYSTEMS AND CULTURE CONFIGURATIONS

In our survey of psychological techniques we found psychoanalysis best suited to our needs because it established certain laws governing mental processes not accounted for by other psychologies. A great deal of stress was laid on the genetic aspects, because if we must study integrational systems we must begin at the beginning. The value of the whole genetic approach lies in its being able to show us how certain integrational systems come into being; and we made it our special concern to track down those systems we designated as projective, in contrast to those of taught or rational origin on the basis of which scientific systems are built. In every society studied we found evidences of these two systems. The empirical reality systems we found in the manipulation and making of tools, the knowledge of planting, and so forth; the projective systems in religion, folklore, and many other systems.

These two types of mental process depend upon different orders of experience. The differentiating feature is not that one has an emotional constituent and the other not. Both have emotional components. Rational thinking is driven by curiosity and has such goals as mastery and utility. The emotional component of projective thinking is made up of all those affects which accompany human relations. In the systems built on a projective basis the conclusions drawn do not depend on any fixity in nature, but on sequences which are contingent on institutionalized practices conveyed by parents or other people in the environment of the growing child. Hence our interest in the genetic aspects. The experiential base of a projective system is generally forgotten; its only remains in the personality are to be found in the conditioned perceptions, meanings, affects, psychosomatic reactions, and behavior. It is a feature of such projective systems that they are capable of extension upon situations which have no actual resemblance to the experiences on which they were based. This may be called *symbolic extension*. Projective systems are established under the influence of the pleasure principle, avoidance of pain, or expediency. The conclusions on which projective systems are based are not inherent but are the record of traumatic experiences. Projective systems are therefore excrescences developed from nuclear traumatic experiences within the growth pattern of the individual. Just as the character structure of the individual has a large component of these projective systems, so the basic personality in any culture contains them. The fewer the anxieties in the growth pattern, the simpler the projective system (Comanche). It is these systems which have given rise to the complaints about the "irrational" factors in society. Their purpose is adaptive, to relieve the mutilating effect of painful tensions. In practice they often miscarry in ways which will be specified.

The interconnections between these two systems are not simple.[7] In infancy the two are connected at the point of maternal care. Good care which fosters growth leaves the child more enterprising and self-confident, free to exercise curiosity and manipulative capacities. Too great dependency on the mother paralyzes the development of curiosity and manipulative skills. It is not infrequent that one finds very pathological characters with brilliant intellects; yet the intellect is saddled with the task of solving these problems involving the projective systems, without success. But the record of the attempt is written into the symptoms the subject brings. Among primitive peoples it does not follow that where maternal care is good, the child is always enterprising. Other factors are apparently responsible. The two systems can be represented thus:

SCHEMATIC REPRESENTATION OF PROJECTIVE SYSTEMS

Nuclear experiences which define apperceptions and emotionally directed interests, e.g., punishment for delinquency

Abstraction and generalization
e.g., "If I am obedient I will suffer no pain."

Projection and systematization
e.g., "I am ill, therefore I have wronged."

Rationalization = ideology = a system to overcome tensions

"There is a supreme being who observes my behavior. He has the attributes of omnipotence and omniscience, etc. If I do wrong I will be punished. If I suffer I will be reinstated." Once this system is accepted as a reality, any number of rational systems can be devised to "prove" it, to modify it, or to render it workable.

SCHEMATIC REPRESENTATION OF RATIONAL SYSTEMS

Perception by sense-organ combinations and motor coördinations
= meaning = utility

Objective = to exploit, avoid, manipulate, destroy

Attitude to object = interest, curiosity, systematization
= knowledge = science

No projective mechanism used and no repression required for correction; no social obstacles put in its way today (there were in the Middle Ages)

The projective and rational systems each furnish a basis for cultural configurations or institutional patterns. We are much less concerned with the morphological aspects of these institutional patterns than we are with the problem of dynamics of social change and of social stability. All societies have institutional patterns based on both projective and rational systems; no culture can be dominated by either one to the exclusion of the other. But it makes a great deal of difference for cultural stability and change whether the institutions are polarized toward either one or the other system.

Furthermore, in the practical thinking of everyone in every society a mental mechanism is used which is compounded of both projective and rational components—that is, rationalization. This term merely means a logical or "reasonable" series of arguments to support an unconscious motive, drive, or interest. The simplest form of rationalization is the "explanation" offered by a person who has just carried out a post-hypnotic suggestion. The most complicated forms of rationalization are to be found in social ideologies. This does not mean that every ideology is a rationalization; it can approximate the scientific only when freed of bias or defense of interest.

If we consider a culture like Tanala, dominated by projective systems, we find that these systems define the nature of the outer world, man's personal fate, and supernatural beings and methods for dealing with them. These were all derived from constellations established in connection with training begun in infancy and consistently followed throughout life. This is the psychological definition of *animism*, a term which has by usage been narrowed to connote the projection of human attributes on inanimate objects. This latter phenomenon is the most naïve expression of this tendency to projection, but by no means its only form.

The importance of this whole system is its derivation from *actual experience*. Why do the Tanala believe that no remedy is effectual unless accompanied by some compulsive ritual? Because their actual experience has led them to the conviction that all good things happen after obedience to some arbitrary command. This constellation is created in the Tanala by experience beginning at six months, when they are expected to have complete sphincter control and are beaten if they fail, and is followed by similar disciplines throughout their normative years. This means in effect that a conclusion of limited application is generalized to encompass the whole of reality and that this reality is evaluated and reacted to on the basis of a pain-avoiding principle, obedience, which not only furnishes no reliable picture of external reality but prevents the formation of any other. The fact is that in this culture obedience actually brings rewards in the form of comfort and security. This nuclear constellation, a logical deduction, creates an unconscious base from which any number of projective systems can arise; hence it becomes a part of their common sense; and to expect that phenomena in the outer world will follow the same pattern is not unreasonable, but it is not rational empiricism. The Tanala also have a firm belief in fate, which can to some extent be altered by magic. This idea, which looks like pure "ideology," is likewise derived from experience. The authority of the father is absolute and status is so fixed within the family that there is no escape from it. This situation is so universal that anyone who did not hold this belief would be decidedly out of contact with the socially effective realities. But this relationship between the derivatives and the original experience is completely unconscious. Such a belief in fate is not held by the Alorese; their experience conduces to no such idea. In other words the ideologies of primitive peoples are generalizations and abstractions of actual experience and not the product of unbridled imagination. That these ideologies give the impression of being wanton and arbitrary is due to the fact that we do not have the key to understand them.

There is still another important sequel to these considerations among the Tanala. This personality with its peculiar common sense is attuned to a particular set of institutions and adjusted to a particular type of economy accompanied by special techniques suited to the environment—the dry cultivation of rice. When the exhaustion of jungle compelled the abandonment of the dry-rice method for the wet method, a great many unpleasant consequences followed. For the first time there was a scramble for the fertile valleys, the family organization was broken up, and the old communal ownership of land gave way to private ownership. Since the personality was not geared to these new conditions, the consequence was that there was a great increase in anxiety, in mutual rivalry and hostility, in black magic and hysterical illnesses, created by the absence of adaptive techniques in the face of new and insistent realities.

We can draw the conclusion from Tanala that a culture in which external reality is evaluated by projective systems, the adaptability of the society is much impaired The external reality can be manipulated in a limited number of ways if perceived in accordance with the analogy of an all powerful father and an obedient child. When the father's power gives out, as it did in Tanala, only disorganized aggression and panic could ensue. The individual who deals with the outer world on the basis of obedience can develop no sense of responsibility for his own fate and cannot therefore develop those manipulative powers of which he is capable. The intensity and cruelty of an exacting superego is no surrogate for responsibility for oneself. All the suffering the individual inflicts on himself as a consequence of superego demands have no relevancy to the external world, or to the difficulties within the social order.

Another illustration of the principle found in Tanala occurs in medieval cosmology. Thomism is a conception of the world based upon the same principle as in Tanala—a powerful father whose commands are natural law. But here a new factor is introduced in the system, not present in the Tanalan cosmology, a conception of natural law. But it stands under the aegis of divine command. This idea is compounded of two elements: of an empirical reality system—natural law—and a projective system; but this empirical system is drawn under the influence of projective constellations. It may be called a compromise. But if natural law is only another of the many instances of divine will, the attitude of the individual to natural law is not modified. It is no invitation to manipulate natural law to the needs of the individual; nor does it augment his sense of responsibility in dealing with natural law. As long as natural law is only a new manifestation of divine will, then one's security does not depend on manipulating reality, but on submission to divine will. The projective screen may be mistaken for reality and important changes in adaptation will be attempted by way of this projective screen, while the social realities are either ignored or they drift aimlessly.

When natural law was finally freed from its contingency on divine will—and the lives of Galileo, Descartes or Pascal are witness to the fact that this was not an easy task—it is reasonable to expect that it would have altered man's conception of himself, his relations to deity, and to the outer world. Under the impact of these alterations in responsibility for oneself, a new freedom to exercise investigative and exploratory impulses must take place. With it there must be a redefinition of the relations to deity, a new allocation of the superego or conscience mechanisms. In the face of these alterations new social changes were bound to follow. But all this does not necessarily mean that natural law was interpreted to mean that the social order itself came under the domination of scientific thinking. The social order would have to improvise its organization as it went along under the impact of the new interpretation of the outer world and its mastery.

We have noted some high points in the accomplishments of that movement in Western history which began with the Renaissance, through the Reformation, down to the present. The social order was never regarded as coming under the influence of natural law. The abortive attempts to make natural law apply to the social order in the so-called Age of Reason were unconsciously polarized in the direction of justifying the expediencies which accident had provided.

The social order, and its institutions, is the source of all projective systems, and when a conception of external reality is based upon this source it is not to be expected that we can derive from it any implements which can serve us as a critique of the very sources from which it originates. This is like trying to lift oneself by the bootstraps. The only hope lies in subjecting the social order to the same kind of critique that was applied to the outer world with so much success. This and only this would mean a triumph for scientific over projective techniques.

That a society which is dominated by projective techniques lacks adaptability can be amply illustrated by contrasts found in the cultures described in this book. In Comanche we have a culture which is least dominated by projective thinking. Their religion is devoid of complex ideologies, though a superior being is recognized. These thin ideologies are completely devoid of any power to affect the stability of the society. Their mythology is largely a carry-over of the culture from which it originated. Otherwise it consists largely of the exploits of former war chiefs. The poverty of projective systems is due not to their lack of imagination but rather to the accidental fact that in the growth pattern of the individual no serious tension points are created which cause the formation of compensatory systems to overcome the mutilation of expressive impulses, sexual or otherwise. In Alor we see a culture in which projective systems are poor in organization because too many and confusing tension points are created in the growth pattern so that the individual is overwhelmed by them and can never create any effective organization. In our culture, like that of Tanala, we find a very rich excrescence of projective systems which are highly organized and capable of influencing stability because the growth pattern has numerous tension points, though not enough to overwhelm the individual. There are also in our culture, as in Comanche, strong ego fortifying factors.

When a society has a highly elaborate projective system, there is the strong temptation to change adaptation by alterations in the projective screen. This is generally no more effective than for a patient who has a phobia for subways to use the bus instead; doing so does not remove the phobia and leaves all the factors which cause the phobia untouched. Such adaptive maneuvers abound in the history of Western society. In certain areas the adoption of Christianity originally was such a maneuver. It altered the projective system, but left completely alone the social realities which cause this particular system to be formed, just as the cult of Osiris left the sufferings of the agrarian proletariat alone while it offered an illusory deferred compensation in the form of a boon collectable after death. In short the adaptation is crippled by the apparent validity of illusory compensations as compared with real ones. The fantasy or projective screen hides social realities, and one cannot come to grips with them because the fantasy screen itself becomes the chief object of preoccupation and is mistaken for the reality to be dealt with. By the same token gratifications in the projective system can be accepted for real ones—for a while, at any rate.

The question as to which of these mental processes predominates forms a crucial chapter in the history of Western society. Generally it can be said that since the Renaissance the projective systems have been much altered, when compared with early Christianity. Why is this factor so important? The alteration of the life of Western man is not limited to the more accurate knowledge of the outer world. This greater scientific knowledge brought with it great alterations in the basic personality of Western man. It gave rise to a new conception of man in relation to himself, as well as to the outer world. This new conception is not describable in terms of freedom or liberty alone; it augmented the responsibilities of man for his own welfare, and helped to define this welfare in new terms, and so to define new social and personal objectives. This story of the changes is not, however, without its comic and tragic aspects. This change not only redefined relations to the deity; through its promotion of mercantilism and manufacture it indirectly had a hand in setting in motion forces which eventually led to the elimination of feudalism and to promote the predominance of the bourgeoisie with all the accompanying blessings and evils. But these were all indirect results. The most significant consequence was the alteration of the whole superego system. All this was not a planned change, but an unconsciously systematized series of alterations, in connection with which some significant oversights were committed which did not come home to roost for hundreds of years.

The development of scientific reality systems had therefore a powerful influence in altering not only the manipulation of the outer world but the social order as well, which had to accommodate itself to the new goals. These social changes which make Western history of the past four hundred years were not planned but were improvised.

In our work in this book we can put the projective screen to good use as a diagnostic indicator of changes in the social order. Much of recorded history follows the fate of this fantasy screen rather than the social realities of which they are merely the shadow.

What was once true of the projective screen is now true of the history of social ideologies. But in evaluating social ideologies we are no longer working with a pure product of projection, but rather with a rational system polarized in the direction of unconscious motivations. The more free an ideology is of the latter, the more likely its validity and the more closely it can approximate scientific conclusions. These are the operational principles to be used in surveying two primitive cultures and one segment of Western society.

NOTES

1. In a seminar at Columbia University.
2. Marquesan, Tanala, Comanche, Pomo, Alor, Navaho, Plainville, Tapirape, Sikh, and Ojibwa.
3. A recent effort to account for social dynamics on the basis of direct learning processes has been made by J. W. M. Whiting, *On Becoming a Kwoma* (New Haven: Yale University Press, 1942). This approach would be valid if man did not *integrate experience*. It therefore presents a one-dimensional picture of mental processes on the basis of which no dynamic of social stability or change can be formulated.
4. To this point we can add a comment of Dr. Robert K. Merton: "It is not, of course, only the projective systems which polarize reality systems. Patterned experiences, differing according to social class, will also make certain beliefs 'meaningless' and 'unacceptable.' A particular type of belief in redemption through suffering and atonement will not spread among the upper social strata of a society, but will have rapid diffusion among the lower strata of the same society. It can also be shown that certain social and economic views or certain scientific systematizations spread rapidly at one time and slowly at another because they are compatible with the generalized personal experience of certain segments of the population. I have found, for example, among seventeenth-century physical scientists, that the Puritan projective system patently exercised a selective influence, such that an undue proportion of these scientists derived from Puritan circles. . . . The English century of genius is not unrelated to Puritanism." (Personal communication.)
5. The inclusion of taboo systems was suggested by Dr. Linton.
6. John Dollard, *Criteria for the Life History* (New Haven: Yale University Press, 1935).
7. There is one additional point that must be noted about projective and rational systems: that there is no difference between the actual logical or ratiocinative processes in the two systems. The difference between them lies rather in the subject matter on which these mental processes are exercised.

PART
THREE
STRUCTURE, FUNCTION, and RECIPROCITY

Émile Durkheim 1858–1917

BACKGROUND

Émile Durkheim was the greatest of French social scientists —he took the sociology of Comte and turned it into a subject at once scientific and human. And—all the more astonishing—he did so without a concept of culture. For, although the idea of culture illuminates Durkheim's work, certainly Durkheim's work illuminates the concept of culture and the entire discipline of anthropology that is based on it.

Durkheim was born in a village in Lorraine, not far from Strasbourg, of a long line of rabbis. It was assumed throughout his youth that he, too, would become a rabbi. He studied Hebrew, acquired a familiarity with the Old Testament and with Talmudic scholarship—and became an agnostic. Durkheim started out with a brilliant record in school, but when he went to the Lycée in Paris to prepare for the university, he got bored and questioned the value of much of the work, though he did work very hard at what he was interested in. When he finally got in, he found the university a disappointment, and claimed later in his life that the essentially literary training of the French universities was the reason that the science of society was backward. Because of his belligerent attitude toward literature and the humanities he had almost as much trouble getting out of the university as he had had getting in, and when the list of successful candidates appeared in 1882, his name was second from the bottom. His time at the university, however, had given him an acquaintance with Fustel de Coulanges, a lasting influence, and had allowed him to master such social thinkers as St. Simon and Comte.

In the years after his graduation, Durkheim taught in several lycées in different parts of France; spent a year studying philosophy in Germany, where he came under the influence of Wilhelm Wundt and where he read Spencer for the first time; and wrote reviews for the *Revue philosophique*, which made him quite well known in the French academic world.

In 1887 a professorship in sociology and education was created for Durkheim at Bordeaux—the first university chair in sociology in France. His teaching duties augmented rather than interrupted the flow of scientific articles, and he published three major books in quick succession: *The Division of Labor in Society* in 1893, *Rules of the Sociological Method* in 1896, and *Suicide* in 1897. These three works and his later book on religion had a tremendous impact in France at the time and in Britain later, eventually providing one dimension of the basic orientation for the British school of social anthropology.

Durkheim was also the force behind the journal *L'année sociologique,* one of the most influential annuals ever published in social science. His goal was systematically and methodically to review the state of all social science, and he came quite close to achieving it. The first *L'année* appeared in 1898, and for the next twelve years we have a summary of what was going on in social science that is still of great use. Each volume contained one or more original articles and a vast number of reviews, each section being covered by an expert.

In 1902 Durkheim was "called," as the French put it, to a professorship of sociology and education at the Sorbonne. There he gathered a distinguished group of young scholars: Henri Berr; Robert Hertz; Marcel Granet; François Simiand; his nephew, Marcel Mauss; and his son, André. His teaching, their research and writing, and the *L'année* were all of a piece. His thoughts on religion developed in this milieu; in 1903 he wrote a piece entitled "Primitive Classification" with Mauss and in 1906 one called "The Determination of Moral Facts." Society was, for Durkheim, a "moral system," giving the word "moral" its extended French meaning, which includes the English "morale." The upshot was *Elementary Forms of the Religious Life* in 1912.

The education part of Durkheim's professorship was not neglected, for in 1904 he began a course at the Sorbonne that was published posthumously as a two-volume history of French education, *L'evolution pedagogique en France,* probably the most comprehensive work on that subject to this date.

During World War I Durkheim gave himself over to patriotism and propaganda; social science seems always to fall to pieces in wartime. He published a study (obviously not a very good one) of the "German mentality," which purported to explain the morbid, pathological character of a mental and moral system that could produce a slogan like *Deutschland Über Alles.* He also wrote hortatory "Letters to all Frenchmen" in the face of the disastrous defeats on the Eastern Front in the summer of 1915.

All of Durkheim's students except Mauss were killed in World War I, and just before Christmas of 1915 his only son, André, died in a hospital in Bulgaria from wounds received during the retreat from Serbia. Durkheim kept up his patriotic work, but he never recovered from this loss. His health was considerably weakened, and in December of 1916 he suffered the first of a series of heart attacks. He began the task of arranging his papers and manuscripts for publication, and in the summer of 1917 he retired to Fontainebleau to begin a planned work on ethics. In November, at the age of fifty-nine, he died.

INTRODUCTION

The work of Durkheim has had a profound influence on the discipline that, in English-speaking countries only, is subdivided into sociology and anthropology. The scope and depth of his work includes some of the earliest statistical studies and some of the earliest cognitive studies in both disciplines (he did not, of course, make the distinction). The main theme that Durkheim worked on throughout his life was that of social solidarity. He wanted to understand, more than anything else, how a social unit holds its members together—in today's stylish language, how alienation is prevented. His use of such concepts as organic solidarity and "conscience collective" was always in response to that question.

Durkheim's doctoral dissertation, "The Division of Labor in Society" (1893), concentrates on the norms of a society that express social solidarity. He regards increased specialization of individuals as the key to greater social solidarity. Societies that have a great amount of specialization possess "organic solidarity," in that each of these highly distinct individuals must cooperate with others in order to survive. On the other hand, societies that have no differentiation of this type are held together by "mechanical solidarity," which means that the individuals have a strong sense of sharing common experiences, but each does not need to cooperate with the other in order for that experience to occur—for all that having it in common is what makes it a binding force.

Later Durkheim added another kind of explanation of social solidarity: that which centers around *conscience collective.* (We have, at the moment, left the phrase in French because of the difficulty of translating *conscience*—it means consciousness, conscience, and whatever it is one is aware of. "Shared awareness" or "common understanding" is about the meaning of the phrase in English; it denotes a view of classifications of the world and society.)

For Durkheim, "sociological knowledge" cannot be derived from the individual; it could not be even if the psychologist who studied him were omniscient. Rather, society must be studied by studying "social facts." For Durkheim "social facts" are what anthropologists understand to be culture. (The concept *conscience collective* is also an inept way of expressing the concept of culture, although for some purposes it has advantages.)

Durkheim's influence on anthropology has been widespread. Three of the most important social anthropologists in the discipline—Mauss, Radcliffe-Brown, and Lévi-Strauss—have been heavily influenced by him. Many others have reacted importantly to him—Benedict negatively, Malinowski positively.

15 RULES FOR THE EXPLANATION OF SOCIAL FACTS

The establishment of species is, above all, a means of grouping facts in order to facilitate their interpretation. But social morphology is only an introduction to the truly explanatory part of the science. What is the proper method of this part?

I.

Most sociologists think they have accounted for phenomena once they have shown how they are useful, what role they play, reason-

Reprinted from Émile Durkheim, *Rules of Sociological Method* (Chicago: University of Chicago Press, 1938) by permission of the publisher. Copyright 1938 by the University of Chicago Press.

ing as if facts existed only from the point of view of this role and with no other determining cause than the sentiment, clear or confused, of the services they are called to render. That is why they think they have said all that is necessary, to render them intelligible, when they have established the reality of these services and have shown what social needs they satisfy.

Thus Comte traces the entire progressive force of the human species to this fundamental tendency "which directly impels man constantly to ameliorate his condition, whatever it may be, under all circumstances";[1] and Spencer relates this force to the need for greater happiness. It is in accordance with this principle that Spencer explains the formation of society by the alleged advantages which result from co-operation; the institution of government, by the utility of the regularization of military co-operation;[2] the transformations through which the family has passed, by the need for reconciling more and more perfectly the interests of parents, children, and society.

But this method confuses two very different questions. To show how a fact is useful is not to explain how it originated or why it is what it is. The uses which it serves presuppose the specific properties characterizing it but do not create them. The need we have of things cannot give them existence, nor can it confer their specific nature upon them. It is to causes of another sort that they owe their existence. The idea we have of their utility may indeed motivate us to put these forces to work and to elicit from them their characteristic effects, but it will not enable us to produce these effects out of nothing. This proposition is evident so long as it is a question only of material, or even psychological, phenomena. It would be equally evident in sociology if social facts, because of their extreme intangibility, did not wrongly appear to us as without all intrinsic reality. Since we usually see them as a product purely of mental effort, it seems to us that they may be produced at will whenever we find it necessary. But since each one of them is a force, superior to that of the individual, and since it has a separate existence, it is not true that merely by willing to do so may one call them into being. No force can be engendered except by an antecedent force. To revive the spirit of the family, where it has become weakened, it is not enough that everyone understand its advantages; the causes which alone can engender it must be made to act directly. To give a government the authority necessary for it, it is not enough to feel the need for this authority; we must have recourse to the only sources from which all authority is derived. We must, namely, establish traditions, a common spirit, etc.; and for this it is necessary again to go back along the chain of causes and effects until we find a point where the action of man may be effectively brought to bear.

What shows plainly the dualism of these two orders of research is that a fact can exist without being at all useful, either because it has never been adjusted to any vital end or because, after having been useful, it has lost all utility while continuing to exist by the inertia of habit alone. There are, indeed, more survivals in society than in biological organisms. There are even cases where a practice or a social institution changes its function without thereby changing its nature. The rule, *Is pater quem justae nuptiae declarant,*[3] has remained in our code essentially the same as it was in the old Roman law. While its purpose then was to safeguard the property rights of a father over children born to the legitimate wife, it is rather the rights of children that it protects today. The custom of taking an oath began by being a sort of judiciary test and has become today simply a solemn and imposing formality. The religious dogmas of Christianity have not changed for centuries, but the role which they play is not the same in our modern societies as in the Middle Ages. Thus, the same words may serve to express new ideas. It is, moreover, a proposition true in sociology, as in biology, that the organ is independent of the function—in other words, while remaining the same, it can serve different ends. The causes of its existence are, then, independent of the ends it serves.

Nevertheless, we do not mean to say that the impulses, needs, and desires of men never intervene actively in social evolution. On the contrary, it is certain that they can hasten or retard its development, according to the circumstances which determine the social phenomena. Apart from the fact that they cannot, in any case, make something out of nothing, their actual intervention, whatever may be its effects, can take place only by means of efficient causes. A deliberate intention can contribute, even in this limited way, to the production of a new phenomenon only if it has itself been newly formed or if it is itself a result of some transformation of a previous intention. For, unless we postulate a truly providential and pre-established harmony, we cannot admit that man has carried with him from the beginning—potentially ready to be awakened at the call of circumstances—all the intentions which conditions were destined to demand in the course of human evolution. It must further be recognized that a deliberate intention is itself something objectively real; it can, then, neither be created nor modified by the mere fact that we judge it useful. It is a force having a nature of its own; for that nature to be given existence or altered, it is not enough that we should find this advantageous. In order to bring about such changes, there must be a sufficient cause.

For example, we have explained the constant development of the division of labor by showing that it is necessary in order that man may maintain himself in the new conditions of existence as he advances in history. We have attributed to this tendency, which is rather improperly named the "instinct of self-preservation," an important role in our explanations. But, in the first place, this instinct alone could not account for even the most rudimentary specialization. It can do nothing if the conditions on which the division of labor depends do not already exist, i.e., if individual differences have not increased sufficiently as a consequence of the progressive disintegration of the common consciousness and of hereditary influences.[4] It was even necessary that division of labor should have already begun to exist for its usefulness to be seen and for the need of it to make itself felt. The very development of individual differences, necessarily accompanied by a greater diversity of tastes and aptitudes, produced this first result. Further, the instinct of self-preservation did not, of itself and without cause, come to fertilize this first germ of specialization. We were started in this new direction, first, because the course we previously followed was now barred and because the greater intensity of the struggle, owing to the more extensive consolidation of societies, made more and more difficult the survival of individuals who continued to devote themselves to unspecialized tasks. For such reasons it became necessary for us to change our mode of living. Moreover, if our activity has been turned toward a constantly more developed division of labor, it is because this was also the direction of least resistance. The other possible solutions were emigration, suicide, and crime. Now, in the average case, the ties attaching us to life and country and the sympathy we have for our fellows are sentiments stronger and more resistant than the habits which could deflect us from narrower specialization. These habits, then, had inevitably to yield to each impulse that arose. Thus the fact that we allow a place for human needs in sociological explanations does not mean that we even partially revert to teleology. These needs can influence social evolution only on condition that they themselves, and the changes they undergo, can be explained solely by causes that are deterministic and not at all purposive.

But what is even more convincing than the preceding considerations is a study of actual social behavior. Where purpose reigns, there reigns also a more or less wide contingency; for there are no ends, and even fewer means, which necessarily control all men, even when it is assumed that they are placed in the same circumstances. Given the same environment, each individual adapts himself to it according to his own disposition and in his own way, which he prefers to all other ways. One person will seek to change it and make it conform to his needs; another will prefer to change himself and moderate his desires. To arrive at the same goal, many different ways can be and actually are followed. If, then, it were true that historic development took place in terms of ends clearly or obscurely felt, social facts should present the most infinite diversity; and all comparison should be almost impossible.

To be sure, the external events which constitute the superficial part of social life vary from one people to another, just as each individual has his own history, although the bases of physical and moral organization are the same for all. But when one comes in contact with social phenomena, one is, on the contrary, surprised by the astonishing regularity with which they occur under the same circumstances. Even the most minute and the most trivial practices recur with the most astonishing uniformity. A certain nuptial ceremony, purely symbolical in appearance, such as the carrying-off of the betrothed, is found to be exactly the same wherever a certain family type exists; and again this family type itself is linked to a whole social organization. The most bizarre customs, such as the couvade, the levirate, exogamy, etc., are observed among the most diverse peoples and are symptomatic of a certain social state. The right to make one's will appears at a certain phase of history, and the more or less important restrictions limiting it offer a fairly exact clue to the particular stage of social evolution. It would be easy to multiply examples. This wide diffusion of collective forms would be inexplicable if purpose or final causes had the predominant place in sociology that is attributed to them.

When, then, the explanation of a social phenomenon is undertaken, we must seek separately the efficient cause which produces it and the function it fulfils. We use the word "function," in preference to "end" or "purpose," precisely because social phenomena do not generally exist for the useful results they produce. We must determine whether there is a correspondence between the fact under consideration and the general needs of the social organism, and in what this correspondence consists, without occupying ourselves with whether it has been intentional or not. All these questions of intention are too subjective to allow of scientific treatment.

Not only must these two types of problems be separated, but it is proper, in general, to treat the former before the latter. This sequence, indeed, corresponds to that of experience. It is natural to seek the causes of a phenomenon before trying to determine its effects. This method is all the more logical since the first question, once answered, will often help to answer the second. Indeed, the bond which unites the cause to the effect is reciprocal to an extent which has not been sufficiently recognized. The effect can doubtless not exist without its cause; but the latter, in turn, needs its effect. It is from the cause that the effect draws its energy; but it also restores it to the cause on occasion, and consequently it cannot disappear without the cause showing the effects of its disappearance.[5]

For example, the social reaction that we call "punishment" is due to the intensity of the collective sentiments which the crime offends; but, from another angle, it has the useful function of maintaining these sentiments at the same degree of intensity, for they would soon diminish if offenses against them were not punished.[6] Similarly, in proportion as the social milieu becomes more complex and more unstable, traditions and conventional beliefs are shaken, become more indeterminate and more unsteady, and reflective powers are developed. Such rationality is indispensable to societies and individuals in adapting themselves to a more mobile and more complex environment.[7] And again, in proportion as men are obliged to furnish more highly specialized work, the products of this work are multiplied and are of better quality; but this increase in products and improvement in quality are necessary to compensate for the expense which this more considerable work entails.[8] Thus, instead of the cause of social phenomena consisting of a mental anticipation of the function they are called to fill, this function, on the contrary, at least in a number of cases, serves to maintain the pre-existent cause from which they are derived. We shall, then, find the function more easily if the cause is already known.

If the determination of function is thus to be delayed, it is still no less necessary for the complete explanation of the phenomena. Indeed, if the usefulness of a fact is not the cause of its existence, it is generally necessary that it be useful in order that it may maintain itself. For the fact that it is not useful suffices to make it harmful, since in that case it costs effort without bringing in any returns. If, then, the majority of social phenomena had this parasitic character, the budget of the organism would have a deficit and social life would be impossible. Consequently, to have a satisfactory understanding of the latter, it is necessary to show how the phenomena comprising it combine in such a way as to put society in harmony with itself and with the environment external to it. No doubt, the current formula, which defines social life as a correspondence between the internal and the external milieu, is only an approximation; however, it is in general true. Consequently, to explain a social fact it is not enough to show the cause on which it depends; we must also, at least in most cases, show its function in the establishment of social order.

II.

Having distinguished between these two approaches, we must determine the method by which they may be developed. At the same time that it is teleological, the method of explanation generally followed by sociologists is essentially psychological. These two tendencies are interconnected with one another. In fact, if society is only a system of means instituted by men to attain certain ends, these ends can only be individual, for only individuals could have existed before society. From the individual, then, have emanated the needs and desires determining the formation of societies; and, if it is from him that all comes, it is necessarily by him that all must be explained. Moreover, there are in societies only individual consciousnesses; in these, then, is found the source of all social evolution.

Hence, sociological laws can be only a corollary of the more general laws of psychology; the ultimate explanation of collective life will consist in showing how it emanates from human nature in general, whether the collective life be deduced from human nature directly and without previous observation or whether it must be related to human nature after the latter has been analyzed.

These terms are almost literally those used by Auguste Comte to characterize his method. "Since," says he, "the social phenomenon, conceived in its totality, is fundamentally *only a simple development of humanity, without the creation of any special faculties whatsoever*, as I have established above, all the effective dispositions that sociological investigation will successively discover will therefore be found at least in the germ in this primordial type which biology has constructed in advance for sociology."[9] According to him, the predominant fact in social life is progress; and moreover, progress depends on an exclusively psychological factor, namely, the tendency which impels man to perfect his nature more and more. Social facts would then be derived so directly from human nature that during the first phases of history they might be directly deduced from it without the necessity of having recourse to the observation of society.[10] It is true that, as Comte confesses, it is impossible to apply this deductive method to the more advanced periods of evolution. But this impossibility is purely a practical one. It is due to the fact that the distance between the point of departure and the point of arrival becomes so considerable that the human mind risks going astray, if it undertakes to traverse it without a guide.[11] But the relation between the fundamental laws of human nature and the ultimate products of social progress does not cease to be intimate. The most complex forms of civilization are only a development of the psychological life of the individual. Thus, while the theories of the psychology are insufficient as premises for sociological reasoning, they are the touchstone which alone can test the validity of propositions inductively established. "A law of social succession," says Comte, "even when indicated with all possible authority by the historical method, ought to be finally admitted only after having been rationally related to the positive theory of human nature, either in a direct or indirect way."[12] Psychology, then, will always have the last word.

Such is likewise the method followed by Spencer. Indeed, according to him, the two primary factors of social phenomena are the external environment and the physical and social constitution of the individual.[13] Now, the former can influence society only through the latter, which thus becomes the essential force of social evolution. If society is formed, it is in order to permit the individual to express his nature; and all the transformations through which this nature has passed have no other object than to make this expression easier and more complete. It is by reason of this principle that, before proceeding to his research in social organization, Spencer thought it necessary to devote almost the entire first volume of his *Principles of Sociology* to the study of the physical, emotional, and intellectual aspects of primitive man. "The science of sociology," he says, "sets out with social units, conditioned as we have seen, constituted physically, emotionally, and intellectually, and possessed of certain early acquired notions and correlative feelings."[14] And it is in two of these feelings—fear of the living and fear of the dead—that he finds the origin of political and religious government.[15] He admits, it is true, that once it is formed society reacts on individuals.[16] But it does not follow that society itself has the power of directly engendering the smallest social fact; from this point of view it exerts an effect only by the intermediation of the changes it effects in the individual. It is, then, always in human nature, whether original or acquired, that everything is based. Moreover, this action that the social body exercises on its members cannot be at all specific, since political ends have no separate existence but are simply a summary statement of human needs.[17] It can then be only a duplication of private activity. In industrial societies, particularly, we are unable to see where social influence has a place, since the object of these societies is, precisely, to liberate the individual and his natural impulses by ridding him of all social constraint.

This principle is not only at the basis of these great doctrines of general sociology, but it likewise fathers an equally large number of specific theories. Thus, domestic organization is commonly explained by the sentiment parents have for their children, and children for their parents; the institution of marriage, by the advantages it presents for the married pair and their progeny; punishment, by the anger which every grave attack upon his interests causes in the individual. All economic life, as economists of the orthodox school especially conceive and explain it, is definitely dependent upon a purely individual factor, the desire for wealth. In morality, the duty of the individual toward himself is made the basis of all ethics. As for religion, it becomes a product of the impressions which the great forces of nature or of certain eminent personalities awaken in man, etc.

But, if such a method is applied to social phenomena, it changes fundamentally their nature. To prove this, let us recall the definition we have given. Since their essential characteristic is their power of exerting pressure on individual consciousness, it follows that they are not derived from the latter and, consequently, that sociology is not a corollary of individual psychology. For this power of constraint is evidence of the fact that social phenomena possess a different nature from ours, since they control us only by force or, at the very least, by weighing upon us more or less heavily. If social life were merely an extension of the individual being, it would not thus ascend toward its source, namely, the individual, and impetuously invade it. If the authority before which the individual bows when he acts, feels, or thinks socially governs him to this extent, it does so because it is a product of social forces which transcend him and for which he, consequently, cannot account. The external impulse to which he submits cannot come from him, nor can it be explained by what happens within him. It is true that we are not incapable of self-control; we can restrain our impulses, habits, and even instincts and can arrest their development by an act of inhibition. But these inhibitory movements should not be confused with those constituting social constraint. The process of the former is centrifugal; of the latter, centripetal. The former are elaborated in the individual consciousness and then tend to externalize themselves; the latter are at first external to the individual, whom they then tend to fashion in their image from without. Inhibition is, if you like, the means by which social constraint produces its psychological effects; it is not identical with this constraint.

When the individual has been eliminated, society alone remains. We must, then, seek the explanation of social life in the nature of society itself. It is quite evident that, since it infinitely surpasses the individual in time as well as in space, it is in a position to impose upon him ways of acting and thinking which it has consecrated with its prestige. This pressure, which is the distinctive property of social facts, is the pressure which the totality exerts on the individual.

But, it will be said that, since the only elements making up society are individuals, the first origins of sociological phenomena cannot but be psychological. In reasoning thus, it can be established just as easily that organic phenomena may be explained by inorganic phenomena. It is very certain that there are in the living cell only molecules of crude matter. But these molecules are in contact with one another, and this association is the cause of the new phenomena which characterize life, the very germ of which cannot possibly be found in any of the separate elements. A whole is not identical with the sum of its parts. It is something different, and its properties differ frcm those of its component parts. Association is not, as has sometimes been believed, merely an infertile phenomenon; it is not simply the putting of facts and constituent properties into juxtaposition. On the contrary, it is the source of all the innovations which have been produced successively in the course of the general evolution of things. What differences are there between the lower and higher organisms, between highly organized living things and proto-plasm, between the latter and the inorganic molecules of which it is com-posed, if not differences in types of association? All these beings, in the last analysis, resolve themselves into the same elements, but these elements are here in mere juxtaposition, there in combination, here associated in one way, there in another. One may even inquire whether this law does not apply in the mineral world and whether the differences separating inorganic bodies are not traceable to this same origin.

By reason of this principle, society is not a mere sum of individuals. Rather, the system formed by their association represents a specific reality which has its own characteristics. Of course, nothing collective can be pro-duced if individual consciousnesses are not assumed; but this necessary condition is by itself insufficient. These consciousnesses must be combined in a certain way; social life results from this combination and is, conse-quently, explained by it. Individual minds, forming groups by mingling and fusing, give birth to a being, psychological if you will, but constituting a psychic individuality of a new sort.[18] It is, then, in the nature of this collec-tive individuality, not in that of the associated units, that we must seek the immediate and determining causes of the facts appearing therein. The group thinks, feels, and acts quite differently from the way in which its mem-bers would were they isolated. If, then, we begin with the individual, we shall be able to understand nothing of what takes place in the group. In a word, there is between psychology and sociology the same break in continuity as between biology and physicochemical sciences. Consequently, every time that a social phenomenon is directly explained by a psychological phenome-non, we may be sure that the explanation is false.

Our critics will perhaps maintain that although society, once formed, is the proximate cause of social phenomena, the causes determining its forma-tion may still be psychological in nature. They grant that, when individuals are associated, their association can give rise to a new form of life; but they claim that the new form can take place only for reasons inherent in individuals. But, in reality, as far back as one goes in history, the principle of association is the most imperative of all, for it is the source of all other compulsions. As a consequence of my birth, I am obliged to associate with a given group. It may be said that later, as an adult, I acquiesce in this obligation by the very fact that I continue to live in my country. But what difference does that make? This "acquiescence" is still imperative. Pressure accepted and submitted to with good grace is still pressure. Moreover, let us look more closely at the nature of my acquiescence. For the present, it is most certainly imposed upon me, for in the vast majority of cases it is materially and morally impossible for us to strip off our nationality; such a change is generally considered apostasy. Likewise in the past, which determines the present, I could not have given my free consent. I did not desire the education I received, which, more than any other thing, fixes me to my native soil. Finally, for the future, I cannot give my acquiescence, for I cannot know what the future is to be. I do not know all the duties which may be incumbent upon me at some future time in my capacity as a citizen. How could I acquiesce in them in advance?

We have shown, then, that the source of all that is obligatory is outside the individual. So long, then, as we do not desert the facts, the principle of association presents the same character as the others and, consequently, is explained in the same manner.

Moreover, as all societies are born of other societies without a break in continuity, we can be certain that in the entire course of social evolution there has not been a single time when individuals determined by careful deliberation whether or not they would enter into the collective life or into one collective life rather than another. In order for that question to arise, it would be necessary to go back to the first origins of all societies. But the questionable solutions which can be brought to such problems could not, in any case, affect the method by which we must treat the facts given in history. Therefore, we do not need to discuss them.

But one would be strangely mistaken about our thought if, from the foregoing, he drew the conclusion that sociology, according to us, must, or even can, make an abstraction of man and his faculties. It is clear, on the contrary, that the general characteristics of human nature participate in the work of elaboration from which social life results. But they are not the cause of it, nor do they give it its special form; they only make it possible. Collective representations, emotions, and tendencies are caused not by certain states of the consciousnesses of individuals but by the conditions in which the social group in its totality is placed. Such actions can, of course, materialize only if the individual natures are not resistant to them; but these individual natures are merely the indeterminate material that the social factor molds and transforms. Their contribution consists exclusively in very general attitudes, in vague and consequently plastic predispositions which, by themselves, if other agents did not intervene, could not take on the definite and complex forms which characterize social phenomena.

What an abyss, for example, between the sentiments man experiences in the face of forces superior to his own and the present religious institution with its beliefs, its numerous and complicated practices, its material and moral organization! What a contrast between the psychic states of sympathy which two beings of the same blood experience for one another,[19] and the detailed collection of legal and moral regulations that determine the structure of the family, the relations of persons among themselves, of things with persons, etc.! We have seen that, even where society is reduced to an unorganized crowd, the collective sentiments which are formed in it may not only not resemble, but even be opposed to, the sentiments of the average individual. How much greater must be the difference between them when the pressure exerted on the individual is that of a well-organized society, in which the action of the traditions of former generations is added to that of contemporaries! A purely psychological explanation of social facts cannot fail, therefore, to allow all that is characteristic (i.e., social) in them to escape.

What has blinded most sociologists to the inadequacy of this method is that, taking effect for cause, they have very often designated as determining the conditions of social phenomena certain psychological states that are relatively definite and distinctive but which are, after all, only the consequence of these social phenomena. Thus a certain religious sentiment has been considered innate in man, a certain minimum of sexual jealousy, filial piety, paternal love, etc. And it is by these that religion, marriage, and the family have been explained.

History, however, shows that these inclinations, far from being inherent in human nature, are often totally lacking. Or they may present such variations in different societies that the residue obtained after eliminating all these differences—which alone can be considered of psychological origin—is reduced to something vague and rudimentary and far removed from the facts that need explanation. These sentiments, then, *result* from the collective organization and are not its *basis*. It has not been proved at all that the tendency to gregariousness has been an inherited instinct of the human species from its beginnings. It is much more natural to consider it a product of social life, which was slowly developed within us; for it is a fact of observation that animals are or are not gregarious according to whether their habits oblige them to live a common life or to avoid it. We must add that the difference between even the more definite tendencies and social reality remains considerable.

There is, moreover, a way to isolate the psychological factor almost completely in such a manner as to determine precisely the extent of its action, viz., to see how race affects social evolution. Indeed, ethnic characteristics are organicopsychological in type. Social life must, therefore, vary when they vary, if psychological phenomena have on society the effects attributed to them. But no social phenomenon is known which can be placed in indisputable dependence on race. No doubt, we cannot attribute to this proposition the value of a principle; we can merely affirm it as invariably true in practical experience.

The most diverse forms of organization are found in societies of the same race, while striking similarities are observed between societies of different races. The city-state existed among the Phoenicians, as among the Romans and the Greeks; we find it in the process of formation among the Kabyles. The patriarchal family was almost as highly developed among the Jews as among the Hindus; but it is not found among the Slavs, who are, however, of the Aryan race. On the other hand, the family type met among Slavs also exists among the Arabs. The maternal family and the clan are observed everywhere. The detail of legal procedure and of nuptial ceremonies is the same among peoples most dissimilar from the ethnic point of view.

If all these things are true, it is because the psychological factor is too general to predetermine the course of social phenomena. Since it does not call for one social form rather than another, it cannot explain any of them. There are, it is true, a certain number of facts which are customarily attributed to the influence of race. In this manner is explained, notably, the rapid and intensive development of arts and letters in Athens, so slow and mediocre in Rome. But this interpretation of the facts, although classical, has never been scientifically demonstrated; it seems, indeed, to derive all its authority solely from tradition. The possibility of a sociological explanation of the same phenomena has not been explored, but we are convinced that it could be attempted with success. In short, when the artistic character of Athenian civilization is related with such facility to inherited aesthetic faculties, we show as little insight as did scholars in the Middle Ages when they explained fire by phlogiston and the effects of opium by its dormitive property.

Finally, if social evolution really had its origin in the psychological constitution of man, its origin seems to be completely obscure. For we would then have to admit that its motivating force is some inner spring of human nature. But what could this be? Is it the sort of instinct Comte speaks of, which impels man more and more to express his nature? But that is begging the question and explaining progress by an innate "tendency toward progress" —a metaphysical entity of the very existence of which there is no demonstration. Even the highest animal species are not at all activated by the need to progress, and among human societies there are many which are content to remain indefinitely stationary.

Or is this motivating force, as Spencer seems to believe, the urge for greater happiness which the increasingly complex forms of civilization are designed to satisfy more and more completely? We would then have to establish the fact that happiness increases with civilization, and we have elsewhere described all the difficulties to which this hypothesis gives rise.[20] But further, even if one or the other of these two postulates were admissible, historical development would not thereby be rendered intelligible, for the explanation which would result from it would be purely teleological. We have shown above that social facts, like all natural phenomena, are not explained by the simple consideration that they serve some end. When it has been proved satisfactorily that the progressively more intelligent social organizations which have succeeded one another in the course of history have had the effect of satisfying more and more certain of our fundamental desires, we have not shown at all how these social organizations have been produced. The fact that they were useful does not tell us how they originated. Even if we were to explain how we came to imagine them and how we planned them in advance so as to picture to ourselves their services to us—a somewhat difficult problem in itself—the desires which called forth their existence do not have the power of drawing them out of nothing. In a word, admitting that social organizations are the necessary means to attain a desired goal, the whole question remains: From what source and by what means have these been created?

We arrive, therefore, at the following principle: *The determining cause of a social fact should be sought among the social facts preceding it and not among the states of the individual consciousness.* Moreover, we see quite readily that all the foregoing applies to the determination of the function as well as the cause of social phenomena. The function of a social fact cannot but be social, i.e., it consists of the production of socially useful effects. To be sure, it may and does happen that it also serves the individual. But this happy result is not its immediate cause. We can then complete the preceding proposition by saying: *The function of a social fact ought always to be sought in its relation to some social end.*

Since sociologists have often misinterpreted this rule and have considered social phenomena from a too psychological point of view, to many their theories seem too vague and shifting and too far removed from the distinctive nature of the things they are intended to explain. Historians who treat social reality directly and in detail have not failed to remark how powerless these too general interpretations are to show the relation between the facts; and their mistrust of sociology has been, no doubt, partly produced by this circumstance. We do not mean to say, of course, that the study of psychological facts is not indispensable to the sociologist. If collective life is not derived from individual life, the two are nevertheless closely related; if the latter cannot explain the former, it can at least facilitate its explanation. First, as we have shown, it is indisputable that social facts are produced by action on psychological factors. In addition, this very action is similar to that which takes place in each individual consciousness and by which are transformed the primary elements (sensations, reflexes, instincts) of which it is originally constituted. Not without reason has it been said that the self is itself a society, by the same right as the organism, although in another way; and long ago psychologists showed the great importance of the factor of association in the explanation of mental activity.

Psychological training, more than biological training, constitutes, then, a valuable lesson for the sociologist; but it will not be useful to him except on condition that he emancipates himself from it after having received profit from its lessons, and then goes beyond it by special sociological training. He must abandon psychology as the center of his operations, as the point of departure for his excursions into the sociological world to which they must always return. He must establish himself in the very heart of social facts, in order to observe them directly, while asking the science of the individual mind for a general preparation only and, when needed, for useful suggestions.[21]

III.

Since the facts of social morphology are of the same nature as physiological phenomena, they must be explained by the principle just enunciated. All the preceding argument points to the fact that they play a preponderant role in collective life, and hence in sociological explanations.

In fact, if the determining condition of social phenomena is, as we have shown, the very fact of association, the phenomena ought to vary with the forms of that association, i.e., according to the ways in which the constituent parts of society are grouped. Since, moreover, a given aggregate, formed by the union of elements of all kinds which enter into the composition of a society, constitutes its internal environment (just as the aggregate of anatomic elements, together with the way in which they are disposed in space, constitutes the internal milieu of organisms), we can say: *The first origins of all social processes of any importance should be sought in the internal constitution of the social group.*

It is possible to be even more precise. The elements which make up this milieu are of two kinds: things and persons. Besides material objects incorporated into the society, there must also be included the products of previous social activity: law, established customs, literary and artistic works, etc. But it is clear that the impulsion which determines social transformations can come from neither the material nor the immaterial, for neither possesses a motivating power. There is, assuredly, occasion to take them into consideration in the explanations one attempts. They bear with a certain weight on social evolution, whose speed and even direction vary according to the nature of these elements; but they contain nothing of what is required to put it in motion. They are the matter upon which the social forces of society act, but by themselves they release no social energy. As an active factor, then, the human milieu itself remains.

The principal task of the sociologist ought to be, therefore, to discover the different aspects of this milieu which can exert some influence on the course of social phenomena. Until the present, we have found two series of facts which have eminently fulfilled this condition; these are: (1) the number of social units or, as we have also called it, the "size of a society"; (2) the degree of concentration of the group, or what we have termed the "dynamic density." By this last expression must not be understood the purely physical concentration of the aggregate, which can have no effect if the individuals, or rather the groups of individuals, remain separated by social distance. By it is understood the social concentration, of which the size is only the auxiliary and, generally speaking, the consequence. The dynamic density may be defined, the volume being equal, as the function of the number of individuals who are actually having not only commercial but also social relations, i.e., who not only exchange services or compete with one another but also live a common life. For, as purely economic relations leave men estranged from one another, there may be continuous relations of that sort without participation in the same collective existence. Business carried on across the frontiers which separate peoples does not abolish these frontiers.

Social life can be affected only by the number of those who participate effectively in it. That is why the dynamic density of a people is best expressed by the degree of fusion of the social segments. For, if each partial aggregate forms a whole, i.e., a distinct individuality separated by barriers from the others, the action of the members, in general, remains localized within it. If on the contrary, these partial societies are, or tend to be, all intermingled within the total society, to that extent is the radius of social life extended.

As for physical density—if is understood thereby not only the number of inhabitants per unit area but the development of lines of communication and transmission—it progresses, *ordinarily,* at the same rate as the dynamic density and, *in general,* can serve to measure it. If the different parts of the population tend to draw closer together, it is inevitable that they will build roads which permit it. From another angle, relations can be established between distant points in the social mass only if distance is not an obstacle, i.e., if it is bridged. However, there are exceptions,[22] and we would lay ourselves open to a serious error if we always judged the social concentration of a society by the degree of its physical concentration. Roads, railroads, etc., can serve for commerce better than for the fusion of populations, of which they are only a very imperfect index. Such is the case in England, whose physical density is greater than that of France, but where the coalescence of social areas is much less advanced, as is proved by the persistence of local spirit and regional life.

We have shown elsewhere how all growth in the volume and dynamic density of societies modifies profoundly the fundamental conditions of collective existence by rendering social life more intense, by extending the horizon of thought and action of each individual. We need not return to the application we then made of this principle. Let us add only that it has helped us to treat not only the still very general question that was the object of this study but many other more special problems, and that we have thus been able to verify its correctness by a considerable number of experiments. Nevertheless, we are far from claiming that we have found all the peculiarities of the social medium which may contribute to the explanation of social facts. All that we can say is that these are the only ones we have observed and that we have not been led to seek others.

But the significance attributed by us to the social and, more particularly, the human milieu does not imply that we must see in it a sort of ultimate and absolute fact beyond which there is no reason for inquiry. It is evident, on the contrary, that its condition at each moment of history is itself a result of social causes, some of which are inherent in the society itself, while others depend on interaction between this society and its neighbors. Moreover, science is not concerned with first-causes, in the absolute sense of the word. For science, a fact is primary simply when it is general enough to explain a great number of other facts. Now, the social milieu is certainly a factor of this kind, since the changes which are produced in it, whatever may be their causes, have their repercussions in all directions in the social organism and cannot fail to affect to some extent each of its functions.

What has just been said of the general social milieu can be repeated for the special milieus of each of the partial groups it comprises. For example, according as the family is large or small or lives a life more or less complete, domestic life will vary. Similarly, if professional groups extend their function over an entire territory instead of remaining restricted, as formerly, to the limits of a city, their professional activity will be very different from what it was formerly. More generally, professional life will be quite different according to whether the milieu of each profession is strongly restricted or whether it is unrestrained, as it is today. Nevertheless, the action of these particular milieus could not have the importance of the general milieu, for they are themselves subject to the influence of the latter. We must always return to the general milieu. The pressure it exerts on these partial groups modifies their organization.

This conception of the social milieu, as the determining factor of collective evolution, is of the highest importance. For, if we reject it, sociology cannot establish any relations of causality. In fact, if we eliminate this type of cause, there are no concomitant conditions on which social phenomena can depend; for if the external social milieu, i.e., that which is formed by the surrounding societies, can take some action, it is only that of attack and defense; and, further, it can make its influence felt only by the intermediary of the internal social milieu. The principal causes of historical development would not be found, then, among the concomitant circumstances; they would all be in the past. They would themselves form a part of this development, of which they would constitute simply older phases. The present events of social life would originate not in the present state of society but in prior events, from historical precedents; and sociological explanations would consist exclusively in connecting the present with the past.

It may seem, it is true, that this is sufficient. Indeed, it is currently said that history has for its object precisely the linking of events in their order of succession. But it is impossible to conceive how the stage which a civilization has reached at a given moment could be the determining cause of the subsequent stage. The stages that humanity successively traverses do not engender one another. We understand that the progress achieved at a given epoch in the legal, economic, political field, etc., makes new progress possible; but how does it predetermine it? It is a point of departure which permits of further progress; but what incites us to such progress?

Are we to admit an inherent tendency which impels humanity ceaselessly to exceed its achievements either in order to realize itself completely or to increase its happiness; and is the object of sociology to rediscover the manner in which this tendency developed? Without returning to the difficulties such a hypothesis implies, in any case laws which would express this development cannot be at all causal, for relation of causality can be established only between two given facts. Now, this tendency, which is supposed to be the cause of this development, is not given; it is only postulated and constructed by the mind from the effects attributed to it. It is a sort of motivating faculty that we imagine as underlying movement, in order to account for it; but the efficient cause of a movement can only be another movement, not a potentiality of this kind.

All that we can observe experimentally in the species is a series of changes among which a causal bond does not exist. The antecedent state does not produce the subsequent one, but the relation between them is exclusively chronological. Under these circumstances, all scientific prevision is impossible. We can, indeed, say that certain conditions have succeeded one another up to the present, but not in what order they will henceforth succeed one another, since the cause on which they are supposed to depend is not scientifically determined or determinable. Ordinarily, it is true, we admit that evolution will take the same direction as in the past; but this is a mere postulate. Nothing assures us that the overt phenomena express so completely the nature of this tendency that we may be able to foretell the objective to which this tendency aspires as distinct from those through which it has successively passed. Why, indeed, should the direction it follows be rectilinear?

This is the reason for the restricted number of causal relations or laws established by sociology. With a few exceptions, of whom Montesquieu is the most illustrious example, the older philosophers of history tried solely to discover the general direction in which humanity orients itself, without seeking to relate the phases of this evolution to any concomitant condition. However great the services Comte has rendered to social philosophy, the terms in which he has stated the sociological problem do not differ from the preceding philosophers. Thus his famous law of the three stages of history has no relation of causality; if it is true, it is, and can be, only empirical. It is a bird's-eye view of the elapsed history of the human species. It is entirely arbitrary to consider the third stage as the definitive state of humanity. Who knows whether another will not emerge from it in the future?

Likewise the law which predominates in Spencer's sociology does not seem to be any different in its nature. If it were true that we tend at present to seek our happiness in an industrial civilization, nothing assures us that, in epochs to follow, we shall not seek it elsewhere. The prevalence and persistence of this method may be accounted for by the fact that we have usually seen in the social milieu a means by which progress is realized, not the cause which determines it.

From another angle, it is again with relation to this same milieu that the utility or, as we have called it, the function of social phenomena must be measured. Among the changes caused by the social milieu, only those serve a purpose which are compatible with the current state of society, since the milieu is the essential condition of collective existence. From this point of view again, the conception we have just expounded is, we believe, fundamental; for it alone enables us to explain how the useful character of social phenomena can vary, without however depending on a volitional social order. If we represent historic evolution as impelled by a sort of vital urge which pushes men forward, since a propelling tendency can have but one goal, there can be only one point of reference with relation to which the usefulness or harmlessness of social phenomena is calculated. Consequently, there can, and does, exist only one type of social organization that fits humanity perfectly; and the different historical societies are only successive approximations to this single model. It is unnecessary to show that, today, such a simple view is irreconcilable with the recognized variety and complexity of social forms. If, on the contrary, the fitness or unfitness of institutions can only be established in connection with a given milieu, since these milieus are diverse, there is a diversity of points of reference and hence of types which, while being qualitatively distinct from one another, are all equally grounded in the nature of the social milieus.

The question just treated is, then, closely connected with that of the constitution of social types. If there are social species, it is because collective life depends, above all, on concomitant conditions which present a certain diversity. If, on the contrary, all the principal causes of social events were in the past, each society would no longer be anything but the prolongation of its predecessor, and the different societies would lose their individuality and would become only diverse moments of one and the same evolution. Since, on the other hand, the constitution of the social milieu results from the mode of composition of the social aggregates—and these two expressions are essentially synonymous—we now have the proof that there are no more essential characteristics than those assigned by us as the basis of sociological classifications. Finally, we must now understand, better than previously, how unjust it would be for our critics to point to these words, "external conditions" and "milieu," as an accusation that our method seeks the sources of life outside the living being. On the contrary, the considerations just stated lead us back to the idea that the causes of social phenomena are internal to society. Rather, we ourselves could more justly criticize the theory which derives society from the individual for trying to extract the internal from the external (since it explains the social being by something other than itself) and the greater from the smaller (since it undertakes to deduce the whole from the part). So little have our principles misinterpreted the spontaneous character of every living being that, if we apply them to biology and psychology, we shall have to admit that there also the individual life is entirely developed within the individual.

IV.

A certain conception of society and collective life emerges from the group of rules just established. But first let us set forth the contrary theories which divide opinion on this point. For some, such as Hobbes and Rousseau, there is a break in continuity between the individual and society. Man is thus naturally refractory to the common life; he can only resign himself to it when forced. Social ends are not simply the meeting-point of individual ends; they are, rather, contrary to them. Thus, to induce the individual to pursue them, it is necessary to constrain him; and the social task consists par excellence in the institution and organization of this constraint. Since, however, the individual is regarded as the sole reality of the human realm, this organization, having for its object to hinder and confine him, can only be conceived as artificial. It is not founded in nature, since this organization is destined to do human nature violence by preventing it from behaving in an antisocial manner. It is a work of art, a machine constructed entirely by hand of man, which, like all products of this kind, is only what it is because men have willed it so. A decree of the will created it; another can transform it.

Neither Hobbes nor Rousseau seems to have realized how contradictory it is to admit that the individual is himself the author of a machine which has for its essential role his domination and constraint. At least, it seemed to them sufficient for the elimination of this contradiction that it be disguised in the eyes of those who are its victims, by the clever artifice of the social contract.

It is from a quite different idea that the philosophers of natural law, the economists, and, more recently, Spencer[23] have taken their inspiration. For them social life is essentially spontaneous and society is a natural phenomenon. But, if they confer this character upon it, it is not because they find in it a specific nature but merely because they find its basis in the nature of the individual. No more than the aforementioned thinkers do they see in it a system of things existing separately, by reason of causes peculiar to itself. But, whereas the former conceived of it only as a conventional arrangement which is attached by no bond to reality and is supported in mid-air, so to speak, Spencer and the economists give as its bases the fundamental instincts of human nature. Man is naturally inclined to the political, domestic, and religious life, to commerce, etc.; and it is from these natural drives that social organization is derived. Consequently, wherever it is normal, it has no need to impose itself. When it has recourse to constraint, it is because it is not what it ought to be or because the circumstances are abnormal. In principle, we have only to leave individual forces to develop freely and they will tend to organize themselves socially. Neither one of these doctrines is ours. To be sure, we do make constraint the characteristic of all social facts. But this constraint does not result from more or less learned machinations, destined to conceal from men the traps in which they have caught themselves. It is due simply to the fact that the individual finds himself in the presence of a force which is superior to him and before which he bows; but this force is an entirely natural one. It is not derived from a conventional arrangement which human will has added bodily to natural reality; it issues from innermost reality; it is the necessary product of given causes. Also, recourse to artifice is unnecessary to get the individual to submit to them of his entire free will; it is sufficient to make him become aware of his state of natural dependence and inferiority, whether he forms a tangible and symbolic representation of it through religion or whether he arrives at an adequate and definite notion of it through science. Since the superiority of society to him is not simply physical but intellectual and moral, it has nothing to fear from a critical examination. By making man understand by how much the social being is richer, more complex, and more permanent than the individual being, reflection can only reveal to him the intelligible reasons for the subordination demanded of him and for the sentiments of attachment and respect which habit has fixed in his heart.[24]

It would be only a singularly superficial criticism, therefore, that would attack our concept of social constraint by restating the theories of Hobbes and Machiavelli. But if, contrary to these philosophers, we say that social life is natural, our reason is not that we find its source in the nature of the individual. It is natural rather because it springs directly from the collective being which is, itself, a being in its own right, and because it results from special cultivation which individual consciousnesses undergo in their association with each other, an association from which a new form of existence is evolved.[25] If, then, we agree with certain scholars that social reality appears to the individual under the aspect of constraint, we admit with the others that it is a spontaneous product of reality. The tie which binds together these two elements, so contradictory in appearance, is the fact that this reality from which it emanates extends beyond the individual. We mean to say that these words, "constraint" and "spontaneity," have not in our terminology the meaning Hobbes gives to the former and Spencer to the latter.

To summarize, the objection can be raised to most of the attempts which have been made to explain social facts rationally that they have lost sight of all ideas of social discipline or have maintained it only by deceptive subterfuges. The principle we have just expounded would, on the contrary, create a sociology which sees in the spirit of discipline the essential condition of all common life, while at the same time founding it on reason and on truth.

NOTES

1. *Cours de philosophie positive,* IV, 262.
2. *Principles of Sociology,* II, 247.
3. Legal marriage with the mother establishes the father's rights over the children.
4. *Division du travail social,* Book II, chaps. iii and iv.
5. We do not wish to raise here questions of general philosophy, which would not be in place. Let us say, however, that, if more profoundly analyzed, this reciprocity of cause and effect might furnish a means of reconciling scientific mechanism with the teleology which the existence, and especially the persistence, of life implies.
6. *Division du travail social,* Book II, chap. ii, notably pp. 105 ff.
7. *Ibid.,* pp. 52–53.
8. *Ibid.,* pp. 301 ff.
9. *Op. cit.,* IV, 333.
10. *Ibid.,* p. 345.
11. *Ibid.,* p. 346.
12. *Ibid.,* p. 335.
13. *Principles of Sociology,* Vol. I, Part I, chap. ii.
14. *Ibid.,* p. 437.
15. *Ibid.*
16. *Ibid.,* p. 14.
17. "Society exists for the benefit of its members; not its members for the benefit of society. . . . the claims of the body politic are nothing in themselves, and become something only in so far as they embody the claims of its component individuals" (*ibid.,* Part II, pp. 461–462).
18. In this sense, and for these reasons, one can, and must, speak of a collective consciousness distinct from individual consciousnesses. In order to justify this distinction, it is not necessary to posit for the former a separate personal existence; it is something special and must be designated by a special term, simply because the states which constitute it differ specifically from those which constitute the individual consciousnesses. This specificity comes from the fact that they are not formed from the same elements. The latter result from the nature of the organicopsychological being taken in isolation, the former from the combination of a plurality of beings of this kind. The resultants cannot, then, fail to differ, since the components differ to that extent. Our definition of the social fact, moreover, only drew in another way this line of demarcation.
19. We may suppose that this exists in lower social groups. See, on this point, Espinas, *Sociétés animales,* p. 474.

20. *Division du travail social,* Book II, chap. i.
21. Psychological phenomena can have only social consequences when they are so intimately united to social phenomena that the action of the psychological and of the social phenomena is necessarily fused. This is the case with certain sociopsychological facts. Thus, a public official is a social force, but he is at the same time an individual. As a result he can turn his social energy in a direction determined by his individual nature, and thereby he can have an influence on the constitution of society. Such is the case with statesmen and, more generally, with men of genius. The latter, even when they do not fill a social function, draw from the collective sentiments of which they are the object an authority which is also a social force, and which they can put, in a certain measure, at the service of personal ideas. But we see that these cases are due to individual accidents and, consequently, cannot affect the constitutive traits of the social species which, alone, is the object of science. The restriction on the principle enunciated above is not, then, of great importance for the sociologist.
22. We made the mistake, in our *Division du travail social,* of presenting material density too much as the exact expression of dynamic density. Nevertheless, the substitution of the former for the latter is absolutely legitimate for whatever concerns the economic effects of the latter, e.g., the division of labor as a purely economic fact.
23. The position of Comte on this matter is a rather ambiguous eclecticism.
24. This is why all constraint is not normal and why that constraint which corresponds to some social superiority, i.e., intellectual or moral, alone merits the name. But that which one individual exercises over the other because he is stronger or wealthier, especially if this wealth does not express his social value, is abnormal and can only be maintained by violence.
25. Our theory is even more unlike that of Hobbes than that of natural law. For the partisans of this latter doctrine, collective life is natural only in the measure in which it can be deduced from individual nature. Now, only the most general forms of social organization can, strictly speaking, be derived from this origin. As for the details of social organization, they are too much removed from the extreme indeterminateness of psychological traits to be connected to them; they appear, then, to the disciples of this school quite as artificial as they appear to their adversaries. For us, on the contrary, all is natural, even the most peculiar social order; for all is grounded on the nature of society.

INTRODUCTION

Elementary Forms of the Religious Life is a study of the relationship of religion to society. Here Durkheim claims that the primal sacred object, totem, is a representation by which society symbolizes itself. The sacred object is the society rationalized through religion. The object that is a totem is in itself neutral, according to Durkheim. What sanctifies this object is the belief bestowed upon it by society. Such a belief implies that a totem, like any other symbol, is a "collective representation."

Elementary Forms of the Religious Life is also important for epistemology. It claims that individual knowledge results neither from the "mind" nor from the senses; rather, we know what we know because we learn socially devised "collective representations." This interpretation of epistemology is said to give the student of the theory a third alternative in addition to the two to be found in traditional philosophy—idealism and empiricism. Some later writers have seriously misunderstood Durkheim by thinking of him as a mystic and idealist simply because he was not a "materialist."

16 ELEMENTARY FORMS OF THE RELIGIOUS LIFE

. . . [O]ur study is not of interest merely for the science of religion. In fact, every religion has one side by which it overlaps the circle of properly religious ideas, and there, the study of religious phenomena gives a means of renewing the problems which, up to the present, have only been discussed among philosophers.

For a long time it has been known that the first systems of representations with which men have pictured to themselves the world and themselves were of religious origin. There is no religion that is not a cosmology at the same time that it is a speculation upon divine things. If philosophy and the sciences were born of religion, it is because religion began by taking the place of the sciences and philosophy. But it has been less frequently noticed that religion has not confined itself to enriching the human intellect, formed beforehand, with a certain number of ideas; it has contributed to forming the intellect itself. Men owe to it not only a good part of the substance of their knowledge, but also the form in which this knowledge has been elaborated.

At the roots of all our judgments there are a certain number of essential ideas which dominate all our intellectual life; they are what philosophers since Aristotle have called the categories of the understanding; ideas of time, space,[1] class, number, cause, substances, personality, etc. They correspond to the most universal properties of things. They are like the solid frame which encloses all thought; this does not seem to be able to liberate itself from them without destroying itself, for it seems that we cannot think of objects that are not in time and space, which have no number, etc. Other ideas are contingent and unsteady; we can conceive of their being unknown to a man, a society or an epoch, but these others appear to be nearly inseparable from the normal working of the intellect. They are like the framework of the intelligence. Now when primitive religious beliefs are systematically analysed, the principal categories are naturally found. They are born in religion and of religion; they are a product of religious thought. This is a statement that we are going to have occasion to make many times in the course of this work.

This remark has some interest of itself already; but here is what gives it its real importance.

The general conclusion of [*Elementary Forms of the Religious Life*] is that religion is something eminently social. Religious representations are collective representations which express collective realities; the rites are a manner of acting which take rise in the midst of the assembled groups and which are destined to excite, maintain or recreate certain mental states in these groups. So if the categories are of religious origin, they ought to participate in this nature common to all religious facts; they too should be social affairs and the product of collective thought. At least—for in the actual condition of our knowledge of these matters, one should be careful to avoid all radical and exclusive statements—it is allowable to suppose that they are rich in social elements.

Even at present, these can be imperfectly seen in some of them. For example, try to represent what the notion of time would be without the processes by which we divide it, measure it or express it with objective signs, a time which is not a succession of years, months, weeks, days and hours! This is something nearly unthinkable. We cannot conceive of time, except on condition of distinguishing its different moments. Now what is the origin of this differentiation? Undoubtedly, the states of consciousness which we have already experienced can be reproduced in us in the same order in which they passed in the first place; thus portions of our past become present again, though being clearly distinguished from the present. But howsover important this distinction may be for our private experience, it is far from being enough to constitute the notion or category of time. This does not consist merely in a commemoration, either partial or integral, of our past life. It is an abstract and impersonal frame which surrounds, not only our individual existence, but that of all humanity. It is like an endless chart, where all duration is spread out before the mind, and upon which all possible events can be located in relation to fixed and determined guide lines. It is not *my time* that is thus arranged; it is time in general, such as it is objectively thought of by everybody in a single civilization. That alone is enough to give us a hint that such an arrangement ought to be collective. And in reality, observation proves that these indispensable guide lines, in relation to which all things are temporally located, are taken from social life. The divisions into days, weeks, months, years, etc., correspond to the periodical recurrence of rites, feasts, and public ceremonies.[2] A calendar expresses the rhythm of the collective activities, while at the same time its function is to assure their regularity.[3]

It is the same thing with space. As Hamelin has shown,[4] space is not the vague and undetermined medium which Kant imagined; if purely and absolutely homogeneous, it would be of no use, and could not be grasped by the mind. Spatial representation consists essentially in a primary co-ordination of the data of sensuous experience. But this co-ordination would be impossible if the parts of space were qualitatively equivalent and if they were really interchangeable. To dispose things spatially there must be a possibility of placing them differently, of putting some at the right, others at the left, these above, those below, at the north of or at the south of, east or west of, etc., etc., just as to dispose states of consciousness temporally there must be a possibility of localizing them at determined dates. That is to say that space could not be what it is if it were not, like time, divided and differentiated. But whence come these divisions which are so essential? By themselves, there are neither right nor left, up nor down, north nor south, etc. All these distinctions evidently come from the fact that different sympathetic values have been attributed to various regions. Since all men of a single civilization represent space in the same way, it is clearly necessary that these sympathetic values, and the distinctions which depend upon them, should be equally universal, and that almost necessarily implies that they be of social origin.[5]

Besides that, there are cases where this social character is made manifest. There are societies in Australia and North America where space is conceived in the form of an immense circle, because the camp has a circular form;[6] and this spatial circle is divided up exactly like the tribal circle, and is in its image. There are as many regions distinguished as there are clans in the tribe, and it is the place occupied by the clans inside the encampment which has determined the orientation of these regions. Each region is defined by the totem of the clan to which it is assigned. Among the Zuñi, for example, the pueblo contains seven quarters; each of these is a group of clans which has had a unity: in all probability it was originally a single clan which was later subdivided. Now their space also contains seven quarters, and each of these seven quarters of the world is in intimate connection with a quarter of the pueblo, that is to say with a group of clans.[7] "Thus," says Cushing, "one division is thought to be in relation with the north, another represents the west, another the south," etc.[8] Each quarter of the pueblo has its characteristic colour, which symbolizes it; each region has its colour, which is exactly the same as that of the corresponding quarter. In the course of history the number of fundamental clans has varied; the number of the fundamental regions of space has varied with them. Thus the social organization has been the model for the spatial organization and a reproduction of it. It is thus even up to the distinction between right and left which, far from being inherent in the nature of man in general, is very probably the product of representations which are religious and therefore collective.[9]

Analogous proofs will be found presently in regard to the ideas of class, force, personality and efficacy. It is even possible to ask if the idea of contradiction does not also depend upon social conditions. What makes one tend to believe this is that the empire which the idea has exercised over human thought has varied with times and societies. To-day the principle of identity dominates scientific thought; but there are vast systems of representations which have played a considerable rôle in the history of ideas where it has frequently been set aside: these are the mythologies, from the grossest up to the most reasonable.[10] There, we are continually coming upon beings which have the most contradictory attributes simultaneously, who are at the same time one and many, material and spiritual, who can divide themselves up indefinitely without losing anything of their constitution; in mythology it is an axiom that the part is worth the whole. These variations through which the rules which seem to govern our present logic have passed prove that, far from being engraven through all eternity upon the mental constitution of men, they depend, at least in part, upon factors that are historical and consequently social. We do not know exactly what they are, but we may presume that they exist.[11]

This hypothesis once admitted, the problem of knowledge is posed in new terms.

Up to the present there have been only two doctrines in the field. For some, the categories cannot be derived from experience: they are logically prior to it and condition it. They are presented as so many simple and irreducible data, imminent in the human mind by virtue of its inborn constitution. For this reason they are said to be *a priori*. Others, however, hold that they are constructed and made up of pieces and bits, and that the individual is the artisan of this construction.[12]

But each solution raises grave difficulties.

Is the empirical thesis the one adopted? Then it is necessary to deprive the categories of all their characteristic properties. As a matter of fact they are distinguished from all other knowledge by their universality and necessity. They are the most general concepts which exist, because they are applicable to all that is real, and since they are not attached to any particular object they are independent of every particular subject; they constitute the common field where all minds meet. Further, they must meet there, for reason, which is nothing more than all the fundamental categories taken together, is invested with an authority which we could not set aside if we would. When we attempt to revolt against it, and to free ourselves from some of these essential ideas, we meet with great resistances. They do not merely depend upon us, but they impose themselves upon us. Now empirical data present characteristics which are diametrically opposed to these. A sensation or an image always relies upon a determined object, or upon a collection of objects of the same sort, and expresses the momentary condition of a particular consciousness; it is essentially individual and subjective. We therefore have considerable liberty in dealing with the representations of such an origin. It is true that when our sensations are actual, they impose themselves upon us *in fact*. But *by right* we are free to conceive them otherwise than they really are, or to represent them to ourselves as occurring in a different order from that where they are really produced. In regard to them nothing is forced upon us except as considerations of another sort intervene. Thus we find that we have here two sorts of knowledge, which are like the two opposite poles of the intelligence. Under these conditions forcing reason back upon experience causes it to disappear, for it is equivalent to reducing the universality and necessity which characterize it to pure appearance, to an illusion which may be useful practically, but which corresponds to nothing in reality; consequently it is denying all objective reality to the logical life, whose regulation and organization is the function of the categories. Classical empiricism results in irrationalism; perhaps it would even be fitting to designate it by this latter name.

In spite of the sense ordinarily attached to the name, the apriorists have more respect for the facts. Since they do not admit it as a truth established by evidence that the categories are made up of the same elements as our sensual representations, they are not obliged to impoverish them systematically, to draw from them all their real content, and to reduce them to nothing more than verbal artifices. On the contrary, they leave them all their specific characteristics. The apriorists are the rationalists; they believe that the world has a logical aspect which the reason expresses excellently. But for all that, it is necessary for them to give the mind a certain power of transcending experience and of adding to that which is given to it directly; and of this singular power they give neither explanation nor justification. For it is no explanation to say that it is inherent in the nature of the human intellect. It is necessary to show whence we hold this surprising prerogative and how it comes that we can see certain relations in things which the examination of these things cannot reveal to us. Saying that only on this condition is experience itself possible changes the problem perhaps, but does not answer it. For the real question is to know how it comes that experience is not sufficient unto itself, but presupposes certain conditions which are exterior and prior to it, and how it happens that these conditions are realized at the moment and in the manner that is desirable. To answer these questions it has sometimes been assumed that above the reason of individuals there is a superior and perfect reason from which the others emanate and from which they get this marvellous power of theirs by a sort of mystic participation: this is the divine reason. But this hypothesis has at least the one grave disadvantage of being deprived of all experimental control; thus it does not satisfy the conditions demanded of a scientific hypothesis. More than that, the categories of human thought are never fixed in any one definite form; they are made, unmade and remade incessantly; they change with places and times. On the other hand, the divine reason is immutable. How can this immutability give rise to this incessant variability?

Such are the two conceptions that have been pitted against each other for centuries; and if this debate seems to be eternal, it is because the arguments given are really about equivalent. If reason is only a form of individual experience, it no longer exists. On the other hand, if the powers which it has are recognized but not accounted for, it seems to be set outside the confines of nature and science. In the face of these two opposed objections the mind remains uncertain. But if the social origin of the categories is admitted, a new attitude becomes possible, which we believe will enable us to escape both of the opposed difficulties.

The fundamental proposition of the apriorist theory is that knowledge is made up of two sets of elements, which cannot be reduced into one another, and which are like two distinct layers superimposed one upon the other.[13] Our hypothesis keeps this principle intact. In fact, that knowledge which is called empirical, the only knowledge of which the theorists of empiricism have made use in constructing the reason, is that which is brought into our minds by the direct action of objects. It is composed of individual states which are completely explained[14] by the psychical nature of the individual. If, on the other hand, the categories are, as we believe they are, essentially collective representations, before all else, they should show the mental states of the group; they should depend upon the way in which this is founded and organized, upon its morphology, upon its religious, moral and economic institutions, etc. So between these two sorts of representations there is all the difference which exists between the individual and the social, and one can no more derive the second from the first than he can deduce society from the individual, the whole from the part, the complex from the simple.[15] Society is a reality *sui generis*; it has its own peculiar characteristics, which are not found elsewhere and which are not met again in the same form in all the rest of the universe. The representations which express it have a wholly different content from purely individual ones and we may rest assured in advance that the first add something to the second.

Even the manner in which the two are formed results in differentiating them. Collective representations are the result of an immense co-operation, which stretches out not only into space but into time as well; to make them, a multitude of minds have associated, united and combined their ideas and sentiments; for them, long generations have accumulated their experience and their knowledge. A special intellectual activity is therefore concentrated in them which is infinitely richer and complexer than that of the individual. From that one can understand how the reason has been able to go beyond the limits of empirical knowledge. It does not owe this to any vague mysterious virtue but simply to the fact that according to the well-known formula, man is double. There are two beings in him: an individual being which has its foundation in the organism and the circle of whose activities is therefore strictly limited, and a social being which represents the highest reality in the intellectual and moral order that we can know by observation—I mean society. This duality of our nature has as its consequence in the practical order, the irreducibility of a moral ideal to a utilitarian motive, and in the order of thought, the irreducibility of reason to individual experience. In so far as he belongs to society, the individual transcends himself, both when he thinks and when he acts.

This same social character leads to an understanding of the origin of the necessity of the categories. It is said that an idea is necessary when it imposes itself upon the mind by some sort of virtue of its own, without being accompanied by any proof. It contains within it something which constrains the intelligence and which leads to its acceptance without preliminary examination. The apriorist postulates this singular quality but does not account for it; for saying that the categories are necessary because they are indispensable to the functioning of the intellect is simply repeating that they are necessary. But if they really have the origin which we attribute to them, their ascendancy no longer has anything surprising in it. They represent the most general relations which exist between things; surpassing all our other ideas in extension, they dominate all the details of our intellectual life. If men did not agree upon these essential ideas at every moment, if they did not have the same conception of time, space, cause, number, etc., all contact between their minds would be impossible, and with that, all life together. Thus society could not abandon the categories to the free choice of the individual without abandoning itself. If it is to live there is not merely need of a satisfactory moral conformity, but also there is a minimum of logical conformity beyond which it cannot safely go. For this reason it uses all its authority upon its members to forestall such dissidences. Does a mind ostensibly free itself from these forms of thought? It is no longer considered a human mind in the full sense of the word, and is treated accordingly. That is why we feel that we are no longer completely free and that something resists, both within and outside ourselves, when we attempt to rid ourselves of these fundamental notions, even in our own conscience. Outside of us there is public opinion which judges us; but more than that, since society is also represented inside of us, it sets itself against these revolutionary fancies, even inside of ourselves; we have the feeling that we cannot abandon them if our whole thought is not to cease being really human. This seems to be the origin of the exceptional authority which is inherent in the reason and which makes us accept its suggestions with confidence. It is the very authority of society,[16] transferring itself to a certain manner of thought which is the indispensable condition of all common action. The necessity with which the categories are imposed upon us is not the effect of simple habits whose yoke we could easily throw off with a little effort; nor is it a physical or metaphysical necessity, since the categories change in different places and times; it is a special sort of moral necessity which is to the intellectual life what moral obligation is to the will.[17]

But if the categories originally only translate social states, does it not follow that they can be applied to the rest of nature only as metaphors? If they were made merely to express social conditions, it seems as though they could not be extended to other realms except in this sense. Thus in so far as they aid us in thinking of the physical or biological world, they have only the value of artificial symbols, useful practically perhaps, but having no connection with reality. Thus we come back, by a different road, to nominalism and empiricism.

But when we interpret a sociological theory of knowledge in this way, we forget that even if society is a specific reality it is not an empire within an empire; it is a part of nature, and indeed its highest representation. The social realm is a natural realm which differs from the others only by a greater complexity. Now it is impossible that nature should differ radically from itself in the one case and the other in regard to that which is most essential. The fundamental relations that exist between things—just that which it is the function of the categories to express—cannot be essentially dissimilar in the different realms. If, for reasons which we shall discuss later, they are more clearly disengaged in the social world, it is nevertheless impossible that they should not be found elsewhere, though in less pronounced forms. Society makes them more manifest but it does not have a monopoly upon them. That is why ideas which have been elaborated on the model of social things can aid us in thinking of another department of nature. It is at least true that if these ideas play the rôle of symbols when they are thus turned aside from their original signification, they are well-founded symbols. If a sort of artificiality enters into them from the mere fact that they are constructed concepts, it is an artificiality which follows nature very closely and which is constantly approaching it still more closely.[18] From the fact that the ideas of time, space, class, cause or personality are constructed out of social elements, it is not necessary to conclude that they are devoid of all objective value. On the contrary, their social origin rather leads to the belief that they are not without foundation in the nature of things.[19]

Thus renovated, the theory of knowledge seems destined to unite the opposing advantages of the two rival theories, without incurring their inconveniences. It keeps all the essential principles of the apriorists; but at the same time it is inspired by that positive spirit which the empiricists have striven to satisfy. It leaves the reason its specific power, but it accounts for it and does so without leaving the world of observable phenomena. It affirms the duality of our intellectual life, but it explains it, and with natural causes. The categories are no longer considered as primary and unanalysable facts, yet they keep a complexity which falsifies any analysis as ready as that with which the empiricists content themselves. They no longer appear as very simple notions which the first comer can very easily arrange from his own personal observations and which the popular imagination has unluckily complicated, but rather they appear as priceless instruments of thought which the human groups have laboriously forged through the centuries and where they have accumulated the best of their intellectual capital.[20] A complete section of the history of humanity is resumed therein. This is equivalent to saying that to succeed in understanding them and judging them, it is necessary to resort to other means than those which have been in use up to the present. To know what these conceptions which we have not made ourselves are really made of, it does not suffice to interrogate our own consciousnesses; we must look outside of ourselves, it is history that we must observe, there is a whole science which must be formed, a complex science which can advance but slowly and by collective labour, and to which the present work brings some fragmentary contributions in the nature of an attempt. Without making these questions the direct object of our study, we shall profit by all the occasions which present themselves to us of catching at their very birth some at least of these ideas which, while being of religious origin, still remain at the foundation of the human intelligence.

NOTES

1. We say that time and space are categories because there is no difference between the rôle played by these ideas in the intellectual life and that which falls to the ideas of class or cause (on this point see Hamelin, *Essai sur les éléments principaux de la représentation,* pp. 63, 76).
2. See the support given this assertion in Hubert and Mauss, *Mélanges d'Histoire des Religions (Travaux de l'Année Sociologique),* chapter on *La Représentation du Temps dans la Religion.*
3. Thus we see all the difference which exists between the group of sensations and images which serve to locate us in time, and the category of time. The first

are the summary of individual experiences, which are of value only for the person who experienced them. But what the category of time expresses is a time common to the group, a social time, so to speak. In itself it is a veritable social institution. Also, it is peculiar to man; animals have no representations of this sort.

This distinction between the category of time and the corresponding sensations could be made equally well in regard to space or cause. Perhaps this would aid in clearing up certain confusions which are maintained by the controversies of which these questions are the subject.

4. *Op. cit.*, pp. 75 ff.
5. Or else it would be necessary to admit that all individuals, in virtue of their organo-physical constitution, are spontaneously affected in the same manner by the different parts of space: which is more improbable, especially as in themselves the different regions are sympathetically indifferent. Also, the divisions of space vary with different societies, which is a proof that they are not founded exclusively upon the congenital nature of man.
6. See Durkheim and Mauss, *De quelques formes primitives de classification,* in *Année Sociologique,* VI, pp. 47 ff.
7. *Ibid.,* p. 34.
8. *Zuñi Creation Myths,* in *13th Rep. of the Bureau of Amer. Ethnol.,* pp. 367 ff.
9. See Hertz, *La prééminence de la main droite. Etude de polarité religieuse,* in the *Revue Philosophique,* Dec., 1909. On this same question of the relations between the representation of space and the form of the group, see the chapter in Ratzel, *Politische Geographie,* entitled *Der Raum in Geist der Völker.*
10. We do not mean to say that mythological thought ignores it, but that it contradicts it more frequently and openly than scientific thought does. Inversely, we shall show that science cannot escape violating it, though it holds to it far more scrupulously than religion does. On this subject, as on many others, there are only differences of degree between science and religion; but if these differences should not be exaggerated, they must be noted, for they are significant.
11. This hypothesis has already been set forth by the founders of the *Völkerpsychologie.* It is especially remarked in a short article by Windelbrand entitled *Die Erkenntnisslehre unter dem Volkerpsychologischen Gesichtspunke,* in the *Zeitsch. f. Volkerpsychologie,* viii, pp. 166 ff. Cf. a note of Steinthal on the same subject, *ibid.,* pp. 178 ff.
12. Even in the theory of Spencer, it is by individual experience that the categories are made. The only difference which there is in this regard between ordinary empiricism and evolutionary empiricism is that according to this latter, the results of individual experience are accumulated by heredity. But this accumulation adds nothing essential to them; no element enters into their composition which does not have its origin in the experience of the individual. According to this theory, also, the necessity with which the categories actually impose themselves upon us is the product of an illusion and a superstitious prejudice, strongly rooted in the organism, to be sure, but without foundation in the nature of things.
13. Perhaps some will be surprised that we do not define the apriorist theory by the hypothesis of innateness. But this conception really plays a secondary part in the doctrine. It is a simple way of stating the impossibility of reducing rational knowledge to empirical data. Saying that the former is innate is only a positive way of saying that it is not the product of experience, such as it is ordinarily conceived.
14. At least, in so far as there are any representations which are individual and hence wholly empirical. But there are in fact probably none where the two elements are not found closely united.
15. This irreducibility must not be taken in any absolute sense. We do not wish to

say that there is nothing in the empirical representations which shows rational ones, nor that there is nothing in the individual which could be taken as a sign of social life. If experience were completely separated from all that is rational, reason could not operate upon it; in the same way, if the psychic nature of the individual were absolutely opposed to the social life, society would be impossible. A complete analysis of the categories should seek these germs of rationality even in the individual consciousness. All that we wish to establish here is that between these indistinct germs of reason and the reason properly so called, there is a difference comparable to that which separates the properties of the mineral elements out of which a living being is composed from the characteristic attributes of life after this has once been constituted.

16. It has frequently been remarked that social disturbances result in multiplying mental disturbances. This is one more proof that logical discipline is a special aspect of social discipline. The first gives way as the second is weakened.

17. There is an analogy between this logical necessity and moral obligation, but there is not an actual identity. To-day society treats criminals in a different fashion than subjects whose intelligence only is abnormal; that is a proof that the authority attached to logical rules and that inherent in moral rules are not of the same nature, in spite of certain similarities. They are two species of the same class. It would be interesting to make a study on the nature and origin of this difference, which is probably distinguished between the deranged and the delinquent. We confine ourselves to signalizing this question. By this example, one may see the number of problems which are raised by the analysis of these notions which generally pass as being elementary and simple, but which are really of an extreme complexity.

18. The rationalism which is imminent in the sociological theory of knowledge is thus midway between the classical empiricism and apriorism. For the first, the categories are purely artificial constructions; for the second, on the contrary, they are given by nature; for us, they are in a sense a work of art, but of an art which imitates nature with a perfection capable of increasing unlimitedly.

19. For example, that which is at the foundation of the category of time is the rhythm of social life; but if there is a rhythm in collective life, one may rest assured that there is another in the life of the individual, and more generally, in that of the universe. The first is merely more marked and apparent than the others. In the same way, we shall see that the notion of class is founded on that of the human group. But if men form natural groups, it can be assumed that among things there exist groups which are at once analogous and different. Classes and species are natural groups of things.

    If it seem to many minds that a social origin cannot be attributed to the categories without depriving them of all speculative value, it is because society is still too frequently regarded as something that is not natural; hence it is concluded that the representations which express it express nothing in nature. But the conclusion is not worth more than the premise.

20. This is how it is legitimate to compare the categories to tools; for on its side, a tool is material accumulated capital. There is a close relationship between the three ideas of tool, category and institution.

Marcel Mauss 1872–1950

BACKGROUND

Marcel Mauss is less known than he might have been had his work appeared in a more compact form—it is scattered widely, most of it is short, and much of it is in collaboration, so that the value of his truly unusual contribution is hard to assess, although present-day social science is shot through with the results of his thinking.

Mauss was born in the same town in Lórraine as his mother's brother, Émile Durkheim. Like Durkheim, he grew up within a close-knit, pious, and orthodox Jewish family, but he was not religious and reacted against Judaism. His main interests being in philosophy, he studied under his uncle at Bordeaux and met there two other philosophers who were influential—Octave Hamelin, a rationalist, and Alfred Victor Espinas, who was at that time concerned with the collective origin of arts, customs, and technology.

When Mauss placed third in the national *agrégation* competition of 1895, he decided to devote himself to research. He began by studying religion in the École Pratique des Hautes Études in Paris, and soon he had close friends there. In 1897–1898 he made a study tour of Leiden, Breda, and Oxford, where he worked with Tylor for a short time. Then from 1900 to 1902 he studied Sanskrit and Indian texts and taught the history of religion and a course in the philosophy of pre-Buddhist India. During that time he also succeeded to the chair in the history of the religions of "noncivilized" people in Paris.

Throughout Durkheim's life, Mauss worked very closely with him. Besides their "Primitive Forms of Classification" (1903), Mauss compiled the statistical tables for Durkheim's *Suicide* and wrote dozens of reviews for *L'année.* Their collaboration usually meant that Durkheim had the theoretical idea, to which Mauss added concrete and illuminating detail. All of Mauss' work from this period was in collaboration, mostly with Henri Hubert, such as "Essay on the Nature and Function of Sacrifice" (1899). He also edited for some years the section of *L'année* devoted to the sociology of religion.

After the death of Durkheim and so many of his students, Mauss tried twice to revive *L'année,* once in the 1920s and once in the 1930s, but without signal success; there was no longer a like-minded group of scholars who could work in close collaboration. Mauss spent much of his time editing and publishing works by Durkheim, Hertz, and Hubert—to the cost, apparently, of his own output.

In 1925 he helped to found, and then became joint director of, the Institut d'Ethnologie of the University of Paris, whose courses and publications hastened the development of field work by young French anthropologists. Although there are good early nonprofessional ethnographic accounts by French travelers and administrators, ethnography and social science remained longer separated institutionally in France than they did in Germany, Britain, or America. Mauss lectured at the Institut, as well as at the College de France, until 1939.

The work Mauss did after World War I falls into two categories: (1) major ethnological studies, of which the most important is *The Gift,* a short book that all but lays the foundation for economic anthropology, although the challenge was not taken up for some decades; and (2) several short programmatic works of methodology, of which "Fragment d'un plan de sociologie generale descriptive" (1934) is probably the best.

Mauss' career ended suddenly and prematurely with World War II and the German occupation of France. The shock of the occupation, of being deprived by war of his friends and colleagues for the second time, as well as domestic troubles and other personal problems, affected his mind. He survived until 1950, but he did no more work. Several projected studies—on money, on prayer, and on the nation—were never completed (the manuscripts were probably destroyed). His work remains fragmentary and scattered—but many-sided and affecting many of the tributaries, as well as the mainstream, of anthropology.

INTRODUCTION

Two aspects of Mauss' works that have had a major influence on anthropologists are his analysis of gift giving and his analysis with Durkheim of primitive classifications. His work on primitive classifications seems to have influenced most especially Lévi-Strauss, and his work on gift exchange has profoundly influenced economic anthropology, as well as Lévi-Strauss and all the structural school.

Mauss and Durkheim saw "primitive" classifications of categories of phenomena as being the first scientific classifications known to man. They regarded such classificatory systems as systems of cognitive classes, organized into hierarchies. The main function of these classifications was to make the relationship between phenomena understandable, not to facilitate action. Classifications were regarded as the connecting points between concepts and the basis for the unity of knowledge.

Mauss' masterpiece, *The Gift,* is an analysis of gift exchanges, or prestations, in simple societies. With this work he became one of the first authors to recognize that (as he put it) the social fabric is nondifferentiated in simple societies. That is, that in such societies economic and political purposes are fulfilled by kinship relationships, making gift giving "a total social phenomena which finds an expression in all aspects of social life and institutions such as the religious, the moral and the economic." This, of course, does not mean that the religious and the economic are intertwined; the point is rather that they have not been differentiated.

Mauss also recognized that gifts are not volitional, but are part of a network of social obligations. In other words, gift giving and the repayment of gifts represent obligations within the social fabric. This is an important realization, once again proving that an ethnocentric view of human activity can be worse than misleading.

17 GIFTS AND RETURN GIFTS

I have never found a man so generous and hospitable that he would not receive a present, nor one so liberal with his money that he would dislike a reward if he could get one.

Friends should rejoice each others' hearts with gifts of weapons and raiment, that is clear from one's own experience. That friendship lasts longest—if there is a chance of its being a success—in which friends both give and receive gifts.

A man ought to be a friend to his friend and repay gift with gift. People should meet smiles with smiles and lies with treachery.

Know—if you have a friend in whom you have sure confidence and wish to make use of him, you ought to exchange ideas and gifts with him and go to see him often.

If you have another in whom you have no confidence and yet will make use of him, you ought to address him with fair words by crafty heart and repay treachery with lies.

Further, with regard to him in whom you have no confidence and of whose motives you are suspicious, you ought to smile upon him and dissemble your feelings. Gifts ought to be repaid in like coin.

Generous and bold men have the best time in life and never foster troubles. But the coward is apprehensive of everything and a miser is always groaning over his gifts.

Better there should be no prayer than excessive offering; a gift always looks for recompense. Better there should be no sacrifice than an excessive slaughter.

HAVAMAL, vv. 39, 41–42, 44–46, 48 and 145, from the translation by D. E. Martin Clarke in *The Havamal, with Selections from other Poems in the Edda,* Cambridge, 1923.

The foregoing lines from the *Edda* outline our subject-matter.[1] In Scandinavian and many other civilizations contracts are fulfilled and exchanges of goods are made by means of gifts. In theory such gifts are voluntary but in fact they are given and repaid under obligation.

This work is part of a wider study. For some years our attention has been drawn to the realm of contract and the system of economic prestations between the component sections or sub-groups of 'primitive' and what we might call 'archaic' societies. On this subject there is a great mass of complex data. For, in these 'early' societies, social phenomena are not discrete; each phenomenon contains all the threads of which the social fabric is composed. In these *total* social phenomena, as we propose to call them, all kinds of institutions find simultaneous expression: religious, legal, moral, and economic. In addition, the phenomena have their aesthetic aspect and they reveal morphological types.

We intend in this book to isolate one important set of phenomena: namely, prestations which are in theory voluntary, disinterested and spontaneous, but are in fact obligatory and interested. The form usually taken is that of the gift generously offered; but the accompanying behaviour is formal pretence and social deception, while the transaction itself is based on obligation and economic self-interest. We shall note the various principles behind this necessary form of exchange (which is nothing less than the division of labour itself), but we shall confine our detailed study to the enquiry: *In primitive or archaic types of society what is the principle whereby the gift received has to be repaid? What force is there in the thing given which compels the recipient to make a return?* We hope, by presenting enough data, to be able to answer this question precisely, and also to indicate the direction in which answers to cognate questions might be sought. We shall also pose new problems. Of these, some concern the morality of the contract: for instance, the manner in which today the law of things remains bound up with the law of persons; and some refer to the forms and ideas which have always been present in exchange and which even now are to be seen in the idea of individual interest.

Thus we have a double aim. We seek a set of more or less archaeological conclusions on the nature of human transactions in the societies which surround us and those which immediately preceded ours, and whose exchange institutions differ from our own. We describe their forms of contract and exchange. It has been suggested that these societies lack the economic market, but this is not true; for the market is a human phenomenon which we believe to be familiar to every known society. Markets are found before the development of merchants, and before their most important innovation, currency as we know it. They functioned before they took the modern forms (Semitic, Hellenic, Hellenistic, and Roman) of contract and sale and capital. We shall take note of the moral and economic features of these institutions.

We contend that the same morality and economy are at work, albeit less noticeably, in our own societies, and we believe that in them we have discovered one of the bases of social life; and thus we may draw conclusions of a moral nature about some of the problems confronting us in our present economic crisis. These pages of social history, theoretical sociology, political economy and morality do no more than lead us to old problems which are constantly turning up under new guises.[2]

THE METHOD FOLLOWED

Our method is one of careful comparison. We confine the study to certain chosen areas, Polynesia, Melanesia, and North-West America, and to certain well-known codes. Again, since we are concerned with words and their meanings, we choose only areas where we have access to the minds of the societies through documentation and philological research. This further limits our field of comparison. Each particular study has a bearing on the systems we set out to describe and is presented in its logical place. In this way we avoid that method of haphazard comparison in which institutions lose their local colour and documents their value.

PRESTATION, GIFT AND POTLATCH

This work is part of the wider research carried out by M. Davy and myself upon archaic forms of contract, so we may start by summarizing what we have found so far.[3] It appears that there has never existed, either in the past or in modern primitive societies, anything like a 'natural' economy.[4] By a strange chance the type of that economy was taken to be the one described by Captain Cook when he wrote on exchange and barter among the Polynesians.[5] In our study here of these same Polynesians we shall see how far removed they are from a state of nature in these matters.

In the systems of the past we do not find simple exchange of goods, wealth and produce through markets established among individuals. For it is groups, and not individuals, which carry on exchange, make contracts, and are bound by obligations;[6] the persons represented in the contracts are moral persons—clans, tribes, and families; the groups, or the chiefs as intermediaries for the groups, confront and oppose each other.[7] Further, what they exchange is not exclusively goods and wealth, real and personal property, and things of economic value. They exchange rather courtesies, entertainments, ritual, military assistance, women, children, dances, and feasts; and fairs in which the market is but one element and the circulation of wealth but one part of a wide and enduring contract. Finally, although the prestations and counter-prestations take place under a voluntary guise they are in essence strictly obligatory, and their sanction is private or open warfare. We propose to call this the system of *total prestations*. Such institutions seem to be best represented in the alliance of pairs of phratries in Australian and North American tribes, where ritual, marriages, succession to wealth, community of right and interest, military and religious rank and even games[8] all form part of one system and presuppose the collaboration of the two moieties of the tribe. The Tlingit and Haida of North-West America give a good expression of the nature of these practices when they say that they 'show respect to each other'.[9]

But with the Tlingit and Haida, and in the whole of that region, total prestations appear in a form which, although quite typical, is yet evolved and relatively rare. We propose, following American authors, to call it the *potlatch*. This Chinook word has passed into the current language of Whites and Indians from Vancouver to Alaska. *Potlatch* meant originally 'to nourish' or 'to consume'.[10] The Tlingit and Haida inhabit the islands, the coast, and the land between the coast and the Rockies; they are very rich, and pass their winters in continuous festival, in banquets, fairs and markets which at the same time are solemn tribal gatherings. The tribes place themselves hierarchically in their fraternities and secret societies. On these occasions are practised marriages, initiations, shamanistic seances, and the cults of the great gods, totems, and group or individual ancestors. These are all accompanied by ritual and by prestations by whose means political rank within subgroups, tribes, tribal confederations and nations is settled.[11] But the remarkable thing about these tribes is the spirit of rivalry and antagonism which dominates all their activities. A man is not afraid to challenge an opposing chief or nobleman. Nor does one stop at the purely sumptuous destruction of accumulated wealth in order to eclipse a rival chief (who may be a close relative).[12] We are here confronted with total prestation in the sense that the whole clan, through the intermediacy of its chiefs, makes contracts involving all its members and everything it possesses.[13] But the agonistic character of the prestation is pronounced. Essentially usurious and extravagant, it is above all a struggle among nobles to determine their position in the hierarchy to the ultimate benefit, if they are successful, of their own class. This agonistic type of total prestation we propose to call the "potlatch."

So far in our study Davy and I had found few examples of this institution outside North-West America,[14] Melanesia, and Papua.[15] Everywhere else—in Africa, Polynesia, and Malaya, in South America and the rest of North America—the basis of exchange seemed to us to be a simpler type of total prestation. However, further research brings to light a number of forms intermediate between exchanges marked by exaggerated rivalry like those of the American North-West and Melanesia, and others more moderate where the contracting parties rival each other with gifts: for instance, the French compete with each other in their ceremonial gifts, parties, weddings, and invitations, and feel bound, as the Germans say, to *revanchieren* themselves.[16] We find some of these intermediate forms in the Indo-European world, notably in Thrace.[17]

Many ideas and principles are to be noted in systems of this type. The most important of these spiritual mechanisms is clearly the one which obliges us to make a return gift for a gift received. The moral and religious reasons for this constraint are nowhere more obvious than in Polynesia; and in approaching the Polynesian data in the following chapter [of *The Gift*] we shall see clearly the power which enforces the repayment of a gift and the fulfillment of contracts of this kind.

NOTES

1. Cassel in his *Theory of Social Economy*, Vol. II, p. 345, mentions this text.
2. I have been unable to consult Burckhard, *Zum Begriff der Schenkung*, pp. 53 ff. But for Anglo-Saxon law our immediate point has been noted by Pollock and Maitland, *History of English Law*, Vol. II, p. 82: 'The wide word "gift" . . . will cover sale, exchange, gage and lease.' Cf. pp. 12, 212–214: 'Perhaps we may doubt whether . . . a purely gratuitous promise . . . would have been enforced.' See also the essay by Neubecker on the Germanic dowry, *Die Mitgift*, 1909, pp. 65 ff.
3. 'Foi Jurée'; see bibliography in Mauss, 'Une Forme archaique de Contrat chez les Thraces' in *Revue des Etudes Grecques,* 1921; R. Lenoir, 'L'Institution du Potlatch' in *Revue Philosophique,* 1924.
4. M. F. Samlo, *Der Güterverkehr in der Urgesellschaft,* Institut Solvay, 1909, has some sound discussion on this, and on p. 156 suggests that he is on the lines of our own argument.
5. Grierson, *Silent Trade,* 1903, argued conclusively against this view. See also Von Moszkowski, *Wirtschaftsleben der primitiven Völker,* p. 1911; although he

considers theft to be primitive and confuses it with the right to take. A good exposition of Maori data is to be found in W. von Brun, 'Wirtschaftsorganisation der Maori' in *Beiträgungen Lamprecht,* 18, 1912, in which a chapter is devoted to exchange. The most recent comprehensive work on so-called primitive economics is Koppers, 'Ethnologische Wirtschaftsordnung', in *Anthropos,* 1915–1916, pp. 611–651 and 971–1079; strong on presentation of material but for the rest rather hair-splitting.

6. We wrote recently that in Australia, especially on a death, there is the beginning of exchange on a tribal basis, and not merely amongst clans and phratries. Among the Kakadu of the Northern Territory there are three mortuary ceremonies. During the third the men have a kind of inquest to find out who is the sorcerer responsible for the death. Contrary to normal Australian custom no feud follows. The men simply gather with their spears and state what they require in exchange. Next day the spears are taken to another tribe, e.g., the Umoriu, who realize the reason for the visit. The spears are piled and in accordance with a known scale the required objects are set before them. Then the Kakadu take them away (Baldwin Spencer, *Tribes of the Northern Territories,* 1914, p. 247). Spencer then states that the objects can then be exchanged for spears, a fact we do not fully understand. But he fails to see the connection between the mortuary ceremony and the exchange of gifts, adding that the natives themselves do not see it. But the custom is easy enough to understand. It is a pact which takes the place of a feud, and which sets up an inter-tribal market. The exchange of objects is simultaneously an exchange of peace pledges and of sentiments of solidarity in mourning. In Australia this is normally seen only between clans and families which are in some way associated or related by marriage. The only difference here is that the custom is extended to the tribal basis.

7. Pindar, *Olympiads,* VIII, 4, reflects the kind of situation we are describing. The themes of the gift, of wealth, marriage, honour, favour, alliance, of shared food and drink, and the theme of jealousy in marriage are all clearly represented.

8. See specially the remarkable rules of the ball game among the Omaha: Fletcher and la Flesche, 'Omaha Tribe' in *A.R.B.A.E.,* 1905–1906, pp. 197 and 366.

9. Krause, *Tlingit Indianer,* pp. 234 ff., notes the character of the festivals and rituals although he did not call them 'potlatch'. Boursin in *Eleventh Census,* pp. 54–66, and Porter, ibid., p. 33, saw and named the reciprocal glorification in the potlatch. Swanton, however, has the best commentary, in 'Social Conditions . . . of the Tlingit Indians' in *A.R.B.A.E.,* XXVI, 345. Cf. our notes in *A.S.,* XI, 207 and in *Foi Jurée,* p. 172.

10. On the meaning of the word potlatch, see Barbeau, *Bulletin de la Société de Géographie de Québec,* 1911, and *Foi Jurée,* p. 162. It seems to us, however, that Davy does not take into account the original meaning of the word. Boas, admittedly for the Kwakiutl and not the Chinook, uses the word 'feeder', although the literal meaning is 'Place of getting Satiated'—*Kwa. T.,* II, p. 43; cf. *Kwa. T.,* I, pp. 255, 517. But the two meanings suggested, gift and food, are not exclusive since the usual content of the gift, here at any rate, is food.

11. The legal aspect of potlatch has been discussed by Adam in his articles in the *Zeitschrift für vergleichende Rechtswissenschaft* starting 1911, and in the *Festschrift* to Seler, 1920, and by Davy in *Foi Jurée.* The economic and ritual aspects are no less important and merit the same detailed study. The religious nature of the people involved and of the objects exchanged or destroyed have a bearing on the nature of the contracts, as have the values attributed to them.

12. The Haida call it 'killing wealth'.

13. See Hunt's documents in *Eth. Kwa.,* p. 1340, where there is an interesting description of the way the clan brings its potlatch contributions to the chief, and

a record of some of the discourses. The chief says: 'It will not be in my name. It will be in your name, and you will become famous among the tribes, when it is said that you have given your property for a potlatch' (p. 1342).

14. The potlatch is not confined to the tribes of the North-West. We consider also the 'Asking Festival' of the Alaskan Eskimo as something more than a mere borrowing from neighbouring Indian tribes.

15. See our observations in *A.S.,* XI, 101 and XIII, 372–374, and *Anthropologie,* 1920. Lenoir notes two clear potlatch traits in South America, 'Expéditions Maritimes en Mélanésie' in *Anthropologie,* Sept. 1924.

16. Thurnwald, in *Forschungen,* Vol. III, 1912, p. 8, uses this word.

17. *Revue des Etudes Grecques,* XXXIV, 1921.

Bronislaw Malinowski 1884–1942

BACKGROUND

Bronislaw Malinowski was one of the great field workers, in spite of the psychic and physical suffering that he—like many anthropologists—underwent in the course of it. His diaries, published years after his death, reveal a sensitive, compulsive man, lonely and driven. The diaries are of interest primarily to field workers and psychiatrists—but the magnificent courage to face himself with enough awareness to write it all down gives some measure of the man.

Malinowski was born and educated in Cracow, Poland. His family was aristocratic and cultured; his father was a college professor and well-known Slavic philologist. From an early age, it was assumed that Bronislaw would become an academic. The University of Cracow granted him a doctorate in mathematics and physical sciences in 1908. During his university years he had also developed a strong interest in folk psychology, having worked carefully through the writings of the German psychologist Wilhelm Wundt.

Illness prevented Malinowski from plunging into a career as a mathematician—and so did his recuperation, for it was during that time that he read *The Golden Bough* as his "first attempt to read an English masterpiece in the original." Whatever we may think of his judgment of that book as a masterpiece, we can be grateful that it inspired him—for he never looked back. England was the European center of anthropology, so in 1910 Malinowski began graduate work at the London School of Economics, where he obtained a D.Sc. in 1916. *The Family Among the Australian Aborigines* (1913) and "The Natives of Mailu" (1915) were presented in lieu of a thesis.

At first he worked with Charles Gabriel Seligman and Eduard Westermarck, the great Finnish social scientist who wrote *The History of Human Marriage.* To Seligman especially he owed training, encouragement, financial assistance, and active intercession for his jobs and field work support (although they later drew apart because of different ideas about the scope and aims of anthropology). Malinowski's first published work in English was an article (1912) on economic anthropology in a volume commemorating Westermarck's fiftieth birthday. Malinowski's work was also influenced by W. H. R. Rivers, whom he viewed critically. Malinowski felt that Émile Durkheim and Sebald Rudolf Steinmetz, along with Westermarck, were the founders of "empirical sociology," as social anthropology was then called.

In 1914, with the help of Seligman, Malinowski undertook field work in New Guinea. He spent several months with the Mailu but returned to Australia in February 1915 because of financial difficulties, which he settled only with Seligman's help. He returned to New Guinea in May and planned to go on to Dobu and Rossel Island, but on the way he stopped in the Trobriand Islands and decided to stay there.

World War I broke out while Malinowski was in the field. This might have proved troublesome, since he was an Austro-Hungarian subject and technically an enemy alien, but with their accustomed common sense in such matters, British officials bent the regulations so that he could stay in the field instead of being rounded up. For two years he did intensive field work in the Trobriands, collecting material on which his later classics were built: *Argonauts of the Western Pacific* (1922), *Crime and Custom in Savage Society* (1926), *The Sexual Life of Savages* (1929), and *Coral Gardens and Their Magic* (1935).

In 1918 he returned to Australia, where he lived for a while in Melbourne and married Elsie Masson, daughter of Sir David Orme Masson, professor of chemistry at Melbourne University. When they returned to Europe, he was threatened with a return of tuberculosis, so they spent a year in Tenerife. Not until 1921 did he begin to teach, as occasional lecturer in sociology at the London School of Economics. He began full-time teaching there as reader in social anthropology in 1924, and was made the school's first professor of anthropology in 1927.

Malinowski was a great teacher—loved by some, hated by as many. His seminars in London overflowed. Like Franz Boas, he trained a whole generation: E. E. Evans-Pritchard, Raymond Firth, Meyer Fortes, Ian Hogbin, Phyllis Kaberry, Hilda Kuper, Hortense Powdermaker, Audrey Richards, and Isaac Schapera. Under his influence, standards of field work zoomed higher; he and his students contributed prominently to the reorganization of anthropology that occurred in the 1920s and 1930s.

Malinowski also traveled extensively, lecturing in Geneva, Vienna, Rome, and Oslo, and spending summers in his villa at Obergozen in the South Tyrol. In 1926 he visited the United States to lecture at the University of California and stopped off to see the Pueblo Indians. In 1933 he returned to deliver the Messenger Lectures at Cornell. And in 1936 came again, as a delegate of the University of London to the Harvard Tercentenary celebrations, in the course of which he received an honorary D.Sc.

The last years of his life were overshadowed by the ill health of his wife, who died in 1935, and by his own health, which had never been robust. He came to the United States on sabbatical leave in 1938, going immediately to Tucson in an attempt to find some improvement, and when World War II broke out he remained in America. In June of 1940 he became a visiting professor at Yale. He was married again, this time to artist Valetta Swann. During summer vacations he carried out field studies of peasant marketing systems among the Zapotec of Oaxaca. In 1942 he was appointed permanently as professor at Yale. But he died in May of that year, in the course of a public lecture, before he could take up his appointment in September.

INTRODUCTION

Malinowski was one of the greatest anthropological field workers of all time. His description of his own field work, in the Introduction to *Argonauts of the Western Pacific* (1922) is fascinating reading—but unfortunately it is too long to be reprinted here. The ideals that Malinowski set up for field work go well beyond the ideals set up by Boas for such research. Malinowski learned to speak the language of the Trobrianders whom he studied; he lived among them and recorded much of his data in their language. His description of his own experience in the Trobriands is the most influential primary source for the succeeding decades, and it sets standards that are still not met by most ethnographers.

The archfunctionalist of anthropology, Malinowski is regarded, with Radcliffe-Brown, as a founder of modern functionalism in anthropology (in economics, the idea came earlier). Malinowski's functionalism is biologically and psychologically oriented. His understanding of functionalism as a transformation of the needs of the individual into secondary social needs underlies this point of view. It must be noted that this biopsychological approach to functionalism is very different from Radcliffe-Brown's approach, which pays no attention to the individual and emphasizes the functions of the social system.

Malinowski's functionalism is founded on what he regards as the seven basic needs of man: nutrition, reproduction, bodily comforts, safety, relaxation, movement, and growth. The individual needs are satisfied by derived cultural and social institutions, whose functions are to satisfy those needs. In other words, every social institution has a need to satisfy, and so does every cultural item. Malinowski's view of culture is also based on basic human biosocial needs—he regards culture as a tool that responds to the needs of human beings in a way that is above any adaptation.

One contribution by Malinowski that is too seldom mentioned by commentators is his idea of the institution. The reason may be that, in calling it an institution, he encouraged people to underplay it, for that word is widely and variously used. Nevertheless, the basic idea is very helpful, not only in ethnographic description, but in comparative studies as well. An institution, Malinowski says, is a group of people united or organized for a purpose. They have a charter, or explanation, and they have the technology with which to achieve, or strive to achieve, that purpose. This view of the institution underlies the following late description by Malinowski of his functionalist position.

18 THE GROUP AND THE INDIVIDUAL IN FUNCTIONAL ANALYSIS

PERSONALITY, ORGANIZATION, AND CULTURE

It might seem axiomatic that in any sociological approach the individual, the group, and their relations must remain the constant theme of all observations and argument. The group, after all, is but the assemblage of individuals and must be thus defined—unless we fall into the fallacy of "group mind," "collective sensorium," or the gigantic "Moral Being" which thinks out and improvises all collective events. Nor can such conceptions as individual, personality, self, or mind be described except in terms of membership in a group or groups—unless again we wish to hug the figment of the individual as a detached, self-contained entity. We can, therefore, lay down as an axiom—or better, as an empirical truth—that in field work and theory, in observation and analysis, the *leitmotiv* "individual, group, and their mutual dependence" will run through all the inquiries.

But the exact determination of what we mean by "individual," or how he is related to his "group," the final understanding of the terms "social organization" or "cultural determinism" presents a number of problems to be discussed. I would like to add that over and above individual mental processes and forms of social organization it is necessary to introduce another factor, which together with the previous ones makes up the totality of cultural processes and phenomena. I mean the material apparatus which is indispensable both for the understanding of how a culturally determined individual comes into being and, also, how he co-operates in group life with other individuals.

In what follows I shall discuss some of these questions from the anthropological point of view. Most of my scientific experiences in culture are derived from work in the field. As an anthropologist I am interested in primitive as well as in developed cultures. The functional approach, moreover, considers the totality of cultural phenomena as the necessary background both of the analysis of man and that of society. Indeed, since in my opinion the relation between individual and group is a universal motive in all problems of sociology and comparative anthropology, a brief survey of the functional theory of culture, with a special emphasis on our specific problem, will be the best method of presentation.

Functionalism differs from other sociological theories more definitely, perhaps, in its conception and definition of the individual than in any other respect.[1] The functionalist includes in his analysis not merely the emotional as well as the intellectual side of mental processes, but also insists that man in his full biological reality has to be drawn into our analysis of culture. The bodily needs and environmental influences, and the cultural reactions to them, have thus to be studied side by side.

Reprinted from the *American Journal of Sociology* 44 (1939) by permission of the publisher. Copyright 1939 by the American Journal of Sociology.

The field worker observes human beings acting within an environmental setting, natural and artificial; influenced by it, and in turn transforming it in co-operation with each other. He studies how men and women are motivated in their mutual relations by feelings of attraction and repulsion, by co-operative duties and privileges, by profits drawn and sacrifices made. The invisible network of social bonds, of which the organization of the group is made up, is defined by charters and codes—technological, legal, customary, and moral —to which every individual is differentially submitted, and which integrate the group into a whole. Since all rules and all tribal tradition are expressions in words—that is, symbols—the understanding of social organization implies an analysis of symbolism and language. Empirically speaking the field worker has to collect texts, statements, and opinions, side by side with the observation of behavior and the study of material culture.

In this brief preamble we have already insisted that the individual must be studied as a biological reality. We have indicated that the physical world must be part of our analysis, both as the natural milieu and as the body of tools and commodities produced by man. We have pointed out that individuals never cope with, or move within, their environment in isolation, but in organized groups, and that organization is expressed in traditional charters, which are symbolic in essence.

THE INDIVIDUAL ORGANISM UNDER CONDITIONS OF CULTURE

Taking man as a biological entity it is clear that certain minima of conditions can be laid down which are indispensable to the personal welfare of the individual and to the continuation of the group. All human beings have to be nourished, they have to reproduce, and they require the maintenance of certain physical conditions: ventilation, temperature within a definite range, a sheltered and dry place to rest, and safety from the hostile forces of nature, of animals, and of man. The physiological working of each individual organism implies the intake of food and of oxygen, occasional movement, and relaxation in sleep and recreation. The process of growth in man necessitates protection and guidance in its early stages and, later on, specific training.

We have listed here some of the essential conditions to which cultural activity, whether individual or collective, has instrumentally to conform. It is well to recall that these are only minimum conditions—the very manner in which they are satisfied in culture imposes certain additional requirements. These constitute new needs, which in turn have to be satisfied. The primary —that is, the biological—wants of the human organism are not satisfied naturally by direct contact of the individual organism with the physical environment. Not only does the individual depend on the group in whatever he achieves and whatever he obtains, but the group and all its individual members depend on the development of a material outfit, which in its essence is an addition to the human anatomy, and which entails corresponding modifications of human physiology.

In order to present our argument in a synoptic manner, let us concisely list in Column A of [the following table] the basic needs of the individual. Thus "Nutrition (metabolism)" indicates not only the need for a supply of food and of oxygen, but also the conditions under which food can be prepared, eaten, digested, and the sanitary arrangements which this implies. "Reproduction" obviously means that the sexual urges of man and woman have to be satisfied, and the continuity of the group maintained. The entry "Bodily comforts" indicates that the human organism can be active and effective only within certain ranges of temperature; that it must be sheltered from dampness and drafts; that it must be given opportunities for rest and sleep. "Safety" again refers to all the dangers lurking in the natural environment, both for civilized and primitive: earthquakes and tidal waves, snowstorms and excessive isolation; it also indicates the need of protection from dangerous animals and human foes. "Relaxation" implies the need of the human organism for a rhythm of work by day and sleep at night, of intensive bodily exercise and rest, of seasons of recreation alternating with periods of practical activity. The entry "Movement" declares that human beings must have regular exercises of muscle and nervous system. "Growth" indicates the fact that the development of the human organism is culturally directed and redefined from infancy into ripe age.

SYNOPTIC SURVEY OF BIOLOGICAL AND DERIVED NEEDS AND THEIR SATISFACTION IN CULTURE

A Basic needs (individual)	B Direct responses (Organized, i.e., collective)	C Instrumental needs	D Responses to instrumental needs	E Symbolic and integrative needs	F Systems of thought and faith
Nutrition (metabolism)	Commissariat	Renewal of cultural apparatus	Economics	Transmission of experience by means of precise, consistent principles	Knowledge
Reproduction	Marriage and family				
Bodily comforts	Domicile and dress	Charters of behavior and their sanctions	Social control		
Safety	Protection and defense			Means of intellectual, emotional, and pragmatic control of destiny and chance	Magic Religion
Relaxation	Systems of play and repose	Renewal of personnel	Education		
Movement	Set activities and systems of communication				
Growth	Training and apprenticeship	Organization of force and compulsion	Political organization	Communal rhythm of recreation, exercise, and rest	Art Sports Games Ceremonial

It is clear that the understanding of any one of these entries of Column A brings us down immediately to the analysis of the individual organism. We see that any lack of satisfaction in any one of the basic needs must necessarily imply at least temporary maladjustment. In more pronounced forms, nonsatisfaction entails ill-health and decay through malnutrition, exposure to heat or cold, to sun or moisture; or destruction by natural forces, animals, or man. Psychologically the basic needs are expressed in drives, desires, or emotions, which move the organism to the satisfaction of each need through systems or linked reflexes.

The science of culture, however, is concerned not with the raw material of anatomical and physiological endowment in the individual, but with the manner in which this endowment is modified by social influences. When we inquire how the bodily needs are satisfied under conditions of culture, we find the systems of direct response to bodily needs which are listed in Column B. And here we can see at once the complete dependence of the individual upon the group: each of these cultural responses is dependent upon organized collective activities, which are carried on according to a traditional scheme, and in which human beings not merely co-operate with one another but continue the achievements, inventions, devices, and theories inherited from previous generations.

In matters of nutrition, the individual human being does not act in isolation; nor does he behave in terms of mere anatomy and unadulterated physiology; we have to deal, instead, with personality, culturally molded. Appetite or even hunger is determined by the social milieu. Nowhere and never will man, however primitive, feed on the fruits of his environment. He always selects and rejects, produces and prepares. He does not depend on the physiological rhythm of hunger and satiety alone; his digestive processes are timed and trained by the daily routine of his tribe, nation, or class. He eats at definite times, and he goes for his food to his table. The table is supplied from the kitchen, the kitchen from the larder, and this again is replenished from the market or from the tribal food-supply system.

The symbolic expressions here used—"table," "kitchen," etc.—refer to the various phases of the process which separates the requirements of the organism from the natural sources of food supply, and which is listed in Column B as "Commissariat." They indicate that at each stage man depends on the group—family, club, or fraternity. And here again we use these expressions in a sense embracing primitive as well as civilized institutions, concerned with the production, preparation, and consumption of nourishment. The raw material of individual physiology is found everywhere refashioned by cultural and social determinism. The group has molded the individual in matters of taste, of tribal taboos, of the nutritive and symbolic value of food, as well as in the manners and modes of commensalism. Above all, the group, through economic co-operation, provides the stream of food supply.

One general point which we will have to make throughout our analysis is that the relation is not of the individual to society or *the* group. Even in matters of commissariat a number of groups make their appearance. In the most primitive society we would have the organization of food-gatherers, some institutions through which the distribution and apportionment of food take place, and the commensal group of consumers—as a rule, the family. And were we to analyze each of these groups from the point of view of nutrition, we would find that the place of the individual in each of them is determined by the differentiation as to skill, ability, interest, and appetite.

When we come to the cultural satisfaction of the individual impulses and emotions of sex and of the collective need for reproduction, we would see that human beings do not reproduce by nature alone. The full satisfaction of the impulse, as well as the socially legitimate effect of it, is subject to a whole set of rules defining courtship and marriage, prenuptial and extra-connubial intercourse, as well as the life within the family (Col. B, "Marriage and family"). The individual brings to this, obviously, his or her anatomical equipment, and the corresponding physiological impulses. He also contributes the capacity to develop tastes and interests, emotional attitudes and sentiments. Yet in all this the group not only imposes barriers and presents opportunities, suggests ideals and restrictions, and dictates values, but the community as a whole, through its system of legal rules, ethical and religious principles, and such concepts as honor, virtue, and sin, affects even the physiological attitude of man to woman. Take the most elementary physical impulse, such as the attraction of one sex by another. The very estimate of beauty and the appreciation of the bodily shape is modified by traditional reshaping: lip plugs and nose sticks, scarification and tattooing, the deformation of feet, breasts, waist, and head, and even of the organs of reproduction. In courtship and in selection for marriage such factors as rank, wealth, and economic efficiency enter into the estimate of the integral desirability and value of one mate for the other. And again the fullest expression of the impulse in the desire for children is affected by the systems of legal principle, economic interest, and religious ideology, which profoundly modify the innate substratum of human physiology.

Enough has been said to point out that here once more any empirical study of the reproductive process in a given culture must consider both the individual, the group, and the material apparatus of culture. The individual, in this most personal and subjective concern of human life, is submitted to the influence of tradition which penetrates right down to the processes of internal secretion and physiological response. The selective business of choice and of mating are constantly directed and influenced by the social setting. The most important stages (i.e., marriage and parenthood) have to receive a social hallmark in the contract of marriage. The legitimacy of the fruits of their bodily union depends upon whether they have conformed or not to the systems evolved in the community by traditional dictates.

Yet here once more we do not deal with the group and the individual, but we would have to consider a whole set of human agglomerations: the group of the two principal actors (i.e., marriage), the prospective family, the already developed families of each mate, the local community, and the tribe as the bearer of law, tradition, and their enforcement.

We must survey the other items of Column B more rapidly. The whole cultural system which corresponds to the necessity of keeping the human organism within certain limits of temperature, to the necessity of protecting it from the various inclemencies of wind and weather, obviously implies also the parallel consideration of individual and group. In constructing and maintaining even the simplest habitation, in the keeping of the fire alive, in the upkeep of roads and communications, the individual alone is not enough. He has to be trained for each task in technological and co-operative abilities, and he has to work in conjunction with others.

From the biological point of view the group acts as an indispensable medium for the realization of individual bodily needs. The organism within each culture is trained to accommodate and harden to certain conditions which might prove dangerous or even fatal without this training.

Here, therefore, we have again the two elements: the molding or conditioning of the human anatomy and physiology by collective influences and cultural apparatus, and the production of this apparatus through co-operative activities. Safety is achieved by organized defense, precautionary measures, and calculations based on tribal knowledge and foresight.

The development of the muscular system and the provision of movement are again provided for by the training of the individual organism and by the collective production of means of communication, of vehicles of transport, and of technical rules which define their use. The physical growth as guided by the influence of the group on the individual shows directly the dependence of the organism upon his social milieu. It is also a contribution of the individual to the community in that it supplies in each case an adequate member of one or several social units.

THE INSTRUMENTAL IMPERATIVES OF CULTURE

In glancing at our chart and comparing Columns A and B, we recognize that the first represents the biological needs of the individual organism which must be satisfied in every culture. Column B describes briefly the cultural responses to each of these needs. Culture thus appears first and foremost as a vast instrumental reality—the body of implements and commodities, charters of social organization, ideas and customs, beliefs and values—all of which allow man to satisfy his biological requirements through co-operation and within an environment refashioned and readjusted. The human organism, however, itself becomes modified in the process and readjusted to the type of situation provided by culture. In this sense culture is also a vast conditioning apparatus, which through training, the imparting of skills, the teaching of morals, and the development of tastes amalgamates the raw material of human physiology and anatomy with external elements, and through this supplements the bodily equipment and conditions the physiological processes. Culture thus produces individuals whose behavior cannot be understood by the study of anatomy and physiology alone, but has to be studied through the analysis of cultural determinism—that is, the processes of conditioning and molding. At the same time we see that from the very outset the existence of groups—that is, of individuals organized for co-operation and cultural give and take—is made indispensable by culture.

But this first approach still remains chaotic and incomplete. On the one hand it is easy to see that certain fundamental types of human grouping, such as family, village community, the politically organized tribe, or the modern state, appear almost everywhere in Column B. The family is not merely the reproductive group, it is also almost invariably a unit playing the more or less dominant part in the commissariat. It is associated with the domicile and often with the production of clothing and other means of bodily protection (Col. B, "Domicile and dress"). The tribe or state which is primarily associated with protection and defense is also the group which takes cognizance of marriage law and family organization, which has its collective financial systems, and which at times organizes nutritive exploits on a large scale. Nor could we eliminate the role of the village community from any of the items listed in Column B, for this also functions at times as a food-producing group, or at least plays some part in the commissariat. It is an assemblage of households or tents providing the social setting for courtship and communal recreations. Thus a further analysis of the integrated responses listed in Column B appears inevitable from the point of view of the organization into concrete units of collective activity—that is, institutions.

Our list is also incomplete in so far as certain institutions have not yet been listed. The church, for instance, to which in primitive communities there may correspond a totemic clan or a kinship group worshiping a common ancestor, is not yet on the map. Institutions corresponding to rank and hierarchy, to occupation, and to free association into groups, secret societies, and charitable insurance groups, have not yet been connected with any part of our argument.

Another element of confusion becomes apparent were we to cut short our analysis at this stage: for certain types of activities—economic, educational, or normative—run right through every one of the cultural responses of Column B.

Our further analysis thus branches off into a double line of argument. We can, on the one hand, consider the organization of human activities into certain concrete and, as we shall see, universal forms such as the family, the clan, the tribe, the age-grade, the association (club, secret society), the occupational group (professional or economic), or the church, and the status group of hierarchy in rank, wealth, or power. We have designated such organized groups, connected with definite purposeful activities and invariably united by special reference to environment and to the material apparatus which they wield, by the term "institution."

On the other hand, we can concentrate on the type and character of the activity and define more fully the several aspects of culture, such as economics, education, social control, knowledge, magic, and religion.

Let us start with a brief analysis of this second point. Man's anatomical endowment—which obviously includes not only his muscular system and his organs of digestion and reproduction, but also his brain—is an asset which will be developed under any system of culture when the individual is trained into a full tribesman or citizen of his community. The natural endowment of man presents also, we have seen, a system of needs which are, under culture, satisfied by organized and instrumentally adjusted responses. The empirical corollary of our analysis of basic needs has been that, under conditions of culture, the satisfaction of every organic need is achieved in an indirect, complicated, roundabout manner. It is this vast instrumentalism of human culture which has allowed man to master the environment in a manner incomparably more effective than any animal adaptation.

But every achievement and advantage demands its price to be paid. The complex cultural satisfaction of the primary biological needs imposes upon man new secondary or derived imperatives. In Column C of our table we have ιbriefly listed these new imperatives. It is clear that the use of tools and implements, and the fact that man uses and destroys in the use—that is, consumes—such goods as food produced and prepared, clothing, building materials, and means of transportation, implies the necessity of a constant "renewal of the cultural apparatus."

Every cultural activity again is carried through co-operation. This means that man has to obey rules of conduct: life in common, which is essential to co-operation, means sacrifices and joint effort, the harnessing of individual contributions and work to a common end, and the distribution of the results according to traditional claims. Life in close co-operation—that is, propinquity—offers temptations as regards sex and property. Co-operation implies leadership, authority, and hierarchy, and these, primitive or civilized, introduce the strain of competitive vanity and rivalries in ambition. The rules of conduct which define duty and privilege, harness concupiscences and jealousies, and lay down the charter of family, municipality, tribe, and of every co-operative group, must therefore not only be known in every society, but they must be sanctioned—that is, provided with means of effective enforcement. Thus the need for code and for effective sanction is another derived imperative imposed on every organized group ("Charters of behavior and their sanctions," Col. C).

The members of such groups have to be renewed even as the material objects have to be replaced. Education in the widest sense—that is, the development of the infant into a fully fledged member of his group—is a type of activity which must exist in every culture and which must be carried out specifically with reference to every type of organization ("The renewal of personnel," Col. C). The need for "Organization of force and compulsion" (Col. C) is universal.

In Column D we find briefly listed the cultural systems to be found in every human group as a response to the instrumental needs imposed by the roundabout type of cultural satisfactions. Thus "Economics," that is, systems of production, of distribution, and of consumption; organized systems of "Social control"; "Education," that is, traditional means by which the individual is brought up from infancy to tribal or national status; and "Political organization" into municipality, tribe, or state are universal aspects of every human society (cf. Col. D).

Let us look at our argument and at our table from the point of view of anthropological field work or that of a sociological student in a modern community—that is, from the angle of empirical observation. Our table indicates that field research on primitive or developed communities will have to be directed upon such aspects of culture as economics, legal institutions, education, and the political organization of the unit. Our inquiries will have to include a specific study of the individual, as well as of the group within which he has to live and work.

It is clear that in economic matters the individual member of a culture must acquire the necessary skills, learn how to work and produce, appreciate the prevalent values, manage his wealth, and regulate his consumption according to the established standard of living. Among primitive peoples there will be in all this a considerable uniformity as regards all individuals. In highly civilized communities, the differentiation of labor and of functions defines the place and the productive value of the individual in society. On the other hand, the collective aspect—that is, the organization of economics—is obviously one of the main factors in defining the level of culture and in determining a great many factors of social structure, hierarchy, rank, and status.

As regards social control, anthropological field work in primitive communities has in my opinion missed two essential points. First of all, the absence of clearly crystallized legal institutions does not mean that mechanisms of enforcement, effective sanctions, and at times complicated systems by which obligations and rights are determined are absent. Codes, systems of litigation, and effective sanctions are invariably to be found as a by-product of the action and reaction between individuals within every group—that is, institution. The legal aspect is thus in primitive societies a by-product of the influence of organization upon individual psychology.

On the other hand, the study of the legal problem from the individual point of view reveals to us that the submission to tribal order is always a matter of long and effective training. In many primitive communities, the respect for the rule and the command is not inculcated very early in life—that is, parental authority is, as a rule, less rigidly and drastically forced upon children among so-called savages than among civilized peoples. At the same time there are certain tribal taboos, rules of personal decency, and of domestic morality that are impressed not so much by direct castigation as by the strong shock of ostracism and personal indignation which the child receives from parents, siblings, and contemporaries. In many communities we find that the child passes through a period of almost complete detachment from home, running around, playing about, and engaging in early activities with his playmates and contemporaries. In such activities strict teaching in tribal law is enforced more directly and poignantly than in the parental home. The fact remains that in every community the human being grows up into a law-abiding member; and he is acquainted with the tribal code; and that, through the variety of educational influences and considerations of self-interest, reasonable give and take, and balance of sacrifices and advantages, he follows the rulings of his traditional system of laws. Thus the study of how obedience to rules is inculcated in the individual during his life-history and the study of the mutualities of give and take within organized life in institutions constitute the full field for observation and analysis of the legal system in a primitive community. I would like to add that the science of modern juris- prudence could become inspired by anthropology in treating legal phenom- ena within the context of social life and in conjunction with other norms of conduct.

As regards education, we need only point out that this is the very process through which the total conditioning of the individual is accomplished, and that this always takes place within the organized groups into which the individual enters. He is born into the family, which almost invariably supplies his earliest and most important schooling in the earliest exercise of bodily functions, in the learning of language, and in the acquisition of the simplest manners of cleanliness, conduct, and polite behavior. He than may, through a system of initiation, enter into a group of adolescents, of young warriors, and then of mature tribesmen. In every one of his technical and economic activities he passes through an apprenticeship in which he acquires the skills as well as the legal code of privilege and obligation of his group.

THE PLACE OF THE INDIVIDUAL IN ORGANIZED GROUPS

So far we have been speaking of the instrumental aspects of culture. Their definition is essentially functional. Since in every community there is the need for the renewal of the material apparatus of tools and imple- ments and the production of goods of consumption, there must exist orga- nized economics at every level of development. All the influences which trans- form the naked infant into a cultural personality have to be studied and recorded as educational agencies and constitute the aspect which we label "education." Since law and order have to be maintained, there must be a code of rules, a means of their readjustment and re-establishment when broken or infringed. In every community there exists, therefore, a juridical system. This functional approach is based on the empirical summing-up of the theory of derived needs and their relation to individual biology and cultural co-operation alike.

What is the relation between these functional aspects of culture and the organized forms of activities which we have called "institutions"? The aspects define the type of activity; at the same time every one of them is carried out by definite groups. Co-operation implies spatial contiguity. Two human beings of different sex who are engaged in the business of reproduction, and who have to rear, train, and provide for their offspring cannot be separated by a great distance in space. The members of the family are subject to the require- ment of physical contiguity in the narrow sense. They form a household, and, since the household needs food, implies shelter, and the whole apparatus of domestic supply, it must not only be a reproductive but also an economic as well as as educational group united by the physical framework of habita- tion, utensils, and joint wealth.

Thus we find that one of the universal institutions of mankind, the family, is not merely a group of people thrown together into a common nook and shelter of the environment, wielding conjointly the definite apparatus of domicile, of material equipment, and a portion of productive territory, but also bound by a charter of rules defining their mutual relations, their activities, their rights, and their privileges. The charter of the family, moreover, invariably defines the position of the offspring by reference to the marriage contract of the parents. All the rules of legitimacy, of descent, of inheritance, and succession are contained in it.

The territorial principle of integration produces yet another group: the village community, municipal unit, horde, or territorial section. People unite into villages or migratory hordes, roaming together over a joint territory— partly because there are many tasks for which the workers have to unite; partly because they are the natural groups for immediate defense against animals and marauders; partly also because daily contact and co-operation develop the secondary bonds of acquaintance and affection. And here also, apart from the territorial unity with its rules of land tenure, corporate or individual, apart from the joint ownership of certain instruments such as communal buildings, apart from the permanent personnel of which such a group consists, we have also mythological, legal, and legendary charters from which the sentiments that enter into the bonds of membership are largely derived.

Another institution determined by the spatial principle and united through it on a variety of functions is the widest territorial group, the tribe. This unit as a rule is organized on the joint wielding of collective defense and aggression. It presents, even in the most primitive forms, a differentiation and hierarchy in administrative matters, in ceremonial proceedings, and in military or legal leadership.

In many parts of the world political organization on the territorial basis and cultural identity have to be distinguished. We have in our modern world the minority problem; in primitive communities the symbiosis of two races or two culturally different communities under the same political regime. Thus, identity of language, of custom, and of material culture, constitutes another principle of differentiation, integrating each component part, and distinguishing it from the other.

We see, thus, that the actual concrete organization of human activities does not follow slavishly or exclusively the functional principles of type activities. This refers more specifically to primitive groups. As civilization develops, we find that law, education, and economics tend more and more to become separated from such forms of organization as the family, the village, or the age-grade. They become institutionalized and bring into being specialized professions, spatially set off, with constructions such as factories, courts, and schools. But even in more primitive groups we find that certain occupations each tend to become incorporated into a definite organization. Such groups as magicians, shamans, potters, blacksmiths, or herdsman fall into natural teams, receiving, at least on certain occasions, a spatial unit—that is, specific rights to portions of the territory and to a material oufit that they have to wield under a differential charter of rules and traditional prerogatives. On occasions they work and act together and in separation from the rest of the community.

The analysis into aspects and the analysis into institutions must be carried out simultaneously, if we want to understand any culture completely. The study of such aspects as economics, education, or social control and political organization defines the type and level of the characteristic activities in a culture. From the point of view of the individual, the study of these aspects discloses to us the totality of motives, interests, and values. From the point of view of the group it gives us an insight into the whole process by which the individual is conditioned or culturally formed and of the group mechanism of this process.

The analysis into institutions, on the other hand, is indispensable because they give us the concrete picture of the social organization within the culture. In each institution the individual obviously has to become cognizant of its charter; he has to learn how to wield the technical apparatus or that part of it with which his activities associate him; he has to develop the social attitudes and personal sentiments in which the bonds of organization consist.

Thus, in either of these analyses the twofold approach through the study of the individual with his innate tendencies and their cultural transformation, and the study of the group as the relationship and co-ordination of individuals, with reference to space, environment, and material equipment, is necessary.

THE CULTURAL DEFINITION OF SYMBOLISM

One more addition, however, we shall have to make to our analysis. Right through our arguments we have implied the transmission of rules, the development of general principles of conduct and of technique, and the existence of traditional systems of value and sentiment. This brings us to one more component of human culture, symbolism, of which language is the prototype. Symbolism must make its appearance with the earliest appearance of human culture. It is in essence that modification of the human organism which allows it to transform the physiological drive into a cultural value.

Were we to start from the most tangible aspect of culture and try to imagine the first discovery and use of an implement we would see that this already implies the birth of symbolism. Any attempt to reconstruct concretely and substantially the beginnings of culture must remain futile. But we can analyze some of the cultural achievements of early man and see what each of them implies in its essence.

Imagine the transition from subhuman to human management of any environmental factor: the discovery of fire, the use of such a simple unfashioned implement as a stick or a stone. Obviously, the object thus used becomes an effective element in culture only when it is permanently incorporated into collective use, and the use is traditionally transmitted. Thus the recognition of the principle of its utility was necessary, and this principle had to be fixed so as to be communicable from one individual to another and handed on to the next generation. This alone means that culture could not originate without some element of social organization—that is, of permanent relations between individuals and a continuity of generations—for otherwise communication would not be possible. Co-operation was born in the actual carrying-out of any complex task, such as making fire and keeping it, and the use of fire for the preparation of food, but co-operation was even more necessary in the sharing and transmission even of the simplest principles of serviceability in production or use.

Incorporation and transmission implied one more element—the recognition of value. And it is here that we meet for the first time the mechanism of symbolization. The recognition of value means that a deferred and indirect mechanism for the satisfaction of an urge becomes the object of emotional response. Whether we imagine that the earliest human beings communicated by elementary sounds or by gesture and facial expression, embodied and connected with manual and bodily activity, symbolism was born with the first deferred and indirect satisfaction of any and every bodily need.

The urges of hunger and sex, the desire for personal comfort and security were refocused and transferred onto an object or a process which was the indirect means to the end of satisfying a bodily need. This transference of physiological urge on the secondary reality was in its essence symbolic. Any of the signs, gestures, or sounds which led to the definition of an object, to the reproduction of a process, to the fixation of technique, utility, and value were in essence as fully symbolic as a Chinese pictogram or a letter in our alphabet. For symbolism from its very inception had to be precise, in the sense that it provided a correct formula for the permanent incorporation and transmission of the cultural achievement. It had to be effective in that the drive of the physiological need was transferred and permanently hitched upon the object, which adequately though indirectly subserved the satisfaction of this drive. The sign, sound, or material presentation, the cultural reality to which it referred, and the bodily desire which was indirectly satisfied through it became thus integrated into a unity through the process of conditioned reflex and conditioned stimulus which has become the basis of our understanding of habit, custom, and language through the researches of Pavlov and Bechtyerev.

This analysis proves again that the most important and elementary process—the creation of cultural symbolism and values—cannot be understood without direct reference to individual psychology and physiology. The formation of habits, skills, values, and symbols consists essentially in the conditioning of the human organism to responses which are determined not by nature but by culture.

On the other hand, the social setting is indispensable, because it is the group which maintains and transmits the elements of symbolism, and it is the group which trains each individual and develops in him the knowledge of technique, the understanding of symbols, and the appreciation of values. We have seen also that organization—that is, the personal bonds which relate the members of a group—are based on the psychology and physiology of the individual, because they consist in emotional responses, in the appreciation of mutual services, and in the apprenticeship to the performance of specific tasks by each man within the setting of his group.

THE INDIVIDUAL CONTRIBUTIONS AND GROUP ACTIVITIES
IN KNOWLEDGE AND BELIEF

The understanding of the symbolic process allows us to consider another class of necessities imposed upon man by culture. Obviously, the member of any group has to be able to communicate with his fellow-beings. But this communication is never, not even in the highly differentiated groups of today, a matter of detached, abstract transmission of thought. In primitive communities, language is used even more exclusively for pragmatic purposes. Early human beings used language and symbolism primarily as a means of co-ordinating action or of standardizing techniques and imparting prescriptions for industrial, social, and ritual behavior.

Let us look more closely at some of these systems. To every type of standardized technique there corresponds a system of knowledge embodied in principles, which can be imparted to those who learn, and which help to co-operate those who are already trained. Principles of human knowledge based on true experience and on logical reasoning, and embodied in verbal statements, exist even among the lowest primitives. The view that primitive man has no rudiments of science, that he lives in a world of mystical or magical ideas, is not correct. No culture, however simple, could survive unless its techniques and devices, its weapons and economic pursuits, were based on the sound appreciation of experience and on a logical formulation of its principles. The very first human beings who discovered and incorporated fire-making as a useful art had to appreciate and define the material to be used, its conditions, as well as the technique of friction and of fanning the spark in the tinder. The making of stone implements, and even the selection of useful stones, implied a body of descriptive rules which had to be communicated from one person to another, both in co-operation and in transmission from those who had the experience to those who had to acquire it. Thus we can list in Column E of our chart the necessity of general symbolic principles, which are embodied as a rule not merely in verbal statements but in verbal statements associated with the actual demonstration of technique and material, of physical context, and of utility and value (Col. E, "Transmission of experience by means of precise, consistent principles"). Thus knowledge, or a body of abstract symbols and verbal principles containing the capacity to appear as empirical fact and sound reasoning, is an implication of all cultural behavior even in its earliest beginnings.

In Column F we thus list knowledge as one of the systems of symbolic integration. By knowledge we mean the whole body of experience and of principle embodied in language and action, in techniques and organized pursuits—in food-gathering, with all it implies of natural history, in agriculture, hunting and fishing, sailing and trekking. Knowledge also implies, at every stage of development, the familiarity with the rules of co-operation and with all social obligations and privileges.

But once we realize that even the most primitive human beings developed systems of thought—that is, of foresight, of calculation, and of systematic planning—we are led to another psychological necessity connected with the cultural satisfaction of primary needs. The use of knowledge not only shows man how to achieve certain ends, it also reveals to him the fundamental uncertainties and limitations of his existence. The very fact that man, however primitive, has to think clearly, has to look ahead and also remember the successes and failures of his past experience makes him realize that not every problem can be solved, not every desire satisfied, by his own efforts.

From the point of view of individual psychology we see that reasonable processes and emotional reactions intertwine. The very calculations, and the fact that the principles of knowledge have to be built up into systems of thought, subject man to fear as well as to hope. He knows that his desire is often thwarted and that his expectations are subject to chance.

It is enough to remember that all human beings are affected by ill-health and have to face death ultimately, that misfortune and natural catastrophes, and elements disturbing the favorable run of food-providing activities, always loom on man's mental horizon. The occurrence of such acts of destiny engender not merely reflection, thought, and emotional responses; they force the human group to take action. Plans have to be reorganized whenever a natural catastrophe occurs. The group becomes disintegrated by the death of one of its members, especially if he is a leading individual. Calamity or misfortune thus affects the individual, even as it disorganizes the group.

Which is the new, highly derived, yet emotionally founded need or imperative which these considerations entail? We see that acting as he always does within an atmosphere of uncertainty, with his hopes raised and fears or anxieties aroused, man needs certain positive affirmations of stability, success, and continuity. The dogmatic affirmations of religion and magic satisfy these needs. Whether we take such early beliefs as totemism, magic, or ancestor worship; or these beliefs more fully developed into the concept of providence, a pantheon of gods, or one divinity; we see that man affirms his convictions that death is not real nor yet final, that man is endowed with a personality which persists even after death, and that there are forces in the environment which can be tuned up and propitiated to the trend of human hopes and desires.

We can thus realize the dogmatic essence of religion by the analysis of individual mental processes. But here also the group enters immediately and no purely physiological or psychological analysis of the human organism is sufficient. In the first place, the reaction of man to death and disaster cannot be understood merely in terms of his concern with himself. It is the care for those who depend on him, and the sorrow for those to whom he was attached and who disappear, that provide as much inspiration to religious belief as does the self-centered concern for his own welfare.

Religion, however, does not end or even begin with dogmatic affirmations. It is a system of organized activities, in ritual as well as in ethics. Belief at no stage, certainly not the primitive levels, is a mere metaphysical system. It is a mode of ritual activity which allows man, whether by constraint or persuasion, to manage the supernatural world brought into being by his desires, hopes, fears, and anticipations. All ritual behavior, whether at burial and mourning, at commemorative ceremony and sacrifice, or even in a magical performance, is social. It is social in the sense that often men and women pray, worship, and chant their magic formula in common. Even when a magical act is performed in solitude and secrecy, it invariably has social consequences. Ritual is also social in the sense that the end to be obtained. the integration of the group after death, the conjuring-up of rain and fertility, of a rich haul in fishing and hunting, or of a successful sailing expedition, concerns the interests not of a single person but of a group.

Even sorcery and black magic conform with the stipulations of our argument. In the first place, sorcery, though carried out in secret, produces powerful though negative social results. Again, sorcery is in correct functional interpretation, a primitive type of explaining and accounting for ill-health and death. The whole system of magical counteraction and cure, which is a regular counterpart of the belief in black magic, is the manner in which primitive man satisfies his individual cravings for some means of controlling a really uncontrollable evil. Sociologically it brings about the mobilization of the group consisting of the kinsmen, friends, and followers of the victim. Thus sorcery and the magical means of combating it again satisfy certain psychological needs and are accompanied by a sociological byplay of collective effort to deal with the disaster.

In all this we see once more that a parallel consideration of individual and organized group is indispensable in order to give us insight into the foundations, as well as the forms, of magic and religion. The structure of these cultural realities entails dogmatic thought—that is, positive affirmations about the existence of good and evil, or benevolent and hostile forces, residing in the environment and capable of influencing some of its responses. Such dogmatic affirmations contain recipes as to how the supernatural forces can be controlled through incantation and prayer, through ritual, sacrifice, and collective or individual sacrament.

Since religion consists by and large of collective efforts to achieve ends beneficent to one and all, we find that every religious system has also its ethical factors. Even in a magical ceremony, performed for a successful war or sailing expedition, for the counteracting of sorcery, or for the fertility of the fields, every participating individual and the leader of the performance is carrying out a task in which he subordinates his personal interest to the communal welfare. Such ceremonies carry with them also taboos and restrictions, duties and obligations. The ethics of a magical system consist in all these rules and restrictions to which the individual has to submit in the interests of the group.

The duties of mourning and burial, of communal sacrifice to ancestor ghosts or to totemic beings, also entail a number of rules, regulations, and principles of conduct which constitute the ethical aspect of such a ritual act. The structure of religion, therefore, consists in a dogmatic system of affirmations, in the technique of ritual, and in the rules and precepts of elementary ethics, which define the subordination of the individual to group welfare.

If we had time more fully to analyze the source of tribal rhythm, of emotional and bodily recreation, as well as their cultural satisfaction in artistic creation, in sports, games, and tribal ceremonial, we would find also that the need for any such cultural activity can only be understood by reference to individual psychology and to the needs of the individual organism. The type of satisfaction for each special need, however, implies immediately the elements of tradition, organization, and material equipment—that is, elements which cannot be discussed, still less understood, without the analysis of group life and group organization.

The gist of the foregoing argument has been condensed in our chart by the entry "Means of intellectual, emotional, and pragmatic control of destiny and chance" (Col. E), and in the corresponding entry of "Magic and religion" (Col. F). Again, the need for a "Communal rhythm of recreation, exercise, and rest" (Col. E) is satisfied by such cultural responses as "Art, sports, games, ceremonial" (Col. F).

SUMMARY AND CONCLUSIONS

This brief outline of the functional approach to anthropological field work and comparative theory of culture shows that at every step we had to study, in a parallel and co-ordinated manner, the individual and the group, as well as their relations. The understanding of both these entities, however, must be supplemented by including the reality of environment and material culture. The problem of the relation between group and individual is so pervading and ubiquitous that it cannot be treated detached from any question of culture and of social or psychological process. A theory which does not present and include at every step the definitions of individual contributions and of their integration into collective action stands condemned. The fact that functionalism implies this problem constantly and consistently may be taken as a proof that, so far as it does, it does not neglect one of the most essential problems of all social science.

Indeed, functionalism is, in its essence, the theory of transformation of organic—that is, individual—needs into derived cultural necessities and imperatives. Society by the collective wielding of the conditioning apparatus molds the individual into a cultural personality. The individual, with his physiological needs and psychological processes, is the ultimate source and aim of all tradition, activities, and organized behavior.

The word "society" is used here in the sense of a co-ordinated set of differentiated groups. The juxtaposition and opposition of "the individual" and "the society," as an undifferentiated mass, is always fictitious and therefore fallacious.

From the structural approach we have found that social organization must always be analyzed into institutions—that is, definite groups of men united by a charter, following rules of conduct, operating together a shaped portion of the environment, and working for the satisfaction of definite needs. This latter defines the function of an institution.

Here, once more, we see that every institution contributes, on the one hand, toward the integral working of the community as a whole, but it also satisfies the derived and basic needs of the individual. Thus the family is indispensable to society in supplying its members, training them, and safeguarding their early stages. At the same time to consider the role of the family without reference to individuals in their sex drive, in their personal affections, as between husband and wife, parents and children, or to study the early stages of life-history of the individual outside the domestic circle would be absurd. The local group, as the organization for the joint use of an apportioned territory, as the means of collective defense, and as the medium for the primary division of labor, works as a part of society and as one of its indispensable organs. At the same time, every one of the benefits just listed is enjoyed by every individual member. His role and membership in that group have to be stated from the point of view of psychology, education, and also of the physiological benefits derived by each from the joint activities. The tribe and state carry out a collective policy in war and peace, in conquest and intertribal or international trade; but the very existence of tribe or state depends on the quality of citizenship, which is an individual fact and which consists in the contributions toward, and the benefits derived from, the participation of the individual in group life.

Were we to consider such institutionalized activities as those dependent on age, which are organized into primitive age-grades or the age hierarchies of our civil service, military organization, or professional work, we would find again that the problem must be stated in terms both of individual life-history and of age as a principle of social differentiation and integration.

In the genetic approach, the functionalist demands that, in field work and theory alike, the formation of such collective aptitudes and formed dispositions as taste, skill, principle, dogma, and value be stated in terms of both individual and group. No mental attitude or bodily skill can be understood without reference both to the innate individual and organic endowment and to the cultural influences by which it is shaped.

We have, in this article, followed the gradual transformation of biological needs into cultural imperatives and satisfactions. We have seen that, starting from the individual organism thereof, we come upon instrumental and integrative imperatives. In every culture there corresponds to these such types of organized activities as economics, education, political organization, and legal system; and again organized religion and magic, as well as artistic and recreational activities.

If space would allow we could show that, since every one of these integrative pursuits is carried on by a group, whether this be family, clan, or congregation; since dogma, mythology, and sacred history provide its charters; since every ritual implies a liturgical apparatus; and since the activities are integrated around a definite purpose or function, the communion with the supernatural—we would find that the integrative aspects of culture are again carried on in institutions, religious, magical, artistic, ceremonial, and recreational. The church, the congregation, the totemic clan, the magical or shamanistic corporations, as well as sporting teams and organizations of musicians, dancers, and actors, are examples of such institutions.

The individual, both in social theory and in the reality of cultural life, is the starting-point and the end. The very beginning of human civilization consists in acts of rudimentary mastery of implements, of production of goods, and of the incorporation of special achievements into a permanent tradition by means of symbolism. Society and its component groups are the carriers of verbal—that is, symbolic—tradition, the guardians of communal wealth, and the joint operators of the material and spiritual achievements of a culture. But in all this the ultimate modifying power, the creative inspiration, and all impulse and invention come from the individual.

Culture remains sound and capable of further development only in so far as a definite balance between individual interest and social control can be maintained. If this balance be upset or wrongly poised, we have at one end anarchy, and at the other brutal dictatorship. The present world is threatened in its various parts and through different agencies both with anarchy and with the brutal oppression in which the interests of the state, managed by small gangs with dictatorial powers, are made completely to overrule the elementary rights and interests of the individual. The theoretical discussion of the relation between the individual and the group has thus in our present world not merely an academic but also a deep philosophical and ethical significance. It cannot be too often repeated that any culture which kills individual initiative, and relegates the interests of most of its members to complete insignificance at the expense of a gang-managed totalitarian state, will not be able to develop or even to preserve its cultural patrimony.

NOTE

1. When I speak of "functionalism" here I mean the brand which I have produced and am cultivating myself. My friend Professor R. H. Lowie of Berkeley has in his last book, *The History of Ethnological Theory* (1937), introduced the distinction between "pure" and "tempered" functionalism—my brand being the pure one. Usually Professor Radcliffe-Brown's name is linked with mine as a representative of the functional school. Here the distinction between "plain" and "hyphenated" functionalism might be introduced. Professor Lowie has, in my opinion, completely misunderstood the essence of "pure" functionalism. The substance of this article may serve as a corrective. Professor Radcliffe-Brown is, as far as I can see, still developing and deepening the views of the French sociological school. He thus has to neglect the individual and disregard biology. In this article functionalism "plain and pure" [is] briefly outlined with special reference to the problem of the group and the individual.

A. R. Radcliffe-Brown 1881-1955

BACKGROUND

A. R. Radcliffe-Brown was so much a rival of Malinowski in the eyes of his students (though never, probably, in his own eyes) that when a memorial volume for Malinowski was published in the 1960s some anthropologists clucked that Radcliffe-Brown's name appeared in it more often than did that of Malinowski himself. The remark would have pleased him. Radcliffe-Brown was more austere and "scientific" in his thinking, less flamboyant and adventurous in his field work, than Malinowski. For Radcliffe-Brown to have exposed himself in a presumably secret diary, as Malinowski did, would have been unthinkable. Seen from today's vantage, it is a little difficult to appreciate what the two were arguing about professionally. Yet they seem to have been designed to put each other off.

Alfred Reginald Brown was born in England in 1881. His childhood was one long fight with tuberculosis. When he was well enough to go to school he was educated, first at a public school in Middlesex, then as a foundation scholar at King Edward's High School in Birmingham.

In 1901 he was admitted to Trinity College, Cambridge. He intended to study natural science, but his tutor convinced him to turn to the "moral sciences," which at that time included experimental psychology and economics as well as philosophy. He met W. H. R. Rivers, Alfred Haddon, and John Myers, anthropologists who (with C. G. Seligman) had been members of the 1898 Cambridge expedition to the Torres Straits, which introduced the practice of field research by professionals into European anthropology. These men led him into anthropology.

From Haddon, who later became his most enthusiastic sponsor, Brown acquired an interest in morphology. Haddon introduced him to the idea that inductive generalization must be done on the widest possible base and that strict use of the comparative method requires intensive field study of particular societies. It was with Haddon that he first became critically aware of the systemic interdependence of social phenomena—something that opened the way for his later interest in Émile Durkheim.

While at Cambridge, Brown acquired a reputation for "dash, extravagance, and overbrilliance" that he never lost. As he grew older he became more sedate and somewhat withdrawn, but he remained a controversial personality.

In 1906–1908 he did field research in the Andaman Islands. His fellowship thesis for Trinity was a conventional reconstruction of Andamanese cultural history. He began almost immediately to rewrite it, and during this process he was led to the French sociologists, especially Durkheim and Marcel Mauss. The final version of *The Andaman Islanders* (1922) is dedicated to Haddon and Rivers, but it bears the unmistakeable mark of *L'année sociologique*. This amalgam provided the basis for the structural-functional school of anthropology, of which Radcliffe-Brown was the principal exponent.

In 1910 he returned to the field. Two years in Australia wrestling with the intricacies of kinship and social organization among the Kariera also gave him new insights into totemism and myth. "Three Tribes of Western Australia" was published in 1913.

When World War I broke out, Brown was made director of education for the island of Tonga. He disliked the job, but from it he learned firsthand the pitfalls of applied anthropology, a pursuit he came to disdain.

Most of his working life was spent as something of a wanderer in Africa, Australia, and the United States. From 1920 to 1923, while he held the chair of social anthropology at Cape Town, he organized the successful School of African Life and Language. When he moved to Australia in 1926 he developed a similar program at Sydney with even greater success. He helped found the journal *Oceania* and completed a major synthesis of his earlier researches, "The Social Organization of Australian Tribes" (1930–1931).

In 1926 he legally changed his name by deed poll. Using his mother's family name of Radcliffe, he became double-barreled Radcliffe-Brown. Before long he became known throughout the profession as R-B.

In 1931 he went to the University of Chicago. During this time he worked on primitive law and social sanction, laid the foundation for the modern treatment of the lineage, and systematized and expanded his conception of social anthropology as a "natural science of society" in a series of brilliant lectures and seminars.

As a teacher, he was a spellbinder, master of both his subject and oratory. Although he never actively sought disciples, circles formed around him. Several generations of American anthropologists found him inspirational. As usual, the reactions he inspired were mixed: he filled some with devotion, some with hostile dismay. Many older American anthropologists resented his influence and the "rejection of history" that was falsely ascribed to him. Lowie had a lengthy exchange with him, and we have already noted his public debates with Linton. Radcliffe-Brown was given to instructing other scholars in their own subjects (one professor of Chinese was particularly bitter)—a trait that became intensified as his notions of social anthropology led him to call into question the autonomy and status of other disciplines.

In 1937 he returned to England to occupy the newly created chair of social anthropology at Oxford. This fulfillment was short-lived; the beginning of World War II brought teaching there to an end. R-B spent 1942–1944 in São Paulo on a cultural mission. Back in England, he helped set up postwar programs for research in Africa and Asia, but he could never take part in them because he was retired, very much against his will, when he reached the statutory age limit of sixty-five.

He was on the loose again. From 1947 to 1949 he was professor of social sciences at Farouk I University in Alexandria; from 1951 to 1954 he held a special appointment at Rhodes University in South Africa. In 1950 he and Daryll Forde edited *African Systems of Kinship and Marriage*, and in 1952 a cellection of his essays was published as *Structure and Function in Primitive Society.*

A serious fall that broke several ribs sent him back to England. Between bouts of pneumonia he continued his work, still carrying on old controversies about his favorite topic, "local groups in Australia." His old lung trouble had by now become serious. He died in 1955. His English and American students and admirers published his *Natural Science of Society* after his death.

INTRODUCTION

Radcliffe-Brown has had considerable influence in both anthropology and sociology. The functionalist aspect of Radcliffe-Brown's work, combined with its structuralist approach, reflects the structural functionalism in sociological thought as well as in social anthropology. In a period when anthropology was putting increased emphasis on field work, Radcliffe-Brown's interests remained theoretical. Even in his field work he was more interested in generalizations about social events than in what happened to individuals. His approach to anthropology was also very different from others of that period. His two major methodological positions were generally disputed by most contemporary American anthropologists. One of these—that the individual is of no account and that it is the social system alone that matters—came when culture and personality more or less dominated American anthropology. The other—the use of the organic analogy to make important theoretical points—was also controverted by American anthropologists.

There are three vital concepts often used by Radcliffe-Brown: process, function, and structure. Social process refers to a unit of social activity; it is the regularities of social processes that are important. Such processes are regarded as being synchronic processes, as opposed to diachronic processes, which refer to changes over longer periods of time.

Radcliffe-Brown derived his concept of function from physiology. He believed that the term "function" in the social sciences denoted the same process as in physiology—the connection between structure and life. In the case of society, the connection was between social structure and social life. Function, then, refers to the relationship between process and social structure. A different way of putting this is to say that function is the contribution an element makes to the whole social system. The difference between Radcliffe-Brown and Malinowski is, then, that Malinowski started with the individual. Individual needs were incidental to Radcliffe-Brown, who regarded the system of human interactions rather than human beings as being central in a functionalist approach to society.

The term "structure" refers to a kind of organized arrangement of parts. In the social structure these parts are individual persons who participate in social life, occupying statuses in the social network. The social network is made up of social relationships between individuals of a society, who are controlled by norms or patterns. In his use of the idea of structure, Radcliffe-Brown was a leader. It was on this aspect of his work that his successors in British social anthropology built.

19 ON THE CONCEPT OF FUNCTION IN SOCIAL SCIENCE[1]

The concept of function applied to human societies is based on an analogy between social life and organic life. The recognition of the analogy and of some of its implications is not new. In the nineteenth century the analogy, the concept of function, and the word itself appear frequently in social philosophy and sociology. So far as I know the first systematic formulation of the concept as applying to the strictly scientific study of society was that of Émile Durkheim in 1895. (*Règles de la Méthode Sociologique*).

Durkheim's definition is that the 'function' of a social institution is the correspondence between it and the needs (*besoins* in French) of the social organism. This definition requires some elaboration. In the first place, to avoid possible ambiguity and in particular the possibility of a teleological interpretation, I would like to substitute for the term 'needs' the term 'necessary conditions of existence', or, if the term 'need' is used, it is to be understood only in this sense. It may be here noted, as a point to be returned to, that any attempt to apply this concept of function in social science involves the assumption that there *are* necessary conditions of existence for human societies just as there are for animal organisms, and that they can be discovered by the proper kind of scientific enquiry.

For the further elucidation of the concept it is convenient to use the analogy between social life and organic life. Like all analogies it has to be used with care. An animal organism is an agglomeration of cells and interstitial fluids arranged in relation to one another not as an aggregate but as an integrated living whole. For the biochemist, it is a complexly integrated system of complex molecules. The system of relations by which these units are related is the organic structure. As the terms are here used the organism is *not* itself the structure; it is a collection of units (cells or molecules) arranged in a structure, i.e., in a set of relations; the organism *has* a structure. Two mature animals of the same species and sex consist of similar units combined in a similar structure. The structure is thus to be defined as a set of relations between entities. (The structure of a cell is in the same way a set of relations between complex molecules, and the structure of an atom is a set of relations between electrons and protons.) As long as it lives the organism preserves a certain continuity of structure although it does not preserve the complete identity of its constituent parts. It loses some of its constituent molecules by respiration or excretion; it takes in others by respiration and alimentary absorption. Over a period its constituent cells do not remain the same. But the structural arrangement of the constituent units does remain similar. The process by which this structural continuity of the organism is maintained

Reprinted with permission of Macmillan Publishing Co., Inc., from *Structure and Function in Primitive Society* by A. R. Radcliffe-Brown. First published by The Free Press in 1952. British rights granted by Routledge & Kegan Paul Ltd.

is called life. The life-process consists of the activities and interactions of the constituent units of the organism, the cells, and the organs into which the cells are united.

As the word function is here being used the life of an organism is conceived as the *functioning* of its structure. It is through and by the continuity of the functioning that the continuity of the structure is preserved. If we consider any recurrent part of the life-process, such as respiration, digestion, etc., its *function* is the part it plays in, the contribution it makes to, the life of the organism as a whole. As the terms are here being used a cell or an organ has an *activity* and that activity has a *function.* It is true that we commonly speak of the secretion of gastric fluid as a 'function' of the stomach. As the words are here used we should say that this is an 'activity' of the stomach, the 'function' of which is to change the proteins of food into a form in which these are absorbed and distributed by the blood to the tissues.[2] We may note that the function of a recurrent physiological process is thus a correspondence between it and the needs (i.e., necessary conditions of existence) of the organism.

If we set out upon a systematic investigation of the nature of organisms and organic life there are three sets of problems presented to us. (There are, in addition, certain other sets of problems concerning aspects or characteristics of organic life with which we are not here concerned.) One is that of morphology—what kinds of organic structures are there, what similarities and variations do they show, and how can they be classified? Second are the problems of physiology—how, in general, do organic structures function; what, therefore, is the nature of the life-process? Third are the problems of evolution or development—how do new types of organisms come into existence?

To turn from organic life to social life, if we examine such a community as an African or Australian tribe we can recognise the existence of a social structure. Individual human beings, the essential units in this instance, are connected by a definite set of social relations into an integrated whole. The continuity of the social structure, like that of an organic structure, is not destroyed by changes in the units. Individuals may leave the society, by death or otherwise; others may enter it. The continuity of structure is maintained by the process of social life, which consists of the activities and interactions of the individual human beings and of the organised groups into which they are united. The social life of the community is here defined as the *functioning* of the social structure. The *function* of any recurrent activity, such as the punishment of a crime, or a funeral ceremony, is the part it plays in the social life as a whole and therefore the contribution it makes to the maintenance of the structural continuity.

The concept of function as here defined thus involves the notion of a *structure* consisting of a *set of relations* amongst *unit entities,* the *continuity* of the structure being maintained by a *life-process* made up of the *activities* of the constituent units.

If, with these concepts in mind, we set out on a systematic investigation of the nature of human society and of social life, we find presented to us three sets of problems. First, the problems of social morphology—what kinds of social structures are there, what are their similarities and differences, how are they to be classified? Second, the problems of social physiology—how do social structures function? Third, the problems of development—how do new types of social structure come into existence?

Two important points where the analogy between organism and society breaks down must be noted. In an animal organism it is possible to observe the organic structure to some extent independently of its functioning. It is therefore possible to make a morphology which is independent of physiology. But in human society the social structure as a whole can only be *observed* in its functioning. Some of the features of social structure, such as the geographical distribution of individuals and groups, can be directly observed, but most of the social relations which in their totality constitute the structure, such as relations of father and son, buyer and seller, ruler and subject, cannot be observed except in the social activities in which the relations are functioning. It follows that a social morphology cannot be established independently of a social physiology.

The second point is that an animal organism does not, in the course of its life, change its structural type. A pig does not become a hippopotamus. (The development of the animal from germination to maturity is not a change of type since the process in all its stages is typical for the species.) On the other hand a society in the course of its history can and does change its structural type without any breach of continuity.

By the definition here offered 'function' is the contribution which a partial activity makes to the total activity of which it is a part. The function of a particular social usage is the contribution it makes to the total social life as the functioning of the total social system. Such a view implies that a social system (the total social structure of a society together with the totality of social usages in which that structure appears and on which it depends for its continued existence) has a certain kind of unity, which we may speak of as a functional unity. We may define it as a condition in which all parts of the social system work together with a sufficient degree of harmony or internal consistency, i.e., without producing persistent conflicts which can neither be resolved nor regulated.[3]

This idea of the functional unity of a social system is, of course, a hypothesis. But it is one which, to the functionalist, it seems worthwhile to test by systematic examination of the facts.

There is another aspect of functional theory that should be briefly mentioned. To return to the analogy of social life and organic life, we recognise that an organism may function more or less efficiently and so we set up a special science of pathology to deal with all phenomena of dysfunction. We distinguish in an organism what we call health and disease. The Greeks of the fifth century B.C. thought that one might apply the same notion to society, to the city-state, distinguishing conditions of *eunomia*, good order, social health, from *dysnomia*, disorder, social ill-health. In the nineteenth century Durkheim, in his application of the notion of function, sought to lay the basis for a scientific social pathology, based on a morphology and a physiology.[4] In his works, particularly those on suicide and the division of labour, he attempted to find objective criteria by which to judge whether a given society at a given time is normal or pathological, eunomic or dysnomic. For example, he tried to show that the increase of the rate of suicide in many countries during part of the nineteenth century is symptomatic of a dysnomic or, in his terminology, anomic, social condition. Probably there is no sociologist who would hold that Durkheim really succeeded in establishing an objective basis for a science of social pathology.[5]

In relation to organic structures we can find strictly objective criteria by which to distinguish disease from health, pathological from normal, for disease is that which either threatens the organism with death (the dissolution of its structure) or interferes with the activities which are characteristic of the organic type. Societies do not die in the same sense that animals die and therefore we cannot define dysnomia as that which leads, if unchecked, to the death of a society. Further, a society differs from an organism in that it can change its structural type, or can be absorbed as an integral part of a larger society. Therefore we cannot define dysnomia as a disturbance of the usual activities of a social type (as Durkheim tried to do).

Let us return for a moment to the Greeks. They conceived the health of an organism and the eunomia of a society as being in each instance a condition of the harmonious working together of its parts.[6] Now this, where society is concerned, is the same thing as what was considered above as the functional unity or inner consistency of a social system, and it is suggested that for the degree of functional unity of a particular society it may be possible to establish a purely objective criterion. Admittedly this cannot be done at present; but the science of human society is as yet in its extreme infancy. So that it may be that we should say that, while an organism that is attacked by a virulent disease will react thereto, and, if its reaction fails, will die, a society that is thrown into a condition of functional disunity or inconsistency (for this we now provisionally identify with dysnomia) will not die, except in such comparatively rare instances as an Australian tribe overwhelmed by the white man's destructive force, but will continue to struggle toward some sort of eunomia, some kind of social health, and may, in the course of this, change its structural type. This process, it seems, the 'functionalist' has ample opportunities of observing at the present day, in native peoples subjected to the domination of the civilised nations, and in those nations themselves.[7]

Space will not allow a discussion here of another aspect of functional theory, viz., the question whether change of social type is or is not dependent on function, i.e., on the laws of social physiology. My own view is that there is such a dependence and that its nature can be studied in the development of the legal and political institutions, the economic systems, and the religions of Europe through the last twenty-five centuries. For the preliterate societies with which anthropology is concerned, it is not possible to study the details of long processes of change of type. The one kind of change which the anthropologist can observe is the disintegration of social structures. Yet even here we can observe and compare spontaneous movements towards reintegration. We have, for instance, in Africa, in Oceania, and in America the appearance of new religions which can be interpreted on a functional hypothesis as attempts to relieve a condition of social dysnomia produced by the rapid modification of the social life through contact with white civilisation.

The concept of function as defined above constitutes a 'working hypothesis' by which a number of problems are formulated for investigation. No scientific enquiry is possible without some such formulation of working hypotheses. Two remarks are necessary here. One is that the hypothesis does not require the dogmatic assertion that everything in the life of every community has a function. It only requires the assumption that it *may* have one, and that we are justified in seeking to discover it. The second is that what appears to be the same social usage in two societies may have different functions in the two. Thus the practice of celibacy in the Roman Catholic Church of today has very different functions from those of celibacy in the early Christian Church. In other words, in order to define a social usage, and therefore in order to make valid comparisons between the usages of different peoples or periods, it is necessary to consider not merely the form of the usage but also its function. On this basis, for example, belief in a Supreme Being in a simple society is something different from such a belief in a modern civilised community.

The acceptance of the functional hypothesis or point of view outlined above results in the recognition of a vast number of problems for the solution of which there are required wide comparative studies of societies of many diverse types and also intensive studies of as many single societies as possible. In field studies of the simpler peoples it leads, first of all, to a direct study of the social life of the community as the functioning of a social structure, and of this there are several examples in recent literature. Since the function of a social activity is to be found by examining its effects upon individuals, these are studied, either in the average individual or in both average and exceptional individuals. Further, the hypothesis leads to attempts to investigate directly the functional consistency or unity of a social system and to determine as far as possible in each instance the nature of that unity. Such field studies will obviously be different in many ways from studies carried out from other points of view, e.g., the ethnological point of view that lays emphasis on diffusion. We do not have to say that one point of view is better than another, but only that they are different, and any particular piece of work should be judged in reference to what it aims to do.

If the view here outlined is taken as one form of 'functionalism', a few remarks on Dr. Lesser's paper become permissible. He makes reference to a diffrence of 'content' in functional and nonfunctional anthropology. From the point of view here presented the 'content' or subject-matter of social anthropology is the whole social life of a people in all its aspects. For convenience of handling it is often necessary to devote special attention to some particular part or aspect of the social life, but if functionalism means anything at all it does mean the attempt to see the social life of a people as a whole, as a functional unity.

Dr. Lesser speaks of the functionalist as stressing 'the psychological aspects of culture'; I presume that he here refers to the functionalist's recognition that the usages of a society work or 'function' only through their effects in the life, i.e., in the thoughts, sentiments and actions of individuals.

The 'functionalist' point of view here presented does therefore imply that we have to investigate as thoroughly as possible all aspects of social life, considering them in relation to one another, and that an essential part of the task is the investigation of the individual and of the way in which he is moulded by or adjusted to the social life.

Turning from content to method Dr. Lesser seems to find some conflict between the functional point of view and the historical. This is reminiscent of the attempts formerly made to see a conflict between sociology and history. There need be no conflict, but there is a difference.

There is not, and cannot be, any conflict between the functional hypothesis and the view that any culture, any social system, is the end-result of a unique series of historical accidents. The process of development of the race-horse from its five-toed ancestor was a unique series of historical accidents. This does not conflict with the view of the physiologist that the horse of today and all the antecedent forms conform or conformed to physiological laws, i.e., to the necessary conditions of organic existence. Palaeontology and physiology are not in conflict. One 'explanation' of the race-horse is to be found in its history—how it came to be just what it is and where it is. Another and entirely independent 'explanation' is to show how the horse is a special exemplification of physiological laws. Similarly one 'explanation' of a social system will be its history, where we know it—the detailed account of how it came to be what it is and where it is. Another 'explanation' of the same system is obtained by showing (as the functionalist attempts to do) that it is a special exemplification of laws of social physiology or social functioning. The two kinds of explanation do not conflict, but supplement one another.[8]

The functional hypothesis is in conflict with two views that are held by some ethnologists, and it is probably these, held as they often are without precise formulation, that are the cause of the antagonism to that approach. One is the 'shreds and patches' theory of culture, the designation being taken from a phrase of Professor Lowie[9] when he speaks of 'that planless hodge-podge, that thing of shreds and patches called civilisation'. The concentration of attention on what is called the diffusion of culture-traits tends to produce a conception of culture as a collection of disparate entities (the so-called traits) brought together by pure historical accident and having only accidental relations to one another. The conception is rarely formulated and maintained with any precision, but as a half-unconscious point of view it does seem to control the thinking of many ethnologists. It is, of course, in direct conflict with the hypothesis of the functional unity of social systems.

The second view which is in direct conflict with the functional hypothesis is the view that there are no discoverable significant sociological laws such as the functionalist is seeking. I know that some two or three ethnologists say that they hold this view, but I have found it impossible to know what they mean, or on what sort of evidence (rational or empirical) they would base their contention. Generalisations about any sort of subject matter are of two kinds: the generalisations of common opinion, and generalisations that have been verified or demonstrated by a systematic examination of evidence afforded by precise observations systematically made. Generalisations of the latter kind are called scientific laws. Those who hold that there are no laws of human society cannot hold that there are no generalisations about human society because they themselves hold such generalisations and even make new ones of their own. They must therefore hold that in the field of social phenomena, in contradistinction to physical and biological phenomena, any attempt at the systematic testing of existing generalisations or towards the discovery and verification of new ones, is, for some unexplained reason, futile, or, as Dr. Radin puts it, 'crying for the moon'. Argument against such a contention is unprofitable or indeed impossible.

NOTES

1. This paper, which is based on comments that I made on a paper read by Dr. Lesser to the American Anthropological Association, is reprinted from the *American Anthropologist*, Vol. XXXVII, p. 3, 1935, where it accompanied Dr. Lesser's paper.
2. The insistence on this precise form of terminology is only for the sake of the analogy that is to be drawn. I have no objection to the use of the term function in physiology to denote both the activity of an organ and the results of that activity in maintaining life.
3. Opposition, i.e., organised and regulated antagonism, is, of course, an essential feature of every social system.
4. For what is here called dysnomia Durkheim used the term anomia (*anomie* in French). This is to my mind inappropriate. Health and disease, eunomia and dysnomia, are essentially relative terms.
5. I would personally agree in the main with the criticisms of Roger Lacombe (*La Méthode Sociologique de Durkheim*, 1926, ch. iv) on Durkheim's general theory of social pathology, and with the criticisms of Durkheim's treatment of suicide presented by Halbwachs, *Les Causes du Suicide*.
6. See, for example, the Fourth Book of Plato's *Republic*.
7. To avoid misunderstanding it is perhaps necessary to observe that this distinction of eunomic and dysnomic social conditions does not give us any evaluation of these societies as 'good' or 'bad'. A savage tribe practising polygamy, cannibalism, and sorcery can possibly show a higher degree of functional unity or consistency than the United States of 1935. This objective judgment, for such it must be if it is to be scientific, is something very different from any judgment as to which of the two social systems is the better, the more to be desired or approved.
8. I see no reason at all why the two kinds of study—the historical and the functional —should not be carried on side by side in perfect harmony. In fact, for fourteen years I have been teaching both the historical and geographical study of peoples under the name of ethnology in close association with archaeology, and the functional study of social systems under the name of social anthropology. I do think that there are many disadvantages in mixing the two subjects together and confusing them. See 'The Methods of Ethnology and Social Anthropology' (*South African Journal of Science*, 1923, pp. 124–147).

9. *Primitive Society*, p. 411. A concise statement of this point of view is the following passage from Dr. Ruth Benedict's 'The Concept of the Guardian Spirit in North America' (*Memoirs*, American Anthropological Association, 29, 1923), p. 84: 'It is, so far as we can see, an ultimate fact of human nature that man builds up his culture out of disparate elements, combining and recombining them; and until we have abandoned the superstition that the result is an organism functionally interrelated, we shall be unable to see our cultural life objectively, or to control its manifestations.' I think that probably neither Professor Lowie nor Dr. Benedict would, at the present time, maintain this view of the nature of culture.

20 ON SOCIAL STRUCTURE

It has been suggested to me by some of my friends that I should use this occasion to offer some remarks about my own point of view in social anthropology; and since in my teaching, beginning at Cambridge and at the London School of Economics thirty years ago, I have consistently emphasised the importance of the study of social structure, the suggestion made to me was that I should say something on that subject.

I hope you will pardon me if I begin with a note of personal explanation. I have been described on more than one occasion as belonging to something called the 'Functional School of Social Anthropology' and even as being its leader, or one of its leaders. This Functional School does not really exist; it is a myth invented by Professor Malinowski. He has explained how, to quote his own words, 'the magnificent title of the Functional School of Anthropology has been bestowed by myself, in a way on myself, and to a large extent out of my own sense of irresponsibility'. Professor Malinowski's irresponsibility has had unfortunate results, since it has spread over anthropology a dense fog of discussion about 'functionalism'. Professor Lowie has announced that the leading, though not the only, exponent of functionalism in the nineteenth century was Professor Franz Boas. I do not think that there is any sense, other than the purely chronological one, in which I can be said to be either the follower of Professor Boas or the predecessor of Professor Malinowski. The statement that I am a 'functionalist' would seem to me to convey no definite meaning.

There is no place in natural science for 'schools' in this sense, and I regard social anthropology as a branch of natural science. Each scientist starts from the work of his predecessors, finds problems which he believes to be significant, and by observation and reasoning endeavours to make some contribution to a growing body of theory. Co-operation amongst scientists results from the fact that they are working on the same or related problems.

Reprinted with permission of Macmillan Publishing Co., Inc., from *Structure and Function in Primitive Society* by A. R. Radcliffe-Brown. First published by The Free Press in 1952. British rights granted by Routledge & Kegan Paul Ltd.

Such co-operation does not result in the formation of schools, in the sense in which there are schools of philosophy or of painting. There is no place for orthodoxies and heterodoxies in science. Nothing is more pernicious in science than attempts to establish adherence to doctrines. All that a teacher can do is to assist the student in learning to understand and use the scientific method. It is not his business to make disciples.

I conceive of social anthropology as the theoretical natural science of human society, that is, the investigation of social phenomena by methods essentially similar to those used in the physical and biological sciences. I am quite willing to call the subject 'comparative sociology', if anyone so wishes. It is the subject itself, and not the name, that is important. As you know, there are some ethnologists or anthropologists who hold that it is not possible, or at least not profitable, to apply to social phenomena the theoretical methods of natural science. For these persons social anthropology, as I have defined it, is something that does not, and never will, exist. For them, of course, my remarks will have no meaning, or at least not the meaning I intend them to have.

While I have defined social anthropology as the study of human society, there are some who define it as the study of culture. It might perhaps be thought that this difference of definition is of minor importance. Actually it leads to two different kinds of study, between which it is hardly possible to obtain agreement in the formulation of problems.

For a preliminary definition of social phenomena it seems sufficiently clear that what we have to deal with are relations of association between individual organisms. In a hive of bees there are the relations of association of the queen, the workers and the drones. There is the association of animals in a herd, of a mother-cat and her kittens. These are social phenomena; I do not suppose that anyone will call them cultural phenomena. In anthropology, of course, we are only concerned with human beings, and in social anthropology, as I define it, what we have to investigate are the forms of association to be found amongst human beings.

Let us consider what are the concrete, observable facts with which the social anthropologist is concerned. If we set out to study, for example, the aboriginal inhabitants of a part of Australia, we find a certain number of individual human beings in a certain natural environment. We can observe the acts of behaviour of these individuals, including, of course, their acts of speech, and the material products of past actions. We do not observe a 'culture', since that word denotes, not any concrete reality, but an abstraction, and as it is commonly used a vague abstraction. But direct observation does reveal to us that these human beings are connected by a complex network of social relations. I use the term 'social structure' to denote this network of actually existing relations. It is this that I regard it as my business to study if I am working, not as an ethnologist or psychologist, but as a social anthropologist. I do not mean that the study of social structure is the whole of social anthropology, but I do regard it as being in a very important sense the most fundamental part of the science.

My view of natural science is that it is the systematic investigation of the structure of the universe as it is revealed to us through our senses. There are certain important separate branches of science, each of which deals with a certain class or kind of structures, the aim being to discover the characteristics of all structures of that kind. So atomic physics deals with the structure of atoms, chemistry with the structure of molecules, crystallography and colloidal chemistry with the structure of crystals and colloids, and anatomy and physiology with the structures of organisms. There is, therefore, I suggest, place for a branch of natural science which will have for its task the discovery of the general characteristics of those social structures of which the component units are human beings.

Social phenomena constitute a distinct class of natural phenomena. They are all, in one way or another, connected with the existence of social structures, either being implied in or resulting from them. Social structures are just as real as are individual organisms. A complex organism is a collection of living cells and interstitial fluids arranged in a certain structure; and a living cell is similarly a structural arrangement of complex molecules. The physiological and psychological phenomena that we observe in the lives of organisms are not simply the result of the nature of the constituent molecules or atoms of which the organism is built up, but are the result of the structure in which they are united. So also the social phenomena which we observe in any human society are not the immediate result of the nature of individual human beings, but are the result of the social structure by which they are united.

It should be noted that to say we are studying social structures is not exactly the same thing as saying that we study social relations, which is how some sociologists define their subject. A particular social relation between two persons (unless they be Adam and Eve in the Garden of Eden) exists only as part of a wide network of social relations, involving many other persons, and it is this network which I regard as the object of our investigations.

I am aware, of course, that the term 'social structure' is used in a number of different senses, some of them very vague. This is unfortunately true of many other terms commonly used by anthropologists. The choice of terms and their definitions is a matter of scientific convenience, but one of the characteristics of a science as soon as it has passed the first formative period is the existence of technical terms which are used in the same precise meaning by all the students of that science. By this test, I regret to say, social anthropology reveals itself as not yet a formed science. One has therefore to select for oneself, for certain terms, definitions which seem to be the most convenient for the purpose of scientific analysis.

There are some anthropologists who use the term social structure to refer only to persistent social groups, such as nations, tribes and clans, which retain their continuity, their identity as individual groups, in spite of changes in their membership. Dr. Evans-Pritchard, in his recent admirable book on the Nuer, prefers to use the term social structure in this sense. Certainly the existence of such persistent social groups is an exceedingly important aspect of structure. But I find it more useful to include under the term social structure a good deal more than this.

In the first place, I regard as a part of the social structure all social relations of person to person. For example, the kinship structure of any society consists of a number of such dyadic relations, as between a father and son, or a mother's brother and his sister's son. In an Australian tribe the whole social structure is based on a network of such relations of person to person, established through genealogical connections.

Secondly, I include under social structure the differentiation of individuals and of classes by their social role. The differential social positions of men and women, of chiefs and commoners, of employers and employees, are just as much determinants of social relations as belonging to different clans or different nations.

In the study of social structure the concrete reality with which we are concerned is the set of actually existing relations, at a given moment of time, which link together certain human beings. It is on this that we can make direct observations. But it is not this that we attempt to describe in its particularity. Science (as distinguished from history or biography) is not concerned with the particular, the unique, but only with the general, with kinds, with events which recur. The actual relations of Tom, Dick and Harry or the behaviour of Jack and Jill may go down in our field note-books and may provide illustrations for a general description. But what we need for scientific purposes is an account of the form of the structure. For example, if in an Australian tribe I observe in a number of instances the behaviour towards one another of persons who stand in the relation of mother's brother and sister's son, it is in order that I may be able to record as precisely as possible the general or normal form of this relationship, abstracted from the variations of particular instances, though taking account of those variations.

This important distinction, between structure as an actually existing concrete reality, to be directly observed, and structural form, as what the field-worker describes, may be made clearer perhaps by a consideration of the continuity of social structure through time, a continuity which is not static like that of a building, but a dynamic continuity, like that of the organic structure of a living body. Throughout the life of an organism its structure is being constantly renewed; and similarly the social life constantly renews the social structure. Thus the actual relations of persons and groups of persons change from year to year, or even from day to day. New members come into a community by birth or immigration; others go out of it by death or emigration. There are marriages and divorces. Friends may become enemies, or enemies may make peace and become friends. But while the actual structure changes in this way, the general structural form may remain relatively constant over a longer or shorter period of time. Thus if I visit a relatively stable community and revisit it after an interval of ten years, I shall find that many of its members have died and others have been born; the members who still survive are now ten years older and their relations to one another may have changed in many ways. Yet I may find that the kinds of relations that I can observe are very little different from those observed ten years before. The structural form has changed little.

But, on the other hand, the structural form may change, sometimes gradually, sometimes with relative suddenness, as in revolutions and military conquests. But even in the most revolutionary changes some continuity of structure is maintained.

I must say a few words about the spatial aspect of social structure. It is rarely that we find a community that is absolutely isolated, having no outside contact. At the present moment of history, the network of social relations spreads over the whole world, without any absolute solution of continuity anywhere. This gives rise to a difficulty which I do not think that sociologists have really faced, the difficulty of defining what is meant by the term 'a society'. They do commonly talk of societies as if they were distinguishable, discrete entities, as, for example, when we are told that a society is an organism. Is the British Empire a society or a collection of societies? Is a Chinese village a society, or is it merely a fragment of the Republic of China?

If we say that our subject is the study and comparison of human societies, we ought to be able to say what are the unit entities with which we are concerned.

If we take any convenient locality of a suitable size, we can study the structural system as it appears in and from that region, i.e., the network of relations connecting the inhabitants amongst themselves and with the people of other regions. We can thus observe, describe, and compare the systems of social structure of as many localities as we wish. To illustrate what I mean, I may refer to two recent studies from the University of Chicago, one of a Japanese village, Suye Mura, by Dr. John Embree, and the other of a French Canadian community, St. Denis, by Dr. Horace Miner.

Closely connected with this conception of social structure is the conception of 'social personality' as the position occupied by a human being in a social structure, the complex formed by all his social relations with others. Every human being living in society is two things: he is an individual and also a person. As an individual, he is a biological organism, a collection of a vast number of molecules organised in a complex structure, within which, as long as it persists, there occur physiological and psychological actions and reactions, processes and changes. Human beings as individuals are objects of study for physiologists and psychologists. The human being as a person is a complex of social relationships. He is a citizen of England, a husband and a father, a bricklayer, a member of a particular Methodist congregation, a voter in a certain constituency, a member of his trade union, an adherent of the Labour Party, and so on. Note that each of these descriptions refers to a social relationship, or to a place in a social structure. Note also that a social personality is something that changes during the course of the life of the person. As a person, the human being is the object of study for the social anthropologist. We cannot study persons except in terms of social structure, nor can we study social structure except in terms of the persons who are the units of which it is composed.

If you tell me that an individual and a person are after all really the same thing, I would remind you of the Christian creed. God is three persons, but to say that He is three individuals is to be guilty of a heresy for which men have been put to death. Yet the failure to distinguish individual and person is not merely a heresy in religion; it is worse than that; it is a source of confusion in science.

I have now sufficiently defined, I hope, the subject-matter of what I regard as an extremely important branch of social anthropology. The method to be adopted follows immediately from this definition. It must combine with the intensive study of single societies (i.e., of the structural systems observable in particular communities) the systematic comparison of many societies (or structural systems of different types). The use of comparison is indispensable. The study of a single society may provide materials for comparative study, or it may afford occasion for hypotheses, which then need to be tested by reference to other societies; it cannot give demonstrated results.

Our first task, of course, is to learn as much as we can about the varieties, or diversities, of structural systems. This requires field research. Many writers of ethnographical descriptions do not attempt to give us any systematic account of the social structure. But a few social anthropologists, here and in America, do recognise the importance of such data and their work is providing us with a steadily growing body of material for our study. Moreover, their researches are no longer confined to what are called 'primitive' societies, but extend to communities in such regions as Sicily, Ireland, Japan, Canada and the United States.

If we are to have a real comparative morphology of societies, however, we must aim at building up some sort of classification of types of structural systems. That is a complex and difficult task, to which I have myself devoted attention for thirty years. It is the kind of task that needs the co-operation of a number of students and I think I can number on my fingers those who are actively interested in it at the present time. Nevertheless, I believe some progress is being made. Such work, however, does not produce spectacular results and a book on the subject would certainly not be an anthropological best-seller.

We should remember that chemistry and biology did not become fully formed sciences until considerable progress had been made with the systematic classification of the things they were dealing with, substances in the one instance and plants and animals in the other.

Besides this morphological study, consisting in the definition, comparison and classification of diverse structural systems, there is a physiological study. The problem here is: How do structural systems persist? What are the mechanisms which maintain a network of social relations in existence, and how do they work? In using the terms morphology and physiology, I may seem to be returning to the analogy between society and organism which was so popular with medieval philosophers, was taken over and often misused by nineteenth-century sociologists, and is completely rejected by many modern writers. But analogies, properly used, are important aids to scientific thinking and there is a real and significant analogy between organic structure and social structure.

In what I am thus calling social physiology we are concerned not only with social structure, but with every kind of social phenomenon. Morals, law, etiquette, religion, government, and education are all parts of the complex mechanism by which a social structure exists and persists. If we take up the structural point of view, we study these things, not in abstraction or isolation, but in their direct and indirect relations to social structure, i.e., with reference to the way in which they depend upon, or affect, the social relations between persons and groups of persons. I cannot do more here than offer a few brief illustrations of what this means.

Let us first consider the study of language. A language is a connected set of speech usages observed within a defined speech-community. The existence of speech-communities and their sizes are features of social structure. There is, therefore, a certain very general relation between social structure and language. But if we consider the special characteristics of a particular language—its phonology, its morphology and even to a great extent its vocabulary—there is no direct connection of either one-sided or mutual determination between these and the special characteristics of the social structure of the community within which the language is spoken. We can easily conceive that two societies might have very similar forms of social structure and very different kinds of language, or vice versa. The coincidence of a particular form of social structure and a particular language in a given community is always the result of historical accident. There may, of course, be certain indirect, remote interactions between social structure and language, but these would seem to be of minor importance. Thus the general comparative study of languages can be profitably carried out as a relatively independent branch of science, in which the language is considered in abstraction from the social structure of the community in which it is spoken.

But, on the other hand, there are certain features of linguistic history which are specifically connected with social structure. As structural phenomena may be instanced the process by which Latin, from being the language of the small region of Latium, became the language of a considerable part of Europe, displacing the other Italic languages, Etruscan, and many Celtic languages; and the subsequent reverse process by which Latin split up into a number of diverse local forms of speech, which ultimately became the various Romance languages of today.

Thus the spread of language, the unification of a number of separate communities into a single speech-community, and the reverse process of subdivision into different speech-communities are phenomena of social structure. So also are those instances in which, in societies having a class structure, there are differences of speech usage in different classes.

I have considered language first, because linguistics is, I think, the branch of social anthropology which can be most profitably studied without reference to social structure. There is a reason for this. The set of speech usages which constitute a language does form a system, and systems of this kind can be compared in order to discover their common general, or abstract, characters, the determination of which can give us laws, which will be specifically laws of linguistics.

Let us consider very briefly certain other branches of social anthropology and their relation to the study of social structure. If we take the social life of a local community over a period, let us say a year, we can observe a certain sum total of activities carried out by the persons who compose it. We can also observe a certain apportionment of these activities, one person doing certain things, another doing others. This apportionment of activities, equivalent to what is sometimes called the social division of labour, is an important feature of the social structure. Now activities are carried out because they provide some sort of 'gratification', as I propose to call it, and the characteristic feature of social life is that activities of certain persons provide gratifications for other persons. In a simple instance, when an Australian blackfellow goes hunting, he provides meat, not only for himself, but for his wife and children and also for other relatives to whom it is his duty to give meat when he has it. Thus in any society there is not only an apportionment of activities, but also an apportionment of the gratifications resulting therefrom, and some sort of social machinery, relatively simple or, sometimes, highly complex, by which the system works.

It is this machinery, or certain aspects of it, that constitutes the special subject-matter studied by the economists. They concern themselves with what kinds and quantities of goods are produced, how they are distributed (i.e., their flow from person to person, or region to region), and the way in which they are disposed of. Thus what are called economic institutions are extensively studied in more or less complete abstraction from the rest of the social system. This method does undoubtedly provide useful results, particularly in the study of complex modern societies. Its weaknesses become apparent as soon as we attempt to apply it to the exchange of goods in what are called primitive societies.

The economic machinery of a society appears in quite a new light if it is studied in relation to the social structure. The exchange of goods and services is dependent upon, is the result of, and at the same time is a means of maintaining a certain structure, a network of relations between persons and collections of persons. For the economists and politicians of Canada the potlatch of the Indians of the north-west of America was simply wasteful foolishness and it was therefore forbidden. For the anthropologist it was the machinery for maintaining a social structure of lineages, clans and moieties, with which was combined an arrangement of rank defined by privileges.

Any full understanding of the economic institutions of human societies requires that they should be studied from two angles. From one of these the economic system is viewed as the mechanism by which goods of various kinds and in various quantities are produced, transported and transferred, and utilised. From the other the economic system is a set of relations between persons and groups which maintains, and is maintained by, this exchange or circulation of goods and services. From the latter point of view, the study of the economic life of societies takes its place as part of the general study of social structure.

Social relations are only observed, and can only be described, by reference to the reciprocal behaviour of the persons related. The form of a social structure has therefore to be described by the patterns of behaviour to which individuals and groups conform in their dealings with one another. These patterns are partially formulated in rules which, in our own society, we distinguish as rules of etiquette, or morals and of law. Rules, of course, only exist in their recognition by the members of the society; either in their verbal recognition, when they are stated as rules, or in their observance in behaviour. These two modes of recognition, as every field-worker knows, are not the same thing and both have to be taken into account.

If I say that in any society the rules of etiquette, morals and law are part of the mechanism by which a certain set of social relations is maintained in existence, this statement will, I suppose, be greeted as a truism. But it is one of those truisms which many writers on human society verbally accept and yet ignore in theoretical discussions, or in their descriptive analyses. The point is not that rules exist in every society, but that what we need to know for a scientific understanding is just how these things work in general and in particular instances.

Let us consider, for example, the study of law. If you examine the literature on jurisprudence you will find that legal institutions are studied for the most part in more or less complete abstraction from the rest of the social system of which they are a part. This is doubtless the most convenient method for lawyers in their professional studies. But for any scientific investigation of the nature of law it is insufficient. The data with which a scientist must deal are events which occur and can be observed. In the field of law, the events which the social scientist can observe and thus take as his data are the proceedings that take place in courts of justice. These are the reality, and for the social anthropologist they are the mechanism or process by which certain definable social relations between persons and groups are restored, maintained or modified. Law is a part of the machinery by which a certain social structure is maintained. The system of laws of a particular society can only be fully understood if it is studied in relation to the social structure, and inversely the understanding of the social structure requires, amongst other things, a systematic study of the legal institutions.

I have talked about social relations, but I have not so far offered you a precise definition. A social relation exists between two or more individual organisms when there is some adjustment of their respective interests, by convergence of interest, or by limitation of conflicts that might arise from divergence of interests. I use the term 'interest' here in the widest possible sense, to refer to all behaviour that we regard as purposive. To speak of an interest implies a subject and an object and a relation between them. Whenever we say that a subject has a certain interest in an object we can state the same thing by saying that the object has a certain value for the subject. Interest and value are correlative terms, which refer to the two sides of an asymmetrical relation.

Thus the study of social structure leads immediately to the study of interests or values as the determinants of social relations. A social relation does not result from similarity of interests, but rests either on the mutual interest of persons in one another, or on one or more common interests, or on a combination of both of these. The simplest form of social solidarity is where two persons are both interested in bringing about a certain result and co-operate to that end. When two or more persons have a *common interest* in an object, that object can be said to have a *social value* for the persons thus associated. If, then, practically all the members of a society have an interest in the observance of the laws, we can say that the law has a social value. The study of social values in this sense is therefore a part of the study of social structure.

It was from this point of view that in an early work I approached the study of what can conveniently be called ritual values, i.e., the values expressed in rites and myths. It is perhaps again a truism to say that religion is the cement which holds society together. But for a scientific understanding we need to know just how it does this, and that is a subject for lengthy investigations in many different forms of society.

As a last example let me mention the study of magic and witchcraft, on which there is an extensive anthropological literature. I would point to Dr. Evans-Pritchard's work on the Zande as an illuminating example of what can be done when these things are systematically investigated in terms of the part they play in the social relations of the members of a community.

From the point of view that I have attempted briefly to describe, social institutions, in the sense of standardised modes of behaviour, constitute the machinery by which a social structure, a network of social relations, maintains its existence and its continuity. I hesitate to use the term 'function', which in recent years has been so much used and misused in a multitude of meanings, many of them very vague. Instead of being used, as scientific terms ought to be, to assist in making distinctions, it is now used to confuse things that ought to be distinguished. For it is often employed in place of the more ordinary words 'use', 'purpose', and 'meaning'. It seems to me more convenient and sensible, as well as more scholarly, to speak of the use or uses of an axe or digging stick, the meaning of a word or symbol, the purpose of an act of legislation, rather than to use the word function for these various things. 'Function' has been a very useful technical term in physiology and by analogy with its use in that science it would be a very convenient means of expressing an important concept in social science. As I have been accustomed to use the word, following Durkheim and others, I would define the social function of a socially standardised mode of activity, or mode of thought, as its relation to the social structure to the existence and continuity of which it makes some contribution. Analogously, in a living organism, the physiological function of the beating of the heart, or the secretion of gastric juices, is its relation to the organic structure to the existence or continuity of which it makes its contribution. It is in this sense that I am interested in such things as the social function of the punishment of crime, or the social function of the totemic rites of Australian tribes, or of the funeral rites of the Andaman Islanders. But this is not what either Professor Malinowski or Professor Lowie means by functional anthropology.

Besides these two divisions of the study of social structure, which I have called social morphology and social physiology, there is a third, the investigation of the processes by which social structures change, of how new forms of structures come into existence. Studies of social change in the non-literate societies have necessarily been almost entirely confined to one special kind of process of change, the modification of the social life under the influence or domination of European invaders or conquerors.

It has recently become the fashion amongst some anthropologists to treat changes of this kind in terms of what is called 'culture contact'. By that term we can understand the one-sided or two-sided effects of interaction between two societies, groups, classes or regions having different forms of social life, different institutions, usages and ideas. Thus in the eighteenth century there was an important exchange of ideas between France and Great Britain, and in the nineteenth century there was a marked influence of German thought on both France and England. Such interactions are, of course, a constant feature of social life, but they need not necessarily involve any marked change of social structure.

The changes that are taking place in the non-literate peoples of Africa are of a very different kind. Let us consider an African colony or possession of a European nation. There is a region that was formerly inhabited by Africans with their own social structure. Europeans, by peaceful or forceful means, establish control over the region, under what we call a 'colonial' regime. A new social structure comes into existence and then undergoes development. The population now includes a certain number of Europeans—government officials, missionaries, traders and in some instances settlers. The social life of the region is no longer simply a process depending on the relations and interactions of the native peoples. There grows up a new political and economic structure in which the Europeans, even though few in numbers, exercise dominating influence. Europeans and Africans constitute different classes within the new structure, with different languages, different customs and modes of life, and different sets of ideas and values. A convenient term for societies of this kind would be 'composite' societies; the term 'plural' societies has also been suggested. A complex example of a composite society is provided by the Union of South Africa with its single political and economic structure and a population including English-speaking and Afrikaans-speaking peoples of European descent, the so-called 'coloured people' of the Cape Province, progeny of Dutch and Hottentots, the remaining Hottentots, the 'Malays' of Cape Town, descendants of persons from the Malay Archipelago, Hindus and Mohammedans from India and their descendants, and a number of Bantu tribes who constitute the majority of the population of the Union taken as a whole.

The study of composite societies, the description and analysis of the processes of change in them, is a complex and difficult task. The attempt to simplify it by considering the process as being one in which two or more 'cultures' interact, which is the method suggested by Malinowski in his Introduction to Memorandum XV of the International Institute of African Language and Culture on 'Methods of Study of Culture Contact in Africa' (1938), is simply a way of avoiding the reality. For what is happening in South Africa, for example, is not the interaction of British culture, Afrikander (or Boer) culture, Hottentot culture, various Bantu cultures and Indian culture, but the interaction of individuals and groups within an established social structure which is itself in process of change. What is happening in a Transkeian tribe, for example, can only be described by recognising that the tribe has been incorporated into a wide political and economic structural system.

For the scientific study of primitive societies in conditions in which they are free from the domination by more advanced societies which result in these composite societies, we have unfortunately an almost complete lack of authentic historical data. We cannot study, but can only speculate about, the processes of change that took place in the past of which we have no record. Anthropologists speculate about former changes in the societies of the Australian aborigines, or the inhabitants of Melanesia, but such speculations are not history and can be of no use in science. For the study of social change in societies other than the composite societies to which reference has been made we have to rely on the work of historians dealing with authentic records.

You are aware that in certain anthropological circles the term 'evolutionary anthropologist' is almost a term of abuse. It is applied, however, without much discrimination. Thus Lewis Morgan is called an evolutionist, although he rejected the theory of organic evolution and in relation to society believed, not in evolution, but in progress, which he conceived as the steady material and moral improvements of mankind from crude stone implements and sexual promiscuity to the steam engines and monogamous marriage of Rochester, N.Y. But even such antievolutionists as Boas believe in progress.

It is convenient, I think, to use the term 'progress' for the process by which human beings attain to greater control over the physical environment through the increase of knowledge and improvement of technique by inventions and discoveries. The way in which we are now able to destroy considerable portions of cities from the air is one of the latest striking results of progress. Progress is not the same thing as social evolution, but it is very closely connected with it.

Evolution, as I understand the term, refers specifically to a process of emergence of new forms of structure. Organic evolution has two important features: (1) in the course of it a small number of kinds of organisms have given rise to a very much larger number of kinds; (2) more complex forms of organic structure have come into existence by development out of simpler forms. While I am unable to attach any definite meaning to such phrases as the evolution of culture or the evolution of language, I think that social evolution is a reality which the social anthropologist should recognise and study. Like organic evolution, it can be defined by two features. There has been a process by which, from a small number of forms of social structure, many different forms have arisen in the course of history; that is, there has been a process of diversification. Secondly, throughout this process more complex forms of social structures have developed out of, or replaced, simpler forms.

Just how structural systems are to be classified with reference to their greater or less complexity is a problem requiring investigation. But there is evidence of a fairly close correlation between complexity and another feature of structural systems, namely, the extent of the field of social relations. In a structural system with a narrow total social field, an average or typical person is brought into direct and indirect social relations with only a small number of other persons. In systems of this type we may find that the linguistic community—the body of persons who speak one language—numbers from 250 to 500, while the political community is even smaller, and economic relations by the exchange of goods and services extend only over a very narrow range. Apart from the differentiation by sex and age, there is very little differentiation of social role between persons or classes. We can contrast with this the systems of social structure that we observe today in England or the United States. Thus the process of human history to which I think the term social evolution may be appropriately applied might be defined as the process by which wide-range systems of social structure have grown out of, or replaced, narrow-range systems. Whether this view is acceptable or not, I suggest that the concept of social evolution is one which requires to be defined in terms of social structure.

There is no time on this occasion to discuss the relation of the study of social structure to the study of culture. For an interesting attempt to bring the two kinds of study together I would refer you to Mr. Gregory Bateson's book *Naven*. I have made no attempt to deal with social anthropology as a whole and with all its various branches and divisions. I have endeavoured only to give you a very general idea of the kind of study to which I have found it scientifically profitable to devote a considerable and steadily increasing proportion of my time and energy. The only reward that I have sought I think I have in some measure found—something of the kind of insight into the nature of the world of which we are part that only the patient pursuit of the method of natural science can afford.

PART
FOUR
EVOLUTION
and
STRUCTURALISM

Julian Steward 1902–1972

BACKGROUND

Julian Steward was born in Washington, D.C., the second child of the chief of the Board of Examiners of the U.S. Patent Office.

As a freshman at the University of California in 1921, he took an introductory course in anthropology taught by Alfred Kroeber, Robert Lowie, and Edward Winslow Gifford. The next year he transferred to Cornell, where he got his B.A. The president of Cornell, Livingston Farrand, himself an anthropologist, advised him to return to California. He did so, and at Berkeley Steward and his fellow students (including William Duncan Strong, Lloyd Warner, and Ralph Beals) gained a concern for the role of physical environment in culture from Carl Sauer of the geography department.

Steward spent his summers in archaeological and ethnographic studies along the Columbia River and in the Owens Valley. During this period he discovered the Eastern Mono practice of systematically irrigating wild seed plants and tubers, even though they did no planting or cultivation.

During 1929 he compiled a description and trait analysis of petroglyphs in California, Nevada, Utah, Arizona, and Lower California. His analysis uncovered indications of chronology and function, but the tedious work discouraged further interest in the culture trait approach. The same year he finished his doctorate with a dissertation entitled *The Ceremonial Buffoon of the American Indian* (published in 1931).

Steward spent the years of the Great Depression at the universities of Michigan, Utah, and California. He worked primarily on Great Basin archaeology, especially cave sites on the ancient terraces of the Great Salt Lake Region.

In 1934 he married Jane Cannon, and they began two years of ethnographic research on Shoshonean cultures. This work resulted in a large monograph, *Basin-Plateau Aboriginal Sociopolitical Groups* (1938), two large inventories of localized cultural detail, and a number of papers.

In 1935, when Steward was appointed Associate Anthropologist in the Bureau of American Ethnology, he had a chance to widen his sphere of work. He did applied anthropology under John Collier, the Commissioner of Indian Affairs, and field work in highland Ecuador and Peru and among the Carrier Indians of British Columbia.

In 1936, in *The Economic and Social Basis of Primitive Bands* he compared the ecology, population density, band size, and marriage rules of hunting and gathering societies as foundation for a theory of primary social organization.

In 1940 Steward summarized one phase of his work in "Native Cultures of the Intermontane (Great Basin) Area" and began his comprehensive survey of South American Indian cultures. A by-product was the formation of the Inter-American Society of Anthropology and Geography, with a journal, *Acta Americana*. He set up, and became the first director of, the Institute of Social Anthropology, established within the Smithsonian Institution to teach in Mexico, Peru, Brazil, and Colombia and to conduct field research on practical aspects of contemporary Latin American cultures.

In 1946, after the *Handbook of South American Indians* was completed and the institute had been turned over to a new director, Steward took a professorship at Columbia University. In 1947 he and a number of collaborators began a project on Puerto Rico, the final report for which appeared in 1956. An offshoot of this study was his book *Area Research: Theory and Practice* (1950).

Between 1952 (when he became research professor at the University of Illinois) and 1959 he wrote up and edited a large backlog, an important collection of works: *Theory of Culture Change* (1955), *The People of Puerto Rico* (1956), and *Native Peoples of South America* (1959 with Louis Faron). During this period he also edited the symposia *Irrigation Civilizations* (1955) and *Perspectives on Plantations* (1957).

A Ford grant in 1956 allowed Steward to begin a new research program on cross-cultural regularities, in which he described and analyzed the culturally leveling and differentiating consequences of industrialization and urbanization on a variety of societies—northwestern Mexico, the central Andes, West Africa, East Africa, Indonesia, and Japan. In 1957 came the start of extensive field work by a team of anthropologists, including Stanley Diamond in Nigeria, Edward Winter and Thomas Beidelman in Tanganyika, Robert Manners in Kenya, Frederic Lehman in Burma, Richard Downs in Malaya, Toshinao Yoneyama in Japan, Charles Erasmus in Mexico, and Sol Miller and Louis Faron in Peru. Steward and his wife spent 1957–1958 visiting the teams operating in Tanganyika, Kenya, Malaya, and Japan.

In 1959 Steward was appointed as one of the first five members of the University of Illinois Center for Advanced Study. With Oscar Lewis and John McGregor, he helped set up the independent Department of Anthropology at that school. He remained at the University of Illinois until his death early in 1972 of a circulatory ailment.

INTRODUCTION

Steward worked in an era, and on a set of problems, that presented him with a difficult contradiction: the fascination of anthropologists had turned almost totally from culture to culture*s*, and the pendulum away from evolution had swung as far as it would go. Steward's problem was to find an acceptable view of evolution without removing the "s" from "cultures." This problem made Steward unconventional in evolutionary theory.

Steward's emphasis on ecology, cultural types, and multilinear evolution gave the anthropology of the 1930s and 1940s a viable alternative to the "traditional" approaches to cultural evolution. Unlike the classical evolutionists, Steward's work stresses the individuality of different cultures. He claims that the whole of human experience can never be reduced to a few distinct stages of cultural development.

"Multilinear evolution," as Steward called his approach, does not maintain that universal stages of development exist. It is a methodology concerned with regularity in social change, the goal of which is to develop cultural laws empirically.

Multilinear evolution is organized around parallel patterns of development, which are regarded as cultural types. The types have cross-cultural validity and show the following characteristics: (1) they are made up of selected cultural elements rather than cultures as wholes; (2) these cultural elements must be selected in relationship to a problem and to a frame of reference; and (3) the cultural elements that are selected must have the same functional relationships in every culture fitting the type. Some known cultural types are feudalism, Oriental despotism, and the patrilineal band.

The patrilineal band was first recognized as a cultural type by Steward himself. It has the following selected elements: (1) patrilineality, (2) patrilocality, (3) exogamy, (4) land ownership, and (5) a certain type of lineage composition. These selected cultural elements are, according to Steward, cross-culturally recurrent. They are to be found in the Bushmen of South Africa, the Australians, the Tasmanians, some Shoshonean groups, and a variety of other cultures.

The cultural core that is basic to the patrilineal band as a type is a result of environmental adaptation. Uniformity of the type results from similar exploitation of the environment by all these groups. The number of cultural types may be huge, and it cannot be organized in broad evolutionary categories.

Cultural types, then, came about as cultural adaptations to the environment, each representing a level of sociocultural integration. Man's adaptation to his environment, however, is different from that of other living organisms. Man adapts much more rapidly through his culture, which is a superorganic entity, than he does through his organism.

Steward's concepts of cultural adaptation are theoretically important in that they break the circular argument that only culture can explain culture, which in a sense remains true. The key to the adaptation of a culture is its technology; the method of cultural ecology developed by Steward stresses technology. The method of cultural ecology has three aspects: (1) the analysis of the methods of production in the environment must be analyzed, and (2) the pattern of human behavior that is part of these methods must be analyzed in order to (3) understand the relationship of production techniques to the other elements of the culture. However, Steward does emphasize that the extent to which productive activities influence a culture is always an empirical problem.

Julian Steward has had a powerful impact, both on evolutionary thinking and on ecological approaches to society. Much of his thinking underlies the anthropology of the 1970s.

21 THE CONCEPT AND METHOD OF CULTURAL ECOLOGY

OBJECTIVES IN ECOLOGICAL STUDIES

At the risk of adding further confusion to an already obscure term, this chapter undertakes to develop the concept of ecology in relation to human beings as an heuristic device for understanding the effect of environment upon culture. In order to distinguish the present purpose and method from those implied in the concepts of biological, human, and social ecology, the term *cultural ecology* is used. Since cultural ecology is not generally understood, it is necessary to begin by showing wherein it differs from the other concepts of ecology and then to demonstrate how it must supplement the usual historical approach of anthropology in order to determine the creative processes involved in the adaptation of culture to its environment.

The principal meaning of ecology is "adaptation to environment." Since the time of Darwin, environment has been conceived as the total web of life wherein all plant and animal species interact with one another and with physical features in a particular unit of territory. According to Webster,[1] the biological meaning of ecology is "the mutual relations between organisms and their environment." The concept of adaptive interaction is used to explain the origin of new genotypes in evolution; to explain phenotypical variations; and to describe the web of life itself in terms of competition, succession, climaxes, gradients, and other auxiliary concepts.

Although initially employed with reference to biotic assemblages, the concept of ecology has naturally been extended to include human beings since they are part of the web of life in most parts of the world. Man enters the ecological scene, however, not merely as another organism which is related to other organisms in terms of his physical characteristics. He introduces the super-organic factor of culture, which also affects and is affected by the total web of life. What to do about this cultural factor in ecological studies has raised many methodological difficulties, as most human and social ecologists have recognized (Alihan 1938). The principal difficulty lies in the lack of clarity as to the purpose of using the concept of ecology. The interaction of physical, biological, and cultural features within a locale or unit of territory is usually the ultimate objective of study. Human or social ecology is regarded as a subdiscipline of its own right and not as means to some further scientific end. Essentially descriptive, the analysis lacks the clear objectives of biology, which has used ecology heuristically to explain several kinds of biological phenomena. If human or social ecology is considered an operational tool rather than an end in itself, two quite different objectives are suggested: first, an understanding of the organic functions and genetic variations of man as a purely biological species; second, a determination of how

Reprinted from Julian Steward, *Theory of Culture Change* (Urbana, Ill.: University of Illinois Press, 1955), pp. 30–42, by permission of the publisher.

culture is affected by its adaptation to environment. Each requires its own concepts and methods.

The first, or biological objective, involves several somewhat different problems, all of which, however, must view man in the web of life. Since man is a domesticated animal, he is affected physically by all his cultural activities. The evolution of the Hominidae is closely related to the emergence of culture, while the appearance of *Homo sapiens* is probably more the result of cultural causes than of physical causes. The use of tools, fire, shelter, clothing, new foods, and other material adjuncts of existence was obviously important in evolution, but social customs should not be overlooked. Social groups as determined by marriage customs as well as by economic activities in particular environments have undoubtedly been crucial in the differentiations of local populations and may even have contributed to the emergence of varieties and subraces of men.

The problem of explaining man's cultural behavior is of a different order than that of explaining his biological evolution. Cultural patterns are not genetically derived and, therefore, cannot be analyzed in the same way as organic features. Although social ecologists are paying more and more attention to culture in their enquiries, an explanation of culture per se has not, so far as I can see, become their major objective. Culture has merely acquired greater emphasis as one of many features of the local web of life, and the tools of analysis are still predominantly borrowed from biology. Since one of the principal concepts of biological ecology is the community—the assemblage of plants and animals which interact within a locality—social or human ecology emphasizes the human community as the unit of study. But "community" is a very general and meaningless abstraction. If it is conceived in cultural terms, it may have many different characteristics depending upon the purpose for which it is defined. The tendency, however, has been to conceive of human and biological communities in terms of the biological concepts of competition, succession, territorial organization, migration, gradients, and the like. All of these derived fundamentally from the fact that underlying biological ecology is a relentless and raw struggle for existence both within and between species— a competition which is ultimately determined by the genetic potentials for adaptation and survival in particular biotic-environmental situations. Biological co-operation, such as in many forms of symbiosis, is strictly auxiliary to survival of the species.

Human beings do not react to the web of life solely through their genetically derived organic equipment. Culture, rather than genetic potential for adaptation, accommodation, and survival, explains the nature of human societies. Moreover, the web of life of any local human society may extend far beyond the immediate physical environment and biotic assemblage. In states, nations, and empires, the nature of the local group is determined by these larger institutions no less than by its local adaptations. Competition of one sort or another may be present, but it is always culturally determined and as often as not co-operation rather than competition may be prescribed. If, therefore, the nature of human communities is the objective of analysis, explanations will be found through use of cultural historical concepts and methods rather than biological concepts, although, as we shall show, historical methods alone are insufficient.

Many writers on social or human ecology have sensed the need to distinguish between biological and cultural phenomena and methods, but they have not yet drawn clear distinctions. Thus, Hollingshead recognizes a difference between an "ecological order [which] is primarily rooted in competition" and "social organization [which] has evolved out of communication" (Hollingshead 1940; Adams 1935). This attempt to conceptualize competition as a category wholly distinct from other aspects of culturally determined behavior is, of course, artificial. Bates (1953), a human biologist, recognizes the importance of culture in determining the nature of communities, but he does not make clear whether he would use human ecology to explain the range of man's biological adaptation under environmental-cultural situations or whether he is interested in man's culture. The so-called Chicago school of Park, Burgess, and their followers were also primarily interested in communities of human beings, especially urban communities. Their methodology as applied to Chicago and other cities treats the components of each as if they were genetically determined species. In analyzing the zoning of a modern city, such categories as retail businesses, wholesale houses, manufacturing firms, and residences of various kinds, and even such additional features as rate of delinquency, are considered as if each were a biological species in competition with one another for zones within the urban area. Such studies are extremely enlightening as descriptive analysis of spacial distributions of kinds of activities within a modern Euro-American city. They do not, however, necessarily throw any light on world-wide ecological urban adaptations, for in other cultures and periods city zoning followed very different culturally prescribed principles. For example, most of the cities of ancient civilizations were rather carefully planned by a central authority for defensive, administrative, and religious functions. Free enterprise, which might have allowed competition for zones between the institutions and subsocieties arising from these functions, was precluded by the culture.

A fundamental scientific problem is involved in these different meanings attached to ecology. Is the objective to find universal laws or processes, or is it to explain special phenomena? In biology, the law of evolution and the auxiliary principles of ecology are applicable to all webs of life regardless of the species and physical environments involved. In social science studies, there is a similar effort to discover universal processes of cultural change. But such processes cannot be conceptualized in biological terms. The social science problem of explaining the origin of unlike behavior patterns found among different societies of the human species is very different from the problems of biological evolution. Analyzing environmental adaptations to show how new cultural patterns arise is a very different matter than seeking universal similarities in such adaptation. Until the processes of cultural ecology are understood in the many particulars exemplified by different cultures in different parts of the world a formulation of universal processes will be impossible.

Hawley, who has given the most recent and comprehensive statement of social ecology (Hawley 1950), takes cultural phenomena into account far more than his predecessors. He states that man reacts to the web of life as a cultural animal rather than as a biological species. "Each acquisition of a new technique or a new use for an old technique, regardless of the source of its origin, alters man's relations with the organisms about him and changes his position in the biotic community." But, preoccupied with the totality of phenomena within the locale and apparently with a search for universal relationships, Hawley makes the local community the focus of interest (Hawley 1950: 68). The kinds of generalizations which might be found are indicated by the statement: "If we had sufficient knowledge of a preliterate peoples to enable us to compare the structure of residence groups arranged in order of size from smallest to largest, we should undoubtedly observe the same phenomena —each increment in size is accompanied by an advance in the complexity of organization" (Hawley 1950:197). This is the kind of self-evident generalization made by the unilinear evolutionists: cultural progress is manifest in increasing populations, internal specialization, over-all state controls, and other general features.

Hawley is uncertain in his position regarding the effect of environmental adaptations on culture. He states: "The weight of evidence forces the conclusion that the physical environment exerts but a permissive and limiting effect" (Hawley 1950:90), but he also says that "each habitat not only permits but to a certain extent necessitates a distinctive mode of life" (Hawley 1950: 190). The first statement closely conforms with the widely accepted anthropological position that historical factors are more important than environmental factors, which may be permissive or prohibitive of culture change but are never causative. The second is nearer to the thesis of this paper that cultural ecological adaptations constitute creative processes.

CULTURE, HISTORY, AND ENVIRONMENT

While the human and social ecologists have seemingly sought universal ecological principles and relegated culture in its local varieties to a secondary place, anthropologists have been so preoccupied with culture and its history that they have accorded environment only a negligible role. Owing in part to reaction against the "environmental determinists," such as Huntington and Semple, and in part to cumulative evidence that any culture increases in complexity to a large extent because of diffused practices, the orthodox view now holds that history, rather than adaptive processes, explains culture. Since historical "explanations" of culture employ the culture area concept, there is an apparent contradiction. The culture area is a construct of behavioral uniformities which occur within an area of environmental uniformities. It is assumed that cultural and natural areas are generally coterminous because the culture represents an adjustment to the particular environment. It is assumed further, however, that various different patterns may exist in any natural area and that unlike cultures may exist in similar environments.

The cultural-historical approach is, however, also one of relativism. Since cultural differences are not directly attributable to environmental differences and most certainly not to organic or racial differences, they are merely said to represent divergences in cultural history, to reflect tendencies of societies to develop in unlike ways. Such tendencies are not explained. A distinctive pattern develops, it is said, and henceforth is the primary determinant of whether innovations are accepted. Environment is relegated to a purely secondary and passive role. It is considered prohibitive or permissive, but not creative. It allows man to carry on some kinds of activities and it prevents others. The origins of these activities are pushed back to a remote point in time or space, but they are not explained. This view has been best expressed by Forde, who writes:

Neither the world distributions of the various economies, nor their development and relative importance among the particular peoples, can be regarded as simple functions of physical conditions and natural resources. Between the physical environment and human activity there is always a middle term, a collection of specific objectives and values, a body of knowledge and belief: in other words, a cultural pattern. That the culture itself is not static, that it is adaptable and modifiable in relation to physical conditions, must not be allowed to obscure the fact that adaptation proceeds by discoveries and inventions which are themselves in no sense inevitable and which are, in any individual community, nearly all of them acquisitions or impositions from without. The peoples of whole continents have failed to make discoveries that might at first blush seem obvious. Equally important are the restrictions placed by social patterns and religious concepts on the utilization of certain resources or on adaptations to physical conditions (Forde 1949:463).

The habitat at one and the same time circumscribes and affords scope for cultural development in relation to the pre-existing equipment and tendency of a particular society, and to any new concepts and equipment that may reach it from without (Forde 1949:464).

But if geographical determinism fails to account for the existence and distribution of economies, economic determinism is equally inadequate in accounting for the social and political organizations, the religious beliefs and the psychological attitudes which may be found in the cultures based on those economies. Indeed, the economy may owe as much to the social and ritual pattern as does the character of society to the economy. The possession of particular methods of hunting or cultivating, of certain cultivated plants or domestic animals, in no wise defines the pattern of society. Again, there is interaction and on a new plane. As physical conditions may limit the possibilities of the economy, so the economy may in turn be a limiting or stimulating factor in relation to the size, density and stability of human settlement, and to the social and political unit. But it is only one such factor, and advantage may not be taken of the opportunities it affords. The tenure and transmission of land and other property, the development and relations of social classes, the nature of government, the religious and ceremonial life—all these are parts of a social superstructure, the development of which is conditioned not only by the foundations of habitat and economy, but by complex interactions within its own fabric and by external contacts, often largely indifferent to both the physical background and to the basic economy alike (Forde 1949:465).

CULTURAL ECOLOGY

Cultural ecology differs from human and social ecology in seeking to explain the origin of particular cultural features and patterns which characterize different areas rather than to derive general principles applicable to any cultural-environmental situation. It differs from the relativistic and neo-evolutionist conceptions of culture history in that it introduces the local environment as the extracultural factor in the fruitless assumption that culture comes from culture. Thus, cultural ecology presents both a problem and a method. The problem is to ascertain whether the adjustments of human societies to their environments require particular modes of behavior or whether they permit latitude for a certain range of possible behavior patterns. Phrased in this way, the problem also distinguishes cultural ecology from "environmental determinism" and its related theory "economic determinism" which are generally understood to contain their conclusions within the problem.

The problem of cultural ecology must be further qualified, however, through use of a supplementary conception of culture. According to the holistic view, all aspects of culture are functionally interdependent upon one another. The degree and kind of interdependency, however, are not the same with all features. Elsewhere, I have offered the concept of *cultural core*—the constellation of features which are most closely related to subsistence activities and economic arrangements. The core includes such social, political, and religious patterns as are empirically determined to be closely connected with these arrangements. Innumerable other features may have great potential variability because they are less strongly tied to the core. These latter, or secondary features, are determined to a greater extent by purely cultural-historical factors—by random innovations or by diffusion—and they give the appearance of outward distinctiveness to cultures with similar cores. Cultural ecology pays primary attention to those features which empirical analysis shows to be most closely involved in the utilization of environment in culturally prescribed ways.

The expression "culturally prescribed ways" must be taken with caution, for its anthropological usage is frequently "loaded." The normative concept, which views culture as a system of mutually reinforcing practices backed by a set of attitudes and values, seems to regard all human behavior as so completely determined by culture that environmental adaptations have no effect. It considers that the entire pattern of techology, land use, land tenure, and social features derive entirely from culture. Classical illustrations of the primacy of cultural attitudes over common sense are that the Chinese do not drink milk nor the Eskimo eat seals in summer.

Cultures do, of course, tend to perpetuate themselves, and change may be slow for such reasons as those cited. But over the millennia cultures in different environments have changed tremendously, and these changes are basically traceable to new adaptations required by changing technology and productive arrangements. Despite occasional cultural barriers, the useful arts have spread extremely widely, and the instances in which they have not been accepted because of pre-existing cultural patterns are insignificant. In pre-agricultural times, which comprised perhaps 99 per cent of cultural history, technical devices for hunting, gathering, and fishing seem to have diffused largely to the limits of their usefulness. Clubs, spears, traps, bows, fire, containers, nets, and many other cultural features spread across many areas, and some of them throughout the world. Later, domesticated plants and animals also spread very rapidly within their environmental limits, being stopped only by formidable ocean barriers.

Whether or not new technologies are valuable is, however, a function of the society's cultural level as well as of environmental potentials. All pre-agricultural societies found hunting and gathering techniques useful. Within the geographical limits of herding and farming, these techniques were adopted. More advanced techniques, such as metallurgy, were acceptable only if certain pre-conditions, such as stable population, leisure time, and internal specialization were present. These conditions could develop only from the cultural ecological adaptations of an agricultural society.

The concept of cultural ecology, however, is less concerned with the origin and diffusion of technologies than with the fact that they may be used differently and entail different social arrangements in each environment. The environment is not only permissive or prohibitive with respect to these technologies, but special local features may require social adaptations which have far-reaching consequences. Thus, societies equipped with bows, spears, surrounds, chutes, brush-burning, deadfalls, pitfalls, and other hunting devices may differ among themselves because of the nature of the terrain and fauna. If the principal game exists in large herds, such as herds of bison or caribou, there is advantage in co-operative hunting, and considerable numbers of peoples may remain together throughout the year. . . . If, however, the game is nonmigratory, occurring in small and scattered groups, it is better hunted by small groups of men who know their territory well. . . . In each case, the cultural repertory of hunting devices may be about the same, but in the first case the society will consist of multifamily or multilineage groups, as among the Athabaskans and Algonkians of Canada and probably the pre-horse Plains bison hunters, and in the second case it will probably consist of localized patrilineal lineages or bands, as among the Bushmen, Congo Negritoes, Australians, Tasmanians, Fuegians, and others. These latter groups consisting of patrilineal bands are similar, as a matter of fact, not because their total environments are similar—the Bushmen, Australians, and southern Californians live in deserts, the Negritoes in rain forests, and the Fuegians in a cold, rainy area—but because the nature of the game and therefore of their subsistence problem is the same in each case.

Other societies having about the same technological equipment may exhibit other social patterns because the environments differ to the extent that the cultural adaptations must be different. For example, the Eskimo use bows, spears, traps, containers and other widespread technological devices, but, owing to the limited occurrence of fish and sea mammals, their population is so sparse and co-operative hunting is so relatively unrewarding that they are usually dispersed in family groups. For a different but equally compelling reason the Nevada Shoshoni . . . were also fragmented into family groups. In the latter case, the scarcity of game and the predominance of seeds as the subsistence basis greatly restricted economic co-operation and required dispersal of the society into fairly independent family groups.

In the examples of the primitive hunting, gathering, and fishing societies, it is easy to show that if the local environment is to be exploited by means of the culturally-derived techniques, there are limitations upon the size and social composition of the groups involved. When agricultural techniques are introduced, man is partially freed from the exigencies of hunting and gathering, and it becomes possible for considerable aggregates of people to live together. Larger aggregates, made possible by increased population and settled communities, provide a higher level of sociocultural integration, the nature of which is determined by the local type of sociocultural integration. . . .

The adaptative processes we have described are properly designated ecological. But attention is directed not simply to the human community as part of the total web of life but to such cultural features as are affected by the adaptations. This in turn requires that primary attention be paid only to relevant environmental features rather than to the web of life for its own sake. Only those features to which the local culture ascribes importance need be considered.

THE METHOD OF CULTURAL ECOLOGY

Although the concept of environmental adaptation underlies all cultural ecology, the procedures must take into account the complexity and level of the culture. It makes a great deal of difference whether a community consists of hunters and gatherers who subsist independently by their own efforts or whether it is an outpost of a wealthy nation, which exploits local mineral wealth and is sustained by railroads, ships, or airplanes. In advanced societies, the nature of the culture core will be determined by a complex technology and by productive arrangements which themselves have a long cultural history.

Three fundamental procedures of cultural ecology are as follows:

First, the interrelationship of exploitative or productive technology and environment must be analyzed. This technology includes a considerable part of what is often called "material culture," but all features may not be of equal importance. In primitive societies, subsistence devices are basic: weapons and instruments for hunting and fishing; containers for gathering and storing food; transportational devices used on land and water; sources of water and fuel; and, in some environments, means of counteracting excessive cold (clothing and housing) or heat. In more developed societies, agriculture and herding techniques and manufacturing of crucial implements must be considered. In an industrial world, capital and credit arrangements, trade systems and the like are crucial. Socially-derived needs—special tastes in foods, more ample housing and clothing, and a great variety of appurtenances to living—become increasingly important in the productive arrangement as culture develops; and yet these originally were probably more often effects of basic adaptations than causes.

Relevant environmental features depend upon the culture. The simpler cultures are more directly conditioned by the environment than advanced ones. In general, climate, topography, soils, hydrography, vegetational cover, and fauna are crucial, but some features may be more important than others. The spacing of water holes in the desert may be vital to a nomadic seed-gathering people, the habits of game will affect the way hunting is done, and the kinds and seasons of fish runs will determine the habits of riverine and coastal tribes.

Second, the behavior patterns involved in the exploitation of a particular area by means of a particular technology must be analyzed. Some subsistence patterns impose very narrow limits on the general mode of life of the people, while others allow considerable latitude. The gathering of wild vegetable products is usually done by women who work alone or in small groups. Nothing is gained by co-operation and in fact women come into competition with one another. Seed-gatherers, therefore, tend to fragment into small groups unless their resources are very abundant. Hunting, on the other hand, may be either an individual or a collective project, and the nature of hunting societies is determined by culturally prescribed devices for collective hunting as well as by the species. When surrounds, grass-firing, corrals, chutes, and other co-operative methods are employed, the take per man may be much greater than what a lone hunter could bag. Similarly, if circumstances permit, fishing may be done by groups of men using dams, weirs, traps, and nets as well as by individuals.

The use of these more complex and frequently co-operative techniques, however, depends not only upon cultural history—i.e., invention and diffusion —which makes the methods available but upon the environment and its flora and fauna. Deer cannot be hunted advantageously by surrounds, whereas antelope and bison may best be hunted in this way. Slash-and-burn farming in tropical rain forests requires comparatively little co-operation in that a few men clear the land after which their wives plant and cultivate the crops. Dry farming may or may not be co-operative; and irrigation farming may run the gamut of enterprises of ever-increasing size based on collective construction of waterworks.

The exploitative patterns not only depend upon the habits concerned in the direct production of food and of goods but upon facilities for transporting the people to the source of supply or the goods to the people. Watercraft have been a major factor in permitting the growth of settlements beyond what would have been possible for a foot people. Among all nomads, the horse has had an almost revolutionary effect in promoting the growth of large bands.

The third procedure is to ascertain the extent to which the behavior patterns entailed in exploiting the environment affect other aspects of culture. Although technology and environment prescribe that certain things must be done in certain ways if they are to be done at all, the extent to which these activities are functionally tied to other aspects of culture is a purely empirical problem. I have shown elsewhere . . . that the occurrence of patrilineal bands among certain hunting peoples and of fragmented families among the Western Shoshoni is closely determined by their subsistence activities, whereas the Carrier Indians are known to have changed from a composite hunting band to a society based upon moieties and inherited statuses without any change in the nature of subsistence. In the irrigation areas of early civilizations . . . the sequence of sociopolitical forms or cultural cores seems to have been very similar despite variation in many outward details or secondary features of these cultures. If it can be established that the productive arrangements permit great latitude in the sociocultural type, then historical influences may explain the particular type found. The problem is the same in considering modern industrial civilizations. The question is whether industrialization allows such latitude that political democracy, communism, state socialism, and perhaps other forms are equally possible, so that strong historical influences, such as diffused ideology—e.g., propaganda—may supplant one type with another, or whether each type represents an adaptation which is specific to the area.

The third procedure requires a genuinely holistic approach, for if such factors as demography, settlement pattern, kinship structures, land tenure, land use, and other key cultural features are considered separately, their interrelationships to one another and to the environment cannot be grasped. Land use by means of a given technology permits a certain population density. The clustering of this population will depend partly upon where resources occur and upon transportational devices. The composition of these clusters will be a function of their size, of the nature of subsistence activities, and of cultural-historical factors. The ownership of land or resources will reflect subsistence activities on the one hand and the composition of the group on the other. Warfare may be related to the complex of factors just mentioned. In some cases, it may arise out of competition for resources and have a national character. Even when fought for individual honors or religious purposes, it may serve to nucleate settlements in a way that must be related to subsistence activities.

THE METHODOLOGICAL PLACE OF CULTURAL ECOLOGY

Cultural ecology has been described as a methodological tool for ascertaining how the adaptation of a culture to its environment may entail certain changes. In a larger sense, the problem is to determine whether similar adjustments occur in similar environments. Since in any given environment, culture may develop through a succession of very unlike periods, it is sometimes pointed out that environment, the constant, obviously has no relationship to cultural type. This difficulty disappears, however, if the level of sociocultural integration represented by each period is taken into account. Cultural types, therefore, must be conceived as constellations of core features which arise out of environmental adaptations and which represent similar levels of integration.

Cultural diffusion, of course, always operates, but in view of the seeming importance of ecological adaptations its role in explaining culture has been greatly overestimated. The extent to which the large variety of world cultures can be systematized in categories of types and explained through cross-cultural regularities of developmental process is purely an empirical matter. Hunches arising out of comparative studies suggest that there are many regularities which can be formulated in terms of similar levels and similar adaptations.

NOTE

1. *New International Dictionary* (2nd ed., unabridged, 1950).

REFERENCES

Adams, C. C.
    1935   "The Relations of General Ecology to Human Ecology." *Ecology*, XVI, 316–335.
Alihan, Milla Aissa
    1938   *Social Ecology.* New York: Columbia University Press.
Bates, Marston
    1953   "Human Ecology," in *Anthropology Today: An Encyclopedic Inventory.* Ed. A. L. Kroeber. Chicago: University of Chicago Press.
Forde, C. Daryll
    1949   *Habitat, Economy and Society.* London: Methuen.
Hawley, Amos H.
    1950   *Human Ecology: A Theory of Community Structure.* New York: The Ronald Press.
Hollingshead, A. B.
    1940   "Human Ecology and Human Society," *Ecological Monographs,* X.

Leslie A. White 1900–

BACKGROUND

Leslie White for years stood alone in his conviction that evolutionary theory as expounded by Herbert Spencer, Lewis H. Morgan, and Edward Tylor was the beginning of the right track for a science of culture. He can now look about him in full awareness that the whole field knows he was right.

White was born in Colorado. Even before he entered high school, in Louisiana, he knew he wanted to become a teacher in either physics or astronomy. He planned to attend Louisiana State University as a physics major, but the entry of the United States into World War I put him in the Navy. He made it to Louisiana State in 1919, but his experience in the war had turned him toward the social sciences: he claimed he discovered in the course of the war that what was taught about society and related subjects was wrong. He determined to find out what was right.

His road to anthropology was a winding one. First he studied history and political science. When he transferred to Columbia University in 1921 he turned to psychology, sociology, and philosophy. His B.A. in 1923 and M.A. in 1924 were in psychology. From 1922 to 1924 he took courses at the New School—economics with Thorstein Veblen, behavioral psychology with John B. Watson, and anthropology with Alexander Goldenweiser. Settling on sociology, he went to the University of Chicago, but there he met Edward Sapir and Fay-Cooper Cole, decided that sociology was all theory and no fact, and changed his field again—this time to anthropology. Today such a program would be called interdisciplinary.

In 1927 White became instructor of sociology and anthropology at the University of Buffalo. His orientation toward anthropology had followed the anti-evolutionary approach of Franz Boas, in accordance with the style of the day. He had studied under students of Boas, and before his doctorate most of what he read was of the Boasian school, with Robert Lowie's *Primitive Society* exerting a special influence.

His conversion to evolutionism began when he had difficulty expounding and defending Boas' theories to his classes. He was further influenced by the philosopher Marvin Farber, his colleague at Buffalo, who had studied some anthropology at Harvard and abroad and was interested in evolution.

White and his students worked on the nearby Seneca reservation, which led him to read Morgan's *League of the Iroquois*. Fascinated, he read all of Morgan's work more thoroughly than he had before, which led him to other early evolutionists. The final step in his conversion was a tour through Russia and Georgia made in 1929, when he read Marx and Engels and became interested in what they had to say about the nature and development of civilization.

In 1930 he moved to the University of Michigan, replacing Julian Steward. The following year he married. Under his guidance the anthropology department at Michigan grew from a one-man affair to one of the outstanding departments in the country. During this time White also served as visiting professor at Chicago, Yale, Columbia, and Harvard; in the fall of 1936 he was at Yenching Institute in Peking.

During his early years at Michigan, White's theoretical writing was devoted to a long and spirited debate with followers of Boas. Because his ideas were at variance with the prevalent currents of theory, he did not greatly influence his peers, but he had a profound effect on his students.

In the years after 1926 he made numerous field trips to the southwestern United States. The results appeared in several monographs: *The Acoma Indians* (1932), *The Pueblo of San Felipe* (1932), *The Pueblo of San Domingo, New Mexico* (1935), and *The Pueblo of Santa Ana, New Mexico* (1942).

Since World War II his major thrust has been toward delimitation of the science of culture that he has called "culturology." *The Science of Culture* (1949) is an introductory treatment of his conceptions of culture, culturology and cultural evolution.

White has carried out intensive investigations of the life and works of Morgan. Not only has he made an exhaustive study of the literary sources on Morgan, but he has also tried literally to retrace Morgan's travels. He has edited *Extracts from the European Travel Journal of Lewis H. Morgan* (1937) and *Pioneers in American Anthropology: The Bandelier-Morgan Letters, 1873–1883* (2 vols., 1940).

In 1959 White published a monumental four-volume work on the development of culture, *The Evolution of Culture: The Development of Civilization to the Fall of Rome.*

INTRODUCTION

The thing about human behavior that makes it human is a function of the use of symbols. To White, all the behavior of man is symbolic behavior, and this is a point close to that of the cognitive anthropologists of our own time. A symbol to White is a phenomenon whose meaning is given to it by the group of people who utilize it. Without symbols man would not be the thinking animal he is. Thus, culture itself, which is dependent on symbols, would not have existed without the ability of man to symbolize. This, however, should not be interpreted to mean that White takes a psychological approach to the understanding of human behavior. Quite the contrary: White's position is one that rejects the individual and psychological explanations in favor of an explanation of human behavior through the superorganic—the symbol. Put another way, the different types of behavior exhibited by different societies are the results of their cultural traditions. The "s" has been put back—at a new level.

22 THE SYMBOL: THE ORIGIN AND BASIS OF HUMAN BEHAVIOR

In the Word was the Beginning . . . the beginning of Man and of Culture.

In July, 1939, a celebration was held at Leland Stanford University to commemorate the hundredth anniversary of the discovery that the cell is the basic unit of all living tissue. Today we are beginning to realize and to appreciate the fact that the symbol is the basic unit of all human behavior and civilization.

All human behavior originates in the use of symbols. It was the symbol which transformed our anthropoid ancestors into men and made them human. All civilizations have been generated, and are perpetuated, only by the use of symbols. It is the symbol which transforms an infant of Homo sapiens into a human being; deaf mutes who grow up without the use of symbols are not human beings. All human behavior consists of, or is dependent upon, the use of symbols. Human behavior is symbolic behavior; symbolic behavior is human behavior. The symbol is the universe of humanity.

INTRODUCTION

White has also made an important contribution to our understanding of the nature and purpose of anthropology as an activity. He has developed a law of the development of the sciences. According to this law, sciences begin and develop fastest in areas where human action is basically unimportant and slowest in areas where human actions are involved. Astronomy was the first area to develop into a science, and the science of culture is the latest to begin and develop. Culturology, as White calls the science of culture, is regarded by him as being the latest step in the evolution of sciences. It is culture as a science, according to White, that can explain more about human behavior than any other science, including sociology and psychology.

The reaction of the Boasians to the comparative school and to evolutionary theory had been so strong that during most of the first half of this century no theory of evolution was developed in the United States. It was White, with his theory of energy in relationship to technology and culture, who brought evolutionary thinking back into American anthropological theory. White, unlike Steward, went all the way in accepting the theory of evolution—and he did so by dropping the "s" from "cultures" and talking again about culture and its evolution.

White is best known for finding a new base for a theory of cultural evolution. This new foundation for evolutionary theory is the expanded use of energy by cultures through the evolution of technology. According to White, the history of human civilization is based on the attempt to control nature by culture, an approach emphasizing the expanded use of energy by cultures through technology over time. The more energy a culture is able to extract from nature, the more evolved a culture is bound to be. This is formulated in a law of cultural evolution stating that cultures evolve either by harnessing more energy from nature or by developing a more efficient technology. The reason that this process results in evolution of culture is that technology and the energy it can harness play a primary role, White says, in determining social organization and ideology. In other words, "a culture" that can harness more energy is going to have, as a result of harnessing that extra energy, a more evolved form of social organization and ideology.

23 ENERGY AND THE EVOLUTION OF CULTURE

The degree of civilization of any epoch, people, or group of peoples, is measured by ability to utilize energy for human advancement or needs . . . —GEORGE GRANT MacCURDY (1933)

. . . the history of civilization becomes the history of man's advancing control over energy . . . —WILHELM OSTWALD (1907)

Having examined the culture process in a number of its aspects, we now turn to a consideration of it as a whole.

As we have already seen, "culture" is the name of a distinct order, or class, of phenomena, namely, those things and events that are dependent upon the exercise of a mental ability, peculiar to the human species, that we have termed "symbolling." To be more specific, culture consists of material objects—tools, utensils, ornaments, amulets, etc.—acts, beliefs, and attitudes that function in contexts characterized by symbolling. It is an elaborate mechanism, an organization of exosomatic ways and means employed by a particular animal species, man, in the struggle for existence and survival.

One of the significant attributes of culture is its transmissibility by non-biological means. Culture in all its aspects, material, social, and ideological, is easily and readily transmitted from one individual, one generation, one age, one people, or one region, to another by *social* mechanisms. Culture is, so to speak, a form of social heredity. We thus view culture as a continuum, a supra-biological, extra-somatic order of things and events, that flows down through time from one age to the next.

We have seen also, in preceding chapters, that since culture constitutes a distinct order of phenomena, it can be described and interpreted in terms of principles and laws of its own. Cultural elements act and react upon one another in their own way. We can discover the principles of behavior of various sub-classes of cultural elements and of cultural systems as a whole; and we can formulate the *laws* of cultural phenomena and systems.

We now propose to sketch the evolution of culture from its beginning upon an anthropoid level to the present time. We may regard the human race —man—as a one. We may likewise think of all of the various cultures, or cultural traditions, as constituting a single entity: the culture of mankind. We may, therefore, address ourselves to the task of tracing the course of the development of this culture from its source to the present day.

Let us return for a moment to a further consideration of the structure and function of the organization of things and processes, the *system,* that we call culture. Culture is an organized, integrated system. But we may distinguish subdivisions within, or aspects of, this system. For our purpose, we shall distinguish three sub-systems of culture, namely, technological, sociological, and ideological systems. The technological system is composed of the material, mechanical, physical, and chemical instruments, together with the techniques of their use, by means of which man, as an animal species, is articulated with his natural habitat. Here we find the tools of production, the means of subsistence, the materials of shelter, the instruments of offense and defense. The sociological system is made up of interpersonal relations expressed in patterns of behavior, collective as well as individual. In this category we find social, kinship, economic, ethical, political, military, ecclesiastical, occupational and professional, recreational, etc., systems. The Ideological system is composed of ideas, beliefs, knowledge, expressed in articulate speech or other symbolic form. Mythologies and theologies, legend, literature, philosophy, science, folk wisdom and common sense knowledge, make up this category.

These three categories comprise the system of culture as a whole. They are, of course, interrelated; each reacts upon the others and is affected by them in turn. But the influence of this mutual interaction is not equal in all directions. The roles played by the several sub-systems in the culture process as a whole are not equal by any means. The primary role is played by the technological system. This is, of course, as we would expect it to be; it could not be otherwise. Man as an animal species, and consequently culture as a whole, is dependent upon the material, mechanical means of adjustment to the natural environment. Man must have food. He must be protected from the elements. And he must defend himself from his enemies. These three things he must do if he is to continue to live, and these objectives are attained only by technological means. The technological system is therefore both primary and basic in importance; all human life and culture rest and depend upon it.

Social systems are in a very real sense secondary and subsidiary to technological systems. In fact a social system may be defined realistically as the organized effort of human beings in the use of the instruments of subsistence, offense and defense, and protection. A social system is a function of a technological system. A ship, says Childe, "and the tools employed in its production symbolize a whole economic system." The technology is the independent variable, the social system the dependent variable. Social systems are therefore determined by systems of technology; as the latter change, so do the former. "The bronze axe which replaces . . . [the stone axe]," again to quote Childe (1936), "is not only a superior implement, it also presupposes a more complex economic and social structure."

Ideological, or philosophical, systems are organizations of beliefs in which human experience finds its interpretation. But experience and interpretations thereof are powerfully conditioned by technologies. There is a type of philosophy proper to every type of technology. The interpretation of a system of experience in which a *coup de poing* is a characteristic feature will, as it must, reflect this kind of experience. It would not be improper to speak of a *coup de poing* type of philosophy as well as of technology. A pastoral, agricultural, metallurgical, industrial, or military technology will each find its corresponding expression in philosophy. One type of technology will find expression in the philosophy of totemism, another in astrology or quantum mechanics.

But the experience of the external world is not felt and interpreted merely at the point of technological articulation; it is filtered through the prism of social systems also. The qualities and features of social, political, ecclesiastical, economic, military, etc., systems are therefore reflected in philosophies.

We may view a cultural system as a series of three horizontal strata: the technological layer on the bottom, the philosophical on the top, the sociological stratum in between. These positions express their respective roles in the culture process. The technological system is basic and primary. Social systems are functions of technologies; and philosophies express technological forces and reflect social systems. The technological factor is therefore the determinant of a cultural system as a whole. It determines the form of social systems, and technology and society together determine the content and orientation of philosophy. This is not to say, of course, that social systems do not condition the operation of technologies, or that social and technological systems are not affected by philosophies. They do and are. But to condition is one thing; to determine, quite another.

We are now in possession of a key to an understanding of the growth and development of culture: technology. A human being is a material body; the species, a material system. The planet earth is a material body; the cosmos, a material system. Technology is the mechanical means of articulation of these two material systems, man and cosmos. But these systems are dynamic, not static; energy as well as matter is involved. Everything—the cosmos, man, culture—may be described in terms of matter and energy.

The Second Law of Thermodynamics tells us that the cosmos as a whole is breaking down structurally and running down dynamically; matter is becoming less organized and energy more uniformly diffused. But in a tiny sector of the cosmos, namely, in living material systems, the direction of the cosmic process is reversed: matter becomes more highly organized and energy more concentrated. Life is a building up process. But in order to run counter to the cosmic current, biological organisms must draw upon free energy in non-living systems, capture it and put it to work in the maintenance of the vital process. All life is a struggle for free energy. Biological evolution is simply an expression of the thermodynamic process that moves in a direction opposite to that specified for the cosmos as a whole by the Second Law. It is a movement toward greater organization, greater differentiation of structure, increased specialization of function, higher levels of integration, and greater degrees of energy concentration.

From a zoological standpoint, culture is but a means of carrying on the life process of a particular species, Homo sapiens. It is a mechanism for providing man with subsistence, protection, offense and defense, social regulation, cosmic adjustment, and recreation. But to serve these needs of man energy is required. It becomes the primary function of culture, therefore, to harness and control energy so that it may be put to work in man's service. Culture thus confronts us as an elaborate thermodynamic, mechanical system. By means of technological instruments energy is harnessed and put to work. Social and philosophic systems are both adjuncts and expressions of this technologic process. The functioning of culture as a whole therefore rests upon and is determined by the amount of energy harnessed and by the way in which it is put to work.[1]

But "the way in which it is put to work" introduces another factor besides energy. Energy by itself is meaningless. To be significant in cultural systems, energy must be harnessed, directed, and controlled. This is of course accomplished by technological means, by means of tools of one kind or another. The efficiency of technological means varies; some are better than others. The amount of food, clothing, or other goods produced by the expenditure of a given amount of energy will be proportional to the efficiency of the technological means with which the energy is put to work, other factors remaining constant.

We may therefore distinguish three factors in any cultural situation or system: (1) the amount of energy harnessed per capita per year; (2) the efficency of the technological means with which energy is harnessed and put to work; and (3) the magnitude of human need-serving goods and services produced. Assuming the factor of habitat to be a constant, the degree of cultural development, measured in terms of amount of human need-serving goods and services produced per capita, is determined by the amount of energy harnessed per capita and by the efficiency of the technological means with which it is put to work. We may express this concisely and succinctly with the following formula: $E \times T \rightarrow C$, in which C represents the degree of cultural development, E the amount of energy harnessed per capita per year, and T the quality or efficiency of the tools employed in the expenditure of the energy. We can now formulate the basic law of cultural evolution: Other factors remaining constant, *culture evolves as the amount of energy harnessed per capita per year is increased, or as the efficiency of the instrumental means of putting the energy to work is increased.* Both factors may increase simultaneously of course. We may now sketch the history of cultural development from this standpoint.

If culture is a mechanism for harnessing energy, it must find this energy somewhere; it may lay hold of natural forces in some form or other if they are to be put to work in the service of man's needs. The first source of energy exploited by the earliest cultural systems was, of course, the energy of the human organism itslf. The original cultures were activated by human energy and by this source and form alone. The amount of power that an average adult man can generate is small, about 1/10 of one horsepower. When women and children, the sick, aged, and feeble are considered, the average power resources of the earliest cultural systems might be reckoned at about 1/20 horsepower per capita. Since the degree of cultural development—the amount of human need-serving goods and services produced per capita—is proportional to the amount of energy harnessed and put to work per capita per year, other factors remaining constant, these earliest cultures of mankind, dependent as they were upon the meager energy resources of the human body, were simple, meager, and crude, as indeed they had to be. No cultural system, activated by human energy alone, can develop very far. Some progress can of course be made by increasing the efficiency of the technological means of putting energy to work, but there is a limit to the extent of cultural advance on this basis. We can form a realistic picture of cultural development within the limits of human energy resources by looking at such modern cultures as those of the Tasmanians, Fuegians, or Andamanese; or the Paleolithic cultures of Europe.

If culture is to advance beyond the limits of maximum technological efficiency and the energy resources of the human body, it must devise new ways to harness additional amounts of energy by tapping natural resources in some new form. In some preliterate cultural systems, fire, wind or water was exploited as a source of energy, but only occasionally and to a very insignificant extent. The conquest of fire was a very early cultural achievement, but it was not until the invention of a practical steam engine that fire became important as a form of energy. Fire was important in early cultures in cooking, providing warmth, frightening wild beasts, and as a symbol, but not as a form of energy. In more advanced cultures, fire was important or essential in the ceramic and metallurgical arts, but here also it is not functioning as a form of energy: i.e., we cannot equate, or substitute, muscle power for fire in any of these contexts. There is one context, however, in which fire functions as energy in some primitive cultures: in hollowing out tree trunks in the manufacture of dugout canoes. Here fire is substituted for muscle power. And there may be a few more similar uses of fire. But, all in all, prior to the invention of the steam engine in modern times, cultural systems made very little use of fire as a form and source of energy which could be substituted for human muscle power.

Primitive peoples could float freight down a flowing stream, but until the invention of the water wheel shortly before the beginning of the Christian era, there was no other way in which moving water could be used as a source of energy for culture building. Wind was not employed as a source of energy until comparatively recent times, and it never has been an important source of power.

Thus, we see that fire, water, and wind were utilized as sources of energy only to a very limited and insignificant extent during the first hundreds of thousands of years of culture history. But there is still another source of energy that was available to primitive man, and eventually we find his cultural systems harnessing it: the energy of plants and animals.

Plants are, of course, forms and magnitudes of energy. Energy from the sun is captured by the process of photosynthesis and stored up in the form of plant tissue. All animal life is dependent, in the last analysis, upon this solar energy stored up in plants. All life, therefore, is dependent upon photosynthesis.

The first men subsisted upon plants and animals as, of course, their pre-human ancestors did before them. The earliest culture systems developed techniques of hunting, fishing, trapping, collecting, gathering, etc., as means of exploiting the plant and animal resources of nature. But merely appropriating natural resources is one thing; harnessing and controlling them is quite another. After some 985,000 years of cultural development, certain plants were brought under the control of domestication and cultivation, and various animal species were brought under control through domestication. The energy resources for culture building were greatly increased as a consequence of this increase in control over the forces of nature. The yield of plant food and other useful plant materials per unit of human labor was greatly increased by the substitution of plant cultivation for wild plant gathering. Improved strains were developed through selective breeding. Cultivation, fertilization and irrigation served to increase the yield per unit of human energy, or labor. Among the plants brought under cultivation, the cereals have been especially important. Tylor has called them "the great moving power of civilization." All of the great civilizations of antiquity were brought into being by the cultivation of cereals; no great culture has ever been achieved independently of the cultivation of cereals.

The domestication of animals, too, increased the energy resources for culture building as a consequence of the increase in control over these forms of energy. Their yield in food and other useful animal products per unit of human labor was greatly increased by the substitution of domestication for hunting. In a hunting economy animals had to be killed before they could be used, and when they were consumed more had to be found and killed. By means of domestication a people could subsist upon its herds and flocks without diminishing their numbers at all; they could even be increased. Animals, like plants, were improved through selective breeding, and, in addition to supplying milk, meat, wool, and hides, some species could be used as motive power, either to carry burdens or to draw plows or vehicles. The domestication of animals thus greatly increased the amount of energy under cultural control and available for culture building.

A great advance in cultural development would be expected, therefore, as a consequence of the great increase in the amount of energy harnessed and controlled per capita per year by means of the agricultural and pastoral arts. And this is exactly what took place. The archeological record bears out our theory fully at this point. In a few thousand years after the inauguration of the arts of domestication and cultivation, the great civilizations of antiquity, of Egypt, Mesopotamia, India, China, and, in the New World, in Mexico, Middle America, and the Andean Highlands, came quickly into being. After hundreds of thousands of years of relatively slow and meager development during the Old Stone Ages, culture suddenly shot forward under the impetus of augmented energy resources achieved by agriculture and animal husbandry. Great cities, nations, and empires took the place of villages, tribes, and confederacies as a consequence of the Agricultural Revolution. Rapid progress was made, especially in the Old World, in all of the arts—industrial, esthetic, and intellectual. Great engineering projects were undertaken and executed; huge architectural edifices erected. The ceramic, textile, and metal-lurgical arts expanded and flourished. Astronomy, writing, and mathematics were developed. Beginnings were made in a rational science of medicine. Impressive works of art were produced, in relief, sculpture, and even in paint-ing. Development and progress took place in all aspects of culture.

But culture did not advance continuously and indefinitely as a conse-quence of increased energy resources won by the techniques of agriculture and animal husbandry. After a period of rapid growth, the upward curve of progress levelled off onto a plateau. The peaks of cultural development in Egypt, Mesopotamia, India, and China were reached prior to 1000 B.C., in some cases considerably earlier, and from that time until the beginning of the Fuel Age, about A.D. 1800, no culture of the Old World surpassed, in any profound and comprehensive way, the highest levels achieved in the Bronze Age. This is not to say, of course, that there was no progress at all from 1000 B.C. to A.D. 1789. There were innovations here and there and many refinements of already existing traits. But, taking cultures as wholes, and measuring them by such yardsticks as size of political unit, size of city, mag-nitude of architectural edifices and engineering works, density of popula-tion, production and accumulation of wealth, etc., the cultures of Europe between the disintegration of the Roman Empire and the rise of the Power Age were in general inferior to those of the ancient oriental civilizations. The reason why cultures did not continue indefinitely to advance under the impetus of an agricultural and stockraising technology is a matter that we shall consider presently.

It appears then that culture had developed about as far as it could on an agricultural and animal husbandry basis before the beginning of the Christian era, at least in the Old World; the New World lagged somewhat behind. And it is reasonable to suppose that culture never would have exceeded the peaks already achieved by this time had not some way been devised to harness additional amounts of energy per capita per year by tapping the forces of nature in a new form. A way was found, however, to do this: energy in the form of coal, and, later, oil and gas, was harnessed by means of steam and internal combustion engines. By tapping the vast deposits of coal, oil, and natural gas, a tremendous increase in the amount of energy available for culture building was quickly effected. The consequences of the

Fuel Revolution were in general much like those of the Agricultural Revolution: an increase in population, larger political units, bigger cities, an accumulation of wealth, a rapid development of the arts and sciences, in short, a rapid and extensive advance of culture as a whole.

But, again, after a very rapid rise, the curve of cultural development began to show some signs of levelling off. We do not wish to intimate that culture had already gone as far as it could on a Fuel basis, for we do not believe it had; we merely believe that we can detect signs of a slowing down of the advance. But before the question of how far cultural development *could* advance on a Fuel-Agricultural-Animal-Husbandry-Human-Energy basis could become anything like a matter of immediate concern, a tremendously significant technological event took place: the energy resources of atomic nuclei were harnessed. For the first time in culture history energy in a form other than solar had been harnessed. No cultural advance has as yet been effected by the utilization of this new form of energy as a source of industrial power. And before it becomes significant in this respect, another fateful question will have to be met and answered, namely, the consequences of the use of atomic energy in warfare.

Thus we trace the development of culture from anthropoid levels to the present time as a consequence of periodic increases in the amount of energy harnessed per capita per year effected by tapping new sources of power. There is, however, another technological factor involved which we have merely mentioned incidentally so far; we must now consider it more fully, namely, the role of tools in the culture process.

Energy is of course neither created nor annihilated, at least not within cultural systems; it is merely transformed. It is harnessed and it is put to work or expended. But this requires tools and machines. The amount of energy harnessed may, and the amount of human need-serving goods produced per unit of energy does, depend upon the efficiency of the tools employed. So far, we have been holding the tool factor constant and varying the energy factor. We now hold the energy factor constant and vary that of tools. We get, then, the following generalization: *the degree of cultural development varies directly as the efficiency of the tools employed, other factors remaining constant.* If, for example, one is engaged in chopping wood, the amount chopped per unit of energy expended will vary with the efficiency of the axe; the amount will increase with the improvement of axes from the Old Stone Age, through the Neolithic, Bronze, and Iron ages up to the finest axe of alloyed steel of the present day. And so it is with other instrumental means, such as saws, looms, plows, harnesses, wheeled vehicles, boats, etc. Cultural advance is effected, therefore, by an improvement of tools as well as by increases in the amount of energy harnessed.

But the efficiency of a tool cannot be increased indefinitely; there is a point beyond which improvement of any given tool is impossible. Thus, a canoe paddle can be too long or too short, too narrow or too wide, too heavy or too light, etc. We may therefore both imagine and realize a canoe paddle of such size and shape as to make any alteration of either result in a decrease of efficiency. Similarly, we may improve bows and arrows, hoes, plows, saws, etc., up to but not beyond a certain point. Perfection, as a practical matter, is either reached or at least closely approximated. No significant improvement has been made in violins in decades. The steam locomotive has apparently come close to its limits of size and speed. To be sure, improvements may be continued for a time by the use of new materials or alloys and by the application of new mechanical principles. But even so, the improvement of any tool or machine approaches closely, if it does not reach, a limit. We cannot expect lomomotives or ocean liners a mile long; they would fall apart of their own weight.

In the culture process therefore, we find that progress and development are effected by the improvement of the mechanical means with which energy is harnessed and put to work as well as by increasing the amounts of energy employed. But this does not mean that the tool and energy factors are of equal weight and significance. The energy factor is the primary and basic one; it is the prime mover, the active agent. Tools are merely the means that serve this power. The energy factor may be increased indefinitely; the efficiency of the tool only within limits. With a given amount of energy, cultural development can progress only so far: to the limits of the efficiency of the tools. When these limits have been reached, no further increases in efficiency can make up for a lack of increase in amount of energy harnessed. But increases in the amount of energy harnessed result in technological progress all along the line, in the invention of new tools and in the improvement of old ones should further improvement be possible. We see, therefore, that important though the tool factor may be, it is merely secondary to the primary and basic factor of energy. And, since increases of energy foster improvement of tools, one may say that it is energy that, at bottom, carries the culture process onward and upward. The general statement that, the environmental factor being constant, the degree of cultural development is proportional to the amount of energy harnessed per capita per year is therefore sound and illuminating.

We turn now to a consideration of social system in the process of cultural development. A social system is, as we have seen it must be, closely related to its underlying technological system. If a people are nomadic hunters— i.e., use certain technological instruments in certain ways in order to obtain food, furs, hides, and other need-serving materials—they will have one type of social system. If they lead a sedentary life, feeding upon rich beds of shellfish, or if they are pastoralists or intensive agriculturalists, or maritime traders, or industrialists, etc., they will have other types of social systems. The process of military offense and defense and the technological means with which it is exercised also act as a determinant of social organization, sometimes a very powerful one. Thus we see that the social system of a people is at bottom determined by the use of the technological means of subsistence and of offense and defense. Those social institutions not directly related to the technology are related indirectly; they serve to co-ordinate the various sectors of society with one another and to integrate them into a coherent whole.

The social systems of primitive peoples vary tremendously in detail because the specific circumstances of natural habitat and technology vary. But all social systems resting upon a human energy (i.e., pre-pastoral, pre-agricultural) basis belong to a common type. They are all relatively small and manifest a minimum of structural differentiation and specialization of function. We find no highy developed societies upon the primitive foundation of a technology powered by human energy alone.

The societies of pastoralists and agriculturalists in the early stages of these technological developments are likewise relatively simple, undifferentiated systems. As a matter of fact we may characterize all human social systems up to a certain point in the development of the agricultural, or farming-and-animal-husbandry, technology as *primitive society:* tribes based upon kinship ties, free access to the resources of nature for all, relatively little social differentiation and specialization, and a high degree of social equality. When, however, a certain point in the development of agriculture was reached, a profound change in social systems took place. This was the *social* aspect of the Agricultural Revolution. Let us trace the course of this social revolution in its main outlines at least.

Agriculture and animal husbandry are means of producing more food and other useful materials per unit of human energy than can be obtained by hunting, fishing, or gathering. When agriculture is combined with stock raising the energy resources for culture building are of course greater than when the cultivation of plants alone is practiced. Not only do flocks and herds supply meat, milk, wool or hides, but their muscle power may be used to carry burdens, draw plows and carts, etc. All of the great civilizations of the Old World grew up on the basis of agriculture and animal husbandry. Since, however, it is the cultivation of cereals that is the basic factor in the new agriculture-and-animal-husbandry technology, we may for the sake of brevity speak of "the social consequences of a developing agricultural technology."

As the agricultural arts developed and matured, as plants were improved through selective breeding, as new techniques of cultivation, irrigation, drainage, rotation of crops, fertilization, etc., were introduced and improved, the amount of food produced increased. As the food supply was enlarged the population increased. Small tribes grew into large tribes and these into nations and empires; villages grew into towns and towns into cities.

Not only was *more food* produced by agricultural techniques than by hunting, fishing, and gathering, but more food per capita, more per unit of human labor expended. And, as the agricultural arts developed, the productivity of human labor in this field increased. It gradually became possible for a portion of the population to produce food for all. This meant that a portion of the population could be diverted from agriculture and turned into other channels, such as the industrial and esthetic arts. As the agricultural technology advanced, more and more of the population could thus be withdrawn from the fields and put to work at other tasks and occupations. Society thus became divided along occupational lines, differentiated structurally and specialized functionally. This led to further social developments as we shall see in a moment.

The mere increase in population had important consequences in another direction also. Tribes and clans were organized upon a basis of kinship ties; social relations were largely exercised in this form. This mechanism worked very well as long as the social units were relatively small; a clan or tribe could be effective as a mechanism of social organization and intercourse as long as its members were not exceedingly numerous, as long as social relations could be *personal*. But when, under the impetus of a developing agricultural technology and an increasing food supply, clan and tribal units grew to huge size, they tended to fall apart of their own weight. Primitive society tended therefore to disintegrate as a consequence of sheer increase of numbers. A new type of social organization was therefore required if chaos was to be averted. This new organization was found in the State. This was another consequence of the Agricultural Revolution.

The developing agricultural technology brought about a profound change in economic organization, also. In tribal society production, exchange, and consumption of wealth took place upon a personal, kinship basis; the economic organization was virtually identified with the kinship system. This type of economic organization worked well in a small society with a minimum of division of labor and with little differentiation of social structure along occupational lines. But as society became extensively differentiated, as a consequence of the increase in productivity of human labor in agriculture, a new type of economic system was required; a way of relating *classes* economically to one another must be devised. This can be done either in a feudal or a monetary-market system. In either case, however, we have a system in which property relations form the basis of social relations rather than the reverse, as was the case in tribal, kinship, society.

On preliterate cultural levels there was of course some fighting between tribal groups. Competition for favored hunting and fishing grounds or other natural resources, vengeance for real or fancied (e.g., magical) injuries, led to a certain amount of intertribal conflict. But the factors necessary for large scale and systematic and sustained warfare were lacking. These were supplied, however, as a consequence of the Agricultural Revolution. A high degree of development of the agricultural, metallurgical, ceramic, and other arts resulted in the production and accumulation of vast amounts of wealth. A rich nation's possessions together with the natural and human resources that made the wealth possible would constitute a rich prize to any people who could conquer it. Warfare became a profitable occupation. Thus we find, especially in Mesopotamia, a condition of almost chronic warfare: nations contending with one another for rich, fertile river valleys, the treasures of palace and temple, one nation conquering and looting another, new empires rising upon the ruins of old.

The social consequences of systematic and chronic warfare are significant: the formation of a professional military class, which in collaboration with political rulers and sometimes even autonomously, may become a powerful political force; the reduction of peoples of conquered nations to the status of slavery or serfdom; and the subordination of the masses at home to the imperatives of prolonged military conflict. Thus warfare tended powerfully to divide society into two major social classes: a relatively small ruling group who organized and directed the campaigns and to whom the overwhelming proportion of the wealth taken as booty went, and a large class who provided the "sinews of war"—the peasants, serfs, the common soldiers, etc. There was often but little difference between the lot of the masses at home and that of the masses of the vanquished nation after conquest and subjugation had been accomplished.

Warfare was not, however, the only means, or social process, that operated to divide societies of the post-Agricultural Revolutionary era into a small, wealthy, powerful, ruling class on the one hand, and a large class of peasants, serfs, or slaves on the other. The peaceful process of commerce, and especially the use of money, operated also to bring about the same end. Trade and commerce are means of concentrating wealth. In this competitive process the big merchants grew at the expense of the small ones. Wealth tended to gravitate into a few hands. Money lending is a particularly rapid and effective means of making the poor poorer and the wealthy richer. When interest rates range from say thirty to one hundred percent or even more, as they did in ancient times, the small borrowers rapidly sink into economic bondage to the money-lenders. It was not at all uncommon in Greece before the reforms of Solon or Kleisthenes for a small farmer to sell his children into slavery in order to pay merely the interest on his loan, let alone the principal. Taxes levied by the ruling class through the mechanism of the state and exorbitant rents levied upon small tenants by large landlords also tended to reduce the masses to a condition of economic bondage and impotence.

Thus we see that the social, political and economic effects of the technological revolution in agriculture were: the dissolution of the old social system of primitive society, the obsolescence of tribe and clan; the division of society into various occupational groups—guilds of artisans and craftsmen; the division of society horizontally into two major classes: a small, powerful, wealthy, ruling class and a large class, governed and exploited by the ruling class and held in bondage in one form or another by them. Civil society based upon property relations took the place of primitive society based upon kinship; the State replaced tribe and clan. The technological revolution in agriculture precipitated and carried through a revolution in the social, political, and economic sectors of culture. As the amount of energy harnessed and put to work per capita per year was increased by the development of the agricultural technology, society became more and more differentiated structurally and increasingly specialized functionally. Concomitant with this trend was the emergence of a special social mechanism of co-ordination of functions and correlation of structures, a mechanism of integration and regulation. This political mechanism had two aspects, secular and ecclesiastic, sometimes closely related, sometimes distinct, but always present. We call this special mechanism of co-ordination, integration, and regulation the State-Church. The evolution of civil society from the early metallurgical era to the present day, passing through a variety of forms of the state and class relations, is a story that we shall turn to presently. At this point we wish to return to a matter touched upon earlier.

If culture evolves when and as the amount of energy harnessed per capita per year increases, why did not culture continue to advance indefinitely as a consequence of the technological revolution in agriculture? As we have already seen, it did not. On the contrary, after attaining certain levels it ceased to advance and thereafter continued on a plateau until a new and powerful impetus came from the Fuel Revolution. Yet, agriculture as a technological process, as a mechanism of harnessing solar energy, was not developed to its technological limits by any means; it has not even yet reached those limits or even approached them very closely according to agronomists. Why, then, did technological progress in agriculture eventually slow down and virtually stop after so rapid a rise?

The answer seems to lie in the relationship between socioeconomic system and technological system established by the Agricultural Revolution. As we have noted, every social system rests upon and is determined by a technological system. But every technological system functions *within* a social system and is therefore *conditioned* by it. The social system created by the Agricultural Revolution affected the technological process so as eventually to "contain it" and to bring further progress in culture as a whole virtually to a standstill. This is how it was done.

The social system of civil society was, as we have seen, divided into a ruling class and an exploited class. The latter produced the wealth; the former appropriated so large a portion of it as to leave the latter with but minimum means of subsistence. No advantage would accrue to the producing class if they enlarged their production through increased efficiency; the increment would only be appropriated by the ruling class. On the other hand, the ruling class were not likely to resort to a long range plan to improve the techniques of agricultural production. If they needed more than they were obtaining at the moment the need was immediate and a long range plan would have been of no use. They would therefore resort to greater exactions from the producing class. But in many, if not most, instances, it would seem, the ruling class had ample for their needs. As a matter of fact, a great deal of evidence indicates that one of the problems they had to contend with was that of overproduction rather than of insufficiency. Thus we see, especially in Egypt but also in Mesopotamia and elsewhere, the ruling class engaging in "conspicuous waste and consumption" and that on a grand scale. Palaces and temples were loaded with wealth and vast treasures were deposited with the dead in tombs. In addition to this, great public works programs—pyramids, monuments, temples, tombs and palaces—were continually being built. It would appear that the ruling class was frequently confronted with the problem of overproduction and the threat of technological unemployment or a surplus of population among the lower classes. Their great public works programs.

the wholesale disposition of wealth in mortuary customs, etc., enabled them to solve both these problems with one stroke. Thus the social system tended to act as a damper on further increase in technological progress once a certain stage of development had been reached. In addition to the factors mentioned above, Childe has pointed out that the social system operated not only to concentrate wealth in the hands of the ruling minority but effectively prevented the fruits of technological progress from being distributed among the masses of the population. There was, consequently, no chance for the technology of production to expand quantitatively or to improve qualitatively.

We see, then, that the new agricultural technology resulted in a tremendous growth of culture in its initial stages. But in effecting this advance a social system was created that eventually curbed and contained the technological system in such a way as to bring progress virtually to a stop, despite the fact that the *technological* limits of agricultural development had not been even closely approximated. We may reasonably conclude, therefore, that human culture would never have gone substantially beyond the peaks achieved prior to the beginning of the Christian era had not the amount of energy harnessed per capita per year been considerably enlarged by tapping the forces of nature in a new form.

The Fuel Revolution was the culmination and synthesis of a number of streams of cultural elements that had been in progress of development for some time just as the Agricultural Revolution was the organized florescence of trends of earlier ages. And, like its predecessor, the Fuel Revolution brought about great social, political, and economic changes as a consequence of greatly augmenting the energy resources for culture building by harnessing solar energy in a new form, this time in coal, oil, and natural gas.

As in the case of the Agricultural Revolution, the new fuel technology resulted in a great increase in population. The population of Europe prior to the Coal Age grew only from 100,000,000 in 1650 to 187,000,000 in 1800. From 1800 to 1900, however, it increased to over 400,000,000. The population of England, to cite the country in which the Industrial Revolution got under way and in which it developed to a very great extent, increased 50 percent between 1700 and 1800. But during the nineteenth century, it increased 260 percent. In the two centuries prior to 1850, the population of Japan increased but 41 percent. In the fifty years following 1872—about the time industrialization began—however, the population increased over 80 percent. Urban development was powerfully stimulated and accelerated by the new technology as it had been by the developing agricultural technology in the Bronze Age. The European feudal system—a rural, aristocratic, agricultural production for use economy—was rendered obsolete and replaced by an urban, parliamentary, industrial, production-for-sale-at-a-profit economy. Social structure became ever more differentiated and functions more specialized. The productivity of human labor increased as technology advanced. Farm populations decreased relatively and in some instances absolutely.

Changes occurred in the class structure of society also. The basic dichotomy—a minority ruling class and the majority of the population in a position of subordination and exploitation—remained, but the composition of these classes underwent radical change. Industrial lords and financial barons replaced the landed aristocracy of feudalism as the dominant element in the ruling class, and an urban, industrial proletariat took the place of serfs, peasants, or slaves as the basic element in the subordinate class. Industrial strife took the place of peasant revolts and uprisings of slaves and serfs of earlier days. And, in a new form, the State-Church functioned as a co-ordinative and regulative mechanism to maintain the integrity of society by containing these class antagonisms and by mobilizing the resources of society for offense and defense.

We may pause at this point to take note of an interesting feature of the process of cultural evolution: *as culture evolves the rate of growth is accelerated.* As we have already seen, the rate of growth in late Neolithic and early Bronze times was much greater than in the Paleolithic and Eolithic ages. The Agricultural Revolution required but a few thousand years to run its course. But the Fuel Revolution is only a century and a half or two centuries old at most, and already greater changes have been effected by it perhaps than by all earlier ages put together. The change is so rapid and we are so much in the midst of it that it is difficult to grasp the situation and to realize the profound and radical nature of the revolution, social and political as well as technological, through which we are passing. Twenty-seven years ago in *New Viewpoints in American History,* Professor A. M. Schlesinger (1922) compared the culture of the United States of Lincoln's day with that of Benjamin Franklin's on the one hand, and with the culture of 1922 on the other. He remarked that the daily life with which Lincoln was familiar was in most respects like that known to George Washington and Franklin. But our culture in 1922 would have been strange and bewildering to Lincoln had he returned to the American scene:

Buildings more than three of four stories high would be new. The plate-glass show windows of the stores, the electric street-lighting, the moving-picture theaters, the electric elevators in the buildings and especially the big department stores would be things in his day unknown. The smooth-paved streets and cement sidewalks would be new to him. The fast-moving electric street-cars and motor vehicles would fill him with wonder. Even a boy on a bicycle would be a curiosity. Entering the White House, someone would have to explain to him such commonplaces of modern life as sanitary plumbing, steam heating, friction matches, telephones, electric lights, the Victrola, and even the fountain pen. In Lincoln's day, plumbing was in its beginnings, coal-oil lamps and gas-jets were coming into use, and the steel pen had only recently superseded the quill pen. The steel rail, the steel bridge, high-powered locomotives, refrigerator cars, artificial ice, the cream separator, the twine binder, the caterpillar tractor, money orders, the parcels post, rural free delivery, the cable, the wireless, gasoline engines, repeating rifles, dynamite, submarines, airplanes—these and hundreds of other inventions now in common use were all alike unknown.

But consider the changes that have taken place—in transportation, medicine, communication, and in technology in general—since Schlesinger wrote in 1922! In warfare perhaps better than in other areas of our culture, is the dizzying rate of technological progress made dramatically apparent. The technology of the first World War looks quaint today, and some of the weapons and techniques introduced for the first time in World War II are already obsolete. One hardly dares to picture the next great military conflict; novelties already unveiled and others only intimated suggest all too vividly the distance that technological progress has gone since the days of Pearl Harbor. And behind the scenes in the theater of Mars are the great research laboratories and proving grounds, working under forced draft to develop and perfect new tools and techniques in all phases of our technology. The rate of cultural advance is now greater than ever before. "Our life," wrote the distinguished physicist, Arthur Holly Compton (1940), "differs from that of two generations ago more than American life of that day differed from the civilized life at the dawn of written history." And, since Compton wrote these words, a profound and awful revolution—perhaps the most significant in all human history—has taken place: the harnessing of atomic energy.

But, even as in the case of the Agricultural Revolution and its aftermath, so in the Power Age the social system created by the new Fuel technology came eventually to act as a brake upon further cultural advance. The price and profit system stimulated production and technological progress as long as the output could find a market. But, like the socio-economic system of the Bronze Age, the new commercialism of the Fuel era had its inherent limitations. No industrial nation had or could have purchasing power sufficient to keep and absorb its own output; the very basis of the Industrial profit system was an excess in value of product over the cost of production in terms of wages paid to the industrial workers. Export of surplus was therefore essential; "we must export or die" is a cry of desperation heard from more than one nation in recent years. For a time new markets could be found abroad. But as the output of industrial nations increased with advances in technology, and as non-European nations such as Japan became industrialized and hence competitors for foreign markets, the international profit system began to bog down. The world market diminished as the industrial output increased. When goods could no longer be sold profitably abroad, production was curtailed at home. Entrepreneurs are disinclined to produce goods that cannot be sold at a profit. Factories, mills, and mines were closed. Millions of workers were thrown out of employment. Surplus goods were destroyed, agricultural production reduced. The awful plague of overproduction and unemployment, "starvation in the midst of plenty," settled upon the land. The social system was strangling the great technological machine of industry and paralyzing the body politic as a whole. The alternatives were stagnation and death or war and revolution. If the social system were able to contain the Fuel technology and the commercial rivalries and class conflicts engendered by it, society would become stabilized in a more or less stagnant form of industrial feudalism. Should, however, the forces inherent in the new technology be able to surmount and overcome the restrictions of the price and parliamentary system, then culture could advance toward higher levels.

There is evidence aplenty that culture, powered by the mighty forces of Fuel technology, is embarking upon the latter course. The first phase of the second great Cultural Revolution—the Industrial Revolution—has run its course and we are now entered upon the second phase, that of social, political, and economic revolution. And, as in the past, war is proving to be an effective means of profound political change. The system of free and individual enterprise in business and commerce is now virtually extinct. The gold standard is merely a memory of an era that is closed. The parliamentary system of government, a device designed to permit the greatest freedom for the growth of industrial and financial enterprise, is practically obsolete also. Private right is no longer significant chiefly as a means of freedom for growth as it was in the early days of commercialism. It now leads toward competitive rivalry, internecine strife, chaos, and paralysis. Concentrations of power without public responsibility among those who own or control vast wealth, or in the ranks of organized labor, are no longer compatible with the degree of unity, integrity, and strength that a nation must have if it is to compete successfully with its rivals in the international arena. The exigencies of national survival require the subordination of private right to general welfare, of part to whole. In short, the State, as the integrative and regulative mechanism of civil society, is destined to acquire ever greater power and to wield more and more control. Social evolution is moving inexorably toward higher levels of integration, toward greater concentrations of political power and control.

On the international level, too, an interesting trend of social evolution can be discerned: movement toward ever larger and larger political units. The Agricultural technology replaced villages with cities, tribes with nations and empires. The modern Fuel technology also is working toward larger political groupings, fewer concentrations of political power. The relatively recent trend toward amalgamation can be seen in the unification of Germany and Italy in the nineteenth century. The Treaty of Versailles attempted, with the "Balkanization of Europe," to oppose the age-old trend of social evolution by breaking the continent up into little pieces. One of the conspicuous and significant aspects of the second World War in its initial phase was a movement toward the unification of Europe. A half-dozen or so World Powers engaged in the first World War; only two great powers emerged from the second. The competition for power narrows as contestants are eliminated. The logical conclusion is, however, not simply the domination of the world by a single nation—this would be but a transitional stage—but a single political organization that will embrace the entire planet and the whole human race. Toward such a denouement is our mighty Power technology rapidly moving us.

But a new and ominous element has recently entered the picture: nuclear atomic energy for military purposes. Here again the significance of this new factor derives from the fact that a new source of energy has been harnessed and in awful form. Once more we are upon the threshold of a technological revolution. But the consequences of this new technological advance may possibly differ radically from those of the Agricultural and the Fuel revolutions. New technologies in the past have rendered old social systems obsolete but they have replaced them with new systems. The new nuclear technology, however, threatens to destroy civilization itself, or at least to cripple it to such an extent that it might require a century, a thousand, or ten thousand, years to regain its present status. At least this is what eminent scientists and military men tell us; as laymen we are in a child's world of ignorance, with almost all the significant facts kept beyond our reach. The destruction of a few score of centers of science and industry in Europe and the United States would just about do for Western civilization and authorities assure us that this is well within the realm of possibility, not to say probability. The hope of the future, therefore, and the salvation of mankind and civilization would seem to lie in the emergence from the next war of a *victor*—not merely a survivor —and one with sufficient power and resources to organize the whole planet and the entire human species within a single social system.

We have thus presented a sketch of the evolution of the culture of mankind from the horizon of our prehuman forebears to the present time. It is a fascinating story of adventure and progress; of a species lifting itself up by its cultural bootstraps from the status of a mere animal to a radically new way of life, a way destined to win mastery over most other species and to exert a powerful and extensive control over the natural habitat. The origin of culture elevated the evolutionary process to a new plane. No longer was it necesary for the human animal to acquire new powers and techniques through the slow process of biological change; he now had an extra-somatic mechanism of adjustment and control that could grow freely of itself. Moreover, advances in one stream of cultural development could diffuse readily to other traditions so that all might share in the progress of each. Thus the story of man becomes an account of his culture.

Technology is the hero of our piece. This is a world of rocks and rivers, sticks and steel, of sun, air, and starlight, of galaxies, atoms, and molecules. Man is but a particular kind of material body who must do certain things to maintain his status in a cosmic material system. The means of adjustment and control, of security and survival, are of course technological. Culture thus becomes primarily a mechanism for harnessing energy and of putting it to work in the service of man, and, secondarily, of channelling and regulating his behavior not directly concerned with subsistence and offense and defense. Social systems are therefore determined by technological systems, and philosophies and the arts express experience as it is defined by technology and refracted by social systems. Cultural systems like those of the biological level are capable of growth. That is, the power to capture any energy is also the ability to harness more and still more of it. Thus cultural systems, like biological organisms, develop, multiply, and extend themselves. The sun is the prime mover; culture, a thermodynamic system operated by it. At least, solar energy has activated all cultural systems of history up to now, and it will continue to do so after terrestrial supplies of fissionable fuels have been exhausted—if civilization should survive and reach this point. But technology is still the leading character in our play, even though it may turn out to be a villain instead of the hero. Technology builds but it may also destroy.

The belief and faith that civilization, won at such great cost in pain and labor, simply cannot go down in destruction because such an end would be too monstrous and senseless is but a naive and anthropocentric whimper. The cosmos does little know nor will it long remember what man has done here on this tiny planet. The eventual extinction of the human race—for come it will sometime—will not be the first time that a species has died out. Nor will it be an event of very great terrestrial significance.

But *man* may survive the coming holocaust of radioactivity even though his culture is tumbled to the level of Neolithic times, only to begin the long climb over again, this time perhaps by a somewhat different route; culture too may be able to profit from experience. But culture may *not* destroy or even critically wound itself with its new powers. Destruction is no more inevitable than salvation. Great though the devastation may—and will—be in the next test of strength in the international arena, the creative powers of the new technology may be sufficiently great to rise up from the ruins and to enclose the whole world in a single political embrace. Then and only then will the curse of war be lifted and the way made free and open for a fuller and richer life.

Our sketch of the evolution of culture is, it will be noted, wholly culturological. It does not resort to race, physical type, intelligence, a moral sense, the dignity of man, the spirit of progress or democracy, the individual—genius or otherwise—the rejection of the father, consciousness of kind, a set of instincts or "drives," social interaction, a basic personality structure, toilet training in infancy, or breast *vs.* bottle feeding and weaning, to account for the behavior and growth of this great extra-somatic tradition. We explain it in terms of culture itself. A thunderstorm or a tornado is explained in terms of antecedent and concomitant meteorological events; a clan or a constitution is likewise accounted for by citing its cultural antecedents and concomitants.

Culture is, as we have pointed out repeatedly, a stream of interacting elements; one trait reacts upon others and is affected by them in return. Some elements become obsolete and are eliminated from the stream; new elements are incorporated into it. New permutations, combinations, and syntheses are continually being formed. Whether we deal with a restricted portion of the cultural continuum such as the evolution of mathematics or the genealogy of the steam engine, or whether we encompass culture in its entirety, the principle of interpretation is the same: culture grows out of culture. In our sketch of the evolution of culture as a whole we deal with large categories: technology, social systems, and philosophies. We break technology down into energy and tool factors. We observe the action of each class of elements, their impact upon others, the effect of technology upon social systems, and the influence of economic and political institutions upon agriculture and steam-driven factories. We note the role that war as a culture process has played in the course of political change. And, finally, we see the fate of civilization delicately balanced in a scales to be tipped this way or that, we know not how, by the modern miracles of nuclear technology.

Culturology is the newest venture of science. After centuries of cultivation in the fields of astronomy, physics, and chemistry; after scores of years of tillage in physiology and psychology, science has at last turned to the most immediate and powerful determinant of man's *human* behavior: his culture. After repeated trials and as many failures it was discovered that culture cannot be explained psychologically; such interpretations are merely anthropomorphisms in scientific clothing. The explanation of culture is and must be culturological. The science of culture is young but full of promise. It is destined to do great things—if only the subject of its study will continue its age-old course: onward and upward.

NOTE

1. The functioning of any particular culture will of course be conditioned by local environmental conditions. But in a consideration of culture as a whole, we may average all environments together to form a constant factor which may be excluded from our formula of cultural development.

REFERENCES

Childe, V. Gordon
    1936   *Man Makes Himself*. London.

Compton, A. H.
    1940   "Science Shaping American Culture," *Proceedings*, American Philosophical Society, 83:573–582.

MacCurdy, G. G.
    1933   *Human Origins*. New York.

Ostwald, Wilhelm
    1907   "The Modern Theory of Energetics," *The Monist*, 17:481–515.

Schlesinger, A. M.
    1922   *New Viewpoints in American History*. New York.

E. E. Evans-Pritchard 1902–

BACKGROUND

Edward Evan Evans-Pritchard—like Bronislaw Malinowski, who was one of his teachers but whom he overtly chose not to emulate—is a brilliantly accomplished ethnographer. There is a story that, when asked whether he collected texts during his field work in Africa (and he collected great bundles of them), he responded, with some scorn for his questioner, "Not really. I always found it easier to learn the language well enough that whenever I needed a text, I could write it."

He was born in England, the second son of the Reverend Thomas Evans-Pritchard. He attended Winchester, then went on as an honors student to Exeter College, Oxford. He began anthropology at the London School of Economics under Charles Gabriel Seligman, who remained his close friend. When ill health prevented Seligman and his wife Brenda from continuing an ethnographic survey they had undertaken for the government of what was then the Anglo-Egyptian Sudan, Seligman arranged for Evans-Pritchard to continue it.

Between 1926 and 1936 E-P (as his friends and students call him) made six expeditions to the Sudan. He did several months' survey work among the Anuak, Ingassana, Moro, and many other peoples. Although he himself wrote on the Shilluk, Anuak, and Luo, he considered that his notes from this trip belonged primarily to the Seligmans. He therefore returned to the Sudan on his own, to make detailed studies first of the Azande and then of the Nuer. The results of all this work were published as papers in *Sudan Notes and Records* in the 1930s. In 1937 *Witchcraft, Oracles and Magic Among the Azande* appeared. Its careful reporting and analysis of a system of empirical reasoning from false premises have made the book basic to all subsequent studies of witchcraft.

The years 1931–1934 were spent in Egypt as professor of sociology at the Egyptian University of Cairo. In 1935 E-P left Egypt to become Research Lecturer in African Sociology at Oxford. This brought him into sustained contact with A. R. Radcliffe-Brown, who had considerable influence on the theoretical side of his work. In 1940 he coedited (with Meyer Fortes) and contributed to a classic in political anthropology, *African Political Systems,* and published the first part of his Nuer trilogy, *The Nuer: A Description of the Modes of Livelihood and Political Institutions in a Nilotic People.*

In 1939 he married. When World War II began the same year, he joined the army. He served first in the Abyssinian campaign, in which he organized the

Azande and other border peoples in an uprising against the Italians in Ethiopia. Then he went as political officer to Syria, where he was one of the few men who had all the requisite languages—English, French, and Arabic.

In November 1942 he was posted as political officer to the British Military Administration in Cyrenaica. He spent two years there, much of the time among the nomadic sections of the Bedouin. Official duties prevented his carrying out what he considered, with his very high standards, to be systematic inquiries into the social anthropology of the Bedouin. Nevertheless, in 1949 he published *The Sanusi of Cyrenaica,* an analysis of the process by which a lineage-based society developed centralized political roles, claimed by many to be a definitive work on this people.

This book is a monument in another way. Unlike most contemporary British and American anthropology, it is a study in culture change that relies heavily on historical material. Evans-Pritchard was trained in history in his undergraduate days at Oxford, and he can be quite eloquent on the social anthropologist's and historian's need for each other.

On returning from the army in 1945, he was appointed Reader in Anthropology at Cambridge. He left Cambridge after a year to take the chair in social anthropology at Oxford upon Radcliffe-Brown's retirement.

Evans-Pritchard's second volume on the Nuer had been planned for 1942, and much of it had actually been written before the war. But military and then academic duty, and then the history of the Sanusi, delayed this volume, *Kinship and Marriage among the Nuer,* until 1951. The third volume, *Nuer Religion,* was published in 1956. It was, perhaps, the first major anthropological work on religion to differ from Émile Durkheim's view that societies worship themselves through worship of some emblem that is the collective expression of the society. Evans-Pritchard's position is that religion does not grow out of social structure, nor is it limited by it. To him what is important in the study of religion is the way men explain to one another the intricacies of the universe in which they live.

In the winter of 1950 he gave a series of lectures on the BBC Third Programme to make the scope and methods of social anthropology better known to the public. The next year these lectures were published as *Social Anthropology.* A second collection of essays and addresses, *The Position of Women in Primitive Society,* appeared in 1956. More of the work from the 1930s in the Sudan appeared as *The Zande Trickster* (1967).

In 1968 he made a lecture tour of the United States, receiving an honorary degree from the University of Chicago. He was knighted in 1971, the year after his retirement from Oxford, where he lives quietly, still working on his Azande materials.

INTRODUCTION

In the body of the following essay, E. E. Evans-Pritchard cites F. W. Maitland's often quoted aphorism that anthropology will one day have a choice of becoming history or nothing. Although the wheel of fortune may turn again, in today's world that notion is backward: history may some day have the choice of becoming anthropology—behavioral science, in any event—or nothing.

The essay begins with a review of the history of anthropology and goes on to represent a view of anthropology that is perennial—and perennially under attack. To take the natural science model for behavioral science is, says Evans-Pritchard, a piece of poor judgment. He might also have said that there is no other European language in which it is possible to squabble, as is almost inevitable in English, about whether anthropology is a "science." Certainly, to put it into German, it is a *Wissenschaft*. When Evans-Pritchard discusses society as a "moral system," and when he claims to be a humanist rather than a natural scientist, he is not making anthropology mystical or less of a *Wissenschaft*—he is, however, changing the criteria by which success in anthropology is to be judged.

This essay is a very early appeal for the kind of thinking that became acceptable in anthropology only ten or fifteen years later, in the "new archaeology" that is, as we write, one of the most interesting of anthropological developments. Evans-Pritchard recognizes that most of the societies the world has ever known are gone and must be studied by historical methods—and that such methods and purposes differ only in detail, and in the activities of the scholar, from classical anthropological method.

Perhaps Maitland would settle for our paraphrasing yet another great man: if history and anthropology do not hang together, they may hang separately.

24 SOCIAL ANTHROPOLOGY: PAST AND PRESENT

The considerable advances made in social anthropology during the last thirty years and the creation of new departments in several universities would seem to require some reflection on what the subject is, and which direction it is taking, or ought to take, for anthropology has now ceased to be an amateur pursuit and has become a profession. There is a division of opinion on these matters among anthropologists themselves, broadly between those who regard the subject as a natural science and those who, like myself, regard it as one of the humanities, and this division, which reflects quite different sentiments and values, is apparent whenever there arises a discussion about the methods and aims of the discipline. It is perhaps at its sharpest when the relations between anthropology and history are being discussed, and since consideration of this difficult question brings out the issues most clearly, I shall devote a large part of my lecture to it. To perceive how these issues have come about it is necessary to cast our eyes back over the period of the genesis and early development of the subject.

EIGHTEENTH-CENTURY ORIGINS

A subject of scholarship can hardly be said to have autonomy before it is taught in the universities. In that sense social anthropology

Reprinted from *Man*, no. 198 (September 1950): 118–124, by permission of the author and the Royal Anthropological Institute of Great Britain and Ireland.

is a very new subject. In another sense it may be said to have begun with the earliest speculations of mankind, for everywhere and at all times men have propounded theories about the nature of human society. In this sense there is no definite point at which social anthropology can be said to have begun. Nevertheless, there is a point beyond which it is hardly profitable to trace back its development. This nascent period of our subject was the middle and late eighteenth century. It is a child of the Enlightenment and bears throughout its history and today many of the characteristic features of its ancestry.

In France its lineage runs from Montesquieu and such writers as d'Alembert, Condorcet, Turgot, and in general the Encyclopaedists, to Saint Simon, who was the first to propose clearly a science of society, and to his one-time disciple Comte, who named the science sociology. This stream of French philosophical rationalism was later, through the writings of Durkheim and his students and Lévy-Bruhl, who were in the direct line of Saint-Simonian tradition, to colour English anthropology strongly.

Our forebears were the Scottish moral philosophers, whose writings were typical of the eighteenth century: David Hume, Adam Smith, Thomas Reid, Francis Hutcheson, Dugald Stewart, Adam Ferguson, Lord Kames and Lord Monboddo. These writers took their inspiration from Bacon, Newton and Locke, though they were also much influenced by Descartes. They insisted that the study of societies, which they regarded as natural systems or organisms, must be empirical, and that by the use of the inductive method it would be possible to explain them in terms of general principles or laws in the same way as physical phenomena had been explained by the physicists. It must also be normative. Natural law is derived from a study of human nature, which is in all societies and at all times the same. These writers also believed in limitless progress and in laws of progress. Man, being everywhere alike, must advance along certain lines through set stages of development, and these stages can be hypothetically reconstructed by what Dugald Stewart called conjectural history, and what later became known as the comparative method. Here we have all the ingredients of anthropological theory in the nineteenth century and even at the present day.

The writers I have mentioned, both in France and England, were of course in the sense of their time philosophers and so regarded themselves. In spite of all their talk about empiricism they relied more on introspection and a priori reasoning than on observation of actual societies. For the most part they used facts to illustrate or corroborate theories reached by speculation. It was not till the middle of the nineteenth century that systematic studies of social institutions were concluded with some attempt at scientific rigour. In the decade between 1861 and 1871 there appeared books which we regard as our early classics: Maine's *Ancient Law* (1861), Bachofen's *Das Mutterrecht* (1861), Fustel de Coulanges' *La Cité antique* (1864), McLennan's *Primitive Marriage* (1865), Tylor's *Researches into the Early History of Mankind* (1865), and Morgan's *The System of Consanguinity* (1871). Not all these books were concerned primarily with primitive societies, though those that were least concerned with them, like *Ancient Law*, were dealing with comparable institutions at early periods in the development of historical societies. It was McLennan and Tylor in this country, and Morgan in America, who first treated primitive societies as a subject which might in itself engage the attention of serious scholars.

NINETEENTH-CENTURY ANTHROPOLOGY

The authors of this decade, like those of the generation before them, were anxious to rid the study of social institutions of mere speculation. They, also, thought that they could do this by being strictly empirical and by rigorous use of the comparative historical method. Using this method they, and those who followed them, wrote many large volumes purporting to show the origin and development of social institutions: the development of monogamous marriage from promiscuity, of property from communism, of contract from status, of industry from nomadism, of positive science from theology, of monotheism from animism. Sometimes, especially when treating religion, explanations were sought in terms of psychological origins as well as in terms of historical origins.

These Victorian anthropologists were men of outstanding ability, wide learning and obvious integrity. If they overemphasized resemblances in custom and belief and paid insufficient attention to diversities, they were investigating a real and not an imaginary problem when they attempted to account for remarkable similarities in societies widely separated in space and time; and much of permanent value has come out of their researches. Nevertheless, it is difficult to read their theoretical constructions today without irritation, and at times we feel embarrassed at what seems complacency. We see now that though their use of the comparative method allowed them to separate the general from the particular, and so to classify social phenomena, the explanations of these phenomena which they put forward amounted to little more than hypothetical scales of progress, at one end of which were placed forms of institutions or beliefs as they were in nineteenth-century Europe and America, while at the other end were placed their antitheses. An order of stages was then worked out to show what logically might have been the history of development from one end of the scale to the other. All that remained to be done was to hunt through ethnological literature for examples to illustrate each of these stages. It is evident that such reconstructions not only imply moral judgments but must always be conjectural; and that in any case an institution is not to be understood, far less explained, in terms of its origins, whether these are conceived of as beginnings, causes or merely, in a logical sense, its simplest forms. For all their insistence on empiricism in the study of social institutions the nineteenth-century anthropologists were hardly less dialectical, speculative and dogmatic than the moral philosophers of the preceding century, though they at least felt that they had to support their constructions with a wealth of factual evidence, a need scarcely felt by the moral philosophers, so that a very great amount of original literary research was undertaken and vast repositories of ethnological detail were stocked and systematically arranged, as, to mention the largest of these storehouses, in *The Golden Bough.*

It is not surprising that the anthropologists of the last century wrote what they regarded as history, for all contemporaneous learning was radically historical, and at a time when history in England was still a literary art. The genetic approach, which had borne impressive fruits in philology, was, as Lord Acton has emphasized, apparent in law, economics, science, theology and philosophy. There was everywhere a passionate endeavour to discover the origins of everything—the origin of species, the origin of religion, the origin of law and so on—an endeavour always to explain the nearer by the farther which, in reference to history proper, Marc Bloch calls '*la hantise des origines.*'

In any case, I do not think that the real cause of confusion was, as is generally supposed, that the nineteenth-century anthropologists believed in progress and sought a method by which they might reconstruct how it had come about, for they were well aware that their schemata were hypotheses which could not be finally or fully verified. The cause of confusion in most of their writings is rather to be looked for in the assumption they had inherited from the Enlightenment that societies are natural systems or organisms which have a necessary course of development that can be reduced to general principles or laws. Logical consistencies were in consequence presented as real and necessary connexions and typological classifications as both historical and inevitable courses of development. It will readily be seen how a combination of the notion of scientific law and that of progress leads in anthropology, as in the philosophy of history, to procrustean stages, the presumed inevitability of which gives them a normative character.

THE TWENTIETH CENTURY

The reaction against the attempt to explain social institutions in terms of parallel, seen ideally as unilinear, development came at the end of the century; and though this so-called evolutionary anthropology was recast and re-presented in the writings of Westermarck and Hobhouse it had finally lost its appeal. It had in any case ceased to stimulate research, because once the stages of human development had been marked out further investigation on these lines offered nothing more exciting than attachment of labels written by dead hands. Some anthropologists, and in varying degrees, now turned for inspiration to psychology, which at the time seemed to provide satisfactory solutions of many of their problems without recourse to hypothetical history. This has proved to be, then and since, an attempt to build a house on shifting sands. If I say no more in this lecture about the relation between psychology and anthropology it is not because I do not consider it important, but because it would require more time than I can spare, and also more knowledge of psychology than I possess, to treat adequately.

Apart from the criticism of evolutionary theory implied in the ignoring of it by these, including Rector Marett, who sought psychological explanations of customs and beliefs, it was attacked from two directions, the diffusionist and the functionalist. Diffusionist criticism was based on the very obvious fact that culture is often borrowed and does not emerge by spontaneous growth due to certain common social potentialities and common human nature. To suppose otherwise and to discuss social change without reference to events is to lapse into Cartesian scholasticism. This approach had, unfortunately, little lasting influence in England, partly, no doubt, on account of its uncritical use by Elliot Smith, Perry and Rivers. The other form of attack, the functionalist, has been far more influential, as it has been far more radical. It condemned equally evolutionary anthropology and diffusionist anthropology, not merely on the grounds that their historical reconstructions were unverifiable, but also, and simply, because both were historical approaches, for in the view of writers of this persuasion the history of a society is irrelevant to a study of it as a natural system.

The same kind of development was taking place at the same time in other fields of learning. There were functional biology, functional psychology, functional law, functional economics and so forth. The point of view was the more readily accepted by many social anthropologists because anthropologists generally study societies the history of which cannot be known. Their ready acceptance was also partly due to the influence from across the Channel of the philosophical rationalism of Durkheim and his school. This influence has had, on the whole, not only a profound but a beneficial effect on English anthropology. It injected a tradition which was concerned with broad general questions into the more piecemeal empirical English tradition, exemplified by the way in which theoretical writers like Tylor and Frazer used their material and by both the many firsthand accounts of primitive peoples written by travellers, missionaries and administrators and the early social surveys in this country. On the other hand, if students are not firmly anchored by a heavy weight of ethnographic fact, they are easily led by it into airy discussions about words, into arid classifications, and into either pretentiousness or total scepticism.

THE FUNCTIONAL THEORY

The functional or organismic theory of society which reigns in social anthropology in England today is not new. We have seen that it was held in their several ways by the early and mid-Victorian anthropologists and by the moral philosophers before them, and it has, of course, a very much longer pedigree in political philosophy. In its modern and more mechanistic form it was set forth at great length by Durkheim and, with special reference to social evolution, by Herbert Spencer. In yet more recent times it has been most clearly and consistently stated by Professor Radcliffe-Brown. Human societies are natural systems in which all the parts are interdependent, each serving in a complex of necessary relations to maintain the whole. The aim of social anthropology is to reduce all social life to laws or general statements about the nature of society which allow prediction. What is new in this restatement of the theory is the insistence that a society can be understood satisfactorily without reference to its past. Almost without exception the eighteenth-century moral philosophers presented their conception of social systems and sociological laws in the form of history in the grand style—a natural history of human societies; and, as we have seen, the enduring passion of their Victorian successors was seeking for origins from which every institution has developed through the working of laws of progress. The modern version of a naturalistic study of society, even if lip-service is sometimes paid to the possibility of a scientific study of social change, claims that for an understanding of the functioning of a society there is no need for the student of it to know anything about its history, any more than there is need for a physiologist to know the history of an organism to understand it. Both are natural systems and can be described in terms of natural law without recourse to history.

The functional orientation, by its insistence on the interrelatedness of things, has been largely responsible for the comprehensive and detailed professional field studies of modern anthropology, such as were entirely unknown to the anthropologists of the nineteenth century, who were content to let laymen collect the facts on which they based their theories. It is also largely due to it that the anthropologist of today sees more clearly than his predecessors than an understanding of human behaviour can only be reached by viewing it in its full social setting. All social anthropologists now accept that the entire activities of primitive societies must be systematically studied in the field, and all have the same holistic approach when they come to set down and interpret their observations.

But a theory may have heuristic value without being sound, and there are many objections to the functional theory. It is no more than an assumption that human societies are systems of the kind they are alleged to be. Indeed in the case of Malinowski the functional theory, in spite of the wide claims he made for it, was little more than a literary device. The theory assumes, moreover, that in the given circumstances no part of social life can be other than what it is and that every custom has social value, thus adding to a native determinism a crude teleology and pragmatism. It is easy to define the aim of social anthropology to be the establishment of sociological laws, but nothing even remotely resembling a law of the natural sciences has yet been adduced. What general statements have been made are for the most part speculative, and are in any case too general to be of value. Often they are little more than guesses on a common-sense or *post factum* level, and they sometimes degenerate into mere tautologies or even platitudes. Also, it is difficult to reconcile the assertion that a society has come to be what it is by a succession of unique events with the claim that what it is can be comprehensively stated in terms of natural law. In its extreme form functional determinism leads to absolute relativism and makes nonsense not only of the theory itself but of all thought.

If for these and other reasons I cannot accept, without many qualifications, the functional theory dominant in English anthropology today, I do not assert, as you will see, that societies are unintelligible or that they are not in some sense systems. What I am objecting to is what appears to me to be still the same doctrinaire philosophy of the Enlightenment and of the stage-making anthropologists of the nineteenth century, with only the concept of evolution substituted for that of progress. Its constructions are still posited dialectically and imposed on the facts. I attribute this to anthropologists always having tried to model themselves on the natural sciences instead of on the historical sciences, and it is to this important issue that I now turn. I must apologize to historians if, in considering it, what I say may seem obvious to them. My observations would be hotly disputed by most of my anthropological colleagues in England.

ANTHROPOLOGY AND HISTORY

In discussing the relations between history and social anthropology it is necessary, if the discussion is to be profitable, to perceive that several quite different questions are being asked. The first is whether a knowledge of how a particular social system has come to be what it is helps one to understand its present constitution. We must here distinguish between history in two different senses, though in a literate society it is not so easy to maintain the distinction as when speaking of non-literate societies. In the first sense history is part of the conscious tradition of a people and is operative in their social life. It is the collective representation of events as distinct from events themselves. This is what the social anthropologist calls myth. The functionalist anthropologists regard history in this sense, usually a mixture of fact and fancy, as highly relevant to a study of the culture of which it forms part.

On the other hand they have totally rejected the reconstruction from circumstantial evidences of the history of primitive peoples for whose past documents and monuments are totally, or almost totally, lacking. A case can be made out for this rejection, though not in my opinion so strong a case as is usually supposed, for all history is of necessity a reconstruction, the degree of probability attending a particular reconstruction depending on the evidence available. The fact that nineteenth-century anthropologists were uncritical in their reconstructions ought not to lead to the conclusion that all effort expended in this direction is waste of time.

But with the bath water of presumptive history the functionalists have also thrown out the baby of valid history. They say, Malinowski the most vociferously, that even when the history of a society is recorded it is irrelevant to a functional study of it. I find this point of view unacceptable. The claim that one can understand the functioning of institutions at a certain point of time without knowing how they have come to be what they are, or what they were later to become, as well as a person who, in addition to having studied their constitution at that point of time, has also studied their past and future is to me an absurdity. Moreover, so it seems to me, neglect of the history of institutions prevents the functionalist anthropologist not only from studying diachronic problems but also from testing the very functional constructions to which he attaches most importance, for it is precisely history which provides him with an experimental situation.

The problem here raised is becoming a pressing one because anthropologists are now studying communities which, if still fairly simple in structure, are enclosed in, and form part of, great historical societies, such as Irish and Indian rural communities, Bedouin Arab tribes, or ethnic minorities in America and other parts of the world. They can no longer ignore history, making a virtue out of necessity, but must explicitly reject it or admit its relevance. As anthropologists turn their attention more to complex civilized communities the issue will become more acute, and the direction of theoretical development in the subject will largely depend on its outcome.

A second question is of a different kind. We ask now, not whether in studying a particular society its history forms an integral part of the study, but whether in making comparative sociological studies, for example of political or religious institutions, we ought to include in them societies as presented to us by historians. In spite of their claim that social anthropology aims at being a natural history of human societies, that is, of all human societies, functionalist anthropologists, at any rate in England, have, in their general distaste for historical method, almost completely ignored historical writings. They have thereby denied themselves access in their comparative studies to the valuable material provided by historical societies structurally comparable to many of the contemporaneous barbarous societies which they regard as being within their province.

A third and to me the most important, question is a methodological one: whether social anthropology, for all its present disregard of history, is not itself a kind of historiography. To answer this question we have first to observe what the anthropologist does. He goes to live for some months or years among a primitive people. He lives among them as intimately as he can, and he learns to speak their language, to think in their concepts and to feel in their values. He then lives the experiences over again critically and interpretatively in the conceptual categories and values of his own culture and in terms of the general body of knowledge of his discipline. In other words, he translates from one culture into another.

At this level social anthropology remains a literary and impressionistic art. But even in a single ethnographic study the anthropologist seeks to do more than understand the thought and values of a primitive people and translate them into his own culture. He seeks also to discover the structural order of the society, the patterns which, once established, enable him to see it as a whole, as a set of interrelated abstractions. Then the society is not only culturally intelligible, as it is, at the level of consciousness and action, for one of its members or for the foreigner who has learnt its mores and participates in its life, but also becomes sociologically intelligible.

The historian, or at any rate the social historian, and perhaps the economic historian in particular, will, I think, know what I mean by sociologically intelligible. After all, English society in the eleventh century was understood by Vinogradoff in quite a different way from the way it would have been understood by a Norman or Anglo-Saxon or by a foreigner who had learnt the native languages and was living the life of the natives. Similarly, the social anthropologist discovers in a native society what no native can explain to him and what no layman, however conversant with the culture, can perceive—its basic structure. This structure cannot be seen. It is a set of abstractions, each of which, though derived, it is true, from analysis of observed behaviour, is fundamentally an imaginative construct of the anthropologist himself. By relating these abstractions to one another logically so that they present a pattern he can see the society in its essentials and as a single whole.

What I am trying to say can perhaps be best illustrated by the example of language. A native understands his own language and it can be learnt by a stranger. But certainly neither the native himself nor the stranger can tell you what are its phonological and grammatical systems. These can only be discovered by a trained linguist. By analysis he can reduce the complexity of a language to certain abstractions and show how these abstractions can be interrelated in a logical system or pattern. This is what the social anthropologist tries to do. He tries to disclose the structural patterns of a society. Having isolated these patterns in one society he compares them with patterns in other societies. The study of each new society enlarges his knowledge of the range of basic social structures and enables him better to construct a typology of forms, and to determine their essential features and the reasons for their variations.

I have tried to show that the work of the social anthropologist is in three main phases or, otherwise expressed, at three levels of abstraction. First he seeks to understand the significant overt features of a culture and to translate them into terms of his own culture. This is precisely what the historian does. There is no fundamental difference here in aim or method between the two disciplines, and both are equally selective in their use of material. The similarity between them has been obscured by the fact that the social anthropologist makes a direct study of social life while the historian makes an indirect study of it through documents and other surviving evidences. This is a technical, not a methodological, difference. The historicity of anthropology has also been obscured by its pre-occupation with primitive societies which lack recorded history. But this again is not a methodological difference. I agree with Professor Kroeber that the fundamental characteristic of the historical method is not chronological relation of events but descriptive intregration of them; and this characteristic historiography shares with social anthropology. What social anthropologists have in fact chiefly been doing is to write cross-sections of history, integrative descriptive accounts of primitive peoples at a moment of time which are in other respects like the accounts written by historians about peoples over a period of time, for the historian does not just record sequences of events but seeks to establish connexions between them. Nor does the anthropologist's determination to view every institution as a functioning part of a whole society make a methodological difference. Any good modern historian aims—if I may be allowed to judge the matter—at the same kind of synthesis.

In my view, therefore, the fact that the anthropologist's problems are generally synchronic while the historian's problems are generally diachronic is a difference of emphasis in the rather peculiar conditions prevailing and not a real divergence of interest. When the historian fixes his attention exclusively on a particular culture at a particular and limited period of history he writes what we would call an ethnographic monograph (Buckhardt's *Culture of the Renaissance* is a striking example). When, on the other hand, a social anthropologist writes about a society developing in time he writes a history book, different, it is true, from the ordinary narrative and political history but in all essentials the same as social history. In the absence of another, I must cite my own book *The Sanusi of Cyrenaica* as an example.

In the second phase of his work the social anthropologist goes a step farther and seeks by analysis to disclose the latent underlying form of a society or culture. In doing so, he goes farther than the more timorous and conservative historians, but many historians do the same. I am not thinking of philosophers of history like Vico, Hegel, Marx, Spengler and Toynbee, not of those who can be exclusively particularized as social historians or writers of the *Kulturgeschichte* school like Max Weber, Tawney, and Sombart or Adam Smith, Savigny and Buckle, but of historians in the stricter and more orthodox sense like Fustel de Coulanges, Vinogradoff, Pirenne, Maitland, or Professor Powicke. It is perhaps worth noting that those historical writings which we anthropologists regard as examples of sociological method generally deal with early periods of history, where the societies described are more like primitive societies than the complex societies of later periods of history, and where the historical documents are not too vast to be grasped and assimilated by a single mind; so that the total culture can be studied as a whole and contained in a single mind, as primitive cultures can be studied and contained. When we read the works of these historians we feel that we and they are studying the same things in the same way and are reaching out for the same kind of understanding of them.

In the third phase of his work the anthropologist compares the social structures his analysis has revealed in a wide range of societies. When a historian attempts a similar study in his own field he is dubbed a philosopher, but it is not, I think, true to say, as it is often said, that history is a study of the particular and social anthropology of the general. In some historical writers comparison and classification are quite explicit; always they are implicit, for history cannot be written except against a standard of some kind, by comparison with the culture of a different time or people, if only with the writer's own.

I conclude therefore, following Professor Kroeber, that while there are, of course, many differences between social anthropology and historiography they are differences of technique, of emphasis and of perspective, and not differences of method and aim. I believe also that a clearer understanding that this is so will lead to a closer connexion between historical and anthropological studies than is at present provided by their meeting points in ethnology and prehistoric archaeology, and that this will be greatly to the benefit of both disciplines. Historians can supply social anthropologists with invaluable material, sifted and vouched for by critical techniques of testing and interpretation. Social anthropologists can provide the historian of the future with some of his best records, based on careful and detailed observations, and they can shed on history, by their discovery of latent structural forms, the light of universals. The value of each discipline to the other will, I believe, be recognized when anthropologists begin to devote themselves more to historical scholarships and show how knowledge of anthropology often illuminates historical problems.

SOCIAL ANTHROPOLOGY AS ONE OF THE HUMANITIES

The thesis I have put before you, that social anthropology is a kind of historiography, and therefore ultimately of philosophy or art, implies that it studies societies as moral systems and not as natural systems, that it is interested in design rather than in process, and that it therefore seeks patterns and not scientific laws, and interprets rather than explains. These are conceptual, and not merely verbal, differences. The concepts of natural system and natural law, modelled on the constructs of the natural sciences, have dominated anthropology from its beginnings, and as we look back over the course of its growth I think we can see that they have been responsible for a false scholasticism which has led to one rigid and ambitious formulation after another. Regarded as a special kind of historiography, that is, as one of the humanities, social anthropology is released from these essentially philosophical dogmas and given the opportunity, though it may seem paradoxical to say so, to be really empirical and, in the true sense of the word, scientific. This, I presume, is what Maitland had in mind when he said that 'by and by anthropology will have the choice between becoming history or nothing.'

I have found, both in England and America, that students are often perturbed at these implications. There is no need for them to be, for it does not follow from regarding social anthropology as a special kind of historiography rather than as a special kind of natural science that its researches and theory are any the less systematic. When therefore I am asked how I think that social anthropology should proceed in the future I reply that it must proceed along much the same lines as does social history or the history of institutions, as distinct from purely narrative and political history. For example, the social historian seeking to understand feudal institutions would first study them in one country of Europe and get to know all he can about them there. He would then study them in other European societies to discover which features were common to European civilization at that time and which were local variations, and he would try to see each particular form as a variation of a general pattern and to account for the variations. He would not seek for laws but for significant patterns.

What more do we do, can we do or should we want to do in social anthropology than this? We study witchcraft or a kinship system in a particular primitive society. If we want to know more about these social phenomena we can study them in a second society, and then in a third society, and so on, each study reaching, as our knowledge increases and new problems emerge, a deeper level of investigation and teaching us the essential characteristics of the thing we are inquiring into, so that particular studies are given a new meaning and perspective. This will always happen if one necessary condition is observed: that the conclusions of each study are clearly formulated in such a way that they not only test the conclusions reached by earlier studies but advance new hypotheses which can be broken down into field-work problems.

However, the uneasiness I have noted is not, I think, on this score, because it must be evident to any student who has given thought to the matter that those who have most strongly urged that social anthropology should model itself on the natural sciences have done neither better research than those who take the opposite view nor a different kind of research. It is rather due to the feeling that any discipline that does not aim at formulating laws and hence predicting and planning is not worth the labour of a lifetime. This normative element in anthropology is, as we have seen, like the concepts of natural law and progress from which it derives, part of its philosophical heritage. In recent times the natural-science approach has constantly stressed the application of its findings to affairs, the emphasis in England being on colonial problems and in America on political and industrial problems. Its more cautious advocates have held that there can only be applied anthropology when the science is much more advanced than it is today, but the less cautious have made far-reaching claims for the immediate application of anthropological knowledge in social planning; though, whether more or less cautious, both have justified anthropology by appeal to utility. Needless to say, I do not share their enthusiasm and regard the attitude that gives rise to it as naive. A full discussion of it would take too long, but I cannot resist the observation that, as the history of anthropology shows, positivism leads very easily to a misguided ethics, anaemic scientific humanism or—Saint Simon and Comte are cases in point—*ersatz* religion.

I conclude by summarizing very briefly the argument I have tried to develop in this lecture and by stating what I believe is likely to be the direction taken by social anthropology in the future. Social anthropologists, dominated consciously or unconsciously, from the beginnings of their subject, by positivist philosophy, have aimed, explicitly or implicitly, and for the most part still aim—for this is what it comes to—at proving that man is an automaton and at discovering the sociological laws in terms of which his actions, ideas and beliefs can be explained and in the light of which they can be planned and controlled. This approach implies that human societies are natural systems which can be reduced to variables. Anthropologists have therefore taken one or other of the natural sciences as their model and have turned their backs on history, which sees men in a different way and eschews, in the light of experience, rigid formulations of any kind.

There is, however, an older tradition than that of the Enlightenment with a different approach to the study of human societies, in which they are seen as systems only because social life must have a pattern of some kind, inasmuch as man, being a reasonable creature, has to live in a world in which his relations with those around him are ordered and intelligible. Naturally I think that those who see things in this way have a clearer understanding of social reality than the others, but whether this is so or not they are increasing in number, and this is likely to continue because the vast majority of students of anthropology today have been trained in one or other of the humanities and not, as was the case thirty years ago, in one or other of the natural sciences. This being so, I expect that in the future there will be a turning towards humanistic disciplines, especially towards history, and particularly towards social history or the history of institutions, of cultures and of ideas. In this change of orientation social anthropology will retain its individuality because it has its own special problems, techniques and traditions. Though it is likely to continue for some time to devote its attention chiefly to primitive societies, I believe that during this second half of the century it will give far more attention than in the past to more complex cultures and especially to the civilizations of the Far and Near East and become, in a very general sense, the counterpart to Oriental Studies, in so far as these are conceived of as primarily linguistic and literary—that is to say, it will take as its province the cultures and societies, past as well as present, of the non-European peoples of the world.

Claude Lévi-Strauss 1908–

BACKGROUND

There was a story current some years ago that Claude Lévi-
Strauss' sister's son and therefore the direct heir of Émile
[...]neal mode of inheritance. It is a pity that the story isn't
[...]orn in Brussels. His father was a middle-class Jewish-
[...]o brought up his son in an atmosphere that combined
[...]m.

[...]as intensely interested in geology. In late adolescence
[...]or interests: psychoanalysis and Marxism, each as a
[...]an as a dogma. He attended the University of Paris
[...]a degree in law, "not because I had any true vocation
[...]mpled other branches of learning and detested them,
[...]n he worked for two years as a student teacher in a
[...]leau-Ponty and Simone de Beauvoir, both of whom
[...]university.

[...]fessor of sociology at the University of São Paulo,
[...]founded by the French (propagating French cul-
[...]c function of the French missions). In Brazil he
[...]By 1937 he had five months' actual field experi-
[...]s view of primitive people. He had expected
[...]culture patterns. Instead he found real people
[...]whom [...] whose ideas of death and society he found
sophisticated.

Lévi-Strauss' first anthropo[...] publication was a forty-five page article on
the social organization of the Bororo, which appeared in 1936. In 1938 he left the
university to spend a year on a more extensive expedition into central Brazil. The
material for his articles on the Nambikwara and Tupi was collected at this time; it
also provided the basis for his travel book, *Tristes tropiques*.

At the outbreak of World War II he returned to France and spent a year in the
military service. After the occupation he made his way to Martinique, then Puerto
Rico, and finally to New York, where a job at the New School had been arranged
for him by Robert Lowie and Alfred Metraux.

Lévi-Strauss made several important acquaintances in New York. Although they
had been students at the same time in Paris, it was in New York that he first met

371

Jean-Paul Sartre, with whom he was to squabble endlessly in the years to come. More important was Roman Jakobson, a member of the Prague school of structural linguistics. The influence of Jakobson's phonemic analysis on the work of Lévi-Strauss is marked. From the structural linguists, Lévi-Strauss developed the idea that universals of culture exist on the level of what he calls "structure," not at the level of manifest fact. In comparative social anthropology, as in comparative linguistics, it is useful to compare patterning of relations that link sets of human behavior, but it is not useful to compare single cultural items as isolates. Much of this thinking appeared in an article, "L'analyse structurale en linguistique et en anthropologie," contributed to Jakobson's journal *Word.* This article is the foundation for much of his subsequent structural anthropology.

After the war Lévi-Strauss remained in the United States for a year as French cultural attaché. When he returned to France he published his major work on kinship, *Les structures élémentaire de la parenté,* in 1949. The *Elementary Structures,* finally translated into English in 1969, touched off an extensive controversy both in the United States and Europe that is still going on.

In 1950 Lévi-Strauss was appointed director of studies at the École Pratiques des Hautes Études at the University of Paris, and in 1953 he was made secretary general of the International Council of Social Sciences, a post he held until 1960.

By that time Lévi-Strauss was the most influential anthropological theorist in France and had attracted a large following. *Structural Anthropology,* which appeared in 1958, was a collection of essays concerned with what he considers to be general principles of thought formation that are valid for all human minds.

Since 1959 his production of books and articles has been impressive. "La geste d'Asdiwal" (1960) is an essay on the analysis of myth; a book on totemism and *La pensée sauvage* appeared in 1962. In the 1960s he began an immense work called *Mythologiques* (all of Lévi-Strauss' work is filled with oblique references, puns, and nuances—to understand the method, you can begin with that title). So far three volumes have appeared: *Le cru et le cuit* (1964), *Du miel aux cendres* (1967), and *L'origine des manières de table* (1969).

INTRODUCTION

The work of Lévi-Strauss is voluminous, multifaceted, and difficult. He calls what he does "structuralism." Structuralism, however, is not a unified school or methodology; Lévi-Strauss does not have a monopoly on structural studies in anthropology, and the basic ideas of structure are far older. A. R. Radcliffe-Brown, George Peter Murdock, and many others have used the word in a different way than he has.

The main aspects of Lévi-Strauss' work can be summarized under three headings: (1) social anthropology and alliance theory, (2) human cognition and mental processes, and (3) structural aspects of mythology.

His theoretical contributions to social anthropology are numerous and important. The best known of these is referred to as "alliance theory." Alliance theory stresses the importance of marriage in society as opposed to the importance of descent. Its basic premise is that the exchange of women between groups of men in a society results in greater social solidarity and a better chance of survival for all members of this society. Lévi-Strauss claims that the regulating of marriages through cultural proscription or preference and the proscription of other types of marriage creates a "flow" of women in simple societies. This flow, accompanied by exchanges of gifts, ensures the cooperation of the members of such societies.

His analysis of the incest taboo is also interesting. He regards this taboo as the link between nature and culture in man. Through it, he says, nature surpasses itself and creates culture, for in this way a human drive—sex—can be regulated by culture, a variation on a point made earlier by Freud. As a result, man has lost his animal nature and become a cultural entity.

The second aspect of Lévi-Strauss' work deals with human mental processes, which are, he says, the same in all cultures, although the manifestations may be very different. Such unity of the mental processes arises from the human brain and the way it functions. As a result of this unity the classification of the universe by "primitive man" has the same basis as when it is done by any other man—interpreting the eternal reality through models. The fact that manifestations of this classification may be different is irrelevant for him.

Lévi-Strauss' work on myth parallels his preoccupation with mental processes —the discovery of unconscious but structured regularities of human thought. Certain structural characteristics, he says, make the comparative study of myth possible. Use of the structuralist analysis of myth allows for the reduction of material to manageable proportions as a result of the insight gained through this use from the stories one is studying. Without a reduction in the bulk of myth material, the proper analysis of myth becomes very difficult. With such reduction, however, cross-cultural studies of myth become possible.

But what are structures? Lévi-Strauss does at least provide us with a definition. First of all, structures are *not* concrete manifestations of reality; they are cognitive models of reality. As such, structures are to be found as mentalistic models in both primitive man and the scientist. The scientist's models are useful in understanding his particular field of study; the mental structures of primitive (or modern) man, which can be conscious or unconscious, help him live out his daily life. According to Lévi-Strauss, man comprehends his universe and orients his behavior on the basis of these mental structures.

25 SOCIAL STRUCTURE

The term "social structure" refers to a group of problems the scope of which appears so wide and the definition so imprecise that it is hardly possible for a paper strictly limited in size to meet them fully. This is reflected in the program of this symposium, in which problems closely related to social structure have been allotted to several papers, such as those on

Reprinted from A. L. Kroeber, ed., *Anthropology Today, An Encyclopaedic Inventory* (Chicago: University of Chicago Press, 1953), **pp. 524–553**, by permission of the publisher.

"Style," "Universal Categories of Culture," "Structural Linguistics." These should be read in connection with the present paper.

On the other hand, studies in social structure have to do with the formal aspects of social phenomena; therefore, they are difficult to define, and still more to discuss, without overlapping other fields pertaining to the exact and natural sciences, where problems are similarly set in formal terms or, rather, where the formal expression of different problems admits of the same kind of treatment. As a matter of fact, the main interest of social-structure studies seems to be that they give the anthropologist hope that, thanks to the formalization of his problems, he may borrow methods and types of solutions from disciplines which have gone far ahead of his own in that direction.

Such being the case, it is obvious that the term "social structure" needs first to be defined and that some explanation should be given of the difference which helps to distinguish studies in social structure from the unlimited field of descriptions, analyses, and theories dealing with social relations at large, confounding themselves with the whole scope of social anthropology. This is all the more necessary, since some of those who have contributed toward setting apart social structure as a special field of anthropological studies conceived the former in many different manners and even sometimes, so it seems, came to nurture grave doubts as to the validity of their enterprise. For instance, Kroeber writes in the second edition of his *Anthropology:*

"Structure" appears to be just a yielding to a word that has a perfectly good meaning but suddenly becomes fashionably attractive for a decade or so—like "streamlining"—and during its vogue tends to be applied indiscriminately because of the pleasurable connotations of its sound. Of course a typical personality can be viewed as having a structure. But so can a physiology, any organism, all societies and all cultures, crystals, machines—in fact everything which is not wholly amorphous has a structure. So what "structure" adds to the meaning of our phrase seems to be nothing, except to provoke a degree of pleasant puzzlement" (Kroeber 1948: 325).[1]

Although this passage concerns more particularly the notion of "basic personality structure," it has devastating implications as regards the generalized use of the notion of structure in anthropology.

Another reason makes a definition of social structure compulsory: from the structuralist point of view which one has to adopt if only to give the problem its meaning, it would be hopeless to try to reach a valid definition of social structure on an inductive basis, by abstracting common elements from the uses and definitions current among all the scholars who claim to have made "social structure" the object of their studies. If these concepts have a meaning at all, they mean, first, that the notion of structure has a structure. This we shall try to outline from the beginning as a precaution against letting ourselves be submerged by a tedious inventory of books and papers dealing with social relations, the mere listing of which would more than exhaust the limited space at our disposal. In a further stage we will have to see how far and in what directions the term "social structure," as used by the different authors, departs from our definition. This will be done in the section devoted to kinship, since the notion of structure has found in that field its main applications and since anthropologists have generally chosen to express their theoretical views also in that connection.

I. DEFINITION AND PROBLEMS OF METHOD

Passing now to the task of defining "social structure," there is a point which should be cleared up immediately. The term "social structure" has nothing to do with empirical reality but with models which are built up after it. This should help one to clarify the difference between two concepts which are so close to each other that they have often been confused, namely, those of *social structure* and of *social relations.* It will be enough to state at this time that social relations consist of the raw materials out of which the models making up the social structure are built, while social structure can, by no means, be reduced to the ensemble of the social relations to be described in a given society.[2] Therefore, social structure cannot claim a field of its own among others in the social studies. It is rather a method to be applied to any kind of social studies, similar to the structural analysis current in other disciplines.

Then the question becomes that of ascertaining what kind of model deserves the name "structure." This is not an anthropological question, but one which belongs to the methodology of science in general. Keeping this in mind, we can say that a structure consists of a model meeting with several requirements.

First, the structure exhibits the characteristics of a system. It is made up of several elements none of which can undergo a change without effecting changes in all the other elements.

In the second place, for any given model there should be a possibility of ordering a series of transformations resulting in a group of models of the same type.

In the third place, the above properties make it possible to predict how the model will react if one or more of its elements are submitted to certain modifications.

And, last, the model should be constituted so as to make immediately intelligible all the observed facts.[3]

These being the requirements for any model with structural value, several consequences follow. These, however, do not pertain to the definition of structure but have to do with the main properties exhibited by, and problems raised by, structural analysis when contemplated in the social and other fields.

A. OBSERVATION AND EXPERIMENTATION

Great care should be taken to distinguish between the observation and the experiment levels. To observe facts and elaborate methodological devices permitting of constructing models out of these facts is not at all the same thing as to experiment on the models. By "experimenting on models," we mean the set of procedures aiming at ascertaining how a given model will react when submitted to change and at comparing models of the same or different types. This distinction is all the more necessary, since many discussions on social structure revolve around the apparent contradiction between the concreteness and individuality of ethnological data and the abstract and formal character generally exhibited by structural studies. This contradiction disappears as one comes to realize that these features belong to two entirely different planes, or rather two stages of the same process. On the observational level, the main—one could almost say the only—rule is that all the facts should be carefully observed and described, without allowing any theoretical preconception to decide whether some are more important and others less. This rule implies, in turn, that facts should be studied in relation to themselves (by what kind of concrete process did they come into being?) and in relation to the whole (always aiming to relate each modification which can be observed in a sector to the global situation in which it first appeared).

This rule together with its corollaries has been explicitly formulated by K. Goldstein (1951:18–25) in relation to psychophysiological studies, and it may be considered valid for any kind of structural analysis. Its immediate consequence is that, far from being contradictory, there is a direct relationship between the detail and concreteness of ethnographical description and the validity and generality of the model which is constructed after it. For, though many models may be used as convenient devices to describe and explain the phenomena, it is obvious that the best model will always be that which is *true*, that is, the simplest possible model which, while being extracted exclusively from the facts under consideration, also makes it possible to account for all of them. Therefore, the first task is to ascertain what those facts are.

B. CONSCIOUSNESS AND UNCONSCIOUSNESS

A second distinction has to do with the conscious or unconscious character of the models. In the history of structural thought, Boas may be credited with having introduced this distinction. He made clear that a category of facts can more easily yield to structural analysis when the social group in which they are manifested has not elaborated a conscious model to interpret or justify them (*e.g.*, 1911:67). Some readers may be surprised to find Boas' name quoted in connection with structural theory, since he was often described as one of the main obstacles in its path. But this writer has tried to demonstrate that Boas' shortcomings in matters of structural studies were not in his failure to understand their importance and significance, which he did, as a matter of fact, in the most prophetic way. They rather resulted from the fact that he imposed on structural studies conditions of validity, some of which will remain forever part of their methodology, while some others are so exacting and impossible to meet that they would have withered scientific development in any field (Lévi-Strauss 1949a).

A structural model may be conscious or unconscious without this difference affecting its nature. It can only be said that when the structure of a certain type of phenomena does not lie at a great depth, it is more likely that some kind of model, standing as a screen to hide it, will exist in the collective consciousness. For conscious models, which are usually known as "norms," are by definition very poor ones, since they are not intended to explain the phenomena but to perpetuate them. Therefore, structural analysis is confronted with a strange paradox well known to the linguist, that is: the more obvious structural organization is, the more difficult it becomes to reach it because of the inaccurate conscious models lying across the path which leads to it.

From the point of view of the degree of consciousness, the anthropologist is confronted with two kinds of situations. He may have to construct a model from phenomena the systematic character of which has evoked no awareness on the part of the culture; this is the kind of simpler situation referred to by Boas as providing the easiest ground for anthropological research. Or else the anthropologist will be dealing, on the one hand, with raw phenomena and, on the other, with the models already constructed by the culture to interpret the former. Though it is likely that, for the reason stated above, these models will prove unsatisfactory, it is by no means necessary that this should always be the case. As a matter of fact, many "primitive" cultures have built models of their marriage regulations which are much more to the point than models built by professional anthropologists.[4] Thus one cannot dispense with studying a culture's "home-made" models for two reasons. First, these models might prove to be accurate or, at least, to provide some insight into the structure of the phenomena; after all, each culture has its own theoreticians whose contributions deserve the same attention as that which the anthropologist gives to colleagues. And, second, even if the models are biased or erroneous, the very bias and types of errors are a part of the facts under study and probably rank among the most significant ones. But even when taking into consideration these culturally produced models, the anthropologist does not forget—as he has sometimes been accused of doing (Firth 1951:28–31)—that the cultural norms are not of themselves structures. Rather, they furnish an important contribution to an understanding of the structures, either as factual documents or as theoretical contributions similar to those of the anthropologist himself.

This point has been given great attention by the French sociological school. Durkheim and Mauss, for instance, have always taken care to substitute, as a starting point for the survey of native categories of thought, the conscious representations prevailing among the natives themselves for those grown out of the anthropologist's own culture. This was undoubtedly an important step, which, nevertheless, fell short of its goal because these authors were not sufficiently aware that native conscious representations, important as they are, may be just as remote from the unconscious reality as any other (Lévi-Strauss 1951).

C. STRUCTURE AND MEASURE

It is often believed that one of the main interests of the notion of structure is to permit the introduction of measurement in social anthropology. This view was favored by the frequent appearance of mathematical or semimathematical aids in books or articles dealing with social structure. It is true that in some cases structural analysis has made it possible to attach numerical values to invariants. This was, for instance, the result of Kroeber's studies of women's dress fashions, a landmark in structural research (Richardson and Kroeber 1940), as well as of a few other studies which will be discussed below.

However, one should keep in mind that there is no necessary connection between *measure* and *structure*. Structural studies are, in the social sciences, the indirect outcome of modern developments in mathematics which have given increasing importance to the qualitative point of view in contradistinction to the quantitative point of view of traditional mathematics. Therefore, it has become possible, in fields such as mathematical logic, set-theory, group-theory, and topology, to develop a rigorous approach to problems which do not admit of a metrical solution. The outstanding achievements in this connection—which offer themselves as springboards not yet utilized by social scientists—are to be found in J. von Neumann and O. Morgenstern, *Theory of Games and Economic Behavior* (1944); N. Wiener, *Cybernetics* (1948); and C. Shannon and W. Weaver, *The Mathematical Theory of Communication* (1950).

D. MECHANICAL MODELS AND STATISTICAL MODELS

A last distinction refers to the relation between the scale of the model and that of the phenomena. According to the nature of these phenomena, it becomes possible or impossible to build a model, the elements of which are on the same scale as the phenomena themselves. A model the elements of which are on the same scale as the phenomena will be called a "mechanical model"; when the elements of the model are on a different scale, we will be dealing with a "statistical model." The laws of marriage provide the best illustration of this difference. In primitive societies these laws can be expressed in models calling for actual grouping of the individuals according to kin or clan; these are mechanical models. No such distribution exists in our own society, where types of marriage are determined by the size of the primary and secondary groups to which prospective mates belong, social fluidity, amount of information, and the like. A satisfactory (though yet untried) attempt to formulate the invariants of our marriage system would therefore have to determine average values—thresholds; it would be a statistical model. There may be intermediate forms between these two. Such is the case in societies which (as even our own) have a mechanical model to determine prohibited marriages and rely on a statistical model for those which are permissible. It should also be kept in mind that the same phenomena may admit of different models, some mechanical and some statistical, according to the way in which they are grouped together and with other phenomena. A society which recommends cross-cousin marriage but where this ideal marriage type occurs only with limited frequency needs, in order that the system may be properly explained, both a mechanical and a statistical model, as was well understood by Forde (1941) and Elwin (1947).

It should also be kept in mind that what makes social-structure studies valuable is that structures are models, the formal properties of which can be compared independently of their elements. The structuralist's task is thus to recognize and isolate levels of reality which have strategic value from his point of view, namely, which admit of representation as models, whatever their kind. It often happens that the same data may be considered from different perspectives embodying equal strategic values, though the resulting models will be in some cases mechanical and in others statistical. This situation is well known in the exact and natural sciences, for instance, the theory of a small number of physical bodies belongs to classical mechanics, but if the number of bodies becomes greater, then one should rely on the laws of thermodynamics, that is, use a statistical model instead of a mechanical one, though the nature of the data remains the same in both cases.

The same situation prevails in the human and the social sciences. If one takes a phenomenon like, for instance, suicide, it can be studied on two different levels. First, it is possible by studying individual situations to establish what may be called mechanical models of suicide, taking into account in each case the personality of the victim, his or her life-history, the characteristics of the primary and secondary groups in which he or she developed, and the like; or else one can build models of a statistical nature, by recording suicide frequency over a certain period of time in one or more societies and in different types of primary and secondary groups, etc. These would be levels at which the structural study of suicide carries a strategic value, that is, where is becomes possible to build models which may be compared (1) for different types of suicides, (2) for different societies, and (3) for different types of social phenomena. Scientific progress consists not only in discovering new invariants belonging to those levels but also in discovering new levels where the study of the same phenomena offers the same strategical value. Such a result was achieved, for instance, by psychoanalysis, which discovered the means to lay out models in a new field, that of the psychological life of the patient considered as a whole.

The foregoing should help to make clear the dual (and at first sight almost contradictory) nature of structural studies. On the one hand, they aim at isolating strategic levels, and this can be achieved only by "carving out" a certain family of phenomena. From that point of view, each type of structural study appears autonomous, entirely independent of all the others and even of different methodological approaches to the same field. On the other hand, the essential value of these studies is to construct models the formal properties of which can be compared with, and explained by, the same properties as in models corresponding to other strategic levels. Thus it may be said that their ultimate end is to override traditional boundaries between different disciplines and to promote a true interdisciplinary approach.

An example may be given. A great deal of discussion has taken place lately about the difference between history and anthropology, and Kroeber and others have made clear that the time-dimension has very little importance in this connection. From what has been stated above, one can see exactly where the difference lies, not only between these two disciplines but also between them and others. Ethnography and history differ from social anthropology and sociology, inasmuch as the former two aim at gathering data, while the latter two deal with models constructed from these data. Similarly, ethnography and social anthropology correspond to two different stages in the same research, the ultimate result of which is to construct mechanical models, while history (together with its so-called "auxiliary" disciplines) and sociology end ultimately in statistical models. This is the reason why the social sciences, though having to do—all of them—with the time-dimension, nevertheless deal with two different categories of time. Anthropology uses a "mechanical" time, reversible and noncumulative. For instance, the model of, let us say, a patrilineal kinship system does not in itself show whether or not the system has always remained patrilineal, or has been preceded by a matrilineal form, or by any number of shifts from patrilineal to matrilineal and vice versa. On the contrary, historical time is "statistical"; it always appears as an oriented and nonreversible process. An evolution which would take back contemporary Italian society to that of the Roman Republic is as impossible to conceive of as is the reversibility of the process belonging to the second law of thermodynamics.

This discussion helps to clarify Firth's distinction between social structure, which he conceives as outside the time-dimension, and social organization, where time re-enters (1951:40). Also in this connection, the debate which has been going on for the past few years between followers of the Boasian anti-evolutionist tradition and of Professor Leslie White (1949) may become better understood. The Boasian school has been mainly concerned with models of a mechanical type, and from this point of view the concept of evolution has no operational value. On the other hand, it is certainly legitimate to speak of evolution in a historical and sociological sense, but the elements to be organized into an evolutionary process cannot be borrowed from the level of a cultural typology which consists of mechanical models. They should be sought at a sufficiently deep level to insure that these elements will remain unaffected by different cultural contexts (as, let us say, genes are identical elements combined into different patterns corresponding to the different racial [statistical] models) and can accordingly permit of drawing long statistical runs.

A great deal of inconvenience springs from a situation which obliges the social scientist to "shift" time, according to the kind of study he is contemplating. Natural scientists, who have got used to this difficulty, are making efforts to overcome it. Very important in this connection is Murdock's contention that while a patrilineal system may replace, or grow out of, a matrilineal system, the opposite process cannot take place (1949:210–220). If this were true, a vectorial factor would for the first time be introduced on an objective basis into social structure. Murdock's demonstration was, however, challenged by Lowie (1948a:44 ff.) on methodological grounds, and for the time being it is impossible to do more than to call attention to a moot problem, the solution of which, when generally accepted, will have a tremendous bearing upon structural studies, not only in the field of anthropology but in other fields as well.

The distinction between mechanical and statistical models has also become fundamental in another respect: it makes it possible to clarify the role of the comparative method in structural studies. This method was greatly emphasized by both Radcliffe-Brown and Lowie. The former writes (1952:14):

Theoretical sociology is commonly regarded as an inductive science, induction being the logical method of inference by which we arrive at general propositions from the consideration of particular instances. Although Professor Evans-Pritchard . . . seems to imply in some of his statements that the logical method of induction, using comparison, classification and generalization, is not applicable to the phenomena of human social life . . . I hold that social anthropology must depend on systematic comparative studies of many societies.

Writing about religion, he states (1945:1):

The experimental method of social religion . . . means that we must study in the light of our hypothesis a sufficient number of diverse particular religions or religious cults in relation to the particular societies in which they are found. This is a task not for one person but for a number.

Similarly, Lowie, after pointing out (1948a:38) that "the literature of anthropology is full of alleged correlations which lack empirical support," insists on the need of a "broad inductive basis" for generalization (1948a:68). It is interesting to note that by this claim for inductive support these authors dissent not only from Durkheim (1912:593): "when a law has been proved by a well performed experiment, this law is valid universally," but also from Goldstein, who, as already mentioned, has lucidly expressed what may be called "the rules of structuralist method" in a way general enough to make them valid outside the more limited field in which they were first applied by their author. Goldstein remarks that the need to make a thorough study of each case implies that the amount of cases to be studied should be small; and he proceeds by raising the question whether or not the risk exists that the cases under consideration may be special ones, allowing no general conclusions about the others. He answers (1951:25): "This objection completely misunderstands the real situation . . . an accumulation of facts even numerous is of no help if these facts were imperfectly established; it does not lead to the knowledge of things as they really happen. . . . We must choose only these cases which permit of formulating final judgments. And then, what is true for one case will also be true for any other."

Probably very few anthropologists would be ready to support these bold statements. However, no structuralist study may be undertaken without a clear awareness of Goldstein's dilemma: either to study many cases in a superficial and in the end ineffective way; or to limit one's self to a thorough study of a small number of cases, thus proving that, in the end, one well-done experiment is sufficient to make a demonstration.

Now the reason for so many anthropologists' faithfulness to the comparative method may be sought in some sort of confusion between the procedures used to establish mechanical and statistical models. While Durkheim's and Goldstein's position undoubtedly holds true for the former, it is obvious that no statistical model can be achieved without statistics, i.e., by gathering a large amount of data. But in this case the method is no more comparative than in the other, since the data to be collected will be acceptable only in so far as they are all of the same kind. Therefore, we remain confronted with only one alternative, namely, to make a thorough study of one case. The real difference lies in the selection of the "case," which will be patterned so as to include elements which are either on the same scale as the model to be constructed or on a different scale.

After having thus clarified these basic questions revolving around the nature of studies in social structure, it becomes possible to make an inventory of the main fields of inquiry and to discuss some of the results achieved so far.

II. SOCIAL MORPHOLOGY OR GROUP STRUCTURE

In this section, "group" is not intended to mean the social group but, in a more general sense, the way according to which the phenomena under study are grouped together.

The object of social-structure studies is to understand social relations with the aid of models. Now it is impossible to conceive of social relations outside a common frame. Space and time are the two frames we use to situate social relations, either alone or together. These space- and time-dimensions are not the same as the analogous ones used by other disciplines but consist of a "social" space and of a "social" time, meaning that they have no properties outside those which derive from the properties of the social phenomena which "furnish" them. According to their social structure, human societies have elaborated many types of such "continuums," and there should be no undue concern on the part of the anthropologist that, in the course of his studies, he may temporarily have to borrow types widely different from the existing patterns and eventually to evolve new ones.

We have already noticed that the time-continuum may be reversible or oriented in accordance with the level of reality embodying strategical value from the point of view of the research at hand. Many other possibilities may arise: the time-dimension can be conceived of as independent from the observer and unlimited or as a function of the observer's own (biological) time and limited; it may be considered as consisting of parts which are, or are not, homologous with one another, etc. Evans-Pritchard has shown how such formal properties underlie the qualitative distinctions between the observer's life-span, history, legend, and myth (1939, 1940). And his basic distinctions have been found to be valid for contemporary societies (Bernot and Blancard, MS.)

What is true of the time-dimension applies equally well to space. It has been Durkheim's and Mauss's great merit to call attention for the first time to the variable properties of space which should be called upon in order to understand properly the structure of several primitive societies (1901–1902). In this undertaking they received their inspiration from the work of Cushing, which it has become fashionable in recent years to belittle. However, Cushing's insight and sociological imagination make him deserving of a seat on Morgan's right, as one of the great forerunners of social-structure studies. The gaps and inaccuracies in his descriptions, less serious than the indictment of having "over-interpreted" some of his material, will be viewed in their true proportions when it is realized that, albeit in an unconscious fashion, Cushing was aiming less at giving an actual description of Zuñi society than at elaborating a model (his famous seven fold division) which could explain most of its processes and structure.

Social time and space should also be characterized according to scale. There is in social studies a "macro-time" and a "micro-time"; the same distinction applies also to space. This explains how social structure may have to do with prehistory, archeology, and diffusion processes as well as with psychological topology, such as that initiated by Lewin or by Moreno's sociometry. As a matter of fact, structures of the same type may exist on quite different time and space levels, and it is far from inconceivable that, for instance, a statistical model resulting from sociometrical studies might be of greater help in building a similar model in the field of the history of cultures than an apparently more direct approach would have permitted.

Therefore, historicogeographical concerns should not be excluded from the field of structural studies, as was generally implied by the widely accepted opposition between "diffusionism" and "functionalism."[5] A functionalist may be far from a structuralist, as is clearly shown by the example of Malinowski. On the other hand, undertakings such as those of G. Dumézil,[6] as well as A. L. Kroeber's personal case of a highly structure-minded scholar devoting most of his time to distribution studies, are proofs that even history can be approached in a structural way.

Since synchronic studies raise fewer problems than diachronic ones (the data being more homogeneous in the first case), the simplest morphological studies are those having to do with the qualitative, nonmeasurable properties of social space, that is, the way according to which social phenomena can be situated on a map and the regularities exhibited in their configurations. Much might have been expected from the researches of the so-called "Chicago school" dealing with urban ecology, and the reasons for the gradual loss of interest along this line of research are not altogether clear. It has to do mostly with ecology, which was made the subject of another paper in this symposium. However, it is not inappropriate to state at this point what kind of relationship prevails between ecology, on the one hand, and social structure, on the other. Both have to do with the spatial distribution of phenomena. But social structure deals exclusively with those "spaces" the determinations of which are of a purely sociological nature, that is, not affected by natural determinants, such as geology, climatology, physiography, and the like. This is the reason why so-called "urban ecology" should have held great interest for the social anthropologist; the urban space is small enough and homogeneous enough (from every point of view except the social one) for all its differential qualitative aspects to be assigned mostly to the action of internal forces accessible to structural sociology.

It would perhaps have been wiser, instead of starting with complex communities hard to isolate from external influences, to approach first—as suggested by Marcel Mauss (1924-1925)—those small and relatively isolated communities with which the anthropologist usually deals. A few such studies may be found (e.g., Firth 1936; Steward 1938; Nadel 1947; Forde 1950), but they rarely and then reluctantly go beyond the descriptive stage. There have been practically no attempts to correlate the spatial configurations with the formal properties of the other aspects of social life.

This is much to be regretted, since in many parts of the world there is an obvious relationship between the social structure and the spatial structure of settlements, villages, or camps. To limit ourselves to America, the camp shapes of Plains Indians have for long demanded attention by virtue of regular variations connected with the social organization of each tribe; and the same holds true for the circular disposition of huts in Gé villages of eastern and central Brazil. In both cases we are dealing with relatively homogeneous cultural areas where important series of concomitant variations may be observed. Another kind of problem results from the comparison of areas where different types of village structures may be compared to different types of social relations, e.g., the circular village structure of the Gé and the parallel-layers structure of the Pueblo. The latter could even be studied diachronically with the archeologist's help, which would raise questions such as the eventual linkage of the transition from semicircular structures to parallel ones, with the shift of village sites from valley to mesa top, of structural distribution of clan houses suggested by many myths to the present-day statistical one, etc.

These few examples are not intended to prove that spatial configuration is the mirror-image of social organization but to call attention to the fact that, while among numerous peoples it would be extremely difficult to discover any such relation, among others (who must accordingly have something in common) the existence of a relation is evident, though unclear, and in a third group spatial configuration seems to be almost a projective representation of the social structure. But even the most striking cases call for a critical study; for example, this writer has attempted to demonstrate that, among the Bororo, spatial configuration reflects not the true, unconscious social organization but a model existing consciously in the native mind, though its nature is entirely illusory and even contradictory to reality.[7] Problems of this kind (which are raised not only by the consideration of relatively durable spatial configurations but also in regard to recurrent temporary ones, such as those shown in dance, ritual, etc.) offer an opportunity to study social and mental processes through objective and crystallized external projections of them.

Another approach which may lead more directly to a mathematical expression of social phenomena starts with the numerical properties of human groups. This has traditionally been the field of demography, but it is only recently that a few scholars coming from different horizons—demography, sociology, anthropology—have begun to elaborate a kind of qualitative demography, that is, dealing no longer with continuous variations within human groups selected for empirical reasons but with significant discontinuities evidenced in the behavior of groups considered as wholes and chosen on the basis of these discontinuities. This "socio-demography," as it was called by one of its proponents (De Lestrange 1951), is "on a level" with social anthropology, and it is not difficult to foresee that in the very near future it will be called upon to provide firm grounds for any kind of anthropological research. Therefore, it is surprising that so little attention was paid in anthropological circles to the study by a demographer, L. Livi, of the formal properties characteristic of the smallest possible size of a group compatible with its existence as a group (1940–1941, 1949). His researches, closely connected with G. Dahlberg's, are all the more important for anthropologists, in that the latter usually deal with populations very near Livi's minimum. There is an obvious relation between the functioning and even the durability of the social structure and the actual size of the population (Wagley 1940). It is thus becoming increasingly evident that formal properties exist which are immediately and directly attached to the absolute size of the population, whatever the group under consideration. These should be the first to be assessed and taken into account in an interpretation of other properties.

Next come numerical properties expressing not the group size taken globally but the size and interaction of subsets of the group which can be defined by significant discontinuities. Two lines of inquiry should be mentioned in this connection.

There is, first, the vast body of researches deriving from the famous "rank-size rule" for cities, which has proved to be applicable in many other social fields, though the original rule remains somewhat controversial (see Davis 1947; Stewart 1947; Zipf 1949).

Of a much more direct bearing on current anthropological research is the recent work of two French demographers, who, by using Dahlberg's demonstration that the size of an isolate (i.e., a group of intermarrying people) can be computed from the frequency of marriages between cross-cousins (Dahlberg 1948), have succeeded in computing the average size of isolates in all French *départements*, thus throwing open to anthropological investigation the marriage system of a complex modern society (Sutter and Tabah 1951). The average size of the French isolate varies from less than 1,000 to over 2,800 individuals. This numerical evaluation shows that, even in a modern society, the network of people united by kinship ties is much smaller than might be expected, of about the same size as in primitive groups. The inference is that, while the absolute size of the intermarrying group remains approximately on the same scale in all human societies (the proportion of the French types in relation to the average primitive types being about 10 to 1), a complex society becomes such not so much because of an expansion of the isolate itself as on account of an expansion of other types of social links (economic, political, intellectual); and these are used to connect a great number of isolates which, by themselves, remain relatively static.

But the most striking result of this research is the discovery that the smallest isolates are found not only in mountain areas, as was expected, but also (and even more) in areas including a large urban center; the following *départements:* Rhone (Lyon), Gironde (Bordeaux), and Seine (Paris) are at the bottom of the list, with the size of their isolates respectively 740, 910, and 980. In the Seine *département,* which is practically reduced to Paris and suburbs, the frequency of consanguineous marriages is higher than in any of the fifteen rural *départements* which surround it (Sutter and Tabah 1951:489).

It is not necessary to emphasize the bearing of such studies on social structure; the main fact, from the point of view of this paper, is that they at the same time make possible the call for an immediate extension on the anthropological level. An approach has been found which enables one to break down a modern complex society into smaller units which are of the same nature as those commonly studied by anthropologists; on the other hand, this approach remains incomplete, since the absolute size of the isolate is only a part of the phenomenon, the other one, equally important, being the length of the marriage cycles. For a small isolate may admit of long marriage cycles (that is, tending to be of the same size as the isolate itself), while a relatively large isolate can be made up of shorter cycles. This problem, which could be solved only with the help of genealogies, points the way toward close co-operation between the structural demographer and the social anthropologist.

Another contribution, this time on a theoretical level, may be expected from this co-operation. The concept of isolate may help to solve a problem in social structure which has given rise to a controversy between Radcliffe-Brown and Lowie. The former has labeled as "a fantastic reification of abstraction" the suggestion made by some anthropologists, mostly in America, that anthropology should be defined as the study not of society but of culture. To him, "European culture is an abstraction and so is the culture of an African tribe." All that exists is human beings connected by an unlimited series of social relations (Radcliffe-Brown 1940b:10–11). This, Lowie says is "a factitious quarrel" (1942:520–521). However, the misunderstandings which lie at its root appear to be very real, since they were born all over again on the occasion of the publication of a book by White (1949) and its criticism by Bidney (1950:518–519; see also Radcliffe-Brown 1949b).

It seems that both the reality and the autonomy of the concept of culture could better be validated if culture were, from an operational point of view, treated in the same way as the geneticist and demographer do for the closely allied concept of "isolate." What is called a "culture" is a fragment of humanity which, from the point of view of the research at hand and of the scale on which it is being carried out, presents, in relation to the rest of humanity, significant discontinuities. If our aim is to ascertain significant discontinuities between, let us say, North America and Europe, then we are dealing with two different cultures; but should we become concerned with significant discontinuities between New York and Chicago, we would be allowed to speak of these two groups as different cultural "units." Since these discontinuities can be reduced to invariants, which is the goal of structural analysis, one sees that culture may, at the same time, correspond to an objective reality and be a function of the kind of research undertaken. Accordingly, the same set of individuals may be considered to be parts of many different cultural contexts: universal, continental, national, provincial, parochial, etc., as well as familial, professional, confessional, political, etc. This is true as a limit; however, anthropologists usually reserve the term "culture" to designate a group of discontinuities which has significance on several of these levels at the same time. That it can never be valid for all levels does not prevent the concept of "culture" from being as fundamental for the anthropologist as that of "isolate" for the demographer. Both belong to the same epistemological family. On a question such as that of the positive character of a concept, the anthropologist can rely on a physicist's judgment; it is Niels Bohr who states (1939:9) that "the traditional differences of [human cultures] in many ways resemble the different equivalent modes in which physical experience can be described."

III. SOCIAL STATICS OR COMMUNICATION STRUCTURES

A society consists of individuals and groups which communicate with one another. The existence of, or lack of, communication can never be defined in an absolute manner. Communication does not cease at society's borders. These borders, rather, constitute thresholds where the rate and forms of communication, without waning altogether, reach a much lower level. This condition is usually meaningful enough for the population, both inside and outside the borders, to become aware of it. This awareness is not, however, a prerequisite for the definition of a given society. It only accompanies the more precise and stable forms.

In any society, communication operates on three different levels: communication of women, communication of goods and services, communication of messages. Therefore, kinship studies, economics, and linguistics approach the same kinds of problems on different strategic levels and really pertain to the same field. Theoretically at least, it might be said that kinship and marriage rules regulate a fourth type of communication, that of genes between phenotypes. Therefore, it should be kept in mind that culture does not consist exclusively of forms of communication of its own, like language, but also (and perhaps mostly) of *rules* stating how the "games of communication" should be played both on the natural and on the cultural level.

The above comparison between the fields of kinship, economics, and linguistics cannot hide the fact that they refer to forms of communication which are on a different scale. Should one try to compute the communication rate involved, on the one hand, in the intermarriages and, on the other, in the exchange of messages going on in a given society, one would probably discover the difference to be of about the same magnitude as, let us say, that between the exchange of heavy molecules of two viscous liquids through a not too permeable film, and radio communication. Thus, from marriage to language one passes from low- to high-speed communication; this comes from the fact that what is communicated in marriage is almost of the same nature as those who communicate (women, on the one hand, men, on the other), while speakers of language are not of the same nature as their utterances. The opposition is thus one of *person* to *symbol*, or of *value* to *sign*. This helps to clarify economics' somewhat intermediate position between these two extremes—goods and services are not persons, but they still are values. And, though neither symbols nor signs, they require symbols or signs to succeed in being exchanged when the exchange system reaches a certain degree of complexity.

From this outline of the structure of social communication derive three important sets of considerations.

First, the position of economics in social structure may be precisely defined. Economics in the past has been suspect among anthropologists. Even in this symposium, no paper was explicitly assigned to economic problems. Yet, whenever this highly important topic has been broached, a close relationship has been shown to prevail between economic pattern and social structure. Since Mauss's pioneer papers (1904–1905, 1923–1924) and Malinowski's book on the *kula* (1922)—by far his masterpiece—every attempt in this direction has shown that the economic system provides sociological formulations with some of their more fundamental invariants (Speck 1915; Richards 1932, 1936, 1939; Steward 1938; Evans-Pritchard 1940; Herskovits 1940; Wittfogel and Goldfrank 1943).

The anthropologist's reluctance originated in the condition of economic studies themselves; these were ridden with conflicts between bitterly opposed schools and at the same time bathed in an aura of mystery and conceit. Thus the anthropologist labored under the impression that economics dealt mostly with abstractions and that there was little connection between the actual life of actual groups of people and such notions as value, utility, profit, and the like.

The complete upheaval of economic studies resulting from the publication of Von Neumann and Morgenstern's book (1944) ushers in an era of closer co-operation between the economist and the anthropologist, and for two reasons. First—though economics achieves here a rigorous approach—this book deals not with abstractions such as those just mentioned but with concrete individuals and groups which are represented in their actual and empirical relations of co-operation and competition. Next—and as a consequence —it introduces for the first time mechanical models which are of the same type as, and intermediate between, those used in mathematical physics and in social anthropology—especially in the field of kinship. In this connection it is striking that Von Neumann's models are borrowed from the theory of games, a line of thought which was initiated independently by Kroeber when he compared social institutions "to the play of earnest children" (1942:215). There is, true enough, an important difference between games of entertainment and marriage rules: the former are constructed in such a way as to permit each player to extract from statistical regularities maximal differential values, while marriage rules, acting in the opposite direction, aim at establishing statistical regularities in spite of the differential values existing between individuals and generations. In this sense they constitute a special kind of "upturned game." Nevertheless, they can be treated with the same methods. Besides, such being the rules, each individual and group tries to play it in the "normal" way, that is, by maximizing his own advantages at the expense of the others (i.e., to get more wives or better ones, whether from the aesthetic, erotic, or economic point of view). The theory of courtship is thus a part of formal sociology. To those who are afraid that sociology might in this way get hopelessly involved in individual psychology, it will be enough to recall that Von Neumann has succeeded in giving a mathematical demonstration of the nature and strategy of a psychological technique as sophisticated as bluffing at the game of poker (Von Neumann and Morgenstern 1944:186–219).

The next advantage of this increasing consolidation of social anthropology, economics, and linguistics into one great field, that of communications, is to make clear that they consist exclusively of the study of *rules* and have little concern with the nature of the partners (either individuals or groups) whose play is being patterned after these rules. As Von Neumann puts it (Von Neumann and Morgenstern 1944:49): "The game is simply the totality of the rules which describe it." Besides that of game, other operational notions are those of play, move, choice, and strategy. But the nature of the players need not be considered. What is important is to find out when a given player can make a choice and when he cannot.

This outlook should open the study of kinship and marriage to approaches directly derived from the theory of communication. In the terminology of this theory it is possible to speak of the information of a marriage system by the number of choices at the observer's disposal to define the marriage status of an individual. Thus the information is unity for a dual exogamous system, and, in an Australian kind of kinship typology, it would increase with the logarithm of the number of matrimonial classes. A theoretical system where everybody could marry everybody would be a system with no redundancy, since each marriage choice would not be determined by previous choices, while the positive content of marriage rules constitutes the redundancy of the system under consideration. By studying the percentage of "free" choices in a matrimonial population (not absolutely free, but in relation to certain postulated conditions), it would thus become possible to offer numerical estimates of its entropy, both absolute and relative.

As a consequence, it would become possible to translate statistical models into mechanical ones and vice versa, thus bridging the gap still existing between population studies, on the one hand, and anthropological ones, on the other, thereby laying a foundation for foresight and action. To give an example, in our own society the organization of marriage choices does not go beyond (1) the prohibition of near kin, (2) the size of the isolate, and (3) the accepted standard of behavior, which limits the frequency of certain choices inside the isolate. With these data at hand, one could compute the information of the system, that is, translate our loosely organized and highly statistical marriage system into a mechanical model, thus making possible its comparison with the large series of marriage systems of a "mechanical" type available from simpler societies. Similarly, a great deal of discussion has been carried on recently about the Murngin kinship system, which has been treated by different authors as a 7-class system, or less than 7, or 4, or 32 (Warner 1930–1931; Lévi-Strauss 1949b; Lawrence and Murdock 1949; Radcliffe-Brown 1951; Elkin, personal correspondence). By getting a good statistical run of actual marriage choices among other excluded possibilities, one could get at a "true" solution. This conception of a class system as a device to reduce the amount of information required to define several hundred kinship statuses was clearly outlined at first by Professor Lloyd Warner (1937b).

In the preceding pages an attempt has been made to assess the bearing of some recent lines of mathematical research upon anthropological studies. We have seen that their main contribution was to provide anthropology with a unifying concept—communication—enabling it to consolidate widely different types of inquiry into one and at the same time providing the theoretical and methodological tools to further knowledge in that direction. The question which should now be raised is: To what extent is social anthropology ready to make use of these tools?

The main feature of the development of social anthropology in the past years has been the increased attention to kinship. This is, indeed, not a new phenomenon, since it can be said that, with his *Systems of Consanguinity and Affinity of the Human Family*, Lewis Morgan's genius at one and the same time founded social anthropology and kinship studies and brought forward the basic reasons for attaching such importance to the latter: permanency, systematic character, continuity of changes (1871). The views outlined in the preceding pages may help to explain this fundamental interest in kinship, since we have considered it as the anthropologist's own and privileged share in the science of communication. But, even if this interpretation were not accepted by all, the fact of the enormous development of kinship studies cannot be denied. It has recently been assessed in various works (Lowie 1948a; Murdock 1949; Spoehr 1950). The latest to appear (Radcliffe-Brown and Forde 1950) has brought together a tremendous wealth of information. Chapters such as Forde's and Nadel's have added the final stroke to unilineal interpretations. However, one may be permitted to regret that the different outlooks of the contributors, their failure to get together and try to extract from their data a small set of significant variations, might become responsible for discouraging potential field workers instead of clearly showing them the purpose of such studies.

Unfortunately, the amount of usable material in relation to that actually collected remains small. This is clearly reflected in the fact that, in order to undertake his survey, Murdock found it possible to retain information concerning no more than about 250 societies (from our point of view, a still overindulgent estimate) out of the 3,000 to 4,000 distinct societies still in existence (Ford and Beach 1951:5); an attempt to add material valid on a diachronic level would considerably increase the last number. It is somewhat disheartening that the enormous work devoted in the last fifty years to the gathering of ethnographic material has yielded so little, while kinship has been one of the main concerns of those undertaking them.

However, it should be kept in mind that what has brought about this unhappy result is not a lack of coverage—on the contrary. If the workable material is small, it is rather on account of the inductive illusion: it was believed that as many cultures as possible should be covered, albeit lightly, rather than a few thoroughly enough to yield significant results. Accordingly, there is no lack of consistency in the fact that following their individual temperaments, anthropologists have preferred one or the other of the alternatives imposed by the situation. While Radcliffe-Brown, Eggan, Spoehr, Fortes, and this writer have tried to consider limited areas where dense information was available, Murdock has followed the complementary (but not contradictory) path of widening the field even at the expense of the reliability of the data, and Lowie (1948a) has tried to pursue a kind of middle road between the two approaches.

The case of the Pueblo area is especially striking, since for probably no other area in the world is there available such an amount of data and of such controversial quality. It is almost with despair that one comes to realize that the voluminous material accumulated by Voth, Fewkes, Dorsey, Parsons, and, to some extent, Stevenson is practically unworkable, since these authors have been feverishly piling up information without any clear idea of what it meant and, above all, of the hypotheses which it should have helped to check. The situation changed with Lowie's and Kroeber's entering the field, but the lack of statistical data on marriage choices and types of intermarriages, which could have been gathered for more than fifty years, will probably be impossible to overcome. This is much to be regretted, since Eggan's recent book (1950) represents an outstanding example of what can be expected from intensive and thorough study of a limited area. Here we find a new instance of the demonstration made under similar conditions by the same author (1937a, b) and elaborated upon by Spoehr, namely, as the latter puts it, "kinship system does preserve the characteristics of a 'system' despite radical changes in type" (1942, 1947:229). The more recent study of the Pueblo's kinship systems by Eggan confirms the results of these earlier, purely diachronic inquiries. Here we observe closely connected forms, each of which preserves a structural consistency, although they present, in relation to one another, discontinuities which become significant when compared to homologous discontinuities in other fields, such as clan organization, marriage rules, ritual, religious beliefs, etc.

It is by means of such studies, exhibiting a truly "Galilean" outlook,[8] that one may hope to reach a depth where social structure is put on a level with other types of mental structures, particularly the linguistic one, as suggested by this writer (1951). To give an example: it follows from Eggan's survey that the Hopi kinship system requires no less than three different models for the time-dimension: there is, first, an "empty" time, stable and reversible, illustrated by the father's mother's and mother's father's lineage, where the same terms are consistently applied throughout the generations; second, a progressive, nonreversible time, as shown in Ego's (female) lineage with the sequence: grandmother > mother > sister > child > grandchild; and, third, and undulating, cyclical, reversible time, as in Ego's (male) lineage with the indefinite alternation between sister and sister's child. On the other hand, these three "straight" frames are clearly distinct from the "curved" frame of Zuñi Ego's (female) lineage, where four terms: mother's mother (or daughter's daughter), mother, daughter, are disposed in a kind of ringlike arrangement, this conceptual grouping being accompanied, as regards the other lineages, by a greater poverty both of terms inside the acknowledged kin and of kin acknowledgment. Since time aspects belong also to linguistic analysis, the questions can be raised whether or not there is a correlation between these fields; if so, at what level; etc. More general problems, though of a similar kind, were raised by L. Thompson (1950) in reference to Whorf's linguistic treatment of Hopi.

Progress in this and other directions would undoubtedly have been more substantial if general agreement had existed among social anthropologists on the definition of social structure, the goals which may be achieved by its study, and the methodological principles to be applied at the different stages of research. Unfortunately, this is not the case, but it may be welcomed as a promising factor that some kind of understanding can be reached, at least on the nature and scope of these differences. This seems an appropriate place to offer a rapid sketch of the attitude of the main contributors to social-structure researches in relation to the working assumptions which were made at the beginning of this paper.

The words "social structure" are in many ways linked with the name of A. R. Radcliffe-Brown. Though his contribution does not limit itself to the study of kinship systems, he has stated the goal of these studies in terms which every scholar in the same field would probably be ready to underwrite: the aim of kinship studies, he says, is (1) to make a systematic classification; (2) to understand particular features of particular systems (a) by revealing the particular features as a part of an organized whole and (b) by showing that it is a special example of a recognizable class of phenomena; (3) to arrive at valid generalizations about the nature of human societies. And he concludes: "To reduce this diversity (of 200 or 300 kinship systems) to some sort of order is the task of analysis. . . . We can . . . find . . . beneath the diversities, a limited number of general principles applied and combined in various ways" (1941:17). There is nothing to add to this lucid program besides pointing out that this is precisely what Radcliffe-Brown has done in his study of Australian kinship systems. He brought forth a tremendous amount of material; he introduced some kind of order where there was only chaos; he defined the basic operational terms, such as "cycle," "pair" and "couple." Finally, his discovery of the Kariera system in the region and with the characteristics inferred from the study of the available data and before visiting Australia will forever remain one of the great results of sociostructural studies (1930–1931). His masterly Introduction to *African Systems of Kinship and Marriage* may be considered a true treatise on kinship; at the same time it takes a step toward integrating kinship systems of the Western world (which are approached in their early forms) into a world-wide theoretical interpretation. Another capital contribution by the same scholar, about the homologous structure of kinship terminology and behavior, will be dealt with later on.

However, it is obvious that, in many respects, Radcliffe-Brown's conception of social structure differs from the postulates which were set up at the outset of the present paper. In the first place, the notion of structure appears to him as a means to link social anthropology to the biological sciences: "There is a real and significant analogy between organic structure and social structure" (1940b:6). Then, instead of "lifting up" kinship studies to put them on the same level as communication theory, as has been suggested by this writer, he has lowered them to the same plane as the phenomena dealt with in descriptive morphology and physiology (1940b:10). In that respect, his approach is in line with the naturalistic trend of the British school. In contra-distinction to Kroeber (1938, 1942:205 ff.) and Lowie (1948a:chap. iv), who have emphasized the artificiality of kinship, he agrees with Malinowski that biological ties are, at one and the same time, the origin of and the model for every type of kinship tie (Radcliffe-Brown 1926).

These principles are responsible for two consequences. In the first place, Radcliffe-Brown's empirical approach makes him very reluctant to distinguish between *social structure* and *social relations*. As a matter of fact, social structure appears in his work to be nothing else than the whole network of social relations. It is true that he has sometimes outlined a distinction between *structure* and *structural form*. The latter concept, however, seems to be limited to the diachronic perspective, and its functional role in Radcliffe-Brown's theoretical thought appears quite reduced (1940b:4). This distinction was thoroughly discussed by Fortes, who has contributed a great deal to the distinction, quite foreign to Radcliffe-Brown's outlook, between "model" and "reality" (see above): "structure is not immediately visible in the 'concrete reality.' . . . When we describe structure . . . we are, as it were, in the realm of grammar and syntax, not of the spoken word" (Fortes 1949:56).

In the second place, this merging of social structure and social relations induces him to break down the former into the simplest forms of the latter, that is, relations between two persons: "The kinship structure of any society consists of a number of . . . dyadic relations. . . . In an Australian tribe, the whole social structure is based on a network of such relations of person to person . . ." (1940b:3). It may be questioned whether such dyadic relations are the materials out of which social structure is built, or whether they do not themselves result from a preexisting structure which should be defined in more complex terms. Structural linguistics has a lot to teach in this respect. Examples of the kind of analysis commended by Radcliffe-Brown may be found in the works of Bateson and Mead. However, in *Naven* (1936), Bateson has gone a step further than Radcliffe-Brown's classification (1941) of dyadic relations according to order: he has attempted to place them in specific categories, an undertaking which implies that there is something more in social structure than the dyadic relations, i.e., the structure itself. This was a significant step toward the communication level (Ruesch and Bateson 1951). Since it is possible to extend, almost indefinitely, the string of dyadic relations,

Radcliffe-Brown has shown some reluctance toward the isolating of social structures conceived as self-sufficient wholes (in this respect he disagrees with Malinowski). His is a philosophy of continuity, not of discontinuity; this accounts for his hostility toward the notion of culture, already alluded to, and his avoiding the teachings of structural linguistics and of modern mathematics.

All these considerations may explain why Radcliffe-Brown, though an incomparable observer, analyst, and classifier, has sometimes proved to be disappointing when he turned to interpretations. These, in his work, often appear vague or circulative. Have marriage prohibitions really no further function than to help perpetuate the kinship system (Radcliffe-Brown 1949b)? Are all the peculiar features of the Crow-Omaha systems satisfactorily accounted for when it has been said that they emphasize the lineage principle (Radcliffe-Brown 1941)? These doubts, as well as many others, some of which will find their place later on in this paper, explain why the work of Radcliffe-Brown, to which nobody can deny a central place in social-structure studies, has often given rise to bitter arguments.

For instance, Murdock has called the kind of interpretation to which Radcliffe-Brown seems to be addicted: "mere verbalizations reified into causal forces (1949:121)," and Lowie expressed himself in similar terms (1937:224–225). As regards Murdock, the lively controversy which has been carried on lately between him and W. H. Lawrence (Lawrence and Murdock 1949), on the one hand, and Radcliffe-Brown (1951), on the other, may help to clarify the basic differences in their respective positions. This was about the so-called "Murngin type" of kinship system, a focal point in social-structure studies not only because of its many intricacies but because, thanks to Lloyd Warner's book and articles (1930–1931, 1937a), we possess a thorough and extensive study of this system. However, Warner's study leaves some basic problems unanswered, especially the way in which marriage takes place on the lateral borders of the system. For Radcliffe-Brown, however, there is no problem involved, since he considers any kind of social organization as a mere conglomerate of simple person-to-person relations and since, in any society, there is always somebody who may be regarded as one's mother's brother's daughter (the preferred spouse among the Murngin) or as standing in an equivalent relation. But the problem is elsewhere: it lies in the fact that the natives have chosen to express these person-to-person relations in a class system, and Warner's description of this system (as acknowledged by himself) makes it impossible in some cases for the same individual to belong simultaneously to the right kind of class and to the right kind of relation. Under these circumstances, Lawrence and Murdock have tried to invent some system which would fit with the requirements of both the marriage rules and a system of the same kind as the one described by Warner. They invented it, however, as a sort of abstract game, the result being that, while their system meets some of the difficulties involved in Warner's account, it also raises many others. One of the main difficulties implied in Warner's system is that it would require, on the part of the natives, an awareness of relationships too remote to make it believable. Since the new system adds a new line to the seven already assumed by Warner, it goes still further in that direction. Therefore, it seems a good hunch that the "hidden" or "unknown" system underlying the clumsy model which the Murngin borrowed recently from tribes with completely different marriage rules is simpler than the latter and not more complicated.

One sees, then, that Murdock favors a systematic and formal approach, different from Radcliffe-Brown's empirical and naturalistic one. But he remains, at the same time, psychologically and even biologically minded, and he can comply with the resulting requirements only by calling upon other disciplines, such as psychoanalysis and behaviorist psychology. Thus he succeeds in unloading from his interpretations of kinship problems the empiricism which still burdens Radcliffe-Brown's work, though, perhaps, at the risk of leaving them uncompleted or having to be completed on a ground foreign to anthropology, if not contradictory to its goals. Instead of seeing in kinship systems a sociological means to achieve a sociological result, he rather treats them as sociological results deriving from biological and psychological premises (1949:131–132).

Two parts should be distinguished in Murdock's combination to the study of social structure. There is, first, a rejuvenation of a statistical method to check assumed correlations between social traits and to establish new ones, a method already tried by Tylor but which Murdock, thanks to the painstaking efforts of his Yale Cross-cultural Survey and the use of a more complex and exacting technique, was able to carry much further than had his predecessor. Everything has been said on the manifold difficulties with which this kind of inquiry is fraught (Lowie 1948a:chap. iii), and, since nobody more than its author is aware of them, it is unnecessary to dwell upon this theme. Let it only be recalled that, while the uncertainty involved in the process of "carving out" the data will always make any alleged correlation dubious, the method is quite efficient in a negative way, that is, to explode false correlations. In this respect Murdock has achieved many results which no social anthropologist can permit himself to ignore.

The second aspect of Murdock's contribution is a scheme of the historical evolution of kinship systems. This suggests a startling conclusion, namely, that the so-called "Hawaiian type" of social organization should be placed at the origin of a much greater number of systems than has generally been admitted since Lowie's criticism of Morgan's similar hypothesis (Lowie 1920: chap. iii). However, it should be kept in mind that Murdock's scheme is not based upon the consideration of individual societies taken as historicogeographical units or as co-ordinated wholes, but on abstractions and even, if one may say so, on abstractions "twice-removed": in the first place, social organization is isolated from the other aspects of culture (and sometimes even kinship systems from social organization); next, social organization itself is broken up into disconnected elements which are the outcome more of the traditional categories of ethnological thought than of the concrete analysis of each group. This being understood, the method for establishing a historical scheme can only be ideological; it proceeds by extracting common elements belonging to each stage in order to define a previous stage and so on. Therefrom it is obvious that systems placed at the beginning can be only those which exhibit the more general features, while systems with special features must occupy a more remote rank. In order to clarify this, a comparison may be used, though its oversimplification makes it unfair to Murdock: it is as though the origin of the modern horse were ascribed to the order of vertebrates instead of to *Hipparion.*

Regardless of the difficulties raised by his approach, Murdock's book should be credited with presenting new material and raising fascinating problems, many of which are new to anthropological thought. It is not doing him an injustice, then, to state that his contribution consists more in perfecting a method of discovering new problems than in solving them. Though this method remains "Aristotelian," it is perhaps unavoidable in the development of any science. Murdock has at least been faithful to the best part of the Aristotelian outlook by demonstrating convincingly that "cultural forms in the field of social organization reveal a degree of regularity and of conformity to scientific law not significantly inferior to that found in the so-called natural sciences" (1949:259).

In relation to the distinctions made in the first section of this paper, it can be said that Radcliffe-Brown's work expresses a disregard for the difference between observation and experimentation, while Murdock shows a similar disregard for the difference between mechanical and statistical models (since he tries to construct mechanical models with the help of a statistical method). Conversely, Lowie's work seems to consist entirely in an exacting endeavor to meet the question (which was acknowledged as a prerequisite for any study in social structure): *What are the facts?* When he became active in research as well as in theoretical ethnology, the latter field was fraught with philosophical prejudices and an aura of sociological mysticism; therefore, his paramount contribution toward assessing the subject matter of social anthropology has sometimes been misunderstood and thought of as wholly negative (Kroeber 1920). But, although this situation made it imperative at that time to state, in the first place, what the facts were *not,* the creative energy liberated by his merciless disintegration of arbitrary systems and alleged correlations has furnished, to a very large extent, the power consumed by his followers. His own positive contributions are not always easy to outline on account of the extreme modesty of his thought and his aversion to any kind of wide-scope theoretical claim. He himself used the words "active skepticism" to outline his position. However, it is Lowie who, as early as 1915, stated in modern terms the role of kinship studies in relation to social behavior and organization: "Sometimes the very essence of social fabric may be demonstrably connected with the mode of classifying kin" (1915, 1929c). In the same paper he was able to reverse the narrow historical trend which, at that time, was blinding anthropological thinking to the universal action of structural forces: exogamy was shown to be a scheme defined by truly genetic characters and, whenever present, determining identical features of social organization, without calling for historicogeographical relations. When, a few years later, he exploded the "matrilineal complex" (1919), he achieved two results which are the fundamentals of social-structure studies. In the first place, by dismissing the notion that every so-called "matrilineal" feature was to be understood as an expression or as a vestige of the complex, he made it possible to break it up into several variables. In the second place, the elements thus liberated could be used for a permutative treatment of the differential features of kinship systems (Lowie 1929a). Thus he was laying the foundation for a structural analysis of kinship on two different levels: that of the terminological system, on the one hand, and, on the other, that of the correlation between the system of behavior and terminology, showing the path which, later on, was to be followed by others (Radcliffe-Brown 1924; Lévi-Strauss 1945).

Lowie should be credited with many other theoretical contributions: he was probably the first one to demonstrate the true bilateral nature of most of the so-called "unilateral" systems (1920, 1929b). He made clear the impact of residence on filiation (1920). He convincingly dissociated avoidance customs from incest prohibition (1920:104–105); his care to interpret social organization not only as a set of institutionalized rules but also as the outcome of individual psychological reactions, which sometimes contradicted or inflected the rules, led to the strange result that the same scholar who was so much abused for his famous "shreds and patches" statement on culture was able to offer some of the most thorough and well-balanced pictures we have of cultures treated as wholes (1935, 1948a:chaps. xv, xvi, xvii). Finally, Lowie's role as a promoter and exponent of South American social anthropology is well known; either directly or indirectly through guidance and encouragement, he has contributed toward breaking a new field.

IV. SOCIAL DYNAMICS: SUBORDINATION STRUCTURES

A. ORDER OF ELEMENTS (INDIVIDUALS OR GROUPS) IN THE SOCIAL STRUCTURE

According to this writer's interpretation, which does not need to be expounded systematically, since (in spite of efforts toward objecjectivity) it probably permeates this paper, kinship systems, marriage rules, and descent groups constitute a co-ordinated ensemble, the function of which is to insure the permanency of the social group by means of intertwining consanguineous and affinal ties. They may be considered as the blueprint of a mechanism which "pumps" women out of their consanguineous families to redistribute them in affinal groups, the result of this process being to create new consanguineous groups and so on. This view results from Linton's classical distinction between "conjugal" and "consanguineous" family (1936:159–163). If no external factor were affecting this mechanism, it would work indefinitely and the social structure would remain static. This is not the case, however; hence the need to introduce into the theoretical model new elements to account for the diachronic changes of the structure, on the one hand, and, on the other, for the fact that kinship structure does not exhaust social structure. This can be done in three different ways.

As always, the first step consists in ascertaining the facts. Since the time when Lowie expressed regret that so little had been done by anthropologists in the field of political organization (1920:chap. xiii), some progress has been made; in the first place, Lowie himself has clarified the issue by devoting most of his recent book to problems of that sort and by regrouping the facts concerning the American area (1927; 1948a:chaps. vi, vii, xii–xiv, 1948b). A recent work has brought together significant data concerning Africa (Fortes and Evans-Pritchard 1940). To this day, the best way to organize the still much confused material remains Lowie's basic distinctions (1948a) between social strata, sodalities, and the state.

The second type of approach would be an attempt to correlate the phenomena belonging to the order first studied, i.e., kinship, with phenomena belonging to the new order but showing a direct connection with the former. This approach raises, in turn, two different problems: (1) Can the kinship structure by itself result in structures of a new type (that is, dynamically oriented)? (2) How do *communication structures* and *subordination structures* interact on each other?

The first problem should be related to education, i.e., to the fact that each generation plays alternately a submissive and a dominant part in relation to the preceding and to the following generation. This aspect has been dealt with chiefly by Margaret Mead;[9] its discussion will probably find a more appropriate place in other papers.

Another side of the question lies in the important attempt to correlate a static position in the kinship structure (as defined by terminology) with a dynamic behavior expressed, on the one hand, in rights, duties, obligations, and, on the other, in privileges, avoidance, etc. It is impossible to go into the discussion of these problems to which many writers have contributed. Especially significant is a protracted controversy between Radcliffe-Brown and others (Radcliffe-Brown 1935, 1940a, 1949a; Opler 1937, 1947; Brand 1948) about the kind of correlaton which exists, if any, between kin terminology and behavior.

According to Radcliffe-Brown's well-known position, such a correlation exhibits a high degree of accuracy, while his opponents have generally tried to demonstrate that this is neither absolute nor detailed. In contrast to both opinions, this writer has tried to establish that the relation between terminology and behavior is of a dialectical nature. The modalities of behavior between relatives express to some extent the terminological classification, and they provide at the same time a means to overcome difficulties and contradictions resulting from this classification. Thus the rules of behavior result from an attempt to overcome contradictions in the field of terminology and marriage rules; the functional unwedging—if one may say so—which is bound to exist between the two orders causes changes in the former, i.e., terminology; and these, in turn, call for new behavior patterns, and so on indefinitely.

The second problem confronts us with the kind of situation arising when the kinship system does not regulate matrimonial exchanges between equals but between members of a hierarchy (either economic or political). Under that heading come the problems of polygamy which, in some cases at least, may be shown to provide a bridge between two different types of guarantees, one collective and political, the other individual and economic (Lévi-Strauss 1944); and that of hypergamy. This deserves much more attention than it has received so far since it is the doorway to the study of the caste system (Hocart 1938; Davis 1941; Lévi-Strauss 1949b:chaps. xxiv–xxvii) and hence to that of social structures based on race and class distinctions.

The third and last approach to our problem is purely formal. It consists in an a priori deduction of the types of structure likely to result from relations of domination or dependency as they might appear at random. Of a very promising nature for the study of social structure are Rapoport's attempts to make a mathematical theory of the pecking order among hens (1949). It is true that there seems to be a complete opposition between, let us say, the pecking order of hens, which is intransitive and cyclical, and the social order (for instance, the circle of kava in Polynesia), which is transitive and non-cyclical (since those who are seated at the far end can never sit at the top). But the study of kinship systems shows precisely that, under given circumstances, an intransitive and cyclical order can result in a transitive and noncyclical one. This happens, for instance, in a hypergamous society where a circulative marriage system with mother's brother's daughter leaves at one end a girl unable to find a husband (since her status is the highest) and at the other end a boy without a wife (since no girl has a lower status than his own). Thus, with the help of such notions as transitivity, order, and cycle, which admit of mathematical treatment, it becomes possible to study, on a purely formal level, generalized types of social structure, where both the communication and the subordination aspects become fully integrated. It is also possible to enlarge the field of inquiry and to integrate, for a given society, actual and potential types of order. For instance, in human societies the actual forms of social order are practically always of a transitive and noncyclical type: if A is above B and B above C, then A is above C; and C cannot be above A. But most of the human "potential" or "ideological" forms of social order, as illustrated in politics, myth, and religion, are conceived as intransitive and cyclical; for instance, in tales about kings marrying lasses and in Stendhal's indictment of American democracy as a system where a gentleman takes his orders from his grocer.

B. ORDER OF ORDERS

Thus anthropology considers the whole social fabric as a network of different types of orders. The kinship system provides a way to order individuals according to certain rules; social organization is another way of ordering individuals and groups; social stratifications, whether economic or political, provide us with a third type; and all these orders can themselves be put in order by showing the kind of relationships which exist between them, how they interact on one another on both the synchronic and the diachronic levels. Meyer Fortes has successfully tried to construct models valid not only for one type of order (kinship, social organization, economic relations, etc.) but where numerous models for all types of orders are themselves ordered inside a total model (1949).

When dealing with these orders, however, anthropologists are confronted with a basic problem which was taken up at the beginning of this paper, i.e., to what extent does the manner according to which a society conceives its orders and their ordering correspond to the real situation? It has been shown that this problem can be solved in different ways, depending on the data at hand.

All the models considered so far, however, are "lived-in" orders: they correspond to mechanisms which can be studied from the outside as a part of objective reality. But no systematic studies of these orders can be undertaken without acknowledging the fact that social groups, to achieve their mutual ordering, need to call upon orders of different types, corresponding to a field external to objective reality and which we call the "supernatural." These "thought-of" orders cannot be checked against the experience to ,which they refer, since they are one and the same thing as this experience. Therefore, we are in the position of studying them only in their relationships with the other types of "lived-in" orders. The "thought-of" orders are those of myth and religion. The question may be raised whether, in our own society, political ideology does not belong to the same category.

After Durkheim, Radcliffe-Brown has contributed greatly to the demonstration that religion is a part of the social structure. The anthropologist's task is to discover correlations between different types of religions and different types of social organization (Radcliffe-Brown 1945). Radcliffe-Brown failed, however, to achieve significant results for two reasons. In the first place, he tried to link ritual and beliefs directly to sentiments; besides, he was more concerned with giving universal formulation to the kind of correlation prevailing between religion and social structure than in showing the variability of one in relation to the other. It is perhaps as a result of this that the study of religion has fallen into the background, to the extent that the word "religion" does not even appear in the program of this symposium. The field of myth, ritual, and religion seems nevertheless to be one of the more fruitful for the study of social structure; though relatively little has been done in this respect, the results which have been obtained recently are among the most rewarding in our field.

Great strides have been taken toward the study of religious systems as co-ordinate wholes. Documentary material, such as Radin's *The Road of Life and Death* (1945) or Berndt's *Kunapipi* (1951), should help in undertaking, with respect to several religious cults, the kind of ordering of data so masterfully achieved by Gladys Reichard for the Navaho (1950). This should be completed by small-scale comparative studies on the permanent and nonpermanent elements in religious thought as exemplified by Lowie.

With the help of such well-organized material it becomes possible, as

Nadel puts it (1952), to prepare "small-scale models of a comparative analysis . . . of an analysis of 'concomitant variations' . . . such as any inquiry concerned with the explanation of social facts must employ." The results thus achieved may be small; they are, however, some of the most convincing and rigorous in the entire field of social organization. Nadel himself has proved a correlation between shamanism and some aspects of psychological development (1946); using Indo-European comparative material borrowed from Iceland, Ireland, and the Caucasus, Dumézil has interpreted an enigmatic mythological figure in relation to specific features of social organization (1948); Wittfogel and Goldfrank have shown how significant variations in mythological themes can be related to the socioeconomic background (1943). Monica Hunter has established beyond doubt that the structure of the magical beliefs may vary in correlation with the structure of the society itself (Hunter-Wilson 1951). These results, together with some others, on which space prevents our commenting, give hope that we may be close to understanding not only what kind of function religious beliefs fulfil in social life (this has been known more or less clearly since Lucretius' time) but how they fulfil this function.

A few words may be added as a conclusion. This paper was started by working out the notion of "model," and the same notion has reappeared at its end. Social anthropology, being in its incipient stage, could only seek, as model for its first models, among those of the simplest kind provided by more advanced sciences, and it was natural enough to seek them in the field of classical mechanics. However, in doing so, anthropology has been working under some sort of illusion since, as Von Neumann puts it (Von Neumann and Morgenstern 1944:14), "an almost exact theory of a gas, containing about 10^{25} freely moving particles, is incomparably easier than that of the solar system, made up of 9 major bodies." But when it tries to construct its models, anthropology finds itself in a case which is neither the one nor the other: the objects with which we deal—social roles and human beings—are considerably more numerous than those dealt with in Newtonian mechanics and, at the same time, far less numerous than would be required to allow a satisfactory use of the laws of statistics and probability. Thus we found ourselves in an intermediate zone: too complicated for one treatment and not complicated enough for the other.

The tremendous change which was brought about by the theory of communication consists precisely in the discovery of methods to deal with objects —signs—which can be subjected to a rigorous study despite the fact that they are altogether much more numerous than those of classical mechanics and much less than those of thermodynamics. Language consists of morphemes, a few thousand in number; significant regularities in phoneme frequencies can be reached by limited counts. The threshold for the use of statistical laws becomes lower, and that for operating with mechanical models higher, than was the case when operating on other grounds. And, at the same time, the size-order of the phenomena has become significantly closer to that of anthropological data.

Therefore, the present conditions of social-structure studies can be summarized as follows: phenomena were found to be of the same kind as those which, in strategies and communication theory, were made the subject of a rigorous approach. Anthropological facts are on a scale which is sufficiently close to that of these other phenomena as not to preclude their similar treatment. Surprisingly enough, it is at the very moment when anthropology finds itself closer than ever to the long-awaited goal of becoming a true science that the ground seems to fail where it was expected to be the firmest: the facts themselves are lacking, either not numerous enough or not collected under conditions insuring their comparability.

Though it is not our fault, we have been behaving like amateur botanists, picking up haphazardly heteroclite specimens, which were further distorted and mutilated by preservation in our herbarium. And we are, all of a sudden, confronted with the need of ordering complete series, ascertaining original shades, and measuring minute parts which have either shrunk or been lost. When we come to realize not only what should be done but also what we should be in a position to do, and when we make at the same time an inventory of our material, we cannot help feeling in a disheartened mood. It looks almost as if cosmic physics was set up to work on Babylonian observations. The celestial bodies are still there, but unfortunately the native cultures where we used to gather our data are disappearing at a fast rate, and what they are being replaced by can only furnish data of a very different type. To adjust our techniques of observation to a theoretical framework which is far more advanced is a paradoxical situation, quite opposite to that which has prevailed in the history of sciences. Nevertheless, such is the challenge to modern anthropology.

NOTES

1. Compare with the statement by the same author: ". . . the term 'social structure' which is tending to replace 'social organization' without appearing to add either content or emphasis of meaning" (1943:105).
2. The same idea appears to underlie E. R. Leach's remarkable study, "Jinghpaw Kinship Terminology" (1945).
3. Compare Von Neumann: "Such models (as games) are theoretical constructs with a precise, exhaustive and not too complicated definition; and they must be similar to reality in those respects which are essential to the investigation at hand. To recapitulate in detail: The definition must be precise and exhaustive in order to make a mathematical treatment possible. The construct must not be unduly complicated so that the mathematical treatment can be brought beyond the mere formalism to the point where it yields complete numerical results. Similarity to reality is needed to make the operation significant. And this similarity must usually be restricted to a few traits deemed 'essential' *pro tempore*—since otherwise the above requirements would conflict with each other" (Von Neumann and Morgenstern 1944).
4. For examples and detailed discussion see Lévi-Strauss (1949b:558 ff.).
5. Never accepted by Lowie; see the Preface in Lowie (1920).
6. These researches were summarized by their author in Dumézil (1949).

7. C. Lévi-Strauss, "Les Structures sociales dans le Brésil central et oriental," in Sol Tax (ed.), *Indian Tribes of Aboriginal America: Selected Papers of the XXIXth Congress of Americanists* (Chicago: University of Chicago Press, 1952).

8. That is, aiming to determine the law of variation, in contradistinction to the "Aristotelian" outlook mostly concerned with inductive correlations; for this distinction, fundamental to structural analysis, see Lewin (1935).

9. In connection with this paper's approach, see particularly Mead (1949).

REFERENCES

Bateson, G.
    1936   *Naven.* Cambridge: At the University Press.

Berndt, R. A.
    1951   *Kunapipi.* New York: International Universities Press.

Bernot, L., and Blancard, R. MS.
                  "Nouville: Un Village français." UNESCO.

Bidney, D.
    1950   Review of White, L. A. *The Science of Culture,* in *American Anthropologist,* LII, No. 4, Part 1, 518–519.

Boas, F. (ed.).
    1911   *Handbook of American Indian Languages.* (Bureau of American Ethnology Bull. 40 [1908], Part I.) Washington, D. C.: Government Printing Office.

Bohr, N.
    1939   "Natural Philosophy and Human Culture," *Nature,* CXLIII, 268–272.

Brand, C. S.
    1948   "On Joking Relationships," *American Anthropologist,* L, 160–161.

Cushing, F. H.
    1896   "Outlines of Zuñi Creation Myths," *Bureau of American Ethnology, 13th Annual Report, 1891–1892,* pp. 325–447. Washington, D. C.: Government Printing Office.

————————
    1920   *Zuni Breadstuff.* ("Indian Notes and Monographs, Museum of the American Indian, Heye Foundation," Vol. VIII.) New York.

Dahlberg, G.
    1948   *Mathematical Methods for Population Genetics.* London and New York: Interscience Publishers.

Davis, K.
    1941   "Intermarriage in Caste Societies," *American Anthropologist,* XLIII, 378–395.

————————
    1947   *The Development of the City in Society: Proceedings of the 1st Conference on Long Term Social Trends, Social Science Research Council.*

Dumézil, G.
    1948   *Loki.* Paris: G. P. Maisonneuve.

————————
    1949   *L'Heritage indo-européen a Rome.* Paris: Gallimard.

Durkheim, É.
    1912   *Les Formes élémentaires de la vie religieuse.* ("Bibliothèque de philosophie contemporaine.") Paris: F. Alcan.

Durkheim, É., and Mauss, M.
    1901–1902   "De quelques formes primitives de classification: Contribution à l'étude des représentations collectives," *Année sociologique*, VI, 1–72.

Eggan, F.
    1937a   "Historical Changes in the Choctaw Kinship System," *American Anthropologist*, XXXIX, 34–52.

————. (ed.)
    1937b   *Social Anthropology of North American Tribes*. Chicago: University of Chicago Press.

————.
    1950   *Social Organization of the Western Pueblos*. Chicago: University of Chicago Press.

Elwin, V.
    1947   *The Muria and Their Ghotul*. Oxford: Oxford University Press.

Evans-Pritchard, E. E.
    1939   "Nuer Time Reckoning," *Africa*, XII, 189–216.

————.
    1940   *The Nuer*. Oxford: Clarendon Press.

Firth, R.
    1936   *We, the Tikopia*. London and New York: G. Allen & Unwin.

————.
    1946   *Malay Fishermen*. London: Kegan Paul, Trench, Trubner & Co.

————.
    1951   *Elements of Social Organization*. London: Watts & Co.

Ford, C. S., and Beach, F. A.
    1951   *Patterns of Sexual Behavior*. New York: Harper.

Forde, D.
    1941   *Marriage and the Family among the Yakö in S.E. Nigeria*. ("Monographs in Social Anthropology," No. 5.) London: London School of Economics and Political Science.

————.
    1950   "Double-Descent among the Yakö." In Radcliffe-Brown, A. R., and Forde, D. (eds.), *African Systems of Kinship and Marriage*. London: Oxford University Press, for the International African Institute.

Fortes, M. (ed.).
    1949   *Social Structure: Studies Presented to A. R. Radcliffe-Brown*. Oxford: Clarendon Press.

Fortes, M., and Evans-Pritchard, E. E.
    1940   *African Political Systems*. Oxford: Oxford University Press, for the International Institute of African Languages and Cultures.

Goldstein, K.
    1951   *Der Aufbau des Organismus*. French translation. Paris: Gallimard.

Herskovits, M. J.
    1940   *The Economic Life of Primitive Peoples*. New York: Knopf.

Hocart, A. M.
    1938   *Les Castes*. ("Annales du Musée Guimet bibliothèque du vulganisation," Vol. LIV.) Paris.

Hunter-Wilson, M.
    1951   "Witch Beliefs and Social Structure," *American Journal of Sociology*, LVI, No. 4, 307–313.

Kroeber, A. L.
1920   Review of Lowie, R. H., *Primitive Society,* in *American Anthropologist,* XXII, No. 4, 377–381.

————.
1938   "Basic and Secondary Patterns of Social Structure," *Journal of the Royal Anthropological Institute,* LXVIII, 299–309.

————.
1942   "The Societies of Primitive Man," *Biological Symposia,* VIII, 205–216.

————.
1943   "Structure, Function, and Pattern in Biology and Anthropology," *Scientific Monthly,* LVI, 105–113.

————.
1948   *Anthropology.* New ed. New York: Harcourt, Brace.

Lawrence, W. E., and Murdock, G. P.
1949   "Murngin Social Organization," *American Anthropologist,* LI, No. 1, 58–65.

Leach, E. R.
1945   "Jinghpaw Kinship Terminology," *Journal of the Royal Anthropological Institute,* LXXV, 59–72.

Lestrange, M. de.
1951   "Pour une méthode socio-démographique," *Journal de la Société des Africanistes,* Vol. XXI.

Lévi-Strauss, C.
1944   "The Social and Psychological Aspects of Chieftainship in a Primitive Tribe: The Nambikuara," *Transactions of the New York Academy of Sciences,* Series II, VII, No. 1, 16–32.

————.
1945   "L'Analyse structurale en linguistique et en anthropologie," *Word,* I, No. 1, 33–53.

————.
1949a   "Histoire et ethnologie," *Revue de métaphysique et de morale,* LIV, Nos. 3–4, 363–391.

————.
1949b   *Les Structures élémentaires de la parenté.* Paris: Presses universitaires de France.

————.
1951   "Language and the Analysis of Social Laws," *American Anthropologist,* LIII, No. 2, 155–163.

Lewin, K.
1935   *A Dynamic Theory of Personality.* New York: McGraw-Hill.

Linton, R.
1936   *The Study of Man.* New York: Appleton-Century.

Livi, L.
1940–1941   *Trattato di demografia.* Padua: Cedam.

————.
1949   "Considérations théoriques et pratiques sur le concept de 'minimum de population,'" *Population,* IV, No. 4, 754–756.

Lowie, R. H.
1915   "Exogamy, and the Classificatory Systems of Relationship," *American Anthropologist,* Vol. XVII, No. 2.

————.
1919   "The Matrilineal Complex," *University of California Publications in American Archaeology and Anthropology,* XVI, No. 2, 29–45.

————.
1920   *Primitive Society.* New York: Liveright.

————.
1927   *The Origin of the State.* New York: Harcourt, Brace.

————.
1929a   "Notes on Hopi Clans," pp. 303–360. ("American Museum of Natural History, Anthropological Papers," Vol. XXX, Part VI.)

————.
1929b   "Hopi Kinship," pp. 361–388. ("American Museum of Natural History, Anthropological Papers," Vol. XXX, Part VII.)

————.
1929c   "Relationship Terms." In *Encyclopaedia Britannica,* pp. 84–89. 14th ed. 1948. Chicago, London, and Toronto: Encyclopaedia Britannica.

————.
1935   *The Crow Indians.* New York: Farrar & Rinehart.

————.
1937   *The History of Ethnological Theory.* New York: Farrar & Rinehart.

————.
1942   "A Marginal Note to Professor Radcliffe-Brown's Paper on 'Social Structure,'" *American Anthropologist,* XLIV, No. 3, 519–521.

————.
1948a   *Social Organization.* New York: Rinehart.

————.
1948b   "Some Aspects of Political Organization among American Aborigines (Huxley Memorial Lecture)," *Journal of the Royal Anthropological Institute,* LXXVIII, 11–24.

Malinowski, B.
1922   *Argonauts of the Western Pacific.* London: George Routledge & Sons.

Mauss, M.
1904–1905   "Essai sur les variations saisonnières dansles sociétés Eskimos: Étude de morphologie sociale," *Année sociologique,* IX, 39–132.

————.
1923–1924   "Essai sur le don, forme archaïque de l'échange," *ibid.,* n.s., I, 30–186.

————.
1924–1925   "Division et proportion des divisions de la sociologie," *ibid.,* n.s., II, 98 ff.

————.
1950   *Sociologie et anthropologie.* Paris: Presses universitaires de France.

Mead, M.
1949   "Character Formation and Diachronic Theory." In Fortes, M. (ed.), *Social Structure: Studies Presented to A. R. Radcliffe-Brown,* pp. 18–34. Oxford: Clarendon Press.

Morgan, L. H.
1871   *Systems of Consanguinity and Affinity of the Human Family.* ("Smithsonian Institution Contributions to Knowledge," Vol. XVII, No. 218.) Washington, D. C.

Murdock, G. P.
   1949   *Social Structure*. New York: Macmillan.
Nadel, S. F.
   1946   "Shamanism in the Nuba Mountains," *Journal of the Royal Anthropological Institute*, LXXVI, Part I, 25–38.

_____.
   1947   *The Nuba*. London and New York: Oxford University Press.

_____.
   1952   "Witchcraft in Four African Societies: An Essay in Comparison," *American Anthropologist*, LIV, Part I, 18–29.
Opler, M. E.
   1937   "Apache Data Concerning the Relation of Kinship Terminology to Social Classification," *American Anthropologist*, XXXIX, No. 2, 201–212.

_____.
   1947   "Rule and Practice in the Behavior Pattern between Jicarilla Apache Affinal Relatives," *American Anthropologist*, XLIX, No. 3, 453–462.
Radcliffe-Brown, A. R.
   1924   "The Mother's Brother in South Africa," *South African Journal of Science*, XXI, 542–555.

_____.
   1926   "Father, Mother, and Child," *Man*, Vol. XXVI, Art. 103, pp. 159–161.

_____.
   1930–1931   "The Social Organization of Australian Tribes," *Oceania*, I, No. 1, 34–63; No. 2, 206–246; No. 3, 332–341; No. 4, 426–456.

_____.
   1935   "Kinship Terminology in California," *American Anthropologist*, XXXVII, No. 3, 530–535.

_____.
   1940a   "On Joking Relationships," *Africa*, XIII, No. 3, 195–210.

_____.
   1940b   "On Social Structure," *Journal of the Royal Anthropological Institute*, LXX, 1–12.

_____.
   1941   "The Study of Kinship Systems," *ibid.*, LXXI, 1–18.

_____.
   1945   "Religion and Society (Henry Meyers Lecture)," *ibid.*, LXXV, 33–43.

_____.
   1949a   "A Further Note on Joking Relationships," *Africa*, XIX, No. 2, 133–140.

_____.
   1949b   "White's View of a Science of Culture," *American Anthropologist*, LI, No. 3, 503–512.

_____.
   1951   "Murngin Social Organization," *ibid.*, LIII, No. 1, 37–55.

_____.
   1952   "Social Anthropology, Past and Present," *Man*, Vol. LII, Art. 14.
Radcliffe-Brown, A. R., and Forde, D. (eds.).
   1950   *African Systems of Kinship and Marriage*. Oxford: Oxford University Press, for the International African Institute.

Radin, P
    1945   *The Road of Life and Death.* New York: Pantheon.
Rapoport, A.
    1949   "Outline of Probabilistic Approach to Animal Sociology," *Bulletin of Mathematical Biophysics,* XI, 183–196, 273–281.
Reichard, G. A.
    1950   *Navaho Religion: A Study in Symbolism.* 2 vols. ("Bollingen Series," No. XVIII.) New York: Pantheon.
Richards, A. I.
    1932   *Hunger and Work in a Savage Tribe.* London: G. Routledge & Sons.

    ————.

    1936   "A Dietary Study in Northeastern Rhodesia," *Africa,* IX, No. 2, 166–196.

    ————.

    1939   *Land, Labour and Diet in Northern Rhodesia.* Oxford: Oxford University Press, for the International Institute of African Languages and Cultures.
Richardson, J., and Kroeber, A. L.
    1940   "Three Centuries of Women's Dress Fashions: A Quantitative Analysis," *Anthropological Records,* V, No. 2, 111–154.
Ruesch, J., and Bateson, G.
    1951   *Communication: The Social Matrix of Psychiatry.* New York: Norton.
Shannon, C. E., and Weaver, W.
    1950   *The Mathematical Theory of Communication.* Urbana: University of Illinois Press.
Speck, F. G.
    1915   *Family Hunting Territories and Social Life of Various Algonkian Bands of the Ottawa Valley.* (Canada Department of Mines, Geological Survey Mem. 70, "Anthropological Series," No. 8.) Ottawa: Government Printing Bureau.
Spoehr, A.
    1942   *Kinship System of the Seminole,* pp. 29–113. ("Anthropological Series, Field Museum of Natural History," Vol. XXXIII, No. 2.)

    ————.

    1947   *Changing Kinship Systems,* pp. 153–235. ("Anthropological Series, Field Museum of Natural History," Vol. XXXIII, No. 4.)

    ————.

    1950   "Observations on the Study of Kinship," *American Anthropologist,* LII, No. 1, 1–15.
Steward, J. H.
    1938   *Basin-Plateau Aboriginal Sociopolitical Groups.* (Bureau of American Ethnology, Smithsonian Institution Bull. 120.) Washington, D. C.: Government Printing Office.
Stewart, J. Q.
    1947   "Empirical Mathematical Rules Concerning the Distribution and Equilibrium of Population," *Geographical Review,* XXXVII, No. 3, 461–485.
Sutter, J., and Tabah, L.
    1951   "Les Notions d'isolat et de population minimum," *Population,* VI, No. 3, 481–489.

Thompson, L.
    1950   *Culture in Crisis: A Study of the Hopi Indians.* New York: Harper.

Von Neumann, J., and Morgenstern, O.
    1944   *Theory of Games and Economic Behavior.* Princeton, N.J.: Princeton University Press.

Wagley, C.
    1940   "The Effects of Depopulation upon Social Organization as Illustrated by the Tapirapé Indians," *Transactions of the New York Academy of Sciences,* Series 2, III, No. 1, 12–16.

Warner, W. L.
    1930–1931 "Morphology and Functions of the Australian Murngin Type of Kinship System," *American Anthropologist,* XXXII, No. 2, 207–256; XXXIII, No. 2, 172–198.

————.
    1937a   *A Black Civilization: A Social Study of an Australian Tribe.* New York: Harper.

————.
    1937b   "The Family and Principles of Kinship Structure in Australia," *American Sociological Review,* II, 43–54.

White, L. A.
    1949   *The Science of Culture.* New York: Farrar, Straus.

Wiener, N.
    1948   *Cybernetics.* Paris: Herman et Cie; New York: Wiley.

Wittfogel, K. A., and Goldfrank, E. S.
    1943   "Some Aspects of Pueblo Mythology and Society," *Journal of American Folklore,* LVI, 17–30.

Zipf, G. K.
    1949   *Human Behavior and the Principle of Least Effort.* Cambridge, Mass.: Addison-Wesley Press.

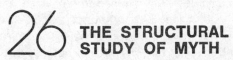

26 THE STRUCTURAL STUDY OF MYTH

It would seem that mythological worlds have been built up only to be shattered again, and that new worlds were built from the fragments. FRANZ BOAS[1]

Despite some recent attempts to renew them, it seems that during the past twenty years anthropology has increasingly turned from studies in the field of religion. At the same time, and precisely because the interest of professional anthropologists has withdrawn from primitive religion, all kinds of amateurs who claim to belong to other disciplines have seized this opportunity to move in, thereby turning into their private playground what we had left as wasteland. The prospects for the scientific study of religion have thus been undermined in two ways.

The explanation for this situation lies to some extent in the fact that the anthropological study of religion was started by men like Tylor, Frazer, and Durkheim, who were psychologically oriented although not in a position to keep up with the progress of psychological research and theory. Their interpretations, therefore, soon became vitiated by the outmoded psychological approach which they used as their basis. Although they were undoubtedly right in giving their attention to intellectual processes, the way they handled these remained so crude that it discredited them altogether. This is much to be regretted, since, as Hocart so profoundly noted in his introduction to a posthumous book recently published,[2] psychological interpretations were withdrawn from the intellectual field only to be introduced again in the field of affectivity, thus adding to "the inherent defects of the psychological school . . . the mistake of deriving clear-cut ideas . . . from vague emotions." Instead of trying to enlarge the framework of our logic to include processes which, whatever their apparent differences, belong to the same kind of intellectual operation, a naïve attempt was made to reduce them to inarticulate emotional drives, which resulted only in hampering our studies.

Of all the chapters of religious anthropology probably none has tarried to the same extent as studies in the field of mythology. From a theoretical point of view the situation remains very much the same as it was fifty years ago, namely, chaotic. Myths are still widely interpreted in conflicting ways: as collective dreams, as the outcome of a kind of esthetic play, or as the basis of ritual. Mythological figures are considered as personified abstractions, divinized heroes, or fallen gods. Whatever the hypothesis, the choice amounts to reducing mythology either to idle play or to a crude kind of philosophic speculation.

In order to understand what a myth really is, must we choose between platitude and sophism? Some claim that human societies merely express, through their mythology, fundamental feelings common to the whole of mankind, such as love, hate, or revenge or that they try to provide some kind of explanations for phenomena which they cannot otherwise understand—astronomical, meteorological, and the like. But why should these societies do it in such elaborate and devious ways, when all of them are also acquainted with empirical explanations? On the other hand, psychoanalysts and many anthropologists have shifted the problems away from the natural or cosmological toward the sociological and psychological fields. But then the interpretation becomes too easy: If a given mythology confers prominence on a certain figure, let us say an evil grandmother, it will be claimed that in such a society grandmothers are actually evil and that mythology reflects the social structure and the social relations; but should the actual data be conflicting, it would be as readily claimed that the purpose of mythology is to provide an outlet for repressed feelings. Whatever the situation, a clever dialectic will always find a way to pretend that a meaning has been found.

Mythology confronts the student with a situation which at first sight appears contradictory. On the one hand it would seem that in the course of a myth anything is likely to happen. There is no logic, no continuity. Any characteristic can be attributed to any subject; every conceivable relation can be found. With myth, everything becomes possible. But on the other hand, this apparent arbitrariness is belied by the astounding similarity between myths collected in widely different regions. Therefore the problem: If the content of a myth is contingent, how are we going to explain the fact that myths throughout the world are so similar?

It is precisely this awareness of a basic antinomy pertaining to the nature of myth that may lead us toward its solution. For the contradiction which we face is very similar to that which in earlier times brought considerable worry to the first philosophers concerned with linguistic problems; linguistics could only begin to evolve as a science after this contradiction had been overcome. Ancient philosophers reasoned about language the way we do about mythology. On the one hand, they did notice that in a given language certain sequences of sounds were associated with definite meanings, and they earnestly aimed at discovering a reason for the linkage between those *sounds* and that *meaning*. Their attempt, however, was thwarted from the very beginning by the fact that the same sounds were equally present in other languages although the meaning they conveyed was entirely different. The contradiction was surmounted only by the discovery that it is the combination of sounds, not the sounds themselves, which provides the significant data.

It is easy to see, moreover, that some of the more recent interpretations of mythological thought originated from the same kind of misconception under which those early linguists were laboring. Let us consider, for instance, Jung's idea that a given mythological pattern—the so-called archetype—possesses a certain meaning. This is comparable to the long-supported error that a sound may possess a certain affinity with a meaning: for instance, the "liquid" semi-vowels with water, the open vowels with things that are big, large, loud, or heavy, etc., a theory which still has its supporters.[3] Whatever emendations the original formulation may now call for,[4] everybody will agree that the Saussurean principle of the *arbitrary character of linguistic signs* was a prerequisite for the accession of linguistics to the scientific level.

To invite the mythologist to compare his precarious situation with that of the linguist in the prescientific stage is not enough. As a matter of fact we may thus be led only from one difficulty to another. There is a very good reason why myth cannot simply be treated as language if its specific problems are to be solved; myth *is* language: to be known, myth has to be told; it is a part of human speech. In order to preserve its specificity we must be able to show that it is both the same thing as language, and also something different from it. Here, too, the past experience of linguists may help us. For language itself can be analyzed into things which are at the same time similar and yet different. This is precisely what is expressed in Saussure's distinction between *langue* and *parole,* one being the structural side of language, the other the statistical aspect of it, *langue* belonging to a reversible time, *parole* being non-reversible. If those two levels already exist in language, then a third one can conceivably be isolated.

We have distinguished *langue* and *parole* by the different time referents which they use. Keeping this in mind, we may notice that myth uses a third referent which combines the properties of the first two. On the one hand, a myth always refers to events alleged to have taken place long ago. But what gives the myth an operational value is that the specific pattern described is timeless; it explains the present and the past as well as the future. This can be made clear through a comparison between myth and what appears to have largely replaced it in modern societies, namely, politics. When the historian refers to the French Revolution, it is always as a sequence of past happenings, a non-reversible series of events the remote consequences of which may still be felt at present. But to the French politician, as well as to his followers, the French Revolution is both a sequence belonging to the past—as to the historian—and a timeless pattern which can be detected in the contemporary French social structure and which provides a clue for its interpretation, a lead from which to infer future developments. Michelet, for instance, was a politically minded historian. He describes the French Revolution thus: "That day . . . everything was possible. . . . Future became present . . . that is, no more time, a glimpse of eternity."[5] It is that double structure, altogether historical and ahistorical, which explains how myth, while pertaining to the realm of *parole* and calling for an explanation as such, as well as to that of *langue* in which it is expressed, can also be an absolute entity on a third level which, though it remains linguistic by nature, is nevertheless distinct from the other two.

A remark can be introduced at this point which will help to show the originality of myth in relation to other linguistic phenomena. Myth is the part of language where the formula *traduttore, tradittore* reaches its lowest truth value. From that point of view it should be placed in the gamut of linguistic expressions at the end opposite to that of poetry, in spite of all the claims which have been made to prove the contrary. Poetry is a kind of speech which cannot be translated except at the cost of serious distortions; whereas the mythical value of the myth is preserved even through the worst translation. Whatever our ignorance of the language and the culture of the people where it originated, a myth is still felt as a myth by any reader anywhere in the world. Its substance does not lie in its style, its original music, or its syntax, but in the *story* which it tells. Myth is language, functioning on an especially high level where meaning succeeds practically at "taking off" from the linguistic ground on which it keeps on rolling.

To sum up the discussion at this point, we have so far made the following claims: (1) If there is a meaning to be found in mythology, it cannot reside in the isolated elements which enter into the composition of a myth, but only in the way those elements are combined. (2) Although myth belongs to the same category as language, being, as a matter of fact, only part of it, language in myth exhibits specific properties. (3) Those properties are only to be found *above* the ordinary linguistic level, that is, they exhibit more complex features than those which are to be found in any other kind of linguistic expression.

If the above three points are granted, at least as a working hypothesis, two consequences will follow: (1) Myth, like the rest of language, is made up of constituent units. (2) These constituent units presuppose the constituent units present in language when analyzed on other levels—namely, phonemes, morphemes, and sememes—but they, nevertheless, differ from the latter in the same way as the latter differ among themselves; they belong to a higher and more complex order. For this reason, we shall call them *gross constituent units*.

How shall we proceed in order to identify and isolate these gross constituent units or mythemes? We know that they cannot be found among phonemes, morphemes, or sememes, but only on a higher level; otherwise myth would become confused with any other kind of speech. Therefore, we should look for them on the sentence level. The only method we can suggest at this stage is to proceed tentatively, by trial and error, using as a check the principles which serve as a basis for any kind of structural analysis: economy of explanation; unity of solution; and ability to reconstruct the whole from a fragment, as well as later stages from previous ones.

The technique which has been applied so far by this writer consists in analyzing each myth individually, breaking down its story into the shortest possible sentences, and writing each sentence on an index card bearing a number corresponding to the unfolding of the story.

Practically each card will thus show that a certain function is, at a given time, linked to a given subject. Or, to put it otherwise, each gross constituent unit will consist of a *relation*.

However, the above definition remains highly unsatisfactory for two different reasons. First, it is well known to structural linguists that constituent units on all levels are made up of relations, and the true difference between our *gross* units and the others remains unexplained; second, we still find ourselves in the realm of a non-reversible time, since the numbers of the cards correspond to the unfolding of the narrative. Thus the specific character of mythological time, which as we have seen is both reversible and non-reversible, synchronic and diachronic, remains unaccounted for. From this springs a new hypothesis, which constitutes the very core of our argument: The true constituent units of a myth are not the isolated relations but *bundles of such relations*, and it is only as bundles that these relations can be put to use and combined so as to produce a meaning. Relations pertaining to the same bundle may appear diachronically at remote intervals, but when we have succeeded in grouping them together we have reorganized our myth according to a time referent of a new nature, corresponding to the prerequisite of the initial hypothesis, namely, a two-dimensional time referent which is simultaneously diachronic and synchronic, and which accordingly integrates the characteristics of *langue* on the one hand, and those of *parole* on the other. To put it in even more linguistic terms, it is as though a phoneme were always made up of all its variants.

Two comparison may help to explain what we have in mind.

Let us first suppose that archaeologists of the future coming from another planet would one day, when all human life had disappeared from the earth, excavate one of our libraries. Even if they were at first ignorant of our writing, they might succeed in deciphering it—an undertaking which would require, at some early stage, the discovery that the alphabet, as we are in the habit of printing it, should be read from left to right and from top to bottom. However, they would soon discover that a whole category of books did not fit the usual pattern—these would be the orchestra scores on the shelves of the music division. But after trying, without success, to decipher staffs one after the other, from the upper down to the lower, they would probably notice that the same patterns of notes recurred at intervals, either in full or in part, or that some patterns were strongly reminiscent of earlier ones. Hence the hypothesis: What if patterns showing affinity, instead of being considered in succession, were to be treated as one complex pattern and read as a whole? By getting at what we call *harmony*, they would then see that an orchestra score, to be meaningful, must be read diachronically along one axis—that is, page after page, and from left to right—and synchronically along the other axis, all the notes written vertically making up one gross constituent unit, that is, one bundle of relations.

The other comparison is somewhat different. Let us take an observer ignorant of our playing cards, sitting for a long time with a fortune-teller. He would know something of the visitors: sex, age, physical appearance, social situation, etc., in the same way as we know something of the different cultures whose myths we try to study. He would also listen to the séances and record them so as to be able to go over them and make comparisons—as we do when we listen to myth-telling and record it. Mathematicians to whom I have put the problem agree that if the man is bright and if the material available to him is sufficient, he may be able to reconstruct the nature of the deck of cards being used, that is, fifty-two or thirty-two cards according to the case, made up of four homologous sets consisting of the same units (the individual cards) with only one varying feature, the suit.

Now for a concrete example of the method we propose. We shall use the Oedipus myth, which is well known to everyone. I am well aware that the Oedipus myth has only reached us under late forms and through literary transmutations concerned more with esthetic and moral preoccupations than with religious or ritual ones, whatever these may have been. But we shall not interpret the Oedipus myth in literal terms, much less offer an explanation acceptable to the specialist. We simply wish to illustrate—and without reaching any conclusions with respect to it—a certain technique, whose use is probably not legitimate in this particular instance, owing to the problematic elements indicated above. The "demonstration" should therefore be conceived, not in terms of what the scientist means by this term, but at best in terms of what is meant by the street peddler, whose aim is not to achieve a concrete result, but to explain, as succinctly as possible, the functioning of the mechanical toy which he is trying to sell to the onlookers.

The myth will be treated as an orchestra score would be if it were unwittingly considered as a unilinear series; our task is to re-establish the correct arrangement. Say, for instance, we were confronted with a sequence of the type: 1,2,4,7,8,2,3,4,6,8,1,4,5,7,8,1,2,5,7,3,4,5,6,8 . . . , the assignment being to put all the 1's together, all the 2's, the 3's, etc.; the result is a chart:

1	2		4			7	8
	2	3	4		6		8
1			4	5		7	8
1	2			5		7	
		3	4	5	6		8

We shall attempt to perform the same kind of operation on the Oedipus myth, trying out several arrangements of the mythemes until we find one which is in harmony with the principles enumerated above. Let us suppose, for the sake of argument, that the best arrangement is the following (although it might certainly be improved with the help of a specialist in Greek mythology):

Cadmos seeks his his sister Europa, ravished by Zeus			
		Cadmos kills the dragon	
	The Spartoi kill one another		
			Labdacos (Laios' father)=*lame* (?)
	Oedipus kills his father, Laios		Laios (Oedipus' father)=*left-sided* (?)
		Oedipus kills the Sphinx	
			Oedipus=*swollen foot* (?)
Oedipus marries his mother, Jocasta			
	Eteocles kills his brother, Polynices		
Antigone buries her brother, Polynices, despite prohibition			

We thus find ourselves confronted with four vertical columns, each of which includes several relations belonging to the same bundle. Were we to *tell* the myth, we would disregard the columns and read the rows from left to right and from top to bottom. But if we want to *understand* the myth, then we will have to disregard one half of the diachronic dimension (top to bottom) and read from left to right, column after column, each one being considered as a unit.

All the relations belonging to the same column exhibit one common feature which it is our task to discover. For instance, all the events grouped in the first column on the left have something to do with blood relations which are overemphasized, that is, are more intimate than they should be. Let us say, then, that the first column has as its common feature the *overrating of blood relations.* It is obvious that the second column expresses the same thing, but inverted: *underrating of blood relations.* The third column refers to monsters being slain. As to the fourth, a few words of clarification are needed. The remarkable connotation of the surnames in Oedipus' father-line has often been noticed. However, linguists usually disregard it, since to them the only way to define the meaning of a term is to investigate all the contexts in which it appears, and personal names, precisely because they are used as such, are not accompanied by any context. With the method we propose to follow the objection disappears, since the myth itself provides its own context. The significance is no longer to be sought in the eventual meaning of each name, but in the fact that all the names have a common feature: All the hypothetical meanings (which may well remain hypothetical) refer to *difficulties in walking straight and standing upright.*

What then is the relationship between the two columns on the right? Column three refers to monsters. The dragon is a chthonian being which has to be killed in order that mankind be born from the Earth; the Sphinx is a monster unwilling to permit men to live. The last unit reproduces the first one, which has to do with the *autochthonous origin* of mankind. Since the monsters are overcome by men, we may thus say that the common feature of the third column is *denial of the autochthonous origin of man.*[6]

This immediately helps us to understand the meaning of the fourth column. In mythology it is a universal characteristic of men born from the Earth that at the moment they emerge from the depth they either cannot walk or they walk clumsily. This is the case of the chthonian beings in the mythology of the Pueblo: Muyingwu, who leads the emergence, and the chthonian Shumaikoli are lame ("bleeding-foot," "sore-foot"). The same happens to the Koskimo of the Kwakiutl after they have been swallowed by the chthonian monster, Tsiakish: When they returned to the surface of the earth "they limped forward or tripped sideways." Thus the common feature of the fourth column is *the persistence of the autochthonous origin of man.* It follows that column four is to column three as column one is to column two. The inability to connect two kinds of relationships is overcome (or rather replaced) by the assertion that contradictory relationships are identical inasmuch as they are both self-contradictory in a similar way. Although this is still a provisional formulation of the structure of mythical thought, it is sufficient at this stage.

Turning back to the Oedipus myth, we may now see what it means. The myth has to do with the inability, for a culture which holds the belief that mankind is autochthonous (see, for instance, Pausanias, VIII, xxix. 4: plants provide a *model* for humans), to find a satisfactory transition between this theory and the knowledge that human beings are actually born from the union of man and woman. Although the problem obviously cannot be solved, the Oedipus myth provides a kind of logical tool which relates the original problem—born from one or born from two?—to the derivative problem: born from different or born from same? By a correlation of this type, the overrating of blood relations is to the underrating of blood relations as the attempt to escape autochthony is to the impossibility to succeed in it. Although experience contradicts theory, social life validates cosmology by its similarity of structure. Hence cosmology is true.

Two remarks should be made at this stage.

In order to interpret the myth, we left aside a point which has worried the specialist until now, namely, that in the earlier (Homeric) versions of the Oedipus myth, some basic elements are lacking, such as Jocasta killing herself and Oedipus piercing his own eyes. These events do not alter the substance of the myth although they can easily be integrated, the first one as a new case of autodestruction (column three) and the second as another case of crippledness (column four). At the same time there is something significant in these additions, since the shift from foot to head is to be correlated with the shift from autochthonous origin to self-destruction.

Our method thus eliminates a problem which has, so far, been one of the main obstacles to the progress of mythological studies, namely, the quest for the *true* version, or the *earlier* one. On the contrary, we define the myth as consisting of all its versions; or to put it otherwise, a myth remains the same as long as it is felt as such. A striking example is offered by the fact that our interpretation may take into account the Freudian use of the Oedipus myth and is certainly applicable to it. Although the Freudian problem has ceased to be that of autochthony *versus* bisexual reproduction, it is still the problem of understanding how *one* can be born from *two:* How is it that we do not have only one procreator, but a mother plus a father? Therefore, not only Sophocles, but Freud himself, should be included among the recorded versions of the Oedipus myth on a par with earlier or seemingly more "authentic" versions.

An important consequence follows. If a myth is made up of all its variants, structural analysis should take all of them into account. After analyzing all the known variants of the Theban version, we should thus treat the others in the same way: first, the tales about Labdacos' collateral line including Agave, Pentheus, and Jocasta herself; the Theban variant about Lycos with Amphion and Zetos as the city founders; more remote variants concerning Dionysus (Oedipus' matrilateral cousin); and Athenian legends where Cecrops takes the place of Cadmos, etc. For each of them a similar chart should be drawn and then compared and reorganized according to the findings: Cecrops killing the serpent with the parallel episode of Cadmos; abandonment of Dionysus with abandonment of Oedipus; "Swollen Foot" with Dionysus' *loxias,* that is, walking obliquely; Europa's quest with Antiope's; the founding of Thebes by the Spartoi or by the brothers Amphion and Zetos; Zeus kidnapping Europa and Antiope and the same with Semele; the Theban Oedipus and the Argian Perseus, etc. We shall then have several two-dimensional charts, each dealing with a variant, to be organized in a three-dimensional order, as shown in [the following figure], so that three different readings become possible: left to right, top to bottom, front to back (or vice versa). All of these charts cannot be expected to be identical; but experience shows that any difference to be observed may be correlated with other differences, so that a logical treatment of the whole will allow simplifications, the final outcome being the structural law of the myth.

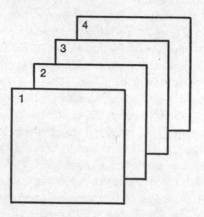

At this point the objection may be raised that the task is impossible to perform, since we can only work with known versions. Is it not possible that a new version might alter the picture? This is true enough if only one or two versions are available, but the objection becomes theoretical as soon as a reasonably large number have been recorded. Let us make this point clear by a comparison. If the furniture of a room and its arrangement were known to us only through its reflection in two mirrors placed on opposite walls, we should theoretically dispose of an almost infinite number of mirror images which would provide us with a complete knowledge. However, should the two mirrors be obliquely set, the number of mirror images would become very small; nevertheless, four or five such images would very likely give us, if not complete information, at least a sufficient coverage so that we would feel sure that no large piece of furniture is missing in our description.

On the other hand, it cannot be too strongly emphasized that all available variants should be taken into account. If Freudian comments on the Oedipus complex are a part of the Oedipus myth, then questions such as whether Cushing's version of the Zuñi origin myth should be retained or discarded become irrelevant. There is no single "true" version of which all the others are but copies or distortions. Every version belongs to the myth.

The reason for the discouraging results in works on general mythology can finally be understood. They stem from two causes. First, comparative mythologists have selected preferred versions instead of using them all. Second, we have seen that the structural analysis of *one* variant of *one* myth belonging to *one* tribe (in some cases, even *one* village) already requires two dimensions. When we use several variants of the same myth for the same tribe or village, the frame of reference becomes three-dimensional, and as soon as we try to enlarge the comparison, the number of dimensions required increases until it appears quite impossible to handle them intuitively. The confusions and platitudes which are the outcome of comparative mythology can be explained by the fact that multi-dimensional frames of reference are often ignored or are naïvely replaced by two- or three-dimensional ones. Indeed, progress in comparative mythology depends largely on the cooperation of mathematicians who would undertake to express in symbols multi-dimensional relations which cannot be handled otherwise.

To check this theory,[7] an attempt was made from 1952 to 1954 toward an exhaustive analysis of all the known versions of the Zuñi origin and emergence myth: Cushing, 1883 and 1896; Stevenson, 1904; Parsons, 1923; Bunzel, 1932; Benedict, 1934. Furthermore, a preliminary attempt was made at a comparison of the results with similar myths in other Pueblo tribes, Western and Eastern. Finally, a test was undertaken with Plains mythology. In all cases, it was found that the theory was sound; light was thrown, not only on North American mythology, but also on a previously unnoticed kind of logical operation, or one known so far only in a wholly different context. The bulk of material which needs to be handled practically at the outset of the work makes it impossible to enter into details, and we shall have to limit ourselves here to a few illustrations.

A simplified chart of the Zuñi emergence myth would read:

CHANGE			DEATH
mechanical value of plants (used as ladders to emerge from lower world)	emergence led by Beloved Twins	sibling incest (origin of water)	gods kill children of men (by drowning)
food value of wild plants	migration by the two Newekwe (ceremonial clowns)		magical contest with People of the Dew (collecting wild food versus cultivation)
		brother and sister sacrificed (to gain victory)	
food value of cultivated plants			
		brother and sister adopted (in exchange for corn)	
periodical character of agricultural work			

war against the
Kyanakwe
(gardeners *versus*
hunters)

food value of
game (hunting)

war led by the two
War-Gods

inevitability of
warfare

salvation of the
tribe (center of
the World found)

brother and sister
sacrificed (to
avoid the Flood)

DEATH   PERMANENCE

As the chart indicates, the problem is the discovery of a life-death mediation. For the Pueblo, this is especially difficult; they understand the origin of
human life in terms of the model of plant life (emergence from the earth). They
share that belief with the ancient Greeks, and it is not without reason that we
chose the Oedipus myth as our first example. But in the American Indian case,
the highest form of plant life is to be found in agriculture which is periodical in
nature, that is, which consists in an alternation between life and death. If this
is disregarded, the contradiction appears elsewhere: Agriculture provides
food, therefore life; but hunting provides food and is similar to warfare which
means death. Hence there are three different ways of handling the problem. In
the Cushing version, the difficulty revolves around an opposition between activities yielding an immediate result (collecting wild food) and activities yielding a delayed result—death has to become integrated so that agriculture can
exist. Parsons' version shifts from hunting to agriculture, while Stevenson's
version operates the other way around. It can be shown that all the differences between these versions can be rigorously correlated with these basic
structures.

Thus the three versions describe the great war waged by the ancestors of
the Zuñi against a mythical population, the Kyanakwe, by introducing into the
narrative significant variations which consist (1) in the friendship or hostility
of the gods; (2) in the granting of final victory to one camp or the other; (3) in
the attribution of the symbolic function to the Kyanakwe, described sometimes
as hunters (whose bows are strung with animal sinews) and sometimes as
gardeners (whose bows are strung with plant fibers).

CUSHING		PARSONS		STEVENSON	
Gods, Kyanakwe	allied, use fiber string on their bows (gardeners)	Kyanakwe, alone, use fiber string	Gods, Men	allied, use fiber string	

VICTORIOUS OVER	VICTORIOUS OVER	VICTORIOUS OVER
Men, alone, use sinew (until they shift to fiber)	Gods, ⎫ allied, use Men ⎭ sinew string	Kyanakwe, alone, use sinew string

Since fiber string (agriculture) is always superior to sinew string (hunting), and since (to a lesser extent) the gods' alliance is preferable to their antagonism, it follows that in Cushing's version, men are seen as doubly underprivileged (hostile gods, sinew string); in the Stevenson version, doubly privileged (friendly gods, fiber string); while Parsons' version confronts us with an intermediary situation (friendly gods, but sinew strings, since men begin by being hunters). Hence:

OPPOSITIONS	CUSHING	PARSONS	STEVENSON
gods/men	−	+	+
fiber/sinew	−	−	+

Bunzel's version is of the same type as Cushing's from a structural point of view. However, it differs from both Cushing's and Stevenson's, inasmuch as the latter two explain the emergence as the result of man's need to evade his pitiful condition, while Bunzel's version makes it the consequence of a call from the higher powers—hence the inverted sequences of the means resorted to for the emergence: In both Cushing and Stevenson, they go from plants to animals; in Bunzel, from mammals to insects, and from insects to plants.

Among the Western Pueblo the logical approach always remains the same; the starting point and the point of arrival are simplest, whereas the intermediate stage is characterized by ambiguity:

LIFE (=INCREASE)

(Mechanical) value of the plant kingdom, taking growth alone into account		ORIGINS
Food value of the plant kingdom, limited to wild plants		FOOD-GATHERING
Food value of the plant kingdom, including wild and cultivated plants		AGRICULTURE
Food value of the animal kingdom, limited to animals	(*but there is a contradiction here, owing to the negation of life =*	
Destruction of the animal kingdom, extended to human beings	*destruction, hence:*)	HUNTING WARFARE

DEATH (=DECREASE)

The fact that contradiction appears in the middle of the dialectical process results in a double set of dioscuric pairs, the purpose of which is to mediate between conflicting terms:

1. 2 divine messengers

   2 ceremonial clowns

   2 war-gods

2. homogeneous pair: dioscuri (2 brothers)

   siblings (brother and sister)

   couple (husband and wife)

   heterogeneous pair: (grandmother and grandchild)

We have here combinational variants of the same function in different contexts (hence the war attribute of the clowns, which has given rise to so many queries).

The problem, often regarded as insoluble, vanishes when it is shown that the clowns—gluttons who may with impunity make excessive use of agricultural products—have the same function in relation to food production as the war-gods. (This function appears, in the dialectical process, as *overstepping the boundaries* of hunting, that is, hunting for men instead of for animals for human consumption.)

Some Central and Eastern Pueblos proceed the other way around. They begin by stating the identity of hunting and cultivation (first corn obtained by Game-Father sowing deer-dewclaws), and they try to derive both life and death from that central notion. Then, instead of extreme terms being simple and intermediary ones duplicated as among the Western groups, the extreme terms become duplicated (i.e., the two sisters of the Eastern Pueblo) while a simple mediating term comes to the foreground (for instance, the Poshaiyanke of the Zia), but endowed with equivocal attributes. Hence the attributes of this "messiah" can be deduced from the place it occupies in the time sequence: good when at the beginning (Zuñi, Cushing), equivocal in the middle (Central Pueblo), bad at the end (Zia), except in Bunzel's version, where the sequence is reversed as has been shown.

By systematically using this kind of structural analysis it becomes possible to organize all the known variants of a myth into a set forming a kind of permutation group, the two variants placed at the far ends being in a symmetrical, though inverted, relationship to each other.

Our method not only has the advantage of bringing some kind of order to what was previously chaos; it also enables us to perceive some basic logical processes which are at the root of mythical thought.[8] Three main processes should be distinguished.

The trickster of American mythology has remained so far a problematic figure. Why is it that throughout North America his role is assigned practically everywhere to either coyote or raven? If we keep in mind that mythical thought always progresses from the awareness of oppositions toward their resolution, the reason for these choices becomes clearer. We need only assume that two opposite terms with no intermediary always tend to be replaced by two equivalent terms which admit of a third one as a mediator; then one of the polar terms and the mediator become replaced by a new triad, and so on. Thus we have a mediating structure of the following type:

INITIAL PAIR	FIRST TRIAD	SECOND TRIAD
Life		
	Agriculture	
		Herbivorous animals
		Carrion-eating animals (raven; coyote)
	Hunting	
		Beasts of prey
	Warfare	
Death		

The unformulated argument is as follows: carrion-eating animals are like beasts of prey (they eat animal food), but they are also like food-plant producers (they do not kill what they eat). Or to put it otherwise, Pueblo style (for Pueblo agriculture is more "meaningful" than hunting): ravens are to gardens as beasts of prey are to herbivorous animals. But it is also clear that herbivorous animals may be called first to act as mediators on the assumption that they are like collectors and gatherers (plant-food eaters), while they can be used as animal food though they are not themselves hunters. Thus we may have mediators of the first order, of the second order, and so on, where each term generates the next by a double process of opposition and correlation.

This kind of process can be followed in the mythology of the Plains, where we may order the data according to the set:

> Unsuccessful mediator between Earth and Sky
> (Star-Husband's wife)
>
> Heterogeneous pair of mediators
> (grandmother and grandchild)
>
> Semi-homogeneous pair of mediators
> (Lodge-Boy and Thrown-away)

While among the Pueblo (Zuñi) we have the corresponding set:

> Successful mediator between Earth and Sky
> (Poshaiyanki)
>
> Semi-homogeneous pair of mediators
> (Uyuyewi and Matsailema)
>
> Homogeneous pair of mediators
> (the two Ahaiyuta)

On the other hand, correlations may appear on a horizontal axis (this is true even on the linguistic level; see the manifold connotation of the root *pose* in Tewa according to Parsons: coyote, mist, scalp, etc.). Coyote (a carrion-eater) is intermediary between herbivorous and carnivorous just as mist between Sky and Earth; as scalp between war and agriculture (scalp is a war crop); as corn smut between wild and cultivated plants; as garments between "nature" and "culture"; as refuse between village and outside; and as ashes (or soot) between roof (sky vault) and hearth (in the ground). This chain of mediators, if one may call them so, not only throws light on entire parts of North American mythology—why the Dew-God may be at the same time the Game-Master and the giver of raiments and be personified as an "Ash-Boy"; or why scalps are mist-producing; or why the Game-Mother is associated with corn smut; etc.—but it also probably corresponds to a universal way of organizing daily experience. See, for instance, the French for plant smut (*nielle*, from Latin *nebula*); the luck-bringing power attributed in Europe to refuse (old shoe) and ashes (kissing chimney sweeps); and compare the American Ash-Boy cycle with the Indo-European Cinderella: Both are phallic figures (mediators between male and female); masters of the dew and the game; owners of fine raiments; and social mediators (low class marrying into high class); but they are impossible to interpret through recent diffusion, as has been contended, since Ash-Boy and Cinderella are symmetrical but inverted in every detail (while the borrowed Cinderella tale in America—Zuñi Turkey-Girl—is parallel to the prototype). Hence the chart:

	EUROPE	AMERICA
Sex	female	male
Family Status	double family (remarried father)	no family (orphan)
Appearance	pretty girl	ugly boy
Sentimental status	nobody likes her	unrequited love for girl
Transformation	luxuriously clothed with supernatural help	stripped of ugliness with supernatural help

Thus, like Ash-Boy and Cinderella, the trickster is a mediator. Since his mediating function occupies a position halfway between two polar terms, he must retain something of that duality—namely, an ambiguous and equivocal character. But the trickster figure is not the only conceivable form of mediation; some myths seem to be entirely devoted to the task of exhausting all the possible solutions to the problem of bridging the gap between *two* and *one*. For instance, a comparison between all the variants of the Zuñi emergence myth provides us with a series of mediating devices, each of which generates the next one by a process of opposition and correlation:

messiah > dioscuri > trickster > bisexual being > sibling pair > married couple > grandmother-grandchild > four-term group > triad

In cushing's version, this dialectic is associated with a change from a spatial dimension (mediation between Sky and Earth) to a temporal dimension (mediation between summer and winter, that is, between birth and death). But while the shift is being made from space to time, the final solution (triad) re-introduces space, since a triad consists of a dioscuric pair *plus* a messiah, present simultaneously; and while the point of departure was ostensibly formulated in terms of a space referent (Sky and Earth), this was nevertheless implicitly conceived in terms of a time referent (first the messiah calls, *then* the dioscuri descend). Therefore the logic of myth confronts us with a double, reciprocal exchange of functions to which we shall return shortly.

Not only can we account for the ambiguous character of the trickster, but we can also understand another property of mythical figures the world over, namely, that the same god is endowed with contradictory attributes—for instance, he may be *good* and *bad* at the same time. If we compare the variants of the Hopi myth of the origin of Shalako, we may order them in terms of the following structure:

$$(\text{Masauwu}: x) \cong (\text{Muyingwu}: \text{Masauwu}) \cong (\text{Shalako}: \text{Muyingwu}) \cong (y: \text{Masauwu})$$

where x and y represent arbitrary values corresponding to the fact that in the two "extreme" variants the god Masauwu, while appearing alone rather than associated with another god, as in variant two, or being absent, as in variant three, still retains intrinsically a relative value. In variant one, Masauwu (alone) is depicted as helpful to mankind (though not as helpful as he could be), and in version four, harmful to mankind (though not as harmful as he could be). His role is thus defined—at least implicitly—in contrast with another role which is possible but not specified and which is represented here by the values x and y. In version two, on the other hand, Muyingwu is relatively more helpful than Masauwu, and in version three, Shalako more helpful than Muyingwu. We find an identical series when ordering the Keresan variants:

$$(\text{Poshaiyanki}: x) \cong (\text{Lea}: \text{Poshaiyanki}) \cong \text{Poshaiyanki}: \text{Tiamoni}) \cong (y: \text{Poshaiyanki})$$

This logical framework is particularly interesting, since anthropologists are already acquainted with it on two other levels—first, in regard to the problem of the pecking order among hens, and second, to what this writer has called *generalized exchange* in the field of kinship. By recognizing it also on the level of mythical thought, we may find ourselves in a better position to appraise its basic importance in anthropological studies and to give it a more inclusive theoretical interpretation.

Finally, when we have succeeded in organizing a whole series of variants into a kind of permutation group, we are in a position to formulate the law of that group. Although it is not possible at the present stage to come closer than an approximate formulation which will certainly need to be refined in the future, it seems that every myth (considered as the aggregate of all its variants) corresponds to a formula of the following type:

$$F_x(a): F_y(b) \cong F_x(b): F_{a-1}(y)$$

Here, with two terms, *a* and *b*, being given as well as two functions, *x* and *y*, of these terms, it is assumed that a relation of equivalence exists between two situations defined respectively by an inversion of *terms* and *relations*, under two conditions: (1) that one term be replaced by its opposite (in the above formula, *a* and *a*–1); (2) that an inversion be made between the *function value* and the *term value* of two elements (above, *y* and *a*).

This formula becomes highly significant when we recall that Freud considered that *two traumas* (and not one, as is so commonly said) are necessary in order to generate the individual myth in which a neurosis consists. By trying to apply the formula to the analysis of these traumas (and assuming that they correspond to conditions 1 and 2 respectively) we should not only be able to provide a more precise and rigorous formulation of the genetic law of the myth, but we would find ourselves in the much desired position of developing side by side the anthropological and the psychological aspects of the theory; we might also take it to the laboratory and subject it to experimental verification.

At this point it seems unfortunate that with the limited means at the disposal of French anthropological research no further advance can be made. It should be emphasized that the task of analyzing mythological literature, which is extremely bulky, and of breaking it down into its constituent units, requires team work and technical help. A variant of average length requires several hundred cards to be properly analyzed. To discover a suitable pattern of rows and columns for those cards, special devices are needed, consisting of vertical boards about six feet long and four and a half feet high, where cards can be pigeon-holed and moved at will. In order to build up three-dimensional models enabling one to compare the variants, several such boards are necessary, and this in turn requires a spacious workshop, a commodity particularly unavailable in Western Europe nowadays. Furthermore, as soon as the frame of references becomes multi-dimensional (which occurs at an early stage, as has been shown above) the board system has to be replaced by perforated cards, which in turn require IBM equipment, etc.

Three final remarks may serve as conclusion.

First, the question has often been raised why myths, and more generally oral literature, are so much addicted to duplication, triplication, or quadruplication of the same sequence. If our hypotheses are accepted, the answer is obvious: The function of repetition is to render the structure of the myth apparent. For we have seen that the synchronic-diachronic structure of the myth permits us to organize it into diachronic sequences (the rows in our tables) which should be read synchronically (the columns). Thus, a myth exhibits a "slated" structure, which comes to the surface, so to speak, through the process of repetition.

However, the slates are not absolutely identical. And since the purpose of myth is to provide a logical model capable of overcoming a contradiction (an impossible achievement if, as it happens, the contradiction is real), a theoretically infinite number of slates will be generated, each one slightly different from the others. Thus, myth grows spiral-wise until the intellectual impulse which has produced it is exhausted. Its *growth* is a continuous process, whereas its *structure* remains discontinuous. If this is the case, we should assume that it closely corresponds, in the realm of the spoken word, to a crystal in the realm of physical matter. This analogy may help us to better understand the relationship of myth to both *langue* on the one hand and *parole* on the other. Myth is an intermediary entity between a statistical aggre-gate of molecules and the molecular structure itself.

Prevalent attempts to explain alleged differences between the so-calle-primitive mind and scientific thought have resorted to qualitative differences between the working processes of the mind in both cases, while assuming that the entities which they were studying remained very much the same. If our interpretation is correct, we are led toward a completely different view—namely, that the kind of logic in mythical thought is as rigorous as that of modern science, and that the difference lies, not in the quality of the intellec-tual process, but in the nature of the things to which it is applied. This is well in agreement with the situation known to prevail in the field of technology: What makes a steel ax superior to a stone ax is not that the first one is better made than the second. They are equally well made, but steel is quite different from stone. In the same way we may be able to show that the same logical processes operate in myth as in science, and that man has always been think-ing equally well; the improvement lies, not in an alleged progress of man's mind, but in the discovery of new areas to which it may apply its unchanged and unchanging powers.

NOTES

1. In Boas' Introduction to James Teit, "Traditions of the Thompson River Indians of British Columbia," *Memoirs of the American Folklore Society*, VI (1898), p. 18.
2. A. M. Hocart, *Social Origins* (London: 1954), p. 7.
3. See, for instance, Sir R. A. Paget, "The Origin of Language," *Journal of World History*, I, No. 2 (UNESCO, 1953).
4. See Émile Benveniste, "Nature du signe linguistique," *Acta Linguistica*, I, No. 1 (1939).
5. Jules Michelet, *Histoire de la Révolution française.* IV, 1. I took this quotation from M. Merleau-Ponty, *Les Aventures de la dialectique* (Paris: 1955), p. 273.
6. We are not trying to become involved with specialists in an argument; this would be presumptuous and even meaningless on our part. Since the Oedipus myth is taken here merely as an example treated in arbitrary fashion, the chthonian nature ascribed to the Sphinx might seem surprising; we shall refer to the testimony of Marie Delcourt: "In the archaic legends, [she is] certainly born of the Earth itself" (*Oedipe ou la légende du conquérant* [Liège: 1944], p. 108). No matter how remote from Delcourt's our method may be (and our conclu-sions would be, no doubt, if we were competent to deal with the problem in depth), it seems to us that she has convincingly established the nature of the Sphinx in the archaic tradition, namely, that of a female monster who attacks and rapes young men; in other words, the personification of a female being with an inversion of the sign. This explains why, in the handsome iconography compiled by Delcourt at the end of her work, men and women are always found in an inverted "sky/earth" relationship.

As we shall point out below, we selected the Oedipus myth as our first example because of the striking analogies that seem to exist between certain aspects of archaic Greek thought and that of the Pueblo Indians, from whom we have borrowed the examples [here]. In this respect it should be noted that the figure of the Sphinx, as reconstructed by Delcourt, coincides with two figures of North American mythology (who probably merge into one). We are referring, on the one hand, to "the old hag," a repulsive witch whose physical appearance presents a "problem" to the young hero. If he "solves" this problem—that is, if he responds to the advances of the abject creature—he will find in his bed, upon awakening, a beautiful young woman who will confer power upon him (this is also a Celtic theme). The Sphinx, on the other hand, recalls even more "the child-protruding woman" of the Hopi Indians, that is, a phallic mother par excellence. This young woman was abandoned by her group in the course of a difficult migration, just as she was about to give birth. Henceforth she wanders in the desert as the "Mother of Animals," which she withholds from hunters. He who meets her in her bloody clothes "is so frightened that he has an erection," of which she takes advantage to rape him, after which she rewards him with unfailing success in hunting. See H. R. Voth, "The Oraibi Summer Snake Ceremony," *Field Columbian Museum,* Publication No. 83, Anthropological Series, Vol. III, No. 4 (Chicago: 1903), pp. 352–353 and p. 353, *n* 1.

7. See *Annuaire de l'École pratique des Hautes Études,* Section des Sciences religieuses, 1952–1953, pp. 19–21, and 1953–1954, pp. 27–29. Thanks are due here to an unrequested but deeply appreciated grant from the Ford Foundation.
8. For another application of this method, see our study "Four Winnebago Myths: A Structural Sketch," in Stanley Diamond (ed.), *Culture in History: Essays in Honor of Paul Radin* (New York: 1960), pp. 351–362.

Marshall D. Sahlins 1930–

BACKGROUND

Marshall Sahlins is really too young to be included in this book—indeed, he is even too young to have much of a biographical sketch. However, the essay we have republished here neatly brings to page the conciliation of Leslie White's and Julian Steward's theories of evolution, which even they had thought to be in conflict. Hence it is an important summarizing statement for an epoch.

Sahlins was born in Chicago in 1930. His undergraduate work was done at the University of Michigan with White, and after his B.A. (1951) and M.A. (1952) he went to Columbia, where he got his Ph.D. in 1954. In that year he married Barbara Vollen and they set out for Fiji, where they lived on the small island of Moala until August 1955. The results of their research were published in *Moala: Culture and Nature on a Fijian Island* (1962).

When he returned from Fiji he became a lecturer at Columbia. Then in 1957, he moved to the University of Michigan. The following year his *Social Stratification in Polynesia* was published; it is an adaptation of Karl Polanyi's concept of redistributive systems to account for variations in social stratification among Pacific island groups.

With Elman Service, a colleague then at Michigan who had been a student of both Steward and White, he edited *Evolution and Culture* in 1960; it is from that book that the present essay was taken.

In 1964 Sahlins returned to the field, this time to New Guinea. In 1968 his book *Tribesman* appeared. He is now at the University of Chicago.

INTRODUCTION

Sahlins dislikes having his work called "neo-evolutionism." He says there is nothing "neo-" about it. Rather, the concept of unilinear evolution, tempered by reference to the work of Steward into "universal evolution," relates the stages of evolution to human culture from a general point of view. We know that all societies did not pass through the same stages, which discredits the theory of unilineal evolution. Yet, in the case of universal evolution, the relationship between existing cultures (with an "s") and evolutionary stages remains uncertain. It is to this aspect of evolutionary theory that Sahlins' hypotheses of specific and general evolution are directed.

According to Sahlins, both biological and cultural evolution move in two directions at the same time. Evolution creates both diversity and progress. Diversity in evolution refers to adaptive changes that evolve new forms out of older forms, while progress, on the other hand, refers to the fact that evolution creates more complex forms. It is general evolution that provides the basis for evolutionary stages in evolution. However, specific and general evolution are regarded not as different facts but as part of the evolutionary process. Specific evolution focuses on the adaptation of a particular culture to its environment, in terms of cultural evolution. General evolution focuses on the ways in which progress in a specific society allows us to consider that society more advanced—and therefore at a higher level of cultural evolution.

27 EVOLUTION: SPECIFIC AND GENERAL

It seems to us that Huxley has been premature in congratulating evolutionary biology on its explicit recognition of the difference between divergence and progress. Despite Huxley's own efforts to make the distinction, and despite the fact that the distinction may well strike a biologist as commonplace should he pause to consider it, it is nevertheless not generally explicated by prominent biologists, and judging from confusion about the character of life's evolutionary progress in recent literature (e.g., Simpson 1950: Chapter XV), it is perhaps not fully understood. On the other hand, the distinction has long existed in the literature of evolutionary anthropology. E. B. Tylor, in the opening chapter of *Primitive Culture* (1871), laid out the study of cultural evolution both "stage by stage" as well as "along its many lines." Yet in this, as in so much else, twentieth-century anthropology did not heed Tylor's advice. The dual character of the evolutionary process was not recognized, and this failing has become the very heart of current confusion and polemical controversy about such terms as "unilinear," "multilinear," and "universal" evolution, as well as about the difference between "history" and "evolution."

It appears almost obvious upon stating it that in both its biological and cultural spheres evolution moves simultaneously in two directions. On one side, it creates diversity through adaptive modification: new forms differentiate from old. On the other side, evolution generates progress: higher forms arise from, and surpass, lower. The first of these directions is Specific Evolution, and the second, General Evolution. But note that specific and general evolution are not different concrete realities; they are rather aspects of the same total process, which is also to say, two contexts in which we may place the same evolutionary things and events. Any given change in a form of life or

Reprinted from Marshall D. Sahlins, *Evolution and Culture* (Ann Arbor: University of Michigan Press, 1960), pp. 12–44, by permission of the publisher.

culture can be viewed *either* in the perspective of adaptation *or* from the point of view of over-all progress. However, the context is very important: a difference in taxonomy is required in examining these two aspects of evolution. Concerned with lines of descent, the study of specific evolution employs phylogenetic classification. In the general evolutionary outlook emphasis shifts to the character of progress itself, and forms are classed in stages or levels of development without reference to phylogeny.

SPECIFIC AND GENERAL BIOLOGICAL EVOLUTION

Life inevitably diversifies. It does so because it is perpetuated by reproduction and inheritance, so that adaptive changes are transmitted only in lines of descent. Thus in evolving—which is to say, moving in the direction of increasing use of the earth's resources or increasing transformation of available energy—life necessarily differentiates into particular (breeding) populations, each adjusted to the exploitation of a given environment. This is the specific aspect of life's evolution, the familiar origin and ramification of species. The much-lauded "modern synthetic theory" of biology, unifying genetic principles with natural selection, is devoted to the unraveling of specific evolution.

The perspective required for understanding specific evolution is a phylogenetic one. We are interested in how one species grows out of another and how the new species gives rise to still other species. We are interested in the precise historical and genetic relations between species, and want to show these connections as well as to explain them by reference to natural selection. Thus we trace out the branching and rebranching of lineages, relating each new line to its ecological circumstances. Inasmuch as our perspective is phylogenetic, so is our taxonomy. While biological taxonomy was not originally phylogenetic, it has come to be primarily so used, indicating again that the decisive concern of evolutionary biology remains specific evolution.

Adaptive specialization of populations is an inevitable aspect of life's evolution, and *advance* is a normal concomitant of adaptive specialization. In the context of specific evolution "advance" means that by adaptive modification the population is enabled to maintain or better itself in the face of a threat induced by changing environment or that it is enabled to exploit the same environment more effectively than before. In any case, in the specific perspective advance is characteristically *relative*—relative to the environmental circumstances. This can be illustrated by looking at adapting species in terms of structure and functioning.

Specific advance is manifest both in improved structure and improved functioning of members of an adapting population, although improved structure usually receives greater attention because it is more easily observed or (for fossils) deduced. There are many possible kinds of functional improvements: in vision, smell, speed, or in temperature control, and so on. Likewise the e are many possible kinds of concomitant structural improvements:

changes in limb structure, in the brain, in the eyes, the development of claws, fins, fur, and the like. But that which is a significant improvement for one species need not be so for another, for they may be adjusting to radically different environments or in radically different ways to the same kind of environment. For some forms in some habitats, increase in size is an adaptive advance, for others, decrease in size is selectively advantageous, and so with all other characteristics. Therefore, no one organism, however high in general standing, has a monopoly on or even necessarily more kinds of adaptive advances than any other. A "higher species," in other words, is not in every respect more "advanced" than a lower: man's color vision may be superior to that of the fish, but he cannot swim as well, nor for that matter is his eyesight the most perfect in the animal kingdom. Moreover, higher organisms are not inevitably more perfectly adjusted to their environments than lower. On the contrary, many higher species die out while lower forms continue to survive in their particular niches for eons. Higher forms are often more generalized, less specialized (adapted) for any particular niche, than lower.

Adaptive improvement is relative to the adaptive problem; it is so to be judged and explained. In the specific context each adapted population is adequate, indeed superior, in its own incomparable way. Considering life's evolution phylogenetically we can be only biological relativists. At this point the cultural anthropologist will probably be unable to refrain from linking the famous axiom of cultural relativism with a specific perspective on cultural change. Such would be a correct historical inference: the philosophy of cultural relativism was elaborated precisely by the historical-particularist school which dominated American anthropology through the first half of this century. But to pursue this further now is to anticipate a later discussion.

In sum, specific evolution is the phylogenetic, adaptive, diversifying, specializing, ramifying aspect of total evolution. It is in this respect that evolution is often equated with movement from homogeneity to heterogeneity. But general evolution is another aspect. It is the emergence of higher forms of life, regardless of particular lines of descent or historical sequences of adaptive modification. In the broader perspective of general evolution organisms are taken out of their respective lineages and grouped into types which represent the successive levels of all-round progress that evolution has brought forth.

Let us first illustrate the difference between general and specific evolution with a diagram. Suppose it is possible to plot the phylogenetic origins of the major lineages of animal life. A good way of doing this graphically would be in the shape of a climbing vine—not a tree, for there is no trunk, no "main line"—each larger branch of the vine representing a major divergence of life through time, and smaller branches representing diversification of major lineages. But the vine has a dimension of height as well as a temporal extension of branches. Suppose that the height is "evolutionary height," that is, that the distance of any form from the base indicates degree of over-all progress according to some agreed-upon criterion. A series of horizontal lines could then be drawn across the vine, with the vertical intervals between them indicating levels of general progress through time. Thus on the diagram, life's evolution is depicted in its lateral, branching dimension as well as in its vertical, progressive one.

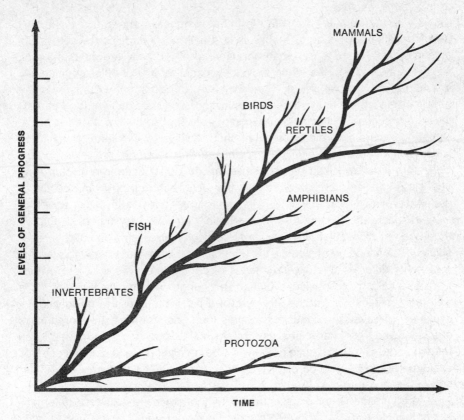

The difference between specific and general evolution can also be illustrated by reference to a familiar group of animals, the primates. The primates are customarily divided into four broad formal categories: prosimian, New World monkeys, Old World monkeys, and hominoid. Each of the latter three, according to Simpson (1950), originated from a different line of prosimian, not one developed out of another. Phylogenetically or specifically, the study of primates consists of tracing the early prosimian radiation, determining how, when, and why each of the other types specialized out, and following the further course of divergence within each line. But it seems obvious and is usually implicitly accepted that the four types of primates, especially their recent representatives, can be arranged to indicate levels of general progress. The hierarchy of over-all standing is, of course: prosimian, New World monkey, then Old World monkey, with hominoid as highest. Although the sequence is a violation of phylogeny, it aids in understanding other consequences of evolution. The heirarchy is commonly used to illustrate general progress in intelligence, social life, and a number of other features. Moreover, a check of history reveals that the levels represented by selected recent specimens are indeed successive. The implication of the last statement deserves to be made explicit: in the taxonomy of general evolution a modern representative of a stage is as "good," i.e., as indicative of the level, as the original and probably extinct representative.

As with the primates, so with life forms in general: a man is more highly developed than a mouse, a mouse than a lizard, a lizard than a goldfish, a goldfish than a crab, a crab than an amoeba. All of these are contemporary, no one is ancestral to the other; they are present termini of different lineages. In what sense can we speak of evolutionary development of one over the other? To anticipate again, the same question appears when we look at contemporary cultures. Eskimo, Sioux Indian, and English culture all exist at the same time and are unrelated to each other. What are the criteria for deciding which is higher on the evolutionary scale, and which lower?

Before an answer can be suggested, another distinction is required. Anyone will recognize the taxonomic shift that occurs in moving from specific to general evolution, a shift from phylogenetic categories to levels of development respectively. But another more subtle shift has also occurred: that is, from species or populations as such to particular organisms as such. In specific evolution the unit of study is the population, the species as a whole, which evolves or differentiates into new kinds of populations. The well-known biological definition of specific evolution, a change in gene frequencies, is a statement explicitly about the structure of a population. In moving to general evolution, however, the concern becomes forms *qua* forms, typical organisms of a class and *their* characteristics. The general taxonomic category, the level, refers to a class of organisms of a given type. It is accurate to say that specific evolution is the production of diverse species, general evolution the production of higher forms.

The difference is not a semantic nicety; it becomes decisive for determining criteria of general progress. It must be recognized that the evolutionary success of a species is often accomplished at the expense of higher development of its individuals. In many situations a species is better maintained by utilizing available energy to produce more of its kind rather than a smaller number of more highly developed specimens (something like modern "higher" education). Specific and general evolution can thus be at cross-purposes, and a measure of the success of a species is not necessarily one of the degree of general development of the particular organisms involved.

Now to a most important point: to embrace general evolution is to abandon relativism. The study of all-round progress requires criteria that are absolute, that are relevant to all organisms regardless of particular environments. The development of higher organisms can be conceived in functional, energy-capturing terms: higher forms harness more energy than lower. Or the criteria of general progress may be structural, the achievement of higher organization.

One common notion of progress can be dismissed out of hand. Most of us have a tendency to equate progress with *efficiency*, which is not altogether surprising because this idea is peculiarly appropriate to a competitive, free-enterprise economy. But an organism's thermodynamic efficiency is not a measure of its general evolutionary status. By efficiency we usually mean some ratio of output to input; thus in rating a machine's efficiency we divide the output of work by the input of energy. Analogously, a measure of the thermodynamic efficiency of a living thing would be the amount of energy captured and used relative to the organism's own expenditure in the process of taking it. But suppose we know the efficiency of an organism as an energy-capturing machine; the use to which the efficiency is put remains unknown. Is it put into build-up and maintenance of its organization? Not necessarily. As pointed out before, the energy taken can be put into the build-up of higher structures *or* into more numerous offspring, each of which concentrates a relatively low amount of energy. The implication is inescapable: an organism can be more efficient than another and yet remain less highly developed.

The difference between higher and lower life forms, it seems to us, is not how efficiently energy is harnessed, but how much. Thermodynamic achievement is the ability to concentrate energy in the organism, to put energy to work building and maintaining structure. Living things take free energy from nature, use it, and dissipate it. In the long run dissipation equals capture, or in terms of entropy, exceeds it—the entropy in the environment in which an organism has lived and died is greater after than before the process. But while alive the organism is trapping energy and transforming it into a higher state, that of protoplasm and its upkeep. It is the amount so trapped (corrected for gross size of the form) and the degree to which it is raised to a higher state that would seem to be the evolutionary measure of life; that would seem to be the way that a crab is superior to an amoeba, a goldfish to a crab, a mouse to a goldfish, a man to a mouse. We put all this in quite qualified form because we lack any competence in physical biology, and do not know how to specify the operations required to ascertain this measure. "A man's reach should exceed his grasp."

But the ability to calculate general progress hardly need remain limited because of our ignorance. General progress can be stated in other, more well-known terms: in terms of organization. Thermodynamic accomplishment has its structural concomitant, greater organization. The relation between energy-harnessing and organization is reciprocal: the more energy concentrated the greater the structure, and the more complicated the structure the more energy that can be harnessed. What is meant by "greater," "higher," or "more complicated" organization? The connotations of these terms are embraced within another, even more formidable one: "level of integration."

The idea of level of integration can be broken down into three aspects. An organism is at a higher level of integration than another when it has more parts and subparts (a higher order of segmentation); when its parts are more specialized; and when the whole is more effectively integrated. Thus general progress in life proceeds in the development of specialized organs and organic subsystems, such as digestive, respiratory, reproductive, and the like, and also in the development of special mechanisms of integration, such as the central nervous system and the brain. When organisms are compared on this basis, over-all progress is clearly seen in the evolutionary record.

And there are still other yardsticks of life's general progress. These are again functional but not put thermodynamically. Huxley's phrase, "all-round adaptability," sums them up. Higher organisms are freer from environmental control than lower, or more precisely, they adapt to a greater variety of particular environments while less bound to any limited niche. It may be that this can also be expressed in terms of greater mobility: higher forms have more, and more complex, motions than lower. More developed organisms are more intelligent also, which is perhaps again only another way of saying that they have more complex motions. Finally, and related to all these aspects of all-round adaptability, higher forms have greater dominance ranges than less developed types.

To recapitulate: specific evolution is "descent with modification," the adaptive variation of life "along its many lines"; general evolution is the progressive emergence of higher life "stage by stage." The advance or improvement we see in specific evolution is relative to the adaptive problem; it is progress in the sense of progression along a line from one point to another, from less to more adjusted to a given habitat. The progress of general evolution is, in contrast, absolute; it is passage from less to greater energy exploitation, lower to higher levels of integration, and less to greater all-round adaptability. Viewing evolution in its specific context, our perspective and taxonomy are phylogenetic, but the taxonomy of general evolution crosscuts lineages, grouping forms into stages of over-all development.

SPECIFIC AND GENERAL CULTURAL EVOLUTION

Culture continues the evolutionary process by new means. Since these cultural means are unique, cultural evolution takes on distinctive characteristics. But still culture diversifies by adaptive specialization and still it successively produces over-all higher forms. Culture, like life, undergoes specific and general evolution.

The cultural anthropologist surveying the ethnographic and archaeological achievements of his discipline is confronted by variety if nothing else. There are myriads of culture types, that is, of the culture characteristic of an ethnic group or a region, and an even greater variety of cultures proper, of the cultural organization of given cohesive societies. How has this come about? In a word, through adaptive modification: culture has diversified as it has filled in the variety of opportunities for human existence afforded by the earth. Such is the specific aspect of cultural evolution. One of the best statements it has received belongs to Herbert Spencer, who, ironically, is commonly and pejoratively categorized today as a "unilinear" evolutionist.

Like other kinds of progress, social progress is not linear but divergent and re-divergent. Each differentiated product gives origin to a new set of differentiated products. While spreading over the earth mankind have found environments of various characters, and in each case the social life fallen into, partly determined by the social life previously led, has been partly determined by the influences of the new environment; so that multiplying groups have tended ever to acquire differences, now major and now minor: there have arisen genera and species of societies (1897: 3, 331).

That culture is man's means of adaptation is a commonplace. Culture provides the technology for appropriating nature's energy and putting it to service, as well as the social and ideological means of implementing the process. Economically, politically, and in other ways, a culture also adjusts to the other cultures of its milieu, to the superorganic part of its environment. Cultures are organizations for doing something, for perpetuating human life and themselves. Logically as well as empirically, it follows that as the problems of survival vary, cultures accordingly change, that culture undergoes phylogenetic, adaptive development.

The raw materials of a culture's phylogenetic development are the available culture traits, both those within the culture itself and those that can be borrowed or appropriated from its superorganic environment. The orienting process of development is adaptation of these traits to the expropriation of nature's resources and to coping with outside cultural influence. In this orienting, adaptive process elements within a culture are synthesized to form new traits, an event we call "invention," and items made available from the outside are incorporated, a process we call "diffusion," or sometimes, "acculturation."

It is time we took stock of the specific evolutionary sophistication of our discipline. The culturological study of the mechanics of invention, diffusion, and cultural adaptation in general—including cultural ecology (cf. Steward 1955)—is fairly well advanced. We need not bow before Huxley's invidious comparison of our understanding of cultural evolution and the "triumphant synthesis" of (specific) evolutionary biology. The synthesis exists in anthropology; it remains only to make it intellectually triumphant.

New cultural traits arising through adaptation can be considered adaptive advances. In this they are similar to structural and functional advances in species, although they are quite different in content. A cultural advance may appear as an innovation in kin reckoning, a "Dionysian" war complex, the elaboration of head-hunting, the development or the redefinition of the concept of mana, or any of a host of other things. Even an efflorescence of stone statuary can be viewed in an adaptive context (among others), as we suggested recently for the stone heads of Easter Island:

> The earliest Easter Islanders arrived from the central Polynesian hearth with a ramage organization [in Fried's (1957) terms, "ranked lineages"] and a tradition of image carving. The organization was suited to and reinforced by communal labor and specialized production [in utilitarian spheres]. Environmental features of the new home largely precluded the use of communal and specialist labor in subsistence production. As a result, these efforts were channelled into an esoteric domain of culture. Perhaps facilitated by a tradition of carving, a limited amount of wood, [yet] the availability of easily worked tuff, the canalization toward esoteric production took the particular direction that resulted in the renowned stone heads of Easter Island (Sahlins 1955:1051).

To cite further examples is unnecessary: recent years have witnessed an abundance of studies demonstrating that special cultural features arise in the process of adaptation. This is the kind of work in which Julian Steward has pioneered.

We are, unfortunately, still accustomed to speak of cultural adaptive modifications such as Easter Island stone images—or Australian section systems, Eskimo technical ingenuity, Northwest Coast potlatching, or Paleolithic cave art—as "cultural bents," manifestations of "cultural interest" or "cultural outlook." But to what purpose? Our understanding has not been enhanced (as usual) by restatement in anthropomorphic terms. In the evolutionary perspective these "bents" are adaptive specializations. So considered they can be interpreted in relation to selective pressures and the available means of maintaining a cultural organization given such pressures. . . .

Adaptive advance is relative to the adaptive problem. In this context a Grecian urn is not a thing of beauty and a joy forever: it is not higher, or better, than a Chinese vase or a Hopi pot; among languages, suffixing tendencies are not more advanced than prefixing; Eskimo kin terminology is no higher than Crow; neither Eskimo nor Crow culture is more developed than the other. *Viewed specifically*, the adaptive modifications occurring in different historical circumstances are incomparable; each is adequate in its own way, given the adaptive problems confronted and the available means of meeting them. No one culture has a monopoly on or even necessarily more kinds of adaptive improvements, and what is selectively advantageous for one may be simply ruinous for another. Nor are those cultures that we might consider higher in general evolutionary standing necessarily more perfectly adapted to their environments than lower. Many great civilizations have fallen in the last 2,000 years, even in the midst of material plenty, while the Eskimos tenaciously maintained themselves in an incomparably more difficult habitat. The race is not to the swift, nor the battle to the strong.

When we look at the specific aspect of culture's evolution we are cultural relativists. But this is not justification for the extension or the distortion of the relativist injunction that says "progress" is only a moral judgment, and all "progress," like all morality, is therefore only relative. Adaptive advances considered as such are relative. Like morals they are to be judged as more or less effective specializations. But general progress also occurs in culture, and it can be absolutely, objectively, and nonmoralistically ascertained.

So far specific cultural evolution has been treated much like specific biological evolution, often in identical terms; but there are also important differences. The fundamental differences stem from the fact that cultural variation, unlike biological, can be transmitted between different lines by diffusion. Separate cultural traditions, unlike separate biological lineages, may converge by coalescence. Moreover, partial phylogenetic continuity sometimes occurs between successive general stages of cultural evolution as backward cultures, borrowing wholesale the achievements of higher forms, push on to new evolutionary heights without recapitulating all intermediate stages of development. By contrast, each new adaptive step is a point of no return for biological populations; they can only (at best) move forward to that full specialization which is ultimately the (dead) end of further progress. In the same connection, replacement of a less highly developed by a more progressive cultural form can be accomplished by diffusion or acculturation, which has the advantage for people that a higher culture may dominate without total destruction of the population, or even loss of ethnic or social integrity, of the lower. . . .

While convergence by diffusion is common in specific cultural evolution, so is parallel independent development, as anthropology has learned well after years of controversy over "diffusion versus independent invention." Perhaps parallel independent development—the consequence of similar adaptation to similar environment—is more common in culture than comparable phenomena seem to be in life because of the limitation on variation imposed by the generic similarity and unity of humanity, the "psychic unity of mankind." In any case, a professional anthropologist can immediately bring to mind a host of parallelisms or "regularities," as Steward calls them, in cultural evolution. Steward, incidentally, virtually equates parallelism with his term, "multilinear evolution," and, furthermore, asserts that multilinear evolution is anthropology's only road to profitable, albeit limited, evolutionary generalization (Steward 1953, 1955). We have something to say about this in the concluding section of the chapter.

Specific evolution is not the whole of cultural evolution. Culture not only produces adaptive sequences of forms, but sequences of higher forms; it has not only undergone phylogenetic development, but over-all progress. In brief, culture has evolved in a general respect as well as a specific one.

General cultural evolution is the successive emergence of new levels of all-round development. This emergent process, however, is not necessarily a historically continuous, phylogenetic one, for new levels of general standing are often achieved in unconnected (or only partially connected) cultural traditions. The relation between general and specific cultural evolution can thus be depicted as we have done before for comparable aspects of biological evolution. *Mutatis mutandis* [the diagram] will serve for both—with the proviso that various culture lines may cross at many points to indicate convergence by diffusion.

The general perspective on cultural evolution has been labelled, by its critics, "universal evolution." Readers other than anthropologists may find this difficult to believe, but the very term "universal" has a negative connotation in this field because it suggests the search for broad generalization that has been virtually declared unscientific (!) by twentieth-century, academic, particularistic American anthropology. Correlatively, "universal evolution" is criticized on the grounds that it *is* universal, i.e., so general as to be vague, obvious, or simply truistic (e.g., Steward 1955). We hope the reader, then, will pardon us for a rather long digression concerning the scientific value of the study of general evolution.

The objectives of general evolutionary research are the determination and explanation of the successive transformations of culture through its several stages of over-all progress. What progressive trends have emerged in warfare, for example, or in economy, in political institutions, or in the role of kinship in society? As the questions we ask are not posed in terms of adaptive modification, neither will our explanations be. In other words, studies of specific and general evolution lead in different directions, as has evolution itself.

Let us take for an example the evolutionary analysis of war. Considered phylogenetically or specifically, variations in warfare are related to the selective circumstances operating on the cultures involved. In this way we examine and explain the development of warfare among Plains Indians in the nineteenth century (see, for example, Secoy 1953), or why it differs from war among California Indians or the Iroquois. Each type of warfare thus considered is a unique, historic type, to be interpreted with reference to its particular historical-ecological circumstances. Using a general perspective, however, we classify types of warfare as representatives of stages in the over-all development of that aspect of culture, and then trace the progressive trends in war as they unfold through these successive stages. (Incidentally, anyone can see from the example we have chosen that "progress" is not here equated with "good.") The progressive trends discovered might include such things as increase in the scale of war, in the size of armies and the numbers of casualties, in the duration of campaigns, and the significance of outcome for the survival of the societies involved. These trends find their explanation not in adaptation but by reference to other developments accompanying them in the general progress of culture, such as increasing economic productivity or the emergence of special political institutions. Our conclusions now are of the form: war changes in certain ways, such as increases in scale, duration, etc., in proportion to certain economic or political (or whatever) trends, such as increasing productivity. It is obvious that the evolution of war has involved both diversification and progressive development, and only the employment of both specific and general perspectives can confront the evolutionary whole.

Distinguishing diversification from progress, however, not only distinguishes kinds of evolutionary research and conclusions, it dissipates longstanding misconceptions. Here is a question typical of a whole range of such difficulties: is feudalism a general *stage* in the evolution of economic and political forms, the one antecedent to modern national economy? The affirmative has virtually been taken for granted in economic and political history, and not only of the Marxist variety, where the sequence slave-feudal-capitalist modes of production originated. If assumed to be true, then the unilineal implications of the evolutionary scheme are only logical. That is, if feudalism is the antecedent stage of the modern state, then it, along with "Middle Ages" and "natural economy," lies somewhere in the background of every modern civilization. So it is that in the discipline of history, the Near East, China, Japan, Africa, and a number of other places have been generously granted "Middle Ages."

But it is obvious nonsense to consider feudalism, Middle Ages, and natural economy as the *general stage* of evolution antecedent to high (modern) civilization. Many civilizations of antiquity that antedate feudalism in its classic European form, as well as some coeval and some later than it in other parts of the world, are more highly developed. Placing feudalism between these civilizations and modern nations in a hierarchy of over-all progress patently and unnecessarily invalidates the hierarchy; it obscures rather than illustrates the progressive trends in economy, society, and polity in the evolution of culture. Conversely, identifying the specific antecedents of modern civilizations throughout the world as "feudalism" is also obviously fallacious and obscures the historic course of development of these civilizations, however much it may illuminate the historic course of Western culture.

> Is not Marx [in the *Communist Manifesto*] in reality beginning with an analysis of the social development of Western Europe and the countries brought from time to time within its orbit from the Dark Ages to the growth of an advanced system of Capitalism, and then trying to apply the results achieved by this analysis to human history as a whole? May not the first of these steps be valid, and the second invalid . . . ? Were the Dark Ages really an advance over the Roman Empire? Civilisation for civilisation, can anyone possibly believe that they were (Cole 1934:38–39)?

Feudalism is a "stage" only in a *specific* sense, a step in the development of one line of civilization. The stage of general evolution achieved prior to the modern nation is best represented by such classical civilizations as the Roman, or by such oriental states as China, Sumer, and the Inca Empire. In the general perspective, feudalism is only a specific, backward form of this order of civilization, an underdeveloped form that happened to have greater evolutionary potential than the others and historically gave rise to a new level of achievement. . . . [T]here is nothing unusual in evolutionary "leapfrogging" of this sort. The failure to differentiate these general and specific facets of the development of civilization can only be a plague on both houses of evolutionary research and a disgrace to the whole evolutionary perspective.

The reader may well feel disturbed, if not deceived, by the preceding discussion. How can an exposition of the course of evolution arbitrarily rip cultures out of the context of time and history and place them, just as arbitrarily, in categories of lower and higher development, categories that are presumed to represent *successive* stages? We are confronting the taxonomic innovation that is required for the study of general evolution.

Perhaps it will help to point out that in biological evolution new forms of low degree are arising all the time, such as new forms of bacteria; in other words, the specific evolution of lower forms does not stop when they are bypassed by higher forms. It follows that the later form is not necessarily higher than the earlier; the *stages* or *levels* of general development are successive, but the particular representatives of successive stages need not be. To return to feudalism, it represents a lower level of general development than the civilizations of China, ancient Egypt, or Mesopotamia, although it arose later than these civilizations and happened to lead to a form still higher than any of them.

The fundamental difference between specific and general evolution appears in this: the former is a connected, historic sequence of forms, the latter a sequence of stages exemplified by forms of a given order of development. In general evolutionary classification, any representative of a given cultural stage is inherently as good as any other, whether the representative be contemporaneous and ethnographic or only archaeological. The assertion is strengthened very much by the knowledge that there is a generic relation between the technical subsystem of a culture and the social and philosophical subsystems, so that a contemporaneous primitive culture with a given technology is equivalent, for general purposes, to certain extinct ones known only by the remains of a similar technology.

The *unit* of general evolutionary taxonomy, it should be noted, is a cultural system proper, that is, the cultural organization of a sociopolitical entity. A *level* of general development is a class of cultures of a given order. But what are the criteria for placing particular cultures in such classes, for deciding which is higher and which lower?

In culture, as in life, thermodynamic accomplishment is fundamental to progress, and therefore would appear useful as a criterion of emergent development. It is well known that revolutionary all-round advance occurs when and where new sources of energy are tapped, or major technological improvements are applied to already available sources (White 1959). But here we enter a caveat similar to that brought up in connection with the thermodynamic development of life: general progress is not to be equated with thermodynamic *efficiency*.

Technological innovation can raise efficiency, i.e., increase the amount of energy captured per unit of human energy expended, yet still not stimulate the progressive development of a culture. Whether or not, or to what extent, a gain in productive efficiency is actually employed in the build-up and maintenance of higher organization depends on local selective circumstances. An increase in efficiency may not be directed toward any advance whatsoever if the existing adaptation cannot accommodate it or the selective pressures remain insufficient to induce it. A people may adopt a technological innovation that theoretically might double output, but instead, they only work half as long (twice as efficiently) as they used to. Such, indeed, is a common outcome of the imposition, however "well-meaning," of Western technology the world over. Or, as Harris has pointed out (1959), a gain in efficiency can as well be put into increasing population as into more goods and services, means of communication, new political systems, or the promulgation of transcendental philosophies, and so forth. A continuation on this course will eventually lead to an expansion of population beyond available social means of organizing it. In an open environment the society will fission into two or more societies, each at a relatively low level of cultural organization, rather than producing one cultural system of a high order of development. Progress is not the inevitable outcome of efficiency.

It seems to us that progress is the total transformation of energy involved in the creation and perpetuation of a cultural organization. A culture harnesses and delivers energy; it extracts energy from nature and transforms it into people, material goods, and work, into political systems and the generation of ideas, into social customs and into adherence to them. The total energy so transformed from the free to the cultural state, in combination perhaps with the degree to which it is raised in the transformation (the loss in entropy), may represent a culture's general standing, a measure of its achievement.

The reader will surmise from the qualified phraseology that we are once more on uncertain ground. It is hardly consolation that we share this unenviable position with our colleagues; it does not appear that any satisfactory and usable method of quantifying the thermodynamic achievements of different cultures has been developed—or even that, with a few exceptions, anyone is very much concerned. Perhaps a start can be made by estimating the total mechanical energy delivered per year by a society. Among primitives, where human beings are usually the sole form of mechanical energy, the calculation would be relatively simple: population size multiplied by average manpower (in energy units) over the year. In societies using nonhuman mechanical energy as well as human, the two are added together—statistics of the amount of nonhuman mechanical energy of many modern societies are available.

Although there is a lack, for the moment, of ready estimations of cultural progress in energy terms, the attempt to measure general standing need by no means be abandoned. There are good structural criteria. As in life, thermodynamic achievement has its organizational counterpart, higher levels of integration. Cultures that transform more energy have more parts and subsystems, more specialization of parts, and more effective means of integration of the whole. Organizational symptoms of general progress include the proliferation of material elements, geometric increase in the division of labor, multiplication of social groups and subgroups, and the emergence of special means of integration: political, such as chieftainship and the state, and philosophical, such as universal ethical religions and science. Long ago, Spencer described all this in painstaking, if not always accurate, detail. Although many social scientists deny that the idea of "progress" is applicable to culture, how can it be denied in the terms we have just stated it? As Greenberg remarks—despite the fact that he rejects the term "progress," after having defined it morally—a theory

which regarded all species as interconnected but which posited some mammalian form as the primeval ancestral type, whence descended in one line all the other vertebrates, in another the ancestor of all non-vertebrate phyla, with Protozoa first appearing in a very recent period, would not be adjudged a representative evolutionary theory (1957: 58–59).

Similarly, culture has not fallen from evolutionary heights; it has risen to them.

The social subsystem of cultures is especially illustrative of progress in organization, and it is often used to ascertain general evolutionary standing. The traditional and fundamental division of culture into two great stages, primitive and civilized, is usually recognized as a social distinction: the emergence of a special means of integration, the state, separates civilization from primitive society organized by kinship. Within the levels *societas* and *civitas*, moreover, further stages can be discriminated on criteria of social segmentation and integration. On the primitive level, the unsegmented (except for families) and chiefless *bands* are least advanced—and, characteristically, preagricultural. More highly developed are agricultural and pastoral tribes segmented into clans, lineages, and the like, although lacking strong chiefs. Higher than such egalitarian *tribes*, and based on greater productivity, are *chiefdoms* with internal status differentiation and developed chieftainship. Similarly, within the level of civilization we can distinguish the *archaic* form—characteristically ethnically diverse and lacking firm integration of the rural, peasant sector—from the more highly developed, more territorially and culturally integrated *nation state*, with its industrial technology.

General progress can also be viewed as improvement in "all-round adaptability." Higher cultural forms tend to dominate and replace lower, and the range of dominance is proportionate to the degree of progress. So modern national culture tends to spread around the globe, before our eyes replacing, transforming, and extinguishing representatives of millennia-old stages of evolution, while archaic civilization, now also falling before this advance, even in its day was confined to certain sectors of certain of the continents. The dominance power of higher cultural forms is a consequence of their ability to exploit greater ranges of energy resources more effectively than lower forms. Higher forms are again relatively "free from environmental control," i.e., they adapt to greater environmental variety than lower forms. . . . (By way of aside, the human participants in this process typically articulate the increasing all-round adaptability of higher civilizations as increase in their *own* powers: the more energy and habitats culture masters, the more man becomes convinced of his own control of destiny and the more he seems to proclaim his anthropocentric view of the whole cultural process. In the past we humbly explained our limited success as a gift of the gods: we were *chosen* people; now we are *choosing* people.)

General cultural evolution, to summarize, is passage from less to greater energy transformation, lower to higher levels of integration, and less to greater all-round adaptability. Specific evolution is the phylogenetic, ramifying, historic passage of culture along its many lines, the adaptive modification of particular cultures.

SOME IMPLICATIONS

We should now like to relate the distinction drawn between specific and general evolution to current scholarly views of evolution, particularly to anthropological views.

But first a word about terms: "specific evolution" and "general evolution" are probably not the best possible labels for the adaptive and over-all progressive aspects of the evolutionary process. Friends and colleagues have suggested others: "lineal," "adaptive," "special," "particular," and "divergent" have been offered for "specific"; "emergent," "progressive," or "universal" for "general." All the alternatives we judge to be somewhat inadequate, for one reason or another, although some were occasionally used in the preceding discussion. In a recent publication, Greenberg (1959) distinguishes "transformism" from "advance" in evolution, which seems to correspond to our "specific" and "general." The reader is free to adopt any of the alternatives. The terms are not the issue; the issue is empirical realities.

. . . when we define a word we are merely inviting others to use it as we would like it to be used . . . the purpose of definition is to focus argument upon fact, and . . . the proper result of good definition is to transform argument over terms into disagreements about fact, and thus open arguments to further inquiry (Mills, 1959: 34).

In biology, the differentiation between general and specific aspects of the evolutionary process has not recently been of great concern. Modern evolutionary biology has chosen to confine itself to the phylogenetic course of life; as noted before, the heralded "modern synthetic theory" is wholly devoted to this. The true "triumphant synthesis" which would unify the particular and general facets of evolution does not exist in biology.

Yet failure to distinguish specific and general evolution, it seems to us, has occasioned some confusion in biology about the nature of evolutionary progress. All-round progress is not detached from relative, specific progression, which apparently leads many biologists, even eminent ones such as Simpson, to virtually deny that progress is a general consequence of evolution. In fact, in a recent article Simpson insists that evolution is only "historical" (i.e., specific) and denies that comparative anatomical studies (i.e., general evolution) are evolutionary at all:

In comparative anatomy some such sequence as dogfish-frog-cat-man is still frequently taught as "evolutionary," i.e., historical. In fact, the anatomical differences among those organisms are in large part ecologically and behaviorally determined, are divergent and not sequential, and *do not in any useful sense form a historical series.* The same objection applies with perhaps even greater force to studies of behavior which state or assume an evolutionary (historical) sequence in, for instance, comparison of an insect ("invertebrate level"), a rat ("primitive mammalian level"), and a man (1958:11; emphasis ours).

Simpson is not willing to rise above the phylogenetic perspective that dominates biology today. The cultural anthropologist will recognize current biological dogmas such as "all progress is relative"—which is false—and "historically divergent forms defy sequential classification by levels of development." They are precisely the dicta that have held back the study of general cultural evolution for the last sixty years. It is almost as if biologists have fallen before a sterile "cultural analogy."

Julian Huxley should be exempted from this stricture, for he has long insisted on separating the over-all progressive from the divergent trends in evolution. Indeed, Huxley considers the former far more important than diversity, which he characterizes as "a mere frill of variety . . . a biological luxury, without bearing upon the major and continuing trends of the evolutionary process" (1942:389). When one considers how much thought, effort, expense, and interest are now vested in biology on a "mere frill of variety," Huxley's assertion is really startling, if not revolutionary. But it is not our intention to begin revolutionary agitations, particularly in what is not our own fatherland.

The traditional evolutionary concerns of anthropology have been precisely the reverse of those in biology, for until recently general evolution rather than specific has occupied first place in evolutionary anthropology. The way the great nineteenth-century cultural evolutionists, Tylor, Spencer, and Morgan,

classied and considered cultures indicates that they were principally interested in general progress. Their procedure was to determine *stages* of development and to exemplify them with contemporaneous cultures.

For this reason alone it would be difficult to support the charge that
evolutionary theory was grafted wholesale from biology onto culture, or that
it was only "biological analogy." It also seems grossly inaccurate, however
frequently it is done, to characterize the perspective of the anthropological
pioneers as "unilinear," which is the idea that every culture in particular
goes through the same general stages. The locus of unilinear evolutionism is
not in anthropology, but, as we have seen with respect to the problem of
feudalism, in "crude Marxism" (this phrase is a kind of current redundancy)
and Bourgeois History . . . strange bedfellows. Considering only their procedures and obvious objectives—and not what they or others have said
ad hoc about these—the nineteenth-century anthropological evolutionists
should be acquitted of the unilinear charge, once and for all. Because the
specific aspect of evolution was not given much attention does not warrant a
criticism which says, in effect, that it was lumped with the general, thus
yielding unilinear evolution. The error, if any, was omission not commission.
And even so, we recall Spencer's words, "Like other kinds of progress, social
progress is *not linear* but divergent and re-divergent" (our emphasis).

But they are dead, and it probably doesn't matter too much if exonerated
or not. What progress has revolutionary anthropology made since the nineteenth century? The current revival of evolutionism in anthropology is, with
the exception of White, decisively specifically oriented. By and large, it is
particularistic and historically oriented, as anthropology in general has been
throughout our century. Steward's "multilinear evolution" is now widely
accepted and respectable. This is a gain, for as a platform, multilinear evolution conceivably embraces all of the specific trends in cultural evolution.
But at what cost shall we secure this gain? In practice, Steward confines his
attention to "regularities," which is to say, parallel developments in unrelated cultural lines (e.g., 1949, 1953, 1955), and at the same time belabors
any more general evolutionary concerns. If anthropology continues on this
theoretical course, then it can only fail to cope with the larger problem of the
origin of diversity, not to mention the whole field of general evolution. Thus
the total effect of widespread approval of Steward's position will mean undue
limitation, a continuation of the reaction against the nineteenth century.

The historical orientation of twentieth-century American anthropology
and of much of its current evolutionism has occasioned a rich controversy
in recent years about the relation between "history" and "evolution." A set
of interconnected issues are involved: (1) Is evolution to be connected with
historical developments in particular cultures or not? (2) Is environment a
relevant, variable factor in the explanation of evolution or an irrelevant, constant factor? (3) Is evolution "history," or are these different real processes?
The chief antagonists in the controversy are Kroeber (1946), Steward (1953,
1955), and White (1945, 1949, 1959a).

White distinguishes history as unique sequences of events located in time and space, whereas evolution is the progression of forms not considered in reference to specific times and places:

> In the evolutionist process we are not concerned with unique events, fixed in time and place, but with a *class* of events without reference to specific times and places . . . The historian—devotes himself to a specific sequence of particular events; the evolutionist, to a sequence of events as a general process of transformation (1945: 238).

Since evolution does not deal with specifics, since it is concerned with classes of cultural forms, culture is considered as a whole and particular environments are not relevant, in White's view:

> The functioning of any particular culture will of course be conditioned by local environmental conditions. But in a consideration of culture as a whole, we may average all environments together to form a constant factor which may be excluded from our formula of cultural development (1949:368).

Not many accept White's attempt to distinguish history from evolution; many profess not to understand it. Perhaps that is why White is labelled a "neo-evolutionary," although, as he says, all he states is the general evolutionary perspective of the nineteenth century.

Kroeber, in an exchange with White, insists that evolution is primarily the historic process, and that historians "do" evolution (1946). Murdock goes Kroeber one better: "The only cultural processes are historical," he writes (1949:116n). And ten years later, ". . . evolution consists of real events, not of abstractions from events, so that evolutionary development is historical in the strictest and most literal sense" (1959:129). Likewise, for Steward (multi-linear) evolution is concerned with, "significant parallels in culture *history* . . . inevitably concerned with historical reconstruction" (1955:28, 18; emphasis ours). In turn, parallel development is parallel adaptation to *environment*; environmental considerations are indispensable (Steward 1955).

The distinction between general and specific evolution is relevant to— and we think, resolves—the debate. The historic development of particular cultural forms is specific evolution, phylogenetic transformation through adaptation. Environment, both natural and superorganic, is obviously essential to the understanding of such processes. The progression of *classes* of forms, or in other words, the succession of culture through stages of over-all progress, is general evolution. This process is neither phylogenetic nor as such adaptive; consequently, environment is "constant," or better, irrelevant. That process which Kroeber labels "history," Steward, "multilinear evolution," and Murdock, "evolution," is the specific aspect of the grand evolutionary movement; that which White names "evolution" is the general aspect. Adopting the grand-movement perspective suggested here, evolution is in one respect "history," but in another not; in one aspect it involves particular events, but in another classes thereof; in one respect environment is relevant, but in another it is to be excluded from consideration. Each of the participants in the controversy is in one respect "right" but in another "wrong"—from our standpoint.

And, if we may be permitted to press home the implications, it seems to us then that evolutionism is the central, inclusive, organizing outlook of anthropology, comparable in its theoretical power to evolutionism in biology, "the great principle that every scholar must lay firm hold of . . . ."

REFERENCES

Cole, G. H. D.
1934   *What Marx Really Meant.* London: Gollancz.
Fried, Morton H.
1957   "The Classification of Corporate Unilineal Descent Groups," *Journal of the Royal Anthropological Society* 87:1–129.
Greenberg, Joseph
1957   *Essays in Linguistics.* Viking Fund Publications in Anthropology 24. New York.
1959   "Language and Evolution," in *Evolution and Anthropology: A Centennial Appraisal,* pp. 61–75. The Anthropological Society of Washington, Washington, D. C.
Harris, Marvin
1959   "The Economy has no Surplus?" *American Anthropologist* 61:185–199.
Huxley, Julian
1942   *Evolution: The Modern Synthesis.* New York and London: Harper.
Kroeber, Alfred L.
1946   "History and Evolution," *Southwestern Journal of Anthropology* 2:14.
Mills, C. Wright
1959   *The Sociological Imagination.* New York: Oxford University Press.
Murdock, George Peter
1949   *Social Structure.* New York: Macmillan.
1959   "Evolution in Social Organization," in *Evolution and Anthropology: A Centennial Appraisal,* pp. 126–143. The Anthropological Society of Washington, Washington, D. C.
Sahlins, Marshall D.
1955   "Esoteric Efflorescence in Easter Island," *American Anthropologist* 57:104.
Secoy, Frank Raymond
1953   *Changing Military Patterns on the Great Plains.* Monographs of the American Ethnological Society 21. New York.
Simpson, George Gaylord
1950   *The Meaning of Evolution.* New Haven: Yale University Press.
1958   "The Study of Evolution: Methods and Present Status of Theory," in *Behavior and Evolution,* Anne Row and G. G. Simpson, eds., pp. 7–26. New Haven: Yale University Press.
Spencer, Herbert
1897   *The Principles of Sociology.* Vol. 3. New York: D. Appleton and Co.
Steward, Julian H.
1949   "Cultural Causality and Law: a Trial Formulation of the Development of Early Civilizations," *American Anthropologist* 51:1–27.
1953   "Evolution and Process," in *Anthropology Today,* A. L. Kroeber, ed., pp. 313–326. Chicago: University of Chicago Press.

1955   *Theory of Culture Change: The Methodology of Multilinear Evolution.* Urbana, Ill.: University of Illinois Press.

Tylor, E. B.
    1871   *Primitive Culture.* 2 vols. London: Murray.

White, Leslie A.
    1945   "History, Evolutionism and Functionalism: Three Types of Interpretation of Culture," *Southwestern Journal of Anthropology* 1:221–248.
    1949   *The Science of Culture.* New York: Farrar, Straus.
    1959a   "The Concept of Evolution in Cultural Anthropology," in *Evolution and Anthropology: A Centennial Appraisal,* pp. 106–125. The Anthropological Society of Washington, Washington, D. C.

PRESS NO. 1

Postlude

Some of the most important elements of anthropological theory—evolution, diffusion, functionalism, and structuralism—have now been traced, as have such concepts as culture, personality, and progress.

We think that, as we write, anthropology stands at a major threshold of change. Therefore any predictions or projections seem ill advised. We will never know where we are going, but we must continue to examine where we are.

Today the unity of our subject, as well as its place in the panoply of behavioral sciences, is unusually clear. And the core problem remains: anthropology continues to be nourished by all other sciences, and it continues to illuminate all other sciences.

ABOUT THE AUTHORS

Paul J. Bohannan is the author of *Social Anthropology* (1963) and coauthor, with Philip Curtin, of *Africa and Africans* (rev. ed., 1971). In addition, he has edited *African Homicide and Suicide* (1960), *Law and Warfare: Studies in the Anthropology of Conflict* (1967), and *Divorce and After* (1970), and has published numerous books and articles on the Tiv of Central Nigeria. He received his B.A. from the University of Arizona and his B.Sc., M.A., and D.Phil. from Oxford University. After teaching at Oxford and at Princeton University, he joined the faculty of Northwestern University. He is now the Stanley G. Harris Professor of Social Science at Northwestern, having taught there since 1959.

Mark Glazer is Assistant Professor of Anthropology at Purdue University, where he has taught since 1970. A native of Turkey, he received his B.A. from Robert College, Istanbul; his M.A. from the University of Istanbul; and his Ph.D. from Northwestern University. His extensive field experience includes participation in archaeological surveys in southern Anatolia, Bogazkoy, Karatepe, Side, and Turlu.

A NOTE ON THE TYPE

The text of this book has been set by linotype in a type face called Helvetica—perhaps the most widely accepted and generally acclaimed sans-serif face of all time. Designed by M. Miedinger in the 1950s in Switzerland and named for its country of origin. Helvetica was first introduced in America in 1963.

The book was composed by Cherry Hill Composition, Pennsauken, N.J.; printed and bound by Halliday Lithograph Corp., West Hanover, Mass.; designed by Marsha Picker.